D0734557

First Lady of Letters

Early American Studies

Series Editors: Daniel K. Richter, Kathleen M. Brown, and David Waldstreicher

Exploring neglected aspects of our colonial, revolutionary, and early national history and culture, Early American Studies reinterprets familiar themes and events in fresh ways. Interdisciplinary in character, and with a special emphasis on the period from about 1600 to 1850, the series is published in partnership with the McNeil Center for Early American Studies.

A complete list of books in the series is available from the publisher.

First Lady of Letters

Judith Sargent Murray and the
Struggle for Female Independence

Sheila L. Skemp

PENN

University of Pennsylvania Press
Philadelphia

Published by
University of Pennsylvania Press
Philadelphia, Pennsylvania 19104-4112

Printed in the United States of America on acid-free paper
10 9 8 7 6 5 4 3 2 1

Library of Congress Cataloging-in-Publication Data
Skemp, Sheila L.
   First lady of letters : Judith Sargent Murray and the struggle for female independence / Sheila L. Skemp.
      p.   cm. — (Early American Studies)
   ISBN: 978-0-8122-4140-2 (alk. paper)
   Includes bibliographical references and index.
   1. Murray, Judith Sargent, 1751–1820.   2. Authors, American—18th century—Biography. 3. Authors, American—19th century—Biography.   4. Feminists—United States—Biography. 5. Feminism and literature—United States—History—18th century.   6. Feminism and literature—United States—History—19th century.   7. Women and literature—United States—History—18th century.   8. Women and literature—United States—History—19th century.   I. Title.
PS808.M8 Z87   2009
818'.209—B 22   2008035356

To Murphy

Contents

Preface

In the early spring of 2002, I attended a conference in Natchez, Mississippi. Before I left Oxford for the coast, I received a call from Jim Wiggins, professor of history at nearby Copiah-Lincoln Community College, who offered to take me, along with two other intrepid souls, on a trip to Judith Sargent Murray's grave. When I eagerly accepted his gracious offer, he made what appeared to me to be a strange request. "You'd better wear your hip boots," he warned. Foolishly shrugging off his sage advice, I came clad in blue jeans and an old pair of sneakers. It had been raining for days, and the sky remained overcast and threatening as we drove toward a site I'd been longing to visit for over a decade. We had barely left Jim's truck and begun our trek when I started to feel as though Natchez and civilization itself were hundreds of miles away. There were no sights or sounds of any other humans as we walked through a field dotted with old Indian mounds before reaching a dense woods. Ducking under branches that were so saturated with water that I imagined they would fall to the earth any minute, clambering over huge logs that were strewn randomly on the ground, we finally reached St. Catherine's Creek. Creek, indeed. If that was a creek, what was a river? My guide informed me that we would have to walk across the rapids. Determined to avoid looking like a cowardly woman (surely Judith would disapprove if my resolve failed!), I plunged gamely into the cold, swiftly moving current. The tennis shoes, I realized were not long for this world. Good sport that I was, I waded determinedly across the creek. I had almost reached the other side when I heard an ominous sucking sound and realized that I was beginning to sink. Not to worry, I told myself as my body continued to descend slowly but steadily and inexorably into the bowels of the earth. My slide did not stop until the water was almost up to my waist. I laughed with ill-concealed relief, Jim pulled me out, and we continued on our way.

We finally made it to the grave site. There, perfectly preserved inside an iron fence, lay the graves of Judith Sargent Murray, her daughter Julia Maria Murray Bingaman, and Judith's granddaughter, Charlotte. Other graves in the enclosure had been destroyed by vandals, but thanks to some unknown providence, the ones that mattered most to me had remained untouched. There had been a time when these graves were easily accessible. Murray was buried in 1821, not far from "Fatherland," the Bingaman family plantation, once a Mecca for Natchez society. Now, however, as we drove back into town, I could not help but think that Judith Sargent Murray—a woman who had always longed for literary fame—remained hidden from public view even in death.

Just as Judith Sargent Murray's grave is inaccessible to all but the most determined and intrepid sojourners, so her work and, even more, the story of her life has remained something of a mystery for decades. In the early 1980s, a few historians and literary scholars read and were intrigued by her "Desultory Thoughts" and her "Observations on Female Abilities."[1] They recognized the author of those essays as someone whose views on women's rights were far more advanced and wide-ranging than those held by any of her more well-known contemporaries. This was a woman who was eager to question what she characterized as "despotic" custom, to demand that gender conventions be judged by their utility and their rationality rather than by outmoded tradition, to examine and probe the limits that circumscribed the opportunities of even the most talented and capable women of her day. A true "Wollstonecraftian," as she characterized herself, Judith was both a contributor to and a product of the transcontinental conversation about gender issues that permeated elite public discourse in the late eighteenth and early nineteenth centuries. And yet, despite her obvious talent and the singularity of her message, her fascinating story remained untold for nearly two centuries. Only Vena Field's brief, obscure, and often inaccurate biography of Murray existed; ironically, that biography—which characterized its subject as a "very minor figure in the history of American letters"—did more harm than good.[2] It repeated as fact the legend that Judith's papers had been stored in an old plantation house in Natchez where they had "decayed and became illegible."[3] For decades, historians took Field's account as gospel, thus assuming that a definitive biography of Judith Sargent Murray was impossible to write. In the 1990s, however, Unitarian-Universalist minister Reverend Gordon Gibson took it upon himself to prove everyone wrong. His persistent detective work led him to Natchez, where he discovered Judith's nine letter books—containing some 2,500 of Murray's personal letters as well as a significant number of unpublished poems and essays—and rescued them from oblivion.

When Judith left Boston for Natchez in 1818, she brought few of her possessions with her. That she was determined to see that the letter books made the arduous journey halfway across the North American continent is a measure of the importance they held for her. They served her as a diary, a record of good times and bad gone for ever. Even more important, she saw them as her final bid for literary immortality. Depressed by her inability to achieve the literary celebrity she had once been convinced would be hers, she still held out hope that subsequent generations would see in her letters and her life something of value that her own contemporaries failed to observe. Those letter books, as well as the not insignificant corpus of her published work, have made this book possible. The letters are an invaluable resource. The first one was a short note to her father, written in 1765 when Judith Sargent was just fourteen years old. The last was written in 1818, as she was preparing to begin the long and dangerous trek to Mississippi with her daughter and granddaughter. Taken as a whole, they provide us with a detailed record of Judith's life. Murray was well connected—at least in Federalist circles—and she corresponded with some of the most important literary and political figures of her day, discussing topics from politics to war, from child care to Universalist theology with a critical and discerning eye. More intriguing still are her personal letters to friends and relatives. While even they lack the spontaneity of friendly notes written in the twenty-first century, they nevertheless offer a tantalizing glimpse into Judith's most intimate and private moments. At the very least, they tell us what she wanted to be, and how she wanted the world to know her. They confirm above all that her concern for women's rights was deep and unwavering. If the letters were works of art, they were also reflections of Murray's hopes and fears—for herself, for the members of her family, and for the new American nation.

It is fair to say that today, Judith remains a virtually unknown commodity. True, as the wife of the first Universalist minister in the mainland colonies, she has always enjoyed a small but dedicated following among Unitarian-Universalists. She is also beginning to receive a modicum of recognition in her own right in the scholarly community. Still, individuals who know at least something of Abigail Adams, Mercy Otis Warren or Phillis Wheatley, draw a complete blank when they hear the name of Judith Sargent Murray. In the early republic, however, Judith was a figure whose work brought her renown in America—especially in her native New England—and at least a measure of international fame. She began writing for publication in 1782, when she agreed to publish a catechism designed to help concerned parents teach their children the basic tenets of the Universalist faith. Soon she was sending her essays and poems to a number of New England magazines under the pen names "Constantia," and "The Gleaner." In 1795, she embarked upon a short-lived career as a playwright when two of her plays appeared briefly at Boston's Federal Street Theater, making her the first woman in America to have a play produced in Boston. Three years later, she published

The Gleaner, a three-volume collection of her writing comprised of new and old poems and essays, including her four-part "Observations on Female Abilities," as well as her two plays. After 1798, Judith continued to publish an occasional essay or poem, writing as the " The Reaper," "Honora," or "Honora Martesia," and she wrote a third play, *The African*, that like her first two efforts was a critical failure. She also helped her husband, John Murray, publish a book of his sermons and other writings, and completed his autobiography for him after his death in 1815.

Judith Sargent Murray was the oldest child of Winthrop and Judith Sargent, both of whom came from wealthy and respected members of the merchant community in Gloucester, Massachusetts. Her elite status gave her a sense of entitlement she never lost, despite the downward social mobility she endured as the result of two financially disadvantageous marriages. Even as a girl she enjoyed intellectual contact with a cosmopolitan world of letters, allowing her to claim with only slight hyperbole that she was a "citizen of the world." Judith took the perquisites of her class position for granted, while at the same time she claimed always to have resented the limitations she faced as a woman. "Custom is a despot," she was fond of pointing out, and her entire life was shaped by her often fruitless efforts to scale the walls that time-honored tradition had erected to impede her progress. Custom denied her the opportunity for a classical education that her younger brothers took for granted. Custom made her a nonperson, a "feme covert," in the political and economic spheres. Even at a time when understandings of femininity and masculinity in America were in a state of flux, when men and women alike struggled to define their roles, their "essential" natures, and their relationships to a new nation where gender, class, and racial identities were being created and contested, women like Judith Sargent Murray continued to occupy a narrowly prescribed sphere.

Judith was determined to transcend the bounds that arbitrary custom had erected. When she began to publish, she refused to confine herself to typical "women's" subjects. She wrote of politics and manners, theology and morals, money and fame. More daringly, she not only demanded equal rights for women, but she questioned the customary meaning and definition of gender itself. She was one of a handful of individuals who disavowed most essential gender differences, emphasizing the human qualities shared by men and women, and arguing that apparent distinctions were the consequence of nurture, not nature. Her Universalist faith, which placed special emphasis on the spiritual unity of all humans, made her particularly suited to construct such an argument. All people, she insisted, whatever their "sect, age, country or even sex" were part of "one grand, vast, collected family of human nature."[4]

Judith's determination to split the mind from the body was essential to her construction of women's identity. Once she assumed that men's and women's minds were equal, even potentially identical, it became possible for her to put pen to paper and enter the world of public discourse on an equal basis. If she was reluctant to thrust herself physically onto the world's stage, if she never demanded the right to vote or hold office for instance, she did insist upon the right to speak to a disembodied audience with a disembodied voice. In style and in substance, her poetry, plays, and especially her essays blurred the intellectual lines dividing men and women. Simply by writing about politics and war as well as charity and piety, she was claiming the right as a citizen to comment directly on public affairs, implying that intelligent women could discuss any topic, that women's intellectual ability knew no bounds. Because she always wrote under a pseudonym, sometimes as a woman and other times as a man, her disguises personified the fluidity of gender identities.

Still, if Murray sought to challenge the "predominate sway of revered opinions" that limited her possibilities if not her aspirations, she unconsciously accepted, even embraced other customs, some of which provided her with a sense of her own worth, others of which actually helped maintain the gender-based barriers that defined and circumscribed her world. In some ways, her pleas for equal rights sound like modern and "enlightened" pleas for equality. In fact, however, she was often as not on the wrong side of history. Her arguments were based as much on understandings of gender identity based on the traditional "one sex" model as they were on the "two sex" model that would characterize the late eighteenth and early nineteenth centuries. Judith was not convinced, in other words, that men and women were opposites, either physically or mentally. More important, as a staunch Federalist, she valued order and decorum, propriety and deference, and frowned upon the more egalitarian notions that were beginning to gain credence throughout the continent. While she believed that gender differences were minor and generally "accidental," she maintained that class differences were real and needed to be preserved. Judith defined class in terms of mental and moral characteristics rather than "mere" physical differences and saw it as a more meaningful and real construct than gender was. Gender differences were irrelevant *because* they were defined in terms of the physical body. Class differences were mental, and hence significant. Such a perspective enabled Judith to demand better education and more opportunities for women like herself, while at the same time allowing her to separate herself from those inferior and disorderly men *and* women who occupied the lower rungs of American society. While she couched her demand for women's rights in universal terms, in fact she assumed that only "naturally" worthy women would enjoy the perquisites of a superior education or the unlimited opportunities that America promised its most deserving men.

Ironically, Judith's embrace of a hierarchical order was both her greatest strength and her most profound weakness. Had she not been so proud of her status as a Sargent, she would never have questioned a world that relegated her to the margins simply because she was a woman. She would not have had the confidence to demand the educational opportunities that her brothers received without question. At the same time, however, her identity as a genteel and respectable woman proved to be her most significant limitation. It blinded her to the problems, dreams, and aspirations of ordinary women. And the more her economic position declined, the more determined she was to be considered a worthy member of elite New England society. Her concern for her own reputation made her reluctant to do anything that would challenge her social superiority. She became more and more cautious, pulling her punches, refusing to do or say or write anything that might undermine her status. Unlike a Mary Wollstonecraft or a Susanna Rowson, she had too much to lose, and thus she did not always follow her own arguments to what appears to be their logical conclusion.

Although Murray challenged the "despotism" of custom in some ways, she deferred to it in others. She proclaimed that unmarried women should never be ashamed of their single status, for instance, but she saw a happy marriage as the most desirable end. She also disapproved of divorce, arguing that once a wife had committed herself to her husband, she could not go back on her word. Moreover, Judith assumed that women were more responsible for marital bliss than men. And while she usually denied any link between bodily attributes and moral or mental characteristics, she nevertheless maintained that women were "naturally" suited to be mothers, indeed that a childless woman was in some fundamental way incomplete. Still, despite shortcomings that seem glaring to a modern sensibility, it is fair to say that to analyze her views is to probe the limits to which any American woman might have aspired in the post-revolutionary age.

A word about organization. This book will follow a pattern that is both analytical and chronological. A chronological perspective is essential, as it helps readers understand when and how and why Judith Sargent Murray's attitudes changed over time. It will also enable them to see the interrelationships between Murray's private life and the changing political and cultural milieu in which she existed. Indeed, all the important public events that dominated the new nation in these years—the American Revolution, the postwar depression, the sectarian challenge to Massachusetts's religious establishment, the beginning of the first two-party system, the gradual decline of the Federalist Party, the westward movement, and the War of 1812—directly affected and intersected with the life of this one, in many ways extraordinary woman.

Nevertheless, like all women, Judith also had a private existence dominated by private concerns, concerns that generally had nothing to do with the "big" issues of the day. There were many times when her own messy life so dominated her thoughts that she scarcely had time even to notice—much less care about—the significant public events that ordered the lives of many elite men. She was a daughter, a sister, a wife, a mother, and an aunt. All of her personal relationships were complicated; some accorded her happiness while others led to sorrow, even despair. That she continued to be aware of public affairs, even while she was simultaneously performing many, often conflicting roles, is a measure of her intellectual and emotional strength as well as her nearly unquenchable literary ambition. While she was overseeing the education of her daughter, her nephews, and one niece, for instance, she was also nursing her ailing husband and defending her brother Winthrop from his political enemies. At the same time, she continued to write—poems, essays, and her third play, *The African*. Thus, while this book maintains a general chronological trajectory, it analyzes Murray's specific experiences within a topical framework.

Part I, "Rebellions: 1769–1784," analyzes Judith's early life in an effort to understand how and why she arrived at her views of gender relations and women's rights. It centers on her decision to embrace the Universalist faith, her conflicted view of America's War for Independence, and her first efforts to develop and put into practice a plan of education that was essentially gender neutral, even as it sought to maintain and reinforce social divisions. Part II, "The Republic of Letters: 1783–1798," analyzes Murray's literary career at its zenith. While it by no means neglects the profound changes in her personal life—the financial collapse and death of her first husband, John Stevens, her controversial marriage to John Murray, and her joy when she finally became a mother—the central focus of this section is Murray's extraordinary literary output in these years. She was already a published author before her little family moved to Boston in 1793, but the heady intellectual atmosphere of the Massachusetts capital nourished her longing for fame and accorded her the contacts she needed to realize her dreams. Her crowning achievement came with the publication of her three-part "miscellaney," *The Gleaner*, in 1798.

Part III, "Retreat: 1798–1821," describes Judith's slow and unsteady withdrawal from the public world, a withdrawal that was never complete and that can be explained in personal as well as historical terms. It is true that both New

England Federalism and arguments for gender equality deteriorated at the beginning of the nineteenth century. Still, Judith Sargent Murray's literary output would have ebbed in these years no matter how receptive the reading public may have been to her views. With her health in decline, she had to face her own mortality and come to terms with the death of some of her closest relatives: her aunt Mary Sargent, her sister Esther Sargent Ellery, and most important, her husband. In these years, as well, she assumed responsibility for the education not only of her daughter, Julia Maria, but for her niece, four nephews, and the sons of three of her brother Winthrop's Natchez friends. Julia Maria's secret marriage to one of those young men, Natchez planter Adam Bingaman, was, at least in the short run, a disaster. Moreover, it ultimately forced mother and daughter to abandon Boston and travel to Mississippi in 1818. Nevertheless, Judith continued to entertain thoughts of literary fame in the face of her many distractions. If she published less often, she did not stop altogether. Only her death led her to lay down her pen.

PART I

Rebellions: 1769–1784

In 1779, Judith Stevens composed a long essay entitled "The Sexes," and tucked it away in a collection of writings that she dubbed her "Repository." The piece was an exposition of her maturing views concerning gender relations, views about which she had been thinking for many years. As early as 1777, Judith had proclaimed her belief that women's presumed intellectual inferiority was the product of nurture. "Education," she had insisted, "not Nature renders us Cowards."[1] That same year, she wrote a piece on "Curiosity." In it she admitted that most people saw women's inquisitive nature as a negative quality, even a "disgusting excrescence." She chose to view it instead as a sign of women's superiority. "If Curiosity were confined to us," she argued, "the Lords of the creation would then be indebted to us for all those improvements of which humanity has been susceptible." Without curiosity, there would be no progress; humankind would remain ignorant; Newton would never have discovered the law of gravity. Rather than denigrate women for their curious natures, she insisted, society should honor them for this characteristic. Thus she hoped that in the future, "Female Curiosity" would "cease to be considered a term of reproach."[2]

"The Sexes" continued in the same vein. Like so many of Judith's literary efforts, the essay reflected an uneasy marriage of the particular and the universal. Murray seldom wrote about constructions of gender without—implicitly or explicitly—referring to her specific experiences, frustrations, and hopes. Yet unlike most of her contemporaries, she had an uncanny ability to transcend her own concerns, to see the obstacles that so "unnaturally" impeded her progress as obstacles limiting all genteel women. In the process, she employed the universal language of human rights as well as the spiritual language of her Universalist faith to attack what she saw as the tyranny of unreasonable and unthinking custom that kept her and women like her from realizing their full potential.

"The Sexes" was Judith's first sustained effort to prove that women were men's intellectual equals. She began with a simple question. Is it logical, she asked, to assume that "one half of the human species is endowed with unquestionable superiority over the other?" Her answer provided the basis for the rest of her argument. I am not convinced, she asserted, "that intellectual inferiority is naturally, or necessarily, annexed to the female mind."[3] Women's apparent weaknesses were purely the product of inferior education. Judith's own experience surely led her to view women's abilities in this way. She often wrote to her brother Winthrop, two years her junior, apologizing for her poor grammar and her syntactical lapses, neither of which she thought reflected her true ability. "I am destitute," she reminded him, "of nearly all those advantages which you so abundantly possess." But even as she asked for Winthrop's tolerance, she insisted that her "pride of sex" did not allow her to believe that her intellectual deficiencies were the result of "radical inferiority." She was capable of learning; she had an insatiable "thirst for intellectual pleasures." It was hardly her fault that she was so ignorant.[4]

In "The Sexes," Judith divided intellectual powers into four categories: imagination, reason, memory, and judgment. In each case, she sought to prove that women were not deficient, indeed that they might well be superior to men.[5] She began, as she had done in "Curiosity," by appearing to accept the conventional negative stereotypes so many of her contemporaries used to limit women's aspirations and to denigrate their ability. In terms of imagination, women were creative enough to devise new fashions and to invent stories about their friends. Everyone knew that the "fertile brain of a female" could destroy the reputation of the best of men. But instead of seeing women's imaginative ability solely in derogatory terms, Judith saw it as an asset. Only a "strong and lively imagination" and a "great activity of mind," she argued, could be so effective. If a tendency to be fanciful was a sign of women's weakness, this was true only because "the sex" lacked the training to use its ability intelligently. Were women equipped with a better education, and given more opportunities to use their talents in a socially productive way, they could put their imaginations to more constructive ends.[6]

Judith also conceded that women were generally "deficient in *reason*," but again that was not evidence of innate inadequacy. "We can only reason from what *we know*," she insisted, and "if an opportunity of acquiring knowledge *has been denied us*, the inferiority of our sex, cannot be fairly deduced from thence."[7] She knew this from her own experience. She also knew it because so many of the women whose literary efforts she had read argued in much the same vein.

Women were, she continued, equal to men in memory. There were as many "loquacious old Women" as there were men who could entertain their friends for hours on end with detailed and accurate stories about events that had occurred decades earlier.[8] Finally, only in judgment women were apparently inferior.[9] Once again, deficiencies were the result of deficient education, not of natural difference. A two-year-old boy was in no way superior in judgment to a two-year-old girl, she observed. But boys quickly surpassed girls because their modes of education were "diametrically opposite." One was "taught to aspire, and the other [was] constantly confined and limited." One was "exalted," the other "depressed." The sister became "wholly domesticated" while the brother was led through "all the flowery paths of science. Grant their minds by nature equal," Judith maintained, "yet who shall wonder at the *apparent* superiority, if it indeed be true, that habit, becomes *second nature*, nay that it supercedes Nature, and that it doth, the experience of every day abundantly evincith." By the time a woman reached adulthood, there was a "void" in her experience that she could never fill. If women did try to fill that void on their own, going to books to improve themselves, they met with derision. They were called "*Learned Ladies*, an opprobrious term" that discouraged all but the heartiest from continuing.[10]

Judith argued that ultimately, women's inadequate education not only hurt women themselves, but it was harmful to society as a whole. Unschooled women were bored and distracted. They exercised their innate intelligence in meaningless—and sometimes destructive—activity. As a result, when a woman married, she was a poor companion to a man who had enjoyed a superior education, even though he might not "by nature" be her superior. She became bitter and self-conscious, and grew to hate both her husband and the "adverse fate" that kept her from realizing her own potential. If, Judith proclaimed, a woman received the same education as her brother, "keeping, however, in view the departments which custom had assigned to each," she would be a contented wife and a rational and productive member of her community. If she had talent, she might even use her abilities to "enrich the world."[11]

Nor would women be "unsexed" by education. A learned woman would not abandon her domestic duties. But it took very little intelligence to learn how to sew and cook and clean. "The employments proper to Women," Judith argued, "leave vacant the intelligent principle." A woman would easily ply the needle while exercising her mind, leaving her "at full liberty for the most elevated and elevating contemplations." Should a "candidate for immortality" be "so degraded," she asked, that she knew nothing more than how to make a pudding or sew a seam?[12]

Significantly, Judith was willing to concede male superiority in one area. While she clung to a belief in women's intellectual equality, she acknowledged that in bodily characteristics women were—at least on average—weaker than men. Still, she insisted, mere "animal powers" were not the true measure of worth. The beasts of the field were stronger than men; yet no one claimed that lions and tigers were the lords of creation.[13] Moreover, she could point to any number of cases where "robust masculine Ladies" were the physical superiors of "effeminate gentlemen." Although Alexander Pope had an "enervated body" and a "diminutive stature," no one questioned his intellect. To the contrary, nature was wise and beneficent, distributing talent according to a just and balanced plan. Often it granted a superior mind in an effort to compensate for an inferior body. If this was the case, then women—if they had just a modicum of education—were in a position to become intellectual giants.[14]

Still, the physical differences that divided the sexes meant that in certain circumstances men and women were called upon to exercise their talents in different ways. This was especially true in wartime, when each sex complemented the other. "You are by nature our Protectors," she told men. "Shield us, we beseech you, from external evils." In return, she promised, "we will transact your domestic affairs" with the care they deserve. A man needed a well-ordered home and a good meal if he were to make his mark on the world; he was distracted and distraught when he suffered the confusion of an ill-regulated family. In the final analysis, the gendered balance of responsibilities was an equal one. Intellectually and spiritually, men and women were identical. When it became necessary to protect or nourish the body, men and women could make their individual contributions to the good of the whole.[15]

Despite her criticisms of the way her own society denigrated women, Judith harbored genuine hopes for a more egalitarian future, as she predicted that in time American women would enjoy the education they both needed and deserved; they would meet the "Despot Man" on even ground; they would transcend their "limits and confines"; they would eschew their "showy exteriors," cultivate their minds, and gain self-confidence. We will, she predicted, learn to "*reverence ourselves*."[16] In the meantime, she herself became increasingly conscious of her identity as a woman and more likely to judge every person she met in terms of his or her views of women's nature.[17]

When she wrote her little manifesto, Judith did not even consider publishing it. She waited until 1790 to revise and submit her essay to the *Massachusetts Magazine*, calling it "On the Equality of the Sexes" and publishing it under her pen name, "Constantia." Although she was not yet ready to share her views with a wider audience, by 1779 Judith had begun to develop a comprehensive perspective on women's rights, a perspective that in its broad outlines she never repudiated. Her essay was in many ways a product of her own experience, especially her resentment of her brother's superior education and her own "confined" position. "The Sexes" may also have reflected her attitude toward her own marriage. Bored, childless, often at loose ends, Judith may well have come to despise the "adverse fate" that confined her to a meaningless existence that neither challenged nor inspired her. More important, although she never said so directly, the essay was in fact designed primarily for elite women. She did not really believe that her servants resented their lack of education or longed for the day when they had the opportunity to improve their minds. Finally, "The Sexes" was a product of her dreams, as Judith dared to imagine that she, herself, might possess the talent to "enrich the literary world."

It was no accident that Judith wrote "The Sexes" at a time when her own world was in turmoil. By 1779, the colonies had declared their independence from England and were engaged in a war to make good on that declaration. Indeed, historians have generally assumed that the American Revolution was the catalyst leading Judith to her systematic and thoroughgoing critique of traditional gender constructions.[18] There is little doubt that her demands for women's equality and her claim that no gender barrier should stand in the way of anyone's right to the pursuit of happiness were inspired by the language of the war for independence. The colonial rebellion against monarchy gave Judith arguments she could use to challenge the patriarchal social and cultural conventions that informed her own world. It also led her to think—and to write—in political terms, to view public affairs in the secular world as legitimate subjects for her consideration. Still, it is worth nothing that in "The Sexes," Judith framed her argument more often by employing spiritual metaphors than she did by embracing the secular rhetoric of independence. Moreover, when the piece did refer—indirectly—to the war effort, it emphasized gender difference rather than the genderless mind. It gave men the role of "Protectors" as it begged them to shield women from "external evils."[19] Ultimately, Judith admitted that war was less kind to women than it was to men.

At least in the short run, Judith's understanding of women's rights was probably more a product of her own decision to embrace the new religion of Universalism than it was a consequence of the war for independence.[20] Throughout the eighteenth century, the church continued to be the most important institution in most women's lives.[21] As a woman, Judith had no real role in the colonies' decision to separate from England. Her decision to leave Gloucester's First Parish Church, however, was one she made for herself. Her first rebellion was religious, not political. Her first published work was a Universalist catechism. It was Universalism that accorded her a concrete experience with an existence lived on the margins of polite society. And it was Universalism that gave her the courage to cut herself off from inherited traditions and to question many of the values of that society. As historian Linda K. Kerber has observed, in the eighteenth century, to leave the church of one's birth was a "central psychological experience." Moreover, when individuals defy expectations in one arena, it sometimes becomes a little easier to defy them in another, to believe that the established wisdom of the ages can be challenged or modified. Religion did not invariably support traditional order. In the right hands, and under the right circumstances, it could be an agent of change.[22]

In the end, it is impossible to disentangle the various threads that combined to create the whole cloth that was the essence of Judith's developing understanding of gender issues. Because her religious conversion occurred at the same time that America was declaring its independence from England, it is especially difficult to argue that either religion or politics was *the* formative influence on her view of gender relations. Both were essential. Universalism led Judith to do everything in her power to eradicate perceptions of intellectual differences dividing men and women. The War for Independence led her to recognize that the new nation was becoming increasingly committed to a social construct that emphasized gender difference. Ultimately, however, the "providential view of history" that was so much a part of the psyche of many New England women of the day made it virtually impossible to draw a distinct line between the secular and religious worlds.[23] For Judith Stevens, each experience, each secular or spiritual perspective, acted upon and reinforced the other, until it became in her view at least a seamless whole. Her rebellion against her religious upbringing and her support for the colonial rebellion against English domination were both essential to her quest for women's rights.

Chapter 1
"This Remote Spot"

"Gloucester possesses for me superior charms—My warmest affections hover round the asylum of my youth—There resideth the indulgently venerable forms of my tender, and even honoured Parents. . . . In that spot rests the ashes of my Ancestors." When Judith Sargent Murray wrote these words in 1790, she planned to live—and die—in Gloucester, Massachusetts. Whenever she wandered through the Sargent family plot, reading the names on the tombstones that marked the lives and deaths of her kinsmen, gazing at "a long line of ancestors marshalled in solemn order," she was comforted by her deep ties to her New England roots. And she assumed that one day she would be laid to rest beside her parents and grandparents, uncles and aunts, brothers and sisters. That never happened. Instead, in 1793 Judith left the town of her birth for the metropolis of Boston. And in 1818 she and her only child, Julia Maria, traveled halfway across the continent to Natchez, Mississippi, to reside with Julia Maria's husband, Adam Bingaman. Judith died there two years later, and it was there, on her son-in-law's plantation, that she was buried. Even as she faced death in this alien frontier settlement, she remembered her connections to Gloucester. In December 1821, her former church announced that the will of "Mrs. Judith S. Murray deceased" left $200 for "the needy, widows & others who are poor of her native place."[1]

Her native place resided at the very core of Judith's identity, tying her at one and the same time to her family heritage and to the social status that was an inextricable part of that heritage, as well as to a wider, more cosmopolitan world and to the secular and religious changes that were sweeping that world in the mid-eighteenth century. Gloucester pulled her in two directions at once. On the one hand, it led her to cherish the values of a traditional, organic society based on order, deference, and hierarchy, imbuing her with a determination to uphold an order that granted her the privileges that were hers by a mere accident of birth. On the other hand, the town provided her with a window on a dynamic Atlantic world. The merchant adventurers who comprised Judith's family and social circle spent much of their lives sailing their vessels along the American coast or setting course for Newfoundland, the West Indies, Europe, or Africa. In the process, they came in contact with customs, attitudes, and beliefs that characterized the denizens of far-flung communities. In mind, as well as in physical reality, these were men whose identity transcended local boundaries, who could claim to belong to "one great family," to be citizens of the world. They became somewhat comfortable with a self-interested and individualistic pursuit of profit, proud of their fearless entrepreneurial spirit and their ability to survive the dangers and vicissitudes of trade, long before their rural counterparts were willing to do so. Paradoxically, while they valued their independence, theirs was not a solitary world. Their livelihood depended upon their ability to develop reciprocal relationships and to communicate with and please others, as they pursued an endless, often intricate round of exchange. They brought new ideas with them whenever they entered their home port at the conclusion of another voyage. As a result, residents of port cities took part in a transatlantic conversation that had begun to cast doubt on the eternal verities of a traditional past. That conversation threatened to substitute egalitarianism for organic hierarchy; it eroded, although it did not destroy, old sources of authority; it questioned ancient religious wisdom, offering thoughtful seekers of spiritual truth the ability to trust their own interpretations of the scriptures instead of relying on received wisdom from ministerial authority; it even destabilized assumptions about "natural" gender roles.[2] Torn by conflicting impulses, valuing traditional order yet championing fundamental changes in that order, Judith Sargent Murray was always a Janus-faced figure, looking both backward and forward as she tried—not always successfully—to carve out a new identity for herself in an uncertain world.

*   *   *

When Judith's great grandfather William Sargent, Sr., sailed into Gloucester in 1678, he was greeted by the sight of a scraggly settlement that could scarcely be called a community. The ethnic, economic, and religious rivalries that had characterized the area during its earliest years were less pronounced by the time he arrived there. People no longer drifted quite so readily in and out of town looking for more hospitable soil and less contentious neighbors. The arrival of Harvard-educated Reverend John Emerson in 1664 had given the village the religious cohesion that so many of its inhabitants desperately desired. Still, Gloucester never resembled anything like the idyllic New England village of popular myth, whose pious inhabitants erected their houses around a centrally located village common. Because the land around Gloucester Harbor was divided by so many inlets, coves, and creeks, the town's residents were forced to settle in discrete clusters, separated from one another by natural barriers as well as by private interest. Even in 1678, Gloucester showed few signs of the commercial prosperity that would one day allow some of its inhabitants to enjoy considerable wealth and exhibit a patina of gentility.[3]

Fortunately for his descendants, William Sargent built a house on two acres of farmland on Eastern Point, overlooking the harbor. Although in the short run, most people saw the location as inferior, by the mid-eighteenth century the Point would be the home of Gloucester's wealthiest and most influential inhabitants. On the face of it, the town seemed to invite, even to demand, that its inhabitants become seafarers. Surrounded on three sides by water, it boasted a deep and well-protected harbor that opened to the east on the Atlantic Ocean. Its cod were said to be more abundant and larger than the fish off Newfoundland. Its dense forests provided early settlers with wood for fuel and houses, but industrious shipbuilders could easily have elected to turn that same wood into sturdy oceangoing vessels, and ambitious merchants could have carried the timber to Boston and reaped a handsome profit from its sale. Conversely, the land around Gloucester was marked by "craggy rocks and steep hills," forcing would-be farmers to remove every boulder and level every ledge before they could prepare the soil for planting. If early settlers were to realize their pastoral dream of a new world dotted by prosperous farms, they would have to conquer and subdue an inhospitable environment. Yet this is exactly what most of them tried to do for the first sixty years or so of the town's existence. So long as farming was the occupation of choice in Gloucester, the Harbor was not an ideal location for anyone.[4]

From the beginning, William Sargent was attracted to the sea. Like his neighbors, he tried to eke out a living from his tiny farm, but by 1693, he was the sole owner of a sloop, one of only three men in town who could claim this distinction. It was, however, William's son Epes—Judith's grandfather—who paved the way for the Sargent family's mercantile fortune. The timing was surely right. By the early eighteenth century, more and more people in Gloucester were drawn to coastwise and even transatlantic trade, and residents in the southern part of town were beginning to enjoy increasing prominence. In 1730, nearly half of Gloucester's inhabitants whose assets put them in the town's wealthiest quartile resided in the Harbor.[5] Epes Sargent was one of those inhabitants.

Born in 1690, Epes built upon the modest foundations his father had laid, steadily amassing property and gaining stature in Gloucester, to the point that one observer exaggerated that before he died, Epes owned "half the town." He was a tough competitor. In 1745, he was hauled before church authorities to answer for his treatment of Ensign John Rowe, who complained—apparently with justification—that Epes had beaten and abused him. While most merchants in town tended to cut debtors some slack, Epes demanded that those who owed him even a pittance be prosecuted to the full extent of the law. Despite his rough edges, he had genteel aspirations. He attended Harvard—although he did not graduate. Still, he was one of a handful of men in the town to have done even that. It was Epes who introduced John Singleton Copley to Gloucester when he invited the peripatetic artist to paint his portrait. The finished product portrays a modest but worldly man, still strong despite his seventy years, confident, relaxed, and nonchalant, the very essence of gentility. His descendants saw in it evidence of the personal achievements of a man who could look back on his life with pride even as he provided his heirs with the means to build their own, even more impressive fortunes. Epes knew how to build a dynasty. He was an aggressive businessman who was willing to take risks to expand his material resources. He also married well. His second wife, Catherine Browne, was his third cousin and the widow of Samuel Browne, far and away the wealthiest merchant in neighboring Salem. When he moved to Catherine's elegant residence in 1744, becoming the owner of the finest and largest residence in the town, he left his children from his first marriage in propitious circumstances.[6]

With his father's departure, Epes's oldest son and namesake became the proprietor of the family's ancestral home. He shared ownership of most of the family's land on the east side of town with his father until Epes, Sr.'s death in 1762. An advantageous marriage to Boston heiress Catherine Osborne solidified his position. But it was his involvement in the cod fishery and the merchant trade that brought Epes his real wealth. Before the American Revolution, he owned more seagoing vessels than anyone in his family. His ships regularly left Gloucester with cod and provisions, sailing to the West Indies or Lisbon in search of sugar, molasses, rum, and coffee, the proceeds of which he reinvested at the end of a successful voyage. Like his father, Epes had pretensions to gentility and he spent money as easily as he made it. He was a frequent customer at Paul Revere's shop in Boston, ordering an engraving of a family coat of arms from the silversmith in 1764. That same year, he imitated his father's example, commissioning Copley to paint likenesses of himself and his wife. The finished portraits reflected their owner's penchant for lavish display. Even the gilt-edged picture frames were elaborate, ornate, and expensive. Epes himself was elegantly dressed, wearing a fashionable, gentleman's wig, as he stood before a Roman column cloaked with dark red draperies. His wife's portrait was a perfect counterpoint to his own. Striking the same pose as her husband, Catherine was clad in a fashionable riding habit graced by gold embroidery. The effect was one of understated opulence. When Epes inherited his father's portrait in 1762, he placed it beside his own and his wife's in the great room of his house.[7]

Across the street from the Sargent family home, on what was known at the time as the Old Shore Path, were the houses of Daniel and Winthrop Sargent. Daniel's skill as a merchant was even more impressive than his older brother Epes's. He, too, married well. His wife, Mary Turner, was known not only for her great beauty, but for her merchant father's wealth. Like so many Gloucester inhabitants, Daniel fled the town and its sagging economy with the coming of the Revolution, moving to Boston where he became, bragged one family chronicler, "the greatest merchant of a family which has produced many successful men of affairs."[8]

Winthrop Sargent, Judith's father, also began his career as a "seafaring man." He was just thirteen when he first set sail on a commercial vessel. While his upward trajectory was not so mercurial as his brothers', he, too, became a prominent merchant and one of Gloucester's leading public figures. Well before the Revolution he stood out. His brig *The King of Prussia* and Epes's *Snow Charlotte* were the only square-rigged vessels in town. Unlike Daniel, Winthrop never abandoned his birthplace. He survived Gloucester's postwar depression, recouped what proved to be temporary losses, and grew steadily more wealthy. He was the kind of merchant typical of the town. Fearful of overextension, he did not embrace change. Stability and continuity were his guides. He may not have been as affluent as either Epes or Daniel, but his resources were considerable and his steady application of tried and true methods of operation served him well over the years. Winthrop married Judith Saunders, daughter of Judith and Thomas Saunders, in 1750. The union did not offer him access to instant wealth as did the marriages of his brothers. Still, his wife's grandfather had arrived in Gloucester in 1702, and her father was a shipbuilder, a sea captain, and a "man of great enterprise."[9] A year after the marriage, on May 5, 1751, Judith Sargent was born.

Wherever she stepped outside her front door, Judith was reminded of her family connections. It is no wonder that her contemporaries described her as a "commanding person," who was always "sought after by the better portion of society." Judith grew up surrounded by uncles, aunts, and an array of cousins whose very presence gave her an easy, unspoken sense of security and privilege. She was proud, but not especially surprised, to see her family name mentioned prominently in Thomas Hutchinson's *History of Massachusetts*. When she attended services at the congregational meetinghouse, located on Middle Street, not far from her childhood home, she was reminded again of her family's importance to the community. Judith certainly knew the history of the First Parish

Church and the part the Sargents played in that history. Her grandfathers had helped finance the building. Her uncle Epes was one of the church's major benefactors. Both the Sargents and John Stevens, Judith's future husband, owned pews in the edifice, an indication of their wealth and, even more important, their claims to gentility. Exclusive rights to pew ownership were hereditary, based as much on lineage as on wealth. They separated the truly genteel from the merely affluent and allowed families to pass their status from one generation to the next, protecting their standing and preserving their connection to Gloucester's historic roots.[10]

Her religion, was as important as her status in forging Judith's identity, connecting her to the intricate network of social and spiritual relationships that shaped her world. That network, like everything else in Gloucester, reflected the colonial assumption that the natural order of things was hierarchical. The very structure of the church bore this assumption out. The pulpit stood on a raised platform, symbolizing the minister's superior position, according him an air of authority that ordinary men could not claim. The first two rows of seats were reserved for deacons and elders. Special seats were also set aside for the "negroes" who attended religious services. Women, too, had their separate pews. If all Christians were equal in the eyes of God, they were not equal when they entered the First Parish Church.[11] But Judith would not have found such an ordered setting unusual. Indeed she probably found it comforting. To sever the ties that bound her to the church would be to abandon the relationships and beliefs that were as much a part of her life as the air she breathed. The church represented her continuity with the past, providing her with yet another reason to value her privileged position as a Sargent.

Town, congregation, family: these were the overlapping institutions that composed the world of most colonial New Englanders. And it was the family that was the glue that held all other relationships together. In pre-Revolutionary America, the family did not constitute a "private" or isolated retreat from a "public world." Rather, it was a semipublic institution. It was an integral part of the social matrix, and its members were inextricably tied to their community through a complex web of connections that defined and gave meaning to their lives. Their paths intersected with other inhabitants at church, in the marketplace, and in the neighborly exchanges that characterized the life of the town. Families were also an essential instrument of socialization. They educated and disciplined their own members, imbued successive generations with the values society found desirable, and were an essential link in the "colonial chain of authority." If all families were important as social and economic units, all families were not equal. Relationships in colonial society were reciprocal, but, as the structure of the First Parish Church signified, they were also hierarchical. The line dividing successful merchants from the sailors and farmers of the town was becoming increasingly rigid by the time Judith was born. Merchants built more elaborate houses and their possessions were more numerous and more expensive, as their ability to provide their families with material goods that proclaimed their rank to the less fortunate men and women around them grew exponentially. Moreover, as wealthy newcomers to the parish soon discovered, gentility in Gloucester was a moral as well as an economic construct. It was possible to be rich and vulgar, or—especially in the case of women—poor and genteel. Gentility was a product of education and training. It required refinement, the ability to carry oneself gracefully—and to do so with apparent ease. To be a Sargent in such circumstances was a considerable asset. After the Revolution, Judith sternly warned her niece Sarah Ellery that no American should boast family distinction. Earned merit, not inherited position, was the only measure by which anyone should be judged. In fact, she never forgot just who she was. Whenever Judith looked outward, she knew that her family's wealth, public service, and lineage determined her place in the social order. As a fourth-generation Sargent, Judith traveled in elite circles. Still, within her family, deference—based on gender and age—was the order of the day.[12]

* * *

Little but the barest of facts exist to tell us about Judith's childhood and youth. What we do know, simply leads to tantalizing, no doubt unanswerable questions. Judith's own accounts are sketchy and of dubious reliability. As a young adult, she carefully sifted through the letters she had saved, destroying everything she wrote before 1774, saving only a few "for the purpose," she explained, "of comparing *myself* with *myself*." Her later references to her childhood are suspect. They reflect the views of an adult whose memories might be faulty, incomplete, or the product of wishful thinking.[13] They reflect, as well, the efforts of a writer who was consciously crafting a useful and compelling version of her life, shaping and refining a coherent narrative that was consistent with the self-image she wished to share with her own readers and perhaps with generations yet unborn.

What do we know about young Judith Sargent? Clearly, being a "Sargent" of Gloucester was at the very core of her identity. Judith grew up surrounded by successful family members who, as she did, took their social position, their wealth, and their heritage—which was impressive by colonial standards—for granted. She had a casual sense of entitlement unknown to most Americans.

While her parents probably did not indulge her with the affection that elite children often enjoyed after the Revolution, there is little doubt that she was secure in their love. They even provided her with dolls, something of a novelty in the mid-eighteenth century, as they allowed her a few years of childish pleasure before she entered the more responsible and demanding adult world. "Their indulgences," Judith claimed, were "extensive." Her mother, in particular, was gentle in her admonitions, correcting her children with verbal reproofs, resorting to corporal punishment only as a last resort. "Never," insisted Judith's second husband, John Murray, "did parents feel a stronger affection for a child than they did for her: never did a child feel a stronger attachment to parents than she did to them."[14]

Such observations have an obviously formulaic and sentimental ring. Judith may have adored her parents, but she did not always agree with them. She claimed to be close to her mother, yet she despised her mother's name. As an adult, she signed all her papers with a "J," and she named her own daughter "Julia," not Judith. Still, the bond between mother and daughter was strong. "I owe everything to you," Judith once told her mother. "You have given me life, and with solicitude truly maternal, you have indefatigably sought to render that life happy." It was her mother, not her father, who first encouraged Judith to write and who showered her literary efforts with fulsome encomiums. It was her mother's "sweet praises" Judith endeavored to earn whenever she completed a bit of fine sewing.[15]

Nevertheless, Judith Saunders Sargent sent mixed messages to her eldest daughter. An elegant, even imposing woman, Judith, Sr., came from a family that valued education. Her brother Thomas had graduated from Harvard, something no one in the Sargent family had yet managed to do. Judith, Sr., could read and write, and she passed her love of learning—along with the books she owned in her own right—to her daughter. Still, she was a conventional woman who expected conventional lives for her children. When Judith, Jr., described her mother in the pages of the family Bible, she emphasized her possession of "excellences which can render interesting and truly acceptable the female character." Judith saw her mother as occupying a series of thoroughly traditional, gender-specific roles. As "daughter, sister, wife, mother, mistress, and matron," her mother knew no equal.[16]

Though Judith loved her mother, it was her father's status that gave her the greatest sense of pride. Thus she reverted to her family name after the death of her first husband. And when she married John Murray she began signing all of her correspondence as "J. Sargent Murray." She was, she explained, fond of the name "Sargent," and she refused to relinquish it and the sense of superiority that accompanied it for a second time. But though she revered her father, she recognized that he was—like his brothers—more comfortable on the docks among Gloucester's sailors and fishermen than he was indulging life's contemplative pleasures. He was literate, and he respected those men who were truly educated. But his own letters were poorly spelled and grammatically incorrect. A man of action, he had an "aversion from his pen" and was certainly "no letter Writer." Moreover, Judith's love of her father was always tempered by her recognition of his power. "My Father," she remarked, "is my superiour and this idea controuls the freedom of my expressions."[17]

If Judith prized her social status, she grew to resent her position as a woman. The one opened up doors for her, offering her a glimpse of the possibilities that awaited those who took advantage of whatever opportunities might come their way, giving her the confidence to challenge the restrictions that circumscribed her world. The other slammed those doors shut. First as a merchant's daughter, then as a merchant's wife, Judith recognized that her position was shaped by gender as well as class. When they were not at sea, colonial merchants were more than mere titular heads of their families. Seeing themselves as superior in body, mind, and spirit, they were authority figures, overseers, benefactors, and guides. They were, in a word, patriarchs. They presided over a world that valued wealth over poverty, age over youth, and men over women. They might be virtuous and philanthropic, sensible and benevolent, as Judith insisted her own father was. But they were also persons of propriety who jealously guarded their "manly dignity." They left no doubt that they alone represented their family's interests to the outside world and that they expected deferential obedience in the home.[18]

The realities of the merchants' trade simultaneously strengthened and undercut New England patriarchy. The wives of merchants saw themselves as dependents whose essential but unpaid work centered on the home. They were, because of the nature of their husbands' work, among the first colonial women who could claim to occupy, at least intermittently, a separate, domestic sphere. The longer they were away from home, the more husbands, fathers, even brothers began to idealize the women they left behind, creating a picture of domestic bliss for themselves that, however comforting, bore only a vague resemblance to the real world. Such pictures led men to demand respect and soft compliance when they returned home, thus reinforcing developing notions of gender difference. Yet because their husbands were away for months on end, these were women who—of necessity—had to be self-reliant and independent. They assumed responsibility for their husbands' business, mollifying impatient creditors and making crucial decisions on their own. In the process, they developed a network of friends and kin to combat their loneliness and help them through difficult times. If they generally looked to men for financial advice, they turned to women for emotional support. Wives knew, whether they talked openly about it or not, that each time their men left port, they might not return.[19]

If Gloucester produced its self-sufficient women, it remained a city as committed to gender hierarchy as it was to a deferential social order. Young Judith Sargent confronted this reality directly in 1753. Until she was two years old, she was an only child. With the birth of her younger brother Winthrop, just four days shy of her own birthday, all that changed. The superiority she took for granted as a member of an elite New England family was diminished by a society that scarcely noticed, much less valued, the intellectual abilities of women. If she grew to expect automatic respect because of her family name, she learned that as a woman her opportunities were limited by time-honored custom.

Judith later claimed that she adored Winthrop, insisting that she never experienced any of the ordinary jealousy that so often weakened the bond between siblings As an adult, she recalled his birth, telling Winthrop that "upon the first hour of your life I pressed your pretty face with the lip of infantile innocence, and fondly lisped my congratulations." Her affection for him, she said, was "interwoven with my existence." In some ways this was surely true. But the relationship was always complicated, fraught with resentment as well as affection. Judith's interactions with her sister Esther, four years her junior, and her brother Fitz William, who was seventeen years younger than she, were often prickly, but less intense. As a girl, Esther did not threaten Judith's position. Esther, moreover, was more conventional than her older sister. She was a wife and mother, a thoroughly affable individual whose "manners were truly feminine." Fitz William was so much younger than Judith that she saw him more as a son than a brother. When he was born, Judith boasted that she, herself, had "grown into importance." She not only nursed her convalescing mother, but she assumed the primary responsibility for her baby brother as well. With Winthrop, however, tension always bubbled beneath the surface. Judith occasionally reminded her brother that she was, indeed, his older sister. At the very least, she liked to think of him as her equal. But she was invariably forced to acknowledge his privileged position and she admitted that in many ways he was both her teacher and her guide. For his part, Winthrop took his superiority as his due, and while he generally saw Judith as his "much beloved sister," he demanded her unswerving loyalty and harshly condemned her in those few instances when she dared defy him.[20]

Judith may or may not have resented her younger brother when he was born. At least by the time she was twelve, his existence forced her to confront the gender-based barriers that would shape the rest of her life. When Winthrop was ten, his parents enrolled him in Boston Latin School, where elite New Englanders sent their sons to acquire the rudiments of a classical education. He never lived in Gloucester again. The wider world, with all its "busy scenes" became his home, as the modest "domestic pleasures" that informed his sister's existence became for him little more than a remote memory. Attendance at Boston Latin School introduced young men to a homosocial society free from the distractions of home and family. It was a sort of male puberty rite for the elite, an apprenticeship that gave able students almost certain access to a Harvard education. There, the study of Greek and Latin prepared them for public life. The classics were a badge of distinction and exclusion, dividing the few—by class and by gender—from the many.[21]

From Boston Latin School, Winthrop took the next logical step, entering Harvard at the age of thirteen. He was somewhat young. Students generally began attending the college anywhere from their mid-teens to their mid-twenties, but the higher a student's social status, the earlier he was likely to matriculate. Perhaps because he was young, perhaps because Harvard was a rowdy place in the mid-eighteenth century, Winthrop did not always focus on intellectual matters during his collegiate years. Judith thought he was more passionate and impulsive than rational, and he no doubt relished the "uncontrolled freedom" of an environment that did not feature even the "shadow of restraint." Like so many Harvard boys of his day, he seized every opportunity to avoid his studies and make life miserable for his tutors. He was nearly suspended his first year, and in 1770 was expelled, the result of his dalliances with "2 women of ill Fame." He returned to school the following year, somewhat chastened, and was the first member of Judith's immediate family to obtain a Harvard degree. Putting his youthful indiscretions behind him, Winthrop left school assuming that he would be one of the moral and intellectual leaders of his generation. Judith could not help but view Winthrop's momentary fall from grace as yet another indication that life was unfair. She, herself, would never have risked losing the opportunity to graduate from Harvard in so cavalier a fashion. But her own education bore no comparison to her brother's—and she knew it.[22]

Even in Puritan New England, where the ability to read the scriptures was at least theoretically necessary for both women and men, women's education had always lagged behind that of their male counterparts. In the seventeenth and early eighteenth centuries, people generally assumed that women were intellectually inferior to men. Their weak minds made them susceptible to temptation, and thus to educate them merely invited trouble. While New England women often learned to read, they did so at their mothers' knees, not by attending whatever schools might have existed in their villages. They seldom learned to write at all. Writing was an active skill and one that was increasingly necessary in the public arena. Merchants, farmers, doctors, and lawyers had to be able to write if they were to make their way in the commercial centers that had begun to characterize New England's economic life. Women did not.[23] Moreover, if formal education was designed to prepare students for a life of virtuous public service, then women—by definition—had no need for such an expensive and time-consuming luxury. Women needed expertise in domestic skills, childbirth, and the nurturing of young children. Because this sort of traditional knowledge could be handed down from generation to generation, in face-to-face encounters between mother and daughter, formal learning looked like a waste of time.[24]

By the middle of the eighteenth century, at least in elite households, that view was beginning to change, especially in commercial centers like Gloucester. Still, even in merchant households, where most people acknowledged that women were intellectually capable, a woman's education generally had different ends than a man's. Many women, for instance, read and admired Dr. John Gregory's *A Father's Legacy to His Daughters*, which advocated learning for women, yet urged those same women to accept their unequal position and to value their softness, their delicacy, and their emotional natures. Most people assumed that genteel women needed to be educated to please elite men, becoming better companions and more gracious hostesses. Thus parents wanted their daughters to be able to write as well as to read and to do simple arithmetic. Beyond that, women needed what society characterized as "ornamental" skills. Girls learned to do fine sewing, to sing or play the piano, to dance with grace, and perhaps to speak a little French. Such skills were not superfluous; they had a practical end. They gave women an all-important edge in the marriage market. But they did not prepare them for public service, nor did they enable women to become economically independent.[25]

Had Judith Sargent been born a decade or so later, she may have enjoyed something approaching a formal education even if that education would have been deficient by male standards.[26] Gloucester erected a permanent grammar school for boys in 1758, but girls did not attend it until after the Revolution, much too late to do Judith any good. The Sargents made a reasonable effort to atone for the town's deficiencies. But while they developed an ambitious plan for Winthrop, they adopted a decidedly haphazard approach for their daughter. Judith's view of her own possibilities owed a great deal to her Aunt Catherine, Epes's wife, who gave her a "zest for *mental* pleasures." She often thought that, had it not been for her aunt's encouragement, the "latent spark" of genius she possessed would have been extinguished. Her formal schooling was scarcely adequate. Her parents briefly placed her under the tutelage of an "ill taught old Woman," who probably gave her reading lessons. The woman's efforts were supplemented by a "superstitious gloomy pastor." Judith also attended what she characterized as a mediocre writing school where, despite the fact that she was her teacher's favorite pupil, she remained for a mere three months. Like most women, she had to learn the rules of grammar on her own. When she was nearly fifty, she encountered Lindley Murray's *Grammar of the English Language* for the first time. Had she had access to such a volume when she was young, she said, and had she enjoyed even a little help from a capable instructor, she would easily have attained a "competent knowledge of the English tongue." As it was, Judith was—like virtually all women her age—intimidated whenever she picked up her pen, fearful that her ignorance would be obvious to a censorious world. Her mathematical skills were deplorable, because, she later explained, in her day it was not "the fashion" to introduce young ladies to unnecessary subjects. The classics, of course, were out of the question. Women had no need to prepare for a virtuous public life. Besides, as John Adams reminded his own daughter, a woman who knew Latin or Greek was not quite respectable. Instead, her parents made sure that Judith had a superficial knowledge of French. She also learned to be a good dancer, got a vague sense of the family business, and had a "pretty extensive acquaintance with a wide variety of needlework." If, however, the Sargents hired a music teacher for their oldest child, they wasted both time and money. She loved music, but was totally unable to carry a tune.[27]

The comparison to Winthrop's education could not have been more striking, and Judith never tired of pointing this out. Her brother, she told a friend, "from his infancy" was accorded the best masters and his mind had been formed for "knowledge and Virtue." She had "begged in vain" to share in his instructions but her "most affectionate parents" never listened. Because they "did homage to the shrine of fashion," letting custom rather than reason guide them, they were only willing to initiate her "into whatever branches of knowledge [were] requisite for a female life." It was, unfortunately, the practice at the time "to confine the female intellect within the narrowest bounds." Thus, Judith was "robbed of the aids of education" and she had to live with the consequences of this "irrational deprivation" forever. Her complaints that she was an "untaught Muse," a "Wild and untutored" child of nature were clearly hyperbolic. But they just as clearly reflected the keen sense of resentment that she claimed to have felt even as a child, a resentment that grew stronger with each passing year. Her parents' refusal to give her the education she wanted so badly—even as Winthrop enjoyed the best schooling the Sargents could buy—served her as a constant reminder of the arbitrary limitations even the most well-born women faced in the mid-eighteenth century. Bright, intellectually alive, and convinced of her own superiority, she never enjoyed the respect or the opportunities she thought she deserved. Instead, she was relegated to the margins, as uneducated and as powerless as the least deserving members of society's lower orders. This was a lesson she never forgot. It became a symbol to her of the artificial barriers that blind obedience to custom erected around all women.[28]

* * *

Like most women on both sides of the Atlantic who yearned to expand their intellectual universe, Judith Sargent was left largely to her own devices. She took advantage of every opportunity, reading whatever books she could buy or borrow, and begging for informal instruction from Winthrop, her male cousins, and her mother. She later remarked that her family encouraged her to read nothing but the Bible, but that was obviously not the case. Judith expended so much energy railing against her inferior education and her confined circumstances that she scarcely recognized her relative good fortune. Though she may have had minimal access to formal schools, for instance, she did enjoy the services of tutors, no matter how "ill taught" or "superstitious." Judith simply saw these advantages as her due. Had she been a child of the seventeenth or even the early eighteenth century, she would probably have read little more than devotional literature and the scriptures. By the mid-eighteenth century, while religious material continued to predominate in American households, the fortunate few, like Judith, could lose themselves in the novels, essays, and poems that catered to the interests of a more complex and more secular society.[29]

That Judith was fortunate goes almost without saying. An appreciation of the value of the printed word was not natural; it had to be inculcated and nurtured. This required time, money, and access to books and newspapers, tracts and pamphlets. Consequently, what historians have dubbed the "reading revolution" appeared earlier and was more pronounced in New England than in other regions of the country, and it hit commercial centers such as Gloucester long before it reached the hinterland. It was, moreover, the province of the elite, only gradually filtering down to the lower and middling sorts. Only members of the elite read simply for their own pleasure, and for them reading was becoming a social necessity. In the eighteenth century, the mere ownership of books was a symbol of taste, affluence, and gentility. Women, in particular, not only read books but discussed and evaluated them. Reading was not just a private and isolated activity; it was part of the cultural discourse, and those who failed to appreciate references to the most popular tomes marked themselves as inferior. Reading separated the privileged few from the rest of society. Because the cost of books was prohibitive, the ownership of reading material represented power. Enterprising individuals could, admittedly, borrow books or in some cases obtain them from the lending libraries that began to pop up in well-populated areas. But for the vast majority of Americans, books remained a luxury. Reading, moreover, required at least some leisure time. Husbands were often preoccupied with work or public affairs. Wives had their children and unending domestic chores to fill their days. Young men were either learning a trade or spending hours on end studying the classics and absorbing the unchanging wisdom of the ages. Only young girls such as Judith Sargent, whose families could afford to indulge their daughters' taste for reading, had time to spend with a good book.[30]

In her youth, Judith was a voracious and undiscriminating reader. As a girl, she pronounced Robert Dodsley's *The Oeconomy of Human Life in Two Parts* "the best book that was ever written." By the time she was a young adult, she had read Shakespeare, of course, and Locke. If she could not read the classics in the original, her letters attest to her familiarity with English translations of the works of Aristotle and Plato. She revered the English poets, especially Alexander Pope and Oliver Goldsmith, and was confident enough of her judgment to express her "own sentiments without hesitation." While she adored Samuel Richardson's *Clarissa*, for instance, she thought Laurence Sterne's *Tristram Shandy* "wounded the delicate ear of chastity." She was impressed with Voltaire, but was less taken with Rousseau's *La nouvelle Héloïse*. She conceded that portions of the book were "entertaining" and even "truly instructive," but she characterized Héloïse as "wanton," not at all suitable as a role model for innocent girls. She disapproved of the cynicism she encountered in Mandeville's *Fable of the Bees*, and attacked another book because it was almost wholly "destitute of propriety." She was more charitable to Addison and Steele's *Spectator*. Addressed to England's middle class, the *Spectator* encouraged its readers to eschew the false gentility of a decadent aristocracy of birth in favor of the genuine sensibility of a more worthy aristocracy based on merit. Such a message was ideally suited to flatter the pretensions of America's merchants and landowners, who saw themselves as naturally superior, but who continually sought to improve their own position.[31] It was a lesson that ambitious women, unhappy with their ascribed status, might take to heart as well.

At least by the outbreak of the American Revolution, Judith had become familiar with a number of women writers whose work led her to think systematically about the role of women in her world. She enjoyed the poetry of Anne

Wharton and Anne Finch. Madame de Scudéry, or "Sapho," "rendered herself eminent by her writings," publishing historical novels whose pages were filled with women who were literate, intelligent, and above all rational. Lady Damaris Masham's *Occasional Thoughts* advocated better education for women. She especially admired Mary Astell. Like Judith, Astell was a political traditionalist who believed in the spiritual and intellectual equality of women. She argued that women only appeared to be inferior to men because they were wrapped "in clouds of ignorance" and "debarred from those advantages with the want of which they are afterward reproached." Her *Serious Proposal to the Ladies*, published in 1697, insisted that educated women did not threaten male authority, nor were they "unsexed," as it argued that learning made women more religious and better mothers and wives.[32]

Long before the publication of Mary Wollstonecraft's *Vindication of the Rights of Woman*, eighteenth-century women were building upon the foundations laid by their seventeenth-century forebears. Poet, essayist, and letter writer Lady Mary Wortley Montagu, one of the founding mothers of England's "bluestockings" bridged the gap between genteel and professional writing. Unlike most women writers of her day, she discussed political as well as domestic affairs. And like Astell, she argued that women were men's intellectual equals, even as she claimed that it was men's prejudices that kept women from realizing their potential. Other English and European women, all roughly equals of Judith Sargent Murray, took up the arguments of their predecessors with varying degrees of enthusiasm. Anna Barbauld and Anna Seward were poets. Hannah Cowley and Elizabeth Inchbald wrote plays. Fanny Burney, Hannah More, and Madame de Genlis were successful novelists. These women were not all cut from the same cloth. More, for instance, accepted the inferior status of women without hesitation. Barbauld argued that women needed to be educated primarily so that they would be better wives and mothers. And Madame de Genlis demanded an equal—though different—education for boys and girls. But no matter what their particular views, these writers all saw the debate over gender roles as a serious issue. Simply by publishing their work, they provided an example that Judith would later use to justify her own literary ambitions.[33]

It is fairly easy to discern a connection between Judith's views on women and the work of writers such as Astell and Montagu. The link between the increasingly popular romantic fiction—most of which came to America from England in the years before the Revolution—and Judith's determination to challenge traditional gender roles in her own time is subtle and much more difficult to prove. As an adult, Judith claimed to disapprove of most "light romances which tend rather to corrupt than instruct a young mind." In fact, however, as a young girl, she whiled away many an hour "weeping over the fanciful embarrassments, and subsequent distresses of some ideal Hero or Heroine, who hath blazed away in the multiplied pages of a romance." Because her mother objected that such fare distracted her from her chores, Judith did much of her reading after everyone else had gone to bed. Even after she married and was mistress of her own household, Judith continued to claim the nighttime hours as her own. Until her eyesight began to fail and she could no longer see by candlelight, she always waited until everyone was in bed and no one was likely to disturb her before turning to her books or her writing.[34]

It is impossible to know what lessons young Judith Sargent garnered from the romances she devoured with such devotion.[35] Novels surely reinforced her desire for a better education. Jonathan Swift was by no means the only writer she encountered who made an explicit case for the moral and intellectual capabilities of women, and who argued that education would benefit both women themselves and society in general. Virtually all fiction of the era was, like Samuel Richardson's *Clarissa*, filled with literate men and women who appeared to take the value of reading and writing for granted.[36] Beyond that, the picture is not so clear. Indeed, the novel's detractors were always troubled by the multiple meanings that fiction might have, especially for the very young.

In some ways, novels by such luminaries as Richardson and Sterne emphasized the importance of gender differences. They depicted a world where women were emotional and men were rational. Thus they implicitly accepted a gendered view of human nature, a view that, if it constructed women as pure, also saw them as weak, defenseless, and often as victims. Still, while some of the literature Judith read was not especially forward looking, and most of it sounds unbearably didactic and moralistic to the modern ear, the very nature of the medium tended to subvert the more obvious message. The act of choosing to read a particular book was in itself empowering. And when Judith claimed the nighttime hours as her own, reading novels she selected for herself, she was asserting her right to control at least a portion of her own life. Those fortunate individuals who read for pleasure entered a realm of infinite possibilities whenever they held a book in their hands. So long as women remained enmeshed in an oral tradition, they inhabited a world where personal authority emanated from on high, from ministers, fathers, and the occasional teacher. These eminences decided not only what their audiences should hear, but how they should interpret what they heard. The world of print was neither so rigid nor so personal. It allowed confident, literate women like Judith to interact directly with the page, to read what they liked and, more important, to construct the meaning of what they read for themselves without the intervention of lofty intermediaries.[37]

Novels were accessible. They were not filled with the Latin and Greek phrases that dotted political and religious tracts, intimidating readers who lacked access to a classical education. And while women were virtually invisible in tracts and sermons, they were likely to be the central figures in romantic literature. To be sure, the earliest novels were usually written by men, but they were often *about* women. They were filled with more or less ordinary people, in what purported to be ordinary situations, who confronted dilemmas to which vulnerable, unmarried girls could relate. Novels described the snares and pitfalls that awaited young women as they confronted a society filled with would-be seducers and unworthy suitors who could destroy their reputations and threaten their happiness. Books allowed girls to imagine different options, to try out a variety of identities, to consider alternative strategies, to entertain myriad possibilities, and to recognize the significance of the mundane reality of their own lives. They invited readers to enter an imaginary world, to interact with the heroes and heroines on the printed page, to analyze, discuss, and even to judge the lessons that authors were trying to impart. And novels gave their readers examples of heroines who acted independently, who triumphed over adversity, and whose ability to reason helped them overcome their weak, emotional natures. Books thus gave girls permission to act on their own authority, allowing them to question the inherited verities of a traditional past. They gave their readers' beliefs and emotions a certain legitimacy. Somewhat ironically, girls—who were the most voracious novel-readers in America in the eighteenth century—had more authority over their texts than did boys who studied the classics. People did not read the classics in order to interpret their meaning for themselves. They read them to receive eternal truths about the human condition. Novels could be liberating in ways that the classics were not.[38]

Finally, reading allowed girls like Judith to travel, at least in their minds, to places they had little chance of seeing on their own. As a merchants's daughter, Judith heard tales about the exotic experiences that awaited men who sailed the seas in search of profit and adventure. She needed only walk along the Harbor shore, gazing at the seemingly endless expanse of ocean before her, to know that other worlds lay just outside her range of vision, virtually begging to be explored. The books she read before the Revolution were written by people who inhabited those other worlds and who wrote with authority about characters who lived fascinating lives in strange and distant locales. They offered an escape from the commonplace, the chance to sample new ideas, and an opportunity to mingle, however briefly, with lords and ladies, kings and queens. They gave Judith her lifelong thirst for adventure, her desire to visit new places and to meet new people. While she often remained confined to her home for days and months on end, books gave her the illusion of freedom, the opportunity to leave her private space for a more public sphere, where, at least in her mind's eye she could briefly transcend her own reality. In some ways, of course, the very books that offered her an entrée to the wider world only exacerbated her sense of deprivation. They gave her a profound sense of the disjunction between the place she inhabited and the one about which she read. "I regret," she wrote from Gloucester, "the shackles of my sex, which chain me to this remote spot—It would be my choice to traverse every part of the habitable globe." If reading gave her access to other worlds, it also sharpened her dissatisfaction with a society that told her not to dream, not to question the customs that defined her legitimate expectations.[39]

✶   ✶   ✶

Reading introduced Judith to the outside world. Writing provided her with the tools she needed if she were to make an impact upon that world. It was her mother who encouraged her to write. In the beginning, she dictated passages to her daughter, telling her what to say and how to form her letters and spell words properly. But one day, "with exquisite tenderness," she urged Judith to compose her own letter to her Uncle Epes. It was an exhilarating but excruciating process. The young girl labored over each word, tearing up countless sheets of paper, finally satisfied with what she hoped was a perfect specimen. But when she showed it to her mother, Judith, Sr., gently pointed out the letter's many deficiencies. Chagrined, Judith corrected her mistakes before posting her little creation to her uncle. The practice of her childhood became her habit as an adult. She had, she explained, a "desire to make my very best appearance" as well as to exhibit "respect for those whom I have addressed" whenever she wrote. She never sent any letter to its final destination until she made at least two copies, improving her handwriting, correcting her punctuation, and altering her substance as well as her style. Indeed, she proclaimed that she could barely write even the most casual letter, "a sketch of which I have not first scribbled upon a separate paper."[40]

Her childish attempts at composing letters gave Judith Sargent her first taste of the exquisite pleasures of writing. Before she was nine, she was a "scribbler." In the beginning, her brother Winthrop, living in far-off Boston, served as her appreciative audience of one. By the time she was fourteen, she had begun writing sonnets. She was soon busily composing what she modestly referred to as a "little work" that she called a "history." Even when an anonymous thief stole the "imbecile effusion," she was not discouraged. Judith's mother, ever mindful of her responsibility to prepare her daughter for her duties as the mistress of a proper household, made sure she never wrote at the expense of "appropriate avocations," but Judith invariably found time to take pen in hand. She wrote poems and essays, sending many of them, along with small gifts, to family and close friends. And she wrote hundreds of letters. She saved some of her efforts, and "consigned to the flames, thousands of pages" more that did not satisfy her increasingly exacting standards. The members of her little circle were impressed by her talent and complimented her efforts. Such praise, even from sympathetic acquaintances, was enough to make her hunger for more. Thus she developed, even as a child, "an inextinguishable thirst for literary fame." Despite reason, she said, "the mania" never died.[41]

Judith's mania marked her as an extraordinary individual. Most women born in the 1750s did not know how to write at all, and if they did write, they did so with great diffidence. Those who may have imagined that they had literary talent often could not afford to satisfy their creative urges, for paper and copybooks were expensive. Judith, however, lived in a household where the ownership of books was taken for granted and where paper was also readily available. Not many colonial women could do as she did, casually destroying hundreds of pages of what most Americans viewed as a precious commodity. If women who wrote at all were exceptional, those who dared write for public consumption were even rarer. A woman or, even more, a young girl who imagined that what she had to say was significant was someone who had a highly developed sense of herself as an autonomous human being who not only possessed considerable self-respect but assumed that she deserved the respect of others.[42]

Judith's confidence in her own self-worth was unusual, but it can be explained. Her social status was surely a significant factor. And if New England was a place that had always valued community and cooperation, it also provided its inhabitants with some sense of their importance as individuals. Puritan churches expected their members to engage in a continual process of self-examination, leading believers to think of themselves as unique persons whose actions and beliefs had very real consequences. New England, moreover, boasted a long tradition of women writers, especially poets. As a rule, these women did not seriously challenge gender conventions. Like Judith, they wrote for friends and relatives, sending little verses along with gifts of baked goods or fine sewing, engaging in the rituals of mutual exchange that were such an integral part of the region's informal domestic economy. But some, even in the seventeenth century, published their efforts. Judith's childhood fantasies of literary fame were unusual, but they were not unthinkable.[43]

Still, even in New England, the highly developed sense of self that writing required was generally associated with men, not women. To write is, above all, an act of assertion. It assumes that the author is an individual whose experiences, emotions, and interpretations of events and of herself deserve a hearing. Writing allows a woman to create her own unique and ever more complex identity, giving her a sense that she is a distinct human being who can leave a significant mark upon her environment. It gives her, as well, a belief in her own agency. It allows her to create a life story that is rational and orderly, that has a beginning, a middle, and an end that conforms to her ideal rather than to her own messy reality. Writing, even more than reading, allows women to go places and do things that their own society declares off limits.[44]

It is probably no accident that Judith's interest in serious writing was first piqued when she began to compose letters. This was the age of the personal letter, and in the eighteenth century most women who wrote, wrote letters. Only for a select few, did informal letter writing lead to more formal, more ambitious efforts. Still, the relationship between private letters and public writing was closer than it might seem. Many of the period's most popular novels were epistolary in form. And women like Judith, who became comfortable writing to close acquaintances, might come to believe that they possessed the skills necessary to emulate a Richardson or a Sterne. In fact, Judith consciously borrowed from the literary devices she encountered in plays or novels. Her missives often read like fiction, as she re-created (or perhaps created out of whole cloth) conversations with friends or devised amusing anecdotes to make her point clearer or more compelling. And they often focused on topics that were common to popular literature—courtship and marriage, social life, and family relationships. Like many women, Judith used her letters as a relatively safe venue from which she could express her opinions, trying them out on sympathetic readers before she dared submit them to an impersonal public.[45]

Letter writing helped Judith develop a distinctive voice. She knew that the "Art of writing" originated in the desire to "record important events, or to snatch from oblivion the sentiment of worth." But in her own day letters were not solely the province of statesmen or literary luminaries. Inexpensive letter manuals, which began appearing in America at the end of the seventeenth century, had helped demystify and democratize the epistolary endeavor. Tradesmen, apprentices, servants, and women of all classes could read these books, learning the rules and imitating the examples of sample letters found in their pages. While many new writers and virtually all women approached their task with trepidation, apologizing in advance for the errors they were sure to make no matter how careful they were, they continued to write. The sense of freedom and power they enjoyed as they tried to capture their own essence on paper, to share themselves, their personalities, their opinions with friends and relatives, made the risk worth taking whenever they took pen in hand.[46]

At one level, of course, a letter was merely a personal conversation between two people. As such, it helped women, in particular, to create emotional "bonds of affection and inclusion," sentimental ties that allowed them to erase the physical space that divided them from distant friends and kin. Personal letters did not speak in universal terms. A correspondent always tried to project her own unique essence on the piece of paper in front of her, sharing her emotions and tailoring her message to fit the needs and interests of a particular individual, living in a particular place, in a particular time. Letters promised writers a safe haven from which they could communicate informally with trusted loved ones, sharing some of their most intimate thoughts without fear that demanding standard-bearers would stand in judgment of their efforts. Because they were more or less private, letters appeared to be true feelings, "spontaneous" effusions that were the unadulterated and authentic representations of a writer's true self.[47]

In the eighteenth century, however, those intimate documents were also semipublic; they were never *just* private conversations. Letters served as a bridge between the public and the private realms, allowing proper women to send a physical representation of themselves to friends—and even strangers—without ever leaving the safety of their own homes. They were liminal projects that transcended the personal, domestic realm, but usually did not become part of formal political discourse. They provided writer and reader alike with a fictive place where people could meet, breaking down their sense of isolation, establishing connections, and sharing beliefs, interests, and experiences. Eighteenth-century letters were public in another sense. Once a letter left her hands, Judith completely lost control of it. It might never get to its destination. It might be opened and read by strangers before it reached its intended recipient. People often shared their correspondence with others, reading it aloud or passing it casually from hand to hand. Judith lent her own letter collection to friends and relatives who enjoyed perusing it almost as much as she did. Like some of her contemporaries, she kept copies of many of her letters, eventually putting them into letter books, which she bequeathed to her daughter, hoping that generations yet unborn would be edified or amused by her efforts. Thus, she wrote with posterity in mind. Letters were in a very real sense her bid for personal immortality.[48]

If this was the case, then Judith, like other genteel women, wanted her letters to be as free from error as possible. When she sent an occasional message to a friend in haste, she demanded its return so that she could correct its mistakes and infelicities of phrase. In those rare instances when she allowed someone to keep a missive that was "warm," "rude," "barely legible," or "undigested," it did not go into her letter book unedited. Rather, she carefully rewrote it before making it a part of her permanent record. Judith did more than simply rewrite her letters until they were nearly perfect. In other ways, as well, she used her correspondence to construct a desirable version of herself.

If Judith's complete collection of letters gives readers the impression that, taken as a whole, it comprises a complete and unified picture of the "real" Judith Sargent Murray, that impression is deceptive at best. The letters present an orderly, "comprehensible narrative," but it is a narrative that tells a particular story from a particular angle. Judith carefully excluded from her permanent collection any number of letters that—for whatever reason—she did not wish to share with anyone. To begin with, she saved no incoming letters. They belonged to someone else, and she always claimed to respect her correspondents' privacy.[49] Fortunately, in her *own* letters Judith freely quoted passages—selectively—from the missives she received, thus preserving parts of them even as she used her excerpts to control her readers' interpretation of events. Moreover, she did not copy all her own letters into her letter books. She omitted many of them, particularly those that were the most personal and most revealing. None of her letters to her first husband, John Stevens, survive, for instance, although Judith wrote to him regularly. Her early letters to John Murray exist, but almost as soon as the two married, her correspondence with him disappears from her letter books' pages. Judith's collection was *hers*. It told her story, from her perspective. If she often found her real world spinning out of control, on the printed page she was able to control the view of herself and her world that future generations would receive.

Judith claimed that all her letters were "clear" and "honest" representations of herself. Perhaps. But she also conceded that an expression of spontaneous friendship had "no merit, save that it was the genuine offspring of sincerity." Apparently sincerity was not enough where her literary reputation was concerned. Even as a child, when she finally created a perfectly worded, orthographically correct missive that looked artless but was achieved only after many drafts and near herculean efforts, Judith understood that letter writing was an art and a performance as much as it was a form of communication.[50] If letters were supposed to reveal something of the "real" person to readers, they were never free of artifice. Judith's letters, especially the ones she wrote as a young matron, were not expressions of her ordinary personality. In her everyday conversations, she surely did not refer casually to "verdant" fields or "halcyon" moments. In the privacy of her home, she gave free rein to her emotions in a relaxed and unrehearsed manner, laughing, crying, even losing her temper without stopping to contemplate the lasting effect her words might have.

Personal letters, however, were designed for effect; writers knew what was expected of them when they put pen to paper, and they did their best to satisfy those expectations. Above all, such missives were expressions of gentility. As such, it was essential that they exhibit a certain polish, that they conform to the rules of polite society, that they appear easy and spontaneous, even though their authors often struggled to achieve that appearance.[51] Correspondents always knew that they were on display, that they were sending a piece of "themselves" whenever a letter left their hands. And the "self" they sent was invariably a version of an idealized self. It was at least somewhat fictive; it was, in effect, literature. Just as novels of the day claimed to be true, so the letters that emulated those novels were often a blend of fact and fiction.

Letters may have been written in the home, but they eventually left for the outside world, going the writer knew not where. Thus even the most personal effort had to be composed with considerable care, forcing self-conscious authors to assume a public face. Letters that might be published—a possibility that Judith later entertained and never completely discarded—had to be constructed even more carefully. In the end, if a letter provided a picture of the writer's self to its readers, that picture was of the self dressed up in its Sunday best. It was not a casual snapshot. Judith explained it well. "No person accustomed to think correctly," she told her cousin Epes, "however conscious of superior work would present himself either unadorned or negligently attired, especially if he was to make his appearance before those whose esteem he was solicitous to conciliate. When ideas are properly cloathed, everything which can possibly be effectuated, is obtained." The clothing, the style, was ultimately as important as the substance. Indeed, no one would pay much attention to the substance if the adornment failed to please. Those who mastered the style, who could use ornamental language correctly and to good effect, and who could toss in the occasional literary allusion for good measure, were able to claim authority over their readers.[52] And while a woman could not transcend her sex in the real world, on paper, if she could write correctly and with some evidence of erudition, she might be able to create her own literary universe where mind ruled and body—sex—was momentarily forgotten.

* * *

But all that was in the future. Judith may have entertained vague fantasies of literary fame as a girl, but her early life was highly conventional. Winthrop could pick and choose among a variety of options upon his graduation from Harvard. His sister, however, could envision only one destiny. She would marry someone whose social status matched or exceeded her own. She would become a mistress of her household and a good mother to her children. She may have vaguely resented the limitations she faced as a woman, but she did not question a world that defined all women as potential wives and mothers.

Judith's early choices were limited, but they were also elevated. Her self-image as well as her expectations were captured on canvas by portraitist John Singleton Copley in 1769. Copley was already "highly esteemed" among the members of Boston's merchant elite. Over the years, the Sargent family's patronage had made him Gloucester's favorite artist, as well. Artists and their products, after all, were part of the commercial society to which the Sargents belonged. To commission a Copley painting was to claim membership in the most rarified circles. Only the wealthiest colonists could afford such a luxury. Only those with a strong sense of their own worth would be audacious enough to advertise their wealth and status in this way. Copley's portraits reflected—and helped constitute—their subjects' position in the colonial hierarchy. Just as people tried to fashion a perfect version of themselves in their letters, so they hoped to present an ideal "social self" to the rest of the world when they sat for their portraits. Portraits often reflected the achievements of their male subjects; or, in the case of young women, they represented their subjects' dreams. And they were often painted at seminal moments in an individual's existence. For girls, not surprisingly, there was a high correlation between marriage and portraiture.[53]

Judith's portrait, painted as she left girlhood behind and prepared to marry merchant John Stevens, was a signifier of both her gender and her class. Especially before the Revolution, elite colonists remained proud of their Anglo-American identity. Thus Judith was eager to note that even London's "principal Nobility" sought the artist out. If her portrait exhibited all the trappings of genteel status, it also created the illusion of idealized sexuality. Copley depicted Judith dressed in a silk wrapping gown that clung in loose, graceful folds about her body as she strolled through a garden. The highlights of her auburn hair were reflected in the freshly cut pink roses she held in her arms. Both the sylvan background and Judith's uncorseted attire spoke to the preference of the age for natural settings. The flowers were a proclamation of Judith's purity, as well as of her hopes for a fruitful marriage. Eighteenth-century women raised both flowers and children, gently nurturing them, helping the little "seeds" realize their full potential. The cultivation of a garden was a feminine accomplishment, a sign of virtue, self-discipline, and class, that proclaimed a young woman's character and articulated her vision for her future. The entire picture evoked a sense of order, assuring viewers that its subject occupied a calm, controlled, and harmonious world.[54]

When Judith Sargent became Judith Stevens she was only eighteen. She was a little young to begin married life. And her husband, ten years her senior, was a little old. In some ways the marriage was predictable. John had even deeper roots in Gloucester than Judith had. His family on both his mother's and father's side had lived there for five generations. He could trace his paternal lineage to ship carpenter William Stevens who arrived in America before 1632 and was in Gloucester by 1643. William was one of the town's first selectmen, and he was elected to the Massachusetts General Court in 1665. John's father, also named William, was both a merchant and farmer who owned at one time or another three fishing schooners, a farm at Eastern Point valued at £800, and another house in the Harbor worth £480. Clearly respected, he carried on family tradition, winning election as both a selectman and a representative to the General Court. Judith followed time-honored practice when she accepted John's proposal. By the eighteenth century, Gloucester's merchant elite formed a tightly knit network. The marriage between John Stevens and Judith Sargent combined the interests of two well-connected and highly venerated families, promising both parties a measure of security and the possibility of accumulating even more wealth in the future.[55]

Unfortunately, John's father had recently fallen on hard times. Like so many Gloucester merchants, including countless members of his own extended family, he suffered from occasional financial embarrassments. His fishing business fell apart, the result to some extent of the recession that hit the town following the French and Indian War. In 1767, just two years before John and Judith married, William died insolvent, owing his creditors nearly twice as much as his estate was worth. John divided what was left—chairs, mirrors, china, books, even a large picture of the Stevens family and the pew in the Harbor Church—among the various claimants. Only Elizabeth Stevens's dower remained intact. That, too, was gone by 1778 when John's mother died. It was up to John to make his own fortune.[56] A marriage to Judith would surely make that process just a little easier. Whether his motives were mercenary or the product of genuine affection—or more than likely some combination of the two—John Stevens focused all of his attention on young Judith Sargent. John was handsome and charming, and Judith was flattered by his interest and utterly enthralled. Only in retrospect did she realize that her decision to marry was not especially wise. She had been too young and inexperienced, she later acknowledged, to know that courtship was a time of artifice when both men and women did all they could to present themselves in the most favorable light. "Specious appearances" and the "enduring credulity of youth" led her to accept John's professions of love at face value. Disappointment under such circumstances was virtually inevitable. The "high minded expectations" with which an innocent girl entered a marriage were, Judith discovered, a "frequent source of conjugal infelicity." Not surprisingly, it became her "firm conviction" that no woman should marry until she was twenty-five. She was troubled whenever she met anyone who married in her teens. Overnight, she observed, a "gay lively Girl" of eighteen would begin acting as though she was a "Matron of Forty." When she was not quite thirty, Judith already saw herself "as *old* in life," as she declared that she had "tasted all the world can give me."[57]

Judith always implied—if she did not overtly admit—that her first marriage was a mistake. "So hasty was I to dawn my matrimonial lot," she once said, that she was totally unprepared for the reality that awaited her. She no doubt thought she knew all she needed to know about her future husband. She was not marrying a stranger. The Sargents and the Stevenses knew each other well. They attended the same church. They moved in the same circles and socialized with one another on a regular basis. It was true that when they wed John was struggling to escape the burden of his father's debts. But Judith knew enough about the vagaries of a merchant's life to realize that occasional ups and downs were not unusual. Indeed, she believed—perhaps because John convinced her that this was the case?—that her future husband's prospects were excellent. She thought he had enough money so that "in almost any business, supposing but moderate success, [he] would have secured a competency." Instead, from the beginning, the Stevenses lived on the brink of insolvency. What assets they had were soon "absorbed in the Vortex of unsuccessful Navigation." While they watched her father begin to build a new, three-story mansion, Judith and her husband were forced to sell John's childhood home. Even the bed they slept in was borrowed, and it was often only Winthrop Sargent's generosity that enabled the couple to stay afloat. During the first few years of her marriage, Judith Stevens lost some of her old sense of self-assurance. When she left the protection of her father's roof, leaving one dependent position for another, she gave up her family name, assumed a new identity, and became a "venerable matron." No longer a Sargent of Gloucester, she was merely the wife of a sea captain who was struggling just to get by.[58]

Judith had assumed that she was marrying well. She also expected her marriage to be emotionally fulfilling. In this, too, she was apparently disappointed. John was a respectable and honest man, she always insisted, and she claimed to be "sensible of his worth." But admiration and love were not the same thing. Perhaps, she thought, she was incapable of love. Perhaps the romantic novels she had read in her youth had given rise to a "heated imagination," raising her expectations to an unreasonably high level. But no matter what the reason, while she dutifully "discharged every obligation" that a wife owed her husband, her feelings for John were almost fraternal; she experienced no "*belle passion*." Judith tended to disagree with those who claimed that the wedded state was "either the highest state of human felicity—or the extreme of wretchedness." Married life, she sighed, was more often than not characterized by "mediocrity." While she agreed that a good marriage was preferable to a single state, she also argued that it was better to remain single than to wed unhappily. The bonds of matrimony, she warned, could be "infinitely more galling than those worn by the slaves confined to a Turkish Galley."[59]

Had Judith wed a generation earlier, she probably would have been less disappointed. By traditional standards, this was a good marriage. John may not have been a soul mate and he was not always the best provider, but he was not a tyrant. He did all he could to protect his wife from financial embarrassments. And if he hated to write even a simple letter, he was nevertheless proud of Judith and supported her literary aspirations. But attitudes toward marriage were changing in the mid-eighteenth century, and many women were beginning to hope for more than security when they entered the bonds of matrimony. In New England, the changes were more a matter of degree than a profound break with the past. While Puritan families had been unquestionably patriarchal, they had always stressed the necessity for reciprocity and friendship in marriage. If wives were required to honor and obey their husbands, husbands had to exercise their authority with love and affection. Still, even in the eighteenth century, if men did not live up to the ideal, women had little practical recourse. No one doubted that the husband was the economic, social, and spiritual head of every family, and as such, he reigned supreme.[60]

By the time Judith and John wed, expectations were slowly beginning to change. Particularly among the elite, people talked increasingly in terms of what historians call "companionate marriage." They put less emphasis on the melding of two families, whose economic and social interests were served by the marriage of two individuals. Instead they urged young people to consider their emotional needs when they married.[61] Clarissa's tragic story surely revealed that to marry for money or social position was a sign of corruption. Decadent aristocrats might put status and material benefit ahead of love. A poor woman might also be forced into a loveless marriage. But an ideal union rested on a foundation of affection, mutual esteem, and personal happiness. Matrimony was, above all, an individual decision. Parents could offer their advice, as Judith and Winthrop Sargent no doubt did, but ultimately, they risked being branded as despots if they did not bow to their children's wishes.[62]

Because they began to put a premium on the satisfaction of their own emotional needs, young people were often disappointed in their marriages. As minister's wife Esther Burr observed, lovers were generally "poor young thoughtless creatures" who "vainly imagine that happiness" came as the automatic consequence of the wedded state. The ideal and the reality were often separated by a broad chasm. Moreover, as Judith Stevens soon discovered, women needed to consider the economic consequences of marriage, no matter what romantic novels might argue to the contrary. A woman was totally dependent upon her husband for her material well-being and for her status. While a man could enter a marriage confident of his ability to earn his fortune, a woman could only pray that her faith in her future husband's prospects was not misplaced. As Judith put it shortly after her wedding day, matrimony was a "union of interests, and of hopes and fears." His failures became her failures; his losses were her losses. Thus no prudent woman would marry a man who promised to lower her status before marriage. And no decent man would ask a woman to do so.[63]

Nor was the "companionate" ideal a recipe for an egalitarian marriage. While men may no longer have overtly claimed the perquisites of patriarchal authority, they remained the heads of their households. In the eighteenth century, the notion of a relationship based on "friendship" was entirely consistent with paternalism. When dependents referred to their patrons as their "friends," for instance, they were not describing an egalitarian bond. From a practical perspective, men had all the advantages. They were generally older than their wives and assumed that they were wiser, that they had more knowledge of the world. Legally, a woman had no identity of her own once she married. Her husband owned and controlled the family's property. He spoke for his wife in political and economic affairs. He was, observed Esther Burr, "her Head and Governor." He fully expected to rule his household, if not with an iron hand, at least with a velvet glove. Judith often insisted that marriage should be based on "similarity of taste," and she looked askance at any wife who, "like Milton's Eve, . . . seems rather to prefer receiving knowledge from her husband, than even from a more elevated source." But in the end, even the most egalitarian eighteenth-century marriage could do little more than soften the rough edges of a patriarchal institution.[64]

It is not surprising that young girls were often frightened by the prospect of matrimony. Their choice of a husband was probably the single most important decision they would ever make. And, as the novels they read told them, a bad choice would be disastrous. The freedom to choose meant the freedom to fail. Ironically, this was especially true when a woman assumed responsibility for choosing her husband instead of relying on her parents to bargain on her behalf. Marriage changed women's lives completely, and not always for the better.

And yet it was a choice most women embraced, even when they acknowledged its risks. If a woman lost her old identity when she wed, she forged a new and socially valuable one based on her relationship to her husband. She may have abandoned one dependent position for another, but as a wife, she gained some authority as mistress of her household. She may have taken on new duties and had less time to call her own, but she expected nothing more. Marriage was her destiny, and most women thought that it helped them fulfill their true nature. It was single women, not their married sisters, who were truly marginalized in the eighteenth century.[65]

Judith may have found her marriage more fulfilling had it not been a failure in a very important way. Almost immediately after she repeated her wedding vows, she began looking forward to nurturing "those innocent pledges of conjugal affection which confirm the happiness of wedded life." Motherhood, not matrimony, was her most cherished dream. But for whatever reason, John and Judith remained childless. John may have been away from home too often, "floating on the world of waters."[66] Judith's lack of passion for her husband may have made sexual relationships for the two a painful experience that they did not like to repeat very often. John may have been infertile. Ultimately it did not matter. Her failure to have children with John was Judith's greatest disappointment, and she never ceased to regret her loss.

A good marriage in the eighteenth century was one that produced children. Motherhood was both a woman's social and biological destiny. While Judith came to believe that matrimony was a social construct, a mere custom that a woman could embrace or avoid at will without losing her "femininity," she always believed that motherhood was central to a woman's identity. The "situation of a childless wife," she sighed, provided a "melancholy contrast" to the joys of motherhood. The longing to bear children, she believed, was instinctive in all women. Even though she was childless, she claimed not to be a "stranger to those emotions which live in the soul of a mother." To be a woman was, by definition, to be a mother. She knew that women would endure the most excruciating physical pain in order to bear children. Her own mother suffered a number of miscarriages and watched four infants die. Yet the "magnitude of her maternal affection" was so great that she never contemplated any effort to avoid yet another pregnancy.[67] Childbirth was painful, even dangerous. But it also promised the sheerest joy and the most profound fulfillment that a woman could ever have.

Once again, timing made Judith's failure to produce children during her first marriage especially devastating. Admittedly, in the seventeenth century a childless marriage was seen as unnatural. Some even saw it as evidence of divine displeasure. And, indeed, it was rare. A mere 10 percent of all colonial marriages were childless. Women typically had their first child about sixteen months after they married, and their last child when they were around forty. There was hardly a time when most mature women were without the presence of children in the home. Even in the late eighteenth century, society viewed pregnancy as natural, barrenness as unnatural. A childless woman cast her own femininity in doubt, and she put her husband's claims to masculinity in jeopardy as well.[68]

But by the mid-eighteenth century, particularly in middling and elite households, motherhood began to take on a peculiarly moral and sentimental character. In earlier days, motherhood was one task among many—and it was not always the most important task, at that. There were always older siblings, servants, and relatives around to watch over younger children. Because virtually all economic activity centered on the household, and because it required a great deal of skill, seventeenth-century women found their work so demanding and time-consuming that they could not lavish much attention on each individual child. Moreover, fathers were at least as responsible for child rearing and religious instruction of their progeny as mothers were. Thus women did not derive any special moral authority from their role as mothers. But as elite women—especially those whose husbands were involved in commercial affairs—began to escape responsibility for some of the more onerous household tasks, hiring servants to do the heavy work and buying items that their own mothers would have produced in the home, they began to focus more attention on their maternal role. Motherhood was, after all, the most "natural" task a woman had. Only women were able to bear and nurse children. It was but a small step for women to claim that a determinative connection existed between their biological, sexual natures and their moral and emotional proclivity for motherhood. More than that, motherhood was viewed as a source of joy, the "route to happiness" for women. Barrenness was painful for husband and wife alike, but in many ways it was a woman's problem.[69]

Judith never submitted gracefully to a fate that robbed her of what she conceived as her natural destiny. She no doubt idealized motherhood all the more because it took her so long to experience it for herself. Ironically, her childlessness may have provided her with a window of opportunity. Granted, she was never a lady of leisure. No eighteenth-century woman was. She may have had servants from time to time. She was able to purchase some necessities that women would once have made themselves. She often dined with her parents, especially when John was away. But she cooked and cleaned, tended the fires and sewed. When guests arrived, she had to see to their every need for days on end.[70] Still, without children to demand her attention from morning 'til night and beyond, she had more discretionary time than most women her age did. When John was gone and she had the house to herself, she enjoyed the opportunity to read and to write. It was a luxury she did not really appreciate until it no longer existed. But by the time her domestic responsibilities became truly onerous, the habits of a lifetime had become ingrained. No matter what, she managed to snatch an hour or two here and there, continuing to enjoy the life of the mind that she began to view as her right and as her real destiny.

Chapter 2
Universal Salvation

On February 11, 1777, the deacons of Gloucester's First Parish Church sent letters to sixteen "delinquent members" of their congregation. Why, they wanted to know, had these once stalwart pillars of church and community chosen to absent themselves from "the worship and ordinances of God in his House?" Among the recipients of the letters were Epes Sargent "and wife," Winthrop Sargent "and wife," and Judith Stevens.[1] The deacons were understandably perplexed. Even in the last quarter of the eighteenth century, religion remained central to the identity of most New Englanders. Whenever communicants signed a church's covenant or attended weekly services at the parish meetinghouse, they were doing much more than declaring their devotion to a particular set of religious principles. The Sargents and Stevenses who filed into their family pews each Sunday were expressing in tangible form their rank and privilege, even as they were affirming their ties to past and present members of Gloucester's religious community. The rites that bound them to their church— baptism, communion, the renewal of the covenant—were all public rituals and participating in them signaled a determination to uphold the values that tied the members of the congregation together. In a society where habit and tradition generally determined individual religious beliefs, where town, family, and church were inextricably intermingled, it was virtually unimaginable for respectable families simply to abandon the church of their birth, much less to embrace an entirely new religion. In theory, religious belief in New England was a voluntary matter. In fact, people like the Stevenses and the Sargents seldom chose their faith. They were born into it, and they expected to die in it as well. Religious diversity in towns like Gloucester was not even a dream for most people. And it surely was not a reality.[2]

All of that began to change the year that Judith Sargent became Judith Stevens and an Englishman by the name of Gregory weighed anchor in Gloucester Harbor. The seaman did not remain there long, but his sojourn dramatically altered the lives of a number of the town's inhabitants. Upon his departure, he left behind a book of sermons written by Welsh minister James Relly, an early proponent of Universalism. Intrigued, a few members of the First Parish Church began meeting quietly together to discuss Relly's work. Although eighteenth-century Gloucester harbored very few dissenters, it is not altogether surprising that some of the town's inhabitants were willing to experiment with new religious ideas in the years immediately preceding the American Revolution. Challenges to received wisdom tended to be met with a warmer welcome in seaport communities than they did in the small villages and farming communities in the hinterland. This was at least in part because merchants often brought more than exotic goods with them when they returned home from their voyages. They brought intriguing foreign ideas, as well. Moreover, coastal residents were more likely than other New Englanders to be comfortable with the competitive ethos that characterized merchant capitalism. If they could entertain thoughts of a free market for material goods, they could at least imagine a world that tolerated a free market for religious views as well. Finally, Gloucester inhabitants were accustomed to the Puritan practice of holding devotional sessions in individual homes during the week. If they knew the tragic story of Anne Hutchinson, they realized that such gatherings could be dangerous. But it is doubtful that anyone was unduly alarmed when the Sargents and their friends began meeting privately to examine their religious beliefs. Gloucester had always enjoyed a tradition of lay-centered control of religion, after all, and from the beginning Puritans had relied on a literate and devout congregation whose members could interpret the Bible for themselves.[3] No one predicted that the Sargents, without whose help the First Parish Church might not even have been built, would spearhead a movement that would disrupt the order and harmony of the congregation.

The study group became potentially more dangerous with the arrival in Gloucester of John Murray, one of James Relly's most talented—his enemies would say notorious—disciples. Born on December 10, 1741, in the English county of Hampshire, Murray spent his formative years in Ireland. There he was raised in a strict Calvinistic household. He later insisted that he always had "more *fear* than *affection*" for his authoritarian father and that he viewed religion as a "subject of terror" as well. "In fact," he said, "I believed that I had nothing to hope, but everything to fear, both from my Creator and my father." John enjoyed a better relationship with his mother, but because she always deferred to her husband, she never intervened on her son's behalf.[4]

John was largely self-educated. When an Episcopal clergyman recognized his potential and offered to give him private lessons in the classics, John's father refused the overture, claiming that his religious scruples forbade a secular education for his son. Thus John was left to fend for himself. Although the elder

Murray never allowed his children access to anything but the Bible and devotional literature, John regularly defied his father's strictures, reading secretly what he could not enjoy in the open. Richardson and Fielding, Addison and Pope, Shakespeare and Parnell allowed him to escape the realities of his own bleak existence and made him hunger for more. In America, where religious groups were proud of their learned clergy, his deficient education gave John's enemies a perfect opening for attack. He was "unstudied" and "totally ignorant of the original languages." How, asked his detractors, could anyone take him seriously?[5]

As a young adult, John grew increasingly religious, briefly embracing Methodism and becoming one of John Wesley's most able lay preachers. But once he escaped his father's roof, he enjoyed life's secular pleasures as well. He moved to London, relishing the plays and music that were available in England's capital. There he met and married Eliza Neale. Unfortunately, her father disapproved of the match. Convinced that John was marrying his daughter for her money, he cut Eliza out of his will. It was while he was in London that John first heard of James Relly. Without ever having met him, Murray despised the Universalist preacher. Arguing that a belief in universal salvation would inevitably lead to a life of debauchery, he assumed that Relly was "a man black with crimes." Only the "dissipated and unprincipled of every class," John insisted, would be drawn to the Universalist faith. In 1757, determined to expose Relly as a fraud, John decided to listen to the minister's sermons for himself. To his surprise, he was totally convinced by Relly's arguments. Soon both he and Eliza became converts to Universalism.[6]

In 1769, shortly after the death of her only child, Eliza succumbed to illness as well. John allowed his bills to pile up as he watched first his son and then his wife sicken and die. Eventually unable to meet his creditors' demands, he wound up in debtor's prison. Upon his release, he decided to leave old England behind. Like many emigrants, he looked to America to offer him a new beginning.[7]

John did not intend to become a minister when his ship ran aground on the New Jersey coast in the fall of 1770. Depressed by the loss of his little family, humiliated by his experience in prison, he longed only for a measure of tranquillity. He came to America, he said, not "in pursuit of bliss, but to avoid if possible a part of [his] misery." But a chance encounter with Thomas Potter, a religious enthusiast who had already experimented with both the Quaker and the Baptist faiths, changed his mind. Potter was enthralled with Murray's Universalist message, and he soon convinced the émigré that it was his destiny to preach to an American populace that hungered for the truth. Thus John Murray became an itinerant minister, traveling throughout New England and the mid-Atlantic colonies. By 1773, interest in his message had become so great that he was invited to preach at Boston's Faneuil Hall.[8]

As his popularity grew, however, so did the size and intensity of his opposition. During his first four years in America, John carefully avoided an explicit discussion of his beliefs and refused to be drawn into theological disputes with other clergymen. He based his sermons on the scriptures—a source with which few colonists disagreed—only hinting at an interpretation of the Bible that directly challenged religious convention. Still, even before they heard his views, established ministers saw him as a threat. No matter how often John insisted that traveling preachers were acting upon the "positive command" of God, many New England clergymen remained unconvinced. They remembered all too well the religious confusion that had spread through New England during the Great Awakening, when itinerants such as George Whitefield and Gilbert and William Tennant had gone from one village to the next, leaving chaos and confusion in their wake. Ministers who had no permanent home were rootless; thus, they appeared to be unscrupulous interlopers, a threat to social and religious stability. They undermined the authority of settled pastors, subverting the relationship between a minister and his flock, leaving a traditional order that privileged both education and breeding vulnerable to attack. Nor did they have "credentials." Evidence of a minister's divine calling and his ability to move audiences, not learning or ordination by a particular church, were the qualifications that mattered most to itinerants and their audiences. Itinerants gave ordinary people choices; they granted once powerless parishioners an opportunity to reject one set of beliefs in favor of another. They expanded the cultural and religious horizons of everyone who listened to them, introducing them to a new body of knowledge that they could make their own.[9]

Some of those who flocked to hear John preach were genuinely seeking religious enlightenment. Others came hoping to be entertained. Murray seldom disappointed. In appearance, he was not especially imposing. Short and stocky, his rough, stern features would never inspire the admiration of a poet. But like George Whitefield, to whom many compared him, Murray had a theatrical flair that he honed to excellent advantage. He invented dialogue, imitated various biblical characters, and modulated his voice for special effect. He never entered the pulpit with a carefully prepared message. Instead, he hit upon a text that was to his liking, "leaving the what and the how to discover itself as I go on." He conceded that he might have been "more coldly correct" had he composed his sermons in advance. But while his efforts lacked a certain polish and they were not always grammatically correct, John's adherents thought that the minister's emotional conviction more than compensated for what cavilers saw as serious flaws.

His humor and warmth, his poetic references, his flowery language, and his ability to think quickly on his feet were enough to dazzle his listeners. What did it matter if he was apt to "fly from the subject" or that he could "never be kept to the point"? If his opponents saw him as incoherent, overbearing, and intolerant, a man who would countenance no interpretation of the scripture but his own, his supporters seldom saw this side of the man—or if they did, they simply did not care.[10]

Unfortunately, there were many established clergymen who did care, especially when they realized that John Murray was not only an itinerant, but that he was preaching universal salvation as well. A few invited John into their churches only to use the occasion to trip him up. Most simply closed their doors to him. Congregational minister Ezra Stiles, normally known for his religious tolerance, accused him of being a papist hypocrite who should be shunned by all right-thinking worshippers. When John demanded a face-to-face interview with the minister so that he could defend himself against such accusations, Stiles refused, insisting that Murray simply could not be trusted. Had he not, after all, tried to hide his Universalist beliefs when he first began to preach? Stiles was convinced that John was an inveterate liar who "had no settled principles either in Politics or Religion."[11]

Wherever he went, John created an "uproar." On occasion he and his followers had to dodge the eggs and stones of hecklers. But though his admirers begged him to flee for his own safety, Murray never budged. He always insisted upon finishing his sermon, much to the delight of an audience whose members welcomed his message and were no doubt entertained by the conflict that his presence evoked. No matter what he did, John was convinced that he could not win. If he declared his beliefs openly, his detractors would label him a blasphemer. If he stuck to the scriptures and avoided doctrinal debate, this was proof of his deceitfulness. Even after he had become somewhat respectable and was ordained as minister of Boston's First Universalist Church, John smarted at the memory of his treatment by the Massachusetts establishment.[12]

In 1774, Gloucester's little group of "Rellyites," as they called themselves, heard stories of a minister who was preaching the doctrine they had tentatively begun to embrace as their own. They sent Epes and Winthrop Sargent, Sr. to Boston to meet with John Murray, hoping to persuade him to come to the port city to minister to them. Murray's visit came at a propitious—some said providential—time. The Rev. Samuel Chandler was old and feeble, and the First Parish Church knew that it would soon have to replace its venerable pastor. When John volunteered to fill the pulpit for a Sunday or two, his supporters viewed his performance as an audition for the job. In the beginning, few objected to Murray's presence. Although he did not come from a settled congregation and no one knew who he was, the enthusiastic recommendation of the Sargents was surely a point in his favor. Still, Chandler was uneasy. When he questioned the newcomer before allowing him to preach, he was profoundly uncomfortable with some of the itinerant's comments. John admitted, for instance, that he "had not been favoured with a liberal education," but insisted that his "extraordinary *call from Heaven*" more than compensated for his deficiencies. Chandler was doubtful, but finally allowed John to fill his pulpit. What harm could one or two sermons do?[13]

John arrived in Gloucester in early November, staying there a little over a week. When he spoke to the members of the First Parish Church, he chose his words carefully, striving not to offend the unsuspecting members of the congregation. Still, while "some admired him, and swallowed all he said with great avidity, others doubted" and many others "were filled with indignation, and said they had been imposed upon." They were particularly offended at John's tendency to speak contemptuously of ministers who did not understand the true message of the gospel. Nevertheless, most members wanted to hear him again. And every evening, John's core supporters gathered in Epes Sargent's parlor where the minister spoke more freely about his beliefs. Already well-versed in Rellyan theology, the little group was enchanted by both the message and the messenger. "Mr. Murray's arguments," wrote Judith Stevens, are "always conclusive—There is no resisting the force of his eloquence." Years later, she still remembered the profound sense of relief she had felt when she heard John's first sermon. Her "days of ignorance" were no more. No longer did she have to ignore the "absurd contradictions" and the irrational inconsistencies of the Calvinist faith. Before she heard Murray speak, she had tried not to dwell on the intellectual problems that Calvinism presented, afraid that if she examined her views closely she would lose her faith entirely. But now, Judith exulted, reason was "emancipated," and John's logical message allowed her to entwine reason and faith once more.[14]

Whether it was John's eloquence or his arguments that were more appealing is hard to say, but Judith was clearly taken by both. Just two days after the minister left Gloucester, she composed her first letter to John Murray. Laying aside "all that awe, and reverence, which his unquestionable superiority demands," she wrote to him with the "freedom of a sister." She was not, of course, accustomed to writing to men. Indeed, she knew that she was violating every rule of decorum when she did so. A woman who corresponded with a member of the opposite sex, particularly a virtual stranger, was flirting with danger. A designing man could use his letters to seduce his innocent prey, appealing first to her intellect, then to her emotions, eventually gaining control of her body. Judith was acquainted with the many novels of the day that showed how easy it was for an epistolary conversation to end tragically. Yet nothing could stop her. Her sense of obligation to John was too great to ignore. He had expanded her understanding of James Relly's theological beliefs. He had disposed of whatever lingering doubts about Universalism she harbored. Moreover, if it was true that in the soul "there be neither male nor female," then she and John could "with the strictest propriety mingle souls upon paper." She predicted that theirs would be a "wholly intellectual" friendship, one that transcended bodily difference and celebrated the spiritual unity of all humans.[15]

The little band of Rellyites became increasingly dependent upon John Murray after his first visit to Gloucester. In mid-December, the minister returned, helping his adherents form a little congregation. Its members met "like the primitive Christians," moving from house to house, worshipping as they pleased. They were delighted as more and more "respectable names" were added to the group's numbers. On occasion, John also preached at the First Parish Church, although by January of 1775, Chandler was warning his congregation against this preacher who attacked "the venerable authority of ancient interpretation." The "seeds of heresy," Chandler warned, "are sowing and sprouting up among us," and many souls in Gloucester were "being seduced into errours." Too sick to defend his parishioners from apostasy, Chandler begged ministers from neighboring churches to do the job for him. In the meantime, he closed his pulpit to Murray. Undeterred, John continued to preach "in a private house," ignoring those who began asking why he remained in Gloucester.[16]

Chandler died in March of 1775, and the Rellyites seized the moment, trying to install John Murray as their permanent pastor. New England's Congregational churches were susceptible to the influence of individuals whose economic and personal prestige, kinship connections, and piety gave them a special place in religious affairs. The Sargents were not totally fanciful if they assumed that they could use their authority to persuade other members of the congregation to embrace John Murray as their own. They no doubt imagined that as leading members of the community, they had the necessary legal, moral, and social standing to have their way. They would not have to rebel *against* the establishment. They would not have to place themselves outside the religious mainstream. They would simply modify the establishment to suit their own purposes.[17]

Unfortunately for them, they were unsuccessful. It did not take New England's religious leaders long to "nip in the Bud," the dangers of Universalism. In August, the congregation engaged the Rev. Eli Forbes as pastor for a trial period of six months. In April of 1776, three-quarters of the members of the First Parish Church voted to make Forbes their permanent minister. On the face of it he was an unobjectionable choice. Charming, erudite, and so traditional that many suspected him of Tory sympathies, he brought a certain gravitas to his position. But some church members were profoundly disappointed. Twenty-six "very reputable gentlemen"—ten of whom were active supporters of John Murray—drew up and signed a letter to Forbes, trying to persuade him to reject the First Church's offer. Winthrop Sargent's name was at the top of a list that included the signatures of Epes Sargent and John Stevens. They painted a bleak picture of Gloucester's economic prospects. Moreover, they darkly predicted that if Forbes came to Gloucester, parish harmony would "entirely be at an end." Forbes thanked the dissidents for their concerns, but he was not dissuaded.[18]

With Forbes's ordination, the dissidents were more disaffected than ever. John Murray, gratified by the adulation of such committed and well-placed supporters, had found a spiritual home, a place to which he could resort on occasion for comfort and affection, girding himself for yet another foray into America's religious wilderness. "Here," he wrote, "my God grants me rest from my toils; here I have a taste of heaven." Thus, although he continued to travel throughout the colonies, he appeared in Gloucester with some regularity, boarding with Winthrop Sargent whenever he was in town. Judith continued to write to John and was so pleased with his replies that when she received one of them she found herself "wishing to swallow the whole with a single glance." She would have been much happier had he decided to remain in Gloucester permanently, but John always reminded her that Universalists had no need of an ordained minister or a formal church organization. Like-minded believers could covenant with one another as the first Christians had done, praying together, and searching for the revealed word of God in scripture. They did not require special ceremonies, church discipline, or even sermons. If other protestant churches saw baptism and communion as central to their faith, and argued at length about the proper way to observe both rites, John thought such matters were merely symbolic and not especially important. It did not matter whether communicants sat, stood, or kneeled when they accepted the bread and wine, nor did it matter who offered these holy gifts. God, he insisted, looked at the "heart, more than the posture."[19]

Whenever their favorite minister was away, the Rellyites struggled along on their own, refusing to attend services at Eli Forbes's church, meeting instead at Winthrop Sargent's house. At those times, they were wrapped in gloom, as there was no one they could count on "to hold forth the word of life." Judith often visited her father's house in John's absence, sitting quietly in Murray's empty room, taking some comfort in her knowledge that he would eventually return to Gloucester where he belonged. On occasion, other Universalist ministers tended to the group's spiritual needs, but everyone agreed that these substitutes were inferior. Sermons of Puritan ministers were even worse. They were little more than long harangues, filled with condemnations of depravity and promises of damnation. Over a year after John first came to Gloucester, Judith claimed that in her mind his words remained as "luminous" as they had been on the day she first heard him.[20] The rest of his adherents agreed.

As Murray's supporters became more committed to Universalism, they gave up any pretense of attachment to the First Parish Church. When their pews remained empty week after week, their absence could not be ignored. To lose the moral and perhaps even the financial support of two of the parish's most respected families was unthinkable. Moreover, it was always possible that influential church members might lead other parishioners astray, creating a schism from which the beleaguered congregation could not recover. Finally, in February of 1777, the church demanded an explanation for the dissidents' behavior. Fifteen of the schismatics responded, saying only that their reasons were "of a religious nature which is wholly between God and our own souls." Jesus, they concluded "is appointed our Judge," and they had no obligation to explain or apologize for their continued absence from church. The First Parish Church insisted that this "contemptuous" response was unsatisfactory, and it continued to demand that the dissenters give some account of themselves. In March the church offered to assemble a council of ministers to act as mediator. Still, the "delinquent Brethren" refused either to appear before the church or to respond to its queries.[21]

Finally, the First Parish Church had enough. On October 16, the members repeated their call for a dialogue, although they suspected that the dissenters would not abandon their "unreasonable, unscriptural, unconstitutional Behavior." They deplored the very idea of a schism, and blamed the Universalists for their plight. You "Dishonor the Christian Name," they said, "offend god, and grieve his People." Even then, they waited almost a year before formally suspending the Universalists in September of 1778. They had hoped, they said in language designed to cause the genteel rebels to squirm, "that the rules of common decency and good Breeding (if no higher Motive) would at length have induced you to make some reply." But clearly that was not to be.[22]

In January of 1779, freed at last from their obligations to the Gloucester establishment, the apostates signed the "Articles of Association," formally creating the Independent Church of Christ in Gloucester, and asking John Murray to be their minister. In keeping with Universalist practice, they neither ordained

Murray nor tried to incorporate their church. Sixty-one people—thirty-one men and thirty women—became members. Judith and John Stevens were included in their number. A year later, they began holding services in their own meetinghouse, a simple building with none of the elegant accoutrements that graced the First Parish Church. Located on property donated by Daniel Sargent, the modest edifice boasted thirty box pews, thirteen of which belonged to various members of the Sargent family. Winthrop Sargent, Sr. assumed most of the financial responsibility for the church's early expenses.[23]

*   *   *

At first blush, it is difficult to understand why John Murray's views appealed to so many members of the Sargent and Stevens families. At its core, Universalism was a democratic faith that challenged the established order. Its ministers were uneducated, at least by standards that New England Congregationalists had come to expect of their religious leaders. While Universalism may not have been the "despised faith" that historian Ernest Cassara describes, neither was it a faith that should logically have found many converts among the colonial elite. In rural areas, to be sure, it attracted a cross section of society. But in the continent as a whole, it drew largely from members of a rising middle class. Impatient and ambitious, they saw themselves as outsiders whose hopes for a better life on this earth were frustrated by a society that seemed determined to deny their expectations. Even if Judith and the other members of her family were not troubled by the democratic implications of Universalism, they surely knew something of the economic hazards they might face as dissenters. When members of the Society of Friends had arrived in the town in the 1660s, they were not welcomed. By 1730, most had left and the rest had been absorbed into the dominant religion—the victims of systematic economic isolation. They had been subject to frivolous lawsuits; they could not secure loans; and townspeople had refused to trade with them. While the Sargents and the Stevenses may have hoped that their exalted position made them immune to such attacks, they could not be sure that this would be the case.[24]

And then, of course, there was simply the matter of inertia, the human tendency to cling to beliefs that were comfortable even when they were not totally satisfying. "I am not pleased with changes," Judith once told John Murray. "They constitute no part of my happiness, even circumstances themselves ineligible, become, by long habit, less painful and I do not wish for an alteration in my situation except I could be [certain?] that the change would decidedly add to my felicity." It could not have been easy for Judith to leave the known for the unknown, to make a deliberate decision to break away from old authority and old friends, to cut herself off from respectable society, and to incur the disdain of individuals whose esteem she had always taken for granted. New England was defined by its Puritan heritage; it was the central organizing principle around which most people in the region formed their identity. To reject that identity was to relinquish a satisfying relationship to the dominant culture and to challenge the vested interests of a community that did not tolerate or even understand dissent. This was a culture, moreover, that had the legal and economic means to maintain its dominance, even against adversaries as well-connected as the Sargents.[25]

Still, there was much about Universalism—at least as it was interpreted by John Murray—that was attractive to those individuals who took their Puritan beliefs seriously. The Calvinism of New England was a harsh and unforgiving faith. It told its adherents that they were tainted with the sin of Adam and Eve and that an all-powerful God had already decided who would be saved or damned. No one could earn salvation. It was God's free gift, a gift, moreover that only a few, fortunate but undeserving individuals would ever receive. "Damnation endless," Judith wrote of the Puritans, "is their darling theme." Fear, not hope, permeated the ethos of Puritanism, and Judith herself could not remember a time when she had not been almost incapacitated when she contemplated the afterlife.[26]

John Murray combined key elements of Calvinism with a dramatically different view of the scriptural promise of salvation. By building upon a familiar theological foundation and relying upon the scriptures as his only authority, he was able to persuade many of Gloucester's faithful to reexamine their beliefs. He denied neither original sin nor predestination. He agreed that all humans deserved damnation, and that Christ alone was the instrument of salvation. He embraced the Puritan insistence on congregational autonomy. Nor did he ever emulate the example of many Universalists who disavowed the doctrine of the Trinity.[27]

For all that, his views were profoundly revolutionary. Murray began with his view of God. His God was all powerful, but he was more accessible than the traditional Puritan deity. In his hands, the Supreme Being was a profoundly compassionate entity who could not bear to see his own creatures suffer. Thus, in "one grand act of amnesty," God had sent his son to die for the sins of all humanity. Indeed, John focused on Christ the redeemer, not God the judge. Christ, in his view, was God's material image. But in the beginning, Christ was simply spirit. More important, all humans were originally spiritual entities as well. And as spirit, before they took on a material form, all humans were one with each other, and one with Christ. They were of common blood and common spirit. As spirit, they were all perfect. It was only in their bodily manifestation that both humans and Christ were imbued with original sin. Once Christ assumed responsibility for the bodily frailty of all humans, that sin was washed away. For if Christ and human were one, Christ's atonement was—by definition—the atonement of humanity. Because Christ died for the sins of all, then it was only logical to assume that all humans were redeemed by his sacrifice. It made no sense to argue that God would redeem some undeserving sinners, while damning most others. All humans were the chosen people. Everyone was elect. This was true, not because humans had earned their salvation, not even because they believed in God's promise, but because of God's overpowering love for his own creation. John agreed with those who argued that all people would reap what they sowed. But, he insisted, it was not reasonable to claim that "when we had sowed in one field, we should reap in another." Human sins would be punished in this world, not in the hereafter. Those like the Puritans, who thought that only a precious few would escape divine punishment, were, he insisted, under "the influence of gloomy superstition and remorseless bigotry." Proud of their own secure position, they arrogantly relegated the rest of humankind to a dismal fate.[28]

Judith Stevens was overjoyed by the promise of Universalism. John arrived in Gloucester in 1774, at a time when her life was in turmoil. She had become a full member of the First Parish Church two years earlier, despite nagging doubts prompted at least in part by her reading of James Relly's sermons. Religion mattered to her. She once declared that she had a mind "strongly tinctured with enthusiasm." So long as she was torn between the faith of her birth and the optimistic message of Universalism, she would remain unhappy, vainly seeking the spiritual assurance she craved. In 1774, she had been married for nearly five years to a husband whose financial prospects were uncertain at best. If an essay she wrote in 1777 was autobiographical, her marriage was a disappointment in other ways, as well. The threads of hymen, she said, could easily become chains, due to the "*blasted expectations*" of both partners. Still childless, Judith had more time than she wanted to dwell on her anxieties. The possibility of war with England hovered ominously in the background, threatening to disrupt the lives of colonists everywhere. Universalism offered her security and a new sense of order. Relying on reason rather than on a disruptive "conversion experience," promising its adherents a sense of community, encouraging them to consider themselves an integral part of a loving universal family, it satisfied both her spiritual and social needs. Above all, it offered a profound sense of relief. The tears and gloom of the faithful disappeared overnight when she realized that salvation was the lot "of every intelligent being." She no longer needed to examine her soul in excruciating detail, searching for any sign of saving grace, fearing that she would discover proof that she did not enjoy God's mercy. It is probably no accident that when her aunt Catherine first told her about the Universalist message, Judith was ill. In the eighteenth century, every illness could mean death. And impending death was always a time for serious soul searching.[29]

For women raised in the Puritan faith, Universalism offered more than freedom from spiritual doubt. While early Universalists were less egalitarian when it came to gender issues than the Quakers were, they still gave more equality to women than the Puritans did. Granted, the messages Judith had received from the pulpit of the First Parish Church were decidedly mixed. In some ways, Puritans actually elevated women. While Catholics and Anglicans both embraced a hierarchical view of religion and society, at least in theory, Puritans did not. They believed that as spiritual equals, all humans were sinners and all enjoyed the same opportunity to be saved. In the end, the soul had no sex, and at least in the eyes of God, men and women were essentially the same. Both had an individual relationship with God that was unmediated by minister, bishop, or king. They both stood alone on judgment day to answer for their sins. When women endeavored to follow God's commandments, they did so as human beings, not as wives, mothers, or even women. In early Massachusetts, the belief in spiritual equality had some practical ramifications. Women and men had both assumed an active role in creating the Bay Colony's first congregations and devising the rules under which those congregations would operate. By 1720, membership in most Puritan churches was dominated by women. Because Congregational churches privileged the laity, ministers were increasingly obligated, whether they wanted to or not, to cater to the spiritual and emotional needs of their women parishioners.[30]

Puritanism also gave women some leverage in their families. In theory, although it viewed marriage as an unequal partnership, it nevertheless demanded a degree of reciprocity between husbands and wives. While it taught women to be submissive to their husbands, it also told them that their ultimate obligation was to God, not man. Their personal relationship to God gave women a sense of spiritual superiority and self-confidence that occasionally allowed them to challenge the dictates of "mere" men. Ordinarily, Puritans celebrated the virtues of obedient wives. But they also honored those extraordinary women who stood alone before the forces of evil, fighting for their faith and disobeying the orders of husbands, fathers, or community leaders who had strayed from the true religion. Finally, long before Benjamin Rush began praising the virtues of republican mothers and wives, Puritan women enjoyed some indirect influence on civil society. The line between religion and politics was fluid and indeterminate in colonial America, and support for the church was also support for the civil order.[31]

Still, no matter what Puritans may have said about spiritual equality, in the real world New England women operated in a society that saw social and gender inequality as natural. Puritanism was, as historian Jeanne Boydston points out, a "patriarchal belief system." Its adherents viewed women as identical to men in all essential—spiritual—ways. But, somewhat illogically, they also tended to link a woman's bodily characteristics to her moral character. In a very real sense, women's biology was their destiny. Indeed, Puritans—like all English people in the seventeenth century—viewed women as biological, not intellectual beings. They assumed that while men dominated, changed, and improved their environments, women, like the physical nature to which they were inextricably linked, simply existed. They did not change, nor did they seek autonomy, power, or status. Women were, in the final analysis, weaker, less rational versions of men. Passionate and susceptible to sexual temptation, and—as the story of Eve in the Garden of Eden surely proved—inherently seductive as well, they were dangerous to themselves and to others. Thus they needed a man to control them, for they had little ability to control themselves. A good woman, then, was demure, chaste, silent, and submissive.[32]

A good woman was also a wife. Indeed, with the loss of both the cult of Mary and the convents where single Catholic women went to pursue a separate and meaningful existence, marriage was the only truly desirable vocation for a Puritan woman. Autonomy was not a viable option. For her own as well as for society's sake, a woman needed to be in the household, subject to the discipline of her intellectually and morally superior husband. In her private relationship to her God, she could speak for herself. But in most other respects, Puritan women were subservient to men. In the family, fathers catechized their children and instructed them in abstruse matters of faith. How, after all, could children—whose reasonable nature was woefully underdeveloped—be curbed by women who were almost as susceptible to passion as they were? In the church, men were the dominant authorities. Sermons and the sacraments were the province of male ministers. By the eighteenth century, women church members were silenced. They were generally excluded from business meetings. They seldom gave public accounts of their conversion before the entire congregation. They had no formal influence on decisions to discipline recalcitrant or unruly parishioners. Not surprisingly, because men defined the terms under which they expected members of the congregation to operate, women tended to be disciplined more often than men. They were punished for absenting themselves from church services, for speaking out in inappropriate ways, and for loose morals or disorderly conduct. Judith needed only peruse the records of her own church to see how throughout the congregation's history women had been censured for "Railing and opprobrious speeches," a "bitter, uncharitable and Censorious spirit," or "unsuitable words and actions."[33]

Universalism did not eradicate women's inequality overnight. Men dominated the ministry in the new church, and the religion's emphasis on the fatherhood of God no doubt gave men an exalted sense of their own importance. While he was generally sympathetic to women's demands for better education, even John Murray remained a product of his time. He could not totally disabuse himself of traditional notions of women as the epitome of evil. "Wickedness," he told one of his acquaintants, "is called a Woman." It was woman "who made the nations drunk with the wine of fornication."[34]

Nevertheless, there were good reasons for the gender imbalance that characterized many early Universalist churches. If leaving the church of one's birth was a painful experience, it could also be liberating. It helped validate one's right to make a deliberate choice, to forge a new identity and a new purpose in life. It allowed women in particular, to challenge the status quo, to reject traditional, man-made law in favor of a higher, spiritual authority. While Judith disdained licentiousness, she embraced religious liberty. In God's hands, liberty was a "moral guide" that allowed his adherents to challenge arbitrary rule wherever they encountered it. A woman's loyalty to God preceded her loyalty to her government, her father, or even her husband. Judith soon learned that by submitting to God's will as she understood it, she could assert her individuality, rejecting the commands and ignoring the criticisms of ordinary mortals. Custom was, she discovered, a "tyrant," and blind conformity to custom could "never be esteemed a social Virtue." Religious custom was "like some rapid torrent" that carried all people before it, so eager were they for mere popular approval. Even when humans knew better, she observed, they were usually so weak that they simply shrank before the "sneer of the gay world, the supercilious smile of contempt." Her newfound religious beliefs made her determined, she said, in words that had a clear double meaning, to "call no *Man* master." Indeed, she insisted that when women faced the choice of obeying either their husbands or their God, they had no real choice at all. Women were not "mere machines" who had to bow meekly to every dictate of their husbands. In the end, their beliefs were "matters between God, and [their] consciences." Women had not only the right but the duty to ignore their husbands when the Lord called upon them to do so.[35]

The actual experience of rebelling against the religious status quo was of inestimable importance in giving Judith Stevens the courage to question conventional gender norms. Her understanding of Universalist theology was at least as important. Of course all Protestant religions privileged the spiritual over the physical, and the notion that the "soul has no sex" was central to the Christian, Renaissance, and neo-Platonist traditions. But the Universalist belief that all humans had originally been united spiritually with Christ led them to place special emphasis on the spiritual nature of humanity. The subsequent acquisition of a body, they insisted, in no way altered an individual's spiritual essence. The body was merely a shell, a temporary and decidedly inferior house for the soul. It was the eternal and genderless soul that mobilized and controlled the body. Mind or spirit—John Murray tended to conflate the two—was "the most, if not the only essential part of being." Universalists also argued that the spiritual unity of humans implied that all humans were tied together on the basis of equality. God's benevolence, said Judith, knew "no bounds" for all people, of whatever "sect, age, country or even sex" were part of "one grand, vast, collected family of human nature." Or, as John put it in a letter to a friend, all humans were at one with one another and with Christ. In essence, he said, there is neither "bond nor free, male nor female, but all is one in the mystical body of our Lord." In the end, all accidental—bodily—differences were "completely swallowed up."[36]

The implications for women of such a perspective were enormous. If spirit was the defining human characteristic, then women and men were not only equal, they were in every area that mattered identical. Universalism led Judith to transcend traditional definitions of feminine and masculine qualities, allowing her to move seamlessly between male and female worlds. It gave her a genderless ideal, even if it did not always offer her a genderless reality. Judith's denigration of the body allowed her readily to concede that men and women were biologically distinct. Men, she said, were generally physically stronger than women. But, as she explained in "The Sexes," strength was merely a bodily characteristic, an ephemeral animal quality. "Men," she maintained, "have from Nature, no other advantage over Women, than what is conferred by muscular strength." And because the essence of humans was spiritual and intellectual, not physical, such an advantage was inconsequential. Judith directly challenged conventional notions that women *were* body, that they could be defined in terms of their physical attachment to birthing, nurturing, and consuming, even as she insisted that in most cases the differences between men and women were irrelevant. At a time when men on both sides of the Atlantic were beginning to put a greater emphasis on physical differences, casting masculinity in bodily terms, emphasizing male health, strength, and virility as their own defining characteristics, Judith was doing everything she could to de-emphasize physical difference and to emphasize common humanity. Indeed, on occasion, she came close to claiming not simple equality for women, but actual superiority. In 1778, she transposed "several chapters" of the book of Isaiah into poetic form. In the margins, she scribbled a note, asking "are not the people often spoke of collectively, in the female character? Is not their Maker said to be their husband, and are they not called the bride, the Lamb's wife?" In *The Gleaner* she would be even more forthright, arguing that "the common Father of the universe manifests himself more readily to females than to males."[37]

*   *   *

Judith was both empowered and debilitated by her decision to embrace Universalism. Her mood swung wildly from ecstasy to despair and back again. But more and more often she celebrated her newfound ability to question the old verities, as she proclaimed that Universalism had given her the ability to "Fearless go forth, nor dread a censuring world." Not long after she first met John, she began her "Repository," a collection of poems and essays she wrote primarily for her own pleasure. Simultaneously, she threw out most of her childhood letters, declaring her independence from her former beliefs, implicitly declaring that she was a new person, both spiritually and intellectually. She grew gradually more confident in her ability to defend her religious views even to strangers. When people asked her to explain an abstruse theological point in writing, she usually offered a pro forma apology, admitting her own inadequacies and indicating that she would prefer to let John Murray answer for her. But then, if John was away from Gloucester, she responded with assurance.[38]

Increasingly comfortable expressing herself on paper, she was always reluctant to present her ideas in person. In the smallest, most informal gatherings she would feel her "face in a glow" when she tried to explain her religious perspective to skeptical acquaintances. "I am not calculated to figure in conversation," she confided to her brother. Whatever merit she had, she said, appears only when "the pen is in my fingers." In the spring of 1778, Judith was in Boston, visiting her uncle Daniel and his wife Mary. She received an invitation from a Mrs. Perkins, asking her to read aloud from one of John Murray's manuscripts. Judith reluctantly agreed after she received assurances that only three or four sympathetic women would be present on the occasion. When she entered the house on the day scheduled for the reading, she was stunned to see a room full of men and women. A "sudden tremor" seized her, as she realized that she would have to speak to a mixed audience composed almost entirely of strangers. Even William Payne, master of one of Boston's best grammar schools, was present.

Unfortunately "there was no receding," and so she took a deep breath and began. At first, her voice was almost inaudible, but after stumbling through two or three pages, she regained her composure. Then a "venerable grey headed Man" entered the room, and again she "absolutely trembled from head to foot." Somehow, she managed to complete her recitation, and her ordeal was over. To her surprise, the entire room "spontaneously" burst forth with praise. As a member of the First Parish Church she would never have been placed in such a position. Only her sense of duty to her newfound faith and her knowledge that she had the support of a small group of believers had enabled her to rise to the challenge.[39] While she never became comfortable speaking before large groups, she was secure in the knowledge that she could do so.

If Universalism empowered her, it also marginalized her. She, who always valued her reputation and had once been entirely confident of her position in Gloucester society, now found herself subject to "ridicule, to slander" after she withdrew from the First Parish Church. She never quite escaped her fear of "Censurers," especially if those critics were socially well placed. No matter how often she insisted that Universalism attracted the most "respectable" adherents, Judith knew that most of her former friends saw the religion as anything but reputable. When she tried to perform her Christian duty, comforting sick and dying friends in spiritual need, she was often turned away by those who disapproved of the message they knew she would bring. When she saw John being "assaulted" with questions from his many detractors, her "cheeks were alternately flushed and pale," and she could "scarcely breathe." Only his "judicious, calm responses" helped her regain her composure.[40]

Universalism separated Judith from old friends, forcing her to exist on the periphery of Gloucester's religious life. Like many proponents of an unpopular faith, she discovered that the bonds of intimacy she shared with other beleaguered worshippers were fiercer, more emotional than they would have been had she remained in the mainstream. This may explain in part the intensity of the relationship that she enjoyed almost immediately with John Murray. The two shared virtually everything. When one of her cousins sent her a letter meant for her eyes alone, Judith thought nothing of reading parts of it to John who was in the room when she received the missive. The two corresponded regularly whenever they were apart. Although Judith would never have admitted it, they behaved like so many young men and women did in the early stages of courtship. She sent John her unpolished "scribblings." On a visit to Newburyport in the summer of 1777, she began keeping a journal, "intended mainly for the amusement of the moment," a copy of which she sent to John for his edification and pleasure. Even her regular letters to him were elaborately ornate and poetic, filled with descriptions of "rich meadows," "verdant forests," "rural and even romantic" vistas, and "labyrinthian woods." In turn, John read and criticized her essays and poetry, and sent her samples of his own literary efforts. If Judith had always longed for a soul mate, she found him in John Murray.[41]

Their mutual admiration was obvious, and their friendship was a comfort to both. When John grew discouraged, convinced that he was making no headway in his efforts to spread the Universalist gospel, Judith urged him to persevere. "Thou Murray," she said, "are engaged in dispersing those . . . clouds, which presumptuously over shadow our intellectual sun." When he wondered what she really thought of him, she was astonished that he needed to ask. "I can never," she declared, "view you in a disadvantageous light." She was so well acquainted with his virtues that she simply could not see him "as an ordinary person." Yet she was comfortable enough in his presence that she dared criticize his conduct. Although she apologized profusely for her "bold and severe" comments, she nevertheless saw her censures as a token of their friendship.[42]

It is tempting to argue that as early as 1779, the friendship between John Murray and Judith Stevens bordered on the romantic. Some observers suspected as much, and John later admitted that he had fallen in love with Judith almost as soon as they met. It is not hard to understand why. She was handsome, intelligent, well read, and a stimulating conversationalist. The fact that a woman who traveled in such exalted circles clearly worshipped him must have been gratifying to a man who was vilified and shunned by respectable colonists everywhere. Judith, however, did not see their relationship in any but the most platonic terms. She was tied to Murray, she insisted, by the "chains or rather the silken bonds of friendship." Most of her early letters to John were not even personal. They were filled with theological questions and observations. Or they were stylized essays describing her travels through the New England countryside. Occasionally she teased John when she suspected him of contemplating a romantic liaison. And she encouraged him to remarry, even as she insisted that if her own husband were to die, she would not marry again. Women, she explained, were "exquisitely delicate" and could not bear the thought of having a "second Lord." Thus she thought that if she were widowed, she would "continue chaste" for the rest of her life.[43] If John was disappointed by her declaration, he prudently refrained from saying so.

*   *   *

Judith's conversion to Universalism opened some doors and closed others. It alienated her from members of her immediate community, even as it brought her into intellectual contact with a small but devout trans-Atlantic community of like-minded believers. Perhaps most important, it gave her the courage to rebel against conventional wisdom by fulfilling her desire to enter the world of letters as a published author. Throughout America's War for Independence, Judith continued to write reams of poetry and a few essays, none of which she considered putting into print. The personal letters she wrote were more likely to be read by strangers than any of her more polished endeavors. Her favorite correspondents were John Murray and her brother Winthrop, both of whom proudly shared her missives with their friends despite Judith's half-hearted attempts to discourage them from doing so. John, in particular, bragged about her talent to everyone he met, describing her work in such glowing terms that Judith begged him to be more circumspect. Her spontaneous and "insignificant time wasters," she insisted, were not meant for the "eyes of the world." Even if John shared her letters with no one, there was always the danger that one of them might go astray, winding up in critical hands. "Efforts acceptable to the bosom of friendship," she pointed out, "the cool eyes of a stranger will methodically examine." Still, when Winthrop asked for permission to share her letters with General Nathaniel Greene, she complied, pointing out that John Murray had already showed the general some of them anyway. He is, laughed Judith, "an old offender in this particular." While she claimed to be irritated by John's behavior, in fact she never stopped him. His indiscretions were not, she admitted, a capital offense, and thus she always gave him clemency, granting him her "imperial forgiveness" whenever he ignored her pleas.[44]

Even as she shared her private effusions with friends and family, Judith continued to protest—perhaps a bit too much—that she had no desire to "exhibit upon a public Theatre." Her pride, she claimed, was "to be unknown," and thus she insisted that she only sought the esteem of a "select Circle." At times when she composed her letters, searching her mind for incidents that would amuse or enlighten a particular reader, she saw herself as another Lady Mary Montagu, whose *Embassy Letters* had won her the literary recognition that Judith both craved and pretended to disdain. But whenever she made such daring and fantastic comparisons, she always retreated. If she dreamed of fame, she tried to keep those dreams firmly in check.[45]

No matter how much she insisted that the praises of her "humble attempts at poetry" that she received from her "very partial friends" were "the only laurels for which I present sigh," Judith relished the adulation her efforts garnered. The more compliments she received, the more she wanted—and the more she tried to hone her talents so that she would be worthy of the approbation that came her way. Applause, she said, was a "sweet incense to my soul," and it stimulated her to improve her talent. When she visited the Reverend Noah Parker in Portsmouth, she was flattered by the attention she received from the Universalist minister's friends. People "absolutely seem to regard me as a being of a superior order," Judith confessed. And when one of her new acquaintances asked her for more samples of her writing she blushed with pleasure. "Thus," she said, " I receive the deference due to talents which few believe I possess."[46]

The compliments of friends, relatives, and even strangers had their effect. By the summer of 1781, Judith was admitting more openly than ever that, if she had the "choice among the various honours which the present state of existence can confer," the "literary crown" would be her most prized possession. To be the "Author of some composition, either sprightly, grave, pathetic, or sublime," she said, was her highest ambition. A writer was a "Creator," who painted a picture of the world that conformed to her ideal vision. An author had authority over her readers, controlling their emotions, and influencing their political, religious, and moral views. Importantly, as an author she could exercise her power in the privacy of her own home, without calling attention to her female body or disrupting the gender conventions of the day. The only real impediment to her ambitions, she said, was her nagging fear that she had no talent. Judith increasingly wished that she could either "*lose the desire* or *acquire the ability to purchase applause.*" Still, she could not stop herself from sending her hastily written endeavors further and further afield, seeking candid criticism even as she dreaded the disdain with which she was sure that impartial readers would view her work.[47]

Some time during the fall or winter of 1781, Judith made what she always considered to be the most momentous decision of her life. It was, she recalled later, nothing less than crossing the Rubicon. It began innocently enough, with her decision to welcome her husband's nieces, Anna and Mary, into her home. Judith believed that she had an obligation to her "orphans," giving them "such ideas as I judge the young mind gradually opening to maturity ought to receive." She did not want her "flowers" to "remain wild and uncultivated." Above all, it was her duty to explain the message of universal salvation to the girls. For Judith, nothing was more natural than putting her religious beliefs on paper, organizing her views, making them as clear as possible. Thus, almost by accident she devised what she began to call a "catechism," designed to teach children the rudiments of the Universalist faith. When her mother saw the finished project, she was so impressed that she urged Judith to show it to Noah Parker. Recognizing its merit, the minister begged her to allow him to publish it. At first, Judith resisted. The manuscript, she pointed out, contained nothing original. Every one of its tenets came from her understanding of John Murray's sermons. Nor was she sure that it was good enough to be shared with anyone outside her own immediate circle. But Parker was insistent. He enlisted other Universalists in his cause, accusing Judith of "ingratitude" to a God who had obviously endowed her with talent for a purpose. At last, grudgingly, she capitulated, demanding as her only concession that the catechism be published without the name of its "adventurous Author."[48]

Judith then began to prepare her piece for the public eye. It was a daunting process, bringing to the surface her own debilitating sense of inadequacy. Repeatedly she threatened to abandon the project altogether, destroying her catechism and destroying as well "every other production of my aspiring pen." Back and forth she went, sometimes saying that reason forbade her from continuing, sometimes acknowledging that her "passion" to publish drove her forward. She tried to convince herself that pride and ambition were laudable emotions—even for women—for they made their possessors strive to "*earn* and to *cherish* the esteem of the worthy." She agreed with those who were beginning to argue that enlightened self-interest, even "*self love*," stimulated ambitious people to seek excellence just as a desire for adulation led them to moral behavior. Thus every individual effort to merit praise, while it might be grounded in selfishness, would ultimately redound to the public benefit. Still, Judith wished that she could distinguish more surely between "a noble emulation and an overweening conceit." She knew that many people viewed writers with suspicion, convinced that they sought to attain distinction, to be part of an exclusive class of intellectuals whose very existence threatened republican notions of an egalitarian society. And always, hovering in the back of her mind, was her fear that by entering the discursive public sphere, partaking in a debate over religious belief, influencing—however tangentially—the behavior and beliefs of total strangers, she was transgressing gender boundaries. As she made the final corrections to her manuscript, Judith continued to hope that John Murray would allow himself to be viewed as the author of the piece.[49]

In the end, the *Catechism* was, as Judith had always insisted it would be, a faithful rendition of the basic tenets of John Murray's understanding of Universalism. It was suffused with scriptural proofs. It proclaimed a belief in original sin and in universal salvation. It denied the need for adult baptism and argued that the Bible "entirely excludes Infant-Baptism." The Lord's Supper, it maintained, had only symbolic importance and was designed primarily to remind participants of the common humanity of all people. Using an analogy of which John Murray was particularly fond, it pointed out that the Eucharist bread was composed of many grains, the wine of many grapes. But it was impossible, once the elements were combined, to distinguish one grain or one grape from another. In the same way were "collected the scattered Individuals of Humanity, forming a complete Man; and constituting the comprehensive Character of our Lord." Hence it was clear that all humans were "descended from the same Stock, and redeemed by the same Emanuel."[50]

Despite its derivative nature, the *Catechism* reflected something of its author's own priorities. It was an obvious rendition of Judith's developing pedagogical beliefs. The book followed a conventional pattern when it took the form of a series of questions and answers about the faith between a teacher and a child. But while Judith's teacher was clearly an authority figure, the relationship between preceptor and pupil was unusually egalitarian. The teacher spoke to the fictive student in words of affection, complimenting her "Tear of Sensibility," and expressing pleasure at the "Blush of Comprehension" on her cheek. The child, in return, praised the teacher's "indulgent Goodness," which gave her the confidence to proceed with her lessons. Most innovative was Judith's decision to invert the traditional order of her *Catechism*, allowing the pupil to question the teacher instead of the other way around. She knew this was not customary. But it was realistic. Children, she explained, were naturally curious. Moreover, by letting the pupils lead the discussion, she was giving them a measure of power. Perhaps, she mused, she should have called her book a "Dialogue" rather than a "Catechism."[51]

The *Catechism* was published in June of 1782. John Stevens, "ever indulgent" and obviously proud of his wife, purchased one hundred copies, planning to distribute them to those Gloucester inhabitants who would appreciate them. The Norwich, Connecticut, newspaper printed the preface verbatim in July. Three months later, Judith enclosed a copy in a letter to Winthrop. She did so with trepidation. She had recently been surprised to learn that although he had once been sympathetic to Universalism, he no longer approved of either John Murray or his faith. Thus she was sure that her brother would not look kindly on her *Catechism*. It was the first time the two had ever clashed about anything so fundamental as religious belief. Still, what was done, was done and there was no way to "keep this little transaction" from him.[52]

Judith's worries about the reaction to her *Catechism* were not solely directed at her brother. As soon as her manuscript was out of her hands, she began to wonder what had possessed her to consent to its publication. "As I reflect upon my temerity," she wrote, "a blush often suffuses my chest." She took comfort knowing that her name appeared nowhere on the manuscript. But in the same breath she confessed that if the publication was good enough to bring her the fame for which she had an "insatiable thirst," she would consent to "expose [herself] to the public eye."[53]

In fact, whether she admitted it or not, Judith had already done just that.

She could not possibly have believed that her identity would remain anonymous. All of Gloucester knew who wrote the *Catechism*. She sent copies of it to her own friends, conceding that her decision to publish was "arrogant." She insisted that she had made sure that her name would be concealed. Yet she advised potential readers to read the apology she had included in her preface.[54] That very apology revealed much more than it hid. By confessing in the very first sentence that the "anonymous" creator of the *Catechism* was a woman, she must have known that at least among Universalists this admission identified her as the author.

Why, if she wanted to hide her identity, did she feel compelled to announce that she was a woman? She had tried to persuade John Murray to take responsibility for her effort. She knew that not one sentence in the *Catechism* was inconsistent with Murray's theology. Had she said nothing about her sex, most people would probably have assumed that Murray was the book's author. In the following years, when she published her essays and poetry, Judith often assumed a male persona, hiding rather than revealing her sexual identity. In this, her first published work, she drew attention to her sex, even as she recognized that whenever a woman "steps without the Line in which Custom hath circumscribed her, she naturally becomes an Object of Speculation." She had, of course, virtually invited such speculation, giving critics plenty of ammunition with which to pillory her and her already suspect sect. Universalism's detractors always sought to marginalize John Murray's faith, associating it with the poor, the illiterate, blacks, and especially women. Eighteenth-century Americans tended to view women as weak, irrational, emotional, and "disorderly," implying that such attributes led almost inevitably to lack of bodily control and even to sexual promiscuity. If disorder and femininity were more or less synonymous, then an attack on the lawless and immoral Universalists always carried with it the heavy baggage of sexual impropriety. The church itself was situated outside the mainstream because of its feminine nature.[55]

Judith had no need to reveal her sexual identity to a potentially hostile world, and every reason not to do so. Yet this is exactly what she did, as her preface boldly defended her decision to publish the *Catechism* in language that left little to the imagination. In 1779, when she wrote "The Sexes" she had argued in abstract terms that women and men were intellectual equals. Two years later, in her *Catechism*, she put the argument to the test. Judith conceded that a good woman was a modest woman, and thus that when she presented her work to the public she was inviting accusations of "Arrogance, Heresy, Licentiousness, etc. etc." But she argued that women could define themselves by more than their modesty. One attribute of the "peculiarly feminine," Judith proclaimed, was "a sacred Attention to those interests that are crowned with Immortality." While the body, that "transient Tenement" reminded everyone of the "Distinction of Male, and Female," in the afterlife the "merely sexual" would no longer exist. Even as she conceded that bodily inferiority incapacitated women in some regards, Judith asserted that in spiritual matters, women were at least equal to men and might actually have the advantage. Women had both the duty and the ability to discuss—even in public—the spiritual truths that they managed to discover.[56]

Judith was not content to claim mere equality for herself, however. She argued that her position as a surrogate mother "in some Sort impelled the arduous Attempt." As she listened to the theological questions of her young charges, she explained, and understood the obligation she had—both as a Christian and as a mother—to prepare her children "to act their Parts, upon the inferior Stage of the Globe," she had no other choice but to acquaint them with the precepts of true religion. She was acting as an obedient servant of the Lord when she first devised her *Catechism*. To offer her insights to other parents was nothing more than her Christian duty. She could, she admitted, have copied her *Catechism* repeatedly, giving it separately to each person who asked for her advice. But that would have been a ridiculous waste of everyone's time. To publish her work was merely to share it with those who needed it most. Judith insisted that she had no interest in controversy. She would not, she said, "enter the lists as a Disputant." Having published her *Catechism*, she intended to return to the privacy of her own family. She would leave the public arena to those—presumably men—who were better prepared than she was to take on the task of defending the Universalist faith.[57]

If Judith constructed herself as a Christian woman who longed only to obey God's commandments, in fact she always hoped that her *Catechism* would bring her a measure of renown. Her poem, "Upon printing my little catechism—1782," which she did not publish, reveals her obvious—and conflicted—desire for literary fame.

Yes there are heights—I ought not to ascend,
My arrogance I never can defend,
Giddy with praise I have too high aspir'd,
My soul by false ambition hath been fir'd—
With modest blushes I should have confest,
The private walks of life for me are best.

Comparing herself to Icarus, whose hubris led to his own demise, she was sure the "Critic's eye" would demolish her arrogant hopes for glory. Her lack of originality, her grammatical errors, and her assumption that a woman had a right to impart her "*female lessons*" to others would all be condemned. Instead of praise, she feared that she would be ridiculed and denounced as an audacious failure.[58]

But still, she persevered. She had, indeed, crossed the Rubicon. As so many friends continued to insist that she was truly talented, she admitted more and more often that if she ever earned her laurels, she hoped to do so as a writer.[59] She had entered the world of print at the service of her God. In the years to come, she would continue to write for public venues with a more personal and ultimately more secular end in mind.

Chapter 3
Independence

From the perspective of Universalism's detractors, John Murray could not have arrived in America at a worse time. Even as Gloucester's religious establishment was trying to avoid a split in the First Parish Church, the town was facing the very real possibility that the colonies would soon declare their independence from England. The divisions in the First Parish Church would have occurred with or without the colonists' quarrel with the mother country, but they surely contributed to Gloucester's anxiety as America edged toward independence. Add to that the downturn in the seaport's economic fortunes, and the town's residents had every reason to feel vulnerable.[1] Order and stability seemed to be under siege from all sides.

There is little evidence that Judith paid much attention to the series of events leading up to the American Revolution. In 1774, she mentioned the destruction of the tea in Boston Harbor, noting that the political world was in "ferment." Reasonable people, she remarked, were right to be worried about the consequences of so rash an act. The following year she praised her father's staunch refusal to supply a British schooner resting in Gloucester's harbor. At the same time, however, she thought many townsmen were behaving impetuously when they fired on the schooner, leaving the seaport open to retribution. As relations between England and America deteriorated, Judith remained ambivalent, admitting that she was a "perfect Chameleon." "Every individual," she sighed, "has the forming of my political creed." When she heard one man brag that British regulars were no match for American volunteers, she solemnly nodded. But when another said just the opposite, she was sure that the colonial army would be crushed by the military might of the redcoats. Generally, at least until the war actually began, she vaguely hoped for rapprochement.[2] Beyond that she wrote very little.

In the end, Judith supported independence, but her criticism of the English government was always muted. Like so many other members of New England's merchant elite, she looked to England as the source of her own identity. While white colonists in New York and Pennsylvania could trace their roots to all parts of Europe, most Gloucester inhabitants were like the Sargents whose ancestors had drawn their "first breath upon the chalky shores of Albion." Judith had been raised to believe that England meant "everything great, everything good," and she could not help but view the coming of the war with sadness. Even in the midst of hostilities, she distinguished between the English parliament—whose actions she deplored—and the English people, with whom she felt a real kinship. She was convinced that most ordinary English men and women were—like John Murray—as opposed to Parliament's tyranny as she was. Describing England as "the home of my soul," she looked forward to a time when the two countries would once again enjoy the blessings of a close relationship.[3]

Likely as not, Judith was emotionally untouched by most of the intricate details of the quarrels over taxation and the rights of Englishmen that absorbed so many of her compatriots throughout the 1760s and 1770s. Just married, worried about her husband's financial position, plagued by doubts about the state of her soul, she may well have seen the oratorical flourishes of those countrymen who decried England's attempts to tax the colonies without representation as irrelevant to her own concerns. As a woman, she was not directly represented in the Massachusetts legislature, much less in Parliament. If men were beginning to value independence, Judith knew that she would remain dependent no matter who ruled America. Moreover, most women—especially young ones—lived lives that were far removed from the political storms that many men found so compelling in these years. When women heard words such as "virtue" or "corruption," biblical rather than classical images sprang most readily to mind.[4] Unless imperial issues directly affected them, their families, or at least their friends, they often had a hard time imagining that those issues were of much importance to them. Some women may have felt "Nationly" when they participated in spinning bees designed to support the occasional nonimportation movement, but others saw such activities, not as a way to politicize household tasks, but as a means of upholding traditional notions of Christian charity and communal piety.[5]

Indeed, as countless historians have pointed out, American women saw the Revolution as essentially Janus-faced. What it promised on one hand, it denied on the other. At times the war seemed to offer them new opportunities, blurring the line between public and private, men and women, challenging, however briefly, traditional notions of gender roles. The rhetoric of the Revolution, with its assault on monarchy, hierarchy, and deference, and its emphasis on the notion of universal, natural rights led women such as Judith Stevens to reconsider—or really to consider for the first time—their rights and obligations in a world where independence and equality were becoming the ideal. As a result, the language of liberty began to come to Judith's lips almost unbidden, even if it often appeared in ways that had few overtly political overtones. Moreover, colonial leaders may have unwittingly magnified women's sense of their own importance when they urged them to purchase colonial goods or to disdain English luxuries. Whenever they begged women to support the resistance, male patriots implicitly acknowledged that women might have their own political views. Ideally, wives deferred to their husbands' opinions, but in fact no one could take women for granted. At the same time, however, it was clear from the start that the very men who celebrated independence and equality in the political arena had no intention of altering the patriarchal and deferential arrangements that shaped their own families. As Judith's observations in "The Sexes" indicate, the war itself deepened and magnified gender differences, leading to an ever more rigid definition of manliness and femininity. And while some women were empowered by their experiences during the war, as they managed to keep their households solvent in their husbands' absence, countless others failed miserably. Even those who succeeded did not always relish their new role. They tended to see themselves as "deputy husbands" who were merely standing in for their menfolk until life returned to its natural rhythms. Despite the radical possibilities inherent in the revolutionary experience, the war reinforced traditional values at least as much as it challenged the old order. For most women, the war represented a burden, not an opportunity.[6]

Despite the generalizations historians make about the meaning of the American Revolution for women, it remains true that even elite women experienced the war in a variety of ways. Each woman had her own story to tell. Abigail Adams, for instance, became the quintessential and reluctant deputy husband. She was responsible for her family's welfare throughout the war years. She struggled in vain to manage the farm and the recalcitrant tenants who operated it. She was only slightly more successful as she tried to avoid the worst effects of an inflated paper currency. But she achieved considerable satisfaction from her experiments as a merchant. She began by selling the goods that John sent her from France. In time she began to take the initiative, requesting supplies she knew would sell, even conducting business directly with French entrepreneur Joseph Guardoqui. She also bought property, sometimes not bothering to seek her husband's advice or approval. Her sacrifices, however modest, were her way of contributing to the American victory. Still, she saw her wartime activities as aberrant, something that she would gladly relinquish once John returned home.[7]

Abigail's good friend Mercy Otis Warren was more direct—and more cerebral—in her efforts to promote independence. Not as successful at managing her family's finances as Abigail, less willing to tolerate her husband's long absences from home, Mercy supported independence with her pen. Known in some circles as the "patriots' muse," she continued to publish throughout the war, and also began her three-volume *History of the American Revolution*. If Abigail's view of the world survived the social changes that accompanied the Revolution, Mercy was shaken by the war's aftermath. The decline in deference and in her husband's political and economic fortunes were all of the same piece in her mind, and by war's end she was convinced that civic virtue was the casualty of a society whose republican values were disappearing.[8]

Although revolutionary ideology may have given Judith the language with which to demand equality for women, the war, itself was a largely negative event in her life. In this, her experience was similar to that of her counterparts. Abigail was an able merchant; Mercy's fame as a poet and playwright grew. Yet despite their achievements, Abigail and Mercy, like Judith, saw the war as an unwelcome disruption, and all three longed for a resumption of the secure and predictable ways of a more uneventful time.

*   *   *

In the spring of 1775 Judith was not aware of any positive implications the Revolution might have for her. She only knew that imperial issues and the threat of war had begun to intrude upon the lives of men and women she loved. While most Gloucester inhabitants grew steadily unhappy with English policy in the mid-1770s, it was becoming obvious to everyone that Judith's uncle Epes was not so disenchanted. In March of 1775, the Gloucester Town Meeting formally questioned Epes's loyalties, sending five men to "waite upon Epes Sargent Esqu and others suspected to be Tories" and asking them to "attend this Meeting at the Adjournment to give the Town Satisfaction." Epes's response echoed his reaction to the First Parish Church's queries about his religious beliefs. While other suspect inhabitants of the town rushed to appear before the elders, insisting that they "highly approved" of the Continental Congress and its defense of American liberties, Epes tersely replied that "his Business would detain him" from giving an account of his views. On March 27, the town meeting decreed that no one in Gloucester should "have any Commerce with any suspected to be Tories nor those connected with them & their Abettors till they give published Satisfaction that they have quite changed their Sentiments." It singled out Epes Sargent as an egregious offender. No longer able to conduct his business, Epes—who had been a Gloucester selectman for the last fourteen years—left town for the comparative anonymity of Boston.[9]

Judith saw her uncle Epes as simply another victim of the new ideological tyranny that pervaded the colonies in the wake of America's independence movement. How, she wondered, could any "friend of genuine Liberty . . . ever wish to countenance or abridge the freedom of thinking, or of rational discussion?" To curb anyone's thought or expression was to her mind "sacrilegious." Putting her views to verse, she asked:

Why forge for liberty the Despots chain,
Why the free range of intellect restrain?[10]

Thus she was prepared to defend her uncle from any aspersion. In June of 1775, she and Esther were traveling to Boston when they encountered a stranger who engaged them in polite conversation. When he discovered that the sisters were from Gloucester, their temporary companion broached the name of Epes Sargent, vilifying him as a Tory. Judith cleverly used gender conventions as a weapon in her uncle's defense. As a mere woman, she demurred, I do not "constitute myself a judge of the contest so unhappily subsisting." As for the terms "Whig and Tory," she continued, "I am free to own I do not understand them." She did know one thing. She refused to judge Epes by his political views. So long as her uncle exhibited an exemplary character and took no active part against the colonies, Judith did not believe he should be persecuted for "mere sentiment, mere opinion."[11]

Epes was by no means the only person dear to Judith Stevens to suffer at the hands of narrow-minded patriots. In part because John Murray was a native of England, even more because he was a Universalist, many in Gloucester questioned the minister's loyalties. John was often greeted with stones and curses as he walked the streets of town. In early 1775, professing to believe that he was an English spy and a papist to boot, the town meeting tried to arrest him for vagrancy. Winthrop Sargent quickly foiled the attempt, giving John enough farmland near town to qualify him as a freeholder. Momentarily thwarted, John's enemies instituted a whispering campaign. "Old slanders were resuscitated," Judith noted, "and new accusations brought forward; tales which had been repeatedly confuted, were new garbed and sent abroad." Inevitably, the steady assault stimulated some people to action. A crowd gathered outside the Sargents' house threatening to remove the minister from town by force if he refused to leave voluntarily. Only the intervention of one of the First Parish Church's elders saved John Murray—and perhaps Winthrop Sargent as well—from physical harm at the hands of an angry mob. Gloucester's treatment of John Murray reaffirmed Judith's belief that "the people" could be as repressive as any government.

Tellingly, she saw attacks on Loyalists as the immoderate product of "passion." As suspicions polluted the atmosphere, as small-minded men sought to "fetter the free born Mind," she predicted that America would pay a heavy price for its bigotry.[12]

John's difficulties did not abate, even after May of 1775 when Nathaniel Greene made the Universalist minister the chaplain of the Rhode Island brigade. Once some of the other army chaplains got wind of Murray's appointment, they begged George Washington to remove him. Instead, the general offered John a commission as chaplain of three of Rhode Island's Continental regiments. Had he accepted it, John would have received a salary and been retired at half pay at war's end. He would, Judith later wrote wistfully, "have commanded his own carriage and servants." But the unworldly John Murray refused the commission, preferring to serve the patriot cause as a simple volunteer.[13]

John did not remain in the Continental army for long. Ill health forced him to resign after only eight months. Determined to prove that his resignation did not indicate doubts about independence, he returned to Gloucester and helped raise money, food, and provisions for the town's poor. Even that gesture did not mollify his enemies. In February of 1777, members of the Committee of Public Safety demanded Murray's appearance before them to account for his political views. Their timing was no accident. Although both John Stevens and Winthrop Sargent, Sr., were members of the committee, neither was in town. Moreover, the First Parish Church had just presented its opening salvo to the Rellyan dissidents. Judith was not alone in her assumption that the secular committee was doing the work of Gloucester's religious establishment, hoping to discredit John Murray and return the town's Universalists to the fold. True, the members insisted that they distrusted the minister because he came from England. They also claimed, no doubt thinking of Epes Sargent, that he associated with some of America's most virulent enemies. But they spent most of their time attacking John's religious beliefs. He preached throughout the colonies "without authority," they said, and his theology was detrimental to the morals of the country. When John protested, saying that "I was not apprized that I was cited before a spiritual court," the committee was unmoved. At the end of a rigorous examination, the members ordered him to leave town by March 1. They would not be held responsible for his safety after that date, they said, as they darkly hinted that if he did not comply, he might become the target of another mob. The town meeting quickly affirmed its support of the committee's order, but John simply ignored it and no one enforced the directive.[14]

Judith was dismayed by Gloucester's intolerance. Taken in conjunction with the town's persecution of Epes and the First Parish Church's refusal to let the Universalists worship in peace, the committee's harassment of John Murray served as a powerful reminder that political and religious issues were easily intermingled in the eighteenth century. It was surely no coincidence that the Committee of Public Safety singled out Epes Sargent and John Murray as objects of its opprobrium. John had actually demonstrated support for the patriot cause. Epes was a Tory, but he was neither a spy nor a member of the king's army, nor was he the only man in town who opposed independence. When Judith began to declare her commitment to freedom of expression, she did so as a religious dissenter as well as a supporter of independence. When she condemned the "tyrannical dominion of prejudice," she never differentiated between religious and secular tyranny.[15]

The coming of war seemed to change everything for Judith, and not for the better. She had once rejoiced that Gloucester provided a refuge from the military drums and bugles that disturbed metropolitan Boston throughout the 1760s. By 1775, even her own sleepy little village was filled with young men parading through the streets, dreaming of heroic military victories, and waving their "instruments of death" in the air. Everywhere, polite discourse was marred by the "rude tumultuous clamours" of a populace that talked of nothing but war. Judith's friends assured her that reconciliation between England and its colonies remained possible, but after the battles of Lexington and Concord, she knew that chances for rapprochement were remote. While Winthrop could scarcely wait to prove his valor on the battlefield, his sister worried about the effects that the "winds of passion" would have on her tranquil existence. It was the encroachment of public affairs on their private lives that led some women to become increasingly political throughout the war. But more often than not they simply resented an unwelcome intrusion that they were powerless to avoid.[16]

Judith could not help but complain about the burdens that the coming of hostilities brought to her everyday life. There were, above all, those uninvited guests who began to find their way to the Stevens abode with maddening regularity. Whenever a privateer captured an enemy vessel near Gloucester Harbor, both passengers and crew were stranded. Ordinary sailors did not expect much hospitality, but genteel officers and passengers were a different story. When refugees showed up unannounced at her doorstep, Judith was often hard-pressed to offer them even the simplest provisions. Oblivious to his wife's distress, John brought home a "constant succession of company." Once Judith returned from Boston to find a house full of strangers—two men, a woman, four children, and two black servants—awaiting her. They had been sailing from Jamaica to England when their vessel had been captured and they were unceremoniously dumped at the nearest port. Judith was often the reluctant hostess of any number of "Jack Tars" who were temporarily stranded in Gloucester, and she, who was "not fond of a croud," was at the beck and call of men—gentlemen to be sure, but still very rough around the edges. She tried to laugh when these "Lords of Creation" stomped into the house, laughing boisterously, demanding her attention. "What a contrast the present winter, to the preceding," she observed in January of 1776. "Need I say," she added wryly, "how greatly I deplore the change."[17]

*   *   *

America did not declare its independence until July of 1776, but Judith had been complaining for a year about the effects of the "present unnatural contest" on her life. "War of any description is particularly oppressive to the inhabitants seated upon the margin of the ocean," she once observed. Thus it is hardly remarkable that the commencement of hostilities had damaged Gloucester's economy in general and the Stevenses' already uncertain prospects in particular. Three-fourths of the town's inhabitants were either fishermen or sailors. Many of them depended directly or indirectly on trade with England for their livelihood. Even those who traded closer to home suffered, as all oceangoing commerce became ever more precarious as the war dragged on. In times past, merchants had been able to call on the English fleet to protect them from pirates and hostile privateers. Now that same fleet was in enemy hands. In 1775, when Captain George Dawson sailed His Majesty's ship into Gloucester, he left without the provisions he demanded, but he did so only after capturing at least fifteen colonial vessels—one of which belonged to Winthrop Sargent.[18] Independence had not been officially embraced, and already deteriorating relationships between England and America were proving costly.

Those who had once been secure were in a precarious position, while the poor were "involved in every species of suffering." Judith and John Stevens were not among the ranks of the poverty stricken. The calling cards Judith preserved—themselves a marker of her elite status—indicate that she enjoyed a full social life in the very years when the colonies were inching toward war. She had a personal maid. She entertained friends with a tea party on the cape. Nevertheless, she had her share of problems. She and John did not have a house or even a horse and chaise they could call their own. In the fall of 1775, her mother and Fitz William fled Gloucester for Chebacco Parish, in Ipswich, a farming community that promised them safety from enemy attack. Others, including Esther, followed in short order. "Friend after friend forsakes this once social spot," Judith sighed. Gloucester was fast becoming a "deserted Village." Everywhere she looked, she saw evidence of the town's transformation. "Are those," she asked plaintively, "the Mansions once so famed for hospitality—where sweet peace, and plenty, went hand in hand?" Judith missed her mother and sister and was as worried as they were that Gloucester might become an enemy target. She always kept an eye on the horizon, watching anxiously for any sign of the approaching enemy. While she hoped that the British fleet would not enter the harbor intent upon destroying the town, she had no faith that the enemy would spare even "so little, so remote a place." At one point, John thought he had secured a tiny house for his wife near Chebacco. It was, observed Judith, a "dreary spot," and the tiny house was suitable only as a temporary retreat.[19] But at least it was relatively safe.

For whatever reason—perhaps because his fortunes were at a particularly low ebb—John failed in his attempts to move even to this unsuitable haven. "We are at a loss," Judith told her sister, "to know what step is next to be taken." They moved briefly to an isolated, inland village, where they planned to occupy a house belonging to a "Mr. C," a friend of Judith's father. Again, the abode was not really desirable, but it did give them some place to store their furniture, which, Judith said, they were "under an absolute necessity" of moving. Their new landlord promised to fix it up enough to make it at least habitable, but in the end Judith returned to Gloucester. By then, the initial panic that led so many to flee the coast seemed like an overreaction. Moreover, Judith thought that if she remained in Gloucester she could help her father, who had boarded up his own house and needed a place to stay whenever he was in town.[20] Many people continued to escape the port city throughout the war, but Judith was not one of them.

Eventually the Stevenses secured "elegant lodgings" in Gloucester but that hardly improved their circumstances. A merchant's daughter, Judith was accustomed to the vagaries associated with trade. Everyone involved in commerce faced peaks and valleys in peace as well as in war. But there was little doubt that war made merchant activity especially risky. In addition to the usual hazards, whenever he left port John now faced the real possibility that he would be captured by the British. That actually happened in the fall of 1779 and while the English crew treated John "with the utmost humanity" on this occasion, Judith knew he might not always be so fortunate. Despite the danger and uncertainty he faced, John's spirits never abated and he was always confident that his next voyage would bring him success. As a result, he seldom remained in Gloucester for long. Although Judith never had to worry about John's death on the field of battle, in many ways her experience replicated the concerns other women had when their husbands marched off to war, leaving their wives behind to deal with the day-to-day struggle to make ends meet.[21]

If Judith worried about her husband, her father, and John Murray, only Murray joined the war effort, and his military career was short-lived. Her oldest brother, whose military service endured throughout the war, gave her many more anxious moments. Judith had seen little of Winthrop since his graduation from Harvard. After he left Cambridge, he had traveled in Europe, broadening his horizons and enjoying a brief respite from all responsibility. Judith envied his freedom, but she also took it for granted. Like everyone else, she assumed that he would eventually do the obvious, becoming a Gloucester merchant alongside his father and uncles. Instead, he returned home in 1775, eager to join the fight for independence. A year later, he accepted a commission as captain-lieutenant in the Continental army. By spring, he had already seen action in Boston and at the Battle of Long Island. Never was Judith so acutely conscious of the differences between men and women as she was when she compared her own prospects with Winthrop's military career. She was proud of her patriot brother. But she could not help but regret his decision. She always feared that he would become a casualty of war. Whenever she witnessed the "wretchedness" of soldiers returning from battle, their hollow cheeks, their emaciated bodies, their ragged clothing all reminded her of the conditions that her own brother endured. Winthrop gently reproved her for her relentless inquiries about his health, his condition, and the state of the American war effort, implying that she was meddling in matters that did not concern her. Judith always defended herself. "I am not," she insisted indignantly, "actuated in my solicitude respecting your movements, by mere female curiosity. To so poor an influence I would rise abundantly superior."[22] Still, her questions did not cease.

Winthrop came home only rarely during the war years; even then, his visits were all too brief. He seldom wrote, and when he did, his letters were often delayed or even lost for good. Living "at a distance from the scene of action," Judith was dependent on secondhand accounts for information from the front lines, and such news was often woefully inaccurate. In 1777, for instance, she was devastated by "premature intelligence" that her brother had died at the Battle of Brandywine, on "plains purple with human gore." When she eventually received a letter from Winthrop dated after the battle had taken place, she was relieved. Yet she always knew that good news was only a respite. She could do nothing to alleviate her foreboding, and so she turned to her pen for comfort, writing reams of poetry to distract herself at least momentarily from the suspense that characterized those "gloomy days" when she awaited word from the her brother.[23]

*   *   *

Her concerns about Winthrop's physical welfare, although serious, were only a small part of the problem. When Judith wrote to her brother, telling him that his own nephew was a virtual stranger to him, and that the young boy spoke of his uncle as though he was "perhaps on the moon," she revealed more than she may have realized about the gendered construction of war. She soon discovered that men and women experienced the Revolutionary War in profoundly divergent ways. As an officer in the Continental army, Winthrop was, in fact, living in a different psychological as well as geographical place than the one she occupied. If war invited challenges to old ways, it also reinforced traditional gender roles. Indeed, as men became immersed in the deadly military game, unleashing their aggressions and repressing their softer inclinations, it seemed more essential than ever for women to remain at home, nurturing the values of the high-minded and orderly civilization for which men were supposedly fighting.[24]

The language of classical "republicanism," which shaped the political views of many elite Americans during the fight for independence, essentially excluded women and their experiences from public discourse, even as it highlighted the importance of military service for men who wanted to prove their masculinity.[25] It emphasized propertied independence, self-reliance, physical strength, and bravery—all framed as manly characteristics, as "virtue." It valued those individuals who eschewed luxury in favor of frugality. It celebrated reason and deprecated unbridled passion. Above all, it glorified those men who behaved as selfless citizens, sacrificing private interest for the public good. There was, of course, no greater sacrifice than the willingness to risk one's life on the battlefield.

Indeed, the characteristics that most people associated with women were precisely those attributes that republicanism framed as especially problematic. If virtue was a man, fortune was a lady. And fortune was fickle and unpredictable. Like fortune, women were passionate, not reasonable. Nor were they able to contain their desire for sexual pleasure or creature comforts. Even Judith conceded that some women's craving for luxury recognized no bounds. In 1778, her aunt became the proud owner of a fashionable gown. Virtually every belle in Boston found some pretext to visit Mary Sargent's home just to touch the dress. One even sent her servant out in a ferocious snowstorm with instructions to borrow it for a day or two so that she could see the wondrous garment for herself. Judith laughed at these luxury-loving women, even as she prayed for her own deliverance from "the bondage of Folly and of Fashion." But she worried that women, more than men, found the material sacrifices they made throughout the war, extremely burdensome. Even more troublesome, she knew that conventional wisdom decreed that women were simply too weak in body and too timid in spirit to join the fight for liberty. Women might be men's equals in their ability to practice private, Christian virtue. They were men's inferiors when public virtue was needed. Married women could not even own property. Consequently, independence, the cornerstone upon which republican virtue was based, could never be theirs.[26]

But it was the *experience* of war, not simply the ideology that informed people's understanding, that had such a gendering effect on the Revolutionary generation. The colonists had been engaged in near perpetual warfare for fifty years when the fight for independence began. As a result, notions of masculinity had already been shaped with military attributes in mind. Not only did war reinforce gender conventions, bringing sexual differences into sharp relief, it offered men certain benefits in return for their service. For Winthrop Sargent, war was an opportunity as well as a sacrifice. Indeed, he saw the two as inextricably intertwined. Officers in the Continental army may have willingly risked their lives for the cause of independence, but they entered military life with hopes for their own prospects. They saw war as a proving ground that would allow them to exhibit valor, to perform heroic deeds, to test their moral and physical courage. And they assumed that if they proved worthy, they would be rewarded. Judith knew that when Winthrop joined the army, he had embarked upon a "Career of fame." He was an "intrepid Soldier," who would earn "the plaudit of every heart" and who would leave the army as "an ornament to his family, to his Country."[27]

Winthrop Sargent did not, as his nephew imagined, live "on the moon." But, as Judith pointed out with increasing frequency, he occupied a world that was far removed from her own. Even before the war, men and women had lived different lives and had markedly different expectations for their futures. Men tended to travel more, to set loftier goals for themselves. To some extent they also hoped to improve their communities, to leave the world a better place than it had been when they entered it. Women seemed more attuned to "natural" rhythms, looking to marriage and childbirth to mark life's important passages, assuming that their daughters would replicate their own experiences in due time. If, like Judith, they longed to widen their horizons, they knew—as she did—that their fantasies of ranging freely over land and sea were "Fairy scenes—Charmingly illusive prospects." The Revolutionary War disrupted the markers with which most women measured their lives. It also highlighted the differences between men's and women's expectations. Judith was quick to note the distinctions. In 1777, Winthrop was in Philadelphia, frustrated because his orders kept him away from his regiment, engaged in meaningless and "inglorious" activity. Judith understood his impatience but was just as happy that her brother was momentarily out of danger. "Thus are our pursuits varied," she observed. While the soldier longs for honor on the battlefield, the wife aches for her husband's return and the mother prays for her son's safety. For her part, she added somberly, she simply wanted to be left to heaven.[28]

Judith barely disguised her resentment when she compared her own life to her brother's. Before the war, Winthrop's knowledge of the world—like her own—had come largely from books. Now he was able to put his abstract beliefs to the test and to profit from his experiences. He was meeting new people and visiting new places. He had, she told him, the opportunity "to ripen your knowledge beyond your years." Even if the war did not give him fame or fortune, it would make him a better person. As an officer, he would learn to demand respect from his inferiors, making the transition from military leader to head of his own household a smooth one. He would also treasure the deep friendships he forged in an environment where like-minded men joined in common cause as they fought to protect their own and their country's precious liberty. As he traveled throughout the land, working side by side with men from all regions and walks of life, he would transcend his parochialism. True, his sacrifices were real. The war was disruptive. It came at the very time when he would ordinarily have been launching his career, forming a family, and establishing ties to his community. But while serving his country forced him to put his plans on hold, Judith had no doubt that if he survived Winthrop would reap the benefits of military service many times over. Whenever she reminded herself that her brother was "actively engaged in struggling for the sacred rights of Mankind," Judith chafed at her own mundane existence. How, she wondered, could she interest him in a single word emanating from her "female pen"? She was "Encircled by one Eternal sameness." Gloucester was just a parochial village. "The manners of its inhabitants," she complained, "render the picture of one day, the delineation of a Century. Revolutions are hardly to be expected among us, we take our sense of public matters from our superiors and we can scarcely boast an idea of our own."[29]

War did more than offer men and women starkly different experiences. From the beginning, Judith almost intuitively recognized that the practice of war was distinctly at odds with her own inclination to blur the lines that separated men and women, masculine and feminine. Instead, it paved the way for an understanding of gender that viewed the sexes as complementary opposites. If Universalism was moving Judith toward an emphasis on the common humanity of men and women, a privileging of mind over body, a virtual denial of the importance of body in defining meaningful human traits, war reminded her that in some cases and in some ways, body was all important. It was, as she recognized in "The Sexes," their physical strength that made men the logical protectors of vulnerable women and children. When government was weak, and anarchy threatened, only the strong had much chance of surviving. Thus, women, who had not voted for independence, and who were not at all certain that an American victory would improve their lives, could also be casualties of war.[30]

*   *   *

Somewhat ironically, a war that divided men from women in some ways brought them together in others. This was a conflict where the physical distance between battlefield and home front was erased, where military might could intrude upon the peaceful domestic sphere and where women, too, faced danger and made sacrifices for their country. While men marched off to fight, determined to protect the women and children at home, they were in fact leaving their dependents more vulnerable than ever. Enemy soldiers could march into town in their absence, confiscate supplies from frightened residents, and destroy the property of rebel sympathizers with abandon. When they faced hostile forces, most women felt helpless, not courageous or empowered.

Judith had a taste of her own vulnerability one evening in September of 1779, when word spread through Gloucester that four enemy men-of-war were approaching the harbor. As the alarm rang out, a few able-bodied men rushed to defend the town while women and children of every age and position tried to quell their panic as they hurriedly grabbed a few possessions before escaping to the interior. Everyone had heard stories of seaport towns that had been burned to the ground simply for the "amusement of an inhuman enemy" and so they expected the worst. John, as usual, was sailing the high seas, and Judith's only servant immediately took flight with no thought of helping her mistress. Judith had no choice but to flee empty-handed. She ran desperately through the woods, encountering an occasional woman staggering under the weight of what few precious items she had picked up as she went out the door. The further Judith ran, the more frightened she became. When a number of "uncivilized barbarians" accosted her with "language the most brutal," she was convinced that she was about to suffer the fate of many unprotected women about whose dreadful experiences she had heard so often. Fortunately, the men "confined their abuse to words," and she reached the house of a friend without incident. Only the following morning did Gloucester's relieved but embarrassed inhabitants discover that their panic had been unnecessary. The English "men-of-war" turned out to be American coasters. For the moment the town was safe. But Judith's sense of vulnerability never abated. She felt a bit foolish on this occasion, but so long as the war lasted, she would never feel totally secure, even in her own home. She may well have had this experience in mind when she wrote "The Sexes." Her need to be protected by strong and able men, was real. Women were, indeed, the "timid Sex," and it was men who "bravely prepared" to fight the enemy.[31]

Most of the time, of course, Judith's wartime experiences were not so dramatic. Like other women, she made any number of quiet sacrifices, sacrifices that underscored her powerlessness, in large part because no one even noticed them. Women endured isolation and loneliness much more than they suffered mind-numbing fear. They made do with less food and worthless money. In port towns such as Gloucester, women spent one monotonous day after another, trudging from shop to shop, vainly hoping to find the barest necessities. And even when those necessities were available, they were often unaffordable, thanks, as Judith remarked cynically, to "the blessed effects of our paper currency." Because seaports were attuned to the market and relied on currency more than the hinterland did, they were particularly hard hit by wartime disruptions. True, the wives of merchants and sailors were accustomed to fending for themselves when their men were away. But this was different. With their economy in shambles and their towns potential targets of the enemy, they endured privations and fears that they had never experienced. Yet, as burdensome as they were, women's contributions to the war effort were almost invariably mundane, almost passive, bringing them no glory and little thanks.[32]

For the most part, Judith's life throughout the Revolutionary War was highly conventional. She did nothing to challenge the perception that she was a proper and dignified young matron, a dutiful helpmate, and a respectable member of her family. But if she was no camp follower and could not envision herself serving as a nurse to soldiers she did not know, she did serve as a dutiful caregiver to members of her own family. Her parents were getting old. Her mother, in particular, suffered from severe rheumatoid arthritis and seldom left home.[33] As the oldest daughter, Judith found it logical to assume the primary responsibility for both parents. She was young and healthy. Unlike Esther, she was childless. When John was away—which was often the case—he did not require her attentions. So she was free to look after her family's needs, a task she embraced without question. Still, if she took a certain pride in her ministrations, she saw her efforts as a duty, not an opportunity.

Only once, in 1780, were Judith's nursing skills needed as a direct result of war. Just two days before Christmas, she received the news she had been both expecting and dreading. Winthrop had fallen ill and was languishing at an inn in Medfield, Massachusetts, some twenty miles outside Boston. Judith and John Stevens were in the capital city visiting Mary and Daniel, but they immediately changed their plans. Ignoring a blinding snowstorm, the two set out for Medfield on Christmas Eve. They met Winthrop, Sr. in Salem, who assured them that his son's condition was not as bad as they had feared. Still, Winthrop was asking for his sister. Somewhat relieved, John went on to Gloucester while Judith rode on with her father, she in a chaise, he on horseback. "Riding at the risk of [their] lives," they struggled through hail, rain, wind, and snow that were so ferocious her father could barely stay in his saddle. Exhausted, wet, and cold, they finally arrived at the inn. Judith entered a "mean room," where Winthrop languished on a "yet meaner bed." It was the first time in two years that she had seen her brother. She scarcely recognized him. He was pale and emaciated. Even his voice had completely changed. Judith pretended to be cheerful, assuring her brother she would make him well and take him home.[34]

Fortunately, Winthrop's condition was not life threatening. By December 26, his fever had broken and the doctor assured Judith that her patient was on the road to recovery. Still, she decided to remain at the inn, despite what she viewed as deplorable conditions, until Winthrop was strong enough to move. Unlike most denizens of public houses, she had her own room. But at night, she was so cold that she could barely hold her pen to write. Her bed was narrow and hard and she claimed she could not turn over without falling on the floor. The partitions dividing one room from another were wafer thin, and the revelry from the tavern kept her awake until two in the morning. She had left Boston so abruptly that she had forgotten to take a change of clothes with her. Which, she wryly observed, was just as well. Fine clothing would have been wasted in such a rude establishment. Moreover, Judith was too busy nursing her brother, cheering him up and trying to keep friends from calling unannounced to think much about her own appearance. When Winthrop's fellow officers dropped by, brimming with good cheer as they returned to camp from the holidays, eagerly sharing stories of their "domestic happiness," her brother grew steadily more depressed.[35]

Judith and Winthrop left for Boston on January 2. There she belatedly celebrated the arrival of another new year with her aunt and uncle, as well as with her husband who arrived in town bearing a parcel of letters from John Murray. The entire party finally set out for Gloucester on the seventh. Their progress was slow, as the "invalid" could not ride long without resting. But that hardly mattered. Winthrop had survived. Unfortunately, he abandoned Gloucester in April, going first to Boston where he remained for almost a month before heading back to "hostile fields of death and carnage." Judith was more than a little hurt when her brother left home with such undisguised eagerness. While she readily acknowledged that her native village offered scant amusement to a single young man, she thought he should be a little more considerate of his mother's feelings. And, no doubt because of his recent illness, she was more concerned than ever about the dangers awaiting him upon his return to duty. Almost as soon as Winthrop left for the front, Judith wrote to him with an urgency that had been lacking in her previous letters. She begged him not to let his "youthful passions" lead him to "hazard *unnecessarily*" his life. "*Rashness*," she lectured, "is not courage."[36]

Winthrop's brush with mortality was something of a turning point for Judith. Admittedly, her account of the ordeal smacked of the melodramatic. It is no doubt revealing that, despite her proclaimed fear for his welfare, she took time to write a poem about her "brother dangerously ill abroad" before she set out for Medfield. She wrote another poem on Christmas day, and continued to scribble away so long as she remained at the inn. Nor were her own or her brother's accommodations at the inn as primitive as she painted them. They both had private rooms—however inadequate—and Winthrop had a servant. Judith herself admitted somewhat shamefacedly that her sacrifices were nothing compared to those suffered by women who had lost loved ones in the war. Still, the incident was a sharp reminder of the dangers of military life. As word from the front became more discouraging, as the Continental army suffered defeat after defeat, as officers were almost daily resigning and unpaid soldiers on the Pennsylvania line mutinied, Judith became convinced that Winthrop had done enough for his country. She conceded that men like her brother were true heroes and "disinterested Patriots" to whom the country owed more than it would ever know.[37] She had always harbored doubts about Winthrop's chosen career. By the spring of 1781, she thought that the time had come for him to retire.

Instead, once his convalescence ended, Winthrop returned to the front. Judith was desolate. Granted, she had not laid eyes on her brother for months, but just knowing that he was in the capital city, out of danger and living with relatives, had been a blessing. His decision to resume active duty, she said, left a "mournful void" in her life. It also meant that her fears returned. Indeed her anxiety was worse than ever. In her waking hours, she imagined her brother lying wounded and mutilated on the field of battle. At night, her sleep was disturbed by dreams that Winthrop had died, "a victim to the mad pride of that Phantom, *Military Glory*." It did not matter that he saw little action after 1781. It was the uncertainty that was so painful. Judith acknowledged that her vivid imagination was her own worst enemy. Because Winthrop's letters home always traveled at an excruciatingly slow pace, she was susceptible to every rumor. "Suspense," she proclaimed, "prepares its tortures."[38]

Judith's unhappiness grew ever more pronounced, her criticisms of the conflict becoming ever more pointed. She attacked on a variety of fronts. Increasingly, she begged her brother simply to resign his position and return to civilian life. He was still frail, and an army camp was no place to mend a broken body. If he clung to his resolve, Judith predicted, he might never recover. But while he occasionally conceded a longing for "domestic sweets" and was disgusted by the way his own countrymen treated the Continental army, Winthrop was determined to "tread the ensanguined paths of death."[39]

Judith eagerly seized upon his every reservation. "Tell me," she demanded, "is it not true that there are times when the *post* of *honour* is a *private station*?" Certainly, after so many years of service, Winthrop had earned the right to return to his books and dreams and to start earning a living for himself. Increasingly, Judith painted mental pictures of her brother no longer clad in "steel and armed with the instruments of death." In her mind's eye she saw him strolling leisurely through a "verdant pasture, stocked with bleating sheep." She only prayed that war had not already so hardened him that he was unsuited for the life of the "humane Philosopher, and the gentle shepherd."[40]

If Winthrop would not quit his post, Judith hoped he would at least perform his duties as humanely as possible. Warfare, she thought, was "barbarous," and it posed a real danger to any soldier's virtue and piety. Private morality, she argued, was the foundation for public virtue. She could not imagine that the rules that guided human relationships in the home or among friends were qualitatively different from the precepts that governed political or military affairs. She knew, for example, that her brother was a strict taskmaster who refused to tolerate the tiniest infraction of his orders. His fellow officers applauded when he ordered the "damned flogging" of a soldier who temporarily deserted his post. But Judith sympathized with "those unhappy beings doomed to suffer the severity of military discipline." Surely, she pleaded, "justice must recoil, when the poor impotent being is led forth to a punishment, sometimes insupportable for crimes which his superior commits with impunity." By what convoluted logic, she wondered, did Winthrop justify his contention that soldiers should obey orders without question, surrendering the very liberty for which they were risking their lives? Did he truly believe that compassion was "altogether confined to the female bosom"? She knew that women were "form'd for tenderness and love, / While man or sinks below, or soars above." Yet she continued to argue that the line dividing female and male attributes could be blurred, that women might exhibit courage and men might be compassionate—even in the midst of war. Surely tenderness was not incompatible with the military character. "The brave are always humane," she insisted, and the ideal soldier possessed "every gentler Virtue."[41]

Judith had no choice but to live with a war that challenged the very spiritual and moral precepts upon which she based her life. The experience of war exacerbated tensions between men and women, setting the manly ideals of bravery, obedience, and spartan self-sacrifice against the values that women such as Judith Stevens held dear. Honesty, charity, benevolence, tenderness, and the willingness to forgive and forget minor transgressions were not, her brother haughtily informed her, useful attributes for an officer. This was something many women could never understand. They viewed war differently than men did, tending to evaluate the military experience from a traditional, usually Christian perspective. A battle won in ways that undercut notions of personal piety or conventional morality was worse than meaningless to women who wanted their men to behave as Christian soldiers.[42]

Judith was no Deborah Sampson, who thrust herself physically into the war effort, joining men like her brother on fields of gore. While history told her that women *could* lead armies courageously and well, this was never a role she sought for herself. As she had acknowledged in "The Sexes," war reminded women that they relied on men for protection. Thus she continued to characterize her own wartime activities in traditional terms. She saw herself as a disinterested observer, whose job it was to urge America's soldiers to observe the religious strictures that made life worth living. By serving as a self-proclaimed—if private—critic of the war, she tried to turn her inferior womanly status into an asset. As an outsider, a mere spectator, as someone who had no direct stake in defending her country's military strategy, Judith felt that she was in a better position than her brother to perceive the moral weaknesses that permeated the American war effort. When she asked men to cultivate their tender nature, thus narrowing the mental and spiritual gap between the sexes that the war itself was widening, she hoped to feminize military life and to soften the men who fought so valiantly in the name of independence.[43]

Unfortunately, the outsider status that Judith thought gave her a certain perspective, put her at a distinct disadvantage. Winthrop disdainfully dismissed her remarks, claiming that "mere women" did not understand war. Such was the case in the fall of 1779 when Judith described a naval battle that ended in England's defeat. The former colonists had achieved their victory by flying the Union Jack, deceiving the "brave English sailors" who fell unwittingly into their trap. Judith could not rejoice in an American triumph that was won so deceptively. She longed for the time when wars were fought by honorable men who scorned disguises and trickery. "I sigh," she wrote John Murray, "for the superior heroism of those ancient times, and I regret that I was not born in the days of other years." In war, she noted sadly, "deceit is deemed a virtue," and he "who can most successfully dissemble is the most renowned Chief." But, as always when she wrote to her brother questioning her country's military tactics, she hesitated, aware that he would be offended by her criticisms and disdain her "womanish fears." She also acknowledged that she wandered from her "proper sphere" whenever she did so.[44] Still, the vague feeling of unease that had haunted her from the beginning of the war, sharpened with each passing year, and she could not always refrain from expressing her concerns.

Judith worried about the effect the war might have on her brother's character. She was also disturbed by the carnage that was the inevitable byproduct of every battle in which soldiers like him engaged. Nowhere, it seemed, could she escape the "rude effects of savage war." A trip to Boston led her through Charleston, decimated by enemy attack and now a desolate shell of its former self. Even a simple family outing to a pond near Gloucester provided no relief. As she roamed the hills with the other women in the party, she knew that the men were fishing for their dinner, "pursuing their murderous purpose" without a thought to the disruption their presence meant in an otherwise peaceful universe. As she observed the efforts to kill the innocent fish, she was reminded of her own countrymen, who were even then filling bloody fields with even more dying bodies.[45]

Where Winthrop celebrated a hard-won victory and moved on, Judith focused on war's human consequences. She never stopped believing that her brother would be rewarded for his heroic sacrifices, but she began to doubt that the prize was worth the cost. Increasingly, she pictured her brother's laurel wreath "steep'd in blood." She asked poetically;

For what can trophied wreaths supply
To drown the desolating cry
That o'er empurple'd fields afar
Proclaims the dread destructive pow'r of war.

Ultimately it did not matter whether soldiers fought for or against independence. All casualties were deplorable. They all created "desolate widows," "destitute orphans," and bereft parents who were innocent victims of war no matter which side of the Atlantic they called home. She conceded that "A state of war, is a natural state to Man," but she began to think that bravery was not a virtue. Rather, it was a "sickness" that led to the destruction of all she cherished.[46]

Never was Judith more critical of the war effort than she was in 1781 when she learned of Benedict Arnold's defection to the British. Like many Americans, she was horrified by George Washington's determination to hang Major John André, whose capture had led to the discovery of Arnold's plot to turn West Point over to the enemy. She had little sympathy for Arnold. She did not question his right to switch sides, for she thought that a distinguishing characteristic of all humans was the "freedom of the intellect." But if Arnold had truly changed his mind, then he should have resigned his commission in the Continental army. Had he openly declared his views he would have merited praise from all but the most prejudiced American. Instead, he had dishonorably betrayed the trust of his countrymen. André, on the other hand, was a gentleman. He had an "elegant mind." Tender and brave, he accepted his fate with dignity. And of course he had deceived no one. He remained from beginning to end, loyal to his sovereign. Yet Washington was determined to treat André with dishonor, refusing the major's request to be shot as a combatant, and hanging him as a spy. Judith was outraged, declaring that Washington was little more than a common murderer "violently seizing a life, which he might have spared." The general's decision, she thought, must have been the temporary consequence of "vindictive rage," a passion to which no just and reasonable man should ever succumb. It was the only time Judith criticized George Washington in writing. But even though it was a singular moment, her anger was genuine, an expression of the fury she experienced whenever she saw the stern hand of military justice at work.[47]

So long as Judith cast doubt on the war effort from a moral perspective she was imitating the example of countless American women who viewed public affairs through the lens of private morality. On occasion, she tread on more strictly political territory. Her observations on specific government policies, however moralistically she framed them, situated her precariously close to the political arena, an arena that proper women entered with trepidation. Even John Murray, who thought Judith could do no wrong, expressed bewilderment at her fascination with political issues. At times, he chided, she sounded like a "female politician," an unnatural species he characterized as an "amphibious animal." Judith acknowledged that her interest was unusual—but she resented John's snide comments.[48] Evidently, a woman could not discuss political issues with the most sympathetic friends or in the bosom of her own family without having her femininity called into question.

Judith was especially uncomfortable with Congress's decision to forge an alliance with France. Each June, Gloucester took part in continent-wide observances marking the birthday of the French dauphin. Towns throughout the land fired cannons, rang bells, beat drums, sported fleurs-de-lis, and displayed fireworks, reminding Judith of a war she had come to hate and of an association she never learned to trust. Such celebrations smacked too much of an unhealthy dependence on the French king. What, she wondered, had happened to "Republican dignity"? Why should America cultivate *any* monarch? Louis was surely no

"Columbian Prince," and she thought that the adulation with which many of her countrymen viewed him came uncomfortably close to "deification." Her own father and grandfather had fought the French. As a young girl she had watched when the First Parish Church became the venue for raising militiamen who marched against the enemy during the French and Indian War. And as the daughter and wife of men whose livelihood depended in large measure upon the cod fishery, she knew that Gallic control of the Newfoundland coast was a barrier to Gloucester's prosperity. True, it was not fair to condemn France "in gross." Not all Frenchmen were alike, and some of them may truly have begun to reject their country's tyrannical past. Still, Judith always remained skeptical of claims that the former enemy had miraculously become an unwavering supporter of American liberty. She was especially taken aback by the attitude of New England's clergy. England had always been the "bulwark of the protestant Religion"; yet Puritan ministers everywhere praised the Catholic Louis XVI as "great and good," as concerned "only with the *liberties of Mankind.*" Judith remained convinced that there was never a "more despotic government than the government of France." When one acquaintance tried to convince her that France's support of independence was truly disinterested while England was determined to turn Americans into slaves, Judith threw up her hands in horror, convinced that the war was "inverting the natural order of things." She wondered at those fickle persons who could so easily praise King George and condemn Louis one moment, and take the opposite position the next. She seized every opportunity to point out the illiberal character of America's newfound friends, maintaining that France spoke with "the tongue of bigotry," not—as the country's misguided defenders proclaimed—the language of freedom.[49]

On occasion, Judith found herself regretting the series of events that had turned England into the enemy, even venturing to question the goal of independence itself. There was, she opined, something prideful and unnatural about such an aim. Society was by its very nature interdependent. All individuals occupied links "in the great chain of being." To destroy the chain, and to proclaim both equality and independence, seemed to challenge God's orderly creation. Most colonists likened the relationship between England and its former colonies to the ties that bound a cruel stepmother to her children, a stepmother who refused to let her progeny grow up and claim the independence that was rightfully theirs. Judith never rejected that familial analogy, but she preferred a different one. The "contending parties," she wrote Winthrop, were of the "same stock." They were brothers and sisters whose parents wept to see their "children engaged in acts of hostility." She recalled that the world's first family had been torn apart when one brother had killed the other. The current conflict, she thought, was simply "the fatal contagion of the first shocking fratricide" that had been handed down from one generation to the next. If the war was little more than humanity's most recent reenactment of the results of original sin, it was hardly surprising that a "tear of regret" ran down Judith's cheek whenever she contemplated the war.[50]

While many Americans despised England and hoped the entire country would be destroyed at the hands of the colonies, Judith was prone to defend the English people—if not the English government. A "few overbearing Men" in Parliament were responsible for the division between England and the colonies, she claimed. Ordinary Englishmen were as unhappy with their government's tyranny as most Americans were. Moreover, even Parliament was not solely to blame for the current state of affairs. If "the parent state was arbitrary and precipitate," she observed, "neither were the offspring totally devoid of blame." All humans were sinners, and the very best Americans were no exception. Judith looked fondly upon the days of her youth, when harmony had existed between England and its colonies, when America's confidence in Great Britain was at its zenith, and when "we acknowledged the sons and daughters of Albion as our nursing Fathers, and our nursing Mothers." Those were the days not only of peace but of prosperity, when colonial warehouses were stocked with goods, and British vessels vigilantly protected American ships from enemy attack. That being the case, Judith looked forward to war's end when reason would triumph and "ties of blood" would again exert their influence. Nothing could change the fact that England and America shared a common religion, tradition, and language. "Mutual interest" alone dictated that the two countries would one day enjoy a "social union," even if their political ties had been broken.[51]

As if to prepare the way for rapprochement, Judith began noting every act of British kindness, even as she deplored the reflexive antipathy with which her own countrymen regarded the "very name of an Englishman." She was especially taken by the tale she heard of the kindness of a British admiral toward a once wealthy American widow and her daughter who had fallen on hard times. The woman never complained of her own misfortune, but she was desolate because she could not "educate her only child in a manner becoming her sex, and that rank in society, to which her birth has given her claim." When the admiral heard of the plight of this "daughter of misfortune," he stepped in to help, even though the woman, supported the rebellion. Together—he by offering financial assistance, she by accepting his offer—the two triumphed over prejudice, forgetting their differences and concentrating on their similarities as compassionate human beings—human beings, Judith hardly needed to add, who shared a common social status, and who were therefore connected by bonds of sympathy.[52]

In 1781, Judith wrote an essay and a poem that were thinly disguised expositions of her basic political beliefs. She chose as her subject Charles I, "the Martyred Prince of England." By refusing to publish the pieces, and by ostensibly writing on a historical topic rather than current affairs, she was partially shielding herself from accusations that she was inappropriately transcending gender boundaries.[53] Just as she evaluated America's military practices in terms of personal morality, so she judged Charles in his private capacity—as a man, not a king. She portrayed him as a decent individual who had been betrayed by the ambitious sycophants around him. Charles was a benevolent patriarch who adored his wife and children and had a "paternal care for the lives of his subjects." Far from being rigid or unbending, he was willing to alter his views if duty and reason demanded it. He was, above all, the victim of an "ill judged education." His own father had implanted "erroneous principles" in his mind at so early an age that it was virtually impossible for him to abandon his kingly claims. Even so, she insisted, Charles had never sought to expand his prerogative but had simply tried to preserve the powers he believed he enjoyed by right and to pass them down unaltered to his beloved son.

Judith conceded that Charles was the wrong king for the time. He never understood that public values had changed considerably since his father's day, that Englishmen were jealous of their liberties and were determined to defend their rights no matter what the cost. But while she might question the king's judgment, she thought it unfair to blame him for the "faults of his instructors" or for the advice of Archbishop Laud and his minions who took advantage of the monarch's innocence for their own nefarious purposes. The true villain of the piece was neither Charles nor Laud, however. It was Oliver Cromwell, the manipulator of the mob whose "treacherous wiles"destroyed a decent man. It was the Puritans, not Charles I, who were unbending and censorious, who unleashed passions unchecked by reason or sympathy, thus destroying the order of a once proud country.

Judith's analysis would surely have raised eyebrows if she had published it in 1781. It was not merely a comment on the value of early education, although it surely was that. Nor was it simply an attack on Puritan intolerance, although it was that as well. It was a defense of all traditional order. Had her musings found their way to the public arena, readers may well have suspected that Judith was defending England and its current king, and condemning American radicals—men like the members of Gloucester's Committee of Public Safety who had treated Epes Sargent and John Murray so shabbily—who were as intolerant and despotic as any monarch. At the very least, she was challenging the conventional wisdom that good ends might justify bad means. If liberty was an appropriate end, the process of achieving that liberty had to be moral, merciful, and rational as well. Judith never actually opposed American independence, but she often found herself questioning the means by which her countrymen—including her own brother—sought to achieve that desirable end.

Judith's view of the war echoed the doubts of many women. Her own nascent literary ambitions, as well as her belief in the intellectual ability of "the sex," both exacerbated and amplified her concerns. America's fight for independence underscored women's physical weakness, highlighting gender differences. War required bodily strength and physical courage, not the assets associated with the mind. It reminded Judith of her own vulnerability, as it forced her to rely on strong men to protect her weak female body from harm. Above all, it denied her a meaningful way to serve her nation. In a world where force, not persuasion, would decide America's fate, her own talents seemed irrelevant.[54]

The American Revolution directly touched the lives of many Americans at one time or another. Still, most people viewed the war through a gendered lens, even if they actually experienced the conflict in ways that made such a perspective more fictional than real. Women as well as men sacrificed to ensure the American victory. Women as well as men were open to enemy attack. Indeed, women's vulnerability led many of them to pay more attention to politics than they had ever done before, as they began to realize that public decisions affected their own private world, that their safety and their quality of life would be determined by the kind of nation in which they lived. But while Judith claimed to be willing to give her life for the cause of liberty, she recognized that it was the sacrifices of soldiers that would be honored at war's end.

The "massy spear" was not meant for women to bear.
Nor was the sword invented for her side,
Her hand could not the deathful weapon guide;
She ne'er assum'd the habiliment of war
The mail assay'd, or sought the bounding core.

If women and men were intellectual equals, men had the advantage where brute strength was needed. Consequently, some argued that those who were weak enough to require physical protection owed obedience to their protectors. Women, in essence, were expected to relinquish some of their rights in exchange for security. No matter how valiantly men strove to hide it, power relations were ultimately based on force—and this was never truer than it was during war. Moreover, throughout the war the infant nation itself took on feminine qualities, as many writers depicted the country as a virgin, helpless before its despoiler. Columbia—figured as a woman—had been "violated," and only the strongest and bravest of men could defend her from further harm.[55]

So long as the war continued, women's attributes—their morality, their intellectual strength, their "tender passions"—would be devalued and ignored. It did little good for Judith to protest that men—even soldiers—could emulate women, to insist that compassion was "not altogether confined to the female bosom." Nor was anyone likely to listen to her claim that the willingness to sacrifice one's life for one's country was only one—and not necessarily the most important—measure of patriotism, that there were other, equally noble ways to serve America, ways that would allow women to express their attachment to the nation and its precepts. As she would later remark in her "Gleaner" essays, "from conspicuous rewards of merit, the female world, seem injudiciously excluded. To man the road of preferment is thrown open—glory crowns the military hero." Women, on the other hand, enjoyed nothing but "*secondary* or *reflected* fame."[56] Always, but especially in wartime, society ignored the private and ordinary efforts that women made everyday. Sadly, if Americans believed that women had contributed nothing of importance to the war effort, no one would argue that they deserved to enjoy the political or economic fruits of victory.

But Judith sensed that the war was about more than heroic deeds on blood-soaked battlefields. It was about the creation of a new nation built upon new principles that denigrated monarchy, hierarchy, and deference in favor of universal natural rights, rights that theoretically devolved upon women as well as men. From the time independence was declared, Judith began trying to create an American identity for herself. Although she burned nearly all of her early letters, she did keep one in which she claimed citizenship for herself as she "gloried" in her knowledge that she was a daughter of Columbia. She read extensively, commenting on the arguments of political observers on both sides of the Atlantic, keeping abreast of the debate over the merits of independence. She believed that women cared about America's future. "The welfare of my Country," she wrote, "the interests of this extensive Continent, I assure you are subjects very near my heart." If everyone—not just men—had an inherent love of liberty, then she did not go out of her sphere when she discussed political matters. No matter how John Murray laughed at her, she never believed she was an "amphibious animal" because she was fascinated by public affairs. "For," she asked rhetorically, "are not our sex interested as wives, as Mothers and as friends" in the welfare of the nation? By framing her question this way, of course, Judith pulled her punches, implying that women were not directly touched by national affairs as *humans*. She appeared to accept the traditional notion that it was indirectly, through their relationships to the men in their lives, that women were "interested" in the public arena.[57]

Still, Judith's experiences throughout the war, as well as her growing if ambivalent desire for literary fame gradually coalesced, leading her to challenge the assumption that women should remain content with "domestic sweets." Women had always confronted arbitrary limits to their ambitions. Judith herself had been denied an adequate education because of her parents' irrational deference to despotic custom. But the war served as a palpable symbol and a constant reminder of the way women were excluded from influencing the most important issues of the day. More than anything else, it made a mockery of Judith's still hesitant desire to be taken seriously on the literary stage. Her letters to Winthrop reveal an undercurrent of envy and resentment that grew stronger with each passing year. She genuinely hoped that her brother would wear the "laurel wreath," and that fame and fortune would be the reward for his sacrifices. But she, too, had begun to admit a hunger for adulation.[58] She knew that so long as the war continued, so long as martial prowess remained the test of public worth and the best if not the only road to glory, her hunger would not be satisfied.

Judith became convinced that only with the return of peace would she be able to devise a socially acceptable way to gain the recognition she craved. She believed that her own chance to contribute something to the public weal and to win the admiration of her fellow citizens would come only after men laid down their arms and turned their attention to domestic affairs. Only then would bodily strength diminish in importance while intellectual capacity and moral rectitude would become the measures of worth. Only then would the line between male and female become less impenetrable and less invidious. Only then would softer virtues prevail—in the bosoms of men as well as women—as the values women held dear would have a chance to gain ascendancy. With war's end, the life of the mind—where men and women were equal—would resume its rightful position; the arts and sciences would be celebrated; poetry would take its place beside military exploits in defining the character of the nation. Then historians would celebrate the victories of American soldiers, so that future generations would appreciate and imitate the sacrifices that had been made in their name. If men had won the war, it would be women's task to write about men's exploits, to keep the soldiers' sacrifices and glorious deeds alive in the nation's memory, and thus to define and preserve the values upon which the new nation was based. Then America would be venerated, not for its military prowess, but for the virtue of its citizens and the superiority of its literature. "Writers of every Class"—and presumably of both sexes—Judith predicted, would "wield the pen." "Imagination would mark the historic page," and talented women would become valued members of their society.[59]

Chapter 4
Creating a Genteel Nation

No one welcomed the end of the war with a greater sense of relief than Judith Stevens. Even before hostilities entirely ceased, her family's fortunes were improving. John's financial position was more secure in the last years of the conflict, and she had no reason to suspect that peace would destroy what war had wrought. Despite her occasional bouts of despair and intermittent illness, Judith found the last years of the Revolutionary War surprisingly productive.[1] Women as a whole may have benefited only marginally if at all by America's independence, but as an individual, Judith had reason to believe that she was in an ideal position to improve her own prospects. Still childless, she was able to sublimate, if not eradicate, her sense of deprivation, when she assumed responsibility for the education of her brother Fitz William and welcomed her husband's nieces, Anna and Mary, into her home. These relationships were far from ideal, but they did allow her to put the finishing touches on her philosophy of education, a philosophy whose basic tenets were an essential component of her developing perspective on gender relations. At a time when the new nation prepared to enjoy the blessings of peace, Judith's always intense but often inchoate views of gender identity began to assume a steadily more coherent form. Her religious faith, the egalitarian ideals that animated the War for Independence, her growing alienation from the ethos of military life, and her abiding belief in the value of education for women all coalesced with breathtaking rapidity in these years, allowing her to begin her career as a public advocate for the rights of "the Sex."

As the war wound down, Judith had to wonder what, if anything, her country's victory meant to her. She believed almost reflexively that a love of freedom was not distinctively male or female. It was "innate in the human Mind."

Dark anger agitates an Infant's breast
When by the hand of full grown power opprest,
The bands of servitude our bosoms scorn.
To liberty our intellect was born.

These sentiments were not especially unusual. For that very reason, postwar Americans wrestled with the contradiction between their declarations of support for equality and universal natural rights and the desire most people had to exclude women from an active political role and to preserve some measure of social and gender hierarchy. At the very least, the new nation had to defend exclusion and inequality in light of its own commitment to the ideals found in the Declaration of Independence. Above all, Americans had to clarify their notion of women's relationship to the state. "Reason allows," Judith sniffed, "a measure of patriotism even to the female bosom." Drawing on Shylock's language in *The Merchant of Venice*, she pointed out that women—like all humans—had eyes and hands, that they ate the same food, were hurt by the same weapons, and suffered from the same tyranny that men did.[2] Thus, women had no less a stake in America's future than any man. Judith said explicitly what many were implicitly suggesting. Women were human. They were neither animals nor slaves. They had rights; they had *some* relationship to the body politic. The Constitution itself recognized white women as part of the public that would be represented in the new government. The framers of that Constitution understood that even if women did not vote or hold office, they nevertheless had an emotional commitment to the nation. Few looked askance when Miss Catherine Davis took part in a public celebration of the election of officers to Boston's artillery company, presenting a flag to the ensign and expressing her hope that the company's members would defend and protect "liberty and Independence." Nor was it unseemly for young women in Judith's own Gloucester to gather and demonstrate their "female patriotism" with a "federal spinning-match" to celebrate the ratification of the Constitution.[3]

If gender roles and identities were contested in the years following the American Revolution, there remained limits, however ill-defined, beyond which the most audacious woman dared not go. Judith had already warned her counterparts not to expect public recognition for the sacrifices they made throughout the war. Women served their country as individuals, not as members of an identifiable collectivity. Thus, few had any understanding of their position *as women*, nor were they able to devise a coherent strategy to improve their lives. Even Judith, who was more aware of the gendered limitations she faced than most women were, did not identify with all members of her sex. While she challenged the limitations that separated her from men of her own class, she invariably distanced herself from men and women of the lower orders.

In this context, Judith struggled to develop an ideological framework that would allow her voice to be heard. The republican ideology that had informed the war was never of much use to women. Deborah Sampson's heroics notwithstanding, women could not point with pride to their military service as a justification for demanding political rights. Rights, after all, were based on duties, and a woman's primary duty was to her husband and children, not to the state. In the short run, the language of Lockean liberalism was only marginally more useful than republican discourse was. True, it theoretically granted natural rights to all humans. But for real women, those rights were seldom political. Besides, Locke had neatly separated the family from the state, implying that the family was the bulwark protecting citizens *against* government, thus preparing the way for a view of the family as an explicitly nonpolitical institution, a haven from a heartless and corrupt world. Finally, America's increasing emphasis on "independence" as a moral value in and of itself also excluded married women from membership in the body politic. As subjects of the king, all colonists—men and women alike—had been "dependents." Gender had been only one basis upon which the colonists had been denied the perquisites of political life. After the Revolution, however, dependence became a pejorative term, associated increasingly with powerlessness and inferiority. As more and more men used their economic independence as evidence that they deserved political rights, the chasm between men and women grew wider and more gender specific.[4]

Women, everyone agreed, did have one place where they belonged: the home. There they performed traditional duties, nurturing their children, supporting their husbands, running their households. Their rights—choosing a husband and maintaining a loving relationship with him, supervising their children's education—were narrow and only vaguely and indirectly political. An educated wife or mother could *influence* the political world, raising patriotic sons and persuading her husband to be virtuous and public-spirited. She could read about and discuss politics with friends. She could even write for public consumption, so long as she discussed appropriate topics in a rational manner. But she could not vote or hold office. She could not enter public forums—Congress, the pulpit, or the courtroom—except as an invited guest or member of the audience. And even her place in the protected family circle existed only at her husband's sufferance. Blind obedience to the king disappeared with the American Revolution. But a war against a patriarchal political order by no means invited an attack on the patriarchal construction of the family.[5]

Indeed, particularly in Federalist circles, the more talk of equality and rights they heard in the aftermath of the Revolution, the more determined elite men were to shore up the remaining barriers that divided the few from the many, men from women, whites from blacks. As a member—by birth and by marriage—of the Gloucester elite, Judith found herself in an anomalous position. While she sought to narrow the gap between men and women, she thoroughly agreed with those who thought that too much democracy would lead to a licentious social order, driven by the "passions of the Mob." The ignorant many, she invariably argued, were apt to be swayed by prejudice rather than reason and to "spread horror, and devastation throughout the Universe." A deferential order was the only natural and safe way to organize society.[6]

*   *   *

Even when her husband's fortunes had been at their lowest ebb, Judith had never lost her sense of her own superiority as a Sargent. By the early 1780s, her confidence was finally validated, as John's brief flirtation with financial success gave her a platform from which to claim her rightful position as a member of Gloucester's elite. "You know," she wrote to Mary Sargent in the spring of 1781, "my life is not gilded by the smiles of affluence." Compared to her parents or to Daniel and Mary, compared to her own expectations, she was no doubt correct. When war between England and its colonies broke out, the Stevenses' already precarious fortunes had plummeted. It was often only the generosity of his father-in-law that enabled John to meet the demands of his creditors. Eventually, the sale of a few parcels of land and, even more, the inflated value of American currency allowed him to pay many of his debts with near worthless continentals. Still, like so many Gloucester seamen, John continued to lose money faster than he made it, sailing on one "disastrous" voyage after another. It was not until a friend sold him a share in a privateer that his fortunes took a turn for the better.[7]

John Stevens was an inveterate optimist, always in "high health and spirits." It took only a success or two to convince him that his future was rosy. In 1782, he seized the moment, beginning construction of a dwelling place that reflected his own and his wife's conception of their proper position in Gloucester society. Judith had once written enviously of her uncle Daniel's house on Boston's Atkinson Street. Whenever visitors entered the Sargent estate through the "neat gate" that set the house and its grounds off from the rest of the town, they left behind the noise, the bustle, and the military parades that continually assaulted the senses of ordinary Bostonians. The gate opened upon a long path leading to a lush garden replete with flowers, fruit trees and vegetables, and a "handsome summer house." From there, they could wander along "serpentine walks" or rest on one of the "highly ornamented seats" that were tastefully scattered throughout the grounds. The elegant "Elysium" offered guests a momentary respite from the cares and confusion of a war-torn world.[8]

At last, Judith could prepare to enjoy her own Elysium. For nearly a year she lived with carpenters, bricklayers, and painters who disrupted her life, giving her little time even to write. The help of two servants—one man, one woman—was barely sufficient to get her through each day.[9] But in the end, it was all worthwhile. She and John would no longer shuttle from one temporary abode to another. The days of sleeping on borrowed beds in rented houses would be nothing more than a faint memory of bad times gone for good. Judith gratefully accepted her father's gift of enough fine furniture to fill an edifice that was, in the words of one visitor, "the largest and most elegant house in town." The three-story wooden structure dominated the landscape, sitting on a hill overlooking Gloucester Harbor, its carefully manicured terraced lawn sloping gently down to the street below. If most New Englanders still resided in two- or three-room, one-story houses, the Stevens residence was a material representation of the genteel pretensions of a merchant class whose members could use their ownership of consumer goods to distance themselves from their social inferiors.[10] Less magnificent than the planters' houses of the Chesapeake, too cramped and narrow for modern tastes, the house was the talk of Gloucester.

The edifice reflected the genteel tastes of the day. While most eighteenth-century Americans lived, ate, cooked, and slept in one "great room," in the Stevens house, rooms were differentiated by function. The front rooms on the first floor were ready to receive guests. More intimate spaces were sheltered from casual visitors, giving John and Judith a measure of privacy that few of their counterparts enjoyed. Rooms that suggested functions related to bodily matters, such as sexual activity or cooking, were entirely hidden from view. When guests entered the front door of the Stevens "mansion," their eyes were immediately drawn to the ornate spiral staircase that invited family members and close friends to leave the area designed for public entertainment and enter the intimate spaces of the dwelling's upper levels. Every room had a large fireplace, topped by an ornate mantelpiece. Delicate wainscoting began at the floors and stretched one-third of the way up the smoothly plastered walls. Thinner, more elaborate molding graced the ceilings. The floorboards on the first level were smooth and narrow, becoming gradually rougher and wider on the second and third tiers of the house. Copley's picture of young Judith Stevens occupied a place of honor in the west parlor, a room that contained other evidences of the owners' taste. There was the matching tea service and the special table that held all "the equipage." The oval looking glass, the mahogany card table, the six leather-bottomed chairs, and two sofas were all props that invited guests to relax with members of their social circle, to exhibit their own gentility—and to appreciate the exquisitely casual refinement of their hosts, as well. There, Judith could read her "sublime poetry" to callers whose sensibilities she deemed refined enough to appreciate her efforts. The east parlor was probably used for small dinner parties. It contained one small and one larger walnut table and an assortment of china. Some of the cups and saucers were "crack'd," but this only proved that they did not belong to an upstart family, desperate to show off its newfound wealth. They were owned by people whose roots stretched back to Gloucester's earliest days. Clearly the first floor was designed to be seen—and to impress.[11]

Most important, there was a place in the new home for John Murray, who had his own room waiting for him whenever he returned to Gloucester. Judith was delighted with this arrangement, although she wished John would avail himself of her hospitality more often. While she knew that he gained emotional sustenance from the eager men and women who thronged to his sermons, she reminded him that Gloucester's parishioners made up in quality what they lacked in quantity. "Reason, deliberation, and sentiment," she argued, "are usually found among the elect few." Moreover, in her household, he could enjoy an ordered existence, studying, writing, and thinking, free from the importunities of a demanding crowd. When John was on the road, the Stevens house felt strangely empty. His room, Judith mourned, was "a dreary desert," his chair was "wildly vacant." At dinner, his place was pointedly empty, unless Agnes, the servant girl, mistakenly set out a plate for him. Still, Judith knew that nothing would keep John tied to one place for long. She had to be content with the moments he shared with his congregation, hoping he would survive the strains his peripatetic career made on his health.[12]

The east bedroom on the second floor was Judith's special refuge. The south window gave her a view of the harbor. From there she could observe vessels sailing in and out of the port or watch for the sight of her husband's sloop making its way home from a profitable voyage. But she prized it most for its "little closet," a tiny room within a room that held her writing desk and chair, allowing her a temporary escape from her household responsibilities, giving her a quiet place to scribble away without interruption. Her pen continued to be her "constant companion" and her most profound pleasure. She prized her closet for another reason. It had one small window, which looked down on the house next door—a residence that had once belonged to Samuel Chandler, the minister who had so effectively poisoned his parishioners' minds against John Murray. How satisfying it must have been, to see from her own lofty perch, the home of a man who had done his best to discredit her religious beliefs not so very long ago.[13]

The Stevenses were finally coming into their own. Their house was the envy of Gloucester. Judith, in particular, enjoyed a social life commensurate with her position. She traveled as much as possible, enjoying genteel conversation and the occasional elaborate ball with "well bred" people she saw as her own kind. No one's company meant more to her than Mary Sargent, her uncle Daniel's wife. Judith and Mary had developed an intense relationship over the years. Whenever they were apart, Judith wrote reams to her aunt, whom she affectionately dubbed "Maria," signing her letters with the pen name "Constantia." In many ways it was an odd match. Maria was nearly ten years Judith's senior, much wealthier, and more fond of luxuries. Nor did she embrace the Universalist faith. But for whatever reason, the two women adored one another. When Maria visited Gloucester, the two women were likely to spend the entire night in Judith's bed, sharing their deepest confidences, not wanting to sleep the precious moments away. Such deep emotional relationships between women were not unusual in the eighteenth century, of course. Indeed, many people argued that women's ability to forge deep friendships reflected their refinement.[14]

Judith relished her position in these years, noting with obvious pleasure each token of respect she garnered from her inferiors, depicting properly arranged scenes that may well have reflected her idealized version of social order as much as they represented her actual circumstances. When, for instance, she embarked on a trip to Boston, she described her departure to John Murray, telling him that the workmen who were putting the finishing touches on her house stopped work and gathered in the yard to see her off. Looking solemn and a little sad, she said, they all "bowed respectfully" as her chaise pulled away from the yard. From Judith's perspective, the truly genteel were confident enough of their status that they could associate with the lower sort without fear of losing face. They knew how to behave, what to wear, and what to say. Providence itself, Judith claimed, "no doubt for wise reasons, established subordination in our World," and thus it would be ungodly to destroy the natural order. Indeed, she thought that people like the Sargents should "seek by every means to preserve legitimate distinctions." Even so, it was essential to rule with a light hand. If subordination was essential, even servants were humans, and Universalists knew better than most that all humans were related. Thus Judith claimed always to give orders with kindness and a gracious smile. Not only was this a mark of gentility, it had salutary practical effects as well. Servants went about their assigned tasks with pleasure when they felt that they were linked to their masters or mistresses by "silken" bonds.[15]

*   *   *

Judith adored her new home and the status it confirmed. But as much as she relished the opportunity to assume her rightful role as mistress of her domain, she was never completely satisfied with a life lived only in the domestic arena. She was determined to find an appropriate way to have an impact on the wider world. Had she been a mother, she may have been content with her lot, believing that her influence, however indirect, was nevertheless real and valuable. But providence had evidently designed her for other ends. If she could not raise her own progeny perhaps she might act as a surrogate mother. She had thought long and hard about the best way to mold and educate children. She believed that mothers, if they performed their duties well were essential to the success of the nation's republican experiment.[16]

Attitudes toward rearing children had changed dramatically in America by the third quarter of the eighteenth century. Gone were the days when pilgrim minister John Robinson could assert without fear of contradiction that "there is in all children . . . a stubbornness and stoutness of mind, arising from natural pride, which must in the first place be broken and beaten down." Enlightened educators were influenced to a large extent by the views of John Locke and his many popularizers. Even when they did not reject the notion of original sin, they softened its implications. They talked increasingly of children who were born innocent, potentially rational, and thus capable of being guided by adults who helped them avoid life's many temptations and prepared them for eventual independence. Most pedagogues believed that sweet reason was more efficacious than corporal punishment, that praise produced better results than stern criticism. Their assumption that humans were almost endlessly malleable led them to argue that "little seeds" needed only a nourishing environment in order to flourish. That environment was most beneficial when it emphasized understanding rather than rote memorization. Emulation, which Judith characterized as "one of the most powerful engines by which those who have the care of young people can operate," worked better than arbitrary precept. Finally, because each child had different needs and inclinations, the wise teacher adapted a curriculum to the "natural Genius" of the individual pupil.[17]

In many respects, Judith was a confirmed Lockean, if for no other reason than that Locke's logic undermined the notion of natural or immutable female inferiority. She freely used all of the English philosopher's common catchphrases. Her letters and essays are dotted with references to the "plasticity" of human nature and the need to teach by example and experience. She was a voracious reader and an eclectic thinker, however, and in the end Judith was influenced as much by her religious beliefs as by her understanding of educational theory. She had read Kames, Ferguson, and Hutcheson as well as Locke, and was fundamentally more comfortable with the Scottish Enlightenment than with its English counterpart. She found the Scottish view of human nature especially appealing because it was more spiritual, less materialistic and mechanistic, than the Lockean variety. Above all, she was drawn to a belief in the "moral sense," a notion that all individuals were born with a knowledge of right and wrong, and that their innate recognition of moral truth helped people evaluate and respond to the sense impressions that constantly bombarded them. It was the moral sense that raised humans above the level of mere animals. Most important, it gave them a "sense of sympathy," a shared affection, which, when properly cultivated, made a good society possible. Natural affinities based on instinct, not education, emotion as much as reason, were the foundations of individual rectitude and the basis of a moral republic.[18]

The implications for women of such a perspective were profound. If the moral sense was the defining characteristic of all humans, if sensibility, not physical strength gave individuals the tools to create a virtuous society, then women had an important role in the new nation. Unlike republican virtue, the moral sense belonged to everyone; it knew no nationality, race, sect, or gender. Insisting that private choices had public consequences, it implied, in the modern vernacular, that the personal was political. If conventional wisdom had it that women were more empathetic, emotional, and affectionate than men, then women were especially qualified to nurture the "social instinct" that lay dormant in every human. A woman could civilize and reform the manners and morals of her husband and children. Conversely, she could judge any culture in terms of the way it treated women. Savage societies viewed women as animals, while civilized ones protected and admired them. At the heart of the Scottish Enlightenment was the notion that virtue was a social rather than a political attribute, an attribute best developed in the home rather than the statehouse or the battlefield. It was in the domestic sphere that children learned compassion and developed the ties of sympathy that held society together. It was the family, and most particularly the mother, that transmitted the habits of civilization from one generation to the next. While men would continue to occupy the seat of government in the new nation, women would be their domestic partners, creating a social environment without which stability and order would disappear.[19]

In an unpublished essay written in 1781, Judith resolutely denied that she was a Lockean, even as she championed (without attribution) the basic tenets of the Scottish Enlightenment. When she first read Locke, she said, she had been aroused by a "daring spirit of opposition," for she simply could not believe that the human mind had ever been a blank slate. From the beginning, she said, the soul animated the mind. Children knew some things instinctively well before they were able to articulate their thoughts to themselves or to anybody else. It is, she proclaimed, as ridiculous to say that babies have no legs because they cannot walk, as it is to say they have no innate ideas because they have not learned to express them. While Judith was not arrogant enough to imagine that she could delineate all innate ideas, she did discuss a few. All people were born with an instinctive knowledge of moral truth. It was the moral sense that differentiated humans from animals, giving them an instinctive "sense of sympathy," which, if properly cultivated, made a moral society possible. Thus, she said, humans were obviously "formed for society, and created social Beings." They also understood the value of property, believed in God, and hungered for knowledge. Children invariably held on to their possessions, protecting them from anyone who tried to take them away. God's existence was obvious to people who had never seen the Bible. Finally, even babies were curious, eager to investigate their environment and to learn more about the world around them. Thus, a desire for knowledge was innate; importantly, it was a human, not a male or a female attribute.[20]

Although she sought to reinforce class differences, Judith simultaneously attempted to make gender distinctions more permeable, to claim her identity as a curious, rational, Christian human being. In fact, she saw the two projects not as contradictory or even paradoxical, but as essential aspects of the same end, for she knew that elite men who sought to accentuate class differences inevitably turned to their female counterparts to help them police the boundaries between themselves and their social inferiors.[21] While she was unapologetic about elite status, she was generally cautious when she tried to assert her prerogatives as a woman, to a large extent because she did not want to undermine her claims to gentility. She exerted her influence in only the most traditional and genteel ways. Shaping her identity as educator and surrogate mother to her own advantage, she tried to demonstrate her right to be taken seriously as a public-spirited member of her society.

In 1780, Judith was twenty-nine; she had virtually abandoned any lingering hope she had that she and John would have children. She had done so with a profound sense of loss, an emotion that was exacerbated as she watched her sister begin a family. She shared in Esther's joy, of course, but it was painful to be a mere onlooker who could only vicariously experience the "White day" that signaled the birth of a child. When Sarah, the Ellerys' daughter was born, friends and relatives gathered to acknowledge Esther's good fortune. Judith, too, rushed to caress her niece, observing her brother-in-law as he celebrated Sarah's birth. "What a melancholy contrast doth the situation of the childless wife exhibit," Judith wrote. "A solitary, a childless Wife—how dreary the idea."[22]

Still, Judith did not totally lack opportunities to act as a mother. It was not uncommon in the eighteenth century for those who could afford to do so to assume responsibility for the children of needy relations or friends. Indeed, to refuse such an obligation without good reason was highly irregular. As a childless couple, the Stevenses were prime candidates for surrogate parenthood. Judith indicated that they had already refused one plea for help due to their precarious financial situation. She may have been glad to have an excuse to avoid what she saw as her duty, but her inability to act as a genteel benefactor was embarrassing nevertheless. By 1780, however, her circumstances had improved and she had no reason to reject another request. On December 1, seven-year-old Anna, John's niece, was ensconced in the Stevens home. And at some point—just when and why is unclear—Mary O'Dell also joined the household.[23]

Judith assumed her new role with trepidation. I "turned every way to avoid it," she later admitted, but her understanding of her duty prevailed. Perhaps she sensed that her decision was an admission, once and for all, that she would never bear a child of her own. She also knew that popular prejudice led many people to view stepmothers with suspicion. Granted, enlightened individuals agreed with Locke that the act of raising children, not the act of giving birth, was the true measure of parenthood. Moreover, a family created by choice, not birth, was a perfect manifestation of the ideals of the American Revolution. Still, Judith felt obligated to marshal as many arguments as possible to bolster her decision. She thought that assuming responsibility for someone else's child gave women a sense of "*self-approbation*" unknown to natural mothers. She also believed that everyone, but especially the truly genteel, felt an innate measure of affection for all dependents. She, herself, had always looked upon her servants as part of her family, treating the younger ones, in particular, almost as if they were her own children. She had, moreover, read her share of novels whose plots revolved around progeny who had been switched at birth and raised by parents who had no biological connection to them. In such cases, the bonds of affection between the putative mother and child were as strong and enduring as they would have been had the mistake not occurred. Surely this was evidence that biology was irrelevant, that attitude mattered more than ties of blood. Those ties were "*corporal*," and had nothing to do with "*the Mind*."[24]

But if blood was irrelevant, character—which began to develop almost at birth—was not. Even virtuous children required early and diligent cultivation. When Anna arrived at the Stevens home, Judith realized that she was not welcoming a newborn babe into her home. Instead, she was raising a girl whose personality and values had to some extent been formed. Nor did the relationship between Judith and Anna begin to replicate the experience of birth mothers and daughters. Judith had not suffered the perils of childbirth; she had not enjoyed the exquisite pleasure of nursing "the innocent." Indeed, in the sense that she came to the Stevens household with her character at least partially molded already, Anna was not an innocent at all. In a poem Judith wrote the year her niece entered her home, the theme of innocence and virginity dominated. She wanted to "cultivate the young, the tender mind, / Unwarp'd by vice—to virtue's path inclin'd." She planned to guard "the spotless Maid," and

to shield her from the wiley flatterer's beguiles,
To warm her heart by honor's sacred fire,
And all the glow of sentiment inspire,
To cherish that sweet roseate virgin blush,
So form'd the daring Libertine to crush.

Judith fervently hoped that Anna would one day win some "manly heart" and become a useful wife and mother. In the meantime, it was her duty to prepare her niece for any eventuality, hoping at the very least that Anna would be a respectable member of society. Above all, she intended to do her utmost to curb her orphan's "passion." Passion led to pride, rancor, and prejudice, and once it obtained a foothold it was nearly impossible to eradicate. Thus she prayed for the wisdom and patience she would need if she were to succeed in disciplining Anna's "ungovern'd mind."[25]

The evening of Anna's arrival, Judith invited some friends to meet the young girl. Judith was comforted to note that a "tear, as I hope of sensibility stole down her cheek." Still, Anna seemed a bit awkward and shy. And no wonder! Surely she sensed that her new guardian was watching her every move for signs of innate intelligence, grace, and character. Somehow, she survived the ordeal. The next morning, Judith summoned her niece to her bedroom, where she laid down the ground rules for the girl's new life. This, Judith told her, would be her home until she married. She would regard Judith as a mother, herself as a daughter. She would not be a servant; her abode would not be the kitchen. She would spend her time reading, visiting, sewing, and performing other unspecified domestic chores. But, Judith hastened to add, Anna must not put on airs simply because she was fortunate enough to have been rescued from a life of drudgery. Remember, she said, that if social distinctions were necessary in this world, in the next equality would reign. Judith promised to reward virtue, to turn "in disgust" from vice, and to correct Anna's faults with "tenderness." In return, Judith was entitled to obedience and honesty. Having completed a speech she had obviously prepared with care, she dismissed Anna, who no doubt left the room a little overwhelmed. "That much," said Judith wryly, "for a beginning."[26]

As she watched Anna settle in to her routine, Judith conceded that she had little to complain about. Her niece had a "docile and uniformly good disposition."

Because she was properly "grateful to her parental friends," she tried hard to please. She was a diligent if not a brilliant student, and her intellectual progress was about what her aunt expected. In time, although she still longed for children of her own, Judith developed a genuine attachment to her ward. When Anna's behavior is pleasing, said Judith, "my heart beats rapturously, pleasure mantles upon my face, and upon my cheek descends the tear of delighted approbation."[27]

Judith constantly peppered her niece with advice. She "instructed," "warned," and "guarded" at every turn, laying out an ambitious and formulaic itinerary that allowed little time for frivolous pleasures. Anna would rise at five. While everyone needed sleep, it was nothing short of debauchery to spend the morning in bed. The hours before eight were her own—but even they needed to be judiciously spent. Judith, herself, "would believe that day lost, in which she imbibed not from books (those repositories of knowledge) information or direction." Thus she advised Anna to devote one hour to reading and another to writing observations on what she had read. At eight, she would eat a light breakfast, and begin the day in earnest. How different this was, Judith pointed out, from the schedule of all too many heedless people. Some laggards actually rose at the decadent hour of nine, and were disorganized and disheveled for the rest of the day. "What a Gothic, what a barbarous murder of time."[28]

While Judith claimed to love Anna unconditionally, always urging her niece to view her as a "maternal friend," her relationship with her ward was always complicated. She was quick to seize upon those occasions when her niece displeased her, obliquely alluding to the vulnerability of helpless orphans—especially girls—that Anna already understood all too well. She pointedly reminded her niece that she had no "natural claim" to Judith's affection. "Circumstances alone" gave Judith an interest in the girl's future. Moreover, Anna was "desolate of fortune, and perhaps less beautiful than many other females." Thus, it was altogether possible that in maturity she would be "friendless and forlorn." This, said Judith, was meant to "stimulate" not to frighten you. But she warned a girl who already knew from experience that the fates could be most unkind, while she and John would endeavor to support her, a merchant's fortunes were precarious. Judith promised Anna that they would never abandon her—unless, of course, they relinquished her to "the protection of some worthy Man." But because she had little to offer in the way of status or wealth, it was incumbent upon her to "lay an early foundation for independence." Anna needed to be proficient at every variety of needlework and to be adept at all household chores. "These," Judith said, "are in female life indispensable requisites, *useful* attainments, without which we are incapable of sustaining with propriety, the character we are called to sustain." Still, she hoped Anna would not be content to stay within the bounds that a narrow-minded world designated as appropriately feminine. Her niece should be able to write, to understand the basic rules of grammar, and to know something of mathematics, geography, geometry, and astronomy. And, after all that, she hoped Anna would be appropriately humble, exhibiting the "dignity of deportment proper to our sex."[29]

Judith's insistence that her niece lay a foundation for independence was the result of her realistic appraisal of Anna's prospects. Unlike her aunt, Anna never viewed a marriage into Gloucester's elite as more or less her due. Indeed, she might not marry at all. When Judith had railed against her own parents, demanding an education commensurate with Winthrop's, she had not done so because she wanted a career or because she expected to support herself. She wanted it because she thought she deserved it and because she loved learning for its own sake as well as for the meaning it had in her world. For her, a knowledge of Latin and Greek, literature and history would have given her the respect and authority she craved in a society where knowledge was power. Anna's circumstances forced Judith, probably for the first time, to consider the practical ends education might offer women who could not rely upon parents or a husband to provide for them. If she was not quite sure what use her niece would make of her ability to read, write, compute, and do fancy needlework, Judith had at least begun to link her demands for equal education to her belief that women needed to be self-reliant.

Perhaps not surprisingly, while Judith claimed to believe that women's education should be equal to men's, her letters to Anna bore little resemblance to the missives she sent Fitz William at roughly the same time. Her advice to her brother was lofty, replete with open-ended descriptions of the many branches of knowledge that lay open to him. She wanted him to be an able merchant, an educated man, and a true gentleman. She hoped he would take his rightful place in the public arena, serving his community and even his country if called upon to do so. Her admonitions to Anna were only tangentially academic. She said little to her niece of the virtues of the studies that she hoped her brother would embrace and that she had so wanted for herself. And she never complained that Gloucester offered no decent schooling for girls. She seemed content to supervise Anna's education herself. For the most part, she focused on shaping Anna's prospects as a moral young lady who would attract appropriate suitors. In later years, Judith would vigorously argue that the "idea of an *old maid*—in its contemptuous sense—it exists not." But if she wanted Anna to be independent if necessary, she always hoped her niece would find a husband to satisfy her emotional and material needs.[30]

Thus, much of Judith's advice to Anna centered on her relationships with men. Imitating the conventional wisdom of her day, she urged her niece to strive for a happy medium, refusing to be either a "prude" or a "coquette." The prude saw evil everywhere, spread rumors about those who failed to meet her exacting standards, and was so censorious and "so outrageously virtuous as to condemn without judge or jury even an exchange of smiles." As a wife, the prude was judgmental and unsociable. But more than likely, she would never marry. She would be a "despised, wretched old Maid" spending her life destroying the innocent pleasures of everyone else. The coquette was no more admirable. Judith had once joked about a "Cruel Girl," of her acquaintance who left "many sighing hearts" in her wake. To Anna, she deplored such heartless behavior. The coquette, she said, was only interested in "dress, equipage and show." She collected and disposed of proposals like badges of honor, seeing each man as nothing more than a potential conquest to be discarded at will. Like her prudish counterpart, she was destined for a lonely and meaningless life. Her beauty would fade quickly. If she married, which was doubtful, she would have nothing of substance to offer husband or children. Fortunately, Judith thought, Anna was too sensible to be proud of her appearance, for she knew that physical beauty was an ephemeral quality, a mere "accidental advantage." Inner qualities represented an individual's true worth, for they depended on merit, not luck. Thus, Judith repeatedly admonished, "be assiduous in furnishing your mind."[31]

Judith thought that the most important advice she offered her new charge was to maintain her reputation for sexual innocence, the prized possession of any elite woman. Anna needed to realize that the assets that society valued in women—emotionalism, sympathy, benevolence—were the very qualities that, carried to extremes, could expose them to temptation and destroy the fragile barriers that kept their sexual appetites in check. It was simply too easy for a woman to become "a victim of sensibility," a virtue that was simultaneously a marker of her superior status and the potential instrument of her downfall. There was, said Judith, "nothing so easily lost, as female reputation," and if she suffered that loss, a girl's future was bleak. Not so for men. Boys, especially, could sow a few wild oats. Like the prodigal son, they could transgress any moral law, repent of their sins, and expect a second chance. A "reformed rake," Judith observed, was intriguing, even admired. Tales of his sexual dalliances might actually enhance his appeal in some circles. For women, this was never the case. Indeed, chastity was "one of the most essential ornaments of female life." Richardson's Clarissa had resisted temptation, yet she was destined to die once the dastardly Lovelace raped her. Even when a woman had sex forced upon her, she was damaged goods and could never overcome her disgrace. Because a single "female deviation" was fatal, a prudent woman had to be vigilant. She knew that "rectitude of heart and unspoiled innocence are insufficient to guard" her. She also knew that Satan found a virtuous target especially challenging and hence the most tempting.[32]

Significantly, Judith did not believe that women were naturally pure. Indeed, she would not have repeated her warnings with such intensity had she thought that Anna was immune to fleshly temptations. She insisted that a woman needed to pretend that she had no desire to engage in illicit sexual activity. But the day had not yet arrived when white, middle-class women in America conceived of themselves as "passionless." In the eighteenth century, the depiction of virtuous women and unscrupulous deceivers was recognized as a literary convention not a reality. Everyone knew how easy it was for a woman's purity to be sullied.[33]

Perhaps because she knew that sexual purity was no more natural to women than it was to men, Judith criticized society's sexual double standard. True enough, she condemned the "idle Hussy" with as much venom as the most catty gossip. And she no doubt recognized that claims to a spotless reputation were an effective way for a woman to claim gentility, to separate herself from lower-class women who could not live up to the chaste ideal. But on the whole, she resented the way her peers singled out weak women for special opprobrium. In 1775, Judith had written an essay on the "melancholy consequences of a single Error," in which she described the fate of an innocent girl whose tender sensibility had led to her seduction. While Judith agreed that "unblemished honour, should be a Woman's shield," she nevertheless thought it unfair that one tiny mistake destroyed a woman's identity as a lady and led automatically to her social death. The "erring female," she maintained, was no more reprehensible than her "destroyer." Both were children of God; both deserved compassion. Just as a rake could reform, so could the "too believing Maid" be taught the error of her ways. Still, Judith never forgot that if her niece defied custom, she would suffer the consequences. In words that would come back to haunt her, she confided that if she ever had a daughter, she would rather see her in an early grave than watch her lose her chastity.[34]

According to Judith, Anna had a variety of ways to maintain her reputation for virtue. She should be a listener rather than a talker, for a woman who could not control her tongue was unlikely to control her passion. Modesty, she continued, was "the most decorous ornament of our sex, and gentleness and affability should be appropriate to womankind." Modesty was the opposite of sexuality. It raised a woman above the level of the animal; it gave her social status. If a woman wore revealing clothing or flirted with abandon, she was indicating that she was receptive to seduction. It was a woman's job, more than a man's, to see that sexual indiscretions did not occur. Women and men did not occupy separate spheres. For that very reason, women needed to be on guard. Thus, as Anna matured, Judith warned her not to indulge in the little freedoms she had enjoyed as a child. There should be no more roughhousing with boys. She needed to act with that "genuine delicacy which should always distinguish the conduct of young Ladies." Proper deportment was desirable for everyone, but women, in particular, needed to "avoid even the appearance of evil." Their conversations should be free of slang, vulgarity, or the suggestive double entendre. Above all, they should never permit a man the "smallest *personal* liberty." A woman could offer her arm to a man, but no lady would permit a coxcomb to kiss her hand. A simple blush or a frown would be sufficient to discourage an offender.[35]

Always, always there was a hint of desperation in Judith's letters. Youth was both the "season of expectation" and the "Age of disappointment." Trust me, she warned Anna, in the spring of 1783, "the disposition of the next five years of your life, will either confirm you a sensible amiable woman, or fix you [as] an insignificant being, merely animal, and wholly unworthy the attention of the refined or sentimental." While Judith always claimed to write to Anna with the "tenderness of a parent," the picture she painted of a life bereft of tenderness, warmth—or a husband—was terrifying.[36]

Just what Anna thought of the torrent of advice she received from her aunt's pen is unclear. But there are indications that she was often overwhelmed by Judith's admonitions. She took refuge in silence, seeing her refusal to answer Judith's letters as her only source of power in an obviously unequal relationship. When she did put pen to paper, she was as brief as possible. Although Judith constantly instructed her niece to write more often and more fully, Anna remained quietly obdurate.[37]

*   *   *

Raising Anna was difficult. Still, her own experiences—as well as her extensive reading on the subject—gave Judith a sense of what women needed to know and how to go about teaching them. Nor did anyone appear to second-guess her efforts—perhaps because no one cared about Anna anyway. When Judith decided to become heavily involved in supervising Fitz William's education, however, she ran up against real obstacles that reminded her of the limits all women faced whenever they exercised authority in even the most conventional ways. She would not even have made the attempt had Winthrop been home. But neither her father nor her mother were educated enough to be confident of their own abilities, and they gladly turned the job over to their daughter. Judith had both the time and the inclination to assume her parents' role, and when Fitz William ultimately rejected her efforts, she was devastated. From her perspective, her failure had political as well as personal ramifications. She believed that if she could do even a little to shape the mind of America's next generation of leaders, she would be performing a valuable service for her country. If she was unsuccessful, however, she would either have to find some other, perhaps less socially acceptable means to serve the new nation, or she would simply have to admit defeat.

As early as 1779, Judith had begun to notice a disturbing change in Fitz William's demeanor. He was melancholy, had trouble sleeping, and frequently dissolved into tears for no apparent reason. When she pressed him for an explanation, he admitted that he despised the "mode of education which is adopted for him." Each day he vainly struggled to complete his Latin lessons. Each night he went to bed dreading the dawn when the torturous process would begin once more. Judith had been Fitz William's earliest teacher, and while he was now venturing into academic areas that were foreign to her, she was determined to help him.[38]

Her reaction to Fitz William's misery was conflicted. While Judith would have given anything to have had the very opportunities that made her brother so miserable, she had already developed firm ideas about pedagogical methods that led her to question her family's determination to give her brother a classical education. She believed that while all children possessed certain general characteristics, each child had unique interests and abilities. If this was the case, then the plan for Fitz William's education was doomed. The boy was simply not designed to be a scholar. "From the first budding of his reason," Judith observed, "his every little action hath portrayed the merchant in miniature." Even as a child, nothing pleased him more than contracting a shrewd bargain. Nor was this surprising. If it was true that all people had an "*innate* tendency to imitation," then it stood to reason that Fitz William would want to follow in his father's footsteps. He was surely not stupid. But he was, she sighed, destined for a "*useful*" rather than a "*splendid* sphere." Judith begged Winthrop to accept his brother as he was. True, the two had very different personalities. But what was wrong with that? "Consider," she said, "were every one formed to fill the same sphere, where would be that beautiful subordination, indispensable in the regular confusion planned and executed by the Deity?"[39]

Still, even the most pragmatic merchant needed a patina of knowledge. While Judith was sure that even without a classical education, Fitz William would hold his own in a small, unpretentious town like Gloucester, she feared that he would be the "subject of ridicule" in the beau monde. Moreover, even if he were content to remain in the provinces, his chosen profession required that he be able to read, write, and do simple arithmetic. A knowledge of French, which was becoming the universal language of commerce, was essential for both "the gentleman and the man of business." But beyond that, he need not go. The boy's own tutor thought that Fitz William should abandon his classical studies. And Judith was convinced that forcing her brother to continue his efforts to master Greek and Latin when there was no rational reason to expect that he would succeed, was both a waste of time and a cruel and unnecessary punishment. Her parents were inclined to agree. But they all deferred to Winthrop—the one college graduate in the family—allowing him to make the ultimate decision.[40]

Winthrop was stern and uncompromising, unmoved by Judith's accounts of Latin lessons bathed in Fitz William's tears. He wanted the best for his brother and to him this meant a grounding in the classics. The rest of the family meekly submitted to his superior judgment. Judith found it difficult to oppose her brother, and whenever she did so, she apologized for her audacity, punctuating her remarks with profuse admissions that she spoke with "great and perhaps uninformed freedom." While she thought that her age gave her a certain amount of wisdom, she knew that her practical experience did not compensate for her ignorance. Thus Fitz William struggled on, while Judith tried to stimulate the unhappy boy's interest in his studies. Not only did she accomplish nothing, she feared that her constant carping would alienate him altogether. She already imagined that he viewed her with fear, even "disgust" whenever she entered the room. In time, she predicted, she would lose her ability to influence him altogether.[41]

Judith was convinced that her efforts to supervise Fitz William's education faced one insuperable obstacle. She was limited by her sex. She was, for instance, unable to secure an assessment of Fitz William's work from his tutors. "As I am a Woman," she explained, "I might be accused of impropriety were I to wait upon his several Preceptors." Nor was she able to judge his progress for herself. Never having studied the classics, she was in no position to dictate terms or advise her brother. She was "scarce mistress of [the] Mother Tongue," she insisted. Her knowledge of French was superficial, and in the dead languages she was simply out of her depth. She lived in dread of the inevitable day when Fitz William would turn on her, telling her she did not know what she was talking about. Ironically, her sense of inferiority gave her the opening she needed to question the strictures that all American women faced. Convinced that women were able—perhaps especially able—to learn Latin and Greek, she wondered why the classics were not an integral part of every elite woman's curriculum. Custom, she pointed out, forced women to lead a more "sedentary" life than men. Thus, they had more time to pursue their studies than men did. Such a pursuit might, she added with more than a small dose of sarcasm, even turn women "from the multifarious scenes of vanity and fashioned into rational beings." Nor would education make women vain or obnoxious, for everyone knew that genuine knowledge led to humility, not pride. She thought that if educated women lost something in delicacy and charm, most members of her sex would gladly exchange "elevation of sentiment" for that "equality to which we were born."[42]

Everyone but Winthrop soon realized that Fitz William would never be a scholar. Isolated from his friends, none of whom was studying the dead languages, having no one whose example he could emulate or who could even join him in complaining about the tedious task he faced each day, Fitz William progressed slowly at best. In December 1779, the family briefly considered sending him to the Governor Dummer Academy in Byfield, Massachusetts, some thirty miles outside Boston. There, at least, he would be surrounded by students who were also studying Latin. Judith had met Samuel Moody, the preceptor of the Academy, a few months earlier, and had been favorably impressed, considering her hours with the Moodys as "among the most pleasurable" she had ever spent. But for whatever reason, Fitz William remained at home under Judith's watchful eye.[43]

No matter what misgivings she had about her own or Fitz William's abilities, once Judith bowed to Winthrop's wisdom, she threw herself into the task of educating her younger brother. "Whether the young rogue will have the audacity to oppose himself to our united authority," she mused, "time must determine." Whenever she felt compelled to bolster her own position, she reminded Fitz William that she was simply following their brother's instructions. But while she tried to present a united front, in fact, she quietly shaped her advice in ways that subtly subverted—even if it did not directly challenge—Winthrop's rigid admonitions. Where Winthrop commanded, Judith appealed to Fitz William's better nature, referring to him as the "dear child of my affection." Nor was she above a little emotional blackmail. Imitating the practice of elite parents everywhere, she reminded him that he occupied a privileged position, that he had opportunities that most young men (and virtually all women?) would never enjoy. His mother and father, she told him, had gladly made numerous sacrifices on his behalf. He was, she added, their "darling boy, their youngest hope," and she hoped he would not disappoint them. Youth, she observed with what must have seemed to Fitz William tiresome regularity, was the "seed time." If he failed to take advantage of his opportunities as a boy, he would never achieve his potential as a man.[44]

Even as she reproved him for his shortcomings, Judith seized every opportunity to praise her younger brother's occasional successes. Unlike Winthrop, she believed that a steady diet of reproaches was likely to convince children that they were incapable of improvement, leading them to give up altogether. Even the most evil person, she explained to John Murray, has "some latent seed of Virtue," and that seed, if "cherished and brought to maturity by the timely influence of well adopted praise," would blossom. Praise would "stimulate to deeds of worth," as students became determined to earn the favor they did not yet deserve. In a poem she wrote in 1779, she expressed her thoughts succinctly. Flattery, she acknowledged, was nothing more than unmerited praise. But if it served as an encouragement, even if the commendation was "not *strictly true*," it was a wise strategy.[45]

Had he read his sister's letters to Fitz William, Winthrop would surely have been less uneasy about Judith's insistence on the value of praise. Whenever she bestowed a compliment on her younger brother, she inevitably followed it with ample criticism. If she told him he was doing well in math, she deplored his slow progress in the sciences. If she praised one of his letters, she immediately inundated him with advice designed to improve both the style and substance of his next missive. To Fitz William, it must have seemed as though he could never satisfy his older sister. Her assurances that one day he would surpass her and be able to correct *her* mistakes were hardly comforting. Indeed, Judith's letters had a lasting—and negative—effect on her brother. He was so traumatized by her criticisms that as an adult he refused to write to any of his siblings unless he had no other choice. Even then, his letters were brief and to the point—and he always complained when Judith sent him one of her long, rambling responses in return. What may have sounded like undue praise to Winthrop's ears did not seem so benign to Fitz William.[46]

If praise was an essential tool in the hands of a perceptive instructor, Judith agreed with Locke that teachers should introduce students to new areas of knowledge as gradually and painlessly as possible. This was especially true when it came to reading. In Judith's mind, reading was so important, it was "so rational, so improving, so superior," that anyone who failed to share her enthusiasm had a "wrong bent—an ill state of body." To correct such a defect, she advised Fitz William to start with light fare—always with the proviso that his meal did not violate the dicta of good taste. Some novels, for instance, were wholesome and might capture the imagination of reluctant pupils; others were "almost wholly destitute, even of the semblance of propriety." From novels, students could graduate to history. History, she said, "abounds with the most entertaining descriptions of Cities, Nations and empires, their Laws, Customs, manners, learning, religion and trade." A study of ancient civilizations led naturally to an examination of the reasons such civilizations declined. It also encouraged students to evaluate the merits of various forms of government, making them useful inhabitants of a nation whose very survival demanded an informed citizenry.[47]

In the fall of 1781, Fitz William moved to Boston, continuing the studies that Winthrop assumed would prepare him for Harvard. Judith seized the opportunity to begin writing to him once a week. Leaving it to others to keep her brother abreast of family news, she used her own letters to "freely advise, suggest, and direct."[48] Each letter was a meticulously designed, self-contained essay that focused on some aspect of her educational program. She regaled her brother with her views on the value of science, history, geography, and literature. She advised him on the importance of proper deportment, honesty, industry, perseverance, and gentility. She evaluated the merits of dueling and dancing. Taken together, the letters represent Judith's first sustained effort to lay out a comprehensive theory of education.

Judith consciously constructed her letters to appeal to Fitz William's practical bent, fully aware that lofty sentiments would be wasted on her brother and might even be counterproductive. The ability to write and an understanding of basic arithmetic, for instance, were essential skills for merchants. Without writing, human beings would be doomed to repeat the mistakes of the past, there would be no progress, and the work of the greatest geniuses would "blaze with momentary splendor" only to be lost forever. Sailors relied on arithmetic to circumnavigate the globe. Merchants needed it to compute costs and balance ledgers. It also served as the basis for other systems of knowledge. Geography, astronomy, and music all relied on mathematical relationships. Thus, she said, "you see the natural connexion or dependence of one branch of science on another." It was all, she exulted, part of "one harmonious chain, so intimately united that to draw the line of distinction becomes difficult, if not impossible."[49]

Despite her effort to be pragmatic, Judith was so convinced of the intrinsic value of learning that she could not always resist pointing out that education meant more than acquiring the skills of a businessman. Above all, even the most secular subjects provided religious lessons. No one could study astronomy, for instance, without coming to the conclusion that some "self-existent Great first cause" had created a vast universe whose bodies operated according to natural law. Similarly, a knowledge of geography led automatically to an appreciation of God's beneficence. "We become acquainted with the various divisions of this ball," she said, "we trace the economy of Deity, and his paternal love in thus proportioning it to the wants and exigencies of his creatures." Nature's variety, she continued, had to "extort, even from the frozen heart of the Atheist, an exclamation of wonder."[50]

No matter how hard she tried, Judith's efforts to educate her younger brother were unsuccessful. At first she tried to assure herself that "youth is the season of whim." But even in the fall of 1782, after he moved in with Daniel and Maria, living under the "eye of affection," exchanging "one parental roof for another" Fitz William continued to be a poor student. Like Anna, he began refusing to respond to his sister's letters. Perhaps he wished to avoid another round of criticism of his spelling, punctuation, and style. Perhaps, as Judith feared, he was beginning to resent her meddling and had decided that unlettered as she was, she had no business acting as his intellectual guide. In the end, Judith had to concede failure, when, in April of 1783, Winthrop Sr. abruptly ordered his son home for good. She was no longer able to send the weekly letters to Boston, which she had so enjoyed composing. Although one can well imagine that Fitz William breathed a hefty sigh of relief at this prospect, his sister missed writing her weekly letters and was devastated by her inability to turn her brother into a scholar.[51]

*   *   *

In most respects, Judith's advice to Fitz William was markedly different from her instructions to her niece, largely because her aims for the two were not the same. She wanted her brother's education to fit him for the public sphere, while she hoped that Anna's schooling would prepare her for private happiness. She seldom discussed heterosexual relationships or marital prospects with Fitz William. Marriage would come in due course, but a boy's education was not really designed to lead him to wedded bliss. Even the most educated girl, however, devoted her life to husband and—if she was fortunate—children. A well-educated young lady would choose her mate wisely. And she would be a good wife and mother because of her intellectual attainments. In one significant way, however, Judith had the same expectations for her brother and her niece. She wanted both to be genteel, sensible, and sympathetic, to meet the expectations of the elite social circles in which she hoped they would travel.[52]

Judith's promotion of gentility and sensibility served two crucial purposes. It helped her to claim the elite status that she saw as her birthright. It also gave her a way to craft a public role for herself, to contribute in an altogether proper way to the creation of a virtuous, orderly nation. Men exercised power and distinguished themselves by voting or holding political office. Judith, by constructing a more expansive and less gendered definition of political activity, thought that women, too, could be valued, even indispensable members of the new nation.

Especially after the Revolution, sensibility, the ability of genteel people to empathize with all humans, to form emotional attachments that reached beyond the family, had significant political connotations. Americans recognized that no society survived long if it was held together by sheer force. Sensibility—more than government—was the glue that held any country, but especially a heterogeneous one like America, together. In an extensive republic, whose members were flying off in all directions, pursuing their interests with little regard for the effect their actions had on others, some countervailing force had to be encouraged if the new nation was not going to disintegrate. The government, the "hard public sphere," was too weak and disorganized to apply the brakes to young, ambitious, autonomous men who focused almost exclusively on their own material prospects. Simply put, ordinary citizens in their private capacity had to do what government could not accomplish. As Judith had noted in her essay on Locke, the social sense was innate. But it needed to be nourished if its effects were to extend beyond the home. She thought that women, whose "affectionate sympathy" was especially strong, were uniquely suited to the task of developing "that subtle, and pervading sensation, which unites and cements consenting minds." It was the "intercourse of Minds," not the "*corporal*" or material bonds, that interested Judith. What eighteenth-century commentators designated as "sociability"—the work of keeping the family together, developing rational friendships, conversing, writing—was what women did best, and this was the foundation upon which the republican experiment ultimately rested. The social order survived only through shared affection, and the development of affection began in the family—the society in miniature—before it spread to the town, the state, the country, and the world—even, thought Judith, to the entire universe. The ascetic values of classical republicanism were well suited to a country at war. But in peacetime, a new ethic of selflessness had to replace one based on martial sacrifice. It was the job of naturally sympathetic women to tame men—not to emasculate them, but to help them retain their "manly vigor" even as they exhibited "humanitarian sentiment."[53]

If sensibility and gentility gave Judith an opportunity to shape the new nation, they also implied hierarchy. Those individuals who occupied the lower orders of the social strata were like animals, too rough, too unpolished, too selfish, and perhaps too insecure to sympathize with others. They, who were often the objects of charity, could not possibly offer charity to those still less fortunate. But members of the elite understood that sensibility was a product of their mind and a measure of their superiority. Thus, Judith constantly called attention to her own sensible character, knowing that by doing so she was exhibiting one of the most important qualities of gentility. "I do really possess a heart capable of feeling for, and sympathizing with every suffering son, or daughter of humanity," she told her uncle. Her heart "bleeds," she wrote another relative, when she confronted evidence of the pain that some people endure. Thus, when she visited the Gloucester almshouse, a "miscellaneous receptacle of suffering," she was moved to tears by the misery of its denizens.[54]

Judith approved of the exclusionary uses to which her sentimental gentility might be put. She longed to establish a rational, sympathetic, and equal connection with men of her own status, but she strove to distance herself from the men and women who occupied the lower tiers of the social order. She clung so tenaciously to her position at least in part because she understood just how precarious it was. She knew from firsthand experience that wealth and position in America could be achieved and lost with alarming speed. All Americans, but especially merchant families, knew that they could not take their position for granted. Thus Judith believed that both Fitz William and Anna had to master the intricate rules that defined proper decorum so that even if they endured economic reverses, they could—as Judith herself did—lay claim to gentility. Manners were not merely trivial reflections of good breeding. Those who knew how to behave were welcome in polite circles everywhere. Those who did not were pariahs. In an enlightened society, manners signified civility and character, separating the "refined or sentimental" from the "merely animal." Even more than the ownership of property, Judith suggested, genteel behavior gave people a sense of their own worth.[55]

Like many of her elite counterparts, Judith saw the performance of gentility as desirable, but she also recognized its dangers. She worried because many members of her own class were beginning to argue that the best way to discourage an egalitarian blurring of bounds was to construct an edifice based upon "natural" gender differences. They suggested that good women should not only behave decorously, but should remain contentedly in the private sphere. At the same time, they argued that women who ignored appropriate boundaries or who were immodest or overtly sexual, who, in other words, imitated the foibles of the lower class, threatened the social order. Judith also knew that because politeness was by definition artificial, even theatrical, it threatened to violate the precepts of honesty, simplicity, and virtue that she prized. The wellborn had to walk a very fine line. While they had to be dignified and cultured, in a republic too much attention to decorum was dangerous. Although both men and women were susceptible to the temptation to be overly refined, common wisdom had it that women were especially vain and hedonistic. Judith argued, however, that men were at least as likely to engage in conspicuous consumption as women. As she declared in her "Sentiments,"

If dress decides—behold the fop,
And each illiberal censure drop.
High powder'd hair with scented snuff,
And every word an empty puff,
His kerchief wafting perfumes mound
With tinsel lace his beaver bound . . .
With bosom pin, and brilliant rings,
Gad's what italian airs he sings![56]

If the practice of gentility always threatened to turn women into selfish coquettes and men into effeminate fops, it presented an even graver danger after the Revolution: the risk of being cast as antidemocratic. Gentility smacked of the very aristocratic order that American soldiers had so recently defeated on the battlefield. Unchecked, it privileged the witty repartee of frivolous and decadent aristocratic pretenders over the quiet decorum of worthy Christians. Yet no one, least of all Judith Stevens, wanted to disregard all gradations. The question, always, was to what extent—and how to justify—class (or gender or racial) difference in a society based on egalitarian values. Hence apologists found it necessary to situate gentility in a republican context. Politeness, they insisted, was useful. It made social relationships more comfortable, and it reminded the genteel of their obligations to the less fortunate. Without it, the world would be chaotic and bellicose and human relationships would founder. Moreover, if gentility was acquired rather than inherited, it actually spoke to the emerging values of the new nation. It gave everyone at least the illusion that they could earn a higher status. Diligent individuals could cultivate civility, restrain their baser instincts, and transcend the limitations of their birth. Even the Irish, Judith acknowledged, could acquire the rudiments of polite behavior. She, herself, had met one such man, a captain in the British army, who had managed to improve himself by reading and traveling, and was therefore "not wholly unpolished." Most important, she had often heard him "express great and respectful devotion to the sex." In Judith's mind, no greater proof of civility existed.[57]

Still, only a relative few would manage to do what the Irish captain had done. Gentility was not natural. It required education, perseverance, and, above all, self-control. Only the most rational beings could control their passions—especially their sexual, bodily desires—with such consistency that circumspect behavior became a habit. Lower-class people could seldom do this. Women, who according to popular wisdom were weak and irrational, also found it difficult to resist bodily temptations. Those who took the trouble to learn proper etiquette and who practiced it with ease, making it *appear* natural, had earned their position.[58]

Judith accepted the value of gentility without question and tried to pass the attributes of sociability down to her niece and brother. Her letters often sounded like the essays on courtesy that dotted the pages of the *Spectator* or that appeared in the didactic passages of Richardson's *Clarissa*. Like these English models, she emphasized the need to respect rank and order, to exhibit bodily restraint, to empathize, and to strive for social harmony. She also recommended a relaxed bearing that made polite behavior appear effortless. Her protégés should be "perfectly easy and genteel, and apparently unconscious of superiority." Well-bred people were graceful, but never affected. A "certain polish" was necessary, for people with rough manners made poor impressions, no matter how intelligent or virtuous they may have been. Judith also wanted Fitz William and Anna to master the "highly sentimental" art of "chit chat." They should steer conversations toward topics that were of general interest, avoiding long, boring discourses or the tendency to be argumentative or didactic. She warned Fitz William, in particular, to curb his predilection for witticisms that degenerated into ridicule. "Cheerful hilarity," she said, was always pleasing. But mocking someone else, even if it led to popularity in the short run, resulted in anguish. Good conversationalists sought to please others. "To give pain," Judith admonished, "is strictly immoral." The key, indeed, was to make everyone comfortable, to make life easy for equals and inferiors alike. Significantly, Judith thought that the best way to do this was to follow established rules. If she believed that custom was a despot when it curtailed women's rights or refused to tolerate religious differences, she knew that it was salutary in social relations. "Nature," she said, "endowed a correct mind, with some rules of self-government." Breaking those rules would lead "to much inconvenience, and create no inconsiderable vexation."[59]

While it was important to be comfortable in polite society, there were dangers awaiting those who frequented the "Beau Monde," with its "insincerity, frivolity, its illusive pleasures." Whenever she returned home from Boston, Judith claimed to be happy to bid adieu to a place "where dissipation sways, / And every night her giddy rule obeys." She insisted that she preferred the rural charms of her native village to the "guileful flattery" and "garish vices" of the metropolis. People should not be rustics of course. But she knew from personal observation that too much time in the city could destroy the character of virtually anyone, especially the young and innocent.[60]

Thus Judith warned both Fitz William and Anna to avoid the foibles of Boston's social scene. While she conceded that the mind "requires unbending," she deplored pleasures that came at someone else's expense. Thus she railed against the practice young people had recently adopted of gathering in small groups, keeping up a "whispering confab," and making outsiders uneasy. Such behavior, Judith pronounced, was "absolutely rude." Private conversations should be reserved for private places. Card playing was another popular activity that Judith found repugnant. People indulged in it, she said, as a way of "*killing time*," the very notion of which she found "Vile, and truly shocking." She could not understand why some people were "devoted to the shuffling, cutting, and dividing fifty-two small bits of parte board—Varregated by black, and red spots." The practice destroyed the health and intellect of all those layabouts who languished at card tables for hours on end. When they played for money, the consequences were still worse. Losers were "stripped of their last dollar" while winners—who were lucky, not virtuous—basked in their own false sense of superiority.[61]

Judith took her obligations to her brother and her niece seriously. She felt that by fulfilling them, she was doing her small part to shape the values of the new nation without risking her own reputation.[62] She was convinced that women could use the domestic realm as a platform for encouraging the harmonious social relations upon which American stability could be built. Even so, something was missing. She enjoyed composing letters of advice to Anna and Fitz William. She continued to scratch away in her little closet, writing poems and essays that she shared with her closest confidants. But she longed for a larger audience, and she wanted to have a direct impact on society. In 1782, she had made her first hesitant foray into the world of letters when she published her *Catechism*. But then she had acted as a servant of God rather than country. And she had acted more-or-less anonymously, claiming—not completely convincingly—to have no intention of using the *Catechism* to obtain the recognition she so obviously desired. In the years to come, she would cast a wider net, becoming increasingly confident and ambitious as she used her talents to shape the trajectory of the new nation and to advance her "career of fame."

PART II

Republic of Letters: 1783–1798

Judith Stevens declared that she had crossed the Rubicon when she published her Universalist catechism in 1782. Still she waited two years before she published anything else. Even after the war between England and its former colonies ended, Judith had a great deal to occupy her. Not only did she—at long last—have a house to run and two orphans to educate, but she was increasingly distracted by the painful realization that her husband's wartime success as a merchant had been only temporary. Moreover, while she continued to scribble away throughout the war years and thereafter, writing reams of poetry and many essays, she needed a venue for her work. Until hostilities ended, there were few publishers who were interested in the effusions of women writers.

In May of 1784, however, Judith's eye was drawn to an announcement in the *Gentleman and Lady's Town and Country Magazine*, one of the many literary journals that appeared throughout America—especially along the New England coast—in the years after the Revolution.[1] Like most magazines of its kind, it was short-lived. Like the others, it appealed to a small but growing audience, hungry for original work, and seemingly eager to patronize the native talent of a very young nation. It was eclectic, casting a wide net, promising to entertain, instruct, and enlighten the men and women who perused its pages. There, readers could find a mix of sentimental stories, essays on manners, political analyses, and edifying poetry. Like other American periodicals, it relied to a large extent on its readers to fill its pages each month. In the very first issue, the editors asked supporters to submit "pieces of Merit" for possible publication. They promised that if they had to reject a submission, they would strive to avoid language that might damage the fragile self-esteem of prospective writers. No "indelicate Censure, or solemn Criticism" would emanate from their desks. Even more tantalizing, the editors appealed to the "Ladies in particular" to "patronize this Work, by adding the elegant polish of the Female Pencil, where purity of sentiment, and impassioned Fancy, are happily blended together."[2] Most magazines sought readers of both sexes. Not all were so pointed in soliciting women writers. As Judith read the editors' invitation, she could not help but hope that they had women like her in mind.

Judith's perusal of the first issue did nothing to discourage her. Admittedly, the volume featured articles on international and national affairs, which most people assumed would attract a male audience. But it also included a number of essays that appealed to women, essays that Judith could have written herself. An essay on friendship, contributed by "Lucia," a "Female Correspondent," condemned vain women who preferred the superficial flattery of coxcombs to the truth from real friends. Another, "The Advantages of mutual Correspondence between the two Sexes," extolled the value of conversations between men and women. Invoking the "complimentarian" language of the day, it argued that women would become more rational, their fund of knowledge more extensive if they conversed with men. At the same time, men who sought out women's company would learn to be polite, cheerful, good-natured, and graceful. Still another essay offered "Advice to a Young Lady, concerning Marriage." It praised a girl who was well-versed in ornamental accomplishments, yet was adept at the skills demanded of a "useful housewife." It argued that women should not marry for money and that, once married, they should enjoy "rational entertainments," rejecting the giddy pleasures of the beau monde. If Judith noted that these were sentiments she had already expressed privately, she could condemn "Rules and Maxims for promoting Matrimonial Happiness, Addressed to the Ladies." The essay urged women to honor their vow to obey their husbands, as it insisted that a wife's power rested solely in her husband's esteem. A woman, it maintained, should avoid arguments, accept her husband's foibles, and submit to his superior judgment.[3]

As early as June of 1784, Judith began contemplating the possibility of submitting a piece of her own to the magazine. She approached her project with anxiety, for the editors of the *Gentleman and Lady's Town and Country Magazine* had already refused to print some offerings, either because they were "imperfect" or because they did not promise to instruct or entertain potential readers. Still, they continued to ask for more. Judith wanted her own piece to be flawless. When a friend praised one of her poems she was pleased, but thought that "at present" it was not ready to present to the public eye. Instead she sat down to write something she hoped was worthy of consideration. Before long she had completed an essay, which she tentatively entitled "Reverence Thy Self."[4]

The essay, which she would publish in a somewhat altered form as "Desultory Thoughts," focused on many of the themes Judith had written about over the years. Assuming that women were as rational as men, it called upon the new nation to educate the fairer sex. It argued that women should be encouraged to utilize their talents, to transcend the obstacles that traditional society and despotic custom had erected in a misguided effort to confine them to a narrow sphere. "Improvements," she said, "are within the grasp of industry." Like her

Catechism, the essay implied that mothers—not fathers—were best equipped to help their daughters develop the innate seeds of rationality. Finally, it maintained that praise was the most powerful engine an instructor had at her disposal. Girls, in particular, were prone to have a "low estimate of *Self*." Such a lack of esteem not only discouraged them from developing their talents; it was positively dangerous. A girl who was not accustomed to compliments would almost surely succumb to the flattery of a conniving seducer. Moreover, if she lacked confidence, she would accept the first marriage proposal she received from the most inappropriate suitor, convinced that she was in danger of being "stigmatized with that dreaded title, an Old Maid."[5] While the first part of the essay pointed to the dangers awaiting women who did not "reverence themselves," the last painted a glowing picture of a society where women were educated for independence and taught to believe that they—like all humans—could make rational choices.

Unfortunately, real life distracted her in the years immediately following the publication of "Desultory Thoughts." The death of her first husband and her marriage to John Murray, two pregnancies—one that ended happily, another that did not—business and pleasure, all intervened and she had neither the time nor the energy to enter the "republic of letters" on a regular basis. But beginning in 1791, she resumed her "career of fame" in earnest, publishing a number of poems and essays in the *Massachusetts Magazine*. She began her famous "Gleaner" essays in 1792, continuing at the same time to write short pieces for "The Repository" under the sobriquet "Constantia." In 1795, after the Murrays moved to Boston with their daughter, Julia Maria, Judith tried her hand at the dramatic arts, seeing two of her plays—*The Medium* and *The Traveller Returned*—performed in the Federal Street Theater in 1795 and 1796 respectively. And in 1798, she published her three-volume magnum opus, *The Gleaner*, a compendium of poems, essays, and plays, as well as her novel-like story of "Margaretta."

Judith hoped that she would merit the applause of America's literary community as she prepared her work for the public arena. She hoped, as well, to become part of that discursive public sphere which occupied a distinct if anomalous position between the nation's formal political structures and the domestic arena. While she recognized that formal politics was the province of elite white men, Judith always strove to find a place at the table for talented women who might contribute to discussions that would shape the social, cultural, and political order of a virtuous nation. Eighteenth-century Americans did not welcome women into the halls of Congress. They were somewhat more receptive to women's efforts to influence the nation through writing. Admittedly, they were happier when women stuck to moral or domestic topics, as Judith did in "Desultory Thoughts." But even discussions of seemingly private issues had a political dimension. They proved, if nothing else, that women were intelligent, rational beings, capable of analyzing their world and offering prescriptions for its improvement. They also gave elite women the opportunity to demand public recognition of whatever social authority they had. Simply writing about domestic affairs was an assertion of the importance of women's activities. Finally, they allowed women to challenge—sometimes directly, usually subtly—their own exclusion from the body politic.[6]

In "Desultory Thoughts" Judith had proclaimed that literary ambition was a "noble" endeavor. In the years following the publication of her first essay, Judith gave full rein to her own ambitions, expanding her efforts to speak in clear, unambiguous political terms, demanding to become a recognized member of the republic of letters. In the end, she was only partially successful, becoming increasingly disappointed and even embittered as she watched her work being denigrated—or worse, simply ignored. But almost until the end of her life, she continued to seek the literary crown.

Chapter 5
"Sweet Peace"

Judith Stevens had eagerly anticipated the end of the war between England and America, assuming that with "sweet peace," the anxieties and turmoil that she had intermittently suffered throughout the long struggle for independence would soon be little more than a faint and unpleasant memory. She took it for granted that the new nation would not alter the stable and hierarchical order that buttressed her own social position. She believed that the new government would eagerly welcome the best men in the country to the corridors of power, allowing men like her brother Winthrop to take their rightful place in a world that recognized their talents and honored their heroic, wartime sacrifices. She, too, might have a place in the new order, and she looked forward to beginning her literary career in earnest, using her pen to shape the values upon which the fortunes of the newly formed United States rested. But if Judith thought that she and people like her would lay the foundations for America's future glory uncontested, she was disappointed. The changes she wanted—changes that would allow women to escape the constraints that relegated them to the private sphere—failed to materialize. If anything, women's sphere actually became smaller. Conversely, the changes she feared most—the democratization of the social order, the diminution of the importance of her New England home—began to appear almost as soon as the war ended. It was not long before she sensed that the nation was moving in directions that would keep her on the margins, making her little more than a bystander who watched helplessly as her own values became increasingly irrelevant.[1]

Judith's sense of personal well-being did not disappear all at once. She refused to accept as permanent some disquieting signs indicating that New England's elite would not enjoy the influence its members had once taken for granted. Nor was it until 1786 that she was forced to admit that her husband's fortunes were steadily declining, putting her on a course that would destroy her self-confidence, leaving her with emotional scars that would eventually pale but never vanish. John was always so optimistic, so sure of himself that Judith was simply unprepared for the disastrous turn his financial affairs took. Thus, in the beginning, she was generally able to enjoy a measure of peacetime tranquility and a social position that she regarded as her due.

* * *

In December of 1784, some of Gloucester's literati formed what Judith called a "society," designed to help its members while away a few hours during the bleak New England winters that stretched endlessly before them. Composed largely of members of the Independent Church, the group's sixteen men and women assembled in one another's houses each Monday night, discussing any book that caught their fancy and feasting on a "cold collation, with a desert of fruit, wine, and lemonade." Judith knew just how difficult it was to find true "sentimentalists" in a spot as secluded as Gloucester, so it was important to cultivate even the rawest material. Conversation, she observed, was "manure to the soul." Sadly, when John Murray became ill, the group disintegrated. Perhaps her native village was simply too provincial to sustain so ambitious an enterprise.[2]

When real life failed to meet her expectations, however, Judith always found succor in books. Gloucester had no bookstore or library, but she borrowed countless volumes from generous friends in York, Maine, Portsmouth, New Hampshire, and Boston. Despite her doubts about the propriety of novels, she continued to weep over the fortunes of many a tragic heroine. *Clarissa* remained one of her favorites, and she recommended it enthusiastically to everyone she knew. Richardson's novels, she proclaimed, were "of essential use in forming the minds of young women." They were "replete with rules proper for young persons, at the most important periods of their lives—nothing, it appears to me, can be added thereto." She also enjoyed Voltaire. And she was thoroughly enchanted by Catharine Macaulay, the "female historian," as she begged her brother Winthrop to tell her as much about the English writer as he could. As for Sterne, he wrote with "brilliancy," but she could never approve his penchant for creating "licentious libertines" whose examples might destroy the innocence of young readers. She was still more conflicted by Rousseau. *Héloïse* was, she granted, well written but hardly faultless. Her "pride of womanhood" would not let her forgive Rousseau for "those sentiments so humiliating to our sex." It was ridiculous to assume, as the Swiss philosopher did, that an educated woman should "relinquish her ideas, not presuming to have an opinion, which shall vary from her Father while under his care, nor clash with those of her Lord and Master, while consigned over as property!!" Women are not "mere machines," she raged. They had a brain, a heart, and a conscience and it was surely their right to think for themselves.[3]

Judith did not always enjoy the life of the mind. Like most merchants' wives, she did little productive work, but this hardly meant she enjoyed a carefree existence.[4] Her one domestic servant probably took over some of the heaviest jobs, but one servant did not make Judith Stevens a lady of leisure. Moreover, there were occasions when she had no household help at all. She did not spin, but there was seldom a day that she did not pick up needle and thread to make new clothes or mend old ones. Every room in her three-story house, was crammed with furniture and glassware that required regular cleaning and dusting. Every fireplace was a source of dirt. Beds had to be made and chamber pots emptied. Rising standards of cleanliness meant that Judith spent more time than she liked on repetitive tasks that she characterized as "trivial" even though they were essential. Like many women of her class, she welcomed guests—both friends and relatives—into her home for days, even weeks on end. And while she enjoyed their company and was proud that she finally had the resources to be a gracious host, she complained that some visitors were impossible to please. She spent hours preserving berries, devising menus, preparing food, and creating the impression that her household affairs were in order, when in fact she thought they had spun out of control. Totally absorbed in the minutia that characterized women's work, she often complained that "joy, intellectual joy" eluded her altogether. Now and then, she rebelled, snatching an occasional moment at her desk, writing a few lines, even though the "turkey burn, or the pudding boil fast to the pot."[5]

At such moments, Judith fantasized about the life she longed to lead. She would be a "Lady" surrounded by many dutiful servants who saw to her every need. She would attend the theater, the ballet, and the opera whenever the spirit moved her. She would own a huge house with open gates, where she could offer hospitality to all. "I should not mean," she hastily added, "to associate indiscriminately, different Classes." After all, she continued, "Providence hath drawn the line, and I should have in view the happiness of my fellow Creatures. Confusion would not promote my purpose, since Order is the Parent of felicity." Thus she would welcome to her salon only those who met the exacting standards of a true "sentimentalist." Her house would be filled with elegantly written classics, whose merits she would judge with a discerning eye. If that scenario was too far-fetched even for her dreams, she imagined that at the very least she would live "upon terms of equality" with a learned lord who would help her evaluate the work that her inferior education kept her from appreciating.[6]

*   *   *

If Judith was relatively pleased with the shape her life had finally assumed, it did not take her long to sense that not all America's leaders shared her values, and that many members of Congress were neither honorable nor virtuous. Her first indication that this was the case came as she saw the government turning its back on the very officers and soldiers who had made independence possible. Again and again she deplored "American Ingratitude" as she watched men like Winthrop fail to receive their just rewards at war's end. In fact, Congress's attitude toward the veterans should not have surprised her. American Whigs had always maintained a complicated relationship with the soldiers who defended their country's liberty. They applauded the republican virtue of those who risked their lives for the public good. Yet they distrusted the career military man and saw officers, in particular, as vain, effeminate, delicate, and hungry for the ribbons and adulation they received from an easily corrupted public.[7]

Winthrop and Judith both discovered just how ungrateful the new nation could be in 1783, when a group of retired Continental army officers announced the creation of the Order of the Cincinnati, a hereditary organization designed to honor America's military leaders. The former officers were blindsided by the outrage that followed. Men such as Samuel Adams—who had never risked their lives in combat—cried that the order violated the very principles for which the war had been waged. They predicted that it would lead irrevocably to the creation of a military aristocracy despite the nation's professed rejection of immutable class differences. Almost immediately, Judith composed a poem—long even by her standards—"On reading the institution of the Cincinnati," defending the organization as the embodiment of everything that was best in the new nation. Its members, she insisted, sought no titles, no "gaudy trappings of nobility." They were merely dedicated to the development of virtue in themselves and in the nation as a whole, and they promised to defend the country from foreigners who would inevitably try to destroy a government whose principles they neither understood nor condoned.[8]

While many Americans saw the roots of a corrupt aristocracy when they viewed the Order of the Cincinnati, Judith was appalled at the egalitarian rhetoric of such critics. "I tremble," she wrote, "as I reflect upon the popular tyranny established under the specious name of a republic." She believed in democracy but she thought efforts to turn America into a classless society were dangerous and nonsensical. In her mind, democracy and equality did not go hand in hand; while the one was desirable, the other was pernicious. Heaven itself was ordered. The natural world, too, was known for its variety, for its small rivers and vast oceans, its craggy mountains and rolling hills, each valuable in its own way, yet each boasting its own unique character. Similarly, there would always be distinctions among people. If the republic were to survive, the many had to submit to the wisdom of the worthy few who alone could guide the nation through the thickets and shoals that might thwart the country's progress. "Peace and consequent happiness," Judith insisted, "are intimately connected with subordination."[9]

In July 1784, Judith put pen to paper once again to express her disgust at her country's treatment of its veterans. Likening America to a virgin whose innocence had been destroyed by a base despoiler, her poem begged the nation to return to virtue before it was too late. She hoped the government would think beyond short-term self-interest and compensate those warriors who had done so much for their country. Clad only in their "naked honor," they had steadfastly fought for principle rather than personal glory. When the war was going badly, a desperate Congress had promised to reward them at war's end. Now that those promises were forgotten, she wondered if anyone would trust the American government again.[10]

Judith made no effort to publish either her ode to the Cincinnati or her poem on "American Ingratitude." Nevertheless, the two pieces signaled her determination to create a niche for herself as a citizen in the new nation. She conceded that her verses were poorly written and barely grammatical, but she resolutely rejected any suggestion that she had gone out of her "own little sphere" when she discussed political matters. America, she assured Winthrop, "is both *your* Country and *mine*." She might not be able to take up arms for the cause of liberty or even vote for her nation's leaders, but she had the right—even the obligation—to use her literary talents to celebrate the achievements of America's warriors and to influence the direction that the country's leaders would take.[11]

If she did not hesitate to comment on public policy in private, when Judith finally dared to reenter the literary world in earnest she selected a topic that was closer to her self-defined province. She would discuss the need to educate women to achieve their full potential. This was an issue about which she had thought a great deal over the years. It was also one with which she had some personal experience. She had done her best to shape her niece Anna into a genteel—but potentially independent—young woman. Perhaps she could offer some guidance to parents everywhere who were trying to do the same thing.

Judith was moved to action in May of 1784, when she read the announcement in the *Gentleman and Lady's Town and Country Magazine*, asking readers to submit their literary efforts for possible publication. Judith had not published anything since her *Catechism* had appeared in 1782. But despite her insistence that she was not especially talented, her literary ambitions had never abated and she could not help but feel that the magazine's appeal for women writers was aimed at her. "Could I persuade all the world to cherish a predilection for me," she admitted, "I should not hesitate to scribble on, to the end of the chapter, while the efforts of my pen should be dispersed far and wide."[12] She immediately began preparing one of her essays for submission. Just five months after the first copy of the *Gentleman and Lady's Town and Country Magazine* appeared, Judith saw her essay in print. She signed her piece "Constantia," the sobriquet she already used when she wrote to Maria Sargent.

Judith opened her piece with a short poem, a convention she continued in all her published essays. Her verse argued that "self-estimation" was essential for all women, even as it protested the "narrow bounds" that currently confined "the Sex." The essay elaborated on the same theme. Maintaining that "ambition is a noble principle," Judith argued that girls should be encouraged to dream, to stretch their minds, to believe that they were capable of succeeding at any endeavor.[13] Anyone who knew her, would have recognized the themes that Judith broached in her first published essay. It contained arguments she had already sounded privately over the years and that she would repeat in public in the decades to come. But if it was not new in philosophy, her decision to publish was a huge step.

Despite her ambitions, Judith submitted her essay to the magazine's editors with real misgivings. When she had published the *Catechism*, she had rationalized that she was doing God's work. In this instance she had no such defense. True, by the end of the eighteenth century, most people did not condemn women whose work appeared in public so long as they discussed appropriate topics and received no money for their work. On both scores, Judith could rest easy. Her essay touched upon a subject—education—that was entirely proper. And she assured her friends that she would never accept pay for the "spontaneous ebullitions of the heart." She hungered only for fame, and her ability to secure a publisher convinced her that she might actually achieve her goal.[14] She was heartened when the editors of the *Gentleman and Lady's Magazine* singled out her essay for commendation, commenting that "The Publishers return their thanks to Constantia for her offered favors, and would take it kind if she would send her Lucubrations early in the month." This was high praise, indeed.

Still, her piece was traditional. Judith's arguments were not out of the mainstream, though the vigor with which she made her points may have surprised some readers. They were arguments, moreover, that she would repeat when she began her "Gleaner" essays for the *Massachusetts Magazine* a few years later. In fact, before she sent her essay to the editors of the *Gentleman and Lady's Magazine*, she actually toned down her rhetoric. She called her published version "Desultory Thoughts upon the Utility of encouraging a degree of Self-Complacency, especially in Female Bosoms." The title implied a level of humility and diffidence that was far removed from the bold, double-underlined assertion of the original essay. Her thoughts were "desultory." They lacked a definite shape or plan. And she advocated only a "*degree* of self-complacency" for women. Her manuscript said she was "certain" of her arguments. The finished project, employing the passive voice, said she was only "persuaded" that they might be true. Her conclusion was more reserved as well. As literary scholar Karen Schiff points out, Judith ends the manuscript version with confidence. She is fairly "bursting with ideas for the betterment of women." In print, however, she apologizes for the "fugitive hints," the mere "hypothesis," of her essay, as she invites an "abler pen to improve thereon."[15]

As excited as she was by the prospect of publishing even more, Judith did not throw herself headlong into writing, in part because she was not entirely pleased with the results of her efforts. Almost a year after her first essay appeared, Judith continued to feel "some pain" whenever she looked at the printers' errors that marred its pages. To be linked to mistakes so obvious that even she recognized them, was "mortifying to a young and timid Author." She would be wise, she often thought, to "shield herself in her native obscurity." In fact, although she continued to write in private, it was some time before Judith published anything again. As John's economic fortunes worsened and her domestic affairs became more discombobulated, she had neither the time nor the energy to enter the republic of letters.[16]

*   *   *

Judith faced many disappointments in the years after the American Revolution, disappointments that made her frustration with printers' errors pale in comparison. To begin with, there was her concern about her brother. Winthrop seemed to make all the wrong decisions at war's end, challenging Judith's understanding of the importance of tradition, family, and even her belief in her beloved New England's central position in the scheme of things. While she clung tenaciously to the values of former days, she saw that Winthrop was determined to leave the town of his birth, to strike out on his own, seeking adventure and fortune elsewhere. Perhaps he recognized that a merchant's life was too uncertain, too likely to end in failure. Perhaps he sensed that America's future did not lay in his native region. He was still young. He was unattached. And he was a man. He could do what his sister could not, pursuing his dreams wherever they might lead him. If most people tended to distrust bachelors, viewing them as rootless men, unconnected to community or family, likely to wander aimlessly, taking unwise risks and succumbing to carnal temptation, Winthrop could turn his apparent defects into assets. He might be lonely and unconnected, he might lack a secure position and a wife and family to govern and give meaning to his life, but he was free in ways that Judith could never be.[17]

Winthrop was in no hurry to return to Gloucester at war's end. In November of 1782, he was in Boston, stubbornly refusing even to write, and discouraging his sister from making the trip to the capital city to see him. Judith occasionally wrote to him on behalf of their "weeping mother," but Winthrop was strangely immune to the effects of her most sentimental language. When he finally arrived in Gloucester in March, he was aloof. He had already warned Judith that his sojourn there would be brief and that he did not plan to visit very often thereafter. When she pushed for an explanation, he tersely responded that the less said, the better. They now lived in different worlds and traveled on different roads, he remarked cryptically. He could no longer share his intimate thoughts with her.[18] If Judith had expected that the end of the war would erase some of the differences between herself and her soldier brother, she was wrong. Instead, the gulf between them had actually widened.

No matter how often she appealed to Winthrop's sense of compassion or duty, her brother remained unmoved. He did not know what he wanted to do with his life, but he could not imagine returning to a place he had not really called home since he left it at the age of ten. In fact, Winthrop was in an anomalous position. In earlier times, he would have agreed with Judith. He would not even have considered defying his parents' wishes, but would have dutifully returned, no matter how stultifying he found his native home. Granted, he would have expected more financial help than his father was willing or able to offer—but if times were hard, thanks to the postwar depression that affected virtually everyone in Gloucester—he would no doubt have made do with reduced circumstances. By the last quarter of the eighteenth century, however, patriarchs were losing some control over their sons. This was in part because fathers like Winthrop, Sr. were unable to promise much security in a world that even in the best of times was risky. It was due, as well, to the values of the American Revolution. As young men fought for independence and celebrated the "pursuit of happiness," the notion that they should disregard their own self-interest and humbly submit to the authority of their elders seemed increasingly archaic. Thus it was now possible, if not desirable, for Winthrop to abandon his family and to achieve his ambitions in his own way.[19]

Winthrop was a product of changes that touched American men long before they began to transform the lives of women. Like his sister, he had been raised to see his identity in terms of his relationship to family and community. His family gave him his social position and a sense of continuity with his past. It also promised him a secure place in the future. In Gloucester, simply being a

"Sargent" was enough to give him respect so long as he served both God and his fellow man. If he had sons of his own, he was expected to teach them the values that had worked from time immemorial to create a peaceful and prosperous community, where each generation would learn anew to appreciate the eternal verities that made life worth living. Even before the Revolution, however, and much more in the last decades of the eighteenth century, the significance attached to family name and community gave way—for men at least—to values based upon individualism and a relatively unfettered and competitive pursuit of profit. Such a view of the world privileged the man who had the courage to free himself from the restraints of the past and who took advantage of the myriad opportunities that awaited those who were strong and intelligent enough to recognize them for what they were.[20]

Winthrop was at loose ends. He had his feet in two worlds. Like Judith, he cherished the order, the predictability, the relative security of the past—and he was proud of the position his family had always enjoyed. Yet he yearned to prove himself and to earn the respect of his contemporaries. Thus, when one door after another slammed in his face, he became disillusioned with an environment that his own exploits on the battlefield had made possible. He wandered aimlessly from Boston to Philadelphia to New York and back again, trying to figure out how to make a living commensurate with his talents and expectations. Like so many officers in the Continental army, he was disappointed by his postwar prospects. He was in poor health. His pension was negligible. The "dastardly" Congress paid him in near worthless paper money that would scarcely last six months. He had fought to free his country from England's yoke, but at the age of thirty-one he was unable to achieve his own independence. Depressed and plagued by a "lassitude of intellect," he wondered if he had lost any chance for happiness.[21]

Although she sympathized with her brother, Judith was convinced that the way he chose to respond to his malaise was wrongheaded, perhaps even immoral. She could not understand why he was considering leaving Gloucester— indeed all of New England—for good. But Winthrop was acknowledging what she, herself, could never accept: New England's prospects were slowly, inexorably, in decline. He was by no means the only footloose young man in these years who was beginning to realize that America's destiny lay, not in the seacoast villages or rocky soil of the Northeast, but in the vast expanses of the nation's hinterland.[22]

Even before the war officially ended, Winthrop was contemplating relocating to Georgia, where good land could be had at an attractive price. Judith was horrified. Georgia's climate was "unfriendly to a northern constitution," she insisted, and a move there would cause immeasurable grief to those who loved him most. If he did not want to live in Gloucester, she asked, what was the matter with Boston? There he would be able to assuage his thirst for variety and adventure. Forgetting that she once had advised him not to trust his fate "to the mercy of the mighty waters," she now wondered why he was not content with the entirely respectable life of the merchant. Such a career might not guarantee great wealth, but it was an occupation for which his entire upbringing had prepared him. The Sargents had always been merchants, not farmers or speculators. Fitz William had already proclaimed that "'the Ocean is my only alternative.'" Jack Ellery, Esther and John's son, was similarly inclined and chafed at his parents' determination to give him a classical education before they allowed him to follow his heart's desire. Winthrop's plans struck Judith as a deliberate rejection of his family and its traditions. It was, moreover, "self banishment," a "voluntary Exile," that would do him little good and might lead him to an early grave. Please, she begged, abandon your "career of ambition" and be content with moderate gains. But Winthrop refused to follow Judith's advice to "pursue some honourable road to complacency."[23]

By the spring of 1786, Winthrop's plans to settle in Georgia had fallen through, much to Judith's relief. His efforts to obtain a government sinecure had also come to nothing. Still, his wanderlust had not abated. In June, while Judith was in New London, Connecticut, she received a letter from her brother informing her that he was leaving Boston for a destination as yet unknown. She soon discovered that Congress had made him one of seven national surveyors of the Ohio country, a vast territory acquired through the Peace of Paris, whose fertile soil promised ambitious men a new start in a "virgin" land. He had already developed an interest in the territory. In March, he had been present when a group of disaffected Continental army veterans—primarily New Englanders—had met in Boston to organize the Ohio Company. He acted as the group's clerk, and soon became one of the company's most effective lobbyists, persuading Congress to sell its members "hundreds of thousands of acres" at a dollar a piece. Winthrop left Boston in June and was captivated at once, enthusiastically—and no doubt hyperbolically—praising the territory's virtues, promising would-be adventurers that they would enjoy "ease & plenty" in a land where corn virtually planted itself.[24]

Judith was not as taken with Ohio's possibilities as her brother was. While she often waxed rhapsodic over the natural beauty of the American landscape, the nature she admired was cultivated, orderly, and tame. She wrote of fields ripe for the harvest, "well planted orchards," and "grazing cattle." The wild and dangerous expanses of the Northwest, a land peopled only by ferocious Indians equipped with the "scalping knife," were utterly foreign to her sensibilities. If Winthrop understood the risks as well as the possibilities that awaited him in Ohio, Judith saw nothing but the "social losses" and heartache her brother would suffer there. But no matter how often she begged and cajoled, Winthrop was undeterred. In 1787, the Confederation Congress appointed him secretary of the Ohio Company, serving directly under Governor Arthur St. Clair. Even then, Judith did not abandon hope that her brother would eventually obtain a more suitable position in his native state. She saw his new post not as an opportunity, but as a retreat. Although Winthrop soon began referring to Ohio as his "*own Country*," she continued to pray that he would tire of his adventure.[25]

Although Judith was honestly convinced that Winthrop should not leave New England, she viewed his adventures with a slight tinge of envy. Just as she had never harbored a hidden desire to join her brother on the field of battle, neither did she really want to imitate his example, abandoning family and friends for a life in the untamed wilderness. Still, she could not help but covet the freedom with which he made his decision. It was a freedom she would never enjoy. Her existence, she complained on more than one occasion, was "one continued round, producing the same object." Everyday, she continued, "I am actually treading the very identical path, which I have so often and so painfully pursued." When John Murray once confided that he was unhappy, she was disbelieving. Like all men, John could travel any time he wanted; wherever he went, he was greeted by throngs of grateful believers; he had a huge influence on the wider world. She, on the other hand, was confined to her house performing the same mindless tasks that made up any woman's life.[26]

Genteel women, it went unsaid, did not roam the countryside by themselves. Even when she had a companion, Judith tried to resist the temptation to spend too much time away from Gloucester. She recognized that a "female repeatedly wandering from her native home, unless she can assign some imposing reason, becomes too eccentric." The circles in which she moved admired a woman who was content "revolving in her own proper sphere" and who regarded "domestic duties as the positive centre of her enjoyments." Judith resented that reality. While the men in her life ranged freely throughout the land or sailed to ports in exotic climes, she was restricted to her house by arbitrary convention. "Often," she said, "do I regret the shackles of my sex, which chain me to this remote spot—It would be my choice to traverse every part of the habitable globe." Instead, she had to be content performing a task that proper women in postwar America had begun to accept as their special province. She would write to Winthrop as often as possible, keeping him informed about the lives of those he left behind. Her letters would travel where she, herself, would never go.[27]

*   *   *

As forlorn as she felt about Winthrop's decision to abandon her, Judith had concerns in these years that threatened her well-being, indeed her very identity, more directly. When she informed her brother that most Gloucester merchants were mired in a postwar depression, she had not been exaggerating. At times the effects of the war had struck uncomfortably close to home. Her uncle Epes was a case in point. His fortunes had steadily declined after 1776, and in 1779, he had succumbed to smallpox, dying insolvent and leaving his wife a "dependent upon the caprice and pride of an ungrateful world." Catherine inherited her widow's dower—a little land, the house in Gloucester, and not much else—to support her in the "evening of her days." Epes's experience was only one example among many.[28]

John Stevens's fortunes had vacillated throughout the war. At first he suffered loss after loss. By the early eighties, however, he had entered into potentially lucrative but extremely risky privateering ventures. Judith had objected to her husband's change of direction on moral grounds, but, she sighed, "Mr. Stevens hath never allowed me to interfere in his business." Moreover, she could not deny that John succeeded as a privateer while he had generally failed as a merchant. Supremely confident of his abilities, relishing the adventure that his new calling offered, he threw all his resources into his endeavors. Where Judith was inclined to be cautious, John thrived on risk. He was enamored of "capricious fortune" and not averse to following "the fickle dame to the other side of the Atlantic." He was a throwback to the daring merchant adventurers of the previous century, and though Judith insisted that he was a "Man of upright intentions," he had no patience with mundane details that might get in the way of success.[29]

Even before the war ended, John was in serious trouble. At one point, he owned parts of ten vessels, all but two of which had either been captured by the enemy or lost at sea. With peace, privateering was no longer an option. Once again, he plunged into debt. He borrowed money, sent his ships on legitimate ventures, ran into more than his share of bad luck, and was soon in danger of losing everything. In former times, he had turned to his father-in-law when his fortunes foundered. But Winthrop, Sr., suffering his own reverses, was unable to rescue him.[30]

By the beginning of 1783, Judith began to suspect that her "temporal prospects" were "involved in darkness." In June, John borrowed enough money to outfit another ship. As always, he was confident, assuring Judith before he left home that she had nothing to worry about. Thus she was both surprised and worried when she opened a letter to John demanding immediate payment of a loan. Like most merchants, whenever John left port, he handed responsibility for his routine financial affairs to his wife. While she conceded that women were "not often qualified to judge, in matters of business" and thus that "it would ill become to dictate," Judith occasionally, with the help of Daniel Sargent, invested in her own small ventures. And she was more than competent to serve as a deputy husband. Such a role did not imply power, of course. It was a duty her husband could grant or rescind as he pleased. It gave her little satisfaction, much anxiety, and no real authority. Even when a husband handled his business affairs badly—as Judith was beginning to fear was the case for John—a wife had no choice but to cope quietly with the mess he had created.[31]

By January of 1784, matters were so hopeless, John's inability to pay his debts so obvious, that Daniel Sargent began complaining, even implying that his niece's husband was trying to defraud him. An accusation of chicanery was an attack on any man's honor, and it was particularly devastating to a merchant, whose very livelihood depended upon his reputation for straight dealing. Judith knew that punctuality was essential to commercial relationships, but she insisted that temporary setbacks in a life dependent upon trade were inevitable and she begged Daniel for patience. Still, in the past year, John had lost about five times more than he owed. Had he taken care of his debts before investing in another ill-advised venture he might have avoided at least some of the difficulties that awaited him.[32]

Judith worried throughout the winter. At the age of thirty-three, she was feeling old. When she saw her reflection in her looking glass she noted that her auburn hair was shot through with silver strands, "mementos" she said, of her "antiquity." Her often frail health deteriorated, a product, perhaps, of her fears. "Dependence," she told Winthrop, "with all its train of mortifications stares me ful in the face." She had once advised Anna to learn to assume responsibility for her own needs, to be independent. She now acknowledged that merchants' wives, too, would do well to cultivate marketable skills. To live at the mercy of her husband's fortunes was to lose control of her life. Money gained through men, even loving fathers or husbands, gave her neither security nor power. Consequently, despite John's insistence that his business was not her concern, Judith found herself drawn ever more deeply into the vortex of her husband's affairs. When, for instance, John prepared to sail for England in hopes of obtaining a line of credit, she conceded that she "*fear*[d] more than she *hope*[d] from Mr. Stevens's voyage." He was, she thought, "making a hazardous experiment, the event of which is involved in clouds." Still, despite her misgivings, she pitched in to help. John needed a letter from someone of "great weight" to testify to his character, and Judith secured it for him.[33]

In May, John came back from England with the credit he sought, and

Judith was momentarily hopeful, resolutely choosing to ignore every disquieting sign. Before he departed, John mortgaged their house to his father-in-law, essentially putting it in Winthrop Sargent's name. This was little more than a paper transaction that was a flimsy and transparent attempt to protect at least some of the Stevens assets from potential creditors. When he returned home, John did not bother to regain title of his possessions. Perhaps he was not as confident as he pretended to be that his difficulties were behind him. Indeed, although he invested the money he had borrowed in England in fishing vessels, his return was not as profitable as he had expected, and thus he could reimburse only a few of his creditors. Those whom he did not pay were frustrated, of course, but at least a few were satisfied. In the short run Judith was relatively sanguine, as John assured her that more lucrative voyages were in the offing.[34]

Although she had no way of knowing it, Judith was enjoying her last, all too brief respite from the financial disasters that characterized so much of her marriage to John Stevens. Relying on John's assurances that his fortunes were on an upswing, she once again began to invite guests to her home. When John Murray dared to criticize her "gay circle," Judith defended herself, forgetting her previous claims that she craved a solitary life. Retirement was a "luxury" she no longer found appealing, and the social whirl was a welcome relief from the seclusion she had endured the previous winter. In fact, when her last visitor left at the end of September, Judith was unaccountably bored and hard-pressed to fill the vacant hours that stretched before her. She even took pleasure in a more fashionable wardrobe, all the while insisting that she had no liking for attire that met the exacting and ever changing standards of the metropolis.[35]

When Gloucester failed to charm, Judith was once more free to travel. In May of 1785, she and John enjoyed an excursion to Lexington. She also visited Daniel and Maria. She had not been to Boston in over a year, but she thought the experience well worth the wait. Granted, the weather was unbearably sultry, leading her to pine for Gloucester's refreshing salty breezes. And it had been so long since she had visited the city that she felt almost like an alien there. But when she strolled through the new mall, she was enchanted. Boston was, she remarked, a "miniature of European taste." She predicted that in time the mall, replete with a banqueting house, the Columbian Museum, and an orchestra hall, would be the center of American culture and sophistication. She remained in the city to observe the celebration of the day that "bestowed independence upon this younger world." All the state's dignitaries joined in the festivities. Members of the much-maligned Order of the Cincinnati were out in full force. Gloucester was a pleasant retreat, but Boston knew how to honor independence in a joyous yet orderly fashion.[36]

Judith's sense of well-being did not last. In November of 1785, she was back in Gloucester. She was "daily emaciating," and her friends predicted that she would not live to see the new year. She linked her poor health to the reappearance of John's financial woes. Even in good times, Judith had begun to regard her husband's affairs as a "never failing source of inquietude." By now she knew that his ventures the previous summer had proved disastrous, and his list of creditors had multiplied. He could answer every demand—or so he claimed—but to do so would leave him "wholly destitute." Whenever she mentioned her fears, Judith was vague about specifics, no doubt because as always, John refused to confide in her. Ignorance, in this case, was not bliss. "Suspense is indeed painfully corroding," she said, and thus she felt more helpless than ever. But although John appeared haggard and withdrawn, he continued to insist that she had nothing to worry about. Clearly that was not true. In September, his creditors began resorting to the Essex County Court of Common Pleas, demanding immediate payment of the debts he owed them. In each case, John failed to appear before the magistrate, leaving authorities no choice but to declare that he had defaulted on his obligations.[37]

On the night of January 3, Judith's world collapsed. It was her father, not her husband, who broke the news on what she later called that "fateful evening." She already suspected, of course, that her husband's position was tenuous, but "from mistaken tenderness," John had always reassured her whenever she questioned him, and she had tried to believe him. "The fear of breaking my peace," she explained, "hath induced Mr. Stevens to draw a veil before my eyes." Her father lifted the veil, informing her that John owed so much to so many people that he could not possibly come to terms with them all. One creditor in particular was demanding immediate payment. Judith was puzzled by the zeal with which the man she had begun to view as her nemesis pursued the matter. John had actually paid him the principal. Only the "*usurious* interest" remained. Still, with everyone clamoring at once, he seemed to have no choice but to declare bankruptcy, parceling out his meager assets among his creditors. Fortunately, the house was no longer in his name and could not be attached. But that was small comfort.[38]

Once Judith comprehended the extent of her husband's arrears, she plunged in to help. John's immediate problem was straightforward enough. As he saw it, if he was to have any chance of paying his debts, he had to continue his merchant activities. His creditors, perhaps understandably, thought that another venture would only throw good money after bad. While they wanted to be paid in full, most would prefer something to nothing. And some no doubt feared that if John left America's shores at this juncture, he might not return.

Unfortunately, John had to secure a "letter of license" from every creditor before he could leave town. If just one refused to sign, he was legally bound to remain in Gloucester. In January, John Murray, acceding to Judith's pleas, rode to Boston in a ferocious snowstorm, using his connections to intercede with Stevens's creditors there. At the same time, John Stevens wrote an "Address to Creditors" begging for "mercy and forbearance." He acknowledged that he might have been too daring in his pursuit of profits, but to attach his property and to threaten him with jail if he left town was not only unfair, but bad business as well. The only chance his creditors had to recoup their losses would be to allow him to set sail in search of his fortune. From the beginning, however, Judith feared that the entire endeavor was a "*fruitless* pursuit."[39]

On Sunday morning, January 22, the family was at breakfast when Mary O'Dell burst into the dining room clutching some papers she had found pinned on the front door. The documents announced for all the world to see that John's goods and estate had been attached. They had barely digested this news, when John's angriest creditor burst into the house without bothering to knock. As everyone stared at him in disbelief, he paced angrily around the room remarking on the fine quality of each piece of furniture, and asking if John had bought it on his latest voyage to England. How, he seemed to be asking, could the Stevenses claim to be destitute when they were living very well, indeed? Judith was indignant. Her husband, she proclaimed, had not bought her so much as a single ribbon in England. This same man had visited them on numerous, happier occasions, and had seen this furniture many times before. It was, she said with asperity, a present from her father—she later referred to it as part of her dowery. It was not evidence of her husband's profligacy.[40]

Most of John's creditors had run out of patience. At the very least, his situation was ironic. By the last quarter of the eighteenth century, especially in merchant communities, business affairs tended to be more impersonal than they once had been. Men borrowed and lent from strangers. Creditors demanded collateral and charged interest on their loans. The relationship between debtor and creditor was becoming essentially economic, not social. Yet John was most successful pleading his case to creditors who were virtual strangers. It was his friends who judged him as wasteful and immoral, not the men whom he scarcely knew. His business connections in Boston were more willing to take a chance on him, evidently agreeing that by allowing John to leave Gloucester they were improving the likelihood of recouping their losses. If it is true that throughout the eighteenth century, people tended to distinguish between "honest" and "dishonest" debtors, then the Gloucester community's refusal to grant John any leeway is revealing. Even in seacoast towns, merchants were often

viewed as deceptive and manipulative. Because they relied so much on their reputation to acquire credit and conduct business, they learned how to present a
false face to the world, hiding their foibles behind a carefully constructed mask.
When a merchant failed, and evidence indicated that he had behaved fraudu-
lently, concealing his assets or lying about his worth, then he seemed to confirm
the suspicions people had about merchant wealth. John Stevens was apparently
found morally wanting by members of his own community, a judgment that Judith found mortifying.[41]

No argument seemed to work. John Murray continued to run into obstacles in his efforts to secure signatures from Boston creditors and by the middle
of February his patience at last ran out. When Judith claimed that she was so ill
that she could not sleep without the aid of laudanum, John exploded. Tired,
frustrated, and more than a little irritated by her constant stream of instructions, he hinted that he doubted that she was as sick as she claimed to be. Judith's reply reeked of self-pity. She assured him that she was as ill as she had ever
been in her life—which, if true, was saying a great deal. At one point she had lain
unconscious for twenty-four hours. For a week thereafter, her death had been
expected momentarily. She lacked good medical care as Dr. Plummer had "un-
generously" moved to Salem, and no one had replaced him. Indeed all her
friends were leaving Gloucester, and no one new or interesting had moved in to
compensate for their loss. Although it was she who had sent him on his fool's
errand, she perversely attacked Murray for abandoning her. Just when she
needed him most, he seemed to prefer his "polite, elegaant, [*sic*] and scientific"
friends in Boston. But the next day, she apologized for involving him in "so intricate a business." She knew that as he tramped through Boston's snowy streets
he was putting his own health at risk.[42] The last thing she needed was to lose
John Murray's friendship.

Judith had begun to feel as though she had committed "some dark crime,"
and she saw her home as less a refuge than a prison. She could not bear to be the
object of her neighbors' scorn or pity, and she suspected that even some Universalists were secretly gloating at the mortifying circumstances of the once proud
Mrs. Stevens. Thus, she quit going to church, dreading the "inquisitive gaze of
the indifferent or censorious" that emanated from the faces of her purported
friends. The short trip to her parents had become an ordeal. She took to visiting
home after night fell so that she could avoid "every curious eye." She locked,
bolted, and barred the front door, and slept with the keys to the house hidden
beneath her pillow. She refused to open the door unless she was positive that the
visitor on the other side was not another creditor. She was so distraught that
when her own father came to the house, she refused to let him in, sure that

someone was imitating his voice in an effort to deceive her. "The enemy," she told a friend, "is constantly laying in ambush for our destruction."[43]

Judith's position was anomalous. At least John could leave the house each day, losing himself in his work, as he struggled to put his affairs back together. Judith, was left home to worry, constrained by both law and custom. After the Revolution as before, married women in America operated within common law tradition. English jurist William Blackstone had explained the system well. In law, if not in reality, husband and wife were one person. He represented her political and economic interests. Her property was his. She could not sue or be sued. She could not enter into contracts without his permission. She was, in the parlance of the day, a "feme covert" and as such she possessed no identity of her own. In Massachusetts, where equity courts did not exist and where traditional notions of family unity did not die easily, coverture had a particular resonance. The Puritans' emphasis on the harmonious family as the essential foundation of the community had unpleasant economic implications for married women. Seventeenth-century divines had simply refused to admit that the interests of husbands and wives might diverge. If a woman was nothing more than a weaker man, she had no reason to disagree with her husband; he could speak for her, "virtually" representing her interests in the public arena. In those rare cases when husbands and wives *did* disagree, wives were expected to submit to their husbands' superior judgment. To give women separate rights would invite confusion. Moreover, because women were characterized as naturally less rational than men, less able to resist temptation or to look after themselves, they needed their husband's protection. What they lost in independence, at least theoretically, they gained in security.[44]

The Revolution did nothing to challenge coverture. The ideology of republicanism may have partially supplanted Puritan theology, but society continued to assume that wives had no separate interests, no will of their own. In the eyes of the law, married women were like privileged children, not responsible adults. Even Judith Stevens, who imbibed more of the revolutionary spirit than many women, did not totally reject the precepts upon which coverture rested. True, she contended that the "love of independence" was "natural to every Mind not absolutely servile." But at the same time, she agreed that her own and her husband's interests were "one." And she understood—if she did not always approve—John's determination to protect her from the knowledge that his affairs were a shambles.[45]

Though Judith may not have been independent, she did want to help. But she soon realized that a wife could easily be as much a detriment as a helpmate. She had to walk a narrow tightrope, trying to support her husband without calling obvious attention to herself or interfering in inappropriate ways. Genteel women could not, of course, enter the workforce. Judith was no Susanna Rowson who supported herself and her ne'er-do-well husband by writing and acting in her own plays. Interestingly, she did not even contemplate using her literary skills to earn money. Proper women wrote for fame, not for profit. There were, however, more subtle and indirect ways by which a woman could contribute to her family's well-being. Judith tried most of them. In January of 1784, she welcomed Sarah Allen—her father's only living sister—into her home. Once affluent, her aunt had recently become an impoverished widow, and both she and her daughter needed a place to stay until her son managed to put the family on solid footing. And so Judith agreed to take the two women into her home as paying boarders. It was a solution no one liked. Despite herself, Judith resented the extra work her aunt's and cousin's presence demanded. She had less time to read and write and never felt comfortable simply retiring to her little closet and escaping the tiresome activities that made up a normal day. Moreover, poverty had turned Aunt Allen, who once had a sweet temper, into a demanding and jealous woman who was impossible to please. For Judith, the entire business was a palpable reminder of just how much her real life diverged from her fantasies. She was far, indeed, from being a cultivated lady of leisure who could distribute her largesse to deserving suppliants with ease. Not so long ago she would have offered her hospitality without expecting payment. To accept money for services rendered instead of to bestow charity on a beloved family member was mortifying, but she had no other option. This was one of the few respectable ways that an eighteenth-century woman could employ to support her family. Women might contribute to the well-being of the household, but elite women in particular did so within very narrowly defined parameters.[46]

There was another way that Judith could help her husband. She could be a thrifty housewife, doing without a personal maid and practicing "strict economy." She could also curtail her penchant for travel. Thus, whenever John's fortunes looked particularly bleak, she rejected every invitation to visit, ignoring Dr. Plummer's advice that a change of scenery and a bit of exercise would do her a world of good. Instead, she assumed the martyr's role, remaining a "close prisoner" in her home. Even a few weeks with her beloved Maria was out of the question. It would not, she said, be "consistent with my duty, by figuring in the Beau Monde." It would give gossips justification to accuse her of living lavishly. Paradoxically, while she could not be seen wasting money, neither could she afford to appear in Boston looking destitute. Because she was temporarily forced to submit to "the most rigid rules of economy," every article of clothing Judith owned was at least two years old. In provincial Gloucester, fashions changed only incrementally. But to appear shabby in Boston, where even after the Revolution the elite kept up with London tastes, would damage her husband's already shaky reputation.[47]

Judith's dilemma was an indication of just how impossible a wife's position could be. She knew that "dress, or at least a decent appearance," acted much like "a title page, to induce us to peruse the volume." But she was conflicted about the way she wanted to present herself to the rest of the world. Inner worth, not outward show, was the most authentic claim to respectability. Still, appearance mattered.[48]

Judith was convinced that the "title page" she presented to Gloucester was an advertisement of her valiant efforts to live economically. From her own perspective, she was thrifty in the extreme. She compared herself to her parents, to Daniel and Maria, and to Esther and John Ellery, all of whom lived much more extravagantly than she and John did. When she had married, she had never imagined that she would face a decline in her social status. To her mind, the fact that she lived well below her expectations, was proof that she was not spending money with wild abandon. Her neighbors saw her differently. They were predisposed to assume that she was, like most women, unable to curb her insatiable passion for luxuries. Unfortunately, Judith gave them the ammunition they needed to prove that she was no exception to the rule. Her three-story mansion was one of the finest and most elegantly furnished houses in all of Gloucester. Even when her husband's business had been collapsing around him, Judith had dressed better than most. She also entertained friends with money her creditors thought should have gone to them. She repeatedly insisted that John's situation was due to *his* bad luck, not *her* "extravagance." If she had a few nice possessions, she said, they were all gifts from "the liberal hands of my indulgent parents" who could not bear to see their daughter want for anything. She had accepted her parents' generosity and "endured the frivolity of fashion," she said, only because she felt that it was her duty to maintain a style commensurate with her rank. Now that she had been deposed from that rank, she would no longer indulge herself. Thus she would be one of those genteel women who—unlike either aristocrats or the members of the lower orders—could control her sensual desires and live a life of republican simplicity.[49]

As John's options steadily narrowed, Judith was forced to make ever more painful sacrifices. She let her servants go. Her nieces could perform most household chores, she said. Because she never left home and had few visitors, new clothes were no longer necessary. Maria did her part, rounding up some sewing jobs and forwarding them to Anna. Judith was grateful to her aunt, but when she returned the finished needlework to Maria, she apologized, fearing that

Anna's efforts might not meet Boston's exacting standards. She hoped that this would not dissuade Maria from sending more work her way. Maria had, Judith added wistfully, so many wealthy friends; surely some of them will be happy to avail themselves of Anna's services. If she ever regained her health, she promised to use her own needle to supplement her niece's efforts.[50]

Judith also contacted some of her husband's creditors, begging them to sign his letter of license. John refused to write to anyone. It was, sighed Judith, a "work of labour" to get him to compose even a sentence on his own behalf. For her, writing was not only second nature, but a source of comfort. At the very least, it gave her something to do. Sitting alone in her house, waiting for the next peremptory knock on the door, was intolerable. Thus she stepped into the breach, always treading carefully, making sure that she did not cross the line between being a helpful wife and an interfering shrew. She knew that she was "presumptuous" to be involved so directly in John's affairs and at times she was amazed by her own "temerity" even as she claimed that she always wrote "in such terms as become my sex." But this was no time to worry about stepping out of her sphere. Indeed, she occasionally used her sex to her advantage. When she wrote Joseph Russell, for instance, she hoped he would "tolerate from a female pen" what he might condemn in her husband.[51]

Many of the men to whom Judith wrote were friends or coreligionists. In those cases she did not hesitate to invoke the "ties of relationship, of neighborhood, and the still more enduring motive, of one Common, one universal faith." She soon learned, however, that such sentiments counted for little in a world where friendship was one thing, but business was quite another. Occasionally she received a positive response. Most of the time she did not. Moreover, whenever she looked at the names of John's creditors, a new one appeared. Her husband always explained these additions away. He owed some of these men only a "trifle," he would say, and so he had been reluctant to worry her by telling her about yet another name on an already daunting list.[52]

While Judith continued to try to secure a letter of license for her husband, John gave up, casting about for an alternative plan. Always impatient when he was idle, he refused to sit quietly, waiting for his creditors' permission to leave town. A respectable man in the eighteenth century had a wife and children for whose material well-being he was responsible. With no children of his own, and his ability to support his little family in doubt, John's self-respect, his very identity was at stake. In a town the size of Gloucester, where everyone knew him and knew that four generations of the Stevens family had lived, worked, and for the most part prospered there, his discomfort must have been excruciating. John thought he had rescued his family name when he moved into his "mansion house." Now, he was about to lose everything in a most public and humiliating manner. Judith may well have unwittingly exacerbated her husband's loss of esteem when she jumped into the fray, writing letters to his creditors, and offering him unsolicited advice.[53]

Even in the best of times, a merchant occupied an awkward position. When he was master of his own ship, his authority was virtually absolute. But when he returned home after a voyage that could easily last two months or more, he was greeted by a wife who had gotten along without him, who had taken care of business in his absence, and who often knew more about his mundane affairs than he did. If he entered port after a failed trip—always a distinct possibility—he was at least momentarily neither a provider nor a protector. He was master of nothing. And defying all logic, eighteenth-century observers tended to evaluate economic failure not as the inevitable consequence of impersonal market forces, but in moral terms. Judith's repeated claims that John was "upright" but unlucky may well have been correct. Indeed, if his voyages had been successful, the world would have praised his skill instead of ranking him with the "fraudulent." But debtors, no matter how blameless, could easily be painted with the brush of self-indulgence and profligacy—characteristics often associated with women. If they refused to pay their debts, many argued that they were "unmanned."[54] As John saw it, another voyage, was his best—perhaps his only—chance to salvage his pride and put his world back together again.

By April of 1786, John was preparing to leave town, with or without his requisite letter of license. He intended to set sail for the West Indian island of St. Eustatius in one of Winthrop Sargent's ships, leaving Judith behind to deal with his angry creditors. Judith argued long and hard against the plan, but she could not prevail against the combined wisdom of her father and husband. There was only so much she could say before she was reminded that John had the power to make all decisions about his financial affairs. "I am now silenced," she told her brother. Her silence, however, did not prevent her from doubting the wisdom of the voyage. "The poor man flatters himself," she said, "that in the course of a few months, he shall be able to return blest with liberty and competency." Judith hoped he was right. As her "dear Exile" left Gloucester for "the hospitable shore, to which the unyielding severity of unfeeling, of heartless Man, hath banished him," she prayed that he would return home safe and solvent. Still, in her heart she knew that John was not a good businessman—nor was he particularly lucky. Once she had relied on his promises. Now she could not hide her misgivings.[55]

Once John left town—family tradition has it that he escaped through a window at the rear of the house while his creditors were pounding on the front door—Judith could do nothing but wait. Strangely, her husband's departure was something of a relief. She had been ill most of the winter, and everyone insisted that the best cure was country air. It went without saying that Anna would go with her. Judith was so weak that she could not even dress without her niece's help, and Anna patiently endured the "little petulencies" in which sick people inevitably indulged. Because Judith's women friends were "wholly domesticated," they could not easily abandon their obligations at home. Most men she knew were busy preparing for another fishing season. Only John Murray, whose work was not dictated by seasonal rhythms and who could preach to the uninitiated wherever he went, was free to accompany her. Thus it was decided that Judith, Anna, and John would travel together, the women in their chaise, John on horseback.[56] They would go to Connecticut, Rhode Island, and New Hampshire, before heading for Boston and then home.

The trip was exactly what Judith needed. Almost as soon as she was on the road, she felt better. Even an occasional night in a dirty public house, where thin, lumpy mattresses crawled with bugs and the noise kept her awake, did nothing to dampen her spirits. In no time she was climbing stairs without help. Wherever she went, she exulted at the crowds that turned out for John's sermons. People "idolize" him, she told her father. After having endured a winter when her husband's every move was met with heads shaking in solemn disapproval, it was a relief to be the companion of someone who was so clearly adored.[57]

There were some unsettling moments along the way, as Judith saw firsthand that Gloucester was not the only New England village that had been disarranged by the American Revolution. Perhaps not surprisingly, Judith thought that women suffered the most from the "Goths and Vandals of our Day." Groton, Connecticut, witnessed the creation of sixty-two widows in a single hour of fighting. In New Haven, the British had not been content until they had destroyed every feather bed in town, leaving the women to put their houses and lives back in order. In Portsmouth, New Hampshire, business was so poor that everyone had an "apprehensive" and "melancholy" countenance. Still, if Judith found evidence of the havoc the British had wreaked throughout New England, there were signs of American perfidy as well. In Boston, she had tea with a Mrs. Knight, a loyalist widow who had fled to England when fighting commenced and had returned home at war's end, only to find that the Massachusetts government had confiscated her estate in her absence. "Doth it square with rectitude," Judith asked, "to wrest property from individuals, merely because their ideas do not exactly coincide with our own?"[58]

No matter how much Judith enjoyed traveling, thoughts of her husband were never far from her mind. Months passed with not so much as a word from

John. When she arrived in Boston at the beginning of August, Judith assured her mother that she would not appear in public so long as she remained in the city. In a separate letter, however, she informed her father that she planned to meet individually with John's creditors, hoping to reassure each one. In private, she was as anxious as the most suspicious creditor, especially after she finally heard from St. Eustatius. John was, characteristically, in good spirits as he begged her to ignore any disquieting news she might have received about him from ill-informed sources. He had opened a warehouse that was piled to the ceiling with vendible goods. Any day now he would be setting sail with rosy expectations of handsome profits. Judith tried not to panic but in fact she "trembled" at the likely outcome of this latest venture. John must have borrowed money to fill his warehouse. Wouldn't this involve him in "new embarrassments"? He was, she repeated in a refrain that had begun to smack of desperation, a good man. But he was "rashly enterprising" and he invariably had "recourse to the most hazardous expedients." Because he was honest, he suspected no one and he had a "disposition prone to confide." She began to think that it was her duty to travel to St. Eustatius, where only her own good sense could save John from disaster. She could "council and restrain" him, and she might yet help him salvage his good name. She had, she all but said, a better head for business than he did.[59]

Judith returned to Gloucester in October, clinging desperately to John's occasional upbeat reports even as she grew steadily uneasy. Thus she continued to consider sailing to the West Indies, although her friends told her such a trip would be foolhardy. They reminded her that she was overcome by nausea whenever she set foot on the deck of a ship. And this would be a dangerous voyage even for a seasoned traveler. Judith refused to be dissuaded. These were "mere trifles" designed to frighten children, not adults. God, she said resolutely, is on the ocean as well as at my writing desk. But if she refused to give in to her fears, in the end she bowed to reality. The islands were expensive; if she went there she might be more a burden than a source of comfort. She had no choice but to live with "corroding uncertainty."[60]

In January 1787, Judith received a packet of letters from her husband. She was happy to learn that in two months' time he would have £200 or so to distribute among his creditors. Unfortunately, her relief was short-lived. She soon learned from other sources "that the enterprising, and confiding disposition of this dear unfortunate Man, hath again ruined all." He had been arrested for debts he had incurred on the island and was languishing in a St. Eustatius jail. Not for the first time, she wished that John would be content with a job as a merchant's clerk. Such a position would not offer him the excitement he craved or the chance for great wealth he thought was his due. But to Judith, security, however modest, looked increasingly inviting. She thought that if she could only speak to him in person, she might persuade John to accept happy mediocrity as his lot. But this was just as fantastic as her dreams of being a great lady once had been. "I am weary," she sighed, "of forming plans, which I am doomed never to execute."[61]

As she often did when her earthly affairs were in disarray, Judith began contemplating her death, deciding how she would dispose of her few material goods. As a rule, married women in Massachusetts and elsewhere did not own much in the way of property, although they did retain possession of some personal items, such as their wearing apparel, that they brought to their marriages. It was her books, not her clothing, that Judith cared about. Some of her volumes had been hers since childhood. All of them were old friends whose value she could not begin to calculate. If her husband's creditors planned to confiscate all John's possessions, she was determined to find some way to keep her books. She admitted that her desire might not correspond with the letter of the law. But she thought that the laws of nature—not to mention the ideals of the American Revolution—were on her side. A "fondness for property is almost one of the first passions we discover," she said. It was only natural that even women would want to control the distribution of their property at their death.[62]

On the evening of March 8, Judith retired early. She sank into a deep slumber and dreamed that John appeared at her bedside, totally silent and "perfectly serene." She began to scream at him, berating him for abandoning her. But he remained mute, simply gazing at her with a superior expression. Awakening with a start, she looked at the clock, and then, going to her night table, she opened her memorandum book. On a clean page, she wrote, *Thursday night, eleven o'clock— eighth of March 1787.* She returned to bed strangely comforted, convinced that her dream was a good omen. Thereafter, she expected John's return at any moment. She knew that his material prospects were "miserably blasted," but she hoped that "the peaceful retreat of his own home" would revive his spirits.[63]

She was thus unprepared when Captain Webber arrived at her door sometime in April to inform her that John would never leave St. Eustatius. He had died on March 8, at 11:00 P.M. Judith was incapacitated by the news. The "repeated shocks" she had endured over the last year and a half were simply too much. She was haunted as much by guilt as by grief. When people die, she told her brother, we invariably forget all their defects. We see instead, every virtue "through the magnifying glass of deep regret." We also see our anger before their death, and wonder why we were not more understanding.[64]

*　　*　　*

At the age of thirty-six, Judith Stevens was a "desolate" widow. "Language cannot furnish another phrase so descriptive of a situation truly forlorn," she said. Judith was not exaggerating. In the past, she had written flippantly about the questionable joys of matrimony. In 1782, for instance, she had penned a poem that described a "very happy couple [who] had dwindled into mere Man and Wife." Marriage, she wrote, inevitably turned passion into "calm indifference." A suitor focused his entire being on the object of his affection, but once the prize was won, the "calls of business" beckoned, and he sought "some *new* amusement to explore," leaving his bride to regret her shattered dreams of marital bliss. Even the most cynical of wives, however, soon learned that the death of a husband was a life-altering experience. Judith was no exception to this rule. Widowhood was often as not emotionally devastating, as it entailed the loss of a way of life and a status to which women had grown accustomed. In earlier days, a widow seldom remained alone for long. But by the last quarter of the eighteenth century, especially in New England, this was no longer true. The American Revolution had exacerbated tendencies long in the making, skewing the sex ratio along the eastern seaboard, making it difficult for a woman to find a first husband, much less a second. The war itself claimed the lives of countless men. After the war, others, like Winthrop Sargent, left the coast in search of prosperity in the nation's hinterland. Moreover, many genteel people—Judith among them—looked down on widows who remarried. To seek another partner was to sully the first marriage and to give credence to the notion that women were lustful creatures who could not live without satisfying their sexual appetites.[65]

Judith was personally acquainted with the tribulations of widows. Men who earned their living on the "fluctuating waves of the Ocean trade" risked their lives as well as their fortunes whenever they left port. Consequently, towns like Gloucester always had more than their share of widows. Judith had spent many a mournful day with women like her own aunt Sarah who had suffered emotionally and materially when their husbands died. They all whiled away the hours talking wistfully of good times gone for good, as they regretted the loss of their once secure place in the social order. A merchant's wife was used to being alone for months on end. But when her husband died, he left a painful void in her life. Even the most prudent men often left their wives in a precarious financial position. If widowhood represented most women's first chance at independence, it also reminded them that if they had neither talent nor resources, independence was a hollow word, indeed.[66]

The general trend for widows throughout the eighteenth century was a decline in their autonomy and material well-being. The ideology of independence did nothing to give women economic security, much less meaningful power.

When revolutionary rhetoric encountered deeply entrenched gendered attitudes about property ownership, tradition invariably triumphed. The founders exhibited considerable concern about the manner in which old inheritance practices might perpetuate an unequal social order, where power and wealth devolved upon a select few. With Blackstone, they agreed that while the right to property was natural, the right to inheritance was an artificial construct that could be altered at will. Thus they passed laws abolishing primogeniture and entail, and forbade the creation of hereditary honors. They enacted no legislation, however, that would mitigate the economic disadvantages widows faced. Before John died, Judith had occasionally dreamed about what she would do if she were left to her own resources and by some "miracle" had "the *sole right*" to the property her husband left behind. As she surely knew, it would take a miracle for her to achieve such authority.[67]

Judith did not have to share her husband's estate with any children, but this by no means implied that she would do with it what she pleased. In most cases, if a man died without issue and left a will, he made his wife the executrix of his estate and gave her most or all of his real and personal property. If, as John Stevens did, a man died intestate, there were certain rules governing the status of his possessions. A wife received the "widow's dower," one third of her husband's real property or the income from that property, for use during her lifetime. Ideally, this satisfied her basic needs. She did not, however, have much control over it. She could not sell, "waste," or "improve" the property. She received a share—somewhere between one half and one third—of her husband's personal estate. The household's "paraphernalia"—clothes, jewelry, and various personal items—was also hers. In essence, while the law was designed to give a widow reasonable security, it did not imagine that she would be either independent or powerful.[68]

The difficulties Judith faced were mind-boggling. Like his father, John had died owing much more than his estate was worth. If creditors could not touch her dower, her personal property—with some exceptions—was fair game. Often judges set aside some items such as furniture, dishes, and cooking utensils that women needed for their subsistence. In most states—but not in Connecticut or Massachusetts—the courts allowed a married woman to have a separate estate, thus enabling her to protect her assets from her deceased husband's creditors. Most ominously for Judith, if a widow appeared to be hiding her assets, she could be sued or even imprisoned. Many of John's creditors already suspected him of chicanery. They would be watching Judith carefully to see that she did not follow in her husband's footsteps. What might have escaped notice in some cases would not be overlooked in hers.[69]

Judith was not as knowledgeable as she thought she was about the legal details that pertained to her own welfare. Thus she was unpleasantly surprised to discover that her husband's death had not even left her with a "competency." I have "scarce anything which I can call my own," she cried, and she feared that she would live the rest of her life in "dependence." She would have resented her situation under any circumstances. It was even harder to bear because all of her siblings were doing so well. Word had it that Winthrop would soon be receiving a respectable salary as secretary of the Ohio Company. In June, Fitz William had returned from a successful voyage and had announced that he was confident he could make a fortune on the high seas. As always, Esther's husband, John Ellery, prospered. His ships never seemed to wind up at the bottom of the ocean. Even Judith's father, while he was hardly out of the woods, thought he saw some indications that the worst of the postwar depression was over. A merchant's fortunes were "ever fluctuating" of course. Still, Winthrop Sr. was guardedly optimistic. Judith tried not to begrudge her relatives' good fortunes. She knew that there were those who were worse off than she was. Noah Parker, for instance, died in the fall of 1787, leaving his wife and daughters destitute. And Isaac Smith, one of the merchants who had once pressed John to make good on his debts, was himself an insolvent debtor. Judith knew that she was not superior to those men who fell on bad times. "One thing I know," she sighed, is "that I have not a right to comment."[70]

As Judith surveyed her few options, only one thing was clear. She was determined not to acquiesce to suggestions from all sides that she move in with her parents. She valued her autonomy too much for that. Dependence, she thought, was for children who were "little superior to mere animals." She was an adult. Moreover, she explained, she had been the "mistress of my own time" for too long and had her own "mode of appropriating my hours." She derived solace from her "beloved *retirement*," and as long as she had her books and her pen, she could be content living alone. Moreover, her parents' house was often chaotic. If Judith moved in, she would never be able simply to retire to her room and ignore the demands of an "ill regulated and entangled" household. It was, she conceded, children's duty to honor "the gray hairs of the Authors of their being." Still, she craved order and quiet. She knew she would have neither if she abandoned that "*one little apartment at least*, which I could consider my own."[71]

Unfortunately, it was no longer really "her" home. Judith had mistakenly assumed that with John's death, the house she had shared with her husband would be hers outright. Instead, her father, who actually owned it, granted her only one third of her home for her use during her lifetime. At her death, because she had no children, it would automatically revert to her father or his heirs.[72]

Meanwhile, Winthrop decreed that Fitz William and Esther—both of whom were far wealthier than Judith—would divide the other two thirds between them. Judith's lawyers assured her that no matter what happened, she could not be evicted. That was at least some comfort. "The idea of property is pleasing," she said, and she felt that as long as she stayed put, she enjoyed a "*kind* of independence." She could live on very little—in fact she had already managed to save some money. She was taking in sewing, and she might accept boarders as well. On the whole, she claimed to be confident. She would, of course, no longer enjoy the "luxuries of life, to which I have perhaps been accustomed," but she hoped her little economies might allow her an occasional "hint of elegance." At least widows who lived in shabby gentility were viewed with sympathy, even if men who fell through the cracks were not.[73]

Judith reluctantly prepared to deal with her husband's creditors, desperately trying to keep as many of "her" belongings as possible. She was especially determined to hold on to the "trifling articles of furniture" her father had given her. Her effort was complicated by John's chicanery. In an effort to raise money and to protect the family's goods from his creditors, John had engaged in a fictitious sale of all the family's furniture to Winthrop, who insisted that he would never consider it as his own. There had been witnesses to the sale. Judith had the receipts to prove that the transaction, however bogus, had occurred. If this was the case, no one could confiscate it. When John's creditors expressed their doubts about the entire transaction, and even a judge informed her that the sale was at the very least "problematical," Judith cast desperately about for some way to keep what she considered morally hers, convinced that she deserved so much more than she had received from her father and her husband. She had, she pointed out, been no more of an expense to John than a "common house keeper," and she had saved him money by assuming the responsibility for teaching his nieces. In the end, her cousin Epes gently dissuaded her, pointing out that she would face "perpetual Law Suits" if she did not end the "heart affecting business." He also suggested a strategy to avoid legal difficulties. She should put all her possessions up for auction and divide the profits among her creditors. The goods would no doubt go cheaply. She might even purchase what she needed—of what she insisted was her own property—for herself. Or some good soul might purchase items for her. Still, Judith balked. Her conscience was clear even if the law did not recognize her claims. Surely, she thought, a woman at least had the right to her own dowry! But perhaps not.[74]

In the end, Judith bowed to the inevitable. The probate judge divided the proceeds of the estate down to the last "joined china tea cup" among her husband's creditors, and by April of 1790 the entire estate had been settled to no one's real satisfaction. John owed over £1,158. The estate, after the deduction of administrative costs, was worth some £53. Judith's father was John's biggest creditor. He was owed £260, and received only £12. But at least, save for a few odds and ends that cropped up with painful irregularity over the years, the ordeal was over.[75]

Not so long ago, Judith had argued that women should be raised for independence. Now, more than ever, she was aware of how important it was for women to be able to take care of themselves. Genteel women, in particular, had little training and few options. They might take in sewing or open their house to boarders, as Judith considered doing. But as productive activity moved from the household to the marketplace, well-bred women discovered that they had few skills that would enable them to earn the most meager living. Teaching was an acceptable profession, but not one for which Judith felt prepared. While some widows took over their husbands' businesses, this had never been common among seafarers. Judith would one day write admiringly of the prowess of a successful "she-merchant," but she never considered this as a course she could follow. Although she was wealthier than most women, her very status limited her options. In the meantime, if the simple life was a republican ideal, then— whether she liked the idea or not—Judith could claim to be an exemplar of republican virtue. Independence was another matter entirely. No one, she wrote a friend as she struggled with the vicissitudes of widowhood, could claim to be truly independent. "A variety of causes, foreign from ourselves, and which are in no sort under our control, may concur to destroy" us.[76]

Still, it was clear that some people were more independent than others.

Chapter 6
A Belle Passion

On March 21, 1788, Judith Stevens wrote to Maria Sargent. "Fitz William is gone," she said. "Every one I love is gone, or *going*, and this place is already sufficiently desolate." For Judith these were trying times, as she struggled to find her footing in a world that seemed to be terribly off-kilter. Nothing was as it should be. Her husband was dead. Her finances were a shambles. She was responsible for the welfare of two female orphans whose prospects seemed even bleaker than her own. Her parents were getting older and more feeble. Esther was preoccupied with her children and husband; Fitz William was often at sea; and Winthrop seldom left the Ohio wilderness. Thus the burden for tending to her mother and father fell as often as not on her shoulders. Adult children of course, often ended up as their parents' keepers, and single women were more likely to be caretakers than men were. Still, it was not pleasant to experience a world turned upside down.[1]

Judith wrote very little in the early 1780s, as her real life dominated her thoughts while the life of the mind receded in importance. Only once, when she joined the battle to defend her church and her minister from attacks by the Massachusetts establishment, did she consider seeking a public audience. Even then, she elected to stay in the background. Proper women did not engage in theological debates, no matter how much their faith meant to them. But if she bowed to convention most of the time, she left her private life open to attack when she married John Murray. Her decision to marry John—an event that surprised her more than it did anyone else—not only incurred her brother Winthrop's wrath but seriously damaged her carefully crafted image of gentility. Judith had always jealously guarded that image. Throughout her first marriage, she had maintained her sense of superiority during the bleakest of times. Now, as rumors about her relationship with John took on a life of their own, her self-esteem suffered a major blow. Still, she never regretted her decision, and her spirits soared, however briefly, when she became pregnant. At last she would be a mother. If she no longer had the energy to publish, she looked forward to serving the public in an entirely acceptable—if more indirect—way. She could raise her child to be a virtuous citizen of the republic. The death of her son in childbirth was a devastating blow, one from which she never fully recovered. Perhaps not surprisingly, by the end of the decade, Judith's letters, normally the epitome of controlled and rational prose, grew ever more frenzied and emotional.

*   *   *

At the same time that Judith Stevens had been trying to help her husband dig his way out of debt, she began doing what she could to defend John Murray and the Independent Church from their many enemies. The Gloucester Universalists had never enjoyed an untroubled existence. But by 1783, Universalists throughout the entire state were under siege. "God and Nature have made us free," insisted the members of one congregation, "and we hope to enjoy Religious Liberty by right, and not by sufferance." They feared, however, that it would not be long before they were not even "suffered" to exist. Arguing that their cause was the "cause of *all* sectarians," they hoped to convince the public that if the Universalists lost their rights, the ability of all Massachusetts inhabitants to worship as they pleased would be in jeopardy.[2]

The third article of the Bill of Rights in the Massachusetts Constitution of 1780 had granted a measure of religious freedom to the state's inhabitants. Nevertheless, the men who designed the new frame of government remained convinced that some connection between church and state was essential to good order. Thus, despite the lip service they gave to religious toleration, they did very little to alter the system that had existed in Massachusetts before the Revolution. For all practical purposes the Congregational church continued to be the established church in every town. Dissenters had to prove that they offered a legitimate alternative to the establishment if they wanted their tax money to support their own minister. The deck was stacked against them, however, for it was the Congregationalists themselves who decided which sects were legitimate and which were not. Not surprisingly, most of them were suspicious of new religious groups that seemed to rise up out of nowhere, attacking received wisdom wherever they appeared. In fact, they recognized only three groups—Anglicans, Baptists, and Quakers—as dissenters for the purposes of tax exemption.[3]

In 1783, a committee of the Independent Church of Gloucester applied to the First Parish Church for a tax abatement. Reeling from the effects of the postwar depression, men like Winthrop Sargent resented seeing their taxes toward the maintenance of a church they no longer attended. But the First Parish Church had never forgiven the Universalists for abandoning it. Moreover, they worried about the precedent they might be setting. "We may expect," they predicted, "that an hundred similar associations will soon be formed, and as many mushroom teachers spring up from the seculency of vice and laziness to take the lead of them." The town would face "anarchy and confusion," were the Universalists' petition to be granted.[4]

The members of the First Parish Church rejected the Universalists' application on two grounds. First, they maintained that because the Independent Church was unincorporated, it had no legal existence. It had not "one single feature of a church of Christ, or any mode of discipline." Second, they directly attacked John Murray as an unlettered opportunist, a "stranger in every sense," whose doctrines had done "more damage to this town than the late war." Because he believed that all people would be saved regardless of the life they led, John did not, by definition, meet the constitutional requirement that a minister be a "teacher of piety, religion and morality." "We beg leave to ask," they said, "Can a man who publickly discards the doctrine of God's moral government—of future rewards and punishments—urge with a good face, or with any hope of success, the practice of 'morality'?" Judith was probably more upset than John by the repeated onslaughts on the minister's character, all of which she characterized as "misrepresentations" and "fabrications." While she insisted that the charges were beneath refutation, she ached to tell the world just how wrong they were.[5]

Not content with rejecting the Universalists' petition, the First Parish Church went on the offensive, trying to undermine the economic position of John Murray and his supporters. In the fall of 1783, Essex County sheriff Michael Farley began confiscating the possessions of the wealthiest Universalists, taking a "silver tankard from one, spoons from a second, porringers from a third, and a variety of shop goods from a fourth." Everything was sold at public auction, the proceeds going to the coffers of the First Parish Church.[6] In December of 1784, Farley brought John Murray before the County Court of Common Pleas, arguing that because he was not ordained, he had no right to perform ministerial functions. Most troublesome, the sheriff insisted that John could not legally conduct marriage ceremonies, and he threatened to levy a fine of £50 for each wedding at which the Universalist minister officiated. When the court agreed with the sheriff's logic, John appealed the decision. He also put his name on another lawsuit aimed at relieving his parishioners from taxation to support the First Parish Church.[7]

Six months later, after "many tedious continuations from term to term," Murray's appeal came before the Supreme Judicial Court at Ipswich. Everyone, including Judith, predicted that he would lose his case, especially after Justice Francis Dana insisted—in an argument that would become standard fare for supporters of the establishment—that only an incorporated church was entitled to tax support. To the surprise of virtually everyone present, the jury ignored Dana's instructions and decided in John Murray's favor. Judith was ecstatic, convinced that in Massachusetts "ignorance" would never again "forge fetters, for the free born mind."[8]

Many Universalists, however, remained uneasy. Instead of directly refuting Dana's instructions, the jury had simply ignored them. Thus John's status remained undefined. On the advice of his lawyers, John appealed the verdict, hoping to establish his legitimacy once and for all. While he awaited another day in court, the Universalists—led by Judith's cousin Epes—published a pamphlet, "An Appeal to the Impartial Publick," designed to win support for their cause. Just how much of a hand Judith had in composing the tract is unclear, but she was surely involved. The "Appeal" employed every argument she had used to justify Universalism over the years. In particular, it echoed her assertion that government had no business interfering in matters of belief. History had proved, she often said, that state-enforced religion destroyed free inquiry and had given "birth to eight hundred years of ignorance and barbarism." The tract also directly addressed Murray's critics, insisting that the Universalist leader was a "teacher of piety, religion, and morality." The charge that Universalism bred immorality was an old one, and Judith had denied it on many occasions. To say that Murray was an enemy to good works was preposterous. Although he did not "thunder out the doctrine of everlasting punishment," he always maintained that God would punish the sin, even if he did not "annihilate" the sinner. Universalism was no more an enemy of morality than Calvinism was.[9]

Whether or not she actually helped Epes compose the "Appeal," Judith was one of the Independent Church members who signed it. She also wrote a "little piece" on the subject. But when Murray suggested publishing an abbreviated version she demurred. Even in its unabridged form she thought it "very imperfect." A "mutilation would of course render it still more incomplete." Still, she left it to others to decide whether her words would serve the Universalist cause. Evidently, no one thought her essay would be of much use, and she never mentioned it again. Clearly, however, she was not the same woman who had declared in her *Catechism* that she had no desire to "enter the lists as a Disputant."[10] If she did not go public in this instance, she was ready to use her pen to uphold her faith if she could find the proper venue.

In June of 1786, the Massachusetts court finally rendered a decision in John Murray's case. The jury gave Judith the only good news she received all year, returning a verdict in John's favor, deciding that he was, as the Constitution required, a preacher of piety and morality. Noting that the court had come down solidly in favor of the principle of separation of church and state, Judith exulted.

"The free born soul, conscious of its native rights, demands emancipation[.] Sweet equality is taking place in the mental world and every one resumes the prerogative with which nature hath invested him—to think for himself." Surely John's difficulties were over.[11]

Unfortunately, this was not the case. While the court had granted standing to unincorporated bodies, it remained silent on the status of ministers who were not ordained. From the perspective of the First Parish Church, John was not a true minister. The Court of Common Pleas agreed, allowing Sheriff Farley to continue fining John for each wedding at which he officiated. This decision rendered the Universalists' other victories meaningless. His lawyers had encouraged John to continue performing marriage ceremonies while his case had wound its way through the courts. And while he was notoriously indifferent to money matters, even John recognized that he could not possibly pay the fines he had already incurred, much less the ones he would face in the future. He had no choice but to leave America temporarily while his supporters petitioned the legislature on his behalf.[12]

Judith was cautiously optimistic. She thought the petition, drawn up by Benjamin Russell, the influential editor of the *Columbian Centinel*, was perfect. If "the signature of any other Woman be affixed," she declared, she would gladly add her own name to the list. Failing that, she worked behind the scenes. As soon as John sailed for England she wrote what purported to be an anonymous letter to Massachusetts supreme court justice Thomas Dawes. Designating herself "A female attached to Mr. Murray by the ties of obligation and esteem," she volunteered to peruse John's papers to see if they contained anything that might influence the legislature. Judith's effort at anonymity was flimsy. What other woman had access to John's private papers? What other woman had the temerity to write to a stranger as she did? Surely she knew that anyone acquainted with the case would know who wrote the letter. Still, she had to *appear* to be reluctant to join the Universalists' battle even if she was eager to do so.[13]

John left Gloucester two days after Christmas; by the end of January he had set sail for London. Judith hated to see him go, but as was so often the case with the men in her life, her wishes went unheeded. She could not resist characterizing the minister's decision in gendered terms, inverting traditional stereotypes in the process. She conceded that some people might attribute his determination to leave America's shores to his "manly fortitude," but she saw it as mere "inflexibility." Paradoxically, it also indicated "inconstancy" a trait she thought described all men. Men, she said, constantly sought change and variety, while women—supposedly the fickle sex—were generally content with life's simpler domestic pleasures.[14]

No matter how she depicted it, Judith was devastated by John's departure. She feared that once he landed on his native shores, he would decide to remain there for good. She had known John for thirteen years, and although she had often complained about his roving ways, she had not gone three weeks without receiving a letter from her beloved itinerant. Now the two were separated by a vast ocean. She had never felt quite so alone. She took some comfort from a note John sent her before he set sail, reading it so often that it became almost illegible, so wet had it become from her tears. She refused even to go near the room John claimed as his own for fear of breaking down completely. For once, neither books nor pen gave her comfort.[15]

Judith's unhappiness was partly the product of the successive shocks that had jolted her over the last few months. Even so, her emotional outburst at John's decision to visit England was, at least on the surface, somewhat puzzling. Her friends—and even more so her enemies—thought they knew why. And they were right. As early as September of 1786, just a few months after her husband had sailed for St. Eustatius, Judith had referred obliquely to the "shafts of slander" that could destroy an innocent reputation due to the "misjudging censures of a malevolent World." A month later, John Murray was in Philadelphia and although he had scarcely left Gloucester, Judith felt compelled to send him a letter. This in itself was not unusual. She indicated, however, that she had tried—for reasons she left hazy—to resist her impulse. Yet she could not stop herself. She had little to say, but she wanted to say it anyway. Judith had not apologized for writing to John Murray since the very first missive she had sent him. Why, suddenly, when she needed comfort the most, did she feel so awkward? In November, Judith was in Boston, when she sent an urgent letter to John Murray, begging him not to visit her there. She predicted that if he ignored her advice, "malicious hearts" would say that he came to see her, not to perform his Christian duty. Being innocent, she lectured, was not enough; they must have the *appearance* of innocence, as well. Judith knew that society simply did not allow a woman to enjoy "an intellectual connexion with an individual of the opposite sex." A woman could "brave the world" if she liked. But she did so at her own risk.[16]

Judith had always known that gossip irrevocably damaged anyone's, but especially a woman's, character. It made no difference whether meddlers spread the truth or lies. Unchecked and in the wrong hands, gossip empowered those who indulged in it and rendered its most innocent victims powerless. Now, malicious tongues were obviously wagging. Although Murray had lived under Judith's roof for years, even staying there on numerous occasions when John Stevens was out of town, everyone sensed that something had changed.

Winthrop was already receiving "officious" letters from not-so-well-meaning tale bearers who urged him to step in to save his sister's good name.[17]

Judith had worried about her precarious position even before her husband's death. Perhaps the journey through New England she had taken with Anna and John had aroused suspicions. Perhaps their time together had awakened Judith's feelings for a man she had always admired.[18] There had always been those who whispered that she and John Murray were more than friends. As a widow she was more vulnerable to idle speculation than ever. A number of people had already observed the "undue interest" Judith had taken in John's legal difficulties. All Gloucester Universalists cared about the fate of their minister, of course, but very few—and certainly no other woman—had thrown themselves into the battle with Judith's zeal. At first, confident of her rectitude, she simply tried to ignore the chatter. She intended to remain single for the rest of her life, she said repeatedly, playing the part of a circumspect widow whose books were her only companions. This was a role that was the "most proper, most ornamental, and most dignifying, to the female character." She had always proclaimed that "*second* marriages, especially of females," were indecorous. One marriage for her was enough. She had no desire to experience the pleasures and pains of matrimony again. Indeed, she fervently wished that the Universalists would follow the Catholic example, offering her a place of seclusion behind cloister walls.[19]

Judith did not imagine for a moment that her single state prohibited her from continuing her "sentimental, virtuous friendship" with John Murray. She shrank from the very idea of "relinquishing his valuable society." It was not long, however, before she had to admit that the gossips were at least partially correct—about her sentiments, if not her behavior. Slowly, and at first only to herself, she conceded that her feelings for John Murray "partook rather too great a degree of tenderness." Initially she tried to deny the force of her own emotions, valiantly suppressing "every rebellious thought." But when John announced that he was leaving for England, she could no longer deceive herself. Her soul "became a scene of tumult." I have, she declared, "become a slave, to the most impetuous of all passions, of which I had erroneously considered myself incapable." Her reason, an attribute she had cultivated so carefully over the years, had lost its ability to control her desires. Bewildered by the strength of her feelings, she was still trying to decide how to proceed when she received John Murray's letter. A "delicate attention" to Judith's "honour, and feelings" had heretofore kept him silent, he said. But he could not leave the country without declaring his sentiments. He admitted that he had fallen in love with her almost as soon as they had met. He had resolutely concealed his feelings, always praising Judith's husband, even working to secure his release from the clutches of his creditors. Before he left for England, however, Murray had to know if "domestic felicity might yet be his." Judith replied immediately in such a way as "to indulge his hopes."[20]

Judith confided in Maria and Anna, but no one else, not even her parents. Her silence complicated matters after the Rev. Eli G. Forbes of the First Parish Church used the rumors swirling about John and Judith for his own purposes. When the Gloucester Universalists denounced Forbes for harrying their minister out of the land, Forbes defended himself by throwing the blame for Murray's departure squarely on Judith. He had it on the best authority, he declared, that John had proposed to Judith, she had refused, and as a result, he had fled the continent, the victim of a broken heart.[21] If Judith denied the accusation she would have to reveal what she resisted discussing in public. To say nothing, would allow the rumors to spread. She nervously followed the latter course.

No matter how often she defended her decision to marry John Murray, Judith had substantial misgivings about it. When she wed her first husband, she had been complacent, assuming that, far from resulting in a loss of status, her new role as wife—and perhaps mother—would elevate her in the eyes of the world. She had no such illusions on this occasion. Moreover, although she urged Winthrop to disregard the "opinion of a misjudging World" and not to be "alarmed by every rude breath of report," she found it almost as difficult to ignore her critics as her brother did.[22]

Still, she was determined to present a brave face to the world. She had already married one inept businessman. John Murray promised to be even worse. Yet at first she tried to deny the obvious. In August of 1787, for instance, she told Winthrop of the wonderful news that John might soon be the proprietor of a French estate worth £500 a year. Even if that did not work out, he had saved "some hundreds of pounds" over the years. Moreover, she was sure that he would soon settle down and make a decent living as the Gloucester church's full-time minister. She also had an answer for those like her brother, who thought that John, an uneducated emigrant with no home, no property of his own, was not worthy of membership in the Sargent family. Determinedly emphasizing the positive, she pointed out that the Christian world granted clergymen "a rank, nay even a precedence in genteel society." Moreover, John was respected by everyone. He was General Nathaniel Greene's friend and confidant, and the great George Washington had appointed him chaplain of three regiments. John and Abigail Adams were both "loud in his praises." Besides, if marriage was increasingly viewed as a private affair, a voluntary contract between two individuals, then the ascribed status of anyone was almost—if not completely—irrelevant.[23]

As worried as she was about the possible ramifications of her marriage, Judith was even more unnerved by the emotions that engulfed her. She had never experienced anything remotely like this. Indeed, she had often suspected that those who claimed to be moved by a "*belle passion*" were deceiving themselves, influenced, perhaps, by too many novels and determined to emulate the heroes and heroines whose incredible romantic raptures appeared with such tiresome regularity on the printed page. At the very least, she had assumed that she, herself was "*incapable* of *love* traced by the pencil of the Poet*.*" She had always held John Stevens in esteem, and she was a dutiful wife, if not a truly loving one. Her feelings were based on friendship, not ardor—and she had been more than comfortable with that.[24]

Indeed, and not only because she was used to it, she actually *preferred* a cool, rational relationship to one that played havoc with her emotions. She had once speculated that friendship might be superior to love. It was more reasonable, less jealous. It was "peaceful and serene," giving birth to "every disinterested sentiment." It also had egalitarian implications. Friends were not helpless slaves to their passions. They made a voluntary and considered determination to enter into a mutually beneficial relationship. Although popular wisdom in the late eighteenth century had begun to emphasize the need for an emotional bond between husband and wife, Judith had never given free rein to her feelings. Affection was necessary, of course. But women, in particular, needed to beware of passions that were "very strong in female bosoms." A woman who married for love risked being so enamored of her husband that she lost her ability to resist his authority, becoming little more than his vassal.[25]

Whenever Judith described the components of an ideal marriage, she spoke in terms of rational and "congenial minds." True love was expansive not selfish, serene not tempestuous. If it were to endure, it came only "when the sensations of the heart, generally the offspring of impassioned fervour, [were] meliorated by reason and authorized by judgment." But when it relied solely on the "fire of fancy," it died as quickly as it appeared. Passion was sexual, the fruit of the fall. Thus Judith was stunned to find that she had become a slave to her emotions—and to the physical desires they revealed—her carefully disciplined feelings temporarily out of control. When Judith talked of her second marriage years later, she said that it "was the result of a strong and holy friendship, founded upon the Rock of Ages; and originating in devout admiration of redeeming love." In the winter of 1788, her feelings were much more chaotic than so prosaic a description revealed.[26]

Judith's distrust of passion was not unique. Eighteenth-century intellectuals sought a balance between reason and passion, sense and sensibility, believing that to indulge one's emotions endangered both the individual and the society.

Reasonable people were public spirited, autonomous, and prudent. Unfortunately, society assumed that reason, like other republican virtues, was more likely to be found in men than in women. Women *could* be rational—just as men could be sentimental—but it did not come easily to them. A good education and unrelenting vigilance would help women harness their emotional tendencies. But only a select few would ever be truly self-controlled, and even they had to work harder than men did to keep their emotions in check.[27]

The binary construction of male and female attributes that increasingly characterized any analysis of gender relations in the late eighteenth century rested largely on two intellectual assumptions. One derived from John Locke, who assumed that people were most likely to act in a reasonable manner—to govern their instincts and calculate their own interests—when they operated in the public domain. The private arena, he argued, was the center of passion and desire. Because women tended to occupy the domestic sphere, it was easy to believe that they were the primary source of emotion. True, there were those who thought that Lockean liberalism offered an escape from the implications of biological determinism. By implying that gender roles were culturally determined, it gave women permission to negotiate a new definition of femininity. What had been done—in the social as well as the political arena—could be undone. In theory, moreover, Locke's social contract implied that all individuals had the capacity to reason and enjoyed identical rights. The neuter body was simply the "location of the rational subject that constitutes the person." Nevertheless, Locke's followers often ignored the egalitarian implications of his philosophy, arguing that in a state of nature men dominated women, and men created the social contract. Thus from the beginning, women were not suited for political activity.[28]

Even more important to a binary perspective was the tendency to regard human nature itself in dualistic terms, privileging mind over body and assuming that women were more captive of their physical selves than men were. Indeed, in the years after the Revolution, as class distinctions were blurred if not eradicated, many Americans were more determined than ever to shore up the boundaries that divided men from women, emphasizing difference and claiming superiority for the values associated with the male world. The pejorative division between mind and body was something that all Christians—and especially all Universalists—had embraced over the years. But it had secular roots as well. Even as Enlightenment thinkers placed rationality and embodiment in opposition, they argued that the rational mind partook of universal qualities while the body was gendered, that it was tied to the particular, to the animal, the sexual. To acknowledge one's lustful nature was to deny one's rational self—and thus not to deserve the rights to which all humans were theoretically entitled. If women found it more difficult than men to control their bodily desires, then it became easier—even necessary—to exclude them from the political world.[29]

Admittedly, the American Revolution had momentarily disrupted traditional notions of gender identity. Its emphasis on universal natural rights had led some to question old constructions of gender and to call for a new paradigm upon which to build human relationships.[30] While most Americans never acknowledged the extent to which the principle of gender equality might be taken, interpretations of femininity and masculinity were in a state of flux in the postwar world, as men and women alike struggled to define their relationship to a nation where gender, class, and racial identities were being re-created and contested. But even as discussions about gender identity took place, observers on both sides of the Atlantic began to adopt a language of scientific discourse that directly linked bodily and emotional traits in order to make a case for qualitative and essential differences between men and women. As they emphasized bodily difference, they also implied that men and women were morally and intellectually distinct, as well. To proclaim difference did not necessarily imply hierarchy. Especially in the beginning, people simply talked of the complementary characteristics of men and women. Each sex supplied what the other lacked, and *if* difference was preserved, then each would complete the other and happiness could result. Gradually, however—but by no means inevitably—many came to the conclusion that men and women were not simply distinct. Rather, especially in matters of the intellect, women were inferior to men. By arguing that nature itself defined masculinity and femininity, these theorists maintained that women were not—as seventeenth-century observers had it—simply weaker versions of men. They were, instead, radically different, even opposites.[31] In the long run, this redefinition of gender difference led to the paradigm of "separate spheres." In both the short *and* long run, it rendered women politically impotent.

This tendency began even before the American Revolution, as elite white men in both England and America claimed "civility" for themselves and cast members of the lower orders as the uncivilized "other." They defined themselves as clean, orderly, rational, and dispassionate, able to rise above their own interests and to serve the public good. The lower sort were everything that independent men were not. They were dirty and disorderly, emotional and thoroughly incapable of acting in the public interest. Lower-class men were in thrall to their beastly selves; they *were* body. Elite men could repress and restrain their bodily selves; they were mind. Because elite American men felt insecure when they compared themselves to their English counterparts, they clung fiercely to their noncorporeal self-definition. Moreover, they searched incessantly for new ways to create and police boundaries between themselves and everyone else. They added blacks and Indians to their list of "others." They also added women, defining women of whatever class or race in terms of their "lust, greed, and lack of control." Women, these men argued, were inextricably bound up in physical processes—they gave birth, they nurtured, they consumed. By linking all women with the lower sort, by establishing a dichotomy grounded in nature that rendered women as cheap, vulgar, disorderly, and irrational, and men as genteel, self-possessed, and reasonable, they created a hierarchical world based on qualitative gender differences, which of necessity denied all women a public voice. As "Lavater," writing in the *Massachusetts Magazine* put it, women were born with "light textures of their fibres and organs," they were characterized by the "irritability of their nerves" and their "incapacity for deep enquiry and firm decision." Women who denied their own nature, he said, who tried to compete with men, were "no longer women but abortions"; they were monsters, more disgusting to behold than a bearded woman.[32]

Judith knew that to submit to her bodily desires, or even to admit their existence, threatened her claims to gender equality. She resisted the very possibility that she could be casually relegated to the same category as those who occupied the lower orders. If she were to be viewed as a member of her status, as someone whose words deserved serious attention, she had to emphasize her rational nature and de-emphasize her bodily reality. Her power, such as it was, lay in her potential for mental activity. Her weakness lay in uncontrolled bodily desire. She recognized that "penetration, depth of judgment and wisdom" were attributed to men, while women were "complimented with imagination, lively fancies, etc. etc." But she always insisted that women—at least exceptional women of a certain status—could become rational beings if they were only given the opportunity. If the body was gendered, the mind was not. She accepted the male standard of excellence, assuming that reason was superior to passion. But as she had argued in "Desultory Thoughts," men and women's minds were equal, potentially identical.[33] Hence, a rational woman could put pen to paper and intrude upon the male world of public discourse on an equal basis. Judith's determination to enter the lists as a serious author, made her more resolved than ever to present herself as a rational being. Thus when she discovered that she was a passionate, sexual creature, she was not only astounded, she was terrified. Still, she could not deny her emotions. Nor, she realized, did she want to do so.

Judith knew from the start that her intention to marry John Murray would draw critics, as she feared that her own words about the pitfalls of wedded bliss might come back to haunt her. Maria totally supported her decision. She thought she could win over her parents, as well. Fitz William and Esther were problematic. But she was most concerned about Winthrop's reaction. Her brother had once praised John with the "highest encomiums." He had occasionally served as the minister's assistant at church. In 1776, he had purchased three copies of Relly's hymnbook. Then, abruptly, with no explanation, his views had altered.[34] Judith had once chosen to ignore her brother's change of mind. She could do so no longer.

She waited until the middle of April 1788 to write to Winthrop. "My heart," she began, "is indeed tenderly, faithfully, irrevocably attached" to John Murray. She would rather live simply and prudently with John than to "be hailed Empress of the Universe." Denying the rumors that had reached Ohio, she insisted that her behavior was unassailable. Until she had been widowed, and hence had become "mistress of myself," her relationship with John had been marked only by the purest friendship. Even when she realized that her feelings had changed, her fear of her brother's disapproval had led her to try to suppress her emotions. In this instance, however, her heart had triumphed over her head, and she had capitulated to the inevitable.[35]

On June 10, Judith finally received the letter from her brother that she had been both anticipating and dreading. While she had feared Winthrop's disapproval, she was totally unprepared for the level of anger his letter revealed. He was "mortified" by her decision, and he accused her of having lied about her feelings for John Murray for years. Again, Judith pleaded her case. If Winthrop was worried about her reputation, she insisted, she was better off getting married than to give gossips continued opportunity to talk about her rational, platonic relationship with John. Winthrop himself, she reminded him, had declared her current situation "improper." He had also accused her of behaving capriciously, as he had urged her to let reason—not passion—guide her. This was obviously not an indictment that Judith could allow to go unanswered. Was it not reasonable, she asked, for her to give herself a "sensible, faithful, and indulgent protector?" She admitted to Maria that she was a slave to her passions. She refused to acknowledge the same thing to Winthrop.[36]

When John finally arrived in Boston in mid-June, Judith momentarily forgot her brother's disapproval and her "pretensions to propriety." Although she was "never fond of being the subject of speculation," she disregarded the disapproval of friends and family and raced to the capital city, joining John on a quick tour through Connecticut. She basked in the praises of the crowds they met along the way, imagining that this was what her life would be like from now on. She and John would travel together up and down the eastern seaboard, greeted warmly by enlightened Christians along the way. She had always resented the strictures that bound an unaccompanied woman to her home. With John at her side, she would no longer be restrained by custom's shackles.[37]

As Judith prepared to return to Gloucester, she girded herself for the trials that lay ahead. She knew that her parents admired John, but they were not sure they wanted him for a son-in-law. They begged their daughter to "look abroad for connexions" that were more appropriate. They had tried so often—and ultimately so fruitlessly—to rescue John Stevens from financial disaster. Winthrop, Sr., had already contributed a great deal to the costs of John Murray's legal battles, and no doubt feared that the minister would be even more likely to require his help if he married Judith. His daughter insisted that John would provide her with an "establishment sufficiently easy." But she also stoutly reminded her parents that a woman could be "rolling in affluence" and still be miserable if wealth came at the expense of love. She had known John intimately for some fourteen years, and their friendship had stood the test of time. She was aware of his faults as well as his virtues. There would be no surprises in this marriage. Moreover, the two shared a "union of mind" based on their religious beliefs and their outlook on the world. Theirs would be a "companionate marriage," an egalitarian union characterized by "love sanctioned by reason," and where "that mortifying distinction, Manly superiority, has no place."[38]

Eventually Judith received her parents' blessing. Her siblings disapproved, however, and many of her friends also viewed the prospect of her marriage with "darkened countenances." Still, she persisted. She knew, of course that she did not *need* anyone's approval. Like many Americans, she believed that marriage was a personal, not a community or even a family decision. While she advised young people to seek advice from their mothers and fathers, she rejected in theory and in practice the notion that parents should influence, much less dictate, their children's choice of a spouse. By definition, the notion of romantic love subverted parental authority. And in the mind of Judith Stevens, this was all to the good. Although passion could be a tyrant, anyone who had read *Clarissa* knew that despotic parents were sure to spell disaster. All individuals were different; only prospective brides and grooms knew their own feelings. If two people wed with "reluctant hearts" they would be "the most wretched of the wretched." Without affection, a woman, in particular, would face her wedding night with "disgust or aversion," for while reason could tame the heart, the heart could never feign an attachment where none existed. A marriage without love was a "union of *persons only*," for it would be a union in which "the heart refuseth to take part."[39]

If, at the age of thirty-seven, Judith did not require her family's approval for her marriage, she wanted it, nevertheless. She was especially distraught by Winthrop's "silence, relative to an event, which looks, with an aspect so important upon my peace." Still, she doggedly forged ahead. When she told one friend—after repeating her usual list of rational justifications for her decision to wed—that in the final analysis, she was going to marry John simply because she could not help herself, she no doubt said more than she realized. All the reasons in the world were ultimately irrelevant. She was swept away by her emotions. To lose such complete control of herself was exhilarating. It was also frightening.[40]

Only her letters to John Murray gave Judith release from the tensions that tormented her. She continued to profess her love for him, composing affectionate little ditties meant for his eyes alone:

In all thy humours whether grave, or mellow,
Thou art such a hasty, testy, pleasant fellow,
Thou hast so much of wit, and spleen about thee,
That there is no living *with thee*—nor *without* thee.

She could not send him the poem—the cost was prohibitive. But writing it brought her some comfort, and in time he would be able to read it in person.[41]

On September 26, 1788, Judith was making last minute preparations to travel to neighboring Manchester where she would meet John Murray, go on to Salem, and be wed. It had been over a year since the two had decided to marry, but even at this late date their plans were fluid. They would have to be content with a civil ceremony. State law prohibited a clergyman from officiating at marriages when neither the bride nor groom was a member of his own parish. Thus, no minister could hear their vows. Still uneasy, Judith begged John to seek "able, friendly, and disinterested council" to make sure that their nuptials would pass legal scrutiny. She wanted to give critics no opportunity to question the legitimacy of her marriage. True, she told John, "when once we have exchanged our solemn vows, the transaction of that solemn hour, will be registered in heaven, and no human authority ought to possess the power to disannul." Nevertheless, she preferred to observe rules designed by "human authority" even if she did not agree with them.[42]

On the evening of September 26, Winthrop, Sr., returned to Gloucester after a short trip. He immediately insisted that John and Judith postpone their ceremony for a week. Judith did not explain her father's reasons—perhaps he still hoped she would change her mind—but she deferred to his wishes. The extra time, she said, would allow her to confirm her "still wavering resolution." She regretted the delay for only one reason. She had an instinctive aversion to October, a month she hated so much that she wished she could remove it from the calendar. Still, she resolved not to be deterred by what she granted was an irrational superstition.[43]

On the evening of October 5, Judith finally arrived in Salem, prepared to wed "with the early dawn," at the same time expressing her sorrow at the disapproval of her siblings as she wondered whether she would be able to summon the courage to accompany John to the altar. A week later, however, Judith wrote exultantly to Maria. She had "passed the Rubicon." Once more, thanks to the "arbitrary rules of custom," she had abandoned the name of Sargent, becoming Judith Murray. But, she said, whether I am Sargent or Stevens or Murray, you must continue to think of me as "Julia" or "Constantia." The ceremony, she reported, was as dignified as it could be under the circumstances. Still, even at the moment when "an eminent justice, cloathed in his magisterial robes" heard their vows, Winthrop's image appeared unbidden before her, and Judith's eyes filled with tears. Nevertheless, she did not regret her decision. To the contrary, she was almost giddy with happiness and relief. She was still nagged by fears that her marriage to John would garner negative attention. But as they began a quick tour through Massachusetts and Rhode Island to allow John the opportunity to fulfill his promise to preach there, Judith tried not to care.[44]

The trip was all that Judith hoped for, perhaps more. She could not resist pointing out that John had friends everywhere who could be ranked among "the first characters" of society. They spent an afternoon with John and Abigail Adams in Braintree, enjoying an easy conversation with two well-traveled and well-read soul mates. Judith saw in Adams the qualities of "the sage, the philosopher, the politician, and the man of unbending integrity." Abigail combined "the domestic as well as the more brilliant virtues." From there they rode on to Rhode Island. In Providence, she saw her first play, a dramatic rendition of the biblical story of David and Goliath. She was transported by the experience. The language was sublime. The acting was so real, she was almost convinced that the protagonist really *was* the shepherd boy. At play's end, the playwright, a Miss Moore, was honored by "universal applause." From that moment on, Judith became a staunch supporter of the dramatic arts.[45]

Judith was caught off guard by the depth of her bliss. Her first marriage had lowered her expectations, and she had come to believe that "happiness is rarely found with the wedded." Once, when she had seen a young husband showering his wife with attention, she had professed surprise, noting that the man in question acted more like a lover than a married man. Now, however, she was willing to concede that marriage might be as fulfilling an institution as the novelists had promised. John, she confided, "is all I wish him, tender, delicate, and manly." Eight months later, she remained ecstatic. "How exquisite are the pleasures resulting from a union with a Man of sense and sentiment," she told John in a letter that was unusually poorly punctuated. "When the sensations of the heart generally the offspring of impassioned fervour are meliorated by reason, and authorized by judgment, how happy how tranquil is that bosom which is their retreat—I bless my beloved Murray I very devoutly bless the hour which made me yours—I bathe your letters with a flow of tears, but they are tears of rapture—such tears as you, best of Men have often caused me to shed." John was, she declared, "the Man of my deliberate choice." Marriage, she happily admitted, did "not always create a tyrant . . . in one instance at least the husband hath continued the Lover."[46]

Despite her joy, all was not perfect, in large part because of Winthrop's continued hostility toward her marriage. Maria tried valiantly to effect a reconciliation between the estranged siblings, and Judith continued to write to Ohio, insisting that each letter would be her last. She was stunned that Winthrop's anger was so strong that he had actually forbade her from moving to Ohio, telling her that he hoped she would remain forever "in the obscure residence of [her] Ancestors." He had written, in words that left no doubt about his feelings, "*I had supposed that all intercourse between us had closed forever—forced into exile from my friends—removed from you, and ever to remain so—I cannot consent that you should come into this Country—We are probably severed forever—I shall never hereafter speak of you in conversation, but should I be tortured with the subject, In common with other pangs, I shall endure it*" (emphasis hers). After she had carefully copied her brother's offending words, Judith burned his letter. "You have," she said tersely, "broken my heart." When she learned that Winthrop planned to marry Rowena Tupper, daughter of General Benjamin Tupper, she immediately wrote to Maria, begging her aunt to tell Winthrop that she prayed for him and his bride every day.[47]

Judith's marriage cost her the affection of other relatives as well. In April, she wrote to her cousin Catherine who had just married Boston merchant William Powell. The two women had once been close, but now their relationship was at an end. Catherine's husband disliked John, and Judith assumed that both women would have to follow the lead of their husbands. Catherine disagreed. True, she agreed with her husband's assessment of John Murray. But why, she wondered, couldn't the two women remain friends? Judith firmly rejected the suggestion. Embracing the language of coverture, she declared that she was no longer an individual. She and John were one person. "I can hardly enjoy a friendship," she maintained, "which is not zested by esteem for the man of my heart."[48]

Judith's marriage to John Stevens had never been easy. It partook more of convenience than love, nor did it bring her the economic security she had expected. To the contrary, she had been pained by the comments of erstwhile friends who seemed to enjoy watching John's fortunes disintegrate. But as a Stevens—and even more as a Sargent—she had somehow felt personally untouched by the disdain of supercilious observers. She saw John's failure as largely accidental, the result of uncontrollable circumstances. Moreover, if blame lay anywhere, it rested on her husband's shoulders. He had never consulted her, never listened when she made suggestions. In the very worst of times, she had felt wronged—but never wrong. Marrying John Murray was different. No matter how often she pointed out that her husband was admired by the best people on both sides of the Atlantic, it was clear that she had crossed the Rubicon in more ways than one when she had wed. "All my life," she had once told Sally Barrell, "[I have] sedulously endeavored to throw a veil over my foibles, and by every possible means to conceal them from the most scrutinizing eye."[49] Yet her marriage to John Murray had irrevocably placed her at the edges of respectable society. She was not as wealthy as she once had been—and she probably never would be. She was attached to a man whose social credentials were doubtful. There were always those who never forgot their suspicions that John and Judith had behaved inappropriately even before John Stevens had died. A whiff of scandal followed her wherever she went.

What else, Congregationalists surely asked one another, could she have expected? If Universalists made no connection between earthly behavior and heavenly reward, would they not inevitably succumb to every imaginable temptation? Moreover, while in fact the rebellious sect represented a cross section of American society, its detractors deliberately situated John Murray's supporters outside the dominant culture, identifying them with other marginal groups: the poor, blacks, and especially with women. Because women were innately irrational, emotional, and "disorderly," traits that led almost inevitably to unrestrained carnality, then sexual misbehavior and femininity were virtually synonymous. When the First Parish Church refused to recognize Universalists as either moral or lawful, the gendered connotation of its accusations lurked just beneath the surface. Not only did such accusations tar the Independent Church with the pejorative brush of femininity, but they implied that dissenting women were especially likely to be slaves to their lustful nature. Judith's relationship with John Murray, even if it was completely innocent, was ready-made to appeal to the prejudices of those who saw Universalism, femininity, and carnality as inseparable.[50]

However concerned about her reputation she was, Judith had to concede that in many ways her life was falling nicely into place. John and the Gloucester Universalists regularized their relationship a month before the wedding, when the male members of the church promised their minister a salary of one hundred pounds a year. They did so in language that paid strict attention to the requirements of the Massachusetts Bill of Rights. While the church recognized "no Master besides God," its members agreed "to yield obedience to every Ordinance of man for Gods sake." The congregation continued to resist incorporation, but on Christmas Day 1788 John Murray was formally ordained minister of the Independent Church of Christ. The church members declared that while John was already their minister, in deference to public opinion they had decided "in perfect conformity to the third article of the declaration of rights," to proclaim—"again"—that they wanted Murray to "inculcate lessons and instructions of piety, religion and morality." Even if Murray continued his itinerant ways, in the eyes of his Gloucester flock, he was their "settled ordained minister." In an emotional speech, John accepted the church's call—as well as the salary that went with it.[51]

John may have reluctantly agreed to accept an annual stipend from the Gloucester church. This did not mean that he had learned to pay much heed to financial matters. He freely admitted that he "was never sufficiently sensible of the value of money to retain it in [his] possession." He was not, he sighed, "designed for a man of business." If John was generous with his money and prone to carelessness as well, Judith claimed to be "rigidly frugal." On one occasion, when she asked her husband to purchase a few necessities, she reminded him not go into debt to do so. Do not, she sternly instructed, act "superior to my directions." At least Murray, unlike her first husband, did not resent her involvement in their financial affairs. "How sweet is the reflection," she smiled, "that I do not run even the smallest risk of offending the Lord of my wishes, by thus dictating in his pecuniary concerns." She had always been proud of her head for business, but where John Stevens had ignored her advice, John Murray welcomed it.[52]

* * *

In January of 1789, Judith's pleasure in her marriage deepened as she began to suspect that, at the age of thirty-eight, she was pregnant. A month later, she was sure, as she happily announced that an "innocent and helpless stranger" would "ere long, make its appearance in this very bad World." She could scarcely believe her good fortune. "The fact is," she said, "I have outlived even the Hope of experiencing those delightful sensations, which are *supposed* peculiar to the maternal bosom—that I should be a Mother is hardly within the chapter of possibilities." Now that she had been proved wrong, her financial position took on monumental importance. Are we not, she asked John, "under obligation to provide for the Being, of whose tortured existence we are the authors, and to whom under God can the little creature look for support if not to us?"[53]

Just as the institution of marriage had changed over the years, so had the meaning of childbearing and motherhood. Seventeenth-century mothers loved their children, of course. But they did not romanticize their role and they took their maternal duties more or less for granted. Motherhood was a biological given, not an experience laden with emotional overtones. It was, moreover, only one of a woman's many duties. In earlier days, women had been so busy cooking meals, weaving cloth, sewing, gardening, making soap and candles, and even on occasion working in the shop or fields, that they had neither the time nor the energy to focus much individual attention on their children. This was especially true for the many women who bore a child approximately every two years. For them, childbearing was as much a burden as a pleasure. Moreover, colonial society did not see the duties of motherhood as particularly demanding or important. Some women may have thought that their ability to endure the pain of childbirth indicated that the "weaker sex" was stronger than conventional wisdom granted. Still, no one claimed that the ability to bear children was a sign of a woman's superiority. In fact, while women tended to the very young, when the shaping of a child's character was at stake, fathers took over. Women, popular wisdom had it, were too weak to rear children in a godly manner. If a child's sinful character was to be curbed if not broken, the qualities of a stern and unbending parent were essential. By the time Judith was of childbearing age, people were no longer so sure this was the case, and they looked to mothers to guide even older children along the path of virtue.[54]

Members of the elite on both sides of the Atlantic began emphasizing the importance of a mother's role for a variety of reasons. At least by the mid-eighteenth century, they embraced the view of human nature advanced by John Locke. Locke had argued that children were not innately sinful creatures who had to be beaten into submission for their own and society's good. Rather, childhood was the "scene of innocence," and if infants were corruptible, they were not intrinsically corrupt. They were impressionable blank slates whose characters would be shaped by their experiences. Significantly, they responded better to rewards than punishment, and learned by example, not precept. Thus, wise parents no longer aimed at abject submission. They sought to develop a child's conscience, preparing their progeny for eventual independence. If that was true, qualities that once seemed to make women unfit for raising children, were now assets. As Judith had argued in "Desultory Thoughts," affection and rational indulgence rather than coercion produced virtuous and independent adults.[55]

Because mothers were especially close to their children during the formative years, commentators began to stress women's role in child rearing. Infancy was a critical period; it was the "seedtime," when the most well meaning parent's mistakes could spell disaster. As Judith saw it, it was a mother's job to form the mind, to "mark the first dawnings of reason, to correct the young idea, and to point to rectitude the expanding intellect." Maria, she noted approvingly, spent her every waking hour in the nursery, never trusting her babies to strangers. Nor, in the circles in which Maria traveled, was her behavior atypical.[56]

Lockean psychology provided the sort of "scientific" basis for valuing mothers that any Western thinker could appreciate. The particular circumstances of post-Revolutionary America guaranteed that Locke's arguments would resonate in the new nation. As they began to devise a constitution that would survive for decades, if not for the ages, the country's leaders tried valiantly to devise structural means to arrest, or at least to impede, the cycle of birth, maturity, degeneration, and decay that had destroyed all republics in the past. But some of them also looked to mothers to do their part. They agreed that if America was to avoid corruption, it had to create a virtuous and educated citizenry. Monarchies could survive without the aid of an educated rank and file; republics would perish if they did not produce successive generations of men who were prepared to forsake their own interests for the public good. Unfortunately, while people believed that familial affection was natural, the same could not be said for national ties. Young men had to be taught to love their country better than themselves, for the bonds that connected citizens to the nation were fragile, artificial, and had to be nourished. The time to produce the first generation of virtuous citizens was at hand. America was a "youthful nation." Like its children, it was "plastic"; it could be molded for good or evil. If it was mothers, in their private capacity, who were in the best position to form the character of succeeding generations of Americans, then the future of the country lay—literally—in their hands.[57]

Most mothers remained more concerned about the fate of their children than the fate of the nation, no matter how many leaders talked about "republican motherhood."[58] Judith was an exception to the rule. Indeed, the duties of mothers were a central motif in the first two pieces that she had submitted for publication. A voracious reader, she simply soaked up the educational theories that permeated American intellectual circles. But she had personal reasons for investing the role of motherhood with special significance. Because she was childless in a world where no marriage was considered complete without children, she may well have invested the role of mother with a romantic aura she would not otherwise have embraced. Moreover, her experience with her orphans not only forced her to take her parental duties seriously, but demanded that she justify her belief that parenthood was more a matter of mind than of body.

By arguing that women were designed by nature for motherhood and even more by advancing an elevated characterization of a role that women had once taken for granted, Judith was erecting an entire ideological edifice upon what had once been merely a biological reality. Most women of her time, even if they began to give more attention to motherhood, did not endow their role with political meaning. They saw themselves as good mothers who served God, husband, and children. Judith, however, invested motherhood with a tenuous and indirect connection to the well-being of the new nation. In this regard, she was one of the most outspoken proponents of republican motherhood. She was always quick to praise—as well as to envy—those women like Maria who produced one healthy child after another, seemingly with little effort. "The community is under vast obligations to you," she told her aunt. "For, if I may trust the prophetic impulse, it will be indebted to you for no less than six of its most valuable Citizens." By embracing some cultural definitions of femininity, Judith imagined that she could use those definitions for her own ends, proclaiming a woman's moral purity, granting importance to the private sphere, giving her a safe base from which to affect (though not to control) the public realm. A mother's influence, she said, touched "generations yet unborn."[59] It was her view of motherhood that afforded her the best ammunition to demand equal education for women. It also allowed her to claim that women were not merely lesser men. Rather they were essential to the very progress of humankind, as they used their unique characteristics to civilize the world. In this sense, civilization and gender difference went hand in hand.

This perspective was not without its ironies. It flew in the face of Judith's usual emphasis on the importance of mind, her insistence that biological difference was unimportant, and her inclination to blur the differences between men and women. It tended to circumscribe the sphere within which a woman operated, encouraging her to make the family—especially her children—the focus of her energies and ambitions. Such a role constricted women's sphere, even though it claimed to elevate women's status. It also de-emphasized the role of housewife, implicitly downplaying women's economic contributions to the economy. It may have allowed women an indirect and mediated influence on the public stage, but it did so without threatening traditional gender conventions. Throughout her life, Judith questioned most such conventions. She could easily understand why some women elected to remain single. She envisioned a time when women might pursue untraditional careers—in business, in politics, even in the military. She never, however, believed that any woman would choose to be childless. Rather, she thought that women's highest calling was motherhood. By defining woman "as mother," Judith accepted an essentialist argument, retreating from her claim that women's ambitions should recognize no boundaries. She was—however unintentionally—providing a justification for those who viewed women as unfit to live a hurly-burly existence in the world of politics or business. By embracing the very duties and values that confined her, she was accepting a view of motherhood that lay at the very heart of the doctrine of separate spheres.[60]

Her understanding of the importance of a mother's role led Judith to separate men and women. It also enabled her to put a certain amount of distance between herself and lower-class women. While she believed that a marriage without children was incomplete, like many of her elite contemporaries she had begun to believe that only women of the lesser orders, who had no control over their own bodily impulses, bore children indiscriminately. While virtually everyone looked at a barren woman as a failure, a happy medium was the ideal, if not the reality. If a woman had fewer children, she could treat each child as an individual with a distinct personality, developing an intense sentimental bond with her "beloved urchins." She entered a child-centered universe, where childhood itself was a discrete stage in life, and where her own rational and intellectual abilities were more important than her physical capacity to produce offspring on cue. Of course, a decline in the quantity of children led to expectations for a better quality of care. Having observed the failures and successes of mothers around her, Judith was convinced that she was prepared to take on a task that she regarded as both the most important and most rewarding that life could offer.[61]

Although Judith was ecstatic at the prospect of becoming a mother, like so many women she feared the experience of childbirth. Everyone was aware of the dangers, especially for a woman of her age. Almost as soon as she knew she was pregnant, Judith began to prepare for the possibility that she might not survive the birthing experience. She secured Maria's promise to raise her child, should that happen. She also urged John to seek "another wedded friend" if "the angel of death" saw fit to visit her. Her anxieties were not unusual, even if they were not especially necessary. Although most American women survived childbirth, virtually everyone knew someone who had not. Even young, healthy women saw pregnancy as a time to prepare for death at the very moment that they looked forward to giving life. "The fear of our sex," Judith had once pointed out, "upon these occasions, too frequently absorbs their hopes." Indeed, most prospective mothers approached their "painful and perilous hour" with trepidation.[62]

John wrote calmly of his wife's condition, in tones that were a stark contrast to Judith's fears. While he dutifully referred to childbirth as the "time of terror," he observed that his wife was healthier than he had ever seen her and that she "suffered as little perhaps from her present circumstances as any one of her sex hitherto." Judith did not agree. Thus she reached out to other women for advice that John was unqualified to offer. In this instance, if in no other, women were the ultimate authorities. Many pregnant women forged deep personal ties with the matrons who supported them as they prepared to give birth. Judith had always been excluded from this network of common experience. If she survived, she would be among those who could share her wisdom with those who faced childbirth for the first time. All too often, however, the women to whom Judith turned offered her "terror," not comfort, as they eagerly embellished the stories of their own physical suffering. The more harrowing the tales became, the more her "coward mind" began to dread her impending ordeal. In March, she contemplated one last trip to Boston, where Maria, at least, would give her the assurance she craved. Eventually she abandoned her plans. My "female acquaintances," she explained, "prognosticate nothing but mischief from my meditated journey." Moreover, her body, already "strangely altered," seemed like an alien being to her and she was increasingly uncomfortable appearing in public.[63]

Even in her own mother's day, women had never been embarrassed to show themselves in mixed company. To the contrary, they were proud of the "big bellies" that proclaimed their fruitfulness. Women like Judith, while they were not yet affected by the exaggerated sense of delicacy that permeated middle-class households in the Victorian era, had become less likely to celebrate the physical changes they experienced during pregnancy. They seldom described themselves as "fruitful" or "big with child." Indeed they tried not to think of their bodies at all. Instead they focused on the "little stranger," the "pledge of love" who would ultimately make their pregnancy worthwhile.[64]

As her "pangful hour" approached, Judith resolutely put her affairs in order. Defying her apprehensions, she asked Maria about the latest styles in shirts and caps for the baby. Such preparations made her feel a little less vulnerable, giving her a sense of control, and taking her mind off her fear. Even so, she began to contemplate the possibility that she might produce an "imperfect or monstrous being." To be the "parent of deformity" was her nightmare vision. Even worse, she worried that her child might not live at all. While she tried to repress such thoughts, they always returned, unbidden.[65] She had watched her own mother experience five successive miscarriages before Fitz William's birth. She did not think she could endure the disappointment if her own baby died.

Never one to await her destiny passively, Judith intended to take any measure to ensure that her ordeal, however excruciating, would have a happy ending. Departing again from her mother's example, she planned to have Dr. Plummer with her once her labor pains began. Childbirth had once been a communal experience and the exclusive province of women. As a woman's time drew near, relatives and neighbors gathered, usually accompanied by a midwife. Men— even husbands—had no place in a ritual that women alone understood. Relying on a combination of folk medicine, experience, and common sense, they offered encouragement, while intervening as little as possible in a process that everyone saw as natural. They filled the birthing room, talking and laughing, eating and drinking, distracting and encouraging the expectant mother. The fate of mother and child was, ultimately, in God's hands. When complications arose, the community comforted the bereaved, helped bury the dead, and humbly submitted to the divine plan.[66]

Increasingly, however, prospective mothers began to take their fate into their own hands. They turned to male doctors, self-styled experts, to help in the birthing process. Doctors were the sole possessors of forceps, whose judicious use could save the lives of mother and child. At first women called for physicians only when they expected a difficult birth. But gradually, in elite circles at least, they turned to doctors almost routinely. They did so for a variety of reasons. They viewed pregnancy and childbirth as a disease, a medical problem that required the skill of college-educated practitioners. Why, they asked, should they leave the most important event of their lives in the hands of uneducated women when well-trained men could provide superior care? They also rejected old religious notions that women's suffering was the unavoidable consequence of Eve's curse. In an enlightened age, when humans were confident of their ability to control their lives in so many instances, it seemed ridiculous to sit quietly and do nothing. Their ability to understand and manipulate the laws of nature, their concern for the comfort as well as the health of the mother, made prospective parents realize just how far civilization had advanced since the Pilgrims had first set foot on American shores. Fashion, the desire to appear genteel, also had a bearing on some women's decision to seek expert help. Lower-class and black women might be able to endure the pains of childbirth with stoicism. Like animals, they were born to breed. But an elite woman was more delicate, less able to withstand tortures that even her own mother had accepted as her lot.[67]

The very delicacy that led women to shrink from the trials of birthing, made many of them uncomfortable with male doctors. Moreover, while they looked to forceps to spare them pain and to ensure a happy outcome, they tended to distrust the very instruments that were designed to alleviate their concerns. But like Judith, who admitted that having a doctor present when she gave birth would do "violence" to her "delicacy," they tried to shunt such worries aside. Convinced that hers would be a difficult birth, Judith wanted all the help she could get. She had waited too long to have a child, and she was determined not to let anything stand in the way of her happiness.[68]

Despite all her efforts, the much anticipated birth of her child ended tragically. On Saturday, August 1, Judith's "hour of danger" finally began. The most harrowing stories of her friends had not prepared her for the unremitting "agonies of a most tremendous kind" that she endured. Years later, she would point to women's ability to survive childbirth as proof of female superiority. Women are, she claimed in *The Gleaner*, "the Enduring Sex. . . . they are subjected to agonies unknown to manhood." In the summer of 1789, however, she was not comforted by thoughts of her own strength. By the fifth day of labor, she was exhausted. Dr. Plummer began to doubt that the baby was even alive and worried that if he did not intervene Judith would follow her child to its grave. As he watched his patient grow ever weaker, he finally produced "*his Instruments*," delivering the child—a boy—who had died in his mother's womb a few hours earlier. Nine months of "cheerful expectation" ended when he placed a "breathless Corpse" in Judith's arms.[69]

It was John's melancholy task to bury his son. They called him George—no doubt a patriotic tribute to George Washington. Judith once would have named him in honor of one of her brothers, but she knew that Winthrop would despise the gesture, and Fitz William would be almost as disdainful. Better to choose a name that no one in the staunchly Federalist family would find offensive. For a long while, John feared that he might lose his wife as well. He had already suffered the death of his first wife and child, and he hoped he was not destined to repeat the experience. For three weeks, Judith's prognosis remained guarded. Three nurses gave her around-the-clock care. Never, John proclaimed, "did woman suffer more than she has suffered." Five weeks after George's birth, she was still unable to sit up, much less to walk. Her legs were so swollen that they were bigger than her father's thigh, and she could not get out of bed without help. In October, when she made the short ride by chaise to her parents' home, the consequences were nearly fatal. At the end of the year, she was still too weak to visit George's grave. Winthrop's stubborn refusal to break his silence even under such distressing circumstances only added to Judith's depression.[70]

Had the end result been different, Judith would gladly have suffered this pain and more. But to have "gone through all this without the gratification she wished for" was intolerable. Only her faith—and the passage of time—alleviated her sorrow. The night after George's birth, she had a strangely soothing dream.

A "host of children" clad in white robes appeared before her, "their beauty beyond description." As they sang and beckoned to her, a curtain rose behind them revealing an indescribably beautiful scene. She had the same dream repeatedly throughout her convalescence. And even after her health returned, she continued to sense that angels surrounded her wherever she went. Her movements of late, she confided to Maria, "seem often to be accompanied by a little Cherub—it goeth up and down with me—It trippeth by my side, and I rarely turn my eyes, but a little attendant being, with a countenance arrayed in smiles, seems actually to meet my glance." If many people were beginning to see babies as cherubs unsullied by sin, then such a vision was understandable and surely comforting.[71]

There was probably nothing even the most skilled physician could have done to save little George. Nevertheless, crushed by her disappointment and convinced that bearing another child was "almost beyond the reach of probability," Judith lashed out, blaming Dr. Plummer, whom she described as an "ignorant butcher"—not God or nature—for her son's death. "Had I been skillfully managed," she insisted, "my infant might have been preserved." Moreover, she was convinced that the doctor and his instruments had turned her into an invalid, "perhaps for life." "To become a mother," she said, "was, I confess, the wish of my soul." It was a wish she now thought she would never fulfill. John, too, was unhappy, but his sunny disposition and his faith in God allowed him to accept his fate. "Let us," he wrote, "not repine. Infinite wisdom cannot err." Judith felt that her inability to bow to her fate revealed a weakness in her faith. As a Universalist she knew that George was in a better place. She tried to view the world with "the eyes of a Poet" who proclaimed with certainty that "from all these seeming evils, *good, eventual Good*" would triumph. But if she accepted this reality intellectually, her heart rebelled.[72]

Judith's criticisms of Dr. Plummer were probably unfair, but they were not especially unusual. Women had once accepted the death of a child as John Murray apparently did, knowing that God directed even the most ordinary daily occurrences. Storms and droughts, war and peace, birth and death were all in his hands. This did not mean, of course, that parents did not grieve over the deaths of their sons and daughters. It did mean, however, that they did not blame themselves or any other human being for an event that was ultimately beyond their control. But just as women were no longer willing to submit to prolonged pain during childbirth, neither could they quite so easily accept the death of newborn infants. They often endured a long grieving process, characterized by sleeplessness, depression, disturbing dreams, a sense of their own vulnerability, and even shame. If motherhood was the focus of their lives, if their very identity was bound up in their ability to bear and raise children, it was not surprising that they suffered so deeply. Moreover, once they had come to believe that humans could at least partly control their own destiny, once they had sought the intervention of physicians, they were no longer able to attribute their loss to providence. Human error was somehow to blame. When the intervention she herself had requested failed, Judith simply could not resign herself to her son's death. She had followed the best advice. She had taken every precaution. She was convinced that somehow the tragedy could have been averted.[73]

Still, Judith could not change the facts. She would be a wife, but not a mother. At least she would be a good wife, married to a man she adored. She would, after all, be free to travel with John as he spread the good news of Universalism. Her expeditions would distract her from her sorrows, even if they did not vanquish her pain. She might even find time to publish again. If she could not give birth to a child of her flesh, she could give birth to the words that enlightened the men and women—strangers as well as friends—who chose to read them.

Chapter 7
A Wider World

Judith Sargent Murray approached the last decade of the eighteenth century with mixed emotions. Still estranged from Winthrop and continuing to mourn the death of her son, she had much to regret. Nevertheless, she was grateful for a great deal. Her marriage to John Murray remained her truest happiness. Her parents, although they were growing older and more feeble, were still alive and remained a source of emotional support. On a grander scale, she was supremely confident of America's prospects. The nation had gotten off to an inauspicious start, but by the fall of 1789, a new Constitution had put the country on more solid footing. Judith was delighted that George Washington was everyone's choice to head the fledgling government. The general's leisurely journey from Virginia to New York where he assumed the duties of the presidency had been nothing short of a triumphal tour, as "both sexes and all ages" gathered to greet him. "The festive board hath been magnificently spread," Judith boasted, "the muses have been exhausted—Countless odes have been composed and set to musick." The war was over. Martial exploits were no longer central to American life. The pen might now be more important than the sword.[1]

No matter how glorious its future might be, the newly formed country was a provincial backwater compared to England or Europe. After her trip to Philadelphia in the summer of 1790, Judith admitted as much. To her, the Pennsylvania capital was elegant and sophisticated, but she suspected that a Londoner would see the American metropolis as little more than a "thrifty Village." More troublesome in her mind, the nation lacked culture, its writers and artists were scarcely in "the dawn of being." Indeed, Judith wrote, "the probability is that Centuries will revolve e'er the fashioning hand of Art will produce anything in this younger World meriting the attention of a European." Still, if that were true, the competition in America for literary laurels might not be so formidable; perhaps her work would be recognized in a country that possessed no Popes or Shakespeares of its own.[2]

*   *   *

If Judith occasionally contemplated a literary career, more often than not her thoughts were closer to home. Her relationship with Esther and even more with Fitz William remained strained. Although her brother began to view John more favorably, he continued to keep his distance from her. Whenever she wrote to him, Judith did her best to honor his preference for short letters; she also tried not to deluge him with unwanted advice. He was, after all, an adult, a man of business, and he deserved to be addressed in the "equal character of a friend." But habits of a lifetime were difficult to break, and her letters often read like the tiresome homilies she had sent him when he was a boy. She urged him to be an honest merchant, to avoid debt, and to be content with the modest fruits of his labor. She even dared to hope that he would one day abandon his hazardous career altogether.[3]

By 1789, Judith was less starry-eyed than she had been when she had wed John Murray. No marriage was perfect. The ideal never measured up to the reality. John was less inclined to insist upon his patriarchal perquisites than her first husband had been. But even an egalitarian union assumed that the husband would be the ultimate authority. A wife might influence her husband, but she dared not dominate him. Moreover, even a woman who exercised too much influence would be viewed as manipulative, dangerous, even unnatural. Thus, Judith was circumspect. If she occasionally tested her limits, she invariably defended herself in conventional terms. When, for instance, she wrote to strangers explaining Universalism's fine points with considerable authority, she always apologized, saying that she was merely complying with her husband's orders to act on his behalf. Marriage may well have been an apt metaphor for republicanism, based on the notion that two individuals freely accepted the terms of the contract that bound them together. But that same contract legitimated a husband's claim to power. Just as "the people" agreed to obey the government of their own creation, so a bride promised to honor her husband's wishes. A husband might, as John Murray generally did, wear his authority lightly. But he need not do so.[4]

Judith was by no means the only woman of her time who noted that the rules of marriage were kinder to husbands than to wives. Granted, Mercy Otis Warren failed to appreciate the difficulties some wives might have. But Abigail Adams spoke for many when she urged her husband to "Remember the Ladies." "Unlimited power" in the hands of men was dangerous, she noted, for all men were "Naturally Tyrannical." Philadelphian Anne Shippen Livingston agreed. She longed for a companionate marriage, but she knew from experience how unlikely it was for a man to "give up the harsh title of master for the more tender & endearing one of a Friend."[5]

Even though many of her friends disapproved of her marriage, Judith did not regret it. Winthrop's fury, however, continued to distress her. After receiving the "fatal letter," in which he had excised her from his life, Judith resolutely stuck to her vow to contact her brother no more. Even when she heard of the death of his wife and baby, she did not break her silence. In the spring of 1790, she could bear the rift no longer. She was in Boston visiting Maria and indulging in nostalgic conversations about "a thousand endearing incidents," all of which reminded her of the affection she and Winthrop once shared. She decided to make one more attempt to repair their relationship, hoping that her brother's recent bereavement might make him more susceptible to her pleas. She, too, had lost a child; she had nearly suffered Rowena's fate. Had she died, brother and sister would never have had the chance to end a quarrel that had lasted two very long years. Employing the sentimental language she thought might move her brother, she declared that no differences were sufficient to destroy "our natural, our long tied, long enduring friendship."[6]

Judith's efforts at reconciliation—something she had once dismissed as "romantic"—were finally rewarded. Winthrop accepted his sister's offer of friendship, even though he refused to concede that he was wrong about her marriage. He also confided that he was planning a brief trip to Gloucester. Judith was overjoyed. When they met at last, her fears that he remained unforgiving vanished. "Our first interview," she wrote Maria, "was tender, and interestingly affecting." Even so, she remained only "half blessed." Winthrop refused to speak to John and so the "honored husband of my most deliberate choice, partook not my joy. The hand of amity is not yet stretched forth to him." Nevertheless, the worst was over and Judith was convinced that Winthrop's irrational hostility would eventually abate.[7]

Once more on speaking terms with every member of her family, Judith settled contentedly into life as a respectable matron. She had almost relinquished any secret hopes she might have had for affluence. But she remained thankful that if she was careful, she need never again face bankruptcy. Usually she was satisfied with that. "I believe," she wrote John, "we are mutually too anxious about pecuniary matters—it would certainly be better, if we *confided* more, and *reflected* less." After all, she added, "we cannot by all our exertions add a single figure to the sum total" of our possessions. Still, while she encouraged John to accept their status, she found it difficult to follow her own advice. She always thought her husband lacked worldly wisdom, and on occasion she exploded. "I regret," she wrote in 1791, "that you are not more uniformly attentive to your interest. . . . At times you appear anxious, and sufficiently economical—but you seem to have no *fixed plan*." It was John's often lackadaisical attitude that occasionally drove Judith to distraction. Moreover, it was she who suffered most when money was scarce. With just one servant at her disposal, she spent more time than she liked on housekeeping, which, she complained, "considerably curtails, and perplexes, those hours which I would gladly devote to employments better suited to my taste."[8]

Not surprisingly, John's haphazard approach to financial matters reminded Judith of the strictures that both law and custom placed on all women. Her first husband had remained supremely confident of his own ability as a provider and had refused even to listen to Judith's advice. John Murray did not resent his wife's "interference." To the contrary, he happily left most decisions in her hands. It was Judith who persuaded John to buy shares in the national bank. It was she who sought out other investment opportunities that would augment her husband's salary. But, as she discovered in the fall of 1791, there were limits beyond which she could never go. The Murrays wanted to sell some land they owned in the Northwest Territory. When Judith asked Winthrop to secure a buyer for her, she assured him that John had agreed to the transaction. "My Brother certainly knows," she added acerbically, "that the law acknowledges no *separate* act of a married Woman."[9]

By assuming a large share of the responsibility for ordering her family's financial affairs, Judith barely nibbled at the edges of respectability. From her own perspective, she put her reputation more squarely on the line in the winter of 1790, when a few young gentlemen of the town put on a play. Gloucester was gloomy and cold in January and the town's inhabitants were eager for any diversion as they impatiently waited for signs of spring. Although she had always longed to attend a theatrical performance, to lose herself for an hour or so in its "variety of wonders," Judith had not seen her first play until she married John Murray. Even then, she had traveled to Rhode Island to do so. She never dreamed that she would see even an amateur production in her own town. In parts of America, and especially in New England, many people viewed the theater with deep suspicion. Judith herself grudgingly admitted that the comedy the Gloucester players chose to perform, George Farquhar's popular *The Recruiting Officer*, was "abundantly supplied with oaths, and obscenity." Thus it was likely to confirm the prejudices of those who saw the theater as an instrument of the devil. Fortunately, the actors sought to disarm some critics when they "corrected" Farquhar's language, eradicating the most risqué passages. Still, Fitz William's Anna refused to attend the first performance.[10]

The Murrays had no such compunctions. John had been a regular theatergoer in London. Judith had been enchanted by her first encounter with the dramatic arts and hungered for more. However, her support for the amateur thespians was based on more than a casual desire to be entertained. At least in Gloucester, she was known for her literary talent. Thus, Gorham Rogers, the group's organizer and the play's leading man, turned to her for an epilogue he could recite at the first performance. Judith hesitated for only a moment. She was, she laughed, "by no means a proficient in the art of refusal." It was pride, she later admitted, that prompted her to accept the challenge. She quickly threw "some lines together," and sent them off. She claimed her feelings would not be hurt if the players rejected them, but she was elated when they pronounced her piece more than acceptable.[11]

Her epilogue was a poetic defense of the theater. Judith linked the little production to American nationalism, asking her listeners to indulge the efforts of rank amateurs and to award their efforts with "sweet applause." In time, she predicted, if critics were not too severe, native performers would become more polished and audiences would be morally improved. Plays were respectable as well as patriotic. There was no risk, she said, in entertaining those worthy souls who spent a few hours reaping the benefits of "joy, chastis'd by wisdom" that the *Recruiting Officer* offered.[12]

When she returned home after the first performance, Judith was giddy with pleasure. Although it was late, she ran straight to her desk and dashed off letters to Maria Sargent and Mrs. Walker. She pronounced the play a complete success. Men had filled all the parts. The actors had no stage, no scenery. But none of that mattered. Even John, who had higher standards than provincial Americans, sang the actors' praises, insisting that only at London's Theatre Royal had he seen a finer production. The rest of the audience clearly agreed. They "laughed, admired, and applauded the performers." Judith was "rendered almost giddy, by clapping of hands." Are we not, she asked in mock horror, "moving toward paths of dissipation?" Better yet, although she modestly claimed it scarcely deserved it, her epilogue had received its share of praise. The theater, even more than the print media, was designed to satisfy Judith's hunger for approval. There, the reward was both direct and public, and she basked in the spontaneous applause of her friends, taking each murmur of approval to heart. More than ever she believed that "were a Theater ever licenced and established among us, it might, as I believe, unquestionably be made a school of morality."[13]

Other Gloucester inhabitants must have agreed. The following winter the "gentlemen Comedians" returned to their makeshift stage. Each play they produced required a prologue and epilogue from the town's resident poet. Judith always claimed to doubt her own talent. When a comedic touch was required, she felt especially out of her depth, and she found it impossible to keep her pieces short and to the point. She also conceded that some of her rhymes were a little off. "Vexation" and "distraction," "appear" and "share," "railers" and "fellows": none of these would do before a truly exacting audience. Still, she never refused a request. Her verses praised American playwrights Royall Tyler and Mercy Otis Warren as excellent examples of native talent. More pointedly, she used her pen to "startle male prerogative," giving "the alarm to sovereign man," as she predicted that American women would soon "ascend the loftiest heights." At a minimum, the plays fulfilled their purpose, giving the town's inhabitants a brief respite from the bleak winter.[14] At most, they encouraged Judith to contemplate seriously once more the possibility of embarking on a literary career.

*   *   *

Judith tried to convince herself that she was happy in Gloucester, but throughout the winter of 1790, she was often morose. She had never recovered either mentally or physically from George's death. "My spirits," she said, "are unequal to the smallest exertion, and I am every moment sinking under the most uncommon, and ill timed depression of Mind." Perhaps because she was childless, perhaps because John was so often on the road, she found her native home increasingly confining. She had come to accept the fact that her husband was constitutionally designed to lead an itinerant's life. Moreover, she thought that their time apart gave a certain zest to their relationship. But in her mind, Gloucester itself, although it was "rapidly advancing in the estimation of many," was becoming less and less attractive. The town seemed more provincial than charming. She had once had many friends there, but the death of some, the departure of others, and her ties to Universalism had all shrunk her tiny circle. Her life was easy enough. Most women would have envied it. But the constant round of visiting, card playing, and gossip seemed so meaningless. While she tried to be content with her lot, she envied John's peripatetic ways. "You have in this respect, as in almost every other," she told him, "the advantage of me, for every excursion is still adding to your original stock of ideas."[15]

   It probably did not help that Judith knew she had some very attractive alternatives. As John's fame grew, many Universalist congregations tried to lure him to their side. Everyone acknowledged their debt to the man some called the father of American Universalism. It was the Gloucester church's decision to separate from the First Parish Church that had been the catalyst for the formation of Universalist congregations throughout New England. It was Murray's legal battles that had won the sect a measure of protection from the whims of Massachusetts's tyrannical majority. Without John Murray, they might all have remained little more than a disorganized group of malcontents. Judith was torn.

She was proud of her husband and impressed by the determination of many churches to persuade him to become their permanent minister. The Universalists at Boston, Philadelphia, and New York were all hinting that they hoped he would settle with them. The advantages of any of these cities were obvious. John often remarked that if he could move to Philadelphia, he would be happy "beyond measure." Judith occasionally indicated that she would follow her husband anywhere.[16] Still, there were times when she felt that leaving her parents, even to go no farther than Boston, was unthinkable.

For awhile, the Murrays postponed any decision. And in the summer of 1790, Judith enjoyed a temporary respite from her routine when she accompanied her husband on a leisurely trip to Philadelphia. It was religious affairs that called John to the nation's most cosmopolitan city. Universalists were guided by the Bible, the Holy Spirit, and little else. As a result, the denomination had broken down into a number of competing factions, and it became clear that its leaders needed to find common ground before the entire movement disintegrated. John was one of the first men to recognize the need for some level of organizational and theological unity. In 1785, he helped convene a general convention in Oxford, Massachusetts, which he hoped would provide the basis for a loosely constructed national organization. The delegates adopted a cumbersome name, the "Independent Christian Society, commonly called 'Universalists,'" and proclaimed their desire to be "cemented in one body, consequently bound by the ties of love to assist each other, at any, and all times when occasion shall require."[17]

While John knew that his church desperately needed a more formal structure, he hesitated. Early Universalists tended to resist doctrinal interference, and efforts to impose any system on the sect would be a thankless task, offering him little honor and even less money. There was a time, he sighed, when he would have been free to ignore practical concerns, but that had been before he had a wife to support. In the summer of 1790, however, church leaders agreed to gather in Philadelphia in an effort to create a unified institution based on whatever principles they shared. From the beginning, John argued that any credo the Universalists adopted had to be cast in the broadest terms. The church, he asserted, was "constituted on such general and generous principles, as to include all who *profess* Salvation in Christ Jesus, and maintain good works."[18] But John, like everyone else, claimed to be more broad-minded than he was, and he often thundered at the apostasy of those who veered from his version of the faith.

Judith and John began their journey on May 4. Twenty-year-old Anna remained behind, first under the watchful eye of Judith's parents, and then in Maine visiting relatives. On occasion Judith complained that she seldom heard from her niece. More often she was amazed at how easy it was to forget the cares she left behind. Everywhere she and John went she met new people and enjoyed new experiences. Travel was exhausting, but seldom dull. They went by land, partly because Judith's seasickness made a trip by water unthinkable, partly because an overland trek allowed John to renew connections with his many friends. Judith never tired of the beauties of the countryside. Her joy was enhanced because she shared it with John, who was captivated by every rock and tree along their way. On her thirty-ninth birthday, he sought to distract her from somber thoughts of aging, picking some wild flowers in a field outside Hartford and presenting them to her with a romantic flourish.[19]

In her poetry, Judith often celebrated the pleasures of hearth and home, insisting that women were happy "in their sphere" and enjoyed their "domestic employments." In reality, she was seldom happier than when she was on the road. The only pastime that pleased her more was writing about her experiences. Thus, just three days out of Gloucester, she announced her plan to maintain a record of her journey. Written as a series of letters to her parents, her journal would keep everyone at home apprised of her progress. At journey's end, she could peruse its pages as often as she liked, reliving her experiences long after the trip itself was a faint memory. She also planned to share the journal with friends and perhaps with strangers, entertaining anyone who might find her musings interesting or instructive.[20]

For Judith, putting pen to paper was as natural as breathing. But "travel writing"—in the form of diaries, journals, or letters—was becoming an especially popular genre for many genteel women by the end of the eighteenth century. It required little learning, allowing women to jot down their observations without worrying about structure or grammar. If they stuck to appropriate topics, writing about morals and manners rather than politics, expressing their emotional reactions to their surroundings, they were doing little to challenge gender conventions. They could even publish their observations without risking disapproval.[21]

The eagerness with which Judith embarked on her trip was not atypical. Travel was the ideal vehicle for proper women who wanted to escape their humdrum routine, to sever—at least momentarily—the bonds that linked them to their homes. Travel was liberating, exhilarating, an adventure. It stimulated the imagination, connecting women to the wider world and affording them pleasant memories long after they had returned to their ordinary lives. At the same time, if a woman obeyed the rules, it was perfectly respectable. Judith went with her husband. She never entered a home without an appropriate introduction. As she walked the streets of unfamiliar towns, rubbed shoulders with strangers, remarked upon—even judged—the people, habits, and institutions she encountered, she never relinquished her claim to gentility. It was perfectly possible, she once had proclaimed, to travel the world over, without losing the character "so ornamental to female life."[22]

While Judith envied the freedom of the men in her life, it never occurred to her to flout convention, nor did she appear to notice that her gentility as much as her gender, restricted her movements, keeping her from traveling without a male chaperone. Consider the experiences of her less well placed contemporaries. Martha Ballard, the midwife whom historian Laurel Thatcher Ulrich has made famous, ranged throughout the countryside around Hallowell, Maine, fording rivers, braving snowstorms, and enduring what she laconically referred to as "very bad wriding." Even more remarkable was Deborah Sampson Gannett, who dressed as a man and fought for American freedom in the last stages of the Revolutionary War. In 1802, Gannett embarked upon a lecture tour that covered well over a thousand miles. She traveled alone, arranging her own itinerary, publicizing her talks, and even staying in an occasional public house when no one would put her up for the night. Deborah wanted to be respectable, but she wanted even more to break loose from the restrictions that confined her as a woman.[23] Unlike Judith, she was willing to reinvent herself, going where she pleased, regardless of the consequences.

Judith could never identify with Martha Ballard or Deborah Gannett. Instead, she was one of a substantial coterie of genteel women who began to see themselves as "tourists" in the late eighteenth and early nineteenth centuries. Especially for the elite, travel in America was becoming less arduous, and as a result people were not only increasingly mobile, but they began to endow their trips with new meaning. Travel was no longer simply an uncomfortable means of getting from one place to another. It was becoming an end in itself, a means of visiting "sights" that local entrepreneurs consciously set up to attract tourists and to advertise the cultural and scientific achievements of a particular country, region, or town. It invited visitors to enter a city, to observe its art and architecture, its manners and mores, to evaluate its virtues and to compare it to the world they left behind. Tourism was entertaining, but it was also useful; it encouraged people to return home with a desire to emulate the "enlightened" example of places situated in other parts of the globe. Perhaps most important, it provided perspective. It helped observers determine what was unique and what was universal about the human experience. It offered proof that custom was accidental and arbitrary and had no more force than people chose to give it.[24] Judith's trip both confirmed and solidified her own preconceptions. She saw the world through Federalist eyes, and thus found ample evidence to support her trust in the value of order and hierarchy. She also encountered proof that religious liberty did not, as Gloucester's First Parish Church argued, lead inevitably to anarchy. She became more convinced than ever that the theater was a school for virtue. And she found that her faith in the value of women's education had not been misplaced.

If Judith was surprised by anything on her journey, it was that Boston was neither so grand nor so cosmopolitan as she had once imagined. She was nearly overwhelmed by her first impressions of New York, where everything, she wrote, "seems upon a larger scale than in the Town of Boston." In area, it was over a third again as large as the Bay Colony's capital; its streets were longer and wider, and were paved "with more exactness." Its public buildings exhibited a certain air of "thriftiness as well as elegance." She was especially enchanted by the spacious stone and marble gallery of the imposing "Federal Edifice" at the head of Broad Street. As she entered the building, she had merely to close her eyes to imagine George Washington taking his oath of office in the resplendent room. She managed to secure a seat in the House of Representatives' women's gallery, where for four hours she watched Congress conduct the nation's business. She was a little disappointed by the spectacle. "My reverential feelings considerably abated," she conceded, "as I observed the apparent negligence of many of the members." They discussed important questions with an eloquence that might have "done honour to a Demosthenes or a Cicero." But in what was already becoming time-honored fashion, most congressmen ignored the rhetoric of their peers. They milled about, reading newspapers, picking their nails, chewing on the heads of their canes, and "examining the beauty of their shoe buckles." Judith was impressed by America's finest orators, but their colleagues were obviously not as serious about the issues of state as they should have been.[25]

If New York was awesome, Philadelphia was more so. Judith's sojourn there was delectable. With John at her side, doors opened to her throughout the city. She saw the moon through David Rittenhouse's telescope, and the paintings of foreign masters and American patriots at the Hall of Exhibition. She visited the "magnificent" State House and the American Philosophical Society. She also attended one of Sally Franklin Bache's levees at Benjamin Franklin's old house on Market Street, where she was especially struck by the doctor's huge library. She had never seen more books in one place except at Harvard. And while she had never attended a Harvard commencement, Judith joined a "numerous and brilliant Audience" for the July graduation exercises at Pennsylvania College. Two of the scholars squared off in a formal debate. Their topic addressed an issue close to Judith's heart: whether or not virtue would survive if there was no future reward or punishment. When the president decided in favor of the "strength and beauty of virtue," two angry clergymen left the hall, but Judith was delighted.[26]

There was, of course, much of Philadelphia that Judith either did not see or chose not to mention. She never, for instance, commented on those bawdy men and women of all classes who enjoyed the "pleasure culture" of the city. She praised the major streets, which were clean, wide, and well lit. Solid brick houses, some "uncommonly lofty," all arranged "exactly in a line," impressed the most critical eye. But in the areas where the poorer sort tended to congregate, the squalor was overpowering; rotting garbage piled up in the streets, emitting a stench that even insensitive noses would find intolerable. If anything, Philadelphia's poverty was becoming more noticeable, and even dedicated philanthropists did little to alleviate the disease and suffering that so many of the city's inhabitants accepted as the natural order of things.[27]

Predictably, Judith made no note of Philadelphia's unfortunate inhabitants when she encountered them in the streets. When she saw them in an institutional setting, she was more interested in their compassionate benefactors than she was in the poor themselves. She was pleased to report that everything at the Philadelphia Hospital was in perfect order. Even the "lunaticks," while they resided in the basement, were housed in lighted and well-ventilated rooms. She chatted with a few of the more lucid inmates and thought that, with such favorable surroundings, they might eventually return to their senses. Like the hospital, Philadelphia's "nobly liberal and benign" almshouse was run by a man who was humane, exhibited "elegant taste and manners," and above all believed in the "beauty of order." A stickler for propriety, even for the most destitute, he divided his charges by sex. He wanted to improve them all, and so he treated his wards with dignity and provided them with adequate food and clothing. Of course, Judith noted approvingly, he did not feed them the strawberries, almonds, and other delicacies that she and John enjoyed during their visit. It would not be advisable to make the inmates so comfortable that they would not want to leave.[28]

It was her trips to Philadelphia's outskirts that made Judith especially aware of the value of an ordered society. She and John rode to the baths at Harrowgate, famed for their healthful waters, their well-appointed gardens, and the "genteel company" they attracted. They twice visited the Schuylkill Gardens—known by Philadelphians as the "American Vauxhall." If the first trip was a pleasure, the second was a disaster. They went on Independence Day, which turned out to be a mistake. Ordinary Philadelphians were there en masse, and, like most Federalists, Judith was uneasy in what she termed "mixed crowds," where black and white, rich and poor mingled freely. When they disembarked from the ferry, the Murrays were confronted with "a view so replete with wild disorder and confused uproar" that they were tempted to retreat at once. "The unlicenced

Mirth, the prevalent anarchy, boisterous manifestations of unbridled joy, and rude elbowing of the promiscuous throng, was really distressing." There was no respite from the disorderly mob. "Upon every seat, and in every embosomed haunt, noisy frolick with rude, unmannered stare had taken its stand," she cried, "and it was well if the thronged croud allowed us to keep our feet." The reason for the near riot was obvious. "All ranks of people were grouped together." Instead of harmony there was anarchy. There was nothing to do but leave. But even that proved problematic, for "thick and lawless ranks lined the gates," blocking their escape at every juncture. Finally, as Judith was about to faint, a kind soul came to their rescue, leading them through a series of subterranean rooms to the street and finally to a carriage and back to Philadelphia. It was an adventure that Judith had no wish to repeat. And she felt vindicated when she later read that the beautiful gardens were nearly destroyed by the mob.[29] When the lower orders transgressed their bounds, disaster was inevitable.

Order was good. Variety, especially in religious matters, was also desirable. Philadelphia had both. Unlike Boston, whose byways had developed in haphazard fashion over the years, Philadelphia's main streets were straight and square. Some people thought the uniformity of the rectangular grid pattern was monotonous. Judith disagreed. "I confess myself so great a Lover of order," she explained, "as to be enamoured of its beauties. . . . To the charms of regularity, every faculty of my soul delights to do homage." Regularity did not lead to a lack of variety. And variety the city had in abundance. Like most observers, Judith was struck immediately by Philadelphia's ethnic heterogeneity. When visitors heard the bewildering cacophony of languages and dialects emanating from every shop, they invariably proclaimed that they understood how the original inhabitants of the tower of Babel must have felt. Judith, of course, was taken by the city's religious diversity. Quakers and Moravians, Catholics and Jews, Presbyterians and Baptists, Universalists and Episcopalians all existed there in perfect peace. Judith was especially intrigued by her experience at a Catholic service. She had always been curious about a religion that was as foreign to her as a "Turkish mosque." In Gloucester, where there was not even an Episcopal congregation, she had no opportunity to satisfy her interest in so exotic a faith. Nor was she disappointed. True, she was confused by the "frequent kneeling and clasping of hands." But the music was beautiful, the service pleasing. Above all she praised the state of Philadelphia for being "indulgent to the unoffending and harmless caprices of its children."[30]

Pennsylvania had always granted religious toleration to its inhabitants. Still, Judith observed that the Quakers dominated the province's culture. Philadelphia's "spirit of equality, or republicanism," she thought, was the product of Quaker influence. Even those genteel Philadelphians who were not members of the Society of Friends avoided "the whims of fashion" that characterized elite self-presentation elsewhere. Moreover, she observed that "every honest, industrious Man, be his calling what it may, obtains respect, and is considered reputable." As a result, opportunities abounded, and it was eminently possible for an industrious mechanic to join the ranks of the city's elite. In time, however, Judith's view became more critical, her understanding of Philadelphia's ambiance more nuanced. She was struck, in particular, by the contradictory manner in which even Friends exhibited their commitment to simplicity. They rode through the streets in the finest carriages, but when Quaker women descended from those elegant conveyances, they were clad in the most austere garments. The exteriors of their homes lacked ornamentation; yet one had to climb marble stairs to reach their front doors and the houses themselves were richly furnished. The Quakers continued to speak the plain language. They were frugal to the point of miserliness. But they were also sociable, and the grandees were part of an interregional aristocracy whose members entertained men and women of similar status from all corners of America. Judith moved easily in such circles, taking tea at the homes of wealthy Philadelphians and mingling with the city's most celebrated residents. In the process, she learned what discerning tourists invariably discovered. First impressions and superficial appearances were deceiving.[31]

Judith's increasingly skeptical attitude toward the Quakers may have been based on one particular disagreement she had with the sect. When she had first contemplated her trip, she looked forward to attending Philadelphia's Chestnut Street Theater. Thus she was devastated to find that despite the city's urbanity, the Universalists there, affected by Quaker prejudice, regarded the dramatic arts with profound suspicion. The most old-fashioned notions, she complained, pervaded a populace that in so many ways was "opulent, and enlightened." In vain the Murrays urged "the morality of a good Play." The response was always the same. "'The Play House is a school for vice. The lives of performers are generally infamous, and by taking a seat at the theatre we countenance, so far as in our power, idleness and debauchery.'" As John Murray's wife, Judith dared not offend anyone. Thus she resigned herself to disappointment.[32]

At last, thanks to the connivance of friends, Judith indulged in an elaborate subterfuge that allowed her one thoroughly enjoyable evening at the theater. Her hosts gave her a large black bonnet that completely covered her face and threw a scarf over her shoulders. They smuggled her, thus disguised, into the building where she eagerly drank in the sights and sounds of a forbidden pleasure. She found everything, from the elevated governor's box to the "hissing, hooping, and stomping" in the gallery, fascinating. The play, Royall Tyler's popular *The Contrast*—written according to the playbill by a "Citizen of the United States"— was, with the exception of one or two scenes, impeccably moral. It was a commentary on the contrast between a "genteel Continental Officer," who was "brave, intrepid, patriotic, manly, and humane," and a "frivolous conceited Coxcomb," who was all too in love with European affectations. While the character of the lowly Jonathan seemed to poke fun at New Englanders, much to the embarrassment of some members of the party who thought she might be offended by an attack on her "country," Judith simply laughed. We are now a "Common Country," she insisted. Far be it from her to take umbrage at a just criticism. To be sure, nothing could have spoiled the night for her. And she regretted again, the bigoted attitudes of those who censured what they did not understand.[33] *The Contrast* provided proof positive that plays could be both patriotic and moral. Nothing would persuade her otherwise.

The highlight of her sojourn was Judith's trip to Bethlehem, located some fifty miles north of Philadelphia. True, the expedition reminded her once again of her childless state, as she lamented that she would never send a daughter to the Moravian seminary for girls located there. But she had never lost her interest in pedagogy and she had always longed to visit a school that was famous for its enlightened approach to women's education. When the seminary opened its doors to outsiders in 1785, it had immediately become a Mecca for some of America's most prominent families. After her tour of the "little Eden," Judith understood why. Bethlehem was founded by Germans, but students came there from all parts of America and Europe. Members of each nationality preserved their own customs even as they observed traditions associated with other cultures. As a result, Bethlehem students were true citizens of the world. No wonder they were totally transformed by their experience—so much so that their own parents scarcely recognized them, after even a short separation.[34]

The seminary's curriculum included virtually every subject a parent could desire. Admittedly, no one taught dancing. But this was something students could pick up easily after they returned home. The academic curriculum was impressive. In addition to reading, writing, composition, and arithmetic, the students mastered English, French, and German—but not Latin or Greek. They could also take lessons in music, painting, geography, and the "rudiments of Astronomy." Judith was especially pleased to discover that the school emphasized the connection between scholarly knowledge and morality, turning the institution into a "Seminary of Virtue." The girls learned to value benevolence and simplicity as well as chastity of deed and mind. Moreover, while they were "shielded from every Vice," they never forgot that there was a world beyond Bethlehem, a world they would one day enter with quiet confidence. They got plenty of exercise, walking near and far—always chaperoned. They also traveled by stage, sampling the pleasures of Lancaster, Elizabethtown, and even Philadelphia.[35]

In keeping with the most advanced theory, students learned by doing. They had no servants and so they kept their rooms spotless, made their own beds, and mended their clothes. While many of the girls would one day oversee large staffs of servants, at Bethlehem they were responsible for all household tasks. Judith noted with approval that although the Moravians were strict disciplinarians, they avoided coercive measures and physical punishment. "Advice and gentle remonstrance" were usually sufficient. A rare incorrigible child would be sent home, her name and the nature of her offense recorded in the school's records.[36]

The seminary's founders boasted that their school prepared young women for life outside the classroom. They assumed, however, without actually saying so, that most girls would end up as homemakers; students were not likely to seek a career or leave "their sphere." Indeed, that was the point. While Latin schools gave boys the academic foundation for *college*, women's boarding schools prepared their charges for traditional roles. Thus Bethlehem girls, like their counterparts elsewhere, learned skills that society deemed appropriate to their sex. They made their own cloth, for instance, becoming so proficient at needlework that their efforts compared favorably to the finest European imports. Nor did Judith ever question this emphasis.[37]

*   *   *

John Murray was disappointed with the negligible results of his convention, but he himself was the gathering's rising star. Almost as soon as he and Judith arrived in Philadelphia, they were bombarded with appealing offers from the city's Universalists. The Murrays received promises of a "genteel house" rent free, and £200 sterling a year, with the possibility that the stipend would go as high as £500. By the time they were ready to head for home, some desperate supporters were saying that no salary was too much. Judith reacted to these offers with the ambivalence she had greeted similar enticements from Boston. She truly liked Philadelphia. There, she could enjoy the status and luxury that she always thought should have been hers. She would be loved by John's supporters and indulged by those who did not share her faith but who cherished the city's tradition of tolerance. A move to Pennsylvania's capital, she predicted, "would crown the Career of our Murray, with both fame and fortune." In the end, however, she could not sever the ties that bound her to her mother and father. A daughter, in particular, was never more "in her proper sphere" than when she was tending to her parents. Gloucester seemed so far away. At times she felt as though an entire continent separated Philadelphia from her home. Had George lived, her attitude may have been different. Then affluence and proximity to good schools would have been overriding considerations. But her son had died and she believed she would never bear another child. Thus a "humble competency," a house near relatives, friends, and the graves of her ancestors, were all she needed. John—perhaps less interested in material matters than his wife—bowed to Judith's reservations and rejected Philadelphia's temptations in favor of "a life of dependence, and embarrassment." Still, Judith suspected that such offers would continue to come their way, and she feared that eventually they would be impossible to refuse.[38]

At the end of July, the Murrays bid Philadelphia farewell. "Forgive me," Judith wrote her parents, "if I acknowledge, that my heart confessed a pang, and that the tear of regret trembled in my eye," as they left town. The couple headed to New Jersey, staying at Mount Place, the home of Michael and Molly Mount with whom John had resided years earlier. Using the residence as a base, John roved throughout the area preaching to huge crowds. No matter how tired he was, he never passed up an opportunity to reach a few more souls. Judith was used to the effect of her husband's sermons, but even she was occasionally swept away by the experience. "Indeed language must ever be inadequate," she said, "to delineate the sensations of a chaste, and tender Wife, as she takes her seat amid the admiring crowd, and hangs with the enlightened multitude, upon the hallowed life of the revered, and beloved Lord of her wishes."[39]

From New Jersey the couple returned to New York. Judith's second visit to the city was even more enjoyable than the first. Although most houses of worship closed their doors to John, he was, of course, welcome at the Universalist church where he gave an address to President Washington. After the sermon, Martha Washington sent Judith a note, inviting her to visit and urging her not to wait until the formal levee day. At 6:00 p.m. on August 10, trembling with nervous excitement, Judith arrived at the Washington residence on Broadway. Her coach was met at the door by a man in livery, and she was soon ushered into the drawing room. It was, Judith noted, furnished in high style, but it was not garish. She had seen furniture every bit as elaborate in Boston and Philadelphia. Although there were a number of women in the room, Martha chose to sit next to Judith. The two were soon engaged in a "familiar and agreeable Chat." They talked of their families. (Martha was, Judith noted, an exemplary mother.) Martha's daughter played the piano and showed them some of her drawings, even promising to paint a flower for Judith before the Murrays left town. But the highlight of the evening came when George Washington entered the room. Judith had never seen the president, but she recognized him immediately. "That dignified benignity, by which he is distinguished," she said, "could not belong to another." He was clad in purple satin, although she thought he required no royal colors to induce everyone to pay him tribute. It was impossible to describe him adequately, which explained, perhaps, why no painter had ever captured his essence. His demeanor was, Judith observed, "elegant beyond what I have ever seen." Washington sought her out, and the two indulged in the kind of small talk that Judith ordinarily found frivolous. All in all, two hours flew by. It was a relaxed visit, nothing like the formal levees about which she had heard so much criticism. There was no receiving line. Guests talked casually to their host and hostess. She had been to tea parties in the country that were more pretentious.[40]

The following day, Judith visited John and Abigail Adams's house located on the banks of the Hudson. She was relieved to discover that despite their exalted station, her hosts were as unassuming as ever. A few days later, Judith was pleasantly surprised when Martha Washington appeared unannounced at her apartment door. "The unmeaning fopperies of ceremony seem to make no part of this Lady," she said approvingly.[41] This was heady stuff indeed for someone whose name had been bandied about the streets of Gloucester, whose husband had been decried as a virtual Antichrist.

On August 14, the Murrays reluctantly left New York, heading for Connecticut before moving toward home. Judith thought the state was as delightful as ever. Its inhabitants were wealthy and happy. It was even more egalitarian than Pennsylvania. No one there made "invidious distinctions." The governor's wife could visit a mechanic's home without inviting comment. Only "irregular or reproachable conduct," not inherited status, kept anyone from mingling in the best company. This was as it should be. In a country founded on the "natural and unalienable rights of Mankind," she said, "Merit will, and ought unquestionably to be regarded, as the only road to preferment." Still, if Judith claimed to admire Connecticut's egalitarian habits, she was pleased when the "best people" (who in her mind were always good and deserving people) welcomed John into their homes.[42]

Connecticut was not perfect. Judith was appalled, for instance, by the ease with which its inhabitants could obtain a divorce. The words "*until death do us part*," she sniffed, should be omitted from the state's marriage contract. Divorces there were "frequent, and the difficulties attendant upon attaining a bill are trivial—almost any pretense is sufficient." It was not necessary, as it was in Massachusetts, to prove that husband or wife had been unfaithful. Simple dissatisfaction with one's spouse was sufficient. Nor, she added, did divorce harm anyone's reputation. It occurred in the best families, and women did not so much as blush when someone asked if they had "obtained a bill." Judith agreed that no one should be forced into a loveless match and argued that neither nature nor religion required unhappy couples to live together. But she drew the line at divorce. Once spouses had committed themselves, they should make the best of their lot.[43]

The Murrays' progress through Connecticut was excruciatingly slow. Many of the roads were virtually impassable. In mid-September, John fell "ill, very ill." Nothing, however, stopped him from preaching, for he knew that the Universalists in the state saw him as "their common Father" and looked to him for inspiration. In October, they finally reached Rhode Island. "Multitudes flock to hear," Judith said, "and the crowds daily increase." They had been on the road nearly six months. Now that they were so close to Gloucester, she was increasingly anxious to see her parents again. Besides, winter was coming and even good roads would soon be unpassable. Judith was finding it difficult to remember that she had ever enjoyed traveling. She had always envied John's peripatetic life, but she had to admit that itinerancy could be exhausting. The "constant succession of objects"and saying goodbye to new acquaintances, took its toll. "Doubtless there are pleasures attendant upon this kind of life," she told her sister, "but it also hath its inquietudes." It rained constantly. Her trunks were lost, and she could not change into dry clothes. Every bone in her body ached, the result of an accident outside Norwich, when her horse fell, pitching her forward, giving her a bloody lip and nose. Sore, tired, and dirty, she began counting the days until she was home.[44]

On October 23, the Murrays arrived in Boston, just in time to celebrate John Adams's birthday. The Federalist city did itself proud. Flags flew, bells rang, cannons fired. Judith sat with Maria in her coach for two hours, watching a military parade wend its way across Boston Common. But even though she enjoyed the pageantry, reveling in the opportunity to express her patriotism in this altogether genteel fashion, she longed to be in Gloucester. More than homesickness made her eager to leave Boston. She had just received a letter from Winthrop, who planned a short visit home before winter set in. She did not want to miss any chance to see her brother.[45]

The final leg of the journey was nearly enough to make Judith resolve never to leave home again. The weary travelers were buffeted by wind and rain. On the way to the Charles River, their chaise locked wheels with a wagon commanded by a careless driver, breaking their axle and forcing them to wait impatiently while their vehicle was repaired. They finally arrived on October 31, spending the night at her father's, before going on to their own house. Almost immediately Judith began to wonder why she had been so desperate to reach home. Perhaps she was simply exhausted. Perhaps her travels made her see her native town from a new perspective. But for whatever reason, she admitted that this "remote and barren" spot no longer possessed its charms. Everything seemed smaller, dingier, more parochial. Her tour had opened her eyes to the possibilities of the wider world. If she could do so without causing her parents untold anguish, she would gladly move elsewhere.[46]

*   *   *

Judith and John had scarcely entered town when they were given a dose of the religious intolerance that still characterized Massachusetts. The contrast to Philadelphia was stark. Less than an hour after their arrival, John received a writ notifying him that he was the object of yet another lawsuit. Gloucester authorities announced that no taxes could be used to support an unincorporated church; consequently, they demanded reimbursement of funds that had erroneously gone to the Universalists. Rather than wage another costly battle, Murray's congregation reluctantly agreed to secure an act of incorporation from the General Assembly. On June 26, the state formally recognized the Independent Christian Church of Gloucester.[47]

John's decision to remain where he was, at least for the time being, by no means meant an end to his travels, and while John was on the road, Judith stayed home. For once she did not chafe at her confinement. She had good reason for her unusual contentment. In November, she wrote to Winthrop, casually remarking that "an additional good" might soon make her joy complete. By the middle of the month, Judith was fairly sure that she was pregnant. To say that she was stunned would be an understatement. When Maria had tried to persuade her that she might yet have a chance to enjoy maternal bliss, she had been unbelieving. "So unskillfully was I managed in the commencement of my late uncommon sufferings," she said, "as to bar a probability of such an event." Her journey to Philadelphia had been designed, in part, to take her mind off her sorrow, but thoughts of George and what might have been had always lurked beneath the surface. Scarcely a day had gone by without a painful reminder of her loss. Usually, her sadness was little more than a dull, persistent ache. Occasionally it was wrenching. Her visit to Charles Willson Peale's Philadelphia museum had proved particularly difficult. She had admired the museum's "curiosities," its paintings, and its collection of stuffed American birds and animals. But she was completely caught off guard when she saw Peale's portrait of his wife Rachel crying over her dead baby, her eyes raised to heaven in mute resignation. "My eyes were wet," Judith informed her parents. "Thus wrapped by icy death, was my darling Babe, in the only view, with which I was favoured of that form, for which I endured unutterable pangs—but enough of this."[48]

Now, against all odds, Judith had another opportunity to become a mother. As rational as she claimed to be, she was subject to "whimsical fancies" and indulged a number of superstitions. She thought, for instance, that gray spiders were a sign of impending disaster while black spiders were harmless. She was delighted whenever she saw a bumble bee. Like George, this baby would enter the world in August. Perhaps this was a bad omen. At any rate, to announce her pregnancy might tempt fate. Thus, as late as March of 1791 she was still referring to her possible good fortune in the vaguest terms, referring only to a "certain event" that put her in a "state of inquietude, and uncertainty."[49]

Judith tried to avoid bad luck. She was also careful to do nothing that might snuff out the little life within her. In March she traveled to Boston. She had ridden as far as Salem, when she fell ill. Luckily, Dr. Plummer had moved to the town and he was able to attend to her. Her condition was serious enough to require bleeding, a service he performed with alacrity before sending her on her way. Once Judith reached Maria's house, she resisted most social pleasures, attending only one party, where she mingled with those "who constitute what is called the bon ton." On those occasions when she ventured outside, she rode in Daniel's closed carriage, which, she insisted, allowed invalids to travel in safety. But by the time she left for Gloucester she was nearly incapacitated. Even writing a short letter exhausted her. Housework was out of the question.[50]

By June, Judith was convinced that she would not survive her second pregnancy. "The probability is, that the Month of August hath in reserve for me my closing scene," she wrote. She was almost forty years old. She suffered chronic ill health and had been "brought to the gates of the grave" on more than one occasion. In two or three months, she would endure pain that would be worse than anything she had suffered before. Nevertheless, she prepared for any eventuality, still insisting that she would accept God's will, no matter what. Even if she died, all was not lost. John would be temporarily grief stricken, of course. But her death would allow him to move to Boston or Philadelphia without worrying about her feelings. He had become increasingly dissatisfied with the Gloucester congregation, and she knew it was in his interest to assume the ministry of one of the country's metropolitan churches.[51]

While Judith had been alternately depressed and frightened in the spring, by July she was eerily sanguine. John and Maria grew more anxious. Gloucester had yet to replace Dr. Plummer. Thus Maria begged her niece to come to Boston where Dr. Lloyd, the town's highly regarded physician, could help her through what would surely be a difficult labor. John seconded Maria's suggestion. But Judith adamantly refused. She had myriad excuses. She feared being a "burden." If her last birthing experience was any indication, she would be bedridden for months, and she might have to remain indefinitely in the house on Atkinson Street. Besides, Boston was unbearably hot in August, while Gloucester's sea breezes were pleasant and refreshing. She disliked living with "strangers," even though Maria, Daniel, and their brood could hardly be ranked in this category. Her parents were increasingly feeble and could not make the trip to Boston to be with her in what might be her dying moments. Perhaps most tellingly, she was not at all sure that she wanted Boston's finest doctor to tend to her. Dr. Plummer's knowledge of her condition, she argued, outweighed his lack of proficiency. True, he lived in Salem. But that was all to the good. She still believed that her first pregnancy had ended badly because of "aid too prompt, and officious." If the doctor failed to reach her bedside, she would deliver her child in a more natural way.[52]

Still, as her fateful hour drew near, Judith was disturbed to learn that Dr. Plummer was near death. Suddenly frightened, she begged Maria to be with her in Gloucester when the baby came. Maria complied, but she took only one look at her niece before insisting that Judith needed all the help she could get, and more. Aunt and husband combined forces, prevailing upon Judith to come to Boston. Even then she wanted to rent some quiet room where she could have her baby without imposing on the Sargents. Maria, of course, vetoed what seemed like either an irrational suggestion or a bid for martyrdom. On August 22, less than a week after Judith reached Boston, she gave birth to a healthy girl. She was, at long last, "a happy Mother." She called her daughter Julia Maria. She had never liked "Judith." Julia was close enough. Maria, of course, deserved the honor of having the child named for her.[53]

Although this was the happy ending for which she had always longed, even Judith was amazed at the depth of her pleasure. She was "delirious of joy." Gone was her distrust of medical intervention. Had Maria not "snatched me from impending danger," she said, she would once again have become "a martyr of inexperience." Dr. Lloyd lived up to his reputation, and Maria had made the week before Julia Maria's birth less frightening than it would otherwise have been. No one would ever again have reason to question the "remarkable attachment so apparently existing between Maria and Constantia," Judith proclaimed, for it was Maria who had enabled her to achieve her most cherished dream.[54]

Once she was safely home, Judith eagerly embraced the duties of motherhood. She seized upon every sign that her daughter was healthy, intelligent, and "good looking." When Julia Maria was barely three months old, Judith declared that her daughter's character was "of the sentimental kind." She listens to me with great attention, she told Maria. If, she laughed, you can trust the suspect judgment of a mother, you should know that "intelligence sparkles in her eyes." To hear Judith tell it, Julia Maria was the center of her universe. Like many elite women of her day, she perused every available book on child rearing, following the dictums of each to the letter. When she saw an article that argued that wine was harmful to children, for instance, she quit serving Julia Maria a mixture of wine and water. Convinced that meat was not healthful, she favored a vegetarian diet for her daughter.[55]

Even though society believed that mothers were naturally designed to raise children, it turned out that motherhood was a truly daunting task that required expertise, energy, and an enormous amount of time. Custom and common sense were never enough. Women had to make a conscious effort to apply modern precepts to a task their mothers had taken for granted. Thus, books on the care and education of children, once addressed primarily to fathers, were now written with mothers in mind. John Locke, himself, had talked of the importance of "parents," not "fathers." By the late eighteenth century, many Americans were beginning to go even further, agreeing with Judith's sentiments in "Desultory Thoughts." Fathers might be the disciplinarians of last resort, but mothers were uniquely imbued with the nurturing qualities that were crucial to a child's development. Punishment assured outward conformity, but it never changed the heart. If Judith thought her vocation demanded knowledge, rationality, and unremitting attention, she saw this as a cause for rejoicing, not complaint. Motherhood was not a chore that society thrust upon her to confine her to the domestic sphere. For her it was evidence of her moral and intellectual superiority. Still, in an uncertain world, where disease and misadventure threatened the lives of the weakest inhabitants, it is hardly surprising that she was frightened as well as empowered by her responsibility.[56]

Had she borne many children, Judith would no doubt have had less time or inclination to focus on any one of them with such relentless determination. She claimed to devote every waking hour to her maternal duties. The instant her daughter woke up, Judith rushed to her side. At night, Julia Maria shared her parents' bed. While she knew that some would disapprove of this "indulgence," Judith disagreed. Children were delicate creatures, and she intended to do everything to keep her daughter healthy. George's death had been traumatic. To lose a second child when she was too old to have another would be devastating. Julia Maria had a weak constitution, and thus Judith greeted each sniffle with alarm, thankful that she lived at a time when remedies unavailable to her ancestors were plentiful. She was especially fond of laudanum, which she doled out in drops at regular intervals. The drug had once been viewed as a "hazardous remedy," but an enlightened age recognized its value.[57]

If Judith resented housework, she relished every aspect of her maternal role. No task was mundane. Above all, she celebrated the pleasures of breast-feeding for both mother and child. Ten months after Julia Maria's birth, she announced that she did not intend to wean her daughter anytime soon. She was blessed with a "plentiful flow" and she thought that nursing was Julia Maria's "highest enjoyment." Nor had she herself ever experienced anything approaching the ecstacy she felt when "the nutritious stream" flowed from her breast. She decided to let her daughter give up nursing on her own. In fact, Julia Maria was nearly two years old before Judith was able to "convince her budding Reason" to abandon mother's milk. The process took just a few days. Significantly, it was Judith who found the "heart affecting work" excruciating. She cried inconsolably while her daughter barely suffered. The "sorrows of the Mother" were much worse than the discomfort of the child.[58]

Again, Judith's approach was typical of elite women in the Atlantic world. Granted, if the advertisements in the *Columbian Centinel* are any indication, many Massachusetts women hired wet nurses. But mothers like Judith Murray viewed such an alternative—always frowned upon in New England anyway—with disapproval. Experts agreed that mother's milk was especially nutritious. But many women had begun to embrace breast-feeding for less pragmatic reasons. As attitudes toward motherhood became romanticized in the late eighteenth century, women claimed that breast-feeding was a pleasurable emotional and physical experience for the *mother*, as much as the baby. It also established a bond between mother and child that could never be broken. Thus Judith pitied those women. like her niece Sarah Ellery, who were unable to "experience all those raptures" associated with breast-feeding. No mother, unless she was utterly devoid of sensibility, would willingly hand this "delightfully interesting employment" to "mercenary hands."[59]

From Judith's perspective, their unique ability to perform a natural physical function was evidence of women's moral superiority. Nursing gave her a sense of power. It was something denied to all men—and some women. It was physically and emotionally satisfying. It allowed her to indulge her daughter, postponing the time when she would have to begin disciplining her instead of satisfying her every need. Men may have used breast-feeding as a means to construct the social order along apparently natural lines, granting women authority in the home while denying them a public role. But Judith never saw it that way. True, breast-feeding highlighted gender differences. It also confined her to the home. But if she claimed that the mind had no gender, Judith was proud of her physical ability to fulfill her destiny as a mother.[60]

* * *

Only one distraction threatened Judith's happiness. The news from the Ohio country was ominous. She could not help wondering if the same God who had given her a child with one hand planned to take her brother away with the other. By 1791, Winthrop's letters home were disconsolate. His wife and daughter were dead. He had served his country long and well and had almost nothing to show for it. His future looked bleak. Judith tried to bolster his spirits. She granted that Winthrop had few immediate prospects. But she thought that anyone who had fought so valiantly for American independence could surmount any adversity. "Will you thus betray a want of courage which, when well directed, is indeed a manly virtue?" she asked. Winthrop needed to subdue his "passions" and "adopt a regular and consistent plan." His claims that no one would miss him if he died, reeked of self-pity. Who knew what pleasures the future held? Despite her brave words, she worried.[61]

In April, Judith became concerned about more than Winthrop's malaise. Newspaper reports indicated that the Indians in western Pennsylvania were on the verge of an uprising. While the government was considering sending troops west to shore up the meager forces already there, Congress was dragging its feet, and no one knew when—or even if—Ohio's settlers would be rescued. Judith did not know whether to be relieved or still more worried when she finally received two letters from Winthrop in mid-June. At least they were evidence that he was alive. But she was distraught to learn that he had resumed his military career, accepting a commission as the adjutant general of the militia in the Ohio Territory. She had always begged her brother to put soldiering behind him. It appeared that he had ignored her advice. Worse, on this occasion he was not facing a civilized foe. "All the perils of a savage and most ferocious war are his," she said. Most disquieting of all, he wrote to her with a certain fatalism, appearing to welcome his own death. He seemed to be "imagining that a sudden and glorious exit, in his present circumstances, may be to him a most desirable ultimatum."[62]

Winthrop did not die, but he did face a blow to his pride and his reputation that nearly destroyed his chances for success in this world, due to his role in what historians have described as the worst defeat ever suffered by white Americans at the hands of the Indians. In the summer of 1791, a motley mix of regulars and militia volunteers assembled under the leadership of Arthur St. Clair, prepared to defend the frontier from almost certain attack. Winthrop arrived at Fort Washington in May to find soldiers and supplies woefully inadequate. It was his job to mold them into a respectable fighting force.[63]

Everything that could go wrong did. Samuel Hodgdon, the quartermaster general, was ineffective at best, corrupt at worst. Once the army left Fort Washington, its progress was painfully slow, morale plummeted, and desertions were rampant. Winthrop did his best, but his "impersonal coldness" made him an ineffective leader. Nor did an "incessant round of floggings for the men and courts-martial for the officers" improve matters. On November 3, the little army pitched camp near the Wabash River. The following morning, they were the victims of a surprise attack that, decimated them in the space of three hours. It was not a battle; it was a rout. "The resistance of the militia deserves not the name of defense," claimed Winthrop. They were all "cowardly in the most shameful degree." Ironically, he reserved what little praise he could muster for camp-following women who showed more courage than most of the men, actually forcing the "skulking militia" to turn and fight.[64]

News traveled slowly from the Ohio country. It was often inaccurate by the time it reached Boston. On December 7, the *Columbian Centinel* announced that the western army was in good shape and "regularly supplied with provisions." Two weeks later, even Gloucester had heard the "petrifying accounts, of the almost general slaughter" in the West. As she had during the American Revolution, Judith feared the worst. She acknowledged that even if Winthrop had somehow managed to escape unharmed, he would be devastated by yet another blow to his reputation. Everyone was saying that the army had behaved recklessly, "that urged by youthful ardor, and ambitious of signalizing themselves by some valorous act, with ill judged bravery they sought the field where they fell a sacrifice to their temerity." Although she had earlier suspected that Winthrop sought his own heroic death, she now valiantly proclaimed that such criticisms could not possibly apply to her own eminently rational brother. For a while, no one was sure what to think, as contradictory stories about the battle swirled around town. Finally Fitz William returned from Boston with what he hoped was credible information. Winthrop had been wounded, but he was safe. Surely, said Judith wistfully, her brother's service would win him the "immortal fame" and earthly reward he sought.[65]

Predictably, brother and sister reacted differently to the debacle. Judith saw it as a blessing. Winthrop, she exulted, would now abandon his military career for good. His life had been spared; his soldiering days had ended "in a manner which is truly honorable." Winthrop, however, was wretched. "He thinks," Judith explained, "that the most glorious close to a life so various would be a death met in the career of honor." Instead, he faced an inquiry from a Congress that was shot through with partisan animus. He thought he deserved a promotion, not an investigation. In the end, Congress exonerated him, and Winthrop returned to Cincinnati, once again serving as St. Clair's lieutenant governor. He bought a large frame house, trying vainly to maintain his standards in the wilderness. He played the role of gentleman farmer, collecting fruit and vegetable specimens and developing an interest in agricultural lore that moved him ever farther from the maritime activity that had once been his vocation.[66]

Both Judith and Winthrop were still searching for purpose and order in their respective worlds. Julia Maria may have been her reason for living, but Judith had not abandoned her literary ambitions. Nor had her determination to help John realize his full potential abated. She felt obligated to remain in Gloucester so long as her parents lived. Beyond that, she refused to commit herself. In the next few years, her life would change dramatically. Both she and John would widen their horizons, and Judith would finally begin her walk along the path of fame.

Figure 1. M. M. Tidd, *View of Gloucester, Mass. from Ten Pound Island.* Courtesy Cape Ann Historical Museum.

Figure 2. Exterior of Judith Sargent Murray's "mansion house" on Middle Street in Gloucester. Courtesy Sargent House Museum.

Figure 3. Interior staircase of Judith Sargent Murray's "mansion house." Courtesy Sargent House Museum.

Figure 4. Artist Unknown, *John Murray*. Courtesy Bostonian Society Library and Special Collections.

Figure 5. John Singleton Copley, *Mrs. James (Mercy Otis) Warren*, c. 1763. Courtesy Museum of Fine Arts, Boston.

Figure 6. Gilbert Stuart, *Mrs. Perez Morton* (no date). Courtesy Library of Congress.

Figure 7. Artist Unknown, *Governor Winthrop Sargent*. Courtesy Mississippi Department of Archives and History, Archives and Library Division.

Figure 8. The Tontine Crescent. Courtesy Bostonian Society and Library and Special Collections.

Figure 9. Henry Sargent, *The Dinner Party*, c. 1821. An interior view of a dining room at the Tontine Crescent. Courtesy Museum of Fine Arts, Boston.

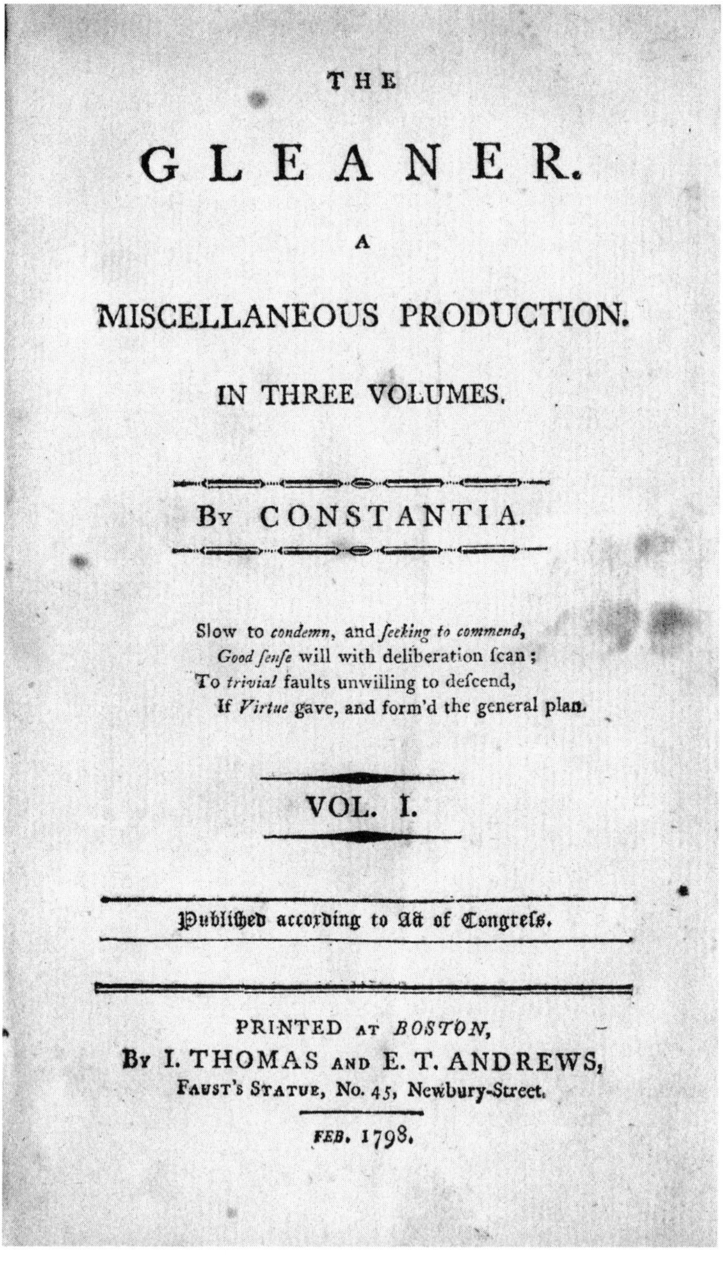

THE

GLEANER.

A

MISCELLANEOUS PRODUCTION.

IN THREE VOLUMES.

By CONSTANTIA.

Slow to *condemn*, and *seeking to commend*,
Good sense will with deliberation scan;
To *trivial* faults unwilling to descend,
If *Virtue* gave, and form'd the general plan.

VOL. I.

Published according to Act of Congress.

PRINTED AT *BOSTON*,
By I. THOMAS AND E. T. ANDREWS,
FAUST'S STATUE, No. 45, Newbury-Street.

FEB. 1798.

Figure 10. Title page of Judith Sargent Murray, *The Gleaner*, published in 1798 by
I. Thomas and E. T. Andrews, Boston. Courtesy Cape Ann Historical Museum.

Chapter 8
A Career of Fame

In the heady days immediately following the Revolution, anything had seemed possible. As they saw homages to equality floating in the air, women like Judith Sargent Murray had reason to hope that the new nation would welcome a social order based on merit rather than birth. If that happened, elite women would be able to compete on an equal basis with their male counterparts, receiving an education that would enable them to soar to the loftiest heights. If, however, growing numbers of men—and women—sought to discourage women from even attempting to fly, then Judith felt obliged to resist. Writing for public consumption, proving by her own example that women were rational creatures who could elevate the level of the nation's discourse, would be her way of doing just that.

Judith summoned the courage to begin her literary career in earnest in 1790. Always, however, her aspirations were limited by her fears. She continued to harbor real doubts about her own talent. She also worried that writing for public consumption would compromise her status as a genteel woman. Above all, she had to convince herself and others that she was not neglecting her all-important maternal duties as she prepared her work for publication. Thus she was always quick to point out that she was a mother first and a writer second. And she leapt to the defense of other women who were criticized for putting their literary careers ahead of their children's needs. But though her anxieties were real, her desire to prove women's intellectual equality with men was strong enough to help her overcome them. She was determined to prove that women could go anywhere, do anything, if only they were given the opportunity to do so.[1]

Judith had never forgotten that the editors of the *Massachusetts Magazine* had included "Constantia" in the list of writers from whom they welcomed submissions. Even so, she periodically insisted that her fervent desire for "the good opinion of every individual" had abated and that she would be content if members of her own small social circle were the only ones who admired her work. Occasionally she threatened to take all her manuscripts and "commit them to the flames." Still, there were times—and they were growing in number and intensity—when she could not deny her "ambitious and presumptuous ideas, ideas which maturer judgment condemns as chimerical." Indeed, she admitted, "my confidence in my own abilities" is truly amazing for one who is "limited by nature, by education, and by a thousand combining circumstances."[2] Perhaps she was learning to "reverence herself."

* * *

Before she began to publish in earnest, Judith needed to take care of a small but irksome business. She had long referred to herself as "Constantia" when she wrote to John Murray and Maria Sargent. She had also used the sobriquet in 1784 when she had published "Desultory Thoughts." Thus she was dismayed five years later, when popular Boston poet Sarah Wentworth Morton claimed the pen name as her own. Judith complained, and the editors of the *Massachusetts Magazine* apologized, promising to affix an asterisk to Morton's signature. When this proved confusing, Morton began signing her work as "Constantia-Philenia," and eventually simply as "Philenia."[3]

Although she won the battle, Judith was dismayed by the entire affair. She knew that the editors of the *Massachusetts Magazine* already favored Morton's work; indeed in 1791 they referred to the Boston poet as the "Sappho of America." Thus, she did not want to appear selfish or competitive, as she assured her editors that she had always been "interested in, and attached to, every female who, in any degree advanced the honour of her sex, by contributing her efforts, to dispense the clouds which, have too long enveloped half of the rational World." To prove her point, she published some effusive "Lines to 'Philenia'" in the *Massachusetts Magazine*. Referring to herself as a "humbler muse," and to her poetry as "lowly verse," she nevertheless admitted that she sought "the glittering wreath of fame." If that were true, the possibility that "the two Constantia's might be thought the same" truly mattered. She may have claimed to be humble, but she did not shrink from admitting her ambitions in public.[4]

When she finally started submitting her efforts to the *Massachusetts Magazine*, Judith proceeded cautiously, sending off some verses and essays she already had on hand. At the moment, she insisted, she was too busy "rocking the cradle of my daughter" to write anything new. She began with "Lines, occasioned by the Death of an Infant," probably written right after her son's death. The description of Bethlehem she had sent to Dorcas Sargent, her cousin Epes's wife, appeared in the spring of 1790. She also polished "On the Domestic Education of Children," an essay she had composed a few years earlier. Repeating her arguments in "Desultory Thoughts," she condemned the harsh methods of the father in favor of a mother's gentler approach. In most ways the essay implicitly denied the importance of gender differences. However, Judith still had to concede that at some point boys had to leave home to complete their education while girls could continue under a mother's tutelage, becoming in the end "worthy and amiable women."[5] If women were especially—essentially?—designed to be their son's teachers, most mothers were not equipped to complete the task for which nature had designed them.

Judith's most ambitious essay was a version of "The Sexes," which she had written in 1779. The new piece appeared in the *Massachusetts Magazine* in March and April 1790. Now entitled "On the Equality of the Sexes," it was her most pointed public declaration of her contention that women and men were intellectual equals. A comparison of the two essays indicates that Judith's view of gender equality had not changed fundamentally in more than a decade. The changes she made were largely cosmetic, but they do shed light on her lack of confidence. She chose each word with excruciating care. Was it better, she wondered, to say, "leave vacant the intelligent principle" or to "leave the intelligent principle vacant"? Would it be more pleasing to say "every" day or "each" day? It is easy to imagine Judith sitting at her desk, painstakingly trying out first one phrase, then another, discarding a word here, adding one there, determined to present her arguments in their best light. If she wanted to plead for women's intellectual equality, her own work had to be faultless. She wrote at a time when persnickety grammarians corrected even Noah Webster's errors. But she was always more sensitive to criticism than most writers. She was convinced that while readers did not view mistakes from a man's pen as signs of male inferiority, they would see her own errors as proof of the "natural incapacity" of women. No matter how often she attributed women's deficiencies to the "false method of cultivation, or perhaps to a total want of advantages, to which, as human beings, they are entitled," Judith knew that many observers were unpersuaded.[6]

If her perspective on women's nature had not changed between 1779 and 1790, Judith sharpened her message in "On the Equality of the Sexes." As usual, she introduced the essay with a poem that captured the essence of her argument. Her verse conceded that not all minds were alike; some were bright, while others were not. She insisted, however, that sex bore no relationship to intellectual merit. Not only were body and mind different, but mind was superior to body. While inferior people were so lacking in intelligence that their souls were "almost with the dull body one," genius rose above the mere animal. Hence a "woman's form" did not, by definition, reflect "a weak, a servile, an inferiour soul." The poem—like the essay that followed—ended on a hopeful note:

Yet haste the era, when the world shall know,
That such distinctions only dwell below;
The soul unfetter'd, to no sex confin'd,
Was for the sholes of cloudless days design'd.
Mean time we emulate their manly fires,
Though erudition all their thoughts inspires,
Yet nature with *equality* imparts,
And *noble passions*, swell e'en *female hearts*.[7]

"On the Equality of the Sexes" differed from "The Sexes" in one significant way. Judith appended a passage to her original essay that refuted Milton's rendition of the biblical creation story, particularly his assertion that the seductive Eve was responsible for original sin. Judith had previously relied on "nature, reason and experience," not scripture, to prove women's ability. Now, she was ready to go public with an argument she had made at least twice in private, to "bend the whole of my artillery against those supposed proofs" that most Christians viewed as axiomatic.[8] She insisted that it was impossible to understand the creation tale without examining Adam's and Eve's motive for succumbing to the devil. Eve was not moved by "sensual"—animal—appetite, but by the serpent's promise of a praiseworthy goal: "a perfection of knowledge." Adam, however, was moved solely by animal instinct. "Blush, ye vaunters of fortitude," she wrote, "ye boasters of resolution; ye haughty lords of the creation; blush when ye remember, that he was influenced by no other motive than a bare pusillanimous attachment to a woman!" It was bodily pleasure, not mental improvement, that Adam sought when he sinned. "Thus," concluded Judith triumphantly, "all the arts of the grand deceiver . . . were requisite to mislead our general mother, while the father of mankind forfeited his own, and relinquished the happiness of posterity, merely in compliance with the blandishments of a female."[9]

"On the Equality of the Sexes," was more daring than anything Judith had published before. True, she had already hinted at her views, especially in her introduction to the *Catechism*. And the essay said nothing that she had not been saying privately for years. But to voice her opinions so forcefully on the printed page was a different matter. Her willingness to let her essay see the light of day is a measure of the increasing assurance with which she began to enter the "republic of letters." While there were many women and men who agreed with her, more and more people on both sides of the Atlantic were beginning to question women's claim to intellectual equality. She may have decided to publish her essay for that very reason.

*   *   *

Judith was reasonably pleased with the reception of her early pieces in the *Massachusetts Magazine*. She had marked out certain themes—the equality of the sexes, the value of education—as her own. She had displayed her talent as a poet and essayist. It was time to move on. Beginning in February 1792, she adopted a new pseudonym and a new approach to her career. Under the name of "The Gleaner," she wrote a series of essays, including her popular novel-like story of Margaretta that appeared nearly every month in the *Massachusetts Magazine* for the next year and a half. While she pretended to be unworthy of comparisons "to the Philenia's and Sabina's of the day," her "Gleaner" essays were an ambitious undertaking designed to challenge the male dominance of her chosen profession and to secure a place for herself in the new nation's pantheon of women writers.[10] They were a reflection of both Judith's ambition and her self-doubt. While the essays repeated her call for women's education, as a whole they treated gender issues in conventional terms. None of the essays was as bold as "On the Equality of the Sexes." As the Gleaner, she was more willing to attack hidebound custom by circumlocution, or when she commented on issues that bore little obvious relationship to women's concerns, than she was to discuss women's place head on.

Her caution is remarkable in any event. It is especially surprising, because at the very time that she was submitting the "Gleaner" essays to the *Massachusetts Magazine*, Judith discovered that she had an ideological soul mate in England. Mary Wollstonecraft had published *A Vindication of the Rights of Woman* in 1792, and by October the *Massachusetts Magazine* had begun to publish excerpts of the book. A year later, Judith sang the English feminist's praises to Sally Barrell. "Of Mary Wollstonecraft," she wrote, "I am a decided admirer, and I wish from my soul that her plans, without an exception, could be adopted." Yet there is little trace of Wollstonecraft in the "Gleaner," especially in the tale of Margaretta, for which Judith gained the most praise. Perhaps she was reluctant to use a novel, a suspect medium to begin with, to argue for women's independence or equality. Or she may have been using Margaretta to "seduce" her readers, to persuade them to read her nonfiction essays, a few of which were much more daring.[11] For whatever reason, the story is designed to ruffle only the most sensitive feathers.

Indeed, the "Gleaner" bows to conventional gender constructs in a variety of ways. In most of the essays, Judith assumes a male persona—usually the Gleaner or "Mr. Vigillius"—and the men in the pieces are clearly in charge. It is they who shape the essays and decide which topics merit gleaning. Only rarely do the women characters speak for themselves. Moreover, on those rare occasions when Mr. Vigillius's wife Mary does speak, her voice is curiously indistinguishable from her husband's, as she adopts the language and style, if not the perspective, of elite white men. Like the *Spectator*, upon which Judith modeled her own essays, her Gleaner is the enlightened ideal, who writes in a detached, impartial, disinterested—and thus in a "male"—manner. The Gleaner's very anonymity grants him authority. He is not a particular person championing a particular cause. He gathers information from all quarters. Thus, he is able to speak for *human* nature, while his wife speaks only for women. As a man, finally, the Gleaner is able to travel where proper women dare not go alone. Judith knew from experience how "awkwardly circumstanced" a woman was if she walked the streets of Boston without an escort. Her narrator has no such difficulties. He wanders at will, sitting alone in public houses, observing the world, listening to the conversations of other men without attracting attention. By portraying the women in her essays as domestic creatures whose influence, such as it is, emanates from the home, and allowing only her men to roam freely, Judith appears to endorse notions of gender hierarchy. Her women's virtues are private, while her men's are public. No matter what she claimed, her essays are hesitant, even apologetic, and often contradictory.[12]

Nearly half of the twenty-seven "Gleaner" pieces are devoted to the tale of Margaretta. Whether she focused on Margaretta's education, courtship, or marriage, Judith's account of her heroine's travails and ultimate triumphs was moralistic, traditional, even hackneyed. If virtually all eighteenth-century novels were didactic, this one was more didactic, more moralistic, less likely to offend, than most.

It is hardly surprising that Judith wanted to use her story as a forum to proclaim the value of women's education. Strangely, however, her depiction of Margaretta's experiences seems actually to subvert her own purpose. The story revolves around an orphan, Margaretta Melworth, adopted by Mr. Vigillius and his wife Mary. Margaretta enchants the childless couple and she rapidly becomes, in the words of Mr. Vigillius, the "child of our affection." The Vigilliuses are determined to prepare their daughter for independence. To that end, Mary devises an "extensive plan of education," designed to allow Margaretta to support herself so that she will not be "*necessarily* condemned to laborious efforts, or to the drudgery of that unremitted sameness, which the routine of the needle presents." Thus, the girl has the advantage of an ambitious curriculum, learning English and French (but not Latin), writing a good hand, and mastering geography, chronology, astronomy, natural philosophy, history, and poetry. Still, Mr. Vigillius hastens to assure his readers that knowledge does not make his daughter unfit "for her proper sphere." She can make the finest puddings, he says, and "in the receipts of cookery she is thoroughly versed, and our linen never received so fine a gloss as when it was ironed, and laid in order by Margaretta." She is also an adept seamstress and is proficient at landscape drawing, the minuet, the cotillion, and the piano. True, these "accomplishments" were not antithetical to a serious education. They were "signifiers of privilege," advertising her worthiness, separating her from the common order of women. When all is said and done, however, it becomes clear that virtuous domesticity is all that this rational and accomplished woman needs to be happy. Her education does not prepare her to be self-reliant or independent. Nor does it improve her judgment. By writing in the public domain, Judith challenged the conventions that gave women a place but not a voice. She did not give her own characters that option.[13]

Margaretta's courtship is a case in point, as it seems to call into question the very value of the education that Mr. and Mrs. Vigillius have offered their daughter. Despite all her advantages and her innate goodness, the girl is defenseless when she encounters the temptations that lurk beyond the home. On a trip to New Haven, far from the protection of her doting parents, she encounters the appropriately named "Sinisterus Courtland," whose charm and sophistication thoroughly enchants the vulnerable Margaretta. Sinisterus, she assures her parents, is "tall, and well made—his address is easy, and commanding; the contour of his face is strikingly agreeable—indeed his whole exteriour is a combination of elegance and dignity—and his manner is confessedly descriptive of the finished gentleman." Just three days after their encounter, Courtland declares his love for Margaretta. There is little doubt that, left to her own devices, Margaretta would have married Sinisterus. Her reason is not strong enough to triumph over her sentimental instincts, nor is she able to penetrate appearances that hide Courtland's true nature. If she is no longer "Eve the seductress," neither has she fully transformed herself into a symbol of unwavering sexual morality. When women lost their seductive nature, they also lost the power they had wielded over men. They could not even use their sexuality to tempt men to do good. Instead, their very sensibility became a weakness, and they became especially subject to the wiles of calculating predators. The right to choose their own husband was a snare as well as an opportunity, and a girl who exercised her newfound freedom without consulting her wiser parents would regret her folly.[14]

Fortunately, Mr. Vigillius knows that Courtland is a mere fortune hunter, an "imposter," who spends his life seeking women who will be deceived by his charms and become the "dupe of her own vanity." The Vigilliuses have done their best to raise their orphan to "reverence herself," to be immune to flattery, and to realize that the passions about which she has read in novels bear no resemblance to true love. Unfortunately, their efforts have not been completely successful. Margaretta is not simply dependent and a little gullible; she is a curiously passive heroine. She faints at the slightest provocation. She makes little effort to assess her own options. In more conventional seduction tales, the heroine struggles alone to resist an attractive rake. She uses her superior reason, her self-control, to overcome her desire, but she is not passionless. Margaretta, however, is not physically attracted to Sinisterus. She is captivated by his mind, not his body. Even so, she is helpless to thwart her pursuer or to take responsibility for her own fate. The conflict is between Mr. Vigillius and Sinisterus. The two men fight *over* Margaretta; she is scarcely involved in the struggle. Ultimately, of course, Mr. Vigillius triumphs, and Margaretta celebrates "her emancipation." Still, it is her worldly wise father, not Margaretta herself, who reveals Sinisterus as the villain he is. Margaretta, it seems, is unable to fend for herself.[15]

As if to reinforce his point, the Gleaner entertains his readers with another case where a good education is not sufficient to protect the best of women. Frances Wellwood is a beautiful, accomplished and wealthy orphan. With no parents to guide her, she, too, falls into the clutches of the ubiquitous Sinisterus, who seduces her with "sophistical arguments," convincing her that marriage is a mere human artifice.[16] The two secretly exchange vows before God—but not before minister or judge—and a short time later, they both disappear. Her friends vaguely wonder what has happened to Frances, but she is "independent," and thus no one feels obligated—or entitled—to interfere. Predictably, Sinisterus runs through her money and abandons her and their children, leaving her to take in needlework to survive. Powerless to reform her seducer, she, too, is saved by Mr. Vigillius, who confronts Sinisterus with the consequences of his selfishness. A legal marriage solves everyone's problem. The rake, who Frances insists is not "naturally bad," but rather is the victim of "a mistaken mode of education," is reformed.[17] Once again, it is the timely intervention of a determined man, not a virtuous woman, that saves the day.

Instead of urging daughters to become self-reliant, to accept responsibility for their own lives, the novel counsels them to seek the guidance of their parents. It assumes that even educated and moral women are too weak to make their own wise decisions. The typical argument for educating women in this period, one that Judith herself often employed, was that women should cultivate their innate propensity for virtue and rationality, not just for their private happiness but for the public welfare. Women had the power to nurture men's best instincts, in effect to seduce men to be good. It was women's moral authority that kept men in line. In this sense, seduction novels had a political message, as they encouraged women to maintain their own virtue in order to keep America virtuous. But the Margaretta story undercuts that message, implying that a superior education may not be enough in a world where men remained powerful. Neither Margaretta nor Frances have any moral authority. They may be "good," but Sinisterus is not moved, much less changed, by their goodness. Nor is anyone else.

Thanks to her father's wisdom, Margaretta is saved from certain misery. She "chooses" to marry the steady, familiar, and androgynous Edward Hamilton, whose heart "is as tender as it is manly." Her love for Edward is "sanctioned by duty, authorized by reason, and borne forward upon the feathery sails of white bosomed hope." But this is not a novel about women's choices.[18] It is, if anything, a cautionary tale, a Federalist warning to Americans who defied proper authority at their own and their country's risk. Just as girls were in danger of yielding to their passions if they failed to heed their parents, so the American public would fall prey to its impulses unless it gave the decision-making power to its superiors.[19]

For Margaretta, marriage to the right man is the happy ending. Moreover, the Gleaner paints a picture of married life that is decidedly traditional, as he urges girls to lower their expectations and warns them not to expect the fire of early love to continue unabated. "The impassioned ardors of the soul must of necessity subside," Mary lectures, as she urges her daughter to be thankful for the "solid pleasures of endearing familiarity." Especially surprising from the pen of one who always celebrated the value of a companionate marriage, the Gleaner's Mary urges Margaretta to be a compliant wife. She insists that she is "not an advocate for undue gentleness, or submissive acquiescence." Still, while she urges her daughter to "reverence herself," she completely subverts the message at the heart of Judith's "Desultory Thoughts." She readily concedes that "custom is a despot," but she indicates that it is "in vain," and perhaps undesirable, to challenge that despotism, to alter the gendered social order that custom has established.[20]

Mary need not worry. Margaretta never questions her duty to comply with her husband's every wish. Almost immediately after her marriage, she learns that Edward faces bankruptcy. A dutiful wife, she accepts her fate, cheerfully preparing to "relinquish the independence of affluence." When Edward prepares to sail for Europe in search of his fortune, he decides to rent his house to strangers, deciding that his wife will return to her parents' home. Interestingly, no one discusses these plans with Margaretta until two days before Edward's departure. Although she has had no part in decisions that will have a profound impact on her life, she acquiesces to her husband's proposal without so much as a murmur. She does not mind losing her independence and abdicating her status as the mistress of her home. Her only concern is that Edward might be lost at sea. Mr. Vigillius and Edward combine to allay her irrational objections. It takes a "few hours," but eventually they win Margaretta's blessing. Her temporary sacrifice will be her sole contribution to the recovery of *Edward's* independence.[21]

Margaretta never asserts her rights; she does not utter the tiniest protest when Edward fails to consult her as he strives to put his affairs in order. She simply trusts her husband to make the right decisions. Nor does her excellent education prepare her to contribute to the family's coffers. She knows how to save money, not to earn it. She is in no way "independent." In March of 1793, Judith had written to Maria, deploring the "degraded" condition in which women found themselves because arbitrary convention rendered most women unable to provide for themselves and their children. Neither the Gleaner nor Margaretta seems to worry about such matters. Margaretta's only contributions to the family's welfare are to avoid luxury and to give up her home, viewing the loss of her position at the head of her own table as of "little or no moment." Hers is not a "companionate marriage." The relationship between Edward and Margaretta is sentimental, bound by ties of emotion rather than reason. Margaretta does not even derive power from her role as wife and mother. Her place is both private and subordinate.[22]

The contrast with Judith's own experience is intriguing. When John Stevens's financial world collapsed, Judith was anything but passive. She wrote to her husband's creditors. She argued vociferously against John's decision to sail to St. Eustatius. She hinted that she was more able than he to handle their finances. She absolutely refused to live with her parents. If the story of Margaretta was autobiographical, even as it "improved" on Judith's own experiences, Margaretta's compliance is especially noteworthy. Did Judith harbor some regrets about her own behavior? Or was she simply giving her readers the message she believed they wanted to hear?

If Judith viewed the Margaretta story as a morality play, then it is fair to ask what lessons she was imparting to her readers. In essence, like so many novels of the day, it accepts a restricted notion of ideal womanhood. While it does not overtly proclaim that men and women are essentially different, it nevertheless praises women who remain in the home and do not challenge gender or class conventions. As a writer, Judith is much more daring than any of the women in her own novel. Yes, the story extolls the virtues of women's education and assumes that women are potentially rational beings. Nevertheless, if Margaretta enjoys the benefits of a liberal education, she puts that education to unexceptional uses. She is a good wife and mother and little more.[23]

Judith's "Desultory Thoughts" and her "On the Equality of the Sexes" were both much more willing to urge readers to transcend gender boundaries than the story of Margaretta was. Admittedly, the tale gives careful readers clues, subtly dropped here and there, that subvert the essays' more obvious gendered message. While Mr. Vigillius is a man whose classical education and worldly experience give him authoritative status, for instance, he nevertheless takes on some stereotypical characteristics of a woman, thus denying that the line between the sexes is obvious or immutable. Like most women—like Judith herself—Mr. Vigillius is confident when he expresses himself in writing, but is nervous and inarticulate speaking in public. And by his own account he is often more "sensible" than rational. He has, he admits, a "violent desire to become a writer." He is, like a woman, a victim of his passions and governed by his "thirst for applause." It is *Mary* who is the rational member of the family, who gently keeps her husband's fanciful tendencies in check. It is also Mary who devises an "extensive plan of education" for Margaretta, despite Mr. Vigillius's (clearly wrongheaded) misgivings. Fortunately, he defers to his wife's superior judgment. Some great writer once said, he explains, that "to the matron is entrusted not only the care of her daughter, but also the forming the first, and oftentimes, the most important movements of that mind which is to inform the future man," and hence the future nation. Of course Mary needs both Mr. Vigillius and the great writer to authorize her plan. Still, it *is* her plan and had it not been for her wisdom, Margaretta's education would have been a traditional—and inferior—one.[24]

Some of the other "Gleaner" essays might have invited controversy had readers known that they emanated from the pen of a woman. Perhaps it was those essays that led Judith to adopt the voice of a male narrator. Granted, only "The Gleaner" number 15 offers anything approaching a direct and sustained argument for women's intellectual equality. And that essay does not achieve the boldness of her earlier publications. Still, appearing as it does just two months after Mr. Vigillius's account of Margaretta's marriage, it offers an intriguing counterpoint to a conventional tale. It is an assault on the constricted goals of girls' education. Women are, says the Gleaner, "bred up with one particular view, with one monopolizing consideration, which seems to absorb every plan that reason might point out as worthy their attention: an establishment by marriage." They learn from the moment they are born that a spinster is a "contemptible being." They accept the first proposal that comes along, fearful that it will be the last. A good education, the Gleaner continues, prepares girls "to procure for themselves the necessaries of life, independence should be placed within their grasp." And, quoting Constantia, he adds, I would teach them to " 'reverence themselves.' " He wants them "to respect a single life, and even to regard it as the *most eligible*" unless they find a man truly worthy of their affection.[25]

The rest of the essay, however, retreats from the original message. It is the familiar story of two sisters, Helen and Penelope Airy, orphans who are separated in their youth, and whose educations prepare them for very different futures. Helen is indulged by her aunt and uncle, and enjoys a constant round of visiting, balls, and plays. She reads "the prettiest sentimental novels." She plays the coquette, attracting, teasing, and rejecting the eager swains who flutter around her. Eventual marriage to a wealthy man is the sole aim of her existence. Her sister Penelope has cultivated her own talents and can support herself with her needlework. She reads history and geography, not novels. "Independence," she insists, is her "ardent pursuit." As for marriage, she refuses to live in anticipation of an event that "may, or may not happen," nor is she convinced that it is a desirable end. Still, in an ironic twist, Penelope's happy ending—like Margaretta's—is marriage; Helen never weds and lives as a "fixed appendage" in her sister's family. Neither sister leads an independent existence.[26]

Interestingly, the "Gleaner" essays that do not deal directly with gender issues are often the most audacious. "The Gleaner" number 4, entitled "The Degeneracy of the Times," is a case in point. It embraces the argument that at least some critics were beginning to make, implicitly questioning the value of the classical curriculum to which elite men of the day enjoyed exclusive access. The Greeks, insists the Gleaner, were barbarous. They made war in ways that would cause "an American savage" to blush. Their religion was a "heap of absurdities." If students left school convinced that the ancients were the font of all wisdom, this was only because they studied the exploits of the Greeks and Romans and nothing else. It was, perhaps, just as well that women were denied access to the classics. They were freed from the despotism of the past and able to appreciate the virtues of a more enlightened age.[27]

At times the Gleaner is more direct in his praise of women. On more than one occasion, for instance, he sings the virtues of a string of literary luminaries. Addison, Swift, Pope, Homer, Virgil, invariably top the list. But mingled casually with the "great men," are Philienia and Mercy Otis Warren, both women, both Americans, both worthy of respect. Judith underscores this point in her fifth "Gleaner" essay, printing a fictional letter from "Modestus Mildmay," who bemoans the dearth of American artists. Too many of the nation's geniuses, argues Mildmay, are so busy eking out meager livings, that they have no time to cultivate their talent. Thus she proposes a constitutional amendment that would empower the government to support "*real genius*, whether it be found in the male or female world." The "road would be open to all, only *real worth* would receive the palm." America would be a true intellectual meritocracy, one that explicitly included women among its members. In his disquisition on the Masons, the

Gleaner repeats this suggestion, urging the benevolent organization to spread its bounty to "every member of the mental *Commonwealth*," offering "powerful patronage to the meritorious of every age, *sex*, and description." None of this, of course, is a demand for women's political or economic equality. But it is central to Judith's belief that the mind has no gender.[28]

However cautiously, the Gleaner makes an occasional case for gender equality. In one essay, he comes close to proclaiming women's superiority to men, even as he seems to undercut the political message of the Margaretta story. "The Gleaner" numbers 22 and 23 offer a Federalist perspective on the dangerous "self *created societies*" organized by Thomas Jefferson's Democratic-Republicans. The Gleaner distinguishes between "liberty"—characterized as a woman—and "licentiousness," a man. In the process, he inverts gender stereotypes. Before and during the American Revolution, colonists commonly saw liberty as a woman, framing her as helpless and fragile, in desperate need of protection from England's seductive power. At war's end, however, Federalists in particular began to fear that unchecked liberty would devolve into licentiousness. Liberty's very fragility made it dangerous in the hands of a people who were vulnerable to the temptations dangled before them by the Sinisterus Courtlands of the world. If the people did not control their passions and accept the authority of their deserving—rational, disinterested, virtuous—superiors, then the American experiment would fail.[29] Just as Margaretta meekly deferred, first to her parents and then to her husband, so the people were to obey their virtuous leaders. They may have been citizens of the republic, but their role was passive.

The Gleaner's gendered depiction of liberty and licentiousness is in line with the Federalist fear of chaos. But by identifying liberty as a woman and licentiousness as a man, he anticipates by some twenty years the departure from the standard metaphor, endowing liberty with traditionally masculine attributes. In his rendition, liberty is neither passive nor in need of protection. She is a "heaven descended goddess, rational and refined." She is the champion of order. She is an "informed, elevated, and well regulated mind." Unlike Margaretta, she needs no guidance from her superiors. She can control herself, and guard the nation that is entrusted to her care. Licentiousness, however, is "unbridled and tumultuous." Like Adam in the Garden of Eden, he is physically strong but morally weak. Worst of all, he wants to "invert the order of nature," to "annihilate every distinction," destroying the new nation almost before it has begun.[30] If woman is "mind" and man is "body," and if, in Judith Sargent Murray's perspective, mind is superior to physical reality, then women have the edge.

The Gleaner's defense of high Federalist thought was neither aberrant nor hypocritical. Like most Federalists, Judith feared anarchy and valued hierarchy.

She did not, as historian Pauline Schloesser suggests, follow the "party line" in order to curry favor with men, so that she could demand a measure of equality for a few qualified women. She saw no inconsistency between her argument for women's equality and her embrace of an ordered society. To the contrary, she saw women as both the beneficiaries and the protectors of such an order. However counterintuitive her perspective sounds to modern ears, her defense of class distinctions and her desire for gender equality depended upon one another and were part of a seamless whole. Her demands for women rested squarely upon her determination to separate body from mind, physical traits from mental potential. Challenging the notion that women of every race and class should be defined by their bodily weaknesses, she rejected a construction of gender that characterized all women as naturally disorderly and irrational, while it described men as genteel, self-possessed, and reasonable. The essence of humans was mental; history provided endless examples to prove the "*independence of intellect, upon any particular combination of matter.*" There was, she told Winthrop, no "corporeal conjunction" between mind and body.[31]

It was at least partly because of her insistence that body was irrelevant that Judith resolutely kept her authorship of the Gleaner essays a secret, dissimulating even to her own husband and her closest friends. Admittedly, those who knew her, must have suspected that Judith was the Gleaner. Her essays surely provided them with enough clues, for she observed that basic dictum of all new authors: write about what you know. They were liberally sprinkled with references to the sea and exhibited much more of their author's familiarity with the sons of Neptune than they did of those heirs of Cincinnatus who earned their living with the plow. Her story of Margaretta was often autobiographical, particularly in its account of her protagonists' financial struggles. That the Hamiltons, unlike John and Judith Stevens, survived their ordeal was beside the point. As an author, Judith could rewrite the past, creating the happy ending for her characters that had eluded her in the real world. The Gleaner's support for women's education and his praise of American writers, may also have led some readers to suspect that Constantia and the Gleaner were one and the same. Above all, the sixteenth installment of "The Gleaner's" bold defense of Universalism would surely have pointed to Judith as the author.

Nevertheless, Judith said she sought anonymity, and the medium of print was a perfect vehicle for this goal, allowing her to hide her identity in ways that would be impossible for someone who wrote by hand. Her friends would, of course, have recognized her handwriting. In the eighteenth century, moreover, cursive writing was gendered. Elite women, who theoretically enjoyed more leisure than men, adopted a particularly ornate hand as a means of claiming their gender and class position. Thus, even strangers would have identified the writer as a woman. Print was by definition impersonal and gave no clue about the gender or status of an author. Writers for magazines who chose to avoid recognition by the public could do so. They could write as abstract citizens who did not—or, in Judith's case, could not—rely on their own authority to carry their arguments. They could let their words speak for themselves.[32]

But the question remains. Why did Judith crave anonymity? Why, in particular, did she hide behind a male persona? It may be true, as Kathryn Shevelow argues, that anonymity protected women writers from accusations of immodesty or indecency. But this was a woman who had waged a public—if genteel—battle to retain her identity as Constantia. This was also a woman who once claimed that "to wear disguises, to assume an appearance foreign to the soul is torture to the ingenuous mind, it is an intellectual slavery."[33] Moreover, at the very time that she was writing as the Gleaner, she was publishing a series of "Repository" essays for the *Massachusetts Magazine* as Constantia.

Judith's reasons were both tactical and principled. To begin with, her practice was hardly unique. Eighteenth-century authors, especially those who wrote for periodicals, often adopted personae such as "The Gleaner" or "The Reaper," as a deliberate strategy for creating a following for their essays. This approach allowed budding writers to experiment with multiple identities and to wrap themselves in mystery, piquing the curiosity of the public and enlarging their readership. Judith's use of the pseudonym "The Gleaner" also offered her some protection. Gleaners, after all, were merely compilers who recognized the value of what they heard, but who had few thoughts of their own. Thus if she claimed authority in her role as a man, she lowered expectations for her work, hiding behind the excuse that she never pretended to be an original thinker. She was, in the end, "but a Gleaner."[34]

Moreover, Judith enjoyed playing games with curious readers. Her sly references to the conversations the Gleaner overheard during his rambles, gently mocked the obsession of those who were determined to discern her identity. She described one such fictitious encounter with her readers in "The Gleaner" number 5. One man thought the Gleaner was a Harvard student, another that this work of "genius" emanated from a "Connecticut pen." Yet a third maintained that he was a "poor, despicably poor—low, pitifully low fellow." No one suggested that he was a woman. In the end, sighed one observer, "he was *any body—every body—or nobody*."[35]

Indeed, that was Judith's point. Her anonymity conveyed a serious lesson. She thought it was "descriptive of the frivolity of the human mind" that people ignored "considerations of real weight" in favor of discerning the identity of the

Gleaner. "A knowledge of the author can be of no moment," she insisted. "The business of the reader is to scan the *intrinsick value* and *general tendency* of the composition." If body was irrelevant and mind was all, then any "body" was as good as any other—or as none at all. Ultimately, the material was immaterial. Readers should evaluate what she said, rather than worry about who said it. Thus Judith wrote with many voices, hiding her identity under a layered variety of aliases in the same way that an actress became a new character by changing her clothes and altering her demeanor. She introduced herself as the Gleaner, but in her story of Margaretta, she became Mr. Vigillius. And there were times when the line between the Gleaner and Mr. Vigillius was so blurred that it was impossible to know who was speaking. To add to the confusion, she created a number of fictional readers—some men, some women—who ask for the Gleaner's advice or beg for news of Margaretta.[36]

But if body did not *in fact* matter, Judith was well aware of the gender conventions of her day, and while she deplored those conventions she was reluctant to challenge them directly. She knew, for instance, that certain subjects were off limits for women. The Gleaner, however, was free to defend his views on religion, the Masons, and politics; his pages were replete with classical references. More important, Judith observed that when a woman writes "she is too often subject [to] the invidious remarks of those who conceive her an imbecile arrogant usurper in a province to which she possesses no natural claim." If readers invariably took sex into account when they evaluated women's work, she needed to transcend her sexual being if she wanted to be taken seriously. Thus she pretended to be a man, hoping that if her deception was successful, she might provide an object lesson that proved women's intellectual ability.[37]

If Judith argued that the body—especially the gendered body—was irrelevant, a mere cultural construct, she maintained that class—which she defined in terms of mental and moral characteristics—was both meaningful and real. Thus, sexual differences were irrelevant *because* they were purely physical. Class differences, at least in America, were achieved; they were thus moral and intellectual. Her own desire for fame demanded a society that took inequality for granted, that assumed superiority—of talent, of morality—of an elite few. She longed for a meritocracy, where the virtuous and intelligent would attain wealth and respect as their due, using their position to rule in a wise and disinterested fashion. To exclude some people from realizing their intellectual potential merely because of artificial sexual differences, was wrong. It was unfair to women like herself, whose elite status accorded them a measure of privilege even as their sex placed them on the margins. Moreover, it deprived society of the benefits of women's wisdom.[38]

Judith's use of a variety of voices in the pages of "The Gleaner" is revealing in this regard. To some extent, it merely reflects the fact that reading, at least in urban areas, was no longer confined to the elite. Shopkeepers, artisans, and sea captains might browse the pages of the *Massachusetts Magazine* along with Judith Murray and her friends. But in Judith's hands, the significance of the voices takes on added meaning. Mary Vigillius and her husband may be virtually identical in style and substance, but when letters from George Seafort, Monimia Castalio, or Rebecca Aimwell appear, the contrast is obvious. The missives are poorly written, marked by egregious grammatical errors and laughable syntactical lapses. The message is clear. Judith is not using these letters to offer an alternative to the authoritative voice of the male elite. Rather, she is asserting that educated men and women speak with one voice, uphold the same standards, and are capable of creating an American literature that will preserve the established order. The lower orders, men and women alike, are a distinct species. Although they may read "The Gleaner" and profit from its message, they are not ready to govern themselves, much less to instruct others. Granted, they have the right to enter the public sphere, but they write as supplicants, reaffirming rather than challenging the hierarchical nature of the writer-reader relationship. The Gleaner remains comfortably above the fray. His understanding of the codes of genteel behavior is proof of his superiority. It is his job to convey those codes to inferior men *and* women.[39]

The Gleaner's defense of hierarchy has often troubled modern scholars. Nowhere is this more the case than in "The Gleaner" number 24, which champions traditional gender roles to make its point. All societies, proclaims the Gleaner, are naturally unequal. So long as all people know their place and inferiors defer to their social superiors, heterogeneity can lead to balance, order, and mutual dependence. To prove his thesis, the Gleaner recounts the experience of a farm family that foolishly disregards the need for deference and order. One fateful morning, the members of the family abandon their conventional roles. The women quit cooking, proclaiming that the men of the house are perfectly capable of feeding themselves. As a result, the meals are ruined, the house is in a shambles, and everyone is miserable. The situation in the fields is even worse. The servants refuse to take orders, each having his own opinion about the best way to farm. Rather than using rational arguments to make their point, they "prepare for a trial of strength" and the fracas quickly leads to fisticuffs. "Bloody noses are the consequence; and the day is sacrificed to discord." By summer's end, the fields are barren and the family faces starvation. No one profits. No one is secure.[40]

A country that abandons its commitment to gradation and order is dangerous for everyone, argues the Gleaner, but it is a particularly unhappy place for the physically vulnerable. In such circumstances, "the strong will invariably oppress the weak; to the lusty arm of athletic guilt, imbecile innocence will fall a prey, and there is no power to redress!" A state of nature is not kind to women and children. Only a society governed by rules will give women security and the chance to realize their potential. Only there, will the arts and sciences survive, and even flourish. Only there will women's voice be heard.[41]

* * *

Judith began submitting her "Gleaner" essays to the *Massachusetts Magazine* in February of 1792. In September, using the familiar name of "Constantia," she started her "Repository" series. These essays, she said—ignoring the fact that she painstakingly wrote and rewrote each one—were "spontaneous reflections," dashed off in the odd hour or two that any cultivated woman enjoyed. But if the pieces were not always serious, she believed that they earned her a permanent spot on the literary landscape. Her words would survive, she said, long after her body had returned to the earth. Paradoxically, she contended that the Repository gave its creator a superior "body" of her own. With the use of the pen, claimed Constantia, "reason assumes a shape—ideas are clothed with bodies, and every thought standeth confessed before us."[42]

"The Repository" pieces were short—often just a paragraph or two— moral essays on a variety of topics. Judith lifted most of them, with just a few changes, from her own private "repository." She wrote about death, spring, nature, and the pain caused by slander. She extolled the virtues of charity, rectitude, and religion. Unlike some of "The Gleaner" essays, none of these pieces was especially controversial in either subject matter or argument. Only one, "The Repository" number 17, was remotely political. Written at the beginning of the American Revolution, this was clearly a historical document, one that would not garner much negative attention in the postwar world.[43]

Even in the Repository Judith could not avoid an occasional reference to gender. In her second essay, she attacked the sexual double standard. Two essays, one on "Friendship" and the other entitled "Platonism," reflected her interest in intellectual relationships, a topic that had always intrigued her. She had written both pieces in 1777, at a time when her friendship with John Murray was blossoming. In "Friendship" she argued that amity did not recognize "sexual distinction." I think, Constantia asserted, "that it may exist in high perfection in those of the same, or different sexes." "Platonism" (originally entitled "Sentiments on Christian Amity") employs similar language to praise the "passionate" yet "wholly intellectual" friendship between individuals of the same sex. As she had once argued to Maria, the joys of friendship produced "those celestial pleasures which await us in the paradise of the blessed." Marriage and family were earthly phenomena, while friendship was immortal.[44]

*   *   *

Although she stopped submitting essays to the *Massachusetts Magazine* in the fall of 1794, Judith had by no means lost her craving for fame. Unfortunately, real life, never as orderly as the existence she designed for her fictional characters, beckoned. John still ranged up and down the entire eastern coast, leaving the responsibilities of their home on her shoulders. Increasingly, he tarried with the Boston Universalists, whose church had steadily gathered adherents over the years. In 1785, the congregation purchased an appropriate building on the corner of North Bennet and Hanover streets. By 1792, it was making plans to apply to the Massachusetts legislature for incorporation, enlarging and redecorating the church, dividing the pews among its parishioners, and creating a "Regular and Orderly" society.[45]

In keeping with their aspirations, the Boston Universalists tried to persuade John to become their pastor. In March, they offered him a salary of four pounds each Sunday if he agreed to preach to them on a part-time basis. The following year, the proprietors voted unanimously to make him their full-time minister, raising his stipend to five pounds a week. John was eager to become the leader of as large and important a congregation of Universalists as existed in America. The Gloucester church, he complained was "small, and rendered still smaller by deaths and removal." Worse, those parishioners who remained had "lapsed into a state of luke-warmness." In Boston, on the other hand, the "commodious meeting-house" could hold up to 1,500 dedicated believers. The Massachusetts capital was, moreover, the hub of the New England universe. To be a minister there was to be the unrivaled leader of the Universalist movement. This was a golden opportunity, one he could not refuse. Thus, on October 24, a "Large Number of Spectators having Assembled," John was installed as the Boston Universalists' minister. Judith was quietly pleased with the proprietors' observation that a "Numerous, Respectable, and Attentive Audience" had witnessed the ceremony. John had come a long way since his first introduction to the town, when a hostile crowd had pelted him with vegetables and stones to the delight of many Boston ministers.[46]

Judith was almost ready to accept the inevitable. Her husband already had the use of a "commodious apartment" near Maria's house. Although for the moment, he continued to divide his time between Boston and Gloucester, she knew he would soon want to call the capital city his home.[47] Nor was a move to the Massachusetts capital as unthinkable as it once had been. The day was fast approaching when leaving Gloucester no longer meant that Judith would be abandoning her parents.

On July 27, 1793, a little less than three months before John's ordination, Judith's mother died. She had been in poor health for years, suffering "excruciating agonies" without complaint. Still, when her time came, it was sudden. His shock at his wife's death turned the once stalwart Winthrop Sargent into a helpless and confused old man almost over night. Judith begged her father to come live with her. When he refused, she offered to move in with him, promising to pay him for any expenses incurred by John or Julia Maria. She was determined that no one thought she was making this suggestion in order to reap an "*undue pecuniary* advantage."[48]

Judith was relieved when both Fitz William and Esther approved her plan. Still, she predicted that her father would reject it. He seemed unable to make any decision, no matter how trivial. Perhaps, she thought, he was simply reluctant to make any changes at this stage in his life. As Winthrop's health steadily deteriorated, Judith took matters into her own hands, moving in with her father, taking her mother's place as mistress of the household. Unfortunately, she could do nothing to slow down Winthrop's decline. On December 3, 1793, he died. Judith did not bother to return home. Together, Fitz William, Esther, and Judith decided to sell her house on Middle Street.[49]

As Judith prepared to leave the town of her birth, she wished she had the power to make her own life as tidy as she did for the characters who inhabited the Gleaner's world. John was right to call their situation "deranged." Even her once emotionally satisfying friendship with Maria was somewhat strained. They had their first real argument—over a packet of letters that John had carelessly mislaid. Only when the missing letters were found was Maria partly mollified. The two women resumed their friendship, trying to pretend that nothing had come between them. Still, the tiff was disquieting. One of the appeals that Boston held for Judith was the opportunity to spend more time with her aunt. She only hoped the incident was not a harbinger of future quarrels.[50]

Family news did not get any better. In August, Anna Maria, Fitz William's four-year-old daughter, died after a short illness. Both parents were devastated. Fitz William almost immediately began talking of leaving Gloucester and all its memories as soon as he could get his affairs in order. John Ellery, Esther's husband, was also contemplating relocating to Boston. There seemed to be little reason for Judith to remain in her ancestral home. Her parents were dead.

Winthrop still resided in the Ohio country and, while he remained frustrated with his dead-end career, he showed no signs of returning to Gloucester. If Esther and Fitz William left town as well, then the time was right for Judith to join her husband. She had always claimed to disdain the beau monde as she had expounded upon the virtues of rural life. But Boston clearly had its assets. It was New England's intellectual and cultural center, an ideal location from which she could strengthen and expand her ties to America's literary world. It had schools for girls. Maria lived there. Esther, and perhaps Fitz William, would soon follow. By the fall of 1794, Judith was ready to bid her native town good-bye.

Chapter 9
"A School of Virtue"

By the spring of 1794, Judith was eager to move to Boston. Her parents were entombed alongside all the other Sargents who had lived and died in Gloucester. The town was almost deserted.[1] Boston promised a better life. John was serving one of the nation's largest and most important Universalist congregations. In time, Julia Maria would enjoy educational opportunities that were far superior to anything Gloucester offered. The political and literary ambiance of the capital city was vibrant, and Judith's intellectual horizons would be broadened there. Fresh from the modest success of her "Gleaner" and "Repository" essays, she hoped that in a new and stimulating environment, where she would have a chance to mingle with America's finest minds, her "career of fame" would rise to new heights. In some ways, her expectations were realized. She published a bit in Robert Treat Paine's *Federal Orrery*. She also embarked on an ambitious career as a playwright. Granted, neither project met her expectations. Timid and self-conscious, afraid of what people would say, determined not to do anything that would be inappropriate for a minister's wife, she tended to soften her message and to retreat in the face of even mild criticism. Still, it was a start.

* * *

Judith was ready to leave Gloucester long before John found appropriate accommodations for the family. Lodging in Boston was expensive. Indeed, everything there cost more than she had expected even in her most extravagant calculations. And John was determined to secure a house that was not, as Judith delicately put it, "less convenient than that to which I have become accustomed." She had always pictured moving to the capital city in terms of upward social mobility. Now she only hoped that she would not be worse off than before.[2]

By midsummer, the Murrays were desperate, and Judith feared that her family might end up in Philadelphia after all. The Universalists there continued to dangle the promise of a "genteel house" rent free. But in August, John announced that he had finally found a suitable place. It was very suitable, indeed. Number 5 Franklin Place was located in Boston's South End, the heart of postwar Federalist society. Before the Revolution, it was the North End, close to public venues such as the State House, that attracted the city's elite. Now, as more and more merchants fled to the capital from dying secondary ports, those who could afford to do so lived some distance from Boston's workaday world. Whether they were old, elite commercial magnates or "businessmen on-the-make," they were not as willing to mingle with the lower orders as their parents had been. Instead, they sought dwellings away from the hoi polloi, surrounding themselves with gardens and parks, creating the illusion of a rural retreat far from the noise and bustle in the center of town. They hoped the poorer sort, whose numbers were multiplying, would stay out of sight altogether. In 1795, the old almshouse was filled to capacity by a population composed "of all ages, sexes, colour and character." The building was dirty, crowded, and bound to turn the worthiest unfortunates into profligate wretches. When a new edifice had to be built, "Civis," writing in the *Columbian Centinel*, asked only that it be erected away from the new State House.[3]

The Murrays' home was far removed from the sounds and stench of the Boston almshouse. Located directly across from the Tontine Crescent, Franklin Place was part of architect Charles Bulfinch's—and Boston's—most ambitious residential project. Begun in 1793, the original plan called for two rows of double houses, sixteen in all, connected in the English style, facing each other across an enclosed park. In the center of the green stood an oolite stone urn dedicated to Benjamin Franklin. The Crescent also included space for the Massachusetts Historical Society and the Boston Library Society. Shares in the houses, sold on the "tontine principle," were offered to the public in 1791, but Bulfinch, more optimistic than pragmatic, began construction before half the shares were sold. Although the project was never a financial success, it was soon the talk of Boston, and for a half a century its houses were among the city's most coveted residences. The buildings' neoclassic style satisfied the century's penchant for order and decorum. Three stories high and 480 feet long, the row of gray brick houses caught the eye of the most oblivious passerby. Contrary to the original plan, the homes on the southern half where Franklin Place was located, were arranged along a straight line. Still, they were as impressive as any abode in Boston. It is not surprising that by 1795, the houses were selling for the princely sum of $8,000, at a time when only one in ten Americans owned a house worth more than $700.[4]

When the Murrays moved in, eight of the projected houses were complete, and eight more were nearly finished. Judith was ecstatic when she described her surroundings. Indoors and out, her home had all the markers of New England gentility. "Furnished in the modern taste," it was "spacious, lofty, commodious, and elegant." It boasted "all possible conveniences for domestic use." We have, she added, "all the necessaries, and many of the elegancies of life." Unlike her Gloucester house, whose interior was the typical simple square divided into rooms of equal size on each floor, Franklin Place had rooms of different dimensions, each designed for a specific function. It had two parlors and an apartment for guests. It even had a dining room, ideal for the dinner parties that Judith might host on occasion. And it had the obligatory two staircases, one for the family, the other for servants. It also had a comforting rural flavor. The first floor window looked out on Thomas Russell's garden. If Judith climbed to the third level, she caught a glimpse of the ocean. While she claimed not to care about such things, Judith proudly called attention to the names of the other inhabitants of the Crescent, virtually all of whom had some claim to fame—at least in elite Federalist circles. Those of her friends who wanted more information, she added, need only consult the February edition of the *Massachusetts Magazine* for a glowing description.[5]

Living in Boston was exciting, but it was also a challenge, especially at first. Chaos reigned when Judith's furniture arrived. "Beds, tables, chairs, looking glasses, pictures, etc. etc." had to be put in their proper places before she was ready to receive visitors. To her dismay, Judith discovered that the Crescent's bushes attracted mosquitoes as well as human admirers, and everyone soon looked as though they were recovering from smallpox. Fortunately, these mosquitoes were not the bearers of the dreaded yellow fever that had struck Philadelphia with devastating force the previous summer.[6]

Judith soon found that there were disadvantages to city living. In Boston, much more than in Gloucester, there was always someone—a relative, a traveler passing through—who took advantage of her hospitality, staying at Franklin Place for weeks, even months on end. Paradoxically, living among strangers was alienating and a little lonely. None of her siblings lived close by, and even after she had been in Boston two years, Judith claimed not to have made a "single *real friend*" there. "Friendship," she suspected, was "a native of the peaceful Hamlet," where it developed "without assuming the disguises which are recommended by cold hearted Caution." Her position was anomalous. Despite her claims to gentility, she was never comfortable in Boston's polite society where she did not have the money to mix in the best circles and even a casual visit demanded "the strict and fatiguing rules of ceremony." Nor did she see as much of Maria as she had hoped. Her aunt lived some distance from Franklin Place, and their relationship became strained over the years in any case.[7] She did enjoy the Mortons and their literary circle. Still, it was only in Gloucester that she completely relaxed.

Judith also understood that if she were to claim elite status, she had to be constantly on guard. In Gloucester, where everyone knew her, she had been able to visit parents or siblings without a male escort. In Boston, proper women moved in refined but restricted circles. They were not seen on the streets, mingling with the crowds, in danger of being run down by the hacks that careened recklessly through town. They surely did not want to be mistaken for those women who drank cheap liquor and wandered the streets in "idleness, poverty, and disgrace," vainly seeking a handout. Even respectable country wives who came to town to sell their wares were inappropriate companions for the sort of lady who inhabited Franklin Place.[8]

Boston was also dangerous. Judith eventually grew used to the clanging of fire bells, as she claimed to be grateful that she and John, unlike Daniel and Maria—whose house on Atkinson Street had recently burned to the ground—had so little to lose. Even so, the Murrays were reluctant to leave their house unattended. Fire was not their only hazard. They also feared the "licentious rabble" who roamed the streets looking for excitement or venting their frustrations by desecrating the property of Boston's high and mighty. Disease was yet another obstacle to their peace of mind. Every summer, the city assumed a "sickly aspect." Boston's narrow streets and "thick compound Atmosphere" were ideally suited to incubate and spread disease, as "dead animals, fishes' heads and entrails, and quantities of vegetables" assaulted the "olfactory nerves" of every inhabitant. No matter how often the local papers warned the city's residents to clean their gutters and to sweep dirt into the center of each avenue, summer always meant death for the unfortunate. In 1795, Judith witnessed the spread of a "contagious fever, and putrid sore throat" that decimated John's congregation. Children and young people were especially vulnerable, and John grimly officiated at the funerals of girls no older than Julia Maria almost daily. Mother and daughter always tried to escape when the heat was at its peak. Most often they went to Gloucester, but on one occasion they traveled to the gentry resort of Fresh Pond, where Judith enjoyed music and mingling with the likes of the *Columbian Centinel*'s Benjamin Russell.[9]

Still, if the city posed hazards, it had much to offer. Granted, while Boston boasted that it was the "Athens of the New World," it could not really compete with Philadelphia or New York. Yet compared to Gloucester, it was a veritable Mecca. It was growing so fast that in 1797 the town meeting considered erecting signs on major streets to help visitors get their bearings. Boston was one of the three leading centers for the American book trade, and Judith loved browsing in the many bookstores whose proprietors advertised in the pages of the *Columbian Centinel*. Circulating libraries also abounded. The Columbian Museum at the head of the mall featured a variety of paintings by native artists. There were also operas and balls, concerts, plays, and "theatrical exhibitions" in such numbers that it was impossible to fit them all in. A year after she arrived in town, Judith attended her first Harvard commencement, as she observed that they did such things better in Philadelphia. Solemn occasions, she opined, "ought not to be marked by riot and intemperance," and she was disgusted by the "hissing, clapping, hallowing, stamping, shrieking" of the raucous audience. Even when the governor and members of the clergy entered the hall, the shameful high jinks continued and the sheriff, himself, could not restore order. Only when Robert Treat Paine, mounted the rostrum to recite a poem he had written for the occasion did the noise lower to a murmur. Still, though the occasion was not perfect, Judith knew that she would not have seen the ceremony at all had she stayed in Gloucester.[10]

Judith was entranced by Boston's cultural treasures. But she was even more excited by the educational opportunities that awaited her daughter in the capital city. In 1789, the town meeting had authorized the creation of three public writing and reading schools. Boys could attend them year round; girls could do so between April and October. More to Judith's liking, a number of private schools for girls were beginning to appear. There were also many tutors who taught reading and writing to "young Ladies." Her fancy must have been especially caught by Francis Nichols's promise to teach up to twenty-five students "of either sex" English, arithmetic, geography, astronomy, moral and natural philosophy—and Latin. Julia Maria would also cultivate those accomplishments that divided merely respectable women from the truly genteel. Mr. Turner, for instance, promised students that his dance classes would "form their manners" and make them "graceful partners." Girls could also learn "drawing in all different branches" at Boston's painting academy. Judith still talked of raising her daughter to be independent. But, now that she lived at Franklin Place, she also wanted Julia Maria to "make a respectable figure in society." Nevertheless, the cost of education was daunting, and while John was a good father, he was not always a good provider. Thus she had to watch every penny.[11]

*   *   *

It is tempting to wonder what the members of his congregation thought as they watched John Murray settle into his luxurious Franklin Place accommodations. Were they proud that he could represent them in such style? Or did they resent knowing that their hard-earned money made that style possible? The Boston Universalists were respectable, but most were members of a rising middle class who counted more craftsmen than merchants in their numbers. They were determined enough to secure John's services to offer him an attractive salary. He deserved, they said, "to be *Decently*, & Comfortably Supported." Still, like many dissenting denominations, they were "aggressively egalitarian in theology and church structure." Thus they strove to make the church's expenses fall equitably upon the "*Society at Large*." That was easier said than done, especially in the face of the periodic downturns that plagued Boston's economy. As the parishioners struggled to survive, they were hardly sympathetic to Judith's complaints that her family was in dire straits. They did their best under difficult circumstances, even raising the price of their pews to meet their obligations. Still, there is little indication that the Universalists regretted making John their minister. He had his detractors of course. But to enjoy the spiritual care of a man of his stature was quite a coup. Moreover, John was a lively preacher. He was open and sociable. And when he was in town he worked hard, officiating at two services on Sunday and giving evening lectures during the week.[12]

John returned his church's affections. He admitted that his congregation was "composed of good, bad, and indifferent," and that people attended his services for a variety of reasons. Some were prompted by their love of spiritual truth. A few came because they despised all other churches. Still others were moved by "the impulse of the moment." He welcomed them all. One of his biographers maintains that John never seriously contemplated leaving Boston for greener pastures. But he did receive occasional invitations to move and did not always reject them out of hand. He had been in Boston only a short time when Judith observed that her husband was already restless and was casting "a languishing eye toward Philadelphia." And while the Murrays never left Massachusetts, neither did John abandon his itinerant ministry. Thus, the Boston Universalists often had to raise money for substitutes, a task they found more and more burdensome with the passage of time.[13]

The social gulf between the Boston Universalists and the Murrays was much wider than it had been in Gloucester. Thus it is not surprising that Judith claimed that she barely knew most members of the Boston church. While she conceded that the congregation had a few "worthy characters," there was only one with whom she could "mingle souls." In fact, her role as minister's wife was not central to the picture of herself that Judith painted in her letters—or at least in those letters she deemed worthy of a place in her letter books. She described herself as a genteel mother, sister, or—less often—helpmate. She was also, of course, a published writer. Still, if she did not derive her identity from her role as a preacher's wife, Judith had to accept the limitations that came from her position. She was always circumspect, knowing that news of her smallest indiscretion would spread quickly.[14] Nor could she escape the time-consuming chores that fell to all women whose husbands were men of the cloth. Her home was open to anyone at virtually any time, and she was expected to accept without complaint the "domestic casualties" that threw the best regulated house into turmoil when parishioners arrived unannounced. She may not have been friendly with the Boston Universalists, but the congregation was large and she surely called on its members. Yet, while she described in loving detail her occasional visits to an elegant residence, writing of homes replete with carpets, pictures, and musical instruments, the houses inhabited by the Boston Universalists merited no such comments.[15]

Judith was generally content in Boston, relieved not to watch as her beloved Gloucester became ever shabbier and more desolate. Her Uncle Epes's old farm was vacant, its buildings in decay. Her father's house, once a source of pride, was also "solitary, forlorn, and rapidly tending to ruin." Nearly all the window panes in the once grand edifice were broken and no one bothered to replace them.[16] Eventually, she thought, both Fitz William and Esther would move to Boston. There, the Sargent children—minus Winthrop—would be reunited.

Unfortunately, Judith's plans for bringing her Gloucester siblings to Boston were never realized. Fitz William moved into his father's abandoned house and indicated that if he did leave, he would settle in Newbury, not the capital city. John Ellery also stayed where he was. Judith was especially frustrated by the Ellerys' change of heart. She had been overjoyed when her brother-in-law made plans to purchase a house on Franklin Place, anticipating a resumption of the relationship she and Esther had enjoyed in Gloucester as they ran in and out of one another's homes, sharing their joys and sorrows as mothers and wives. Although Ellery was a successful entrepreneur who prospered even in dismal times, like many merchants, he tended to overestimate his prospects. He had counted on purchasing his new abode with the earnings from a single voyage, but when his venture was not as profitable as he had expected, he decided to remain in Gloucester. John was proud, Esther explained, and he refused to move to Boston until he could "live as those he would wish to associate with."[17]

When Esther admitted that she was depressed by what she saw as her husband's "failure," Judith was unsympathetic. Scarcely able to disguise her envy, she advised her sister to count her blessings. Although Esther was four years Judith's junior, she was much wealthier. She lived in a "commodious, and even elegant Mansion." She would soon receive her portion of their father's estate and could spend it as she pleased. Meanwhile, the Murrays lived on a "scanty pittance," and even that depended on the health of a frail man. When Judith received *her* share of their father's legacy, she would spend it on necessities; she would have nothing to leave her only child. Still, she continued piously, although she was much poorer than her sister, she never complained. Judith's letter was the first of many such missives she would send over the years. Boston gave John visibility, but it did not offer financial reward. He received no raise after 1795. Yet his expenses steadily grew, and while Judith insisted that she was not "in the habit of bowing down to wealth," she could not help but envy Esther's good fortune, as she struggled to maintain a genteel lifestyle on a minister's stipend. She was as deserving as her siblings. Yet as they prospered, her own circumstances declined.[18]

*   *   *

Despite an occasional disappointment, Judith found Boston more intellectually stimulating than Gloucester had ever been. As The "Gleaner" essays indicate, she had developed a coherent set of political views well before she moved to Franklin Place. But she grew more interested in public affairs in a city where factional warfare was in the very air she breathed. Even celebrations marking American independence, she observed, were "tinctured with the acrimonious spirit of party." Judith was a voracious reader of newspapers, magazines, and pamphlets, all of which had something to say about the issues of the day. Partisan newspapers, such as Judith's favorite, staunchly Federalist *Columbian Centinel*, kept the political pot boiling. There were other sources of news as well. Boston was a lively commercial center, and whenever ships from Europe sailed into the harbor, they brought the latest continental news with them. In such a vibrant atmosphere, Judith could not help but develop a sense of connectedness with the wider world, nor, like many women of the time, could she resist entering the political debate. Women after the Revolution may have occupied the domestic sphere but, as historian Mary Ryan points out, the house was hardly a fortress. A minister's home, in particular, was filled with visitors. Men and women, young and old, rich and poor, brought news and opinions with them whenever they entered Franklin Place.[19]

No topic attracted the attention of Americans in the late eighteenth century like the French Revolution. And while women may have seen the Revolution through a gendered lens, focusing on the personal, moral, and religious repercussions of the Gallic upheaval, they did not shrink from making their views known. Judith arrived in Boston with her opinions on this subject already formed. She had never trusted France, even during the colonial struggle for independence. And while she had smiled on the Revolution in its earlier stages, like most Federalists, by 1793 she viewed French affairs with alarm.[20] She loved liberty, of course, but she disapproved of the "savage barbarity" that she saw as integral to the Paris scene. Her alarm turned to hostility with the beheading of Louis XVI. She compared the king's fate to that of Charles I, "the martyred Prince of England," whose demise she had once described so sympathetically. Both monarchs were victims of "horrid parricides," but Louis was even more blameless than Charles. He was, she declared, "as faultless a Man as ever was invested with royal dignity!!!"[21]

Inevitably, international affairs became entangled in domestic politics, especially after "Citizen Genet" came to America, determined to meddle in his host country's politics. Judith was as disdainful of the French ambassador as any Federalist. "For Genet," she wrote Maria, "but what of Genet—Let him continue to occupy the public prints—he shall not sully this milk white sheet, nor shall his insidious proceedings, have the honor to be noted by me." Robespierre was worse still. A "Savage, and unprecedented Monster," he was responsible for all the crimes and atrocities that the revolutionary regime had perpetrated in his name.[22]

Judith was frightened by the challenge to order, stability, and religion that the French Revolution seemed to portend. Unlike Mary Wollstonecraft—whom in so many respects she admired—Judith disapproved of a county whose citizens were eager to "rally round the Standard of Anarchy." She continued to believe that social leveling would lead to chaos, and that women—at least elite women—would lose much more than they gained were America to imitate the French example. But she refused to take what many Federalists saw as the next logical step. She would not retreat from her belief in gender equality. A society grounded in deference and subordination need not, she insisted, revert to the patriarchal order of old. Learned women were not obliged to remain in their homes. Nor did she see herself as an "amphibious animal" simply because she cared about politics.[23]

To the contrary, Judith's determination to express her political sentiments steadily mounted, as she insisted that a woman could declare her "Amor patria" with as much justice as any man. "Say not that this matter is uninteresting to me!" she told Winthrop when she was commenting on his prospects in Ohio. She cared as a sister of course. But more than that, she had a direct interest, "as a daughter of Columbia," in her country's fate. If she was becoming more political, Judith was also more partisan. In the spring of 1794 the Gleaner had railed against the factionalism of the Democratic-Republicans, arguing that everyone should rise above party affiliation. A year later, Judith defined herself as a Federalist. The first competitive presidential election was eminent. George Washington refused to serve another term. It was anyone's guess who would succeed him. Winthrop's prospects, of course, depended upon a Federalist victory. So, in Judith's mind, did "Peace, Order, and good Government." Everywhere she saw ominous signs. "Impending darkness" she declared, "seems to envelop the political horizon." Reviewing the events of the past year, she reeled off a list of calamities that showed how close to the edge the nation had wandered. "The Indian war, the Pittsburgh insurrection—contested elections, violent Parties, Jacobism etc. etc. etc., these all agitate the public mind beyond description," she said, as the "zeal of ignorance, and bigotry" was destroying American virtue.[24]

Nothing, not the Whiskey Rebellion, not the machinations of Genet, not the rise of Republican clubs, pushed Judith—and many other New Englanders— into the Federalist camp as did the controversy over Jay's Treaty. The Senate ratified the treaty, negotiated in 1794, with relative ease. But the House, where Judith saw "proof positive" of party spirit at work, was outraged by an agreement that appeared overly sympathetic to Great Britain. While it could not vote against the treaty, Congress could refuse the funds to enforce it. Once Republicans appeared ready to adopt this strategy, Jay's Treaty became the center of an intense national debate in which Judith became absorbed. She spent hours scouring the pages of the *Columbian Centinel*, tracking down every rumor, and analyzing every argument.[25]

Everyone, she assured Winthrop, was furious when news of the Republican strategy reached Massachusetts. The effort "astounds and alarms every reflecting Federalist throughout the union." She was convinced that the consequences of the House effort would be dire. All order, she cried, "will be whelmed beneath the waves of confusion!!!" Fortunately, up and down the New England coast, communities rushed to pass resolutions urging male citizens to sign petitions supporting Jay's Treaty. Salem's town meeting did so with only four dissenting votes. Boston would soon follow suit and Judith was sure that the "highly Federal" town of Gloucester would also come on board. Even as she donned a partisan mantle, she returned to her old antifaction rhetoric, accusing the Republicans of "party spirit," while insisting that the Federalists were acting in the "true interest" of the nation. In the end, the Republicans failed to block Jay's Treaty. Her friends thought that the oration by Massachusetts's Fisher Ames, delivered right before the final vote, had saved the day. When the speech appeared in pamphlet form, Judith read all fifty-two pages, noting that Ames's effort was well argued and that its "flowers of rhetoric are judiciously disposed, and many paragraphs are pathetically interesting."[26]

*   *   *

Judith's interest in politics was never entirely disinterested. Yes, she was happy that the decision to enforce Jay's Treaty "preponderated in favour of Order and good government." But personal considerations were uppermost in her mind. American involvement in European wars, which many feared if the treaty failed, always hurt commerce and thus threatened the livelihood of Fitz William and Esther. Her most nagging concern, however, was Winthrop. She was delighted to observe that with the treaty in place, England at last began to evacuate its forts in the Northwest Territory. Surely this would make life in the region less perilous, and it might bring her brother a measure of prosperity as well. By the same token, Judith condemned Congress when it refused to reimburse Winthrop for the expenses he incurred in Ohio. She framed her brother's quarrel with the legislature in moral terms. No government acted with "integrity, honour, and generosity," she said, when it defrauded "the Man of real merit." If Congress continued to be parsimonious with deserving citizens, America would be known for "the worst kind of poverty—a poverty of virtue." Judith conceded that her views were colored by her love for her brother, but she refused to retreat from her belief that she was as able as any man to assess the moral dimensions of public affairs.[27]

Judith and her brother were finally on excellent terms. Winthrop had even begun to look favorably upon her "wedded friend." Although it cost a great deal to send letters west, Judith eagerly took advantage of the thaw. She wrote regularly to Ohio, trying to bolster her brother's spirits. There was a pattern in everyone's life, she said, and what looked like cruel happenstance to mere mortals, was part of an intricate plan whose purpose God would reveal at the proper time. Winthrop no doubt wondered when he might expect his sister's promised pattern to emerge. And even Judith admitted that although he was "high in the estimation of the western world," her brother was living the life of an exile, "entombed alive" and likely to remain so. Under the circumstances, she wished he would simply come home.[28] Unfortunately, the men she most loved were destined to be wanderers.

Winthrop made one of his rare visits to Boston in the autumn of 1795. He did not stay long, but he was there long enough to give Judith time to show off her elegant surroundings. She also enjoyed stepping briefly into her mother's shoes. When her brother had come home in happier times, Judith, Sr. had tended to her oldest son's every need. Now that Judith could assume this role, she was both proud and pleased. Winthrop left the East in the spring of 1796, heading to Detroit and then to Mackinaw before returning to Cincinnati. He had never seemed so far away. Judith could not even trace her brother's movements on a map. Still, she entertained occasional thoughts of visiting him after he reached home. "A progress through the wilds of America, during the continuance of the mild season," she wrote, "provided I could be secure from the assaults of the natives of the Forest, and from Savage Men, would be perfectly to my taste." A trip west would replicate the experiences of her rugged ancestors who had abandoned European civilization for the untamed new world. She probably knew that she was indulging in a fantasy. Still, she loved to travel. She was strong and adaptable. She could learn to be comfortable with only a "Beaver covering" to protect her. But in the meantime, her duties at 5 Franklin Place beckoned.[29]

Winthrop shared one carefully kept secret with his sister during his brief visit to Boston. While Judith could fairly claim that her brother's public integrity was without peer, she knew that his private behavior was not always pristine. He had been crushed by the death of his wife and daughter, sure that domestic bliss was lost to him forever. He had tried to find solace in his work. But life on the frontier was lonely and there were few suitable women to share his leisure hours. It was hard to maintain one's guard all the time. Winthrop had been something of a lady's man in his youth. He had not lost his touch. In January of 1795, he met Sarah Chapese of Redstone Fort, Pennsylvania. Sarah had been abandoned by her husband, Henri. A single woman on the frontier was more vulnerable than any heroine in a romantic novel. Thus, when Winthrop gallantly offered Sarah his protection, she gladly moved in with him. By the middle of February she was pregnant. In June, she returned to Redstone where she gave birth to a girl, Caroline Augusta. Convinced that he could give her a life that would be far superior to anything her mother could offer, Winthrop sought custody of his daughter. But Sarah, while she was often on the verge of agreeing, always reneged at the last moment.[30]

Judith never condemned Winthrop for fathering an illegitimate child. Referring to Caroline Augusta as a "little blossom" and a "tender flower," she indicated that in her life as well as in her fiction, she did not blame children for the sins of their parents. Winthrop, so quick to judge others, could well have expected both Murrays to condemn his own moral lapses. He, after all, had refused to accept John as his brother-in-law for years, declaring that his sister's marriage had dishonored the family. How galling it must have been, when John meekly turned the other cheek and almost immediately volunteered to take Caroline Augusta into his home. Judith, too, begged her brother to send Caroline to Boston, even offering to travel to Redstone to make her case to Sarah in person. She was so confident that her niece would join her family that she began to devise ways to introduce her to Boston society. It might, she thought, be best to say that she was the daughter of Winthrop's deceased wife.[31]

There is no evidence that Caroline Augusta ever visited Boston, although

Judith mentioned the possibility from time to time. She genuinely wanted to raise Winthrop's daughter as her own. Julia Maria was a "solitary little being" who longed for a sister or a brother, and Judith believed she would profit from the "society of a young person of her own standing." Her own life had been immeasurably enriched by the affection she "early felt to the children of my parents." Besides, although she loved her brother dearly, she thought no man was qualified to raise a girl. Nature, she reminded her brother, "although equal in her distributions is nevertheless various in her gifts, and her discriminating lines are perfectly obvious." While no intellectual difference divided the sexes, women were made for motherhood, and there were some tasks for which men were unsuited.[32]

Judith was no doubt sincere whenever she told Winthrop that she hoped his fortunes would improve. Yet at some level it was comforting to know that at least one of her siblings was struggling to make ends meet. She and John had never been wealthy, but in Gloucester they got by on relatively little. Their house was paid for. Judith encountered few enticements to spend John's hard-earned money. But in Boston, prices were high and grew ever higher. Inflation always hurt some people more than others. For those, like John, who lived on a fixed income, it was disastrous. When they bought their shares in Franklin Place, the Murrays had assumed that Judith's share of the sale of the house in Gloucester, added to her patrimonial inheritance, would enable them to purchase their new dwelling outright. Unfortunately, affairs on both fronts moved more slowly than anyone had anticipated. Frederick Gilman offered a respectable price for the house in November of 1795, but the sale was not finalized for over a year. And despite his best efforts, Fitz William took forever to settle his father's estate. Over two years after Winthrop, Sr.'s death, matters remained at a standstill. Meanwhile, the Murrays had to borrow £400 from Fitz William just to get by. It was a considerable sum, and John, whom Judith described as "wholly unacquainted with the forms of business," was reluctant to accept the loan. Judith, however, sailed confidently forward. Mr. Gilman would pay for the Gloucester house in due time, she said, and then she would have her "Widow's dowry." Her patrimony would soon follow. She would reimburse her brother in no time.[33]

Instead, the Murrays' finances deteriorated. Their rent rose by twenty pounds a year. The price of Tontine shares also climbed and the Murrays could no longer afford them. It began to appear as though they would have to leave Franklin Place. Judith resolutely looked on the bright side, pretending not to mind that the house she had planned to live in forever would be just "a temporary abode." She had once declared that her home was perfect. Now she complained that it had not been "the plan of the august Architect to fit it up with every convenience." But although she tried to rationalize her predicament, Judith was determined to remain where she was. Matters grew still more complicated in January of 1796, when Charles Bulfinch and William Scollay, the original proprietors of Franklin Place, declared bankruptcy and control of their holdings went directly into the hands of their many creditors. When she first heard the news, Judith assumed that this development had sealed her family's fate. Now they would definitely have to move. Instead, nearly a year and a half later they were still in their house, although Judith noted that the Crescent's finances continued to be "in a confused situation." She and John had two options. They either had to sell their shares in Franklin Place, and "go to board" or they would "take up a sum sufficient to constitute us *full Proprietors* of our house." They decided on the latter course, borrowing the daunting sum of $2,625 from "a widow woman" at 6 percent interest. Judith expected that as soon as her father's estate was settled, they would be able to repay the entire sum. "I have a presentiment," she said, that "we shall go on charmingly."[34] As a child she had watched her father and uncles weather good years and bad. Her first husband, while he died insolvent, had prospered on occasion. She simply could not believe that John Murray's fortunes would never be materially better and might get much worse.

If Judith was optimistic, John was bewildered. He had not expected his marriage to be so expensive. "I had no idea," he confessed, "ever having any children—[Judith] was married sixteen years without children." Moreover, when they wed, he had planned to remain in Gloucester. Thus he assumed he would never want for any of life's material comforts. Instead, he said, "by little and little," he was "drawn into a labyrinth out of which I cannot find my way— my troubles continually increasing." While he loved his wife—"the best woman in this world"—and doted upon his daughter, he groaned when he recalled his once "Independent life." In the spring of 1798, he faced the ultimate indignity, when the Boston proprietors informed him that he was in arrears some $17 for the family pew.[35]

The Murrays cut corners. John reluctantly canceled their subscription to the *Massachusetts Magazine*, citing the "advanced price of the necessaries of life" as his reason. He also sold some of his sermons and pamphlets. Unfortunately, while some people thought his writing did him "much honor," it did not bring in a lot of money. Judith did her part. Domestic help was expensive so she did most of her own housework. She did all the cooking and dressed Julia Maria herself. She also went without a carriage.[36]

* * *

No matter how burdensome her duties as wife and mother, no matter how worried she was about making ends meet, Judith could turn to her writing for solace. "Many an heavy hour have I beguiled at my pen," she wrote Maria. "Writing has been a source, from which I have still derived through the lengthened night of adversity, essential relief." Because she never neglected her domestic duties, she did not feel it "censurable that I have indulged my leisure moments, in thus soothing my feelings." She could always find time to write an odd poem or two and send it on to friends or relatives. Exchanging letters was also comforting and in some ways superior to face-to-face conversations. In writing, she explained, "the mode of communication in its gift is less material—it partakes the nature of spirit." Letters were ideally suited to give friends separated by distance an account of her "mental arrangements, hopes, fears, and prospects." Of course, she chided Esther, letters were not much use if only one party bothered to write. How could you call it a *correspondence* when there was no give and take?[37]

Personal letters were one thing. Writing for the public was something else. Although she was now a published author, Judith remained uncertain about her ability. Still, she viewed the launching of yet another literary magazine with interest. The *Federal Orrery*, appeared in the fall of 1794. Its editor was Robert Treat Paine, a high Federalist, and one of Boston's literary lights. Like all editors, Paine was always on the lookout for original work. He suspected that Judith was the author of "The Gleaner" essays, and thus asked her to submit her work to his magazine. Judith was thrilled with the editor's praise, even as she halfheartedly denied that she was the Gleaner. "Appearances are frequently deceitful," she pointed out. "Similarity of style, hand writing, sentiment, etc. etc. although strong circumstances—ought not to be regarded as proof positive." She made her usual, by now formulaic apologies for her own lack of talent. Thanks to the prejudices of her day, she had a "stunted and circumscribed female education" and her work suffered as a result. Besides, her days were filled with household chores. Still, if she could "*invigorate* the most imbecile mind," and find a "leisure hour" or two, she promised to send her efforts to Paine.[38]

Judith found a leisure hour very quickly. Five days after her letter to Paine, one of her essays appeared in the first issue of the *Federal Orrery*. Taking the name of "The Reaper," she characterized herself as a dilettante who sought recognition, not fortune. Her essays were pithy and generally unexceptional. Most trod well-worn ground. One essay, "Androgeny," described an exemplary young man who possessed "the elegant and mild virtues generally appropriated to the female world, with all the firmness and solidity which are the supposed prerogatives of Manhood." Another gave a concrete example of the virtues of benevolence, with the story of a child named Julia who shamed her mother into giving money to a hapless beggar. One sentence stands out. The Reaper's admonition that the good life avoided extremes and strove for "the calm and happy medium" would be the theme of Judith's first play.[39]

While he favored Philenia over the Reaper, Paine thought Judith had some talent. But if she had become almost resigned to the fact that Sarah Morton would always be more popular than she was, Judith could not tolerate the way Paine edited her work. She was especially irritated when he substituted one word for another after she had taken great pains to select just the right one, even consulting Johnson's dictionary to make sure her choice was appropriate. She had vainly complained of the same high-handed practice to the editors of the *Massachusetts Magazine*. She knew her ability was modest. Still, she had that "decent kind of pride, which will not permit me to array myself—or to submit to be arrayed, in borrowed plumage," and she refused to allow the "changing or curtailing of sentences, or *even words*." She was always a little sensitive to accusations of plagiarism, firmly believing that women were more likely than men to be the target of such charges. She knew that Rousseau once said that "whenever a female draws the pen, it is well known that some Man of letters sits behind the curtain to guide her hand." The Swiss philosopher was not the only "unmannerly Pedant" to make such an assumption, and she was determined that no one would ever be able to say that her work was not her own.[40]

Judith soon severed her connection with the *Orrery*. Desperate as Paine was for submissions, he actually rejected one of her essays—her very best, she thought—out of hand. Perhaps she was not exaggerating when she claimed to lack confidence. One rejection was enough to make her retreat. In the "face of neglect," she told her cousin Epes, she was no longer interested in trying to "preserve my niche in that paper."[41] But Judith had another reason for discontinuing her "Reaper" essays. She was preparing to embark on her most audacious literary project to date. This project, moreover, was designed not just to win her fame. This time she hoped to make money, as well.

The idea had been percolating in her mind at least since the winter of 1790 when she had written prologues and epilogues for the Gloucester thespians. Her ambition had been reinforced when the *Massachusetts Magazine* published her creations. Even so, had she remained in Gloucester, she may never have summoned the nerve to become a playwright. But Franklin Place was within walking distance of the Federal Street Theater, a constant reminder that fame and perhaps fortune awaited those writers who were ambitious and talented enough to write audience-pleasing plays. In the fall of 1795, "Voltaire," writing in the *Columbian Centinel*, complained that the Boston theater only produced English products, observing that "not one original *drama*, possessing the least particle of merit, has yet gratified the taste of a Patriotic people." Surely, thought Judith, she could help turn that dismal picture around. She had already achieved modest success as a poet, essayist, and writer of fiction. Her own letters were lively and amusing, filled with bits of dialogue and little vignettes that never failed to entertain. She knew the rules of drama as well as anyone. Each play had to have its beginning and its "Catastrophe." It had to have five acts, each subdivided into a number of scenes. Shakespeare's example notwithstanding, she would follow Aristotle's rule of the "three unities." Why not, she asked, take the plunge?[42]

There were many reasons to answer that question in the negative. Judith had always been a supporter of the theater. She knew, however, that throughout America, particularly in Massachusetts, many people viewed the dramatic arts as not quite respectable. The state's Puritan roots had a great deal to do with the hostility. But it was more than that. Countless people saw the theater as un-American, a threat to the very values upon which the new nation was erected. Most plays—and most players—were English, after all. Allowing English vice to exist alongside American virtue made no sense. They also saw the theater as an engine of corruption, leading innocent Americans to embrace luxury, idleness, and dissipation, and they were determined not to let any entertainment destroy the innocent republic.[43]

The end of the war did not mean an end of suspicions. Some regions quickly repealed antitheater laws. New York and Providence did so relatively early. Yet Philadelphia's Chestnut Street Theater did not open until 1789, a year before Judith and John's visit to the city, and that victory did not come without a fight. Massachusetts was slower still. In 1785, the legislature actually reenacted its earlier ban, using arguments with which Judith would ordinarily have sympathized. The theater, said its critics, brought lower-class Americans together in one place, undermining their moral character, arousing their passions, and leading them to engage in all sorts of debauchery—drinking, fighting, even prostitution. They spent their time and their money foolishly, thus leading to idleness, extravagance, and ultimately to the poorhouse. To give the theater the state's blessing would be to guarantee the nation's ultimate decay.[44]

Respectable men were hard put to defend the morality of the theater. Respectable women stood on still shakier ground. The theater in the 1790s was, in the words of one historian, "marginal, provincial, and disreputable." And the bawdy women who frequented certain sections, laughing and shouting, displaying their bodies, selling the use of those bodies, simply confirmed the venue's immorality. True, genteel women attended plays, but never in the numbers that men did. Even then, they always came properly escorted and only attended productions that were above reproach. They pretended not to see, or sometimes actually turned their backs on, the rowdy men and women in the gallery or pit. Even so, they were uneasy. Reading a romantic novel in the safety and privacy of one's home was suspect enough. Appearing in public, mingling—however briefly—with the unwashed multitude in an unprotected space, gave the bravest women pause.[45]

Not all Americans saw the dramatic arts in these terms. There were those, especially among the Federalist intelligentsia, who petitioned the Massachusetts legislature as early as 1791, demanding an end to antitheater legislation. Perez and Sarah Morton, took an active part in the fight, as did the *Centinel*'s Benjamin Russell. Far from seeing the theater as the scene of dissipation, Russell referred to it as a "school of virtue," a perspective that Judith adopted in her essay on the subject in "The Gleaner." Indeed, "The Gleaner" number 21, published just after Massachusetts softened its antitheater legislation, was a compendium of the arguments that appeared in the *Centinel* throughout the early 1790s. Judith agreed with those who linked the prohibition of plays with an assault on the right all citizens had to pursue their own version of happiness. Americans had fought a war to combat tyranny. Why, she asked, did the government insist upon regulating the speech and movements of its own people? Moral theater—surely the only kind Massachusetts would tolerate—blended "entertainment with improvement," educating theatergoers, encouraging them to live a virtuous life. Indeed, even acting was a worthy profession.[46]

The struggle to legalize the theater was ultimately successful. Bowing to reality, the legislature arrived at a compromise in 1793, allowing plays in Boston, while continuing to ban them in the rest of the state. The Federal Street Theater, under the management of English actor Charles Stuart Powell, opened on February 3, 1794. The building itself, designed by Bulfinch, was as grand as anything the New World had seen. Constructed entirely of brick, both its front and rear entrances featured imposing Corinthian columns that appealed to the Federal era's propensity for "strict symmetry." The theater's backers certainly wanted members of every class to attend the productions. Indeed, there were those who argued that plays were a force for national unity because they drew inclusive audiences. Still, there was no reason to mix the social orders indiscriminately. Thus, members of the elite were protected from proximity to ordinary citizens. There were separate entrances for those who purchased seats in the pit, the gallery, and the boxes. Proper women could be found only in the boxes. To be sure, respectable patrons could never entirely avoid the antics of the masses. Boys often gathered outside the main entrance, throwing stones, and creating an uproarious scene. Actors and musicians regularly complained about apples and other projectiles flying from the pit. And theatergoers always risked having their possessions stolen by nimble-fingered pickpockets.[47] Still, the managers did their best to assure patrons that their pleasures would not be marred by any unfortunate incident.

When they first entered the theater, most visitors were awestruck. Owners of the delicately painted straw and lilac boxes entered a wide entryway, strolled through a waiting room, and mounted ornate staircases before arriving at their destination. Once seated, they observed the gilded molding, the crimson silk drapery suspended from the second tier of boxes, and the twelve brass chandeliers hanging from the ceiling. The east side of the building boasted a "richly ornamented" dancing room as well as card and tea rooms, and a number of kitchens. The Federal Street Theater had been well worth the wait.[48]

Judith was one of the theater's most avid supporters. Her defense of the dramatic arts appeared in the *Massachusetts Magazine* in February of 1794, perfectly timed to coincide with the opening production, the tragedy *Gustavus Vasa: The Deliverer of His Country*. She was in the packed house the first night, where she pronounced Robert Treat Paine's prologue a triumph. The play itself was "the very soul of valour, benevolence, patriotism, and every shining virtue." Predictably, some critics pronounced the performance amateurish, but Judith attributed their disappointment to impossibly high expectations. In time, she predicted, "the audience will refine the players, and the players will refine the audience." Judith attended as many performances as she could, often sitting with Maria in her box. She sympathized with Romeo and Juliet, those star-crossed lovers who defied their parents' wishes in pursuit of true love. *The School for Scandal* was also superb.[49] But however fine, these productions were imports. Surely, she thought, Boston had room for local talent.

Still, Judith hesitated. She was comfortable writing for the *Massachusetts Magazine*, where her readers were an "invisible public," existing in her own mind. Magazines were expensive, and thus only the best people were likely to sample her essays. Moreover, they did so in the privacy of their own homes. In contrast, the theater was a public venue, where the vulgar as well as the genteel watched as actors and actresses—themselves often exuding a whiff of scandal— gave bodily form to the written word. Moreover, the theater in the eighteenth century was a highly politicized arena, and thus a venue that women entered at some risk. The Federal Street Theater, for instance, was a Federalist stronghold. The Haymarket, erected in 1796, catered to Republicans. To write for either establishment was to make a partisan statement. Even if women could persuade critics that their work had no party message, their plays were, by definition, political. Most of the new nation's playwrights justified their efforts in patriotic terms, framing their plays as part of an attempt to forge a native literary tradition and to offer an American perspective on the world. Women realized that for them, this justification had some potentially undesirable consequences, as it suggested that they were blurring the line between public and private, male and female.[50]

Judith was convinced that the theater was a virtuous entertainment, no matter what naysayers argued, but she was uneasy about writing for profit. There had been a time when she had hesitated to publish her *Catechism*, but at least then monetary reward had not been her object. She had sought influence, not wealth. She characterized herself as a "lady" who entered the public sphere in a disinterested fashion, writing at her leisure, hoping the public would benefit from her moral lessons. In the mid-nineteenth century, a woman could earn money through her writing without losing status. Eighteenth-century women had to defend such activity, often by pointing to the example of their English counterparts. In England, Hannah More's tragedy *Percy* ran twenty-one nights and earned its author £600. Hannah Cowley and Elizabeth Inchbald were also well-known playwrights. There were a few American women dramatists as well. Anna Kemble Hatton, and Susanna Rowson, both English emigrants, wrote successful plays. Still, if women earned money, they had to prove that they *needed* it to support their children, that they were writing as good mothers, not as self-interested professionals. Even then, to sell their words was to sell themselves. They were, like women who were members of the oldest profession, tainted by their interaction with strangers who paid for their services.[51]

Because Judith hesitated to write "with *pecuniary* views," she fell back on traditional justifications for her decision. She had ambitious plans for Julia Maria's education and thought this was the best, perhaps the only "reputable way" to guarantee her daughter's prospects. John must have shared her misgivings. Years after his wife's plays appeared, although he knew better, he was telling friends that Judith "never will, I am persuaded, write for the stage." She only wrote plays for children to read, he insisted, hoping that young minds, bored by the essays of Addison and Steele, would profit from moral lessons that came in a more palatable form.[52]

Judith guarded her respectability in another way. She refused to appear on stage, even to deliver an epilogue or prologue. She would not imitate the example of America's most successful woman playwright, Susanna Rowson. In many respects, Susanna and Judith had similar stories. Both married unsuccessful businessmen. Both took the egalitarian rhetoric of the American Revolution seriously and applied it to women. Both had an abiding interest in improving women's education. But Susanna's plays, especially *Slaves in Algiers*, were more frankly feminist than Judith's were. Rowson created strong women characters who were brave, intelligent, and actively defended themselves and their rights. Her plays were also unabashedly political. Because she contended that America was a "state of mind" and that anyone could declare allegiance to the country's values, she insisted that foreigners as well as native-born Americans, women as well as men, could be citizens.[53]

While Judith Murray tried to conceal her very identity from the public and never appeared on stage, Susanna Rowson was an actress before she was a playwright. Rowson wanted literally to move herself and other women onto the public stage. This was a dangerous game, one Judith had no desire to play. To display her body before a mixed audience would be to call attention to her sexual nature, to become an object of male fantasy, allowing *herself*—as opposed to her *mind*—to be judged. This was something she could not imagine doing. She had no difficulty in engaging in the "disembodied business of writing." But when she did so, in "The Gleaner" and in her plays, she wore a disguise. She wanted people to appraise her words, not herself.[54]

Judith entered her career as a playwright with high hopes. However suspect, the theater remained one of a limited number of venues for women who wanted to earn a measure of financial independence. Even if their plays were not critical triumphs, writers could earn money by publishing their work, reaching a wider—perhaps a more genteel—audience. True enough, most American playwrights—men and women alike—did not earn a living writing on the stage.[55] But Judith thought that if Boston audiences seriously wanted to promote native talent, she might succeed where others had failed.

On February 26, 1795, the *Federal Orrery* announced that a new comedy, *The Medium, or Happy Tea-Party*, written by a "Citizen of the United States," would be performed at the Federal Street Theater on March 2. As she had done when she published "The Gleaner," Judith submitted her play under a pseudonym that implied male authorship. Most, if not all women playwrights used their own names. But as the wife of Boston's Universalist minister, Judith had to be especially careful. John's detractors had often accused him of delivering sermons that were too theatrical. There was no point in giving critics more ammunition. Thus both John and Judith were distressed when they opened the *Orrery* on March 2. An anonymous observer proclaimed that the evening's play was "the joint production of Mr. and Mrs. Murray." Two days later, John moved to minimize any damage to his reputation, firmly disassociating himself from the play. In a statement to the *Columbian Centinel* he solemnly declared that he never saw a "single sentence, line, or *even word* of the comedy" until it was performed.[56]

Judith was already nervous. The statement in the *Orrery* added to her anxiety. Still, she entered the Federal Street Theater a little before 6:00 p.m. with hope as well as trepidation. The theater's manager, Charles Powell, had assured her that *The Medium* was sure to please. Admittedly, he had rushed the play forward with what Judith thought was "more *dispatch* than *providence*," giving the second-rate cast little time to rehearse. Still, all American productions at the time were slapped together without much preparation. Judith breathed a little easier when the first act received "uncommon applause." Then everything fell apart. One actress forgot her lines, burst into tears, and fled the stage. The rest of the cast barely "hobbled through." It was, if not an unmitigated disaster, a huge disappointment. Powell offered to give the play a second chance, but Judith, humiliated, declined.[57]

Only one person defended *The Medium* in public. On March 11, "Candour" wrote to the *Centinel* asking why the play had not received a second showing, suggesting that Powell was prejudiced against American authors. The "*imperfection* of the performers," he said, did not give it a real chance. It had, he insisted, "all the features of a regular play." The plot was "well laid and interesting." While some of the speeches were a bit long, more suited to the printed page than to the stage, Candour remained convinced of *The Medium*'s merits.[58]

Judith was gratified by her supporter's kind words, but she conceded that her play had not been well received.[59] Even her own relatives were not unstinting in their praise. Winthrop, thin-skinned as always, took umbrage at the character of Captain Flashet, a former soldier whose foppish behavior and laughable pretensions to erudition were intended as comic relief. Judith was taken aback by her brother's reaction. She had used Flashet merely to poke fun at those who *pretended* to valor. Moreover, two of her characters heaped praises on America's true military heroes. Still, she promised never again to treat any soldier so cavalierly. Epes, too, had a few criticisms, most of which Judith thought had some merit. She conceded that some of her "low scenes" were too long. She had lengthened them, she explained, upon the advice of a "*literary* friend" who thought they might please her audience. But Epes was right. Whenever authors strove for effect they ended up adopting "a kind of humour which their judgment cannot approve." Still, when male writers stooped to such techniques, they were praised. Women did not enjoy this luxury.[60]

Amazingly, Judith was undeterred by the embarrassment her play caused John or by the tepid critical response *The Medium* garnered. She convinced herself that the production's reception did not reflect her drama's quality. Like many American playwrights, she blamed the actors for the cloud that hovered over the play. She was also convinced that prejudiced theater managers did their best to "suppress American performances." And besides, everyone knew that a prophet was without honor in his own country. Although she had yet to receive any reward for her efforts except for the use of a box at the Federal Street Theater, Judith moved confidently on a number of fronts.[61]

First, she wrote to Sally Bache, Benjamin Franklin's daughter, hoping to enlist her as the *Medium*'s "protectress." She had met Sally only once and was not even sure that the Philadelphia matriarch would remember her. But surely, she thought, John Murray's name would ring a bell. Judith wanted the Chestnut Street Theater to produce her play. To make sure that audiences would not reject her effort out of hand because of its failure in Boston, she rewrote some of it and changed its title, calling it *Virtue Triumphant*. As usual, she felt compelled to defend her project. "I am free to own," she wrote Bache, "that my *first object as a writer is fame*." Still, because her daughter's education hung in the balance, it was her duty to contribute what she could to the family's coffers. For now she would remain anonymous. If the play was a success, however, she would reveal her identity. She still hoped to "command that celebrity" for which she had "ever been ambitious."[62]

Judith revealed a sophisticated knowledge of what she might expect if her plan succeeded. In England, all proceeds of plays performed on the third, sixth, and twenty-first nights went to the author. Real money, however, came at the end of the season, when plays for the benefit of the actors, the manager, and popular authors were performed. She was willing to accept less generous terms. "America is in its infancy," she admitted, "and the present is by no means the Augustan age of the New World." Thus she would be content—at least for the moment—with modest profits. If *The Medium* was well received, it might create a demand for American drama throughout the land. This would inevitably "open a way to future pecuniary emoluments as well as fame."[63]

Judith's aspirations far outstripped her ability. When Sally Bache did not reply to her request, she enlisted the services of other friends in Philadelphia. She also asked Winthrop, who was in the city lobbying Congress, to visit the Bache residence on her behalf. He did his best, but Sally either would not or could not persuade the managers of the Chestnut Street Theater to give *The Medium* a chance. By May of 1796, Judith admitted defeat. Still, she knew that people like Mercy Otis Warren often published plays that were never performed. Perhaps this would be her best strategy.[64]

Even as she tried to salvage something from her first effort, Judith was hard at work on a second, *The Traveller Returned*. Just two months after the disappointing performance of *The Medium*, Judith sent her manuscript to Charles Powell. "Strange as it may seem," she told him, "my efforts are rather excited than depressed." At least her play had reached the Boston stage, an achievement no other American-born woman could claim. Moreover, it had earned a modicum of praise. Judith was determined to give the *Traveller* a chance to succeed. She had lost control of her first production; she would not do so again. Thus she gave Powell explicit instructions about the way to proceed.[65]

First, if he thought the play was too long, she had marked specific passages for him to cut. If he liked it, she wanted him to take the *Traveller* to Newport, where no one was familiar with her handwriting. There he could pay someone to copy the manuscript. All rehearsals were to be in Newport, and the play had to be performed there at least once, thus assuring her that the actors would know their lines perfectly before they came to Boston. Finally, she hoped that *The Traveller* would open the Federal Street Theater's season. She thought it was sound strategy to show "indifferent pieces" early, when people were eager for any entertainment and were in a less critical frame of mind than they might be later on. Moreover, she was sure that no one would suspect that Powell had chosen to begin the year with a play by Judith Sargent Murray. Once *The Traveller* arrived in Boston, Powell would have to submit it to the censors, who vetted all new plays for violations of moral standards. When you give them the play, Judith admonished, make sure that it is not one in "*my hand writing on any consideration.*" Nor did she want him even to hint that the play was an American production.[66]

Charles Powell accepted Judith's play, even agreeing to her conditions. At first everything went smoothly. But just as the play went into rehearsal, disaster struck. Powell was not an especially capable manager. Rumors that he was incompetent, deceitful, and had lost complete control of his own actors had floated around Boston for some time. Forced to work with second-rate thespians, dogged by criticisms that as an Englishman he never quite understood American sensibilities, and faced with the reality that Boston did not have the large audience base that other cities did, he always lost money. In June of 1795, he was fired, replaced in September by Bostonian John S. Tyler. Powell was "totally deranged" by his ouster. He left Newport, his company dispersed, and Judith's hopes were "entirely lost." When the Federal Street Theater opened in November, it was an English comedy, not *The Traveller Returned*, that welcomed Bostonians to the third season.[67]

Not knowing how to proceed, Judith reluctantly confided in John, who read the play and pronounced it perfect. Forgetting his discomfort when his name had been linked to *The Medium*, he urged his wife to seek the influence of the Mortons. They eventually persuaded Tyler to give the play a chance. As the time for the production loomed nearer, Judith shared her "secret" with more and more people. She asked Epes for his criticisms. Her sister Esther and her sister-in-law Anna both knew all about it. No doubt their husbands were aware of her plans as well. She did not, however, consult Maria, who complained bitterly when she realized that she was excluded from Judith's "select party of friends."[68]

Throughout the early spring of 1796, Judith was alternatively hopeful and panic stricken. Although Tyler had hired New York professionals for the Federal Street Theater's third season, the New Yorkers left town early. Once again her fate was in the hands of inferior actors. "The indifferent opinion which the Town entertained of the remaining performers," Judith said, "operated against the piece," and she tried to persuade Tyler to postpone the production. But the manager had already gone to some expense on her behalf, and the theater's patrons were expecting to see her play. Moreover, prices in Boston were escalating daily, and the Murrays needed the money. Money "as an object in literary productions, is sanctioned by the example even of persons possessing comparative affluence," Judith told her skeptical sister. So long as she earned her reward in a *"reputable"* way, she intended to supplement the paltry stipend upon which her family existed. Thus, when the *Orrery* "prematurely advertised it,"she allowed Tyler to proceed.[69]

Two days before *The Traveller Returned* was slated to appear, Robert Treat Paine, a passionate supporter of the theater, visited 5 Franklin Place. Judith shared her anxieties with the *Orrery*'s influential editor. If, she confided, Boston's Universalists ever suspected that John had written a play, it would "totally ruin his interest among them." Paine's reply was noncommittal, but Judith was convinced that he "well knew from whence the production proceeded." She also believed that he valued her friendship. He was a fellow Federalist. She had often praised his poetry. She had submitted her "Reaper" essays to the *Federal Orrery* at his invitation. She had no reason to suspect that he bore her ill will.[70]

On March 9, Judith once again sat in her box at the Federal Street Theater, anxious, excited, and hoping for the best. The building had been virtually empty since the New York players had left. This night, however, it was filled nearly to capacity. To her relief, the actors did an excellent job. Even more gratifying, the audience seemed to love her play. She blushed with pleasure when the actors were interrupted time and again not just with applause but "loud huzzas." Elated by the apparent success of *The Traveller*, Tyler announced that it would be performed the very next night. Unfortunately, March 10 was not a usual "play evening." Many Bostonians were confused about the starting time. Others had already made plans. Still, attendance was acceptable, and Tyler gave the play "unequivocal marks of approbation." He promised Judith the all important third performance, the proceeds of which would go to her.[71]

Four days after the second performance, the *Orrery*'s "Thespiad"—Paine's pen name—reviewed *The Traveller*, damning it with the faintest of praise. Because it was a homegrown production, he said, it was very well received. The actors performed admirably. The author had modest "dramatic talent" and wrote "many good scenes." As a whole, however, the play was tedious, solemn, pedantic, and substituted "broad humor for wit, and dulness for pathos." The soliloquies needed "a prudent use of the pruning knife." Finally, while American audiences loved patriotic plays, it was possible to overdo a good thing. Stung by criticism from someone she had counted as an ally, Judith wrote to Paine, defending her play. Ignoring her request for confidentiality, Paine published her letter on March 17. Two days later, "Fair Play," writing to the *Columbian Centinel*, answered Thespiad's criticisms in a point by point rebuttal, pronouncing the *Orrery*'s criticisms puzzling and "invidious."[72]

Robert Paine never allowed anyone to question his critical taste. He struck back almost immediately. His first critique of *The Traveller*, he said, was "too lenient." In fact, the public had "universally condemned" the play. It had no "interest, plot, sentiment, or humor." It was "insipid" and moralistic. Nor did the playwright possess any talent. The play was clotted with "turgid phrases," "filched ribaldry," and "forced conceits."[73]

Fair Play replied to Paine's vicious critique, asking with stinging sarcasm, "Has the Traveller Return'd met with *too much success*? Or what has so deeply wounded your feelings?" Three days later, Paine turned his attack on John Murray—or "parson Flummery" as he called him. Murray and Fair Play, he proclaimed, were one and the same. Taking advantage of John's reputation for theatricality, he claimed that when the minister had brought Fair Play's defense to the *Centinel* office, he had read it aloud "before strangers and apprentices, with all that antic grimace, for which it is reported, you were so famous, as a strolling player in Ireland." Paine mocked John's "ungovernable appetite for dramatic form" and his willingness to appeal to all classes with his "SMOOTH CONFECTIONARY STYLE." Most troubling, he hinted that John was the author of *The Traveller Returned*. Once more, John Murray had to defend himself in public. Writing to the *Columbian Centinel* he insisted that he was not Fair Play nor had he written so much as a line of *The Traveller* or any other play. Granted, he thought the production deserved its "general bursts of applause." And he did not "consider it dishonest or dishonorable to appear on the stage." Still, Thespiad needed to check his facts before rushing to print.[74]

Judith was crushed. Instead of receiving adulation, she had drawn herself and John into a demeaning newspaper war. Under the circumstances, she vowed to reject a third showing of *The Traveller Returned*. Even so, the Murrays' battle

with Robert Paine continued. In April, when Paine saw husband and wife standing in front of their house, he accosted them "in a very insulting way," darkly
predicting that John would soon meet with bodily harm. John, oblivious to
Paine's threats, went about his business in his usual carefree fashion. But Judith
sitting at home with Julia Maria—who picked this moment to contract the
measles—let her all too active imagination get the best of her. A few days after
his confrontation with Paine, John left Franklin Place early in the morning,
promising to return shortly. Instead, he was waylaid. When he had failed to return by midnight, Judith was frantic. She set out alone to look for him, half expecting to come upon her husband's lifeless body slumped in an alley. Instead,
she ran into him as he was strolling leisurely toward Franklin Place. As always,
he was cheerful and bemused by her fright. Still, she was convinced that Paine
was a man whose enmity could not be taken lightly. It was no wonder, she
thought, that while many people praised her play privately, no one had the
courage to "produce for the *public prints, a Candid Critique*."[75]

Not only was Judith wounded and frightened by Paine's behavior, she was
bewildered as well. She simply could not account for the "illiberal abuse which
has so copiously proceeded" from Thespiad's pen. Moreover, she said in an obvious understatement, she was not in the habit of ignoring "the opinion of the
world." Among people who knew her, she had a reputation that was above reproach. Indeed, she had heard that many gentlemen in the city—men who were
not especially supportive of John and who did not know her at all—were so disgusted by "the inhuman malice of the Man" that they were determined to have
nothing more to do with Paine. But none of this did her much good. Even
though she firmly believed that she was the injured party in the entire affair, she
knew that the *Orrery* had a wide readership. Complete strangers would read
Paine's critique and be convinced that he was right.[76]

Judith never knew what she had done to incur Paine's animus. Granted, her
critic was more sympathetic to American plays than he was to English imports.
And some of her friends suspected that he was a frustrated playwright who envied *The Traveller*'s success. Judith refused to believe that this was the case, but
had no explanation that made any more sense. Indeed, she had some reason to
be puzzled. Thespiad attacked other performances at the Federal Street Theater,
but he generally criticized the actors rather than the plays.[77] Nor were his cri-
tiques usually quite so venomous.

Still, no matter why Paine was so disdainful of Judith's plays, one fact remains: he was not unduly harsh. A more confident playwright would have ignored the *Orrery*'s editor altogether. Again, the contrast with Susannah
Rowson's experience is instructive. In 1795, Federalist William Cobbett, writing

under the name "Peter Porcupine," leveled a scurrilous assault on both *Slaves in Algiers* and its author. Cobbett's misogynist screed went for the jugular, as he vilified not just Rowson but that "whole tribe of female scribblers and politicians" whose determination to write for money led to the desecration of all women. Compared to this outburst, Paine's criticism was tame stuff, indeed. Moreover, as any experienced author knows, a little publicity is never a bad thing. Rowson shrugged off Cobbett's attacks. Some of her admirers leapt to her defense. And her play drew bigger audiences as people came to see what the fuss was all about. Admittedly, Susanna needed money more than Judith did. She could not afford to be too sensitive. Nor was she inhibited by pretensions to gentility as Judith was. Moreover, Judith was especially hurt because, as a Federalist, Payne was one of her own. He shared her values and did not, as "Porcupine" did, believe that women had no place in the public sphere. Still, she probably should have heeded the words of one of her characters in *The Traveller Returned*. Harriot Montague insisted that she would "rather be paragraphed in a newspaper, than not distinguished at all." Even a vicious attack would prove that she had once existed.[78]

Neither *The Medium*—or *Virtue Triumphant* as Judith ultimately called it—nor *The Traveller Returned* were unusually bad or especially good. Historian George Seilhamer attributed Judith's first play to Royall Tyler, a compliment of sorts. But most modern critics would probably agree with Zoe Detsi-Diamanti's assessment of *Virtue Triumphant* as "stilted and dull." *The Traveller* was only marginally better. Both plays were derivative, filled with humorous stock characters and trite plotlines. Still, Judith's depiction of women was largely her own.[79] And *Virtue Triumphant*, in particular, reflected an interestingly ambivalent attitude toward both marriage and class to which Judith did not usually admit.

The male heroes in both dramas are conventional, one-dimensional, and virtuous to a fault. In *Virtue Triumphant*, Charles Maitland is a cardboard representation of ideal manhood. He is brave, graceful, sympathetic, and sensitive, combining the best attributes of "masculine" and "feminine" virtues. Similarly, *The Traveller*'s Mr. Rambleton is steady, courageous, and willing to sacrifice his all for family and country. Major Camden, his son, gives up a promising merchant career to serve in the Continental army. He is serious, too serious for his intended, Harriot Montague. He even has doubts about the value of romance, claiming that love of country is superior to love for any woman. His feelings for Emily Lovegrove, the true object of his affections, are more rational than passionate, based on the confluence of compatible minds, not sexual attraction.[80]

Judith's female characters are far more interesting than her men, and less conventional than the Gleaner's treatment of women in the Margaretta story. The heroines of both plays are orphans who are virtuous, modest, and self-possessed. Unlike either Margaretta or the unfortunate Frances Wellwood, however, their education has given them the strength to protect their own virtue and remain independent. No one helps either Eliza Clairville of *Virtue Triumphant* or Emily Lovegrove of *The Traveller* conduct courtships that end in marriage on their own terms. Eliza, in particular, knows her own mind and makes her own decisions. Emily is more passive, but—unlike Margaretta—she is able to recognize and reject an immoral choice.[81]

Both plays have their stock female characters, in particular, their stereotypical coquettes who spend each day in a round of "shop-hunting, visiting, cards, balls" and the mindless pursuit of fashion. But *Virtue Triumphant* also has its male counterpart to the coquette in Flashet, the "harmless flutterer" to whom Winthrop had so strenuously objected. More important, if Emily and Eliza are such paragons of virtue that they are ultimately uninteresting, Judith's other characters challenge the gender status quo. Matronia Aimwell, in *Virtue Triumphant*, is the aunt and guardian of Eliza's friend, Augusta Bloomville. Matronia has never married and is in fact the independent woman that Judith admires but never manages to emulate. Unlike the play's circumspect heroine, who shrinks from mingling in "promiscuous company," Matronia is active and powerful. She walks alone through town. Instead of waiting demurely in her own parlor, hoping for the assistance of a noble benefactor, she calls on widower Ralph Maitland, Charles's father, entering his parlor and penetrating his space. Although she knows that "custom hath in some sort interdicted my sex" from conducting financial affairs, she disregards the artificial strictures designed to keep her in her place, borrowing and investing money with ease. Not only is she a competent businessperson, but she is "*more than parent*" to her niece. This spinster reflects Judith's belief that women need not have children of their own to practice their most important profession. Matronia, like Mary Vigillius, is a true "republican mother." But unlike Mary, she is independent as well.[82]

Both plays have their versions of the reformed—female—rake. Theatergoers were used to seeing such characters. But they were, like "The Gleaner's" Sinisterus Courtland, almost always men. Augusta Bloomville appears at first to be little more than a thoughtless coquette. She spends her husband's money with abandon and flits from one meaningless party to another. Still, we are told, she has "innate rectitude." She flirts, but she is never promiscuous. Moreover, she has the good sense to see the virtuous Eliza as a role model. In the end, Matronia helps Augusta mend her evil ways, leading her to become a good and obedient, if not a loving, wife. Like Augusta *The Traveller*'s Mrs. Montague did not

love her husband when she married him. She, too, "engaged in a round of dissipation," and sought the attention of a man who was obviously her husband's
inferior. Her affair, which she later describes as "indiscreet" but not "criminal,"
drove her husband away. Mrs. Montague, too, learns from her mistakes, repudi-
ating her lover and embracing "a life of solitude," determined to atone for her
sins. Even then, she rejects the life of a typical matron. She does not knit or
weave or sew. She reads philosophy and natural science, not frivolous romances.
She is not especially interested in domestic matters, supervising her servants in
a vague, distracted manner. Still, she is a conscientious mother. Above all, unlike
most fallen women in the eighteenth century, she does not lose her status because of her youthful indiscretion. Her experience brings to mind Frances Wellwood in the Margaretta story, not Clarissa Harlowe or Charlotte Temple.[83]

The Traveller's Harriot Montague is arguably the least stereotypical of Judith's creations. Like an airy-headed coquette, she loves fashionable clothes,
adores "society," and refers to her morally superior cousin as a "plodding, sentimental girl." She follows her heart, deceiving her mother and conducting a clan-
destine courtship with Alberto Stanhope. "That I am not, strictly speaking,
within the line of discretion," she says, "I am fully sensible." Still, Harriot has her
admirable qualities. She leads an active life, enjoying her "divine rambles" and
insisting that "exercise is necessary for girls." While she is flirtatious, she is not
immoral. Moreover, while casual observers might see her as frivolous she does
have her "moments of reflection."[84]

As in all sentimental comedies of the period, both plays end with the marriage of the hero and heroine. Yet neither presents marriage as inevitably happy.
As Judith had reminded Winthrop, "the days of wedded life are not all halcyon."
Married or single, all people would discover that "the rose invariably connects a
thorn." Significantly, the one marriage actually depicted in *Virtue Triumphant* is
a troubled one. Augusta married for all the wrong reasons, to follow "the fashion" and because so many other women saw her suitor as a good catch. Matronia's advice to her niece is stern and prosaic. Augusta must relinquish her
romantic notions and make her husband's happiness her life's work. Augusta is
probably not made for the "ungovernable ardours of impetuous love." And that
is just as well. Passion was a despot, and it never lasted in any event. Mrs. Montague echoes Matronia's advice, insisting that love is a "*chimera*" and that the
"passions should always be under the government of reason." Still, the plays
imply that women were wise to hold out for more than esteem. Eliza and
Charles are soul mates who fall in love at first sight.[85] Emily and Harriot
demand—and get—more from marriage than friendship. Reason is fine; but
love is better. It is possible for a marriage built on respect alone to survive. Such

a marriage requires real effort, however, and a union that has affection at its core is more likely to succeed.

Both plays remind audiences that settling for less is not always necessary or even desirable. Although she is single, Matronia's life is complete. She has friends, independence, even power. She is never pitiable. The redoubtable Eliza, too, has learned to "reverence herself." For her, a loveless marriage or one that denies a wife true equality is far worse than virtuous spinsterhood. "There are," she insists, "*joys* and *sorrows* peculiar to every situation in life." And while Harriot loves Alberto, she nevertheless thinks she might never marry. If she does, she plans to postpone such a happy event to a "distant day."[86]

Judith's depiction of marriage as both an attractive and a suspect institution is not out of character. But her ambiguous treatment of class, especially in *Virtue Triumphant*, is intriguing. Both plays depict stereotypical servants who are irrelevant to the plot, existing only for comic effect. They are obviously inferior to their masters. Somehow one suspects that even if they learn to speak without mangling the English language, they will remain outside the bounds of polite society. Mr. Rambleton's landlord and landlady, the villainous Vansittarts, Dutch parvenus in *The Traveller Returned*, surely prove just that. Dorothy vainly aspires to be "jonteel."[87] She is not only a social climber but a shrewish wife, who browbeats her hapless and helpless husband and violates both gender and class conventions. Still, if some of her characters can never transcend their station, Judith creates others whose message is more than a little muddled.

Central to *Virtue Triumphant* is Eliza's erroneous belief that she is the child of destitute parents. Thus she refuses to marry the well-connected Charles Maitland. "I *never, but on equal terms*, will plight my faith with yours," she tells him.[88] "Subordination, rank and degree," she adds, in words that Judith uttered on many occasions, "are of divine original; the lines are justly drawn; and he who breaks the rank assigned him by his Creator, is surely an aggressor." When Augusta gently chides her friend for placing too much value on money, Eliza disagrees. She is only recognizing reality. "I do but submit," she says, "to a necessity which the *despot, Custom, hath rendered irreversible*." In the end, Eliza discovers that she is not only wealthy, but she is of noble birth. She is actually superior to the besotted Charles. Her friends are not completely surprised by this revelation. They have already observed that she is formed to give rather than receive commands.[89] True class, it seems, cannot be disguised. Apparently it cannot be *earned* either. Eliza's character does not change with her knowledge of her noble birth. Yet character alone has not made her comfortable as a member of polite society.

Questions about *Virtue Triumphant*'s rendition of social class abound. Is

Eliza's superiority the product of an excellent education, and thus open to anyone? Or does her nobility enable her to take advantage of that education, giving her the moral strength she would have exhibited under any circumstance? If "subordination, rank and degree" are of "divine" origin, then what are we to do with the depiction of the well-born Dorinda Scornwell? Dorinda is snobbish and supercilious. She refers to the "dirt-sprung Eliza" as "a kind of upper servant," not fit for polite society.[90] She demands—as Eliza apparently does as well—that all people, especially servants, remain firmly in their place. Her behavior reveals her moral defects, and the audience is happy that she gets her due in the end. Still, the play ends on a conflicted—if happy—note. Viewers do not know whether to condone Eliza's original refusal to marry Charles. Nor are they sure if "despotic custom" should be obeyed or ignored.

Unlike Susanna Rowson's *Slaves in Algiers*, neither *Virtue Triumphant* nor *The Traveller Returned* overtly sounds a call for women's political rights. The unsympathetic Dorothy Vansittart is the only woman in either play to utter a political statement, when she argues that "the goods of a tory are free to plunder!" No other female character seems even vaguely interested in public affairs. Still, both plays feature rational, independent, and active women who possess all the qualities of men who are full members of the body politic. If they do not engage in politics narrowly defined, they have the capacity to do so. They are, moreover, free to demand the fruits of the American Revolution, to imagine a better life, and to pursue their own version of happiness. And, as the characters of both Augusta and Mrs. Montague indicate, these are women who reflect the American belief in the ability of all people to learn from their mistakes and to improve themselves. For Judith Sargent Murray, women as well as men can correct their errata.[91]

Despite the embarrassment she suffered as a result of the newspaper controversy over the *The Traveller Returned*, Judith allowed the Federal Street Theater to put on her second play one last time, asking that the proceeds go to the benefit of the poor. By now, everyone knew that Judith was the play's creator. Thus, she wrote an "apology for the author" to be delivered by Mrs. Snelling Powell before the play began. It defended her desire "to seek an honest fame." It also hinted that her critics were so vicious because she was a woman, as it proclaimed explicitly what her plays had only implied: women were men's intellectual equals. If their talents fell a little short, their inferior education, not their innate character, was to blame:

Who would not tolerate a female pen?
Women, perhaps, were born a match for men:
But natal rights by education crampt,

The sex's inequality is stampt.
Yet sure in this celebrious age design'd,
To crown the struggles of the opening mind,
To equal efforts you will point the way,
Nor e'en the emulative wish betray.

But if the "apology" was a forthright plea for women's equality, it ended in a darker tone. Judith claimed that she had only "aim'd to please." Encouraged by the praises her work had received over the years, she had tried to stretch her wings only to see her hopes dashed by a narrow-minded critic. Her play had been destroyed, her ambitions were dead, "beyond resuscitation." Only public encouragement would give her the courage to make another attempt at the dramatic arts. Nearly two years later, Judith remained haunted by her humiliation. Sounding like the determinedly confident and optimistic Harriot, she claimed that Paine was ultimately harmed more by his attack than she was. Still, she admitted, "the conclusion which forces itself upon me, is not in favour of a perseverance in the dramatic line—it is a road infested with thorns." She would have to be "renovated by the genial rays of unequivocal encouragement" before she would risk any more embarrassment.[92] Unfortunately, that encouragement failed to materialize.

If Judith chose to end her career as a playwright, she did not—as she later claimed—accept "obscurity." At least not yet. She could not deny her ambitions.[93] Nor could she deny her family's need for money. Boston was not prepared to recognize her dramatic talents. But even Paine did not deny her ability as a poet and essayist. "The Gleaner" had been well received. Perhaps she could capitalize on its popularity. She could put her essays between the solid covers of a book, add a few more to fill out the collection, and sell them throughout the United States. It would be easy. Done right, it would win her fame as well as fortune, for she would not hide her identity on this occasion. After her very public war of words with Robert Paine, there was no point in dissimulating any longer.

Chapter 10
Federalist Muse

There was a time when Judith Sargent Murray's fame—such as it was—derived almost completely from *The Gleaner*, her three-volume "miscellany" published in 1798. Scholars throughout most of the twentieth century believed that Judith's precious letter books were not only illegible, but that they had also disappeared from view. A few historians were impressed by her entries in the *Massachusetts Magazine* or the *Gentleman and Lady's Town and Country Magazine*, duly observing that their author must have been an extraordinary woman who, more than most of her American contemporaries, demanded intellectual equality for "the sex." Focusing on *The Gleaner*'s four-part "Observations on Female Abilities," they pronounced Murray the "chief theorist of republican womanhood," an "advanced thinker," and one of the "central architects of the new female ideology" of the post-Revolutionary world.[1]

Judith would not have been displeased by such comments. She longed for recognition for her entire corpus, but she harbored particularly high hopes for *The Gleaner*. She began to consider publishing her opus as early as the spring of 1796, having reluctantly conceded that her plays would bring her neither money nor renown. Still, the response to her anonymous "Gleaner" essays had been sufficiently positive to persuade her that "fame and fortune" might yet be hers. She also considered publishing her private letters if her book was well received. She did not think it appropriate for just anyone to share her personal correspondence with the public. A book of letters had to be "preceded by a production which may announce and give a degree of eclat, or importance, to the Author," she said. Judith hoped that where her essays and plays had failed to give her that importance, *The Gleaner* would succeed.[2]

From the beginning, John saw his wife's project as a moneymaking venture. Judith had always been a prodigious writer, he explained to his English friend Robert Redding. However, he added—conveniently forgetting her brief career as a playwright—she had never sought to profit from her talent. They had both come to the conclusion that while John's salary covered their barest expenses, they would not be able to put money aside if they relied on his earnings alone. John was ten years older than Judith, and he would probably die first. Fearing that his little family would be thrown on the mercies of "an unfeeling world" upon his death, he had encouraged Judith to "make this trial."[3]

While she did not disdain money, Judith was always more interested in fame than profit. Her aspirations were lofty, but not necessarily far-fetched. America was still in its infancy. It remained something of a blank tablet whose culture lay waiting to be shaped by a generation of writers who could influence the country's character now and in the future. With the Constitution written, the new government a reality, the economy growing, America's intellectual and material resources seemed ripe for exploitation. Yet with opportunity came peril. Growing partisan conflict, international tensions, and the untested and tenuous nature of all American institutions magnified the importance of every misstep, every controversy. In such an atmosphere, writers understandably believed that the country's very survival was at stake and that their work would define America's character for generations to come. What people *did* or *said* mattered in the short run. What they *wrote* might last forever.

Judith was well aware of the significance of her decision to publish *The Gleaner*. Books were less ephemeral than pamphlets, magazines, or plays. They suggested a certain seriousness and an element of authority with which less weighty efforts could not compete. That very seriousness, their relative permanence, required even more caution than usual. Judith was always tentative and a little insecure when she sent her essays and poems off to her publishers. But never had she exhibited the painstaking attention to detail that she lavished upon *The Gleaner*. This time she made no attempt to hide her identity. To hope for fame while wearing a mask was, she admitted, counterproductive. But with no disguise to protect her, she was laying herself open to an entirely new level of public scrutiny.[4]

Judith's fear of critical failure was genuine. Thus she made every effort to ward off her critics. She had been humiliated by Robert Treat Paine's criticism of her plays. Another, more recent, incident also rankled. Sometime between December and April of 1794, one of the *Massachusetts Magazine*'s readers made Judith the object of "a *serious accusation*," a charge that so upset her that she abruptly stopped writing for the publication. She had assumed that was the end of the matter. Two years later, when she opened an out-of-date copy of the *Massachusetts Magazine*, she was stunned by a reference to her original "Gleaner" essays in a section editor Thaddeus Harris customarily used to communicate with his contributors. Harris announced that he would not print "the strictures of *Impartialis* on the *Gleaner*," but he did not deny their validity. He had simply decided that he was unwilling "to commence a needless controversy, and thus perhaps renew prejudices which are forgotten, or reprobe a closing wound."[5]

In Judith's estimation, Harris's comment had done as much to "reprobe" the wound as a publication of Impartialis's denunciation would have done. She was convinced that Paine was her accuser. Worse, she predicted that he would "probably again point the arrow at my breast." He was not an enemy to be taken lightly. His literary reputation was growing, and most observers thought his work was destined for immortality. Judith wanted to use *The Gleaner* to present her side of their ongoing quarrel. Thus, she decided to include revised editions of her two plays, accompanied by some of the letters from Paine concerning her comedies in the third volume of her opus. She had already composed an essay that put the letters in what she characterized as a proper context. Indeed, she hinted that this, even more than her desire for fame or profit, was her underlying reason for publishing *The Gleaner*. Both John—who seldom criticized his wife for anything—and Epes begged her to reconsider, arguing that printing Paine's letters would only revive a quarrel long since forgotten by everyone. Judith reluctantly deferred to their wisdom, but she was never happy with her decision. Perhaps, she conceded, the public no longer cared about this incident. She, however, did.[6]

*   *   *

Had she known how difficult it would be to publish her three-volume miscellany, Judith may never have embarked upon her project. She would have "*written*," she said, but "I should nevertheless have hesitated much longer before I had *published*, a book." Writing was the easy part. Selling and distributing the book was an arduous undertaking. A mass audience for American productions simply did not exist in the late eighteenth century, nor did the nation boast anything akin to an efficient distribution system. No printer, even if he was dedicated to promoting native writers, would risk his livelihood on a book that might not sell. Thus authors had to fund their own efforts. Unless they were independently wealthy, they were forced to distribute subscriptions to friends, relatives, and strangers before printing could begin. Not surprisingly, American writers tended to idealize the practice of the past, when aristocratic authors were dilettantes and starving artists relied on the support of well-heeled patrons. To deal with the grubby details of the mundane business world was a bit degrading for a man and much more so for a woman.[7] Still, while the process of obtaining subscriptions was arguably more democratic than the old patronage system, it was more genteel than the devices some authors employed. Advertising in the newspapers or asking peddlers to sell their work to nameless customers in the countryside might be effective. But securing subscriptions, however distasteful the task, did give Judith some control over her audience. At least she was not throwing her book upon the questionable mercies of a vulgar and unlettered public.

Whether Judith sought subscriptions to preserve her dignity or because it was the most practical route to success, she embraced the process with zeal. She had always urged women to "reverence themselves" and to be independent. *The Gleaner* itself was designed to prove that women could enter any sphere without apologizing. This was her chance to follow her own advice, to be a respectable yet successful businesswoman. It was as close as she ever came to challenging the strictures that kept proper women from making money. While she did not achieve the triumph she hoped for, given her background and her lack of experience, she was surprisingly successful.

Judith's efforts were unusual. Many American women were sympathetic to demands for women's rights, and even more chafed at their inferior education, but very few were published authors. Fewer still, were involved in the messy business of trade. Abigail Adams was interested in politics and had a quiet confidence in her own intellectual ability, but she had no desire to publish. Abigail's friend Mercy Otis Warren published her political plays, poetry, and her *History of the American Revolution*. But she wrote because the men in her life recognized her talent and encouraged her to do so. It was Dr. James Freeman of Boston's King's Chapel who found a printer for her book and secured her subscribers. Mercy did not write to prove that women were men's intellectual equals, nor was she interested in making money. Moreover, she always insisted that she would gladly resume her ordinary duties as wife and mother if her male admirers withdrew their support.[8]

Sarah Wentworth Morton was proud of her poetry, but until the end of her life, she wrote only for journals. She published just one book, *My Mind and Its Thoughts in Sketches, Fragments, and Essays*, in 1823. True, she sold it by subscription, but, like Warren, she relied upon men to secure sponsors for a very limited edition. Philadelphian Elizabeth Graeme Fergusson had every reason to imitate Judith's example. Although she suffered emotionally and economically when her Tory husband abandoned her during the war, and she faced huge obstacles as she tried to pay her debts and turn her ancestral home into a productive farm, she never seemed to realize that her own circumstances proved that traditional notions of women were both harmful and untrue. She wrote primarily to escape life's disappointments, publishing little, and always relied on men to help her negotiate the alien publishing world.[9]

Only Susanna Rowson's experience came close to Judith's. Rowson tended to rely on patrons when she could, but she was proud of her prowess as a businessperson and did not shrink from the nitty-gritty details that her career as a playwright and novelist demanded. Still, unlike the writers with whom Judith identified, Susanna had few if any elite pretensions. She was driven by necessity, not by a desire for literary laurels. Because she had to support her father, her husband, and her children, she could not afford to worry about how her business affairs might reflect on her character. Significantly, she was an actress before she was a writer, and that in itself meant that she had no genteel reputation to protect.[10]

Judith had few if any role models. She sought the advice of men who were not much more experienced than she. Often as not, she relied on her own instincts as she carefully balanced her need to turn *The Gleaner* into a profitable venture with her determination to maintain her respectability. She began by seeking the endorsements of political and literary luminaries. She was delighted when Massachusetts governor Increase Sumner agreed to purchase a copy, as did Generals Henry Knox and Benjamin Lincoln. Her greatest coup, however, came when she secured the patronage of George Washington and John Adams. She approached both men with apprehension. True, she had already met them, but were hardly friends. Thus she felt obliged to defend her request from any tinge of impropriety, assuring Washington that she was imitating a "variety of precedents" when she summoned the courage to write the "Hero, who should reign unrivalled in the bosom of every American." All she asked of the president was a promise to buy *The Gleaner*. She had more in mind for Adams. She wanted permission to dedicate the book to him. Conscious of her own "inferiority," she told him, she hoped to "give celebrity to my essays by your name."[11]

Judith was relieved when she received a positive response from both men. Of course her triumph had its downside. With the backing of such revered figures, she feared that "much is expected of me." She also knew that her heartfelt admiration for Adams might offend some readers. When he read her paean, Epes—who shared her respect for the newly elected president—tried to tone down her praise, sarcastically asking if she would prefer to address Adams as "sire." She considered her cousin's query with complete seriousness until John gently suggested that Epes thought her draft was a bit too "adulatory." Judith reluctantly agreed. She insisted that Adams deserved any honorific, "but so irrational are the prejudices of a large proportion of the American people," that many would not read beyond the introduction if they encountered language they associated with monarchy. If she sought a wide readership, she could not afford to offend those patrons who supported the Democratic-Republicans. She had no idea, she sighed, that her project would be so complicated. Still, whenever she thought it would help, she reminded prospective customers that

Washington and Adams had subscribed to *The Gleaner*. Washington, she proudly pointed out, had written to her "with his own hand."[12]

Judith also sought the support of literary figures to give her publication weight. Early on, she wrote to Mercy Otis Warren, whom she had never met, praising Warren's talents and referring to herself as a "humble Adventurer in the Career of fame." In 1790, Mercy had published her own miscellany, *Poems, Dramatic and Miscellaneous*, which Judith adopted as something of a model. It, too, included essays, plays, and an eclectic collection of poetry. True, Mercy was a Jeffersonian Republican, but she and Judith were both "daughters of Columbia," who wanted to shape a uniquely American culture. This aim, Judith thought, made up for their political differences. American authors—especially American *women* authors—should support one another. Thus she hoped Mercy would not only purchase a subscription, but would ask her friends to do the same.[13]

Their "predilection for American efforts" made the Mortons obvious customers. Sally Sayward Barrell of York, Maine, was not only a friend but the mother of a novelist. Judith thought that the claims of "sex, neighbourhood, and country" were sufficient to seek approval from that quarter. Anne Bingham of Philadelphia was well connected and celebrated for her promotion of the arts. Jedidiah Morse, author of *American Geography*, had an excellent reputation, as did Federalist Joseph Dennie, editor of the *Lay Preacher* and *Farmer's Weekly Museum*. Although Judith had never written for the *Farmer's Weekly Museum*, she reminded its editor that he had once spoken kindly of "The Reaper." Perhaps, she suggested, he might persuade his acquaintances to purchase *The Gleaner*.[14]

It was useful, perhaps even necessary to secure the support of recognized names. But Judith needed many subscribers if she were to raise enough money to persuade the firm of Thomas and Andrews to embark upon the expensive process of printing her volumes. She hoped she could count on her family to buy copies, but she was curiously apologetic when she wrote to Esther and Winthrop, assuring them that they were under no obligation to do so.[15] Judith need not have worried. The Sargents were well represented among *The Gleaner*'s subscribers. Winthrop, Fitz William, Esther's husband, John, and Anna each bought a copy. Daniel, Maria, and their sons were also purchasers, as were Epes and his two sons.

Family was not enough. Judith exploited any personal connection, however tenuous, to expand her list of subscribers. She reminded one man that he had once remarked that her essays gave him unfeigned pleasure. She told another that they had met at the home of mutual friends. She wrote to a number of people with whom she had lost contact over the years. Recalling the good times they had once enjoyed, she hoped that shared memories would induce old acquaintances to purchase a subscription. Most daringly, she even wrote to people she had never met. Man or woman, friend of a friend, or complete stranger—it did not matter. If reminders of a common past or a mutual acquaintance failed to do the trick, Judith appealed to potential readers' nationalistic sentiments. She assured one acquaintance that his name was among the "uniform patriots." She was sure that he would support any effort, "*however feeble*," that will "prove beneficial to your Country." In her optimistic moments she thought such patriotic rhetoric might work. When she was discouraged, she was not so certain. "The American taste is not in favor of home production," she complained. "Indeed I have sometimes thought, if our citizens are palpably deficient in anything it is in national Attachment."[16]

Judith became a shrewd, relentless, and increasingly aggressive businesswoman. She developed a sophisticated market strategy, creating a wide, interconnected group of friends and relatives who promised to distribute subscription papers and a prospectus of *The Gleaner* to anyone who might be remotely interested. She asked every subscriber to help her reach other customers. Usually she simply asked them to spread the news among their friends. Occasionally she was more specific. She told one Gloucester merchant, for instance, to display her subscription form in his store, to "the succession of persons who almost daily pass in review before you." She also sent some potential customers a few of her essays to help them gauge the quality of her work.[17]

While she did not hesitate to appeal to men, Judith was more comfortable—and more demanding—when she sought women's help. Her dealings with Abby Saltonstall are a case in point. When her cousin agreed to purchase *The Gleaner*, Judith begged her to take on the "disagreeable employ" of securing more subscribers. Abby reluctantly consented. A few months later, Judith began to complain that the girl had obtained a paltry five signatures. The reason was clear. She was seeking subscribers only from "her female acquaintance." Judith did not want to hurt her cousin's feelings, but neither did she want her prospects to be so limited. Finally, she wrote to Abby, coming straight to the point. "I highly respect the natural abilities of my sex," she explained, "esteeming their intellectual endowments fully equal with those who have, through revolving centuries, usurped the superiority." Still, she continued, I am "aware, that education, and that walk in life which is marked out for them, damps the sublime fervour of the soul, too generally arrests their literary progress, bars the avenues of science, and creates an artificial difference to mental pursuits." In the end, while she might deplore the "artificial difference" separating women from men, she could hardly deny that such a difference existed. For the present, she needed the "patronage of those whom custom as well as their own appropriate merit, hath invested with eminence." In other words, she required the help of men. Custom was a despot with whom Judith was sometimes willing to do business.[18]

Judith was relatively gentle with Abby. With older women she was more impatient. She was pleased when Elizabeth Jackson volunteered to act as her chief contact in Philadelphia. I have placed "both my fame and fortune" in your hands, Judith wrote, sending some copies of her prospectus along with a stack of subscription papers. But it was not long before Elizabeth was sending her bad news. Even people like Benjamin Rush, who were fond of Judith, were buying very few copies. Judith refused to give up, immediately suggesting a number of other prospects for Elizabeth to contact. She also told her friend to distribute her prospectus to the city's bookstores. Do not forget, she admonished, to tell them that the names of all the subscribers will appear in the third volume of the book. Even when Judith thanked Elizabeth for her exertions, admitting that her friend had garnered nearly twice as many subscriptions as anyone else, she invariably found something to criticize. What was an act of friendship for Elizabeth Jackson was serious work for Judith Sargent Murray.[19]

While Judith tried to sound confident, she grew steadily more anxious as she prepared to turn her manuscript over to the publishers. In the spring of 1797, she was alternately upbeat and panic stricken. Subscriptions were rolling in, though not as quickly as she would have liked. Now she had another worry. What if the subscribers refused to pay part of the cost in advance? She feared that many unsophisticated people thought that their down payments went straight to her. Nothing could be further from the truth. The printers needed the advance to cover the cost of paper and binding, which was "now very high." To have gone this far, to have committed herself so publicly to *The Gleaner*, and then to fail to collect enough to complete her project would be humiliating. She promised to return every penny to her customers if the printers were not able to proceed, but she never saw this as a serious alternative.[20]

As printing costs continued to rise, Judith feared that she would do little more than break even. In the beginning, the printers had promised that if she obtained 500 subscribers, the firm would produce 1,000 copies of *The Gleaner*. But by July 1797 their calculations changed. Judith needed to come up with ten cents more per copy before they would begin. It was not a large sum, but it was daunting. Adding to her difficulties, her manuscript was running longer than she had predicted. The printers had told her that a few more pages would not increase their cost, and some of Judith's more experienced friends assured her that an extra three shillings per volume should be enough to complete the project. Still, she did not know what to expect.[21]

By midsummer, Judith desperately needed a respite from Boston's heat and her own worries. Thus, she and Julia Maria traveled to Gloucester where they could enjoy the town's salubrious sea breezes and spend a quiet month or two with family and old friends. There would be plenty of time in September to attend to the vexing last minute demands of *The Gleaner*. At first, her vacation was all she had hoped it would be. But at the end of August, Esther's husband began complaining of excruciating headaches. His condition rapidly deteriorated, and while he enjoyed a few lucid moments, they became fewer and farther between. On August 24, just five days after he fell ill, John Ellery died. No one knew why. Ultimately it didn't matter. The suddenness of his death made it all the more difficult to accept. She had been deprived of her husband's company, Esther wrote Winthrop, "without the smallest preparation."[22]

At least Esther was not an impoverished widow. Unlike Judith she enjoyed a "genteel competency." Still, she feared having to live as a boarder in someone else's house. Like Judith before her, she shrank from the prospect of dependence. Anxious to put some distance between herself and the reminders of happier times that haunted her every step, she began looking for suitable accommodations in Boston. Gloucester, she confided to Winthrop, seemed like "*one wide tomb*." She felt a "total void in my heart, and my Spirits so low" that she found it difficult even to go beyond her own front door.[23]

Judith returned to Franklin Place in September, not nearly as refreshed as she would have liked. She had expected to be excited as the publication date for her book drew ever nearer. Instead, she was depressed by her brother-in-law's death and had a hard time concentrating on the task at hand. Still, she girded herself for the next stage of the "laborious, and unprofitable" process of publishing *The Gleaner*. Although the number of subscribers fell short of her aspirations, she was reasonably sure that she would be able to pay the printers, once they agreed to accept reimbursements in regular installments. They asked only that Judith pay for the pages she had added. It was not an unreasonable request and so she nervously complied.[24]

As complicated as the business was, Judith made it more so when she decided—she claimed at the request of friends—to offer her patrons special volumes printed in "high style" for fifty cents more. These would be printed on "wove paper" with gilt edges. The first and last pages of each volume would have the appearance of marble. And there would be an "enwreathed number on the backs."[25] That settled, the printers were finally ready to begin. The first advertisement for *The Gleaner* appeared in the *Columbian Centinel* on October 16. There was still time to secure a subscription, it read. But those who wanted their names to appear in the third volume would have to sign on by the end of November. The price for nonsubscribers would go up by fifty cents.

*   *   *

At the same time that Judith had been seeking subscribers and tending to the myriad details that publication entailed, she had also been editing her manuscript. The task was hard enough in any event, but it was made more difficult because Julia Maria was always at her side, chattering incessantly and demanding her mother's complete attention. If she had not been an only child, she would have been happier. As it was, Judith was mother, often father, and companion all wrapped up in one not very neat package. At times she was so distracted that her pen moved automatically across the page and she had no idea what she was saying.[26]

In an effort to make her book as perfect as possible, Judith asked Epes to read her essays and point out any "glaring error." Unlike her husband, Epes had a college education, and she both respected and envied his knowledge of the English tongue. Women in the eighteenth century were always vulnerable when they put pen to paper, and the most accomplished among them regularly apologized for their deficiencies in composition, penmanship, and grammar. They were especially daunted by punctuation. They did not, in the vernacular of the day, know how to "point." Even Mary Wollstonecraft, whose forceful, "masculine" style earned her respect in literary circles, often ended her sentences with a dash instead of a period. Women's inability to punctuate properly is not surprising. In the eighteenth century, every period, comma, colon, or semicolon was a signal to public speakers, telling them when and how long they should pause between phrases. Women were not orators. Nor did they expect their correspondence to be read aloud in a forum that required elocutionary precision. Their letters were a substitute for informal conversation and their use of the dash actually served as a marker of their private purpose.[27]

That was fine among friends, but it would not do in public discourse. Judith's essays in the *Massachusetts Magazine* had relied on the dash, but a book demanded better. She sensed that punctuation gave writers control over their work. An "author best understands his own meaning," she said, and although her knowledge of punctuation was "extremely superficial," she knew enough to understand that the meaning of an entire paragraph could be changed "by a single comma." Benjamin Rush, one of America's leading supporters of education for women, gave Judith another reason to worry. Whenever he encountered a piece that was "blotted, crooked or illegible," he said, he saw it as "rude and illiberal," the "mark of a vulgar education." Bad grammar, then, meant more than ignorance. It bore the tincture of inferior social status and implied that the writer lacked character. Proper writing was as important as proper manners;

both signified taste and gentility. To ignore the rules was to lose the right to be taken seriously. Federalists, in particular, while they championed the creation of a peculiarly American literature, remained wedded to English standards. They valued literature that was structured, decorous, and polite. As so many Americans challenged all authority, they clung ever tenaciously to traditional forms. Without method, there would be chaos.[28]

Elite women, such as Judith Sargent Murray, who were proud of their social status but lacked the skills that would proclaim their gentility to the reading public, were frustrated. Worse, grammatical errors that might be excused as mere oversights in a man, were seized upon as signs of fundamental inferiority in a woman. Indeed, observers seemed determined to view both reading and writing in terms of gender difference. For instance, while men were nearly as likely to enjoy romances as women were, such novels, especially if their authors were women, were relegated to an inferior separate sphere. Books for and by women were cheap, accessible to the masses, and therefore seen as vulgar and tasteless.[29] Judith was determined to attack head-on the link between women and the lower class that her generation had begun to construct as natural. *The Gleaner* would address serious subjects in a serious manner. She intended to give no one an excuse to view her style or her substance through a gendered lens.

Judith readily deferred to Epes's knowledge of grammar, but she reacted defensively to some of his criticisms. She was particularly hurt by his comments on her poetry. As she had done in the original "Gleaner" essays, she began each piece with a verse. Proud of her talent as a poet, she slaved over each line, but the more she changed, the less satisfied she became. At times she threatened to dispose of them all. When Epes suggested the same thing, however, she bristled. Her poems were important, she maintained, not for their intrinsic beauty but for their meaning. Echoing the complaints of her contemporaries, virtually all of whom felt hemmed in by neoclassic dogma, she wondered if it really mattered that her words did not always rhyme. The "best poets" took similar liberties. Pope, for instance, rhymed "here" with "star" and "plain" with "man." Although she was not confident enough to ignore the rules as often as the English poet did, she occasionally forged ahead. But Epes remained unsatisfied, even suggesting that she substitute the poetry of recognized authors, like Milton and Pope, for her own. Judith balked. It was too late. She would have to scour the libraries for appropriate verses. Meanwhile, the printers would demand compensation for the delay. While she knew that Epes's alternative was the usual practice, she had deliberately broken with convention. She was afraid that if she borrowed from truly great writers, her own work would look that much more amateurish by comparison. Besides, she added somewhat contradictorily, some people "well known to the American literati" preferred her poetry to her prose.[30]

There was no end to the last minute details that demanded Judith's attention. She agonized, for weeks, for instance, over the best way to organize the subscribers' names, before finally hitting upon a complicated scheme. In general, the names would appear alphabetically. But each letter of the alphabet would include an elaborate set of subdivisions. Important subscribers—the governor of Massachusetts, George Washington, and John Adams for instance—would appear at the top of the entire list. They would be followed by Boston purchasers. She would list most of them alphabetically, but again those who were superior in "rank, years, and respectability" went to the head of the line. After the Boston subscribers, came other Massachusetts residents. She listed the rest in terms of their distance from Boston. English customers came first, then residents of the Northwest Territory, and so on, with subscribers from neighboring New Hampshire bringing up the rear. The arrangement was orderly; it recognized "any character which is by the general voice invested with decided superiority." And it immediately drew readers' attention to the literary and political figures who had deigned to purchase *The Gleaner*. Still, she never stopped fretting, wondering if there might be some better way to acknowledge her patrons.[31]

By the end of September, Judith had begun inspecting the proof sheets for the first volume. "There is now," she declared soberly, "no receding." Nearly every day she received another sheet, "generally deformed by errors." She never got used to seeing the egregious mistakes that marred virtually every page. It "throws me into a fit of horrors," she cried. Besides, she spent so much time correcting the proofs that she had no time to "beautify" what remained to be written. More than once she confessed that she was in over her head. The printers complained that she still used too many dashes and that she capitalized words irregularly. They volunteered to clean up the manuscript themselves, but Judith did not really trust them, and so she continued to peruse each page herself.[32]

If Judith occasionally regretted her decision to become "the Writer of a Book," there were probably times when William Manning, the foreman at the firm of Thomas and Andrews, shared her sentiments. She could not seem to stop herself from interfering. While she recognized that she was not the printers' only customer Judith chafed at every delay and constantly tried to "accelerate their movements." Nor did she accept any blame for their leisurely pace. Even after the second volume had been completed, she was still making substantive changes. She constantly wrote to Manning pleading for permission to change a word or two, to transpose an occasional line, to add a parenthesis in one place or a comma in another. Even as she requested alterations, she was deleting some

essays and dividing others in half, as she conceded that somehow her manuscript kept expanding. From the beginning, she had wanted *The Gleaner* to be
composed of 100 essays, and she continued to believe that was an attractive
number.[33]

By March, Judith was putting the finishing touches on *The Gleaner*. She
was relieved that she had found "not a single mistake" in the last set of proofs.
Still, she knew that there would always be some errors, and so she demanded an
errata page, where readers would be sure to see it—perhaps right before the title
page. Finally, on the twenty-first of the month, Judith wrote to Winthrop. *The
Gleaner* was finished. She had obtained 800 advance orders. Thomas and Andrews had made one thousand copies. If all went well, she might even get a second printing. Although she still did not know whether to expect a profit, she was
determined to go forward.[34]

*   *   *

Judith's artistic work ended once her book was ready for distribution, but the
challenges she faced as a businesswoman expanded. She had experienced a hint
of the difficulties she would encounter as early as the fall of 1797, when Elizabeth
Jackson seemed ready to buckle under the strain. Judith appreciated Elizabeth's
endeavors, but she seldom bothered to express her gratitude. To the contrary,
she deluged her friend with an unending stream of instructions and criticisms.
She worried that, like most women, Elizabeth might not have the expertise to
keep accurate records. To "prevent confusion," she urged her friend to keep a detailed list of patrons, noting those who had already paid and those who were in
arrears. Elizabeth also had to seek the safest way to send money to Boston. To
add to her difficulties, Philadelphia was suffering another yellow fever epidemic.
Many people were leaving town. Others faced financial ruin and were trying to
back out of—or at least delay—their payments.[35]

At the end of March, Judith began distributing *The Gleaner*. As she had
done at every stage of the process, she assumed responsibility for the entire operation. Whenever she forwarded copies to distributors, she sent a few extra volumes, hoping her friends would be able to dispose of them. She also asked the
editors of the *Centinel* to announce that readers could order copies at any
Boston bookstore. Despite her efforts, she was often discouraged, finding the
"pecuniary part of this business very toilsome." Somehow, she had amassed a
number of "unexpected charges." *The Gleaner* had surpassed the 900-page limit
upon which she had agreed, and printing costs were $200 more than she had ex-
pected. Worse, some subscribers neglected to pick up or pay for their volumes.

Judith did not shrink from pressing her delinquent customers. She began sending not so gentle reminders to laggards in May. She also instructed distributors to dispose of unclaimed copies by selling them again.[36]

Some of Judith's distributors were able to comply with her instructions. Elizabeth Jackson, however, faced with purchasers who were enduring economic bad times, was ready to rebel, as she hinted that she might have to return half the books in her possession. If Judith was shocked at the "want of punctuality" of so many "people of fortune," Elizabeth had reason to grumble, not only about the onerous task she had undertaken, but about Judith's constant—and changing—demands. No matter what she did, it seemed to be wrong. Because Judith said she needed cash immediately, Elizabeth rushed to send whatever she collected to Boston. Instead of thanking her, Judith pointed out that it was silly to bother with such "small sums." By the end of the year, she took over the Philadelphia operation herself. Elizabeth had moved to Maryland and was happy to wash her hands of an undertaking that had resulted in "unexpected fatigue." The two women finally settled their accounts in February of 1800, even though Judith was sure Elizabeth's records were faulty. Adopting a martyr's tone she conceded that Jackson had done her best. "Although I am unfortunate," she added, "I will yet subscribe, without dispute, to your statement of the matter."[37]

Judith always expected her projects to proceed more smoothly than they did. She kept meticulous records, computing her finances down to the last penny, somehow imagining that her attention to detail would get her what she was due. But the real world was never as orderly or as easily controlled as she thought it should be. One man, for instance, was on the way to Boston with some proceeds from the book when his ship capsized and he—and her money—were lost at sea. Another had all his goods, including the nearly 100 copies of *The Gleaner* she had entrusted to his care, seized by the local sheriff. Many subscribers died, and their relatives refused to pay for a book they did not want. A little less than three months after *The Gleaner* appeared, Judith was depressed. She had, she wrote Esther, "nothing pleasing to transmit." Her hopes for a profit were, "if not prostrate, at least suspended." When John suggested that she send a circular letter to recalcitrant subscribers demanding reimbursement, Judith hesitated, but only because she doubted that reminders would do any good.[38]

From a financial perspective, *The Gleaner* was neither as successful as Judith had desired, nor the failure she claimed that it was. No one in the eighteenth century expected to make a living as an author. Even Susanna Rowson had to supplement her income as a successful playwright and novelist by opening up a girls' school in Boston. Judith's experience was typical. *The Gleaner* did not, as some scholars have suggested, allow her to become the "prime financial mainstay" for her family. She did not even dispose of all 1,000 copies, although money was still trickling in two years after the volumes appeared. She eventually took to giving them away, hoping that new readers would spread the word about her effort. "Vanity is said to predominate in the female bosom," she would say, with just a touch of irony. Still, if *The Gleaner* did not earn a fortune, it made enough to allow Judith to pay off the mortgage on Franklin Place, a debt, she confided to John's mother, "that hath long been a source of uneasiness to me." The final payment, she told Epes, was "the day of our emancipation."[39] In fact, Judith had to be relieved—even pleased—by *The Gleaner*'s receipts. This was, after all, the first money she had ever earned. Her frugality had stretched John's salary over the years. Eventually she received her patrimony, and she also got a third of the profits from the sale of the house in Gloucester. But actually earning money was different and, in the circles in which she traveled, unusual. Her achievement was a sign of her ability to claim a measure of independence for herself and her family. But Judith had hoped that *The Gleaner* would vault her to the very top of America's literary circles. Unfortunately, fame continued to be elusive.

*　*　*

The minute she began distributing *The Gleaner*, Judith experienced serious qualms about its reception. She had worked so hard to secure subscribers. What if her sales pitch had succeeded too well and her readers' expectations had been "too high raised"? While she knew it was unrealistic to expect "universal approbation," she would be mortified if readers thought they had not received value for their money. In fact, Judith had reason to be proud of what was truly a prodigious undertaking. "It is written with care," she told Robert Redding, "in the highest style of elegance, propriety of diction, and chastity of sentiment which I could command." While she referred to *The Gleaner* as a "miscellaneous work," she insisted that all its essays were connected. She had employed a variety of disparate literary forms—fiction, nonfiction essays, poetry, plays, and letters. Still, particularly in the two new volumes, her effort to create a unified vision was largely successful. The book touched on many subjects, but it was clear that its one grand purpose was to prove the intellectual equality of women. Sometimes, especially in the beginning, that purpose was oblique. Yet nearly every essay led steadily and inexorably to the third volume's four-part "Observations on Female Abilities."[40]

Scholars have a tendency to look at eighteenth-century women writers as one means of questioning the traditional formulation of the "master narrative" that once dominated the study of early American letters. They see the presence of women's voices as an emblem of American diversity, proof that authors such as Judith Sargent Murray, Sarah Morton, and Mercy Otis Warren challenged and problematized the elite, white, male control of politics and culture of their age. The very existence of such women helps historians appreciate the disparate views and experiences of those individuals who existed at the nation's margins.[41] In Judith Sargent Murray's case, this perspective is itself problematic. Granted, Murray put women at the center of her story. In this sense, she was a "revisionist historian" who challenged the dominant views of her day. Her understanding of the political and literary world was clearly informed by her experience as a woman. Yet Judith never saw herself as "challenging" the master narrative. To the contrary, she was eager to play by elite, male rules, asking only to be admitted as a member of the literary establishment. She had just one real, albeit fundamental, quarrel with the way that New England's self-proclaimed cultural leaders constructed their reality. She found their refusal to take women's views seriously, to give "the sex" something of the equality that God had granted and the Declaration of Independence had promised, unforgivable. Her ability to see and her willingness to decry the barriers that women faced in their quest for inclusion in the civic conversation about America's future seldom led her to sympathize with other disadvantaged members of society. "Custom," the Gleaner insisted, "has judiciously affixed to the various ranks in society its ascertaining marks, and we cannot see her barriers thrown down, or the rushing together of the different classes of mankind, without regret." While she wanted women—elite women—to be involved in the discussions that shaped America's character, she was not interested in including others, who she thought had yet to earn a place at the table.[42] Unfortunately, her blinkered vision limited her audience and diminished her impact.

The first volume of *The Gleaner* was a slightly altered version of the essays that had originally appeared in the *Massachusetts Magazine*. Thirty-one essays became thirty-four. Judith changed a few words, corrected her grammar, and "pointed" properly. Perhaps to mollify Epes, she shortened some poems and completely replaced others. Still, it was essentially the work with which many readers were familiar. This time, however, they knew from the beginning that they were reading the words of a woman who wrote most often as a man. Judith continued writing as the Gleaner, perfecting her original essays and adding more to her repertoire. But she left no doubt about who she was. She was through with her efforts to hide her identity, coyly dissimulating when friends penetrated her pathetically thin disguise. The title page of *The Gleaner* announced that "Constantia" was the book's author. From the beginning, then, she disrupted the narrative voice of *The Gleaner*, blurring gender differences, proving that women could write with authority even when they commented on "male" topics.[43] Although Mr. Vigillius or the Gleaner assumes control of the narrative on occasion, readers know that Constantia is the "real" intellectual force shaping the book's arguments. The Gleaner is merely a puppet; Constantia is in charge.

Judith's decision to claim authorship for her miscellany was deliberate, central to her desire to challenge gender categories to a much greater extent than she had done in her original essays. Nevertheless, the book's preface lacks the confidence and forcefulness of the original Gleaner's voice. It adopts a conventional tone as far as gender assumptions were concerned, accepting a marginal status for its author and deferring to male standards of excellence—perhaps because Judith assumed that readers expected humility from a woman. She is, she concedes, "solicitous to render myself acceptable." She fears that her critics will see her as "an unpardonable offender against the rules of language, and the elegance and graces of style." Nevertheless, it is her "*ruling passion*" to "stand well in the opinion of the world." Thus she frames her decision to publish *The Gleaner* in an acceptably feminine manner, hoping her book will benefit young people who are preparing to enter the adult world.[44]

If the book's preface is deferential, the conclusion, also signed "Constantia," is less so. In "The Gleaner Unmasked," Judith claims to be "throwing aside the veil," announcing that she is that "identical *Constantia*" whom readers might remember from the *Massachusetts Magazine*. Her revelation is obviously unnecessary. Some eight hundred pages earlier she had already revealed her identity. But she is determined to explain her reasons for having assumed a masculine character throughout the body of *The Gleaner*. She has done so, she says, not because women are unworthy writers, but because of the illogical prejudices against "female productions" that still exist. Her desire to be taken seriously has led her to assume a "borrowed character." To the extent that she had originally fooled her readers, she has already proved her point. There is no intellectual difference between men and women.[45]

Judith has another reason for writing as a man. She is "ambitious of being considered *independent as a writer*." She wants neither her errors nor her achievements to be attributed to anyone else. For that reason, she was always more sensitive to accusations of plagiarism than most eighteenth-century authors were. This was a time when readers did not always expect literature to be original, when authors tried only to improve upon existing models. Yet Judith was frantic when her cousin Epes urged her to get rid of an allusion she had used in her dedication. He had already heard her comparison of John Adams with the prophet Elisha when he had attended Harvard's commencement exercises. He had also seen it in the *Farmer's Weekly Museum*. Judith spiritedly defended herself. She had employed this comparison long before it had appeared elsewhere, she said. Her thoughts might be trite, but they were her own. Thus, her conclusion repeats comments she had made to Robert Treat Paine a few years earlier, as she observes that many people agreed with Rousseau, that whenever a woman "*ostensibly*" held the pen, it was "certain that some man of letters sits behind the curtain to guide its movements." Constantia may have accepted her marginal status in *The Gleaner*'s preface. By the time she reaches her conclusion, she is no longer willing to do so.[46] Indeed, she has neatly turned Rousseau's assertions on their head. In this case, it is a man who "ostensibly" holds the pen, while a woman controls its movements.

*   *   *

The original "Gleaner" essays were probably most popular because of the story of Margaretta. The tale was didactic and predictable, but it was also entertaining. Readers, especially young readers who may not have found moralistic essays appealing, were caught up in the story of the young orphan and her struggles. Margaretta is a presence at the beginning of the second volume of *The Gleaner*, but it is the girl's education, not her effort to find a suitable husband or to be a good wife that is at the heart of the essays. Like Mary Wollstonecraft, Judith had always argued that women's apparent inferiority was the product of inadequate schooling. To prove her point, fifteen of the first eighteen entries in the second volume center on education. Two essays on the subject—both apparently from the pen of Mr. Vigillius—open the second volume. Mr. Vigillius links education with the fate of the American nation, arguing that mothers, in particular, hold the country's future in their hands. Thus even the most ordinary woman has a political role. Mothers, he says, "imprint on the opening mind, characters, ideas and conclusions which time, in all of its variety of vicissitudes, will never be able to erase." For the sake of their country, then, women had to be well educated. Even knowledge of Latin was not "*unsexual*." Still, if girls should learn Latin, boys and girls alike should be able to read and write in their native tongue. Men who graduated from American universities with the highest honors were often unable to pronounce English words correctly and were at a loss when it came to punctuation. They were as poorly prepared for the real world as any woman. Ironically, girls—who customarily had no access to the classics—might actually be better able to meet life's challenges than boys were.[47]

Having set the parameters for the discussion to follow, Mr. Vigillius retires, turning the story over to Mary and Margaretta, in the form of a series of letters between mother and daughter. Granted, Mr. Vigillius lends his authority to Mary's project, as he assures his readers that *he* decides which letters will appear in *The Gleaner* and which will remain private. Still, education is clearly the mother's responsibility. Mary is rational and knowledgeable. She might spend most of her time at home, but her influence travels well beyond the confines of the domestic sphere. The line between private virtue and the health of the republic is virtually nonexistent.[48]

Reflecting the preference of most educators of her day, Mary views the study of history as central to a young woman's education. Carefully chosen novels were fine for the very young, but once they learned that reading could be pleasurable as well as enlightening, girls were ready for substantial fare. In the eighteenth century, good history served moral ends, helping readers to avoid the pitfalls of the past and to imitate the virtuous examples of the heroes of bygone days. The past invariably shaped the present, providing useful examples for virtuous citizens.[49]

Mary's approach to history simply assumes that women are citizens, that they have the capacity to judge political leaders and to challenge authority. Only those rulers who promote education and reward their subjects' virtue deserve veneration. Mary also urges her daughter to revere those leaders who protect the marginal members of society. Religious tolerance, in particular, is an essential component of a good ruler. "Zeal of religion" is never a good thing.[50]

It is not enough, though, to give her daughter the abstract precepts she needs to evaluate the nation's leaders. If Margaretta is going to have the confidence to use history for rational ends, Mary must put women at the center of her narrative. Thus she directs her daughter's attention to the public roles that women have played in the past. More than one good king saw his mother as the source of his virtue. Alfred the Great's mother, for instance, encouraged her son to study English, Latin, and every other branch of knowledge, despite her husband's opposition. Wives, too, had an impact. The justly admired czarina Catherine of Russia was her husband's most valued adviser. Even ordinary women, Mary observes, did not always remain on the sidelines. Thus the Senate in ancient Rome formally recognized all its meritorious women.[51]

Nor were women always appendages to men. Some exercised power directly. Judith was one of many women historians who was fascinated by the story of Elizabeth I and Mary, Queen of Scots. And like her contemporaries, she was ambivalent about the lessons the story imparted. Ironically, she judged the two monarchs as women first, and rulers second. Viewed this way, Mary was infinitely superior. She was proficient in Latin, French, Italian, and Spanish as well as in all ornamental accomplishments. A wise and tolerant ruler, she was also a wife and mother. While she twice married unwisely, she remained loyal and loving to the end. She assumed the Scottish throne, not because she hungered for power but because it was her duty to do so. Women, like men, could sacrifice their own happiness for the good of their country. Elizabeth, although "powerful," was "unsexual, unjust, and infinitely cruel." She had all the characteristics of the worst man. Too selfish to marry or bear children, she was consumed by jealousy when she heard of Mary's womanly achievements. Thus she signed the Scottish queen's death warrant "with an air of levity" that proved how unnatural a woman she was. In the end, motherhood triumphed over brute force. Mary's son James ascended the throne upon the death of the Virgin Queen, uniting England and Scotland and laying the foundations for a powerful British empire.[52]

If *The Gleaner*'s assessment of women rulers had ended with Mary Vigillius's rendition of the struggle between the Scottish and English queens, scholars might validly claim that Judith Sargent Murray's attitude toward women leaders was deeply traditional, even reactionary. To be sure, Mary makes a point of proclaiming women's intellectual equality with men. She argues that women can be virtuous patriots, so long as their contributions to their country's well-being are consistent with their domestic role. Still, she implies that while they may exert their *influence*, as wives and mothers, when they exercise power directly they risk their very identity as women. If an accident of history thrusts leadership upon them, they must accept their role as a sacrifice, as a duty. Once they develop a "passion" for power, they become like Elizabeth, "unsexual," even monstrous.

The rest of *The Gleaner* challenges that perspective. Mary's historical lessons are simply an opening salvo, a means of inserting the question of women's place and women's rights into the debate. Judith had always argued that teachers needed to take their pupils by the hand, gradually acquainting them with increasingly complex and alien concepts. Her organization of *The Gleaner* reflects this strategy. Like the most cunning seducer, she does not assault prejudice head on, but leads her readers slowly, deliberately, toward her ultimate goal—the recognition that in virtually every aspect of human endeavor women are men's equals.

Seven of the remaining fourteen essays in the second volume of *The Gleaner* focus on women or women's concerns. But the centerpiece is the "Observations on Female Abilities," a supplement to "The Equality of the Sexes" that had appeared "some years since, in a periodical publication of a miscellaneous nature." While Constantia is pleased with the progress women have already made, she knows that many Americans still require evidence of women's capabilities. Her proofs begin conventionally enough, as she was by no means the only woman of her day to compile impressive lists to show that, given a chance, women could be artists, authors, soldiers, or rulers. The "Observations" is most persuasive when it proclaims women's intellectual equality with men. Adopting the Lockean belief that nurture usually trumps nature, it insists that "with proper attention to their education and subsequent habits, [women] might easily attain that independence for which a Wollstonecraft hath so energetically contended." Education, then, is not an end in itself. It is the foundation of independence. If only a few talented women aspired to literary greatness, all women longed to "depend on their own efforts." They hoped marriage would be a choice, not a necessity. They wanted, as Eliza Clairville had done in *Virtue Triumphant*, to see marriage as a matter of "*indifference.*" They wanted the expression "helpless widow" to be heard no more.[53]

The "Observations" offers two intriguing examples of women who are independent and self-reliant. Constantia tells the story of an unschooled Massachusetts girl who has never married. As a child, she roams the fields at will, exercising her body, if not her mind. As a result, "her limbs expanded, and she acquired a height of stature above the common size." Upon the death of her parents, she inherits a few acres of land, and in no time is "a complete *husband-woman.*" "Extremely active and wonderfully athletic," she is so successful that she hires and supervises (male) laborers, relishing her ability to provide for her own needs. Equally impressive are the achievements of the Widow Birmingham. The head of a profitable merchant establishment, she "breathed the true spirit of commerce." The redoubtable woman is born with the skills she needs to prosper, but her daughters require education for independence. Thus she teaches them to serve as clerks in their own business. None of them worry about the future; none will be degraded by dependence or forced to marry in order to survive; none is "unsexed" by her experience.[54]

Despite its ringing endorsement of women's ability, the "Observations" retreats to more conventional territory in its closing paragraphs. Women could do anything. That did not mean, however, that what was possible was always desirable. Constantia has no desire "to array THE SEX in martial habiliments." Nor does she believe that women should aspire to be merchants or farmers. Thus, she cedes control of her narrative to Mr. Vigillius, who assures his readers that Constantia is arguing only for the "*capability*" of the sex. She wants women to cultivate their talents, to be proficient at some branch of business, so that if they *must* take care of themselves, they will be able to avoid that dependence "against which the freeborn mind so naturally revolts." Mr. Vigillius has the last word, and he uses it to maintain that a woman's highest happiness derives, not from the equality she shares with men, but from the unique attributes she enjoys as a member of her sex. The exquisite joys of motherhood, which "always have belonged, and always will belong, only to Women," could compare to no other experience.[55]

When she speaks as Constantia, Judith seeks to blur the differences between men and women, to deny—or at least to ignore—any connection between body and essence, anatomy and destiny. But as Mr. Vigillius, she appears to accept the "essential" differences dividing the sexes. Scholars have often expressed disappointment at what appears to be the mixed message of the "Observations." It promises so much, yet—as even Mary Wollstonecraft had done on occasion—appears to relinquish its potential, retreating into a saccharine paean to motherhood. At best, it straddles the fence. Judith claims power because she sees herself as one of the few women who could enter the public sphere, at least on paper, mingling freely and equally with male writers. Yet she also recognizes gender differences, creating a separate sphere where a woman naturally could exercise power over her house and family. Especially troubling, while *The Gleaner* offers its readers examples of "she-merchants" and "husbandwomen," it never even hints that women should demand the vote or the opportunity to hold office. More than one historian has been puzzled by the "failure" of any eighteenth-century American woman to issue a call for formal political rights at a time when more and more men were beginning to equate citizenship with suffrage and to demand formal political rights. They suggest that America's "founding mothers" were simply too marginalized to have an interest in political activity narrowly defined.[56]

In fact, however, Judith's strategy was not a product of her half-formed and tentative sense of consciousness as a woman. Rather, it reflected her view of human nature—women's and men's alike—a view that was central to her understanding of women's political role. She was perfectly aware that republican rhetoric assumed a gendered world, where true citizens were men linked to the nation by their public spirit. She knew as well that "independence" was the necessary requisite for claiming political rights. In this sense, her attempt to prepare future generations of women for independence had radical implications. But above all else, she shared the belief of women like Susanna Rowson that citizenship and patriotism were intellectual categories. Thoroughly attuned to the mind/body dualism of her age, assuming that mind—or spirit, or soul—was superior to body, she believed that she need only convince her readers of women's intellectual ability to exercise her claim as a "daughter of Columbia." Citizenship was a moral phenomenon, the perquisite of the "*good and worthy*." Government was the province of the reasonable, the knowledgeable, and the wise. All people, she had once argued to Winthrop, who were well educated and well bred, and who had attained the ability to "bid adieu to every selfish, every degrading passion," could justly claim a designation as citizen.[57]

The duties of citizenship that Judith (and many of her compatriots) thought were most important centered on the obligation of rational individuals to help the new nation achieve its moral potential. While she accepted the importance of women's ability to bind the nation with ties of love and sensibility, piety and domestic virtue, Judith wanted more for herself. She did not demand a direct role in public affairs. She sought, in terms that Jurgen Habermas has made famous, to be part of an elite "public sphere," a sphere that was neither official nor private, that would utilize women's *unique* talents, and that would value their minds. She wanted to engage other citizens on an equal—disembodied—basis, evaluating and shaping public opinion in an independent, reflective manner. The world of print was an ideal forum through which she could shape her nation's future without violating the rules of decorum. There she could speak clearly, forcefully, and above all rationally to her readers, without calling attention to her physical attributes. Thus, Judith was content sitting in her little closet, speaking with a pure voice to an invisible audience, *hiding* her sex under a variety of aliases. Such a venue did not require her to vote or to hold office; its very existence assumed that it was possible to be political *without* exercising formal political rights. To the contrary, its value lay in the fact that it set itself in opposition to the formal state and its sordid machinations. It demanded only that women be recognized as rational beings.[58]

Judith argued that women and men were virtually identical in mind, even as their minds temporarily resided in dissimilar bodies. Her strategy led her to emphasize her intellectual capabilities while she avoided activities—with the significant exception of motherhood—that might remind her readers of women's fleshly identity. This explains in part why she had no interest in the vote. She, who had an opinion on virtually everything, never once wrote about the femes sole of New Jersey who briefly exercised the franchise in the years after the Revolution. This was not, however, a retreat from citizenship. Judith invariably drew a sharp distinction between governments and nations. The former were generally the province of men, while the latter belonged to everyone. Thus she was not dissimulating when she assured her sister-in-law that she was "no politician." But if she was not a politician, she *was* a citizen. She argued that private individuals were more important than government in defining the moral interests of any country. Politics was little more than a "capability of distinguishing that which will probably advance the real interests of a Community." If politics was at bottom a moral issue, who was more qualified than women to enter any public discussion? They already did so—as Mary Vigillius's example proved—as mothers and teachers of America's children. Some were prepared to go one step further, using their pens to become involved in the debate over the country's future.[59]

If Judith argued that the ability to reason, to make moral choices, to be an *influence* on the body politic was what truly mattered, then it is fair to say that the entire *Gleaner* is a political document, designed to prove that women were valuable members of the republic. Interestingly, in private, she occasionally entertained the possibility of expanding women's direct influence—even women's power—more than she did in public. A letter to Epes Sargent is intriguing. Abigail Adams, she asserted confidently, was her husband's most "valuable auxiliary." It was obvious, she continued, "that *every transaction* of his administration is now laid before her—she is not only his bosom friend, but his aid and his Councellor in every emergency." So far, Judith was describing the ideal republican wife. But she went further, asserting that several highly placed gentlemen in Boston had declared that "was the President called out of time, they should rather see Mrs. Adams in the Presidential chair, than any other character now existing in America." Under the right circumstances, qualified women, even in her own day, could assume the reins of government without endangering their femininity or their country.[60]

Still, Judith was usually content urging women to use their pen to exercise influence. *The Gleaner*'s remaining essays reinforce that point. As the narrator prepares to bring the work to a close, he offers example upon example of the practical and public value of the privately written word. Mr. Vigillius has hinted at this very possibility in the opening essays of the second volume of *The Gleaner*. When one of Margaretta's friends asks why she and her mother make it a practice to write "to each other under the same roof, when they could talk together every hour if they pleased," Mary explains that it does not matter that mere walls separate her physically from her daughter. Once Margaretta is out of her sight she might as well be living in a different country instead of in another room. Spirit is not, she insists, "embarrassed by distance, or assisted by vicinity." In either case, individuals have to use their imaginations to communicate with one another. Moreover, by creating a relationship that depends on *words*, Mary is making a case for the singular value of the mind. She wants no gesture, caress, or frown to distract Margaretta from the force of her argument. Her attempt to form her daughter's character is entirely a mental exercise. She dominates with reason, not her physical presence.[61]

The final essays in *The Gleaner* suggest that even the most reclusive women can extend their influence far beyond their homes. The letters Mary and Margaretta write to one another are never truly private; they touch the minds of countless readers throughout America and beyond. There are other women in the new nation who write more directly for a broader public. Mercy Otis Warren's plays, for instance, are capable of serving as a "powerful engine in forming the opinions and manners of a people." Yet, because Americans tended to ignore the work of their own citizens, "the finished scenes of the correct and elegant Mrs. Warren, have never yet passed in review before an American audience." Given a chance, Warren and many other women would make the nation a better place without risking their status.[62]

Still, those readers who actually plowed through all three volumes of *The Gleaner* were left with an altogether traditional picture of women's influence. The ninety-eighth essay gives the reader one final glimpse of Margaretta. While her husband ranges over the entire world, Margaretta remains in her own rural retreat. She spends each morning at her desk, writing letters that will spread her influence as far as Europe and the West Indies. She uses her pen to plead for the occasional "desolate female" whose plight has come to her attention. She receives strangers in her parlor, listening to each tale of woe with such exquisite sympathy that "she seemed all soul." Every afternoon, she walks in her garden, an enclosed grotto that protects her from the public eye, yet allows supplicants to enter her world and plead for her aid. Because her reputation as an angel of mercy has spread far and wide, she need not go into the world in order to save it.[63]

As readers learn in the final two essays, *The Gleaner* itself has improved the lives of countless individuals. "George Seafort" tells readers that his daughter Molly has found a good husband and continues to heed the advice of *The Gleaner*. "Alfonso," a character from an earlier essay, writes to announce that he has reformed and gives *The Gleaner* credit for the direction his life has taken. "Martha Studious" describes a circle of her friends who gather each week to ply their needles while they discuss the moral lessons that good literature offers and imitate Margaretta's example by collecting money for the deserving poor. If eighteenth-century observers believed that utility was "the essential component of virtuous public texts," the experiences of *The Gleaner*'s readers endow the book with real legitimacy.[64]

Finally, reluctantly, the Gleaner brings his miscellany to a close, even as he hints that he is ready to publish more essays if there is a demand for them. The book concludes with "The Gleaner Unmasked." The final essay reflects Judith's fears about the critical reception of her book. She defends her decision to appear before her readers "in a masculine character." She assures her readers that she has written every word herself. "In this arduous enterprise," she says, "however daring, I have stood alone." Now she sits back to wait, hoping that her "Patrons and Patronesses" will be pleased with what she had done.[65]

*   *   *

Judith had impossibly high hopes for *The Gleaner*. She knew that Wollstonecraft's *Vindication*, published just six years earlier, had been an international triumph, selling over 300,000 copies almost immediately. Was it unrealistic to think that she might achieve the same success? In her most halcyon moments, she thought her book would give her more than fame. It might also change the world. Unfortunately, while the fictional Alfonso and Molly Seafort claimed that their lives were fundamentally altered by *The Gleaner*, in real life such responses were rare. The public reaction to the book was mixed. Judith was especially pleased with George Washington's praises. John Murray had dinner at Mount Vernon not long after *The Gleaner*'s publication. Washington, declared John with obvious pride, referred to Judith as "the first literary Lady as was ever seen in any country." Other readers were not so kind. Judith probably did not know that Sarah Morton, who was one of her earliest subscribers and whom the Gleaner had taken great pains to praise, had privately laughed at her ambition. "Mrs. Murray," Sarah told Joseph Dennie, "has given out Proposals for printing by Subscription *600 Pages* of 'The Gleaner'!!!" What, one wonders, was Sarah's reaction when she learned that the book was one third again as long? John James, Epes's son, called Judith's attention to a review by the "Agawam Critic," which referred in an obliquely negative way to her energetic efforts to secure subscribers. Judith weakly replied that she had suffered much worse attacks in her day and thus was "less susceptible" to them than she once had been. That, however, did not keep her from trying to find out just who her critic was.[66]

Judith also complained that many subscribers dipped briefly into *The Gleaner*, condemning it before they gave it a chance. This was especially true of many Virginia customers, who took one look at the dedication's "expansive effusions" in praise of John Adams and read no further or in some cases refused even to pay for the book. Judith insisted that her praise was not "*lavish, or excessive.*" I should not be "deemed reprehensible" she said, for lauding one "which the majority of the suffrages of a *free people* hath elevated to the first office in the government." She would not retract her acclamation of so exemplary a figure even for a few more sales.[67]

Not surprisingly, some readers were offended by *The Gleaner*'s defense of

Universalism. In 1806, nearly a decade after the book appeared, an anonymous reviewer in the Charleston, South Carolina, *Monthly Register, Magazine and Review of the United States* attacked the book on a number of points. It was much too wordy. Its meaning was often nonsensical and its style was "in general, stiff, forced, inelegant, coarse, affected, and feeble, and oftentimes incorrect." Most egregiously, one of its essays maintained that all humans were destined for a heavenly reward. Just as the Gloucester Puritans once had done, the reviewer insisted that Universalism not only violated scripture, but tended to "confound all the distinctions between right and wrong; to break down all the barriers, which separate virtue from vice."[68]

Judith probably dismissed the reviewer's attack on her religious beliefs with a shrug. She was less able to disregard J. S. J. Gardiner's comments. Gardiner was a Federalist; he tutored her nephews; he was a friend. Still, he had refused to purchase her book, and when Judith made him a gift of all three volumes, Gardiner was dismissive. He acknowledged that many Bostonians "considered *The Gleaner* as a *chef-d'oeuvre* in essay writing." He disagreed. Indeed, he thought that no American production measured up to European standards. To argue otherwise was either the "grossest ignorance or the most insufferable vanity." Judith may have been slightly comforted by Gardiner's claim that no other American displayed much talent either. Still, that was not much solace for someone who had hoped to claim a place in the highest echelons of the literary world. Even more upsetting, some readers compared her— unfavorably—to her contemporaries. Joseph Dennie, for instance, pronounced her literary talent mediocre. In his view, Sarah Morton, Hannah Adams, and Mercy Otis Warren were all far superior.[69]

Criticism was bad enough. Being ignored was worse. "Oblivion," she wrote in *The Gleaner,* was the fate she dreaded above all else. And in later years, it was Judith's sense that no one cared about or even remembered her book that hurt most. "In this my native soil," she wrote, "my aspiring views are blighted by the icy influence of frigid neglect."[70] Judith was both hurt and puzzled by the lack of interest in *The Gleaner*. In fact, the tepid popular and critical response to a work in which she had invested so much hope is not altogether surprising. That her efforts fell well short of her own aspirations says more about the limits of *The Gleaner*, including its centerpiece, "Observations on Female Abilities," than it does about America's failure to support native authors. Although throughout her book Judith insists that her primary purpose is to cast doubt on traditional notions of femininity, in fact she only occasionally—and then very cautiously— challenges established wisdom. Unlike Mary Wollstonecraft, she is all too willing to play it safe. Any argument that might garner criticism is muted, almost hidden from view. Judith's desire for gentility—and perhaps her determination not to embarrass her husband—leads her to avoid making waves. Not willing to risk attack, she ends up ignored, leaving her dream of achieving a prominent place in the nation's "republic of letters" unfulfilled.

The Gleaner's message is circumscribed. "The female world," Judith complains in her fifty-fourth essay, is excluded "from conspicuous rewards of merit," while "to man the road of preferment is thrown open." But if her essay pretends to speak about the entire "female world," in fact the focus of the book is extremely narrow. True, Judith urges all women to leap over arbitrary barriers, to expand their lives and to aspire to the loftiest heights. Almost by definition, however, the women who were most likely to be inspired by such a challenge were a talented and privileged group. It was educated, elite women whom "ignorant or interested men" had systematically excluded from the "road of preferment" and who could expect only *secondary* or *reflected* fame." Almost without exception, the examples Judith employs throughout *The Gleaner* ignore the plight of ordinary women in ordinary circumstances.[71]

This approach is apparent even in the most well-known piece in *The Gleaner* essays, the "Observations on Female Abilities." Like most of the essays, the "Observations" is both expansive and constricted, daring and timid. It urges young women to take advantage of their opportunities, to abandon "the use of the needle" for "studies of a more elevated nature." It rejoices that America is "forming a new era in female history." And it boldly declares that "*The idea of the incapability* of women, is, we conceive, in this *enlightened age* totally *inadmissable.*" Constantia's long list of women whose accomplishments give the lie to stereotypic gender definitions is impressive and wide-ranging. Women have not merely been long-suffering, inventive, loyal, and energetic. They have ridden at the head of entire armies, they have "armed themselves for the combat—they have mingled amid the battling ranks—they have fought heroically." Women, she says, have also "publickly harangued on religion," and they have filled "with equal honour the toils of government." If Judith is anxious to prove women's capabilities, she is even more interested in erasing gender differences. "The sexes," says Constantia, "are congenial; they are copyists of each other." It is mere "contingencies" that explain the differences between men and women.[72]

Still, while women may have been naturally equal to men, the vast majority would search the pages of *The Gleaner* in vain for examples to which they could relate. The women warriors Constantia extols are never common soldiers. They are generals, not privates. She ignores ordinary school girls in favor of the "lady" from Bologna who once delivered an oration in Latin to an assemblage of erudite gentlemen. Her women who challenge male-dominated governments are not the common housewives of Paris who marched on the Bastille demanding bread for their families. They are queens who have inherited their position and whom an accident of history has thrust into the limelight. The poets and playwrights whose accomplishments dominate the "Observations" are similarly genteel. Constantia praises Mercy Otis Warren, Philenia, and Antonia. She neglects Susanna Rowson, whose determination to make money and her brief career as an actress put her beyond the pale of respectable society.[73]

Judith was not deliberately excluding women of the lower orders from her vision of equality. She simply could not see beyond her own experience. While she recognized that women were the "sport of contingencies," she never seemed to realize that lower-class women—and men—were also the product of the accidental restrictions created by their narrow and debilitating environment. It was Mary Wollstonecraft, not Judith Sargent Murray, who resented class as well as gender bias, and who consequently was able to indict her society with a broad and penetrating analysis. Historians continue to put the two women in the same category, whether as "liberals" or "feminists."[74] True, they were both part of the wide-ranging trend toward gender equality that briefly characterized the Atlantic world in the age of the American and French Revolutions. But neither owed much directly to the other. There is no evidence that Mary Wollstonecraft ever heard of Judith Sargent Murray. Judith's "Desultory Thoughts" appeared in 1784, nearly a decade before the *Vindication* was published in America. Both were indebted to historian Catharine Macaulay, whose example provided their inspiration, and whose *Letters on Education* reflected their views. Both were deeply influenced by John Locke's view of human psychology, and both had read and vehemently rejected Jean-Jacques Rousseau's *Emile*. Both thought that education was the key to solving virtually all of women's problems. But despite their similarities, their different experiences led them in very different directions.

Mary came from what today would be called a dysfunctional family. Her father was an improvident and violent alcoholic whose "slide from respectability" put his family's welfare into jeopardy. Her mother, often the target of her husband's drunken rages, was weak and compliant, to the evident frustration of her helpless daughter. While Judith was proud of her family and benefited from her parents' beneficence, Mary learned early on to distrust all authority figures. She later recalled that by the time she was fifteen she had already "resolved never to marry for interested motives, or to endure a life of dependence." Lacking the options that men enjoyed, her respectability was compromised as she struggled to support herself and her sisters, becoming in rapid succession a teacher, a governess, and a paid companion to a crotchety old woman, positions that constantly reminded her that she did not enjoy the education her brother took for granted or the esteem that men and women of the aristocracy accepted as their due. She never forgot that she was a "dependent," that a mere accident of birth had made her a woman *and* someone who had to support herself. She could not afford to worry about her reputation when she agreed to travel to Ireland without an escort to assume a position as governess in a well-placed family. Nor was she free to write merely for pleasure or for fame. From the beginning, she used her pen not only as a way to express outrage at society's injustices, but to make a living. Because she was always an outsider, her critique was harsh and unforgiving. She despised the effete and idle aristocrats whose meaningless lives she witnessed firsthand as a governess. She rebelled against all invidious distinctions, whether they were based on social status or gender, that kept people from realizing their potential. For her, justice required the reconfiguration of the entire social order and the destruction of all oppressive systems. Wollstonecraft's ideal society did not recognize the "subordination of rank" that constituted what Judith saw as "natural." To the contrary, Mary asserted that "the more equality there is established among men, the more virtue and happiness will reign in society." Hierarchy, she added, was "highly injurious to morality."[75]

While their views of women's equality were superficially similar, the two women's emphasis could not have been more different. Mary thought that women could not achieve equality—even within marriage—unless the entire social order was transformed. Thus she supported the French Revolution, and while she deplored the Jacobin terror, she had enough faith in human potential to believe that in time the French people would moderate their excesses and create a stable, more equitable order. Judith, to the contrary, opposed any social leveling. She assumed, moreover, that if women achieved equality in the home, their influence on the public world would surely follow. She took it for granted that if women could prove that they were rational beings, capable of performing a wide variety of political, social, and economic functions, there would be no reason to deny them the opportunity to compete with their male counterparts on an equal basis. If Mary wanted to alter the social structure as well as the role of women, Judith argued simply for a genderless meritocracy, where wellborn women would find their proper place alongside men of their own kind. She firmly resisted any tendency to "throw down barriers, most judiciously erected," as she insisted that order was as necessary for human happiness as equality was.[76]

The irony was profound, and for Judith it had unfortunate implications. It was an English woman who intuitively understood the direction in which Western society—especially in America—was moving. Judith's commitment to an organic social order was not yet obsolete, but it was fast becoming so. Already, her views were in danger of being dismissed as anachronistic, as the nation inched toward an ideology that promised white men a measure of political equality. In another generation, the high Federalists with whom the Sargents identified would lose their national influence altogether. Even more troubling, just as *The Gleaner* appeared in print, America was beginning to experience something of a backlash against women's rights. Judith, it turned out, was on the wrong side of history both as an advocate for women and as a champion of social hierarchy.

If her "Desultory Thoughts" had urged women to "reverence themselves," Judith found it increasingly difficult to follow her own advice after 1798. In time, she thought, critics might recognize her work's merit. Meanwhile, she had to wait. She had other concerns that would more than occupy her time in the next few years. Julia Maria was ready to begin her "extensive" education, and like Mary Vigillius, Judith planned to be her daughter's most attentive tutor. In time, she would welcome other children into her home as well. It would not be long before she would have the opportunity to put her well-honed theories of education to the test.

PART III

Retreat: 1798–1820

Like other New England Federalists, Judith was disenchanted with the egalitarian message that emanated from the pens of so many unworthy and misguided Americans at the end of the eighteenth century. She began to despair of a country whose potential had once seemed so grand but whose inhabitants now made a mockery of order, decorum, and propriety. Especially after 1800, with Thomas Jefferson's elevation to the presidency, many New Englanders felt increasingly alienated from the crass, materialistic, and disorderly society America seemed to have become. More and more often they retired to their little closets, abandoning any attempt to influence society, seeking sanctuary from a noisy and self-interested public that no longer cared about anything they had to say. Judith felt less and less welcome in a world that threatened to destroy class differences, even as it erected ever more sturdy barriers to women's aspirations. Indeed, many historians argue that the "revolution of 1800" destroyed her chances for literary success, banishing her to hearth and home.[1]

It is hardly necessary, however, to look at the changes in American society to explain Judith Sargent Murray's retreat from the public sphere after 1798. To begin with, she did continue to write, and she made a number of attempts—not entirely futilely—to publish the fruits of her labors. Her play *The African* appeared at the Federal Street Theater, receiving the same tepid reviews her earlier dramatic efforts had garnered. She also helped John publish his sermons and his biography. Still, she was not as prolific as she once had been. She was getting older. She was disappointed by the lack of enthusiasm *The Gleaner* had received. But most of all she was preoccupied with other, more demanding, in her mind, perhaps, more important tasks. Indeed, what looks like a "retreat" from the perspective of the twenty-first century did not necessarily look that way to Judith Sargent Murray. If she had not been so disappointed by the results of her efforts to educate her daughter as well as a steady stream of Mississippians who came to Boston to secure the schooling they could not obtain at home, she may well have seen her life after *The Gleaner*'s publication not only as a resounding success, but as her crowning achievement.

These were challenging days for the Murray household. As Julia Maria matured, she demanded all of her mother's attention and Judith tried to give her daughter the most extensive education her limited funds could provide. From time to time, she also assumed responsibility for Winthrop's five children and three sons of Winthrop's neighbors. If *The Gleaner* offered Americans an abstract plan for educating the country's youth, Judith now had a chance to put her ideas to the test—in the case of the boys, with near disastrous results. For a couple of years, Judith's cousin Mary Allen also lived at Franklin Place, eventually leaving to stay with Jack Ellery, whose cosmopolitan lifestyle she found more appealing than the saturnine existence she endured with the Murrays.[2] Then there was John Murray, who endured a succession of debilitating strokes, becoming a virtual invalid before he died after nearly a decade of suffering. Judith had often had an uneasy relationship with the Boston Universalists. As John's condition deteriorated, as he became more a burden than a source of inspiration, his congregation became ever less willing to put up with Mrs. Murray's haughty ways, not to mention her incessant demands for financial support. Judith's complaints about money also put a strain on her relationship with her siblings. Worst of all, she had to deal with the ramifications of Julia Maria's unhappy marriage to Mississippi planter Adam Bingaman, a marriage that eventually forced both mother and daughter to leave Massachusetts, traveling halfway across the continent to Natchez to live their remaining years in a wild and alien country. Under the circumstances, Judith's "failure" to publish much in the way of creative work after 1798 is not surprising. The fact that she continued to write and to yearn for fame is an indication of how much she valued her literary career.

Still, although she had her own particular reasons for retiring from the public stage, Judith was surely distressed by a broad-based hostility to women's aspirations that seemed to be gaining in numbers and credibility with each passing year. There were many reasons for what could aptly be termed a backlash against women's rights. But if observers wanted to point to any one incident to explain the genteel distaste for what passed as American feminism in the late eighteenth century, they would have placed the publication of William Godwin's *Memoirs of the Author of a Vindication of the Rights of Woman* high on their list. Godwin rushed the book into print in 1798, a little more than four months after his wife's death. A year later, the *Memoirs* was reprinted in the United States, and with it Wollstonecraft's reputation—along with the tolerance for women's rights she espoused—plummeted precipitously. From Judith's perspective, the timing could not have been worse. She had praised Wollstonecraft in *The Gleaner*. The arguments of the two women were markedly alike. True, Judith had arrived independently at her belief in the value of women's education and her admiration for women who learned to reverence themselves. Still, she had reason to fear that her work would suffer because of the public's growing aversion to "rights talk" for women.[3]

When Judith published *The Gleaner* she had not imagined that many people would react especially negatively to her praise of Mary Wollstonecraft. Granted, the *Vindication* already had its detractors. Benjamin Russell, editor of the *Columbian Centinel*, with whom Judith generally agreed, was critical of Wollstonecraft from the beginning. There were always those, like Alice Delancey Izard, who asserted that the *Vindication's* author was little more than "a vulgar, impudent Hussey." Still, for every Izard or Russell, there were many more Americans who saw Wollstonecraft as a kindred spirit, viewing her perspective on gender equality as more or less "common sense." If some readers thought Wollstonecraft's language a bit strident, her tendency to blame men for the woes of women a little unfair, her hints that women and men were social as well as intellectual equals somewhat frightening, most Americans ignored the occasional "errors" they found in her book, focusing instead on those insights with which they agreed. Federalist Aaron Burr pronounced the *Vindication* a "work of genius." John Adams was complimenting his wife when he noted that Abigail was a "Disciple of Wolstonecraft." While Elizabeth Drinker thought Wollstonecraft advocated more "independence" for women than was quite proper, she nevertheless proclaimed that the author " '*speaks my mind* ' " in most instances.[4]

All that changed after the appearance of the *Memoirs*. Godwin wrote the book in an admirable but misguided effort to win sympathy for his wife and support for her beliefs. It had just the opposite effect. He portrayed Wollstonecraft as a passionate being who, after denying her innate sexuality for years in a valiant but futile attempt to conform to the dictates of bourgeois morality, finally gave "loose to all the sensibilities of her nature." Her three-year affair with American poet Gilbert Imlay resulted in the birth of an illegitimate daughter, Fanny. After Imlay spurned his lover for another woman, Wollstonecraft, a "female Werter" as Godwin had it, tried twice to end her own life, not, unfortunately, because she repented of her sins, but because she was disconsolate at the loss of her lover. Until the very end, Godwin claimed, "Mary felt an entire conviction of the propriety of her conduct."[5] Clearly Wollstonecraft was unredeemable. Nor did the tale of this female rake end here. She formed a second illicit relationship, this time with Godwin. Once more she became pregnant and only then, with great reluctance, did the two marry. At least the conclusion to Godwin's tragic tale was comforting. God had the last word. Mary Wollstonecraft died a few days after the birth of her second daughter, Mary. If Godwin was to be believed, his wife never discussed God, religion, or the state of her soul as she faced certain death.

Almost overnight, Wollstonecraft's story became an object lesson on the dangers of feminism. The English woman was, said her critics, an "unsex'd female," a "whore whose vices and follies had brought about her providential end." English writer Hannah More, who had refused even to read the *Vindication*, was herself vindicated. Women who let themselves be seduced by Wollstonecraft's views, she said triumphantly, were "female pretenders" who had rejected their God-given role as inferior helpmate. In America, Timothy Dwight and Benjamin Silliman rushed to link the *Vindication* to free love, proclaiming that Wollstonecraft's views were "unnatural," leading inevitably to the subversion of all natural order. She was "polluted" even "*lewd*," and displayed a total "disregard for the boundaries." Her philosophy, they said, would mean the end of marriage, the end—even worse—of motherhood. No one condemned Wollstonecraft with as much relish as Benjamin Russell. Her supporters, he said, "have striven to divest the sex of their ancient character; to banish shamefacedness, and softness, and delicacy, the retired virtues and the domestic attainment; and to invite women to become amazons and states*men*, and directors, and harlots, upon philosophical principles."[6]

Judith never ventured to defend Mary Wollstonecraft in public, but she was eager to do so in private. In 1800 she wrote to her friend, Sally Barrell with a "formidable accusation." You say, Judith began, that you hate "female politicians." Had her friend merely criticized women's "*ostentatious*, or *intrusive display* of patriotism and *political knowledge*," Judith would have understood. But such a sweeping statement threatened to return women to "that affected ignorance, and childish imbecility, which is supposed the characteristic of the female world." Do not, she urged, "confine us to a state of idiotism." She suspected that Sally's views were colored by her reaction to Godwin's *Memoirs*. Judith had been looking for a chance to defend the English writer, and she now seized the opening. Of course she would never be an advocate "for the pernicious doctrines *attributed* to Mary Wollstonecraft." She had, however, read the *Vindication*, and while it was not perfect, it contained "many luminous truths" and was clearly the "offspring of a superior mind." Surely even Sally Barrell, whose own daughter was a widow with children, would sympathize with Wollstonecraft's insistence that all women should be able to take care of themselves and their dependents.[7]

In June of 1800, Sally's daughter, Sally Sayward Barrell Keating published *Julia, and the Illuminated Baron*. Sally wrote four novels after the death of her husband, Richard Keating, in 1783. Like Judith, she was a committed Federalist who saw the French Revolution as a challenge to all that was good and orderly. Unlike Judith, she held very traditional views of the role of women, arguing that women acted most appropriately when they tended to their domestic duties. The passionate Wollstonecraft, who defied all social conventions and who dared to match wits with any man was Sally's nightmare vision of the evil woman.[8]

Judith had tried to get subscribers for *Julia*, but the task was just as formidable as the one her own friends had faced three years earlier when they sought advance purchasers for *The Gleaner*. Some women claimed never to read novels. Others preferred circulating libraries. Still others did not bother to give her any explanation at all. Judith did not have to feign sympathy for her friend's predicament. "This is not the age, or rather *the Country* of literary patronage," she said feelingly, "and Columbian authors, with a very few exceptions, must look to posterity, for that harvest of fame beneath the umbrageous perfume of which they may have hoped to indulge the most exquisite feelings of the soul." Nevertheless, Judith gave the book unqualified praise, and not only because it quoted passages from her own *Gleaner*. It "seized irresistibly upon my faculties," she proclaimed, "and I did not relinquish the volume, until I had devoured every line."[9]

Still, Judith objected to Keating's pointed attacks on Mary Wollstonecraft, and she was determined to defend the English author to her friend. To do so, she had to confront the apparent lessons of Godwin's *Memoirs* directly. She elected to disregard Godwin's depiction of his wife, constructing her own, more sympathetic version of the English writer's biography. She began by grounding herself in conventional morality. If Wollstonecraft was really guilty of the "rancorous delineations of her Caluminators," she declared that she would be as eager as anyone to make her "the object of my detestation." But Judith had her own experience living "under the banner of prejudice." Remembering a time when vicious rumors had swirled around her relationship with John Murray, she knew how eager people were to believe the worst. In this case, she thought that she knew just *why* people were rushing to judgment, exaggerating and even making up stories about Wollstonecraft out of whole cloth. "Her real *crime*," Judith insisted, "*was her able defence of the sex*." Had she not been so outspoken a supporter of women's rights, the world would not have so gleefully attacked her.[10] Critics had claimed that Wollstonecraft was an atheist, an opponent of marriage, and a leveler whose ideas would destroy all order. Judith addressed all three accusations and found them lacking. Significantly, she did not defend Wollstonecraft's right to hold the opinions attributed to her, nor did she countenance those opinions herself. Instead she reinterpreted Wollstonecraft's life and message, framing them in traditional terms.

Judith did not believe that Wollstonecraft was an atheist. To the contrary, she argued that the *Vindication* breathed not only "a spirit of *virtuous* independence" but a "deep sense of religion." Wollstonecraft believed in the existence of a "great First Cause," and described God as the perfect author of all order. She quoted the scriptures with "marked approbation." She believed in the soul's immortality and insisted that women—who were equal before God—should have equal rights before men. Is this, Judith asked rhetorically, the work of an atheist?[11]

Judith faced a more difficult task when she defended Wollstonecraft's view of marriage, but it was a challenge from which she did not shrink. In her hands, the Englishwoman became the supreme advocate of marital rectitude. If I were to believe the charges of a "certain class" of people, she said, I would agree that Wollstonecraft was trying to "disseminate principles the most licentious, demoralizing, and consequently detestable." But the author's own words and even her deeds gave the lie to the accusations that swirled about her. Far from seeking to destroy marriage, Wollstonecraft saw it as the very foundation of virtue. She sought only to secure a safer and more equal place for women within an institution that had traditionally suffered from patriarchal injustice so that she could "render females more respectable as daughters, wives, mothers and members of society." She valued marriages where men and women stood side by side, working together for their mutual happiness and for the good of society. She did not promote education for women because she wanted to turn women into men, but because "by strengthening the body and exercising the mental capacities," women would be "rendered more capable of managing [their] families, of systematizing morality, and of becoming the *friends* of [their] husbands" and the capable mothers of their children.[12]

As for the sordid aspects of Wollstonecraft's life, they were easily explained. If the Englishwoman was guilty of anything, it was an "*excess* of tenderness" and a certain naïveté, qualities, unfortunately, that most women had in abundance. Wollstonecraft believed that she had been spiritually—if not legally—married to Gilbert Imlay, the "wretch" and "miscreant" who took advantage of his lover's innocence. This was, of course, an error, but hardly a mortal sin. Judith was sophisticated enough to know that marriage rites differed throughout the world. The Bible itself prescribed no particular wedding ceremony. Even some Christian communities recognized an announcement of intention to wed as sufficient. And while it was true that God condemned those who broke the marriage contract, it was Imlay, not Wollstonecraft, who dissolved their relationship, abandoning both "wife" and daughter when his fickle passions took him elsewhere. Wollstonecraft's devotion to little Fanny was so profound that she meekly offered to live with Imlay and his new mistress so that her child might have a father. Moreover, she married William Godwin, proof, surely, that she did not oppose marriage. In the end, Wollstonecraft loved only two men; yet she was "charged with a *multiplicity* of amours." Her critics would stop at nothing to smear the unfortunate woman's good name.[13]

Finally, Judith addressed the claim that Wollstonecraft was a leveler. In what was arguably both the most creative and the weakest portion of her argument, she denied the accusation. Wollstonecraft, Judith conceded may have attacked invidious distinctions based on wealth and power. But she never claimed that all people were equal. She supported distinctions based on "*mental excellence.*" Even when she analyzed the relationship between men and women she never denied "*masculine superiority.*" She knew that "Men were designed by providence to attain a greater degree of virtue than women," and she had never demanded full gender equality. She had only insisted "upon a similarity in *quality*, not in the *quantity* of mind." Nor had she conflated "the different pursuits and departments, allotted to Men, and Women." Women should not hunt and fish, nor should men cook and clean. Only in those areas that were "human"— in other words intellectual—should women strive to improve themselves. It was for this reason that they should demand equal educational opportunities as they raised expectations for generations of women to come.[14]

Judith's belief in women's rights was as strong as ever after the publication of Godwin's *Memoirs*. She did not join those critics who attacked Wollstonecraft and her beliefs. Still, she was affected by an intellectual climate that was growing ever more hostile to the rhetoric of gender equality. Even her private comments on Wollstonecraft's merits were defensive and she never discussed the issue in public. Her arguments were more traditional than modern. She was more willing than she once had been to acknowledge gender differences. While she never retreated from her argument that women were intellectually *equal* to men, Judith now readily conceded that this did not mean that women's goals, their careers, their lives would necessarily be the *same* as those of men. There were, she said, "different pursuits, and departments, allotted to Men, and Women."[15]

Even without Godwin's *Memoirs*, supporters of women's rights would have encountered increasing resistance in America by the end of the eighteenth century. On both sides of the Atlantic, many scholars were adopting an increasingly gendered language of scientific discourse to define women's nature, linking bodily and emotional traits to make a case for qualitative, immutable, and essential differences between men and women. Such a linkage was necessary if governments grounded in universal rights were to devise an intellectually defensible way to deny women any formal place in the political arena. By maintaining that nature itself defined masculinity and femininity, these theorists maintained that women were not simply weaker versions of men. Rather, men and women were radically different, even opposites.[16] The window of opportunity for women who hoped to share in the egalitarian promise of the American Revolution, was—if it had ever existed—rapidly closing.

In the years after she published *The Gleaner*, Judith had her own very private and increasingly heavy burdens to bear. Even had she wanted to continue her public fight for women's equality, she probably would have lacked the time to do so. More and more people clamored for her attention, and she had fewer emotional, physical, or financial resources to satisfy the demands of friends and loved ones. Still, while she published very little after 1798, her interest in her literary career diminished only slowly and never completely disappeared. At times she appeared determined to abandon her work altogether, as she expressed her "strong regrets" that she had ever written anything other than letters to her most intimate friends. Even when she was most discouraged, however, she never quit sending occasional verses to friends, even though she proclaimed that she no longer cared what became of her little ditties. As she confided to one acquaintance, "The ardour with which I once desired literary fame being chilled by the torpid influence of continued neglect, I have very little anxiety for their fate."[17] Nevertheless, as she approached the end of her life, she held on to her precious letter books, carrying them with her when she left Boston for Mississippi, hoping that men and women would read them after she died. If she did not achieve fame in her own lifetime, perhaps it was not too late to make a bid for literary immortality.

Chapter 11

"We Are Fallen on Evil Times"

Something had changed in America by the turn of the century. From Judith Sargent Murray's perspective, that something did not bode well. It was not an abrupt change, of course, nor was America as dramatically different as the cries of dismay from New England Federalists would indicate. But for people like Judith, the direction in which the new nation was heading seemed both obvious and alarming. The traditional vision of an organic, relatively static, hierarchical social order was clearly in danger of being replaced by an individualistic, competitive, and dynamic society. It was a time, she observed, when "heads are whirled below, and heels above." In this unnatural environment, even servants no longer knew their place, and as a result, "the aristocracy" had of necessity "descended to the kitchen."[1] While her family found it increasingly difficult to make ends meet, Judith always identified with the elite and not with ordinary Americans.

George Washington's death in December of 1799 signaled to most Americans—and to Federalists in particular—the end of a heroic era. Judith thought that with Washington gone, Columbia itself was an orphan, as she compared her feelings now to the despair that had engulfed her when her own father had died. Most Bostonians agreed. Shops closed, bells tolled, balls and festive amusements were suspended. Throughout the country, there were orations, eulogies, dirges, hymns, and mournful processions. John's pulpit was draped in black, and he nearly broke down during the sermon he gave commemorating Washington's life. Judith, herself, had never felt such a visceral connection to the body politic. As she observed Americans everywhere engaged in rites of mourning, she could not help but "glory in the reflection, that I am an American." At the same time, however, she could hardly deny that Washington's death had ushered in a "revolution in public men and measures" that should be lamented, not celebrated. More than ever, the country was divided into two parties, implanting "in the bosoms of our most upright, and best informed Citizens, all those barbed and corrosive shafts, which are found in the quiver of acrimony." Americans were engaged in a desperate fight, not only over the future of the nation but over their very identity. It was a fight that New England Federalists were destined to lose.[2]

*   *   *

Everything seemed to come to a head with the election of Thomas Jefferson as president a year later. Until then, Judith was reasonably confident that her vision of America would prevail. New England's own John Adams had carried on the tradition of his predecessor, reining in those boisterous and unruly spirits whose lawless impulses threatened to destroy all semblance of order. Adams's good judgment and his commitment to spreading reason and stability to the nation's hinterland was never more obvious than in the spring of 1798, when Judith learned that the president had made Winthrop the first governor of the Mississippi Territory. Her brother's prolonged trial in the Ohio wilderness was finally over. He was elated. He knew that Natchez was the home of the dregs of civilized society, settled by men of a "refractory and turbulent Spirit." Nevertheless, he was sure that he was just the man who could subdue all incendiaries and bring the rule of law to the region so long as he was willing to rule with an iron hand.[3]

When he first arrived in Mississippi, Winthrop was appalled by the territory's climate and the character of its people, feeling at times like the "Veriest Slave in the World."[4] Still, he had not doubted his own ability or questioned his methods. Unfortunately he never got a chance to prove that he was right. From the beginning he faced the steady and determined resistance of the Jeffersonian Republicans who predominated in the Mississippi Territory, men who resented his stiff New England ways and who used all their influence to get him removed from office. So long as Adams remained president, Winthrop was protected. After 1800 he was vulnerable.

As Judith saw it, all order and virtue were at risk once Jefferson assumed office. "Do not," she asked rhetorically, "thick clouds hover over the United States?" She predicted that with Jefferson's election, the "horrors of a revolution" would "usher in the approaching Century." "Apprehension," she added, "predominates in my bosom." Her apprehension was personal. She feared that men—like her brother—"whose political sentiments, are opposed to the system about to be established" would soon lose their positions. She was right. Almost immediately, grumblers began working diligently to remove Winthrop from office. Judith was not a passive observer of her brother's fate. Instead she joined the partisan debate, gathering information about affairs in Mississippi, sending a flurry of letters defending Winthrop to anyone who might have influence in Washington, and encouraging the sale of Epes's "Political Intolerance," a pamphlet that put Winthrop in the best possible light. Even as she marshaled her arguments, Judith suspected that facts were irrelevant. She knew that the attacks on Winthrop were purely partisan. We are, she told Massachusetts congressman Samuel Thatcher, "fallen upon evil times, a certain class of men seem to bear down all opposition, to carry every point." Her brother, she proclaimed, "is detested by the Jacobins," who were determined to convict him of the "high crime of Federalism." There was no point in hoping for a miracle in an age when innocence was no match for slander. In the end, Jefferson, himself removed Winthrop from office, naming Republican William C. C. Claiborne, one of her brother's leading detractors, in his place. The president, observed John Murray, was "determined to be the Fool of the Multitude."[5]

After 1800, like so many New England Federalists, Judith felt increasingly marginalized. "Clouds seem to gather round our political career," she said, "and if we are not on the brink of ruin, the testimony of those statesmen in whom we have confided, unwarrantably aggravates the calamities of our situation." Unable to stop America's leaders from bringing on such calamities, she could only deplore the effect their policies had on the country's economic fortunes. The political influence of the Northeast declined, and its economy was in free fall. European warfare continued to wreak havoc on Boston merchants. The city's streets were clogged with unemployed sailors. Fewer imported goods found their way into the shops, and prices steadily climbed. By the fall of 1806, everyone was complaining that necessities were unaffordable, and luxuries were simply out of the question. All Boston suffered as the English and French stepped up their attacks on American vessels. Even the wealthy members of John's congregation were casualties of the depression. As Judith told Winthrop, "the Commerce of our Country, paralized by a train of events, is prostrate." Not only did John fail to get a raise, but the pernicious effects of inflation meant that in real terms his salary declined.[6]

Judith thought that Jefferson's Embargo Act, passed in 1807, only made matters worse. In letter after letter she decried the way that the legislation decimated Boston's merchants and reduced "our upright Citizens, to subterfuges, which in better times, they would disdain," turning many an ordinary American into a criminal. A vessel from Boston bound ostensibly for New Orleans often sailed instead to an interdicted destination, directly violating legislation that most people in Massachusetts saw as ill-advised in any event. In response to such blatant disregard for government edict, federal authorities stepped up enforcement efforts, demanding bonds from merchants who claimed to be sailing to legal venues. Investors forfeited their money, of course, whenever a vessel failed to arrive at its declared port of call. No wonder Boston observed the first anniversary of the Embargo Act by tying black ribbons around vessels languish-ing in the harbor and flying ships' flags at half-mast. Merchants and sailors alike joined the slow, dirgelike procession through the town, solemnly mourning the death of American commerce. With James Madison's election to the presidency, Washington eased trade restrictions and by May of 1809, Judith was declaring that commerce had been restored to "perfect freedom."[7] Still, if she had ever harbored any doubts that political decisions affected helpless women and chil-dren along with the men who made them, the Embargo Act disabused her of those notions.

In 1812, war broke out between England and America. Again, Judith saw her-self as a victim of policies over which she had no control. Even during the Amer-ican Revolution, whose aims she supported, she had hated the martial ethos the conflict had engendered and deplored the death and destruction that war in-evitably brought in its wake. At least then she had seen her sacrifices as having a noble purpose and she embraced the end of hostilities with optimism, foolishly assuming that she would never live to see a new generation of men marching off to do battle with England. This war was different. For many Americans—especially New Englanders—it entailed suffering to no good purpose. Historians look upon the War of 1812 as America's "second war of independence." For Judith, the conflict simply rendered her more powerless, more dependent than ever. War had been bad enough when she was young. She had passed her sixtieth year when hostilities broke out a second time and there were days when she thought she would not survive this new international conflagration.

Judith had reason to hate the war. Like most New England Federalists she distrusted the motives of Republicans whose virtual party-line vote had made it possible. She knew that hostilities would disrupt commerce and once again Boston's economy would suffer. Ministers throughout the region, who lived on a fixed income and were always at the mercy of their congregations, would be especially hard hit. But the entire coast was affected. Fishing was interrupted. Towns were vulnerable to attack. No one was building houses and "mechanicks of every description" were out of work. Stocks plummeted. Banks, such as the Massachusetts State Bank in which Judith had invested both her own and Winthrop's money, were on the brink of bankruptcy. Even the most prudent Federalists were not immune from bad judgment or worse luck. Dividends, if they came at all, were a fraction of what they once had been. When Judith sent her nephew to the Marine and Fire Insurance Company to inquire about the status of her investment there, the company's agents laughed in his face.[8]

At the same time, prices skyrocketed and no one would lend Judith money when she needed just a little something to tide her over. The price of paper doubled and books were simply unaffordable. She doled out at least ten dollars for a yard of broadcloth that once cost three. Butter, sugar, and flour, tea, milk, and coffee were priced beyond the ability of many people to purchase them. In the Sargent family, only Fitz William emerged relatively unscathed. He had the golden touch and triumphed even in the worst of times. Indeed, he did so well, as his vessels almost magically evaded capture by the British, that he was able to purchase an estate in Newton, Massachusetts, where he moved shortly after hostilities began. For everyone else, the world was "rapidly hastening to destruction."[9]

That destruction appeared eminent in the fall of 1814, when the British invaded Washington, burning most of the city to the ground. Even Judith, usually something of an Anglophile, was outraged. We now have a "new view of British Moderation," she declared. In the aftermath of the razing of the nation's capital, every town on the eastern seacoast prepared for similar attacks. Boston assumed the appearance of a garrison. Soldiers patrolled the streets day and night. Martial music filled the air. Suddenly patriotic, citizens showed up with axes, spades, and provisions to repair and staff the town's fortifications. Harvard students gave up their last day of vacation to do their part strengthening the ramparts.[10]

*   *   *

Even the most committed Federalist celebrated General Andrew Jackson's victory at the battle of New Orleans. In Boston, church bells rang and guns were fired as the town anticipated the better times peace would surely bring. Judith was thrilled that the war that had brought rich as well as poor to ruin was finally over. Still, she did not look upon peace with confidence. Instead, she often found herself "labouring under great depression of spirit." She had not enjoyed truly good health since Julia Maria's birth. What at first had been mere chronic discomfort grew worse as she aged. Her eyesight began to fail and she feared that she was going blind. At one point, she dared to take a dose of laudanum to help her through an especially trying day. It had a positive effect, at least temporarily, allowing her to mingle with a group of strangers "with exhilarated spirits, and tolerable confidence." In her youth, she would have disdained such an artificial stimulant. Now she was glad it was available.[11]

Poor health and a general sense of malaise were bad enough. Being penniless was excruciating. More than once, Judith was ashamed to show her face in the marketplace because she owed so much to so many people. Occasionally, when John left town and the Universalists failed to pay his salary, she considered simply shutting down the house and moving in with friends. It was probably an idle threat. Still, she had reason to be anxious. It seemed as though everything that could go wrong, did so. The Boston Universalists were hard hit by the economic vicissitudes that rocked the New England economy at the turn of the century. As a result, they often could not pay John on time. When the Murrays asked the church to supply their firewood—a perquisite that virtually all Massachusetts ministers enjoyed—they refused. "You would be surprised," John confided to New York Universalist William Palmer, "to see how many there are of a Sunday afternoon in our meeting and how few of that number put a penny into the Box." Increasingly, he hinted that his "connections" in Boston were tenuous, and that his church no longer revered him as it once had done. "I have had," he said, but "slender evidences of their affections in a pecuniary point of view." There were times when he regretted ever having left Gloucester, and Judith predicted that if his congregation continued to neglect him, he would accept one of the offers from other churches that still came his way. Had he been free to follow his impulses, he would probably have left for New York, where he felt more at home than he did any place in America. Unfortunately, John said, "I cannot think for myself wholly." But while he remained in Boston, when he wrote to his New York friends his tears were often so thick that he could scarcely see the paper in front of him.[12]

John may have complained privately about the way the Boston church treated him, but he shrank almost instinctively from arguments over money, fondly remembering those times when he was not obliged even to think about such distasteful matters. He had always been genuinely satisfied to live modestly, trusting in the Lord and his own admirers to satisfy his needs. Now that he had an "expensive family" to support, it was hard to do so. At least, he implied, it was hard when his wife was never satisfied.[13]

While John did his best not to think about his precarious finances, Judith could think of little else. Insecurity invariably brought out the worst in her. Her sense of helplessness as she tried to make sense of the bewildering decisions that faced her, led almost inevitably to arguments over mere trifles. She quarreled with Esther and Fitz William over what she thought they owed her after they finally sold her Gloucester house. At one point, when Judith tried once too often to explain her position, Esther became so angry that she stormed out of Franklin Place.[14]

Judith's own history no doubt made her fears loom especially large. She had once been connected to "a man of sorrow" and had been "doomed to drag the Debtor's length'ning chain." She was frantic when she contemplated the possibility of losing everything once again. She had always complained that her education had not prepared her for independence, and she loathed the thought of living on the charity of friends or relatives. She had seen too many families over the years who floundered when the man of the house became incapacitated or died. Even when widows and daughters were willing to take in sewing, they were often unable to support themselves. She had long argued that legislators should give "pensions adequate to their needs" to widows and orphans. So far, however, Congress had not heeded her advice. Thus Judith feared that she and her daughter would "become the needy dependants, upon caprices which chance may render most unpropitious." Her fears exacerbated her desire to challenge the outworn traditions that circumscribed her reality. "Would it were the custom," she cried, "to qualify Women for exertions, which would enable them to bring forward even in a state of widowhood the children whom they had introduced into being. But lost by the kind of instruction to which we are limited," she continued, "we are in many respects . . . degraded" and are left to "struggle with all the mortifications incident to artificial imbecility." Dependence meant powerlessness, a condition that Judith had resisted throughout her entire adult life, sometimes successfully, more often not. What had once been an abstract desire for equality and independence was now a concrete necessity. While Judith insisted that she was "not in the habit of bowing down to wealth," as Julia Maria matured and John grew more feeble, she was almost obsessed with concerns about her material well-being.[15]

If she was frightened, Judith was also bitter. Fitz William was blessed with good fortune, and even after her husband died, Esther lived comfortably. Once he moved to Mississippi, Winthrop, too, almost forgot that he had ever worried about making ends meet. Judith alone appreciated the steady loss of status that accompanied downward economic mobility. She occasionally boasted that Franklin Place was "the resort of the principal gentry of our Metropolis," but living in such elegant surroundings only made her own position seem worse by comparison. She refused to accept defeat gracefully. Although she steadfastly maintained that she was "never ambitious of disproportionate gains," she was determined to get, as she always saw it, what *we consider as righteously our due.*[16]

There were, unfortunately, few options to which a genteel woman could resort to earn money. A Mary Wollstonecraft or a Susannah Rowson might open a school, but although Judith valued education and enjoyed inspiring young minds, she never considered earning a living in quite so public a way. The time-honored approach, of course, was to live frugally. Judith insisted that she never spent so much as one "superfluous penny" on herself. When she and John visited John and Abigail Adams, for instance, she donned her mother's old coat because she could not afford a respectable one of her own. She also did most of the housework, although this meant that little time remained for intellectual pleasures. It was amazing that "matters so transient, and so trivial" were so time-consuming, stripping matters "of intelligence and of sentiment" of their importance. Judith knew that she should exult in her position as mistress of her home, but in fact she felt "enchained to the kitchen" and had no faith that she would ever again enjoy the life of the mind. Nor was her social life what it once had been. When she refused Maria's dinner invitations, she explained that she preferred intimate groups to "brilliant assemblies." Perhaps. But just as likely, she felt a little out of place in the circles that Daniel and Maria frequented, nor could she return the Sargents' hospitality in an appropriate fashion.[17]

Saving money was not enough to achieve the desired results. Nor did *The Gleaner* earn as much as the Murrays needed. Thus, Judith was constantly on the lookout for other ways to augment John's salary. She had always fancied herself as something of an entrepreneur and was grateful that, unlike her first husband, John trusted her with the family's finances. Because she acted with his blessing, she felt confident that she was not behaving improperly when she began seeking out investments in what she fervently hoped were safe but profitable ventures.[18] So long as things went well, she was circumspect. But when the family's economic position took a decided turn for the worse, and when she found herself hemmed in by the age-old strictures against independent women, she railed against a reality that blocked her every endeavor.

At times she was delighted with her efforts. Over the years necessity had forced her to juggle her accounts and she learned to handle the family's finances with a certain confidence, seeking advice from relatives and friends who could steer her in the right direction. She invested money in loan office certificates and bought and sold stock in banks in both Gloucester and Boston. She borrowed money when she had to, always seeking loans at the lowest interest possible, boasting that she felt as though she was "doing business like a merchant." Unfortunately, she was not invariably successful. When the women in *The Gleaner* assumed control of their own resources, they relished their independence and triumphed over material adversity. Real life was seldom so kind. In 1806, for instance, Judith put $700 in Massachusetts state bonds, assuming that the money would earn 5 percent interest. By the following year, however, the investment was rapidly diminishing in value. Because John was "unacquainted with the nature of publick stocks," Judith took it upon herself to seek expert advice, looking for a venture that was "*permanent* and *productive*," even as she complained that she could not act on her own behalf. Women were not welcome in stockholders' meetings and so she had to work through an intermediary. If she was successful, she intended to surprise her husband "with an unexpected resource." She did not say what she would do should she fail.[19]

Judith's most prolonged experience with the injustices of the economic world was the result of the one occasion when John became directly involved in a speculative venture. When Judith finally received her "patrimonial inheritance" of $2,000, her husband refused to touch even the interest on the bequest. He planned to save the little nest egg for Julia Maria's education. But then he disregarded his usual caution, investing the money in a venture that ended disastrously. In early January of 1797, Philadelphian Samuel Jackson, Elizabeth's husband, was in Boston. When John mentioned Judith's inheritance to his friend, Jackson offered to invest the money. Judith later claimed to have opposed the proposal from the beginning, preferring "*moderate* interest, to exorbitant gains." But, as she had done with John Stevens, she yielded to what she had hoped was her husband's better judgment. Like her first husband, however, John Murray often trusted the wrong people. He readily conceded that because he was artless himself, he "expected no art" in others. Indeed, he was so enchanted by Jackson's promise of easy money easily gained, that he wanted to mortgage Franklin Place to obtain still more capital to invest. To this, said Judith, "I positively refused my assent." That was one decision she never regretted.[20]

Jackson promised to put their money in only the safest ventures. Indeed, he was so confident of his own intuition that he casually remarked that *should* he invest unwisely, he would compensate the Murrays out of his own pocket. His first effort on their behalf, however, which he predicted would earn about $800 a year in interest alone, was disappointing. In July, he put their funds in the Population Company of Pennsylvania. He promised that the investment would be worth $3,000 in no time, and in eighteen months they would double their money. By the time Julia Maria was fifteen, she would be affluent. "I am as sure as I live," he assured the Murrays, "there will be a fortune for your little daughter."[21]

Unfortunately, the Population Company was a highly speculative endeavor. Its backers, most of whom were Federalists, bought land north of the Ohio and west of the Allegheny River at rock-bottom prices, hoping to sell it to settlers who would leap at the opportunity to become independent farmers. The company offered 100 acres to people settling there as tenants. If they improved their holdings they could purchase an additional 300 acres at a moderate price. The investors argued that they were public-spirited citizens as well as shrewd businessmen, for they were keeping the disorderly riffraff at bay, thus guaranteeing Pennsylvania's social stability. Almost immediately, however, some adventurers sensed disaster. Land in Pennsylvania and Ohio was cheap, and stockholders had difficulty securing settlers. Moreover, tenants who initially agreed to the company's terms often refused to pay for their land, claiming ownership by right of settlement.[22]

As early as 1798, disquieting news about the venture began drifting in to

Boston. One of the chief investors, Robert Morris, had declared bankruptcy, and the Murrays heard that Samuel Jackson had gone down with him. Judith wrote to Elizabeth, not Samuel, for reassurance. Samuel immediately returned $1,000 to the Murrays, but he convinced them to keep the rest of their money where it was. Still, John was concerned enough that he traveled to Philadelphia to secure a receipt for his remaining shares. By the time he arrived, however, Samuel was in Tennessee and John returned home empty-handed. Not long thereafter, the Murrays learned that Jackson had sold their shares and pocketed the money. "So," John sighed, "I must live by faith a little longer."[23]

Judith was less able to live by faith than her husband was. Thus she stepped to the fore, scarcely pausing to apologize for intruding where many thought she did not belong. "You may think," she wrote Elizabeth Jackson, "I am out of my sphere in attending to these matters." But she was not. The system of coverture decreed that she and John were one. Thus, she said, "I must suffer equally with my husband." In reality, given their very different personalities and expectations, she surely suffered more.[24]

Judith never quit seeking reimbursement. In 1809, John finally consented to allow her to sue their would-be benefactor. In response, Jackson boldly denied owing the Murrays anything, even as he offered them four shares in the Population Company, worth in his estimation some $1,000. Refusing to be cheated again, Judith did some checking before she accepted the overture. What she discovered made her more furious than ever. Once again, Jackson was taking advantage of her. He did not even own the four shares he had promised her, nor were the shares worth anywhere near his estimate.[25] Most galling, he acted as though Judith did not exist. The matter, he said, was between John and himself. At that, Judith exploded. Of course she knew that "the law acknowledges no *separate* act of a *married* woman." Still, she said, the money we put in Jackson's hands was hers "by a double right." It was a gift from her own father, thus giving her "the right of Nature." It was also hers "by the sanction of my husband, who guaranteed to me the sole, and separate use thereof." Unfortunately, her claims were moral rather than legal. While she wanted "justice, justice, justice," she knew that the law "was not designed for integrity, it only forges fetters for fraud." Besides, by the time John finally agreed to let her sue Samuel Jackson, the Murrays did not have the money to institute proceedings. No matter how many appeals Judith made, no matter how often she repeated her story, piling detail upon detail in a desperate effort to prove her point, she never obtained satisfaction. As late as 1816, she was still writing to Jackson, who no longer bothered to answer her. The problem was one she had confronted in one form or another her entire life. Although her nemesis was a "weak man," he nevertheless feared "nothing from a Woman's pen." He would only "shrink from the serious remonstrances of a determined Man."[26]

*   *   *

Thwarted at every turn by her efforts to earn money for her family, Judith had one more option, one that seemed especially suited to her own ability and inclinations. Despite all of the disappointments she had suffered, she continued to harbor lingering hopes that she might use her talents as a writer to material advantage. She never stopped imagining that she might "still come into possession of that portion of celebrity, to which my humble efforts may be legitimately entitled." In 1799, she contacted the editor of the *Columbian Phoenix*, offering to send some verses to the magazine. She hoped, she said, that like the phoenix itself, she was ready to rise from the ashes. She was especially optimistic in 1806, when Robert Redding made plans to republish *The Gleaner* in England. To be published in London would be a real coup, one most American writers only dreamed about. Redding died, however, before he could get *The Gleaner* in print, and the project died with him. Even then, Judith continued to hope for vindication in the world of letters, writing some poems under the name of "Honoria Martesia" for the *Boston Weekly Magazine*.[27]

Nothing Judith published after *The Gleaner*, however, made much impact. If *The Gleaner* was not as daring as "Desultory Thoughts" or "On the Equality of Sexes" had been, her work after 1798 was even more bland and unobjectionable and, as a result, completely forgettable. Judith may well have wanted simply to play it safe, as she sensed the changing attitude toward women's rights that followed in the wake of Godwin's *Memoirs*. Or she may have been worn down by the indifference her best efforts met. Her belief in her chances for fame was clearly more conflicted than it had been when she was young. True, most of the time she still found writing therapeutic. "The potent little instrument" of the pen, she said, has often "stollen me from myself." It acted like "some magick wand," and she usually rose from her "writing desk, *calm, if not happy.*" But increasingly her mood darkened, as she predicted that "versification and its laws will in future cease to occupy my contemplations." She was convinced that her enemies were determined to discredit her. "So pointed is the cruelty, and so frigid the neglect, which mark the conduct of my contemporaries," she said, that there was no reason to continue. More and more often she threatened to burn all her manuscripts, or at least to hide them away so that no one could ever laugh at her pretensions again. "I am," she told Epes, "induced to conceive, that I possess neither Genius, taste, nor judgment; and when this melancholy conclusion obtains, I am on the point of binding myself, never more to attempt, even a common letter of friendship." The "repeated mortifications, and rebuffs" she had endured made her determined never again to "venture upon so fluctuating an ocean as publick opinion." She would leave it to her survivors to decide whether to publish the poems and essays that remained in her possession, or to have them "consigned to oblivion."[28]

An unusually cruel practical joke played by Maria's son, Lucius Manlius, destroyed what remained of Judith's self-confidence. Her favorite cousin was intelligent and charming. He was also high-spirited and had a propensity for pranks that sometimes got out of hand. In the spring of 1806, Judith became the special object of his "unmanly and unnatural persecution." It started in June, when she received a letter, purportedly from Boston printers Joshua Belcher and Samuel Armstrong, asking for permission to publish some of her essays. As Lucius Manlius had expected would happen, "the bait was greedily swallowed." Judith responded immediately. The "mingling frigidity, and ill-mannered severity, with which my compositions have been received," she explained, had led her to conclude that nothing she wrote was worthy of publication. Perhaps she was wrong. Thus, she gave the firm her cautious permission. She was mortified, however, when the puzzled printers informed her that they had never written to her. Lucius Manlius, she eventually realized, was the author of the "forged letter, designed to perplex, and ridicule me."[29]

At least this embarrassment was relatively private. Judith also suffered public humiliation at her cousin's hands. The August 27 edition of the *Columbian Centinel* included a little ditty signed by "Honora," one of Judith's recent pseudonyms. The poem, which took advantage of Judith's reputation as a shameless publicity seeker, was a florid hymn of praise for "Constantia." While many readers chuckled at the poem's witticisms, Judith was distraught. That anyone would think that she had written her "own panegyric," that she had exhibited such "ridiculous indecorum" was ludicrous. Still, she had her enemies, especially in literary circles, and she was convinced that Lucius Manlius's little joke had made her a laughingstock. Four months later, she was still refusing Maria's invitations to visit, fearing that she might be "an object of ridicule" if she set foot in her aunt's house.[30]

Despite her misgiving and her sense that time had passed her by, Judith was not yet ready to abandon all hope. She made one final effort to achieve a position of prominence in America's literary circles, and perhaps to make a little money as well. In the fall of 1804, she once more sought renown as a playwright. It had been nearly a decade since her very public quarrel with Robert Treat Paine, time enough for old wounds to heal. Besides, the Federal Street Theater seemed more open to homegrown productions than it once had been. Susanna Rowson's *Slaves in Algiers* and her *Americans in England* had both been produced there. And Deborah Sampson Gannett had trod the boards in uniform, describing her military exploits during the Revolutionary War. Judith's fascination with the dramatic arts had never abated. She attended the Federal Street Theater regularly, and she kept the lines of communication open with manager Snelling Powell. Somehow, she had found the time to write a new play, entitled *The African*, which she hoped to see performed. Interestingly, she sent her script to Paine, swearing him to secrecy and asking for his honest assessment of its merits. If he liked it, she asked him to forward it to Powell.[31]

Judith was determined to keep her project a secret. If there really was a "malicious prejudice, in force" against her, then even if her work had true merit, her enemies would see that it was doomed. Thus, with the connivance of Julia Maria and her niece, Anna Williams, Judith devised an elaborate strategy for concealing her identity. The two girls laboriously copied the entire play so that no one would recognize the manuscript's handwriting. Rather than use the post to communicate with Paine, Julia Maria became her mother's private courier. Judith thought her decision to seek Paine's sponsorship was a stroke of genius. No one who knew anything about her quarrel with the *Orrery*'s editor would suspect him of lending her a hand. She had another, more devious motive for seeking Paine's help. She sought, she later admitted, to "disarm my adversary," making it virtually impossible for him to criticize her play.[32]

When Judith began to believe that her comedy might actually be produced, she grew increasingly worried that her disguise would be penetrated. How, she wondered, should she handle newspaper advertisements? If the ads did not mention the author, might this not awaken suspicion? Eventually she hit upon an anagram of "Martenia," a pseudonym she had occasionally adopted, calling herself "M. Maranite." She fretted—no doubt correctly—that the disguise might be too thin, but she hoped it would shield "the trembling Author" from the "scrutinizing glance" of a censorious world.[33]

As was her wont, Judith pretended to have modest aspirations for her play even as she planned meticulously for a resounding success. She insisted that she had written *The African* only because she was in Powell's debt. His Federal Street Theater had endured more than its share of bad luck over the years. In 1798, the edifice had burned to the ground, and even after a new building was erected the company continued to lose money. Still, Powell had put a free box at Judith's disposal and she had used his gift liberally over the years. Humiliated by the snide comments people made about her willingness to accept the manager's charity, she thought that her play, given as a benefit for Powell, would serve as compensation. Nevertheless, while she vowed to remain in the background, she did hope to profit by selling the play's copyright. And if *The African* was a success, she would "consent to throw off the mask" completely.[34]

By February of 1805, Judith was confident that she would soon see *The African* performed. She waited, patiently at first, less patiently as month devolved upon month and her play remained unproduced. There was always some excuse. Paine had not finished editing her manuscript. Powell did not have enough actors at his disposal. Frustrated, she finally demanded an explanation. Either reject *The African*, she said, or produce it. Powell did neither. In the fall of 1806, Judith finally took matters into her own hands. She suspected that the problem lay with actor Thomas Abthorpe Cooper. Viewed as the greatest tragedian to appear on the American stage, he had dazzled audiences throughout America. Powell had pulled off a major coup when he lured the actor to Boston for the 1806 season. Word had it that he was tired of learning new lines and Powell was reluctant to push him. No matter. Judith sent a flurry of letters directly to Cooper, begging him to help her quench "an unextinguishable thirst for literary fame." She appealed to his patriotism (although he was English) as well as to his ego. "America must one day be elevated to literary, as well as civil independence," she said, and Cooper could move this process forward. When the actor read her play and expressed interest in it, Judith felt vindicated. "I complacently indulge a presentment," she told him, "that I am to owe you an essential obligation." Comparing Cooper to David Garrick, she hoped he would do for her, what the great Garrick had once done for Hannah Cowley.[35]

Once again, Judith was on the verge of success. In 1807, the theater was finally poised to produce the play. While she tried to let the actors go about their business, she seemed constitutionally unable to do so. "Propriety" dictated that she not interfere, but when she learned that Mrs. Usher, a "beautiful and deserving Woman," would play the role of a fourteen-year-old girl, Judith was "impelled" to object. She was "tremblingly alive to the fate of a piece, which has for upwards of three years, held [her] soul in suspense." Mrs. Usher needed to be recast. Almost immediately, however, she regretted her remarks, worried that her "imperiously negative" views might lead to still more delays.[36]

Sometime in January of 1808, *The African* made its long awaited debut. Judith sat breathlessly in her box as the curtains rose on opening night. She was stunned by the performance. In 1795, it had been the actresses who forgot their lines and fled the stage in disgrace. This time it was the actors who had apparently not memorized their parts. "You will judge," Judith wrote her niece, "of my suffering." By now, everyone knew the play was hers. Her humiliation was complete. Even so, Judith had a number of excuses to explain the debacle. The theater had been "thinly attended" all year. Boston was suffering the effects of Thomas Jefferson's Embargo Act, everyone lived in fear of a war with England, and no one was in the mood for frivolous amusements.[37]

Judith's failure to wring fame from *The African* marked her last sustained effort to write anything original for public consumption. Although she never laid down her pen for good, the mangled performance and the "gall steeped pen" of an anonymous critic were simply too much to bear. Ridicule, criticism, and—perhaps worse—indifference had taken their toll. Judith had once dreamed of becoming America's literary muse. After 1808, her hopes were dormant, if not dead.[38]

*   *   *

Judith endured more than her share of crises after 1800. Most—the death of loved ones, the family's financial woes—were beyond her control. Her response to those crises, however, often made things worse. One chronic difficulty was her steadily worsening relationship with the Boston Universalists. She had never been especially close to her husband's parishioners. As a result, she did not have a reservoir of good faith upon which to draw when nerves frayed. As the church suffered financially, many members began to resent the time John spent away from Boston. Judith was left to handle any problems that arose during her husband's absences. Lacking her husband's charisma, and not always the soul of tact, she often exacerbated tensions. While she may not have required the Boston church's goodwill in the beginning, in the long run her cool relations with her husband's congregation would have unfortunate consequences.

The Universalists struggled to survive Boston's faltering economy, and many resented what appeared to be the lavish circumstances the Murrays enjoyed at their expense. Moreover, it was Judith, not John, who constantly demanded more than they were willing or able to offer. Judith had once been humiliated when she heard coins drop in the collection box, hating to acknowledge her dependency on the church's parishioners. Now, she had no compunction about haranguing the congregation's elders for her husband's pay. In the fall of 1798, she wrote—almost surely without John's knowledge—to the Universalist proprietors, outlining her family's difficulties. All we ask, she said, is "the *regular* advance of our weekly stipend" as well as payment of all arrears. Two years later, the church continued to drag its feet.[39]

Money was not the only issue that Judith had to negotiate with the Boston congregation. The problem of securing substitutes for John, who was so often on the road, was particularly thorny. In 1799, for instance, the Reverend Hosea

Ballou was filling in while Murray was in Philadelphia. Judith had heard Ballou preach in Gloucester and thought his views were similar to her husband's. Admittedly, the minister was ambitious, impulsive, and a little overbearing, but he was also an excellent speaker. She thought his "want of cultivation" was obvious, but then in her mind no one compared to John.[40]

At first, all went well. Ballou drew large crowds, as Bostonians flocked to his services, eager to hear a new voice or to learn more about the Universalist faith. But then, perhaps sensing that his influence was growing, Ballou overstepped his bounds. Among other things, he implied that Jesus was not divine. He also seemed to be moving dangerously close to Unitarianism. Judith sat frozen in her pew. It had been she who persuaded John, against his own judgment, to invite Ballou to Boston. He would surely blame her if members of his congregation defected to the heretical but charismatic minister. She breathed a little easier when a voice rang out from the back of the room. Brother Balch condemned the sermon, assuring all visitors that this was not the message that usually emanated from John Murray's pulpit. As soon as the service ended, people gathered around the minister's wife, demanding her opinion of Ballou's views. Judith was never at her best when she spoke in public and she was especially nervous in the presence of strangers. "With more warmth than prudence," she later reported, "I asserted that I had never attended a public exhibition of sentiments so deistical, and blasphemous." When some onlookers demanded particulars, Judith trembled, her voice faltered, and she could not utter a single word. Fortunately, a deacon came to her rescue, informing her that her sleigh was waiting outside. Safely tucked away at home, she immediately resorted to form, writing down her objections to Ballou's sermon, and offering a copy to anyone who asked. Luckily, many people assured her that there were no more than four people in the entire church who agreed with Ballou. Not so fortunately, the four were very influential. Still, for the moment the issue faded. The church dismissed Ballou and the pulpit remained empty for the next four Sundays.[41]

*   *   *

More and more, Judith felt alone and isolated, unable to connect with anyone, even on paper, much less in person. Just as her beloved New England became less able to control the larger world, just as the most elite and deserving women began to be relegated to a separate and unequal status, so, even in her own home and among her closest friends and trusted relatives, Judith felt marginalized, nearly invisible. Everywhere she saw signs—some real, some surely imagined—that everyone she loved was abandoning her. She was hurt when Esther came to town and refused to attend services at the Universalist meetinghouse. She was even more distraught because Fitz William's daughters virtually refused to visit Franklin Place. On those rare occasions when they did come, they were extremely cold, seldom stayed more than a quarter of an hour, and approached John "with marked reluctance, and with a kind of a peevish frigidity."[42]

And then there was her quarrel with Anna, her once-devoted orphan. Her niece apparently resented Julia Maria's central place in the Murray household, especially after the family moved to Franklin Place. Anna's "passionate declamations, jarring disputations," and "deforming paroxysms" proved that despite her best efforts, Judith had not raised her niece to be rational or even genteel. Eventually, the young woman left the house altogether. When she asked to return, Judith refused. Even if you were "destitute of a home," she said, she would "rather pay a weekly sum for your board, than receive you again into this house." A household with "two directing females," she added, was as unnatural as a "two headed animal." Judith promised that she and John would try to remember Anna in their will. More than that small gesture, she refused to offer.[43]

If Judith was saddened by her quarrel with her niece, she was disconsolate as she began to sense that she and Maria were drifting apart. When she had moved to Boston, Judith had eagerly anticipated the many leisurely, intimate conversations the two of them would enjoy. She would no longer have to rely on letters and the occasional visit to fulfill her need for a satisfying companion. Instead, almost as soon as she settled in at Franklin Place, Judith noticed that Maria's devotion had cooled. "I could particularize," she said tersely. There were "many little circumstances, in reality trivial," that taken as a whole indicated that her aunt no longer saw her as a soul mate. In fact, Maria noticed the same "appearance of distance." When Judith turned down dinner invitations, claiming to prefer intimate gatherings to the "gayest scenes which the most brilliant assemblies can boast," Maria saw herself as unworthy, assuming that her niece had rejected old relationships in favor of the witty repartee of her new literary friends. She had been especially hurt when Judith did not tell her about her plans to publish *The Gleaner*. The two women eventually brought their mutual fears of rejection to the surface. Judith promised to keep no more secrets and to "*disdain suspicion*." Once more, she and Maria would share "all those plans and prospects, in which a Castle building imagination fondly delight." Still, the relationship between the two was never quite the same. Both women periodically fancied slights. They came together, cried, and made up, and then one would sense a certain constraint in the other and the cycle of suspicion would repeat itself. Perhaps a heartfelt friendship conducted on the written page was more satisfying than one depending upon face-to-face contact.[44]

Judith could not ignore the overwhelming sense of powerlessness with which she seemed destined to struggle. Age had something to do with it, of course. When she glanced in the mirror and saw her gray hair and the ever deepening lines that marked her face, she barely recognized the person who stared back at her in somber disbelief. She had grown plumper over the years, and she only vaguely resembled the sylphlike ingenue that Copley had captured on canvas so long ago.[45] True, maturity had its advantages. Matrons could ignore society's rules without sacrificing their reputation more easily than young women could. They were freer to move about without a male escort and could speak their minds more readily. Still, they could do so only because no one really cared where they went or what they said. Judith had always predicted that in a nation dominated by young people, her prospects would steadily narrow. "Old Age," she once told John, "strips the venerable Man, or Woman, of the energies of youth[.] they are judged too antique for the rest of society, and their presence creates disgust!"[46]

Age alone was not enough to make Judith unhappy. She had reached that time in her life when she was reminded as never before of her own mortality. Her contemporaries were ill or dying, and all too often she found herself sitting at the deathbed of a friend or relative. It was well and good for a Universalist to proclaim that the body meant nothing, that death was an occasion for rejoicing, not sorrow. Like all humans, she found it difficult to let go of those individuals whose lives were inextricably bound up with her own.

Judith's family was becoming ever smaller. Her uncle Daniel, her father's only remaining brother, died in 1806. Seven years later, she sat with Maria as her aunt drew her last breath. More distressing was the death of Esther in 1811 at the age of fifty-six. The sisters had not gotten along over the last few years. They had, Judith noted, "different views, different connexions, and different duties," all of which "seemed in some measure to sever us." In July of 1806, when Esther had moved into 3 Franklin Place, tensions between the two had grown. Judith was competitive, and she could never stop trying to keep up with her younger sister. She especially resented the ease with which Esther was accepted by Boston society. Once, when Esther's family was invited to a grand ball, Judith tersely remarked, "I, and mine, are left out." And when Esther began renovating her new house, converting two parlors into one, and repapering and repainting the entire edifice, Judith immediately embarked upon her own remodeling project. Some people, she conceded, might see her plans as extravagant, but they were wrong. As long as we had to "unroof our little room" anyway, she rationalized, it made sense to enlarge it at the same time.[47] Still, despite her estrangement from Esther—or perhaps because of it—Judith was devastated by yet another break in the web of relationships that had once shaped her identity.

No one, of course, with the exception of Julia Maria, meant as much to Judith as John Murray. Granted, although John always characterized his wife as "one of the best of human Beings," their relationship was not quite what it once had been. When Judith wanted to accompany her husband on his travels, he usually told her that he preferred to go alone. Even when he was home, he was often an unsatisfactory companion. Judith, for instance, enjoyed reminiscing about her parents, but John resolutely refused to join her, complaining that such conversations only reminded him "of enjoyments that he can never hope to reiterate." He preferred to live in the present, happily "losing the remembrance of the past, in the present good." Judith had always worried that her husband had no business sense, but she had never before viewed him as emotionally lacking.[48]

The temperamental distance between husband and wife was disappointing, if predictable. John's failing health was also not surprising but more difficult to accept. He had never enjoyed a robust constitution, but by century's end, he had taken a clear turn for the worse. Throughout the spring of 1799, he suffered repeated colds and had a painful tumor under his left arm. The doctors tried desperately to dissolve the tumor, but instead, the swelling increased and Judith thought her husband's chances for recovery were remote. At the beginning of June, Dr. Lloyd finally operated. When the "very distressing, although safe" procedure was over, John had a wound nearly three inches long in his side. Although by the middle of the month both his body and his spirits had begun to heal, he was never quite the same. Two years later, at the age of sixty, he suffered a "paralytic stroke." Thereafter, his right hand was virtually useless. Not surprisingly, John's thoughts turned increasingly to his native England. He longed to see his home one more time, but he knew that was out of the question.[49]

Although John survived his stroke, nearly everyone conceded that his days were "drawing to a close." The church proprietors granted him a leave of absence whenever he asked for one, and John left Boston as often as possible. He always felt better when he was on the road. But eventually even that no longer did the trick. By the spring of 1808, he could barely hold a pen. Still, he tried to hide his condition from the Boston Universalists. He did not, he explained, want to "blazon my infirmities" abroad. He fooled no one. His sermons got shorter and shorter, as he was too weak to stand at his pulpit for very long. Sometimes Judith refused to face the truth, hinting that if John would just try a little harder, his condition might improve. Usually she conceded that her husband was becoming "more and more enfeebled."[50]

John continued his peripatetic ministry longer than anyone could have predicted. He was happy when he traveled, frustrated and cranky at home. In constant pain, he resented the "*infirmities* of old age." His condition reminded him of just how unimportant money really was. Wealth, he said sadly, "will not make *old folks young*." On October 19, 1809, John suffered a second, massive stroke. While the shock to his system did not kill him, it rendered him "helpless as an infant." His left side was paralyzed and he found the lightest touch excruciatingly painful. Judith determinedly insisted that her husband's intellectual capacity had not diminished, that only his body had been affected by this latest assault on his feeble frame. Still, the letters John managed to write after 1809 indicate that his mind was not as sharp as it once had been. He seldom preached after his stroke. Even the short trip to church was an ordeal.[51]

Judith noted with a certain grim satisfaction that every minister in the city came to Franklin Place to pay respects to a man they had once viewed as a pariah. At first the Boston Universalists were similarly solicitous. The proprietors immediately voted to pay a church member to sit with John during what they assumed would be a short illness followed by a merciful death. A week later, they agreed—"after some debate"—to pay his medical expenses and to continue his salary at a slightly reduced level. But although the doctors expected John's death at any moment, the minister surprised everyone with his tenacity. It did not take long for Judith and the Universalists to begin sniping at one another. Judith, for instance, looked upon the nurse the church hired to help her as little more than a domestic and was annoyed when the woman behaved like a "visiting lady." A stickler for propriety no matter what the circumstances, she insisted upon a well-run household where rank was observed and order prevailed.[52]

The Universalist proprietors soon began balking at Judith's requests and although the church continued to renew the minister's annual contract, it steadily cut John's pay. Thus, even as the family's expenses grew, its income diminished. Doctors were expensive, and their prescriptions were even more costly. They instructed their patient, for instance, to go riding once a day. The Murrays owned no carriage; thus Judith had to hire a hack at the prohibitive price of a dollar an hour on weekdays, and twice that sum on Sunday. The Universalists contributed nothing for what they saw as a luxury. John was too weak to fight for himself or his family, and so Judith entered the breach, exacerbating the resentment that at least some members of the congregation harbored toward a woman who seemed to hold herself above ordinary Universalists. Again and again she wrote to the church, not bothering with her usual apologies for traveling out of her sphere. Yes, she understood the legalities of the church's position. John had never been blessed with "worldly wisdom," and thus while virtually all clergymen in Massachusetts were established for life, he was not. Still, contractual agreements were not everything. Judith insisted that the years her husband had accumulated in the service of Universalism gave him a certain moral standing.

She had no qualms about trying a little emotional blackmail. If the church did not do more, she said, she would have no choice but to humiliate herself—and, she implied, the Boston Universalists as well—by selling her furniture at public auction, renting out Franklin Place, and moving with her invalid husband to a cottage in the country. When Judith heard that the church proprietors would soon quit paying John's salary altogether, giving the family only enough money for firewood, she was distraught. Perhaps, she thought, they wanted her to start a fire and kill her entire family for the entertainment of the town.[53]

Judith was partly to blame for the Universalists' apparent hostility toward her family. Just as John Stevens's creditors had once resented her for going around Gloucester clad in the latest fashions, so the members of the Boston church accused Judith of extravagance because she continued to live at Franklin Place. Many were taken aback by the signs of prosperity, even luxury, that greeted them whenever they visited John. The house, with its separate dining room and two parlors was daunting enough. Its furnishings—the portraits, the books, the magazines, the piano—all bespoke an opulence that most of them would never attain. Few could afford either the time or the money to pose for Gilbert Stuart, America's leading portrait painter. Yet both Judith and Julia Maria had done just that in 1806, announcing to anyone who entered their parlor that, despite Boston's hard times, they could secure the services of an artist whose talent every elite Federalist venerated. No one listened when Judith explained that Winthrop had paid for the paintings. Indeed, some Universalists thought Judith was wealthier than she was. One church member told her, for instance, that everyone believed she possessed $1,500 of her own. She suspected that rumors of her wealth were based on the large sums of money that her brother sent her over the years. But that money was earmarked for Winthrop's children. It was not hers, and she only dipped into it out of sheer necessity. Even then, she planned to reimburse her brother for the occasional liberties she took.[54]

Judith had suffered so many criticisms, endured so many indignities that she began to see intentional efforts to embarrass her everywhere. She even lashed out at her relatives, compiling a careful record of every slight, real or imagined. She could tell Winthrop exactly how many times and for how long each member of her family had visited her since John's stroke. For all practical purposes, she insisted, her relations treated her as a stranger. Church members, too, seemed determined to humiliate her at every turn. They all complained to John about his wife's officious airs. Judith suffered an especially painful public sign of her lost stature when the Reverend Edward Mitchell, John's replacement, arrived in Boston. Mitchell's family immediately took possession of the pew that

Judith assumed would be hers at least until John died. True, Mrs. Mitchell graciously offered to share the pew, but it was not big enough for both families. Julia Maria, who Judith conceded might have been "too highly wrought," was so indignant that she announced that she would never set foot in the church again. Judith's attempts to ease tensions, deciding to sit with her cousin Epes, who had recently moved to Boston, only made matters worse. One member of the congregation berated her with what Judith thought was "more abruptness, and freedom" than someone of his status had a right to exhibit, informing her that she had frequently offended church members, and citing her refusal to sit with Mrs. Mitchell as an example. Judith faintly apologized and returned to her former pew. She had, she thought, surely fallen on "evil times."[55]

Judith was truly shaken in April of 1812 when the Universalists, by a "fearful majority," not only reduced John's salary once more, this time from $12 to $10, but stopped supplying the family's firewood. Even that small sum was a great deal to give a minister who could not fulfill his basic duties. Edward Mitchell had abruptly returned to New York in December of 1811. For a while, the Universalists supplied the pulpit on an ad hoc basis, but they could not do so indefinitely. At one point, they considered disbanding the church altogether. If that happened, of course, John would receive no salary at all. Instead, the church hired Paul Dean as John Murray's "colleague," formally installing him in August of 1813. Dean was young—only thirty years old—a Trinitarian, and an opponent of Hosea Ballou. Still the choice was by no means unanimous. Two years later Judith was still referring to the "breeches" the decision had opened. She bemoaned the loss of "purity, and singleness of faith" the church endured under Dean's care. Eventually she declared that she no longer considered herself a member of the congregation. To abandon the Boston Universalists gave her no pleasure. But she could not look at the pulpit without comparing John's present condition to that of the vibrant man she had married. Moreover, she pointed out, Dean's views varied "essentially from more than one of the principles in the faith which I have embraced." Once Judith left them, most Universalists quit visiting Franklin Place. And in 1815, the church voted to stop paying their minister's salary altogether, barely softening the blow by suggesting that any parishioner who chose to do so might help the family on a voluntary basis.[56]

Judith cut corners where she could, acknowledging that a virtuous and rational wife should exercise self-restraint. She served only the simplest fare. While she enjoyed the services of a cook and hired an occasional domestic, she did most of the household work herself. Except in the coldest months, the family used only three fireplaces, and although she had once begun her day before anyone else had risen, Judith now remained in bed as long as possible to save fuel. She even sold her daughter's "very elegant, handsome, silk saddle." The doctors thought that riding would improve Julia Maria's health, but the family needed to economize.[57]

* * *

Economizing helped. Still, it only saved money. It did not bring money in. In January of 1811, Judith reluctantly turned to what she knew best. After the failure of *The African*, she had vowed never to write another word for general consumption "except my invitation to embark, should be both publick, and unequivocal." Writing took too much time in any event. "I accumulate years," she explained, "and my domestic cares do not lessen." Still, when a few Universalists urged her to help John prepare his papers for publication, she had no choice but to comply. Thus she began to revise and transcribe John's life's work, predicting that when she was finished, the three-volume book would run some thousand pages. The task added yet another burden to her already busy schedule, but if her husband's memory was to be preserved, she was the logical person to do it. Her experience with *The Gleaner* would come in handy. True, her contacts in the literary world were not what they once had been. But she knew something about garnering subscriptions and working with printers. Moreover, she said, her understanding of John's views allowed her to express her husband's thoughts more accurately than anyone else. At least no one could justly accuse her of pride or ambition. This was not a book that would give her the laurels for which she once had yearned. Rather, it was the sort of tribute that any capable wife would be glad to render. Even so, when friends urged her to seek more subscribers, she refused. Delicacy, she demurred, forbade such forward behavior.[58]

In no time, Judith was enmeshed in the myriad details that writing, publishing, and distributing a book entailed. Of course she claimed that profit was not her motive. She and John merely wanted to share the joys of Universalism with the entire world. Still, it went without saying that they were not rich, and the Murrays thought they had a right to the "remuneration of our labours." Whether her goal was money, the spreading of the Universalist good news, or even fame, Judith was destined for yet another disappointment. John's *Letters and Sketches of Sermons* was in print by the end of 1812. However, printer Jonathan Belcher fell victim to the hard times that everyone in Boston faced. In the summer of 1813, his goods were attached by the sheriff, and his creditors took possession of everything—including John's books—that remained in the printer's hands. Desperate to recoup at least some of their losses, the creditors threatened to sell the *Letters and Sketches* at public auction. The Murrays were now in danger of actually losing money on their venture. In the end, they borrowed money to purchase the volumes from Belcher's creditors. Still, Judith remained stubbornly optimistic. The "celebrity of these Volumes," she predicted, may yet give us "fame and fortune."[59]

If that prediction remained unrealized, another opportunity beckoned. In 1815, again at the "earnest solicitation" of John's friends, Judith began helping John with his biography. Yet, even as she was sitting at her husband's side, writing down stories about his youth that she had heard on so many happier occasions, Judith predicted that she would not be listening to his recollections much longer. I am "weary of conjecture," she told Winthrop, "struggling to keep hope from expiring and frequently loathing life." In August, she reported that John was experiencing a "new and distressing complaint." Finally, on September 3, a little less than six years after his final stroke, John Murray died. He was a man, Judith said simply, "to whom from *sentiment* and from *principle*, my heart, my soul was engaged." She was a widow once more. The Universalists assumed responsibility for the minister's funeral expenses, but when Judith asked them to pay for her mourning clothes, the proprietors replied in a terse negative. They did agree to give her $160, the amount she would have received had the church not quit paying John's salary the previous June. Most ministers' wives continued to receive their husband's salaries, for a good part of their widowhood. Judith, however, was on her own. She valiantly struggled to complete her husband's biography, but in the beginning she found the effort almost impossible. The simple act of looking at John's papers resulted, she said, in "confusion or swimming in my head." Eventually she finished the project, although it did not bring the revenue for which she had hoped.[60]

A year after John's death, Judith was still struggling to get accustomed to her new life and to put her finances in order. She was indebted to a number of relatives. She also owed $32 in taxes to the state of Massachusetts, an obligation she especially resented. The government exempted ministers from all taxes, but had recently begun taxing their widows. The "absurdity" of such an inhumane policy was obvious—at least to Judith—but pay she must. If she decided to sell Franklin Place, she would have to make major repairs on the house, thus going still deeper in debt and "forging new fetters" that seemed destined to bind her forever. Even if she managed to sell a few more copies of *The Gleaner* she could do little to diminish her mounting financial obligations. Nothing, she said, was enough to give her the "freedom from debt, for which indeed, and in truth, my heart most ardently pants."[61]

Judith had never felt quite so alone. She had offended countless friends and relatives to whom she might have been able to turn. Many others were dead. Fitz

William was in Newton, seldom left home, and never wrote. Judith recognized that no matter how often Winthrop contemplated the possibility, her brother would never leave Natchez. Perhaps, she thought, happiness was too much to expect in this life. Still, she never quite managed to accept what the fates offered her without a fight. Her aspirations were subdued. They were never completely extinguished.

Chapter 12

Republican Daughters, Republican Sons

Judith Sargent Murray's life became more restricted, her focus on her family more pronounced, in the years after the publication of *The Gleaner*. Although she never lost interest in the outside world, she reluctantly came to the conclusion that she had little chance of becoming the new nation's Federalist muse. Thus she lived more than ever through her daughter. "My every expectation of terrestrial felicity," she once told Julia Maria, "reposes upon you." Uppermost in her mind was "one grand object." If she realized her desire to give her daughter "as extensive an education as the laws prescribed by custom to the female world will admit," none of her disappointments would matter quite so much. In her own mind, her focus on her duties as a mother was not really a retreat. She had always thought that motherhood was any woman's crowning achievement, her most important contribution to a nation's future. If she did her job well, Judith would not only have ensured her daughter's personal happiness, but she would have done her small part to erect a moral foundation for her country. Julia Maria would be a worthy daughter of the republic. By the same token, however, if women served their country best by raising the next generation of republican men and women, then Judith's contribution to the nation's well-being fell far short of her own aspirations.[1]

Judith had, she confided to Sally Barrell, "a theoretick system" of education in mind long before Julia Maria's birth. While she admitted that she had not had much opportunity to put her ideas into practice, she was convinced that her system would benefit not just her own daughter, but generations to come. Referring to the mothers of the new nation, Judith assured Winthrop that "Posterity will reap the benefit of our labours, their salutary effects may ameliorate society, and looking with a benign influence upon the community at large, they may powerfully influence movements the most important, even to the latest period of time." Judith's hopes for her daughter's future as well as for her country's prospects were invested in Julia Maria. If all went according to plan, Julia Maria would be another Margaretta, whose intellectual attainments were both deep and broad-ranging, and whose character was above reproach. She would not only learn to "reverence herself," but she would be independent. She would be able to support herself should she choose not to marry, perhaps imitating Mary Wollstonecraft, becoming "an instructress to the younger part of her sex."[2] If she had children, she would raise them to be the virtuous citizens the new nation needed if it were to avoid a republic's inevitable tendency to decay.

*   *   *

Judith's experience as a "republican mother" failed to live up to her lofty expectations. To begin with, she ended up welcoming a number of other children into her home, all of whom competed with Julia Maria for her attention. When Winthrop moved to Natchez in 1798, he surprised everyone by marrying thirty-three-year-old Mary Williams, a widow with four children, less than two months after he arrived in Mississippi. "My brother's marriage," Judith observed sardonically, "is an event upon which I did not calculate." Winthrop's ready-made family included three young children—two boys and a girl—who desperately needed access to better schooling than primitive Natchez had to offer. The frontier outpost had no public schools, and the only tutor Winthrop could secure was a hopeless alcoholic. It was not long, moreover, before Mary and Winthrop had two sons of their own, both of whom would benefit from New England's excellent educational institutions. Thus they decided, with "many a heart felt pang," to place their children under Judith's care.[3]

Judith welcomed her brother's children as well as the sons of some of Winthrop's Natchez acquaintances into her often crowded little home. Before he died, John had been a little unnerved by the sudden addition of so many rambunctious young people to his household, but he was invariably enchanted whenever he entered the dining room and viewed "the Matron seated at the Table with her Children." It made a fetching tableau. Judith had always regretted the fact that Julia Maria was a "solitary little Being." As she recalled—no doubt through rose-colored glasses—her attachment to her own siblings when she was young, she profoundly regretted that her daughter would never experience a similar pleasure. Her brother's children filled a very large void, even as they gave Judith a sense of connection with her Sargent family roots. The boys were, she said, " bone of my bone, flesh of my flesh."[4] Almost as important, they gave her an opportunity to put her favorite educational theories to the test.

In broad outline, Judith's "theoretick system" reflected the views of most of the day's educators. Over the years, in her private correspondence as well as in her more polished, published work she had repeatedly declared her preference for "gentle methods" and "mild persuasive tenderness." Like John Locke, she argued that praise and shame, not harsh punishment and physical blows, were best suited to turn unformed children into mature, rational, independent adults. Like Frances Hutcheson, she saw each child as a little seed, whose social conscience would blossom if it was cultivated by a firm but loving guardian. Severity, she insisted, should be employed only as a last resort. She would never mete out physical punishment nor would she turn her charges over to anyone who used the rod. Her mother, she fondly remembered, had always "requested" rather than commanded her children. If Judith followed that stellar example, ruling more by "persuasion, and reason, than by despotic arrangements," she had nothing to fear. Still, if she was not unduly severe, neither did she think she ever "improperly indulged" her own or her brother's children.[5]

Judith had always viewed education as the means by which genteel women could surmount the barriers that kept them from realizing their true potential. She assumed that if girls received the same education as their male counterparts, the intellectual differences between the sexes would be blurred if not eradicated. Ironically, in her case, just the opposite occurred. While she strove to think in gender neutral terms, maintaining that all children benefited from the same methods, she soon had to admit that by the end of the eighteenth century, boys and girls had begun to inhabit distinct worlds. No education would enable her charges to disregard the psychological and experiential differences that formed their characters or ordered their goals in life. Moreover, no matter what she argued in theoretical terms, Judith discovered to her dismay that the process of education itself actually widened the gender gap, both reflecting and exacerbating the divide between men and women. What worked for her daughter and niece did not work for her nephews. Boys were educated in different ways and for different ends, and they were judged by different criteria. Ironically, it was the very gentility that Judith prized that in large measure led to the hardening of gender differences in general, and the sexual double standard in particular.

For Judith, the paradoxes she faced were painful. She deplored any limitation on girls' dreams, eagerly allying herself with her daughter and niece, ready to do battle with anyone who stood in their way. With her nephews, the issue was different. Custom never circumscribed boys' aspirations. Rather, it separated Judith both physically and emotionally from her nephews, ultimately turning them all—especially William Sargent—into her adversaries.

Judith confronted another dilemma, one that she never seemed fully to understand or even to acknowledge. She tirelessly urged her daughter and niece to reject a past that kept them firmly in their place and to embrace a future that offered them gender equality and a measure of independence. Where women were concerned, she wanted to change the world. She expected her nephews, how-

ever, to be content with old values that had worked well enough for her brothers, but that were increasingly irrelevant to a new, more egalitarian and competitive age. She was not alone in her inability to adapt to the changing American
scene. Parents everywhere were shaking their heads at their sons' refusal to accept traditional notions of republican virtue. They were uneasy in a society that
privileged individualism and denigrated—especially in men—genteel sympathy. New England Federalists were especially out of touch with a world that
seemed to have lost all appreciation of an organic order where sons deferred to
their elders even as servants acknowledged the superior wisdom of their masters. Judith, like so many elite women of her day, was simply overwhelmed by a
new male society that she neither understood nor approved. As she prepared
Julia Maria and Anna to assume a significant role in a nation that allowed
women to become virtuous citizens, she did not realize that her notion of virtue
was fast becoming obsolete, that even if girls were eager to embrace the old verities, boys would not be similarly bound.[6]

*   *   *

Judith never doubted her ability to understand her daughter or her niece, and
she felt more than qualified to guide both girls through the early stages of their
education. Mothers knew, at least in broad outline, what to expect from girls,
and in turn girls looked to older women as models of what they would become.
Mothers and daughters in the eighteenth century enjoyed a particularly intimate relationship. They lived in the same physical and emotional sphere, identifying with one another's dreams and fears. A mother's wisdom was useful; it
encompassed the skills a daughter would need to become a valued member of
society. Girls continued—"naturally," or so it seemed—to be happy in the
home. They grew older, but no one expected them to change in any fundamental way. Thus, a daughter had little need to proclaim her independence from her
mother in order to forge an identity for herself. She was comfortable replicating
her mother's life, improving upon it, perhaps, but seldom rejecting it. Judith, in
particular, thought that she knew what girls needed to learn; she was also
painfully aware of what they had been denied. If she wanted so much more for
her daughter than she herself had enjoyed, she was nevertheless secure in the
knowledge that her own experience would prove beneficial to Julia Maria. In her
daughter she saw herself. She saw both her own deficiencies and her own potential. By giving Julia Maria the opportunities she had never enjoyed, she hoped to
eliminate the former and augment the latter.[7]

Even after Julia Maria enrolled in Boston's Federal Street school, she spent at the very most only four hours a day in the classroom. The rest of the time she remained with Judith, who heard her lessons and supervised her sewing. After Anna Williams joined the Murray family in the spring of 1801, Judith lavished attention on both girls, spending an inordinate amount of energy supervising what she described as "the flowery part" of their education. In addition to plain sewing and knitting, she wanted the girls to be able to tat Dresden lace and to be familiar with "all the various kinds of muslin work that can be done out of a frame." Throughout the winter of 1805, the cousins spent a full six hours a day on an embroidered depiction of a scene from Shakespeare's *Tempest*.[8]

Such an allocation of valuable time seems unbalanced, even frivolous to modern eyes. But in the late eighteenth century elite girls expected to excel in plain and fine sewing. The former symbolized domesticity, practicality, and usefulness, according girls a chance to serve their families in concrete ways. When Anna and Julia Maria made purses and shirts for James, David, and Winthrop, for instance, they were helping to forge and maintain family ties. Fine sewing, if not so useful, made a public statement about a girl's identity. It was at least as important a marker of femininity, status, and gentility as the ability to write a good hand or to speak French fluently. Girls were justifiably proud of their skills.[9]

Boys were different. Judith always found the education of boys something of a mystery. Her experience with David and James Williams, and William and Washington Sargent did not enlighten her. Instead, it undermined her confidence in herself and her methods. In time she would declare herself "humbled in the dust." "Let no one," she added dramatically, "entrust their children to me."[10]

Judith's experience with her nephews replicated the difficulties that many adults had begun to face. As the chasm that divided men and women, public and private, grew ever wider after the American Revolution, mothers were especially bewildered by their sons. When boys were very young, of course, they accepted their mothers' supervision without protest. They lived in a world characterized by "affection and moral suasion"; they developed strong bonds with their mother, bonds she could manipulate as she struggled to keep their exuberance in check. By the time boys turned ten or eleven, however, they were increasingly prone to rebel against a feminine world that seemed confining, even alien to them and their interests. They rejected the softer values of their mothers, and embraced the competitive individualism they sensed would serve them well as adults. They lived in a society that tended to denigrate the more androgynous male ideal of a bygone age, an ideal that was fast becoming a relic of their own fathers' memories, and so they rejected the feminine attributes to which their mothers remained wedded. Boys had to change; they had to *achieve* maturity and manliness. Unfortunately, their mothers could offer them no practical guidance as they negotiated the treacherous passage from boy to man. To the contrary, as mothers attempted to suppress their sons' boisterous spirits, boys increasingly viewed women as obstacles to be avoided or simply ignored. They fled to the commons or the streets as often as possible, running and shouting and roughhousing, free of the gentle restraints of the women in their lives. The more they saw of domestic life, the less they thought of it. To be feminine was to be fettered; to be masculine was to be free. In such a bifurcated world, women's values did not stand a chance.[11]

For Judith's nephews, the process of maturation was particularly difficult. When they left Mississippi, the boys were separated not only from their father, but from any appropriate male role model who could help them envision their own future. They assumed that they would be planters; yet no one in Massachusetts could show them in any meaningful way what the life of a planter might be. To make matters worse, at Franklin Place they lived in a feminized space, in a household dominated by Judith and Julia Maria. The few men whom they did encounter did not appear worthy of emulation. John was a shadowy figure, and as his health deteriorated he hardly provided an attractive picture of masculine maturity. Nor could they imagine themselves as a writing teacher or a Latin tutor. Like other boys raised primarily by women, they developed an exaggerated and highly stylized notion of masculinity. They saw women as bars to their autonomy, not as helpful agents who could turn them into respectable adults. Moreover, like other boys who left rural areas for the city, they looked romantically on their frontier roots, idealizing what were no doubt stereotypical notions of the rugged and primitive male. Judith was a stern matriarch who had high expectations for her nephews. The more she demanded obedience, the more her nephews rebelled. In the end, they feared her as much as they loved her. She may on occasion have been able to make them feel guilty about their indiscretions, but guilt almost inevitably led to anger and then to self-destructive behavior.[12]

Judith tried to understand her nephews, admitting that boys were inclined to be heedless and a little wild. While Anna and Julia Maria were generally docile, following their parents' instructions without much protest, the boys eagerly escaped to the streets or to Exeter or Harvard where they relished their independence. From the beginning, William Sargent, in particular, was a "Lover of Play," and was "passionately fond of driving a hoop." He was all too prone to flee household and classroom and "bluster through the commons." He never took the shortest route to any destination, tending to loiter, thoroughly enjoying his temporary freedom from adult supervision. But the other boys were not much better. William's younger brother Washington was always happiest when he was outside, walking or playing ball. He loved visiting Fitz William and Anna after they moved to Newton, where he was allowed to race giddily through the countryside. After each such trip, however, both Judith and his tutors were hard pressed to get him to settle down. Above all, he enjoyed tending to his little garden, growing beans, corn, peas, and sunflowers, and imagining that he was the lord of his own miniature plantation.[13]

One of the biggest, and most disturbing bones of contention Judith had with her nephews concerned money. Their claims to independence were meaningless if they could not pay their own way. Winthrop had warned his sister to expect his sons to chafe at an allowance they thought was inadequate. He did not, he assured her, possess "immeasurable wealth." In fact, he had noticed "a custom amongst southern people, to magnify property, and to deceive themselves, too often to their ruin." Even children, he said, "imbibe a very exaggerated idea of *their*, or their parents, property." He was determined to disabuse the boys of their illusions. It was entirely possible, he predicted, that his sons might have to earn their own fortune.[14]

While Anna never seemed to complain about her allowance, none of Winthrop's sons accepted the economic strictures within which their father expected them to live. They did not want to compare unfavorably to their peers, and Judith thought they surrendered far too readily to "the extravagant fancies, and impetuous passions of young people." In Natchez, they had enjoyed status and comparative luxury. Thus they refused to tolerate the Spartan existence that Winthrop thought would develop their character. If they could not afford something, they simply borrowed what they wanted, often wasting time and money on "frivolous amusements." When David Williams visited friends in York, for instance, Judith asked him how he paid for the trip. The boy's answer was not what she expected. He "declared with a supercilious smile this consideration was extremely inconsequential, since there was money enough in the world!"[15]

* * *

If boys and girls had different characters and scholastic experiences, they also had distinct expectations for their future. The most ambitious educators hoped to turn out women who were feminine versions of republican virtue. They wanted girls to be modest, useful, and to shun decadent frivolity. They thought, as Judith put it, that education would furnish a woman, "in whatever situation she may be placed, with resources of profit, and amusement—with an antidote against that ennui of which females are *especially* too often found complaining." They also expected educated women to be good wives and mothers, improving the character and behavior of the men in their lives. "Mothers and Schoolmasters," argued one observer, "plant the seeds of nearly all the good and evil which exist in society." Or, as Benjamin Rush succinctly put it, "let the ladies of a country be educated properly, and they will not only make and administer its laws, but form its manners and character."[16]

Other supporters of education for women, even those who assumed that men and women were intellectual equals, had less expansive goals in mind. Some merely assumed that an accomplished woman would be equipped to compete on the marriage market. Education would also help vulnerable girls resist the blandishments of the Sinisterus Courtlands of the world. They thought that a prudent wife would not exhibit "uncommon" intelligence. Instead, she would "assist her husband" and be "an agreeable companion for a sensible man." Very few commentators suggested, as both Judith Sargent Murray and Mary Wollstonecraft had argued, that women should seek independence. Education was designed to turn girls into better *women*, not self-reliant human beings. It was supposed to make them conventionally "useful," giving them "the power of doing good," nursing the sick and soothing the needy. "Exempted from the duties of publick life," women would be free to make the domestic sphere more pleasant. Women were educated to serve the status quo, not to challenge it. Intellectual equality did not, for Judith or for anyone else, imply an end to social hierarchy.[17]

Most eighteenth-century Americans, then, promoted a certain *kind* of schooling for girls, one that would both reflect and promote the values consonant with republicanism. So long as women's education promoted republican virtue, most people were willing to give it a chance. But, as playwright Royall Tyler warned, an intellectual woman who could not do plain sewing or bake a pie was a threat to the values the new nation held dear. Ironically, the more the country rejected immutable class divisions, accepting—at least in theory—the possibility of upward social mobility, the more it sought to reinforce gender and racial differences. As a result, when girls attended single-sex schools and discovered that their education, however challenging, prepared them for a destiny that was quite different from their brothers', they received a subtle message that sexual identity mattered. Even if they did not agree with Benjamin Rush, who advocated segregated education so that girls would preserve their natural "delicacy," they left their classrooms with a sense that they were unique in some fundamental and unalterable way. At least in theory, Judith went against the grain. While many people were softening class differences and accentuating gender distinctions, her inclination was just the opposite.[18]

Judith embodied the contradictory attitudes of her age. Despite her professed desire to see girls soar to the loftiest heights, for instance, she actively discouraged Anna and Julia Maria whenever they exhibited any tendency to indulge in individualistic rivalries. She had read her Hume and Kames. She knew that humans were social animals who naturally enjoyed and were improved by personal relationships. "Emulation" was the key to creating better people and a better society. It was an "excellent auxiliary—the hope of excelling by comparison renders children abundantly more assiduous" and led people to strive for the highest standards. Unfortunately, like anything else, emulation had its dangers. Even "naturally" sympathetic girls found it hard to prevent emulation "from degenerating into an envious competition." Judith thought that awards encouraged all students to do better. It was for this reason that she had argued in *The Gleaner* that society needed to recognize its literary luminaries. Still, she found it necessary—if difficult—to balance her determination to urge her daughter and niece to excel with her desire to keep them from an unseemly desire to succeed at one another's expense. She wanted no "rivalship" that would result in disaffection.[19]

Judith never disdained traditional and status specific ends for her daughter. She wanted Julia Maria to have "polish," to enjoy that "kind of education, which shall fit her to make a respectable figure in society." She also stressed the value of motherhood. She argued that mothers did not have to write poems, essays, or plays to serve their country, and she presumed that most women would spend considerable time "teaching the young idea how to shoot." Indeed, she probably stressed the public importance of motherhood more than most of her contemporaries did. Still, she always wanted more for her daughter than motherhood. Because of the Murrays' precarious financial circumstances, because John and Judith were older than most parents, it was easy for her to picture Julia Maria "destitute, desolate," without any material resources. Then too, Judith was convinced that the most privileged girl's prospects were by definition dimmer than the most unfortunate boy's. If Judith were to die, she worried, she would "yield a *female* infant uneducated, unportioned, and unprotected, to the cold sympathy of an unfeeling and barbarous world." Julia Maria had to learn to take care of herself. Most daringly, Judith readily entertained the notion that her daughter might not want to marry. An education would give her a choice. She would never be forced to rely on the goodwill of any man.[20]

If Judith made an effort to defend her desire to educate her daughter, allowing for the possibility, at least, of an unconventional future for Julia Maria, she knew that no one questioned the value of education for elite boys. Winthrop and Mary Sargent expected their sons to excel academically, even though they did not appear to have a definite career in mind for any of them. Whether they went to

Exeter, as David and James Williams did, or, like William and Washington Sargent, studied Latin with Boston's John Sylvester John Gardiner, they all saw their early education as a springboard for admission to college. They had a "rank in life to fill above the level of the many," and a college education would prepare them to assume their rightful place in society. Thus, when she took David and James to Exeter, Judith was relieved to note that the school expected "due subordination" from its students. There was, she noted, "no jacobine" at the New Hampshire school. Not only did their education make her nephews "useful and ornamental members of society," but—if Winthrop had anything to say about it—they would develop manly characteristics as well. When, for instance, David and James Williams asked for permission to purchase some violin strings, Winthrop replied with a terse negative. He gladly paid for Anna's piano lessons, but he did not want his sons' time at school to be "*fiddled* away." He regarded "performance upon any musical instrument, as an effeminate occupation."[21]

When Winthrop indicated that he wanted his stepsons to become manly men, he was viewing education through a gendered lens. Judith rejected such conventions in the abstract, but she, too, sensed that the purpose of a boy's education differed from a girl's. Her unpublished essay on education reflects that understanding. In some ways, the piece's vision is not gender specific. But the martial imagery that suffuses its closing paragraphs is clearly not intended for girls. Education, the essay says, is a city, surrounded by enemies. The "Citizens" must defend it at all costs. If the young guards can "man, and strengthen their ramparts, if they are sedulous, systematic and uniform," if they "strain every nerve, nor relax their efforts, until the loud shot of victory is heard in their borders" then they will deserve the honors their country heaps upon them. The soldiers in the piece are defenders of knowledge, not members of imperialistic armies. Nevertheless, the virtues they admire—discipline, industry, and courage—are not measurably different from the ideals of the young men who fought the redcoats a generation earlier.[22]

*   *   *

Their separate educations reflected the different worlds that formed the reality of boys and girls in the early nineteenth century. If they expected their sons to learn to fend for themselves, parents sought to secure their daughters from harm. Judith and John, who had but one living child and would never have another, were probably more watchful than most parents. They were determined to do everything right. Viewing no decision as "trivial," they wanted their daughter to have every material and moral advantage at their disposal. Despite the obvious risk, they decided to innoculate Julia Maria so that she would not succumb to the dreaded smallpox. John plied her with silk cloth from London that he could not afford. She also had plenty of toys, including her favorite doll and the "little Chair" that William Palmer sent her from New York. Judith scarcely let her daughter out of her sight. She washed and dressed her each morning, a task she would not have relinquished to a maid had she been able to afford one. The girl even slept in her parents' bed. Judith admitted that she might be overly protective, worrying that her efforts to insulate her daughter would "enervate her mind, render her peevish, and irritable, and produce her in society an overgrown Baby." But she could not help herself.[23]

Boys and girls had distinct purposes for their education. They also had different, and—despite the progress the new nation had made—inferior opportunities. One of the reasons that Judith had been eager to move to Boston was to take advantage of the city's schools. Of course even in the Massachusetts metropolis, girls lacked the choices boys took for granted. But when Judith compared her daughter's prospects to her own at the same age, she was pleased, if somewhat envious. Boston opened its three public schools to females in 1789, allowing girls to attend classes there about half the year. As she had boasted in *The Gleaner*, America was also home to a growing number of "female academies." Sarah Pierce had opened her school for women in Litchfield, Connecticut, by 1792. Susanna Rowson started her academy in 1797, drawing upon Boston's elite families for her clientele. There was also the Moravian academy at Bethlehem, whose praises Judith had sung in 1790. Unfortunately, she understood that the Pennsylvania seminary's teachers had begun to proselytize, implanting "prejudices" in their pupils that "became a very part of their being." What had once looked like an ideal spot, no longer looked so inviting.[24]

Still, there were other options. In 1801 Judith had helped a Miss McGeorge open a school for young ladies on Federal Street. A year later, she became even more involved in the efforts of Mrs. Saunders and Miss Beach—the former, a relative on her mother's side—who established an academy for girls in neighboring Dorchester. The seminary instructed students in reading, English grammar, French, writing, arithmetic, and geography, "including the use of the Globe." It also offered courses in "painting and hair work upon ivory" and all branches of needlework. And it paid close attention to students' health, manners, and morals. Judith was one of the Dorchester school's most vociferous advocates. She secured the services of a Dorchester native, a Mr. N____, who located a suitable building for the school, and rounded up pupils—fifteen in all—for the venture. She also helped publicize the venture, placing announcements in the *Centinel* and the *Chronicle* and trying unsuccessfully to publish a highly laudatory essay in the *Massachusetts Magazine*, written with Federalist sensibilities in mind. The "great business of education," she said, was the foundation of a social order that relied on "due subordination." The Dorchester school promised to strengthen students' reason by curbing their emotions, and it was dedicated to the inculcation of morality and gentility. Nevertheless, although Judith was pleased with the school's success, and she even allowed Julia Maria to visit Dorchester on occasion, she never considered sending her daughter there—or to any other boarding school. She knew she was selfish, but she cherished every moment she shared with Julia Maria and could not bear the thought of sending her away.[25]

In fact, Judith had developed "insuperable objections" to boarding schools, fearing that children, especially girls, who attended them might, like Rowson's Charlotte Temple, encounter all manner of temptations at a time when they were least able to resist them. Remembering how Fitz William had rebelled when the family had tried to fit him into a mold that had suited his older brother very well, Judith was convinced that the generic approach to education that most schools offered was destined to fail. "I should as soon persuade myself," she said," that one soil, and one method of cultivation, would answer for every description of plants, as that one mode of education should be adopted for every mind." She knew, for instance, that Julia Maria was designed by nature "to feel exquisitely upon every occasion." She was also "volatile in the extreme" and "perhaps more heedless than children of her age usually are." At home, Judith watched her with "unremitting care," making her recite lessons over and over again until she got them right. The "one great object in her education" was to teach her daughter "self command, and a *due regulation of the passions*." Only a mother had the time, knowledge, and incentive to tend to her child's particular needs. Formal schooling was undesirable in another way. When students were thrown together indiscriminately, they learned from bad examples as well as good ones. She observed, for instance, that Anna and Julia Maria listened to their classmates as they read out loud, providing the "worst examples," constantly violating the rules for "cadences, accents, emphasis, and even pauses." Thus Judith had the girls read to her each night, to correct the damage the academy had done.[26]

In the beginning, Judith had enjoyed teaching Julia Maria at home. For all her own deficiencies, she was competent in the lower branches of education. At the age of five, Julia Maria could spell and read, painstakingly sounding out each word one syllable at a time. She had also made some progress with Noah Webster's grammar. And she could sew a plain seam or mend a hem as ably as any adult. Unfortunately, Judith's sense of accomplishment was fleeting. "The attention requisite to the fashioning the mind of my daughter," she said, "gives me *still more feeling to regret*, the custom which, barring the cultivation of the female intellect, during my childhood has, in many respects unqualified me for the pleasing employment of her mind." Her experience was an object lesson in the importance of educating every woman for the demanding role of mother. Thus in the spring of 1798, when Julia Maria turned seven, the day Judith had both anticipated and dreaded finally arrived. She made arrangements for Mr. Nicholls, an "erudite" Englishman, and William Payne, who with his two daughters ran an academy on Federal Street, to assume responsibility for Julia Maria's formal education.[27]

Three years later, when Anna Williams arrived in Boston, she joined her cousin at the Federal Street Academy. Judith never truly trusted anyone at the school to do the job right. She continued her protective ways, writing letter after letter to Eliza Payne, the school's writing teacher, complaining about the girls' lack of progress. "The familiar picture of the hen, with one chick, is often present to my view," she laughed ruefully. Still, she was never able to resist the temptation to second-guess. She was virtually traumatized by her conviction that her daughter, in particular, was losing too many "golden opportunities." The Paynes were not "sufficiently *determined* or *regular*." They accepted sloppy lessons as complacently as perfect ones. When Judith examined Julia Maria's first writing book, she was dismayed. Her daughter had completed the entire book "without exhibiting even a resemblance of those ideas which we wish her to obtain." She was not yet able to form a simple "C." Two years later, Judith was still complaining. Although she thought that by now she surely had a right to "expect some considerable progress," her daughter still exhibited an "awkward stiffness in her letters, particularly in her capital jay." At one point, Eliza simply gave up, declaring that she would no longer be Julia Maria's writing teacher. Judith apologized profusely, claiming that her daughter's "levity, and inattention," not Payne's teaching methods, were the problem. Eliza must have been mollified, for she allowed her pupil to return to class.[28] Still, Judith was always there, coaxing, prodding, watching as her charges added more subjects to their curriculum. Nor did the girls appear to resent the close attention they received. If they did, they never rebelled.

* * *

The same could not be said for Judith's nephews, all of whom endured less supervision but resented it more. Judith may have had a decided preference for home schooling, but for elite boys, the practice of the day dictated a different policy. Winthrop had left home to attend Boston Latin School when he was ten, and he never lived under his parents' roof again. Thus, while he vowed to protect his daughter from the temptations of the *beau monde*, like most parents, he wanted his sons to be free of "the pampered treatment and imprudent fondness of luxurious and indulgent parents." He had once accused Esther of allowing her fondness for her son Jack to cloud her judgment, and he was determined to avoid her mistakes. A boy, he insisted, should enjoy diverse experiences, learn to compete, and become a "man of the world."[29]

Judith argued that even boys were vulnerable. They, too, needed a loving home where mothers in particular could watch over them. They should be introduced, in small doses and under carefully controlled circumstances, to the temptations of a "dissipated" environment. If their guardians taught them to resist those temptations, their experiences would inoculate them, hardening their character and preparing them for a virtuous life as adult members of a stable republic.[30] Unfortunately, she soon discovered that it was much easier to follow this advice with girls than it was with boys. She could easily judge the progress Julia Maria and Anna made as they worked on their knitting or writing; she could not advise or correct her nephews once they began studying the classics. However much she wanted to "point and stimulate their opening faculties," her "sex, and consequent education" rendered her useless.[31]

Had they remained in Mississippi, under Winthrop's care, the boys would still have faced difficulties. By the end of the eighteenth century, the bond between fathers and sons was becoming steadily weaker. When they left home, that bond was more fragile still. Once they left Franklin Place for boarding school or college, they lived in a world that was cut off from parents and siblings, governed by different rules and expectations. So much autonomy led them to become "a little giddy, and a little negligent." Thrown to a large extent on their own resources, insecure and frightened, they felt compelled to prove themselves in a new environment. Alienated and adrift, they spent most of their leisure hours with their friends. True, they wanted to meet their parents' expectations. But they were equally determined to earn the respect of their peers. Neither children nor adults, they resented all rules and circumvented what they saw as arbitrary authority. Academies valued deference and tried to create an environment where rank and decorum were the order of the day. But in fact, students clung tenaciously to their independence, enjoying more freedom than most had ever experienced. Thus, Judith could not help but think that "the chance of children in full schools is very slender." With "no kind friend" who was "constantly at their elbow," they squandered their time and left school as "illiterate pretenders." Judith's nephews fit this pattern perfectly. James and David Williams enrolled at

Exeter almost as soon as they arrived in the East, and Winthrop and Washington Sargent went to Harvard when they were barely in their teens. Under the circumstances, she thought that Winthrop should not have been surprised by his sons' "retrocession." Their backsliding was a "natural event."[32]

Judith had but one consolation as she set out to supervise her nephews' education from afar. In the character of Mary Vigillius, she had argued that written communication was often more effective than face-to-face admonitions. If she was right, she need not worry. She certainly did her best, trying to build the boys' character and to encourage them academically with a continuous flow of letters. Winthrop always complained that his sister was too free with applause, but in fact her compliments were rare. Most of the time, she was stern, mixing an occasional word of encouragement with a heavy dose of criticism. She cajoled, threatened, and shamed. To fail when everyone was counting on them and when they had so many "hereditary advantages," she lectured, would be a "dishonour." Her nephews quickly learned to open her letters with trepidation. Usually, she enclosed long lists of the mistakes they had made in their own missives. On occasion she summarily returned their efforts, demanding that laughable grammar and misspelled words be corrected before she would read them. As a result, the boys were often so discouraged by Judith's litany that they refused to write to her for months at a time.[33]

Despite her efforts, nothing Judith said seemed to make much difference. From the beginning, James Williams, who was never convinced of the value of an education, floundered. When Exeter authorities threatened to "rusticate" him, sending him to study under the tutelage of a rural minister, Judith managed to dissuade them. But although she insisted that James had a sweeter disposition than his older brother, and that he was not "dead to all sense of propriety," he never made much progress. Ultimately he left Exeter, returning briefly to Franklin Place, where he studied Latin for an hour a day, but spent most of his time on math and penmanship and putting a final polish on his social graces. David went on to Harvard, after vainly trying to persuade his father and his aunt to allow him to attend Yale instead. Yale was an "inferior" institution, Judith sniffed. A "greater honour attaches to an education at Harvard." In fact, David would never enjoy the "honour" of a Harvard diploma. He had not been in Cambridge for a quarter when, like his stepfather before him, he began to attract the unwanted attention of college authorities. On December 7, he was fined for staying out all night without permission. Two weeks later, he took an "offensive powder into the reciting room at the time of recitation," throwing it around the room and "making loud, indecent noise till the Officer deemed it necessary to direct him to leave." Not surprisingly, the board of governors rusticated him.[34]

Although David continued his rebellious ways, Judith assumed that her nephew would return to the college once his exile ended. Indeed, she was so convinced that his predicament was the result of one isolated incident, that she did not bother to inform her brother about David's disgrace. Thus she was stunned at the end of August when she received a letter from her nephew. He had taken money she had sent him to pay his bills, absconded to New York, and was preparing to set sail for New Orleans. He offered only one explanation for his behavior. He was simply unable to face his friends at Cambridge "after suffering degradation." Judith was "deeply wounded" by the secretive manner in which David had chosen to leave. She had believed that he trusted her and that he would tell her anything. She had acted as his mother, advising, loving, and protecting him. Surely she deserved better.[35]

If she was disappointed by her efforts to supervise the Williams brothers, Judith was devastated by her experience with William Sargent, Winthrop and Mary's oldest son. Having made a few mistakes with David and James, she thought she had learned her lesson. Thus when everything went awry for a second time, her confidence plummeted and she began to suspect that there was something about boys that she would never understand.

William arrived in Boston with his parents in the spring of 1807. Winthrop, Mary, James, and Anna all returned to Natchez that fall, leaving the homesick little boy behind. William feared that he would never see his parents again, convinced that he could not possibly learn the "ten million things" Winthrop demanded as a condition for returning home. Judith comforted her nephew as best she could. She knew that children who left the "affectionate indulgence" of their family suffered in the beginning. Their parents felt "pangs" as well. Still, as difficult as the process was for everyone, it was for the best. She immediately enrolled William in the Federal Street Academy, begging Eliza Payne to take special care of the "little trembler." She also demanded daily replies to a set of questions she had devised to monitor William's progress.[36]

Judith was confident that she would not experience a repetition of her difficulties with David and James. William was young. He would not go to Exeter to live among strangers. Instead, he would remain under her roof where she could watch his diet, supervise his studies, and guide his hand as he struggled to learn how to write. While she knew she was immodest, she could not help but be proud of William's "advancement in the path of knowledge" so long as he remained under her direct care.[37] But as soon as he began studying the classics with John Sylvester John Gardiner, Judith sensed that she was at a disadvantage.

In the fall of 1812, at the age of thirteen, William entered Harvard as one of the youngest members of his class. Gardiner argued that the boy was simply too immature to attend college, noting that some of his peers were in their mid-twenties. Judith and Winthrop disagreed. Viewing David's experience as a negative reference, they were convinced that William should go to Cambridge as early as possible. He would be easier to control when he was young, for everyone knew that boys had to attain "a certain age" before they were subject to sexual temptation. And if he *did* misbehave, the stigma would be less. Only later did Judith concede that she had made a terrible mistake when she allowed William to leave Franklin Place so soon. When he had lived with her, she knew where he was every second of the day. Like Julia Maria and Anna, he was always watched by a "vigilant Preceptor" or a "tenderly interested Aunt." Then, much too suddenly, he had obtained his freedom. While Judith did not believe that "Vice is a necessary, or uniform appendage to a College life," she knew how easy it was for innocent boys to lose their moral compass at Harvard. They went to Cambridge at a time when their "passions" were strong and their reason was weak. They were in "intimate association" with young men who might be able to control their baser instincts as individuals, but who in a group were far too likely to succumb to temptations of the flesh. If young men who possessed "strong fortitude and exquisite sensibility" were apt to falter, mere boys were even more at risk. Judith tried to prepare her nephew to resist the enticements he would soon encounter. She knew well enough that David Williams's experience was by no means unusual. The college's students came from all parts of the country and from many backgrounds, and while the governors refused to examine a candidate for admission unless a tutor or "some other proper person" vouched for his character, even upright boys soon discovered that Harvard offered all sorts of opportunities to engage in ritualized insubordination, pranks, rebellion, even violence.[38]

Even so, it took a while for William's world to unravel. At first he boarded with Mrs. Webber, whose husband had been Harvard's president until he died suddenly of "Apoplexy." Judith had complete confidence in her nephew's guardian. She also kept a maternal eye on her charge from a distance, writing to Henry Ware, William's tutor, begging him to regard his young pupil with "unremitted vigilance." Education was most effective, she thought, "when parents guardians and Instructors cooperating unite their efforts to one desirable grand point."[39]

Disquieting signs appeared from time to time. William soon took up cigars and was fond of "wine drinking." And it was not long before Mrs. Webber asked William to secure alternative lodgings, because he and her son were at odds.[40] Soon thereafter, President Kirkland informed Judith that William was "*very gay*" and seldom worked to his potential. He tended to see the time when he was not in the classroom as his own and although he was not innately evil he was much too prone to "levity and inattention." William settled down his sophomore year, but Judith knew that he had a "volatile and eccentrick disposition," and she never completely relaxed. She was not wrong to worry. In the fall of 1814, everything fell apart. William was castigated for "neglect of College studies & duties" in October. A month later, he received a formal admonishment from Dr. Ware for "improper & irreverent behavior at public worship." The college informed Judith that if she did not want her nephew to be rusticated, she should pull him out of school.[41]

Once William withdrew from Harvard, his behavior rapidly deteriorated. His aunt was helpless to stop his downward spiral. Even when Judith told him that his father would cut off his allowance if he persisted in his rebellious behavior, William was unmoved. If that happened, he shrugged, he would simply board a privateer and "speedily shape his own fortune." Most ominously, Judith's authority diminished. William was constantly saying, "*I will*" or "*I will not*," and he simply refused to obey her. Significantly, despite his demands for more freedom, he frequently declared that all he really wanted was to go home. For that reason, if for no other, Judith did not want to rusticate him. She feared that if she let him out of her sight, he would imitate David's example and return to Mississippi.[42]

William was determined to rebel. If Judith had argued that her daughter and niece should prepare for independence, she thought her nephew exhibited a "kind of premature independence very improper at his age." A bid for autonomy in the abstract was one thing. In reality, it was disturbing. "I have soothed and supplicated[.] I have even kneeled to him," Judith said. She also "remonstrated with more severity," "commanded," and "threatened." Nothing worked. William left home each morning and when Judith confronted him with "streaming eyes," asking him where he had been, who his friends were, and where he got his money, he "answered with a song." With John too ill to cope with William's aberrant behavior, Judith finally wrote to Fitz William for advice. Her brother merely sent a cryptic note saying that William "was a bad boy and deserved the rod," a suggestion that even under her present circumstances Judith rejected.[43]

William occasionally begged his aunt's forgiveness, attributing his behavior to "a kind of frenzy," and Judith always accepted his apologies "with proper lenity." But he invariably began to act out once more. "To say truth," she told Winthrop, "some of William's actions are descriptive of a species of insanity."[44] One evening, he stripped his pantaloons "piece by piece from his body," and threw his new gown into the fire. He shoveled embers from the kitchen fireplace onto the floor in an apparent effort to burn the house down. On another, even more nightmarish night, he marched around the house for three hours, clad only in his shirt, brandishing a sword before him. When Judith tried to wrench the weapon away from him, her nephew hit her and threatened to stab her if she repeated her effort. Truly frightened, Judith called Dr. Jeffries in for a consultation. Jeffries thought the boy was suffering "a species of distraction, resulting from genius, and talents, inflamed by self conceit, and gaining strength from idleness." But despite his recommendation that William return to Natchez, Judith decided to heed President Kirkland's advice, sending her nephew to a "discreet, humane, firm and well informed Clergyman, remote from this Town." Thus William began a painful and ultimately unsuccessful sojourn, as one clergyman after another accepted responsibility for him. Glowing reports were invariably and rapidly replaced by harsh criticisms, as the boy repeatedly wore out his welcome. Rejecting all adult authority, he frequented taverns and ran up huge debts, which he had no ability to repay, selling his books and pawning his possessions for a fraction of their value. He rented a horse and carriage and paraded through Cambridge, a brazen violation of Harvard's rule that no rusticated student could set foot in the town. Whenever he appeared to be settling down, making enough academic progress so that Judith thought he might be able to return to Cambridge, his "eccentricity, and want of self government involved him in fresh difficulties."[45]

In late winter of 1816, Judith conceded defeat. As she saw it, only one option remained: Winthrop needed to come to Cambridge to assume personal responsibility for his son. Though he agreed with his sister, he was suffering from painful and debilitating gout and was in no position to begin his trip right away. It was not until April that he was able to leave Natchez. He and Mary did not arrive in Boston until the end of May. Almost as soon as he arrived, Winthrop collapsed and was confined to his bed. When William finally passed what Judith characterized as his "arduous" entrance exam, preparing the way for his return to Harvard, his father was not there to witness his triumph.[46]

By September, Winthrop's health improved enough that he moved to Cambridge, renting a magnificent house for $400 a year. Both his sons came with him. Washington entered Harvard for the first time; William was ready to try again. Winthrop literally whipped his sons into shape, ordering his slaves to catch William and Washington when they misbehaved, and applying a horsewhip to their backs himself with grim determination. For years William had romanticized his father and longed to return home. Indeed, his outrageous behavior may well have been designed with that end in mind. Surely this was not the happy reunion he had envisioned.[47]

Even Winthrop's lash could not control William for long. By the spring of 1817, the boy's "aberrations" were growing more frequent and more alarming. Finally, he and a few other members of a club they called "The Chosen Few" posted an advertisement for some festivities their proudly exclusive group was planning. The ad included "portions of scripture, irreverently used." Not wanting his son to be suspended again, Winthrop interceded with the governors, who agreed to let William leave school for the rest of the term and gave him "the promise of a degree."[48] Judith's obligations to her nephews were at an end.

*   *   *

Judith's understanding of her experience with her nephews—especially with William—is revealing. Her letters to Natchez detailing her nephews' escapades were never designed solely to keep her brother abreast of his sons' affairs. They were her attempt to explain and defend her methods to an increasingly skeptical audience, as she clung desperately to her worn and tattered "theoretick plan" of education. The differences Judith had with Winthrop were replicated in many families throughout America in the early nineteenth century. Men, like Winthrop, looked to harsh discipline, "systematic and rigid subordination," and a "strong arm" to subdue their children's passions; women, like Judith, preferred moral suasion. Her nephews were "sweet and docile," she insisted, and "*always accessible* to kindness."[49]

If she refused to believe that her methods were at fault, Judith needed to explain why she failed so abysmally. A child's earliest experiences were, of course, crucial. Thus, although she never said so directly, Judith thought Winthrop and Mary shared some of the blame for their sons' misbehavior. None of the boys had been properly disciplined; none had received much in the way of an education. And their early contact with slaves had introduced them to habits that were nearly impossible to eradicate. Judith wrote almost nothing of the suffering that slaves endured, but she did discuss the negative effects slavery had on slaveholders. Her nephews, she observed, had all enjoyed an early and "uncontested dominion over the degraded African," giving them a "haughty and imperious mode of thinking," weakening their benevolent instincts, and developing in them a stubborn and "unwarrantable pride." Slavery had an especially telling effect on "the infant faculties," leading a vulnerable boy to become a "tyrant in miniature." He soon expected everyone to "do homage to his petit prowess." He developed other bad habits as well. He learned to lie, cultivating "seeds of cunning and duplicity." William's dishonesty might well have been attributable to the lessons he had learned from Mississippi slaves, lessons that were integral to his essence long before he entered Judith's home. The institution of slavery might also explain what all New Englanders viewed as virtually axiomatic, that the unruly students at Harvard, Princeton, and Yale were "principally natives of the southern states."[50]

If contact with slavery was bad for the character, it was especially harmful to children with academic aspirations. "I think," Judith proclaimed, "the almost unavoidable necessity of allowing children upon a plantation to associate for the first eight or ten years of their lives, with uneducated slaves, is truly pernicious." Proximity to slaves "depressed the intellect." Children learned modes of speech, peculiar pronunciation, and all manner of irrational ideas from the superstitious laborers on southern plantations. Washington, she noted with horror, believed in "hobgoblins." He also refused to become a lawyer because if he did so, he solemnly assured her, "the black man will tear my soul from my body, and carry it to his dark hole, where he will keep it everlastingly burning." Judith was convinced that her nephew could only have learned such nonsensical notions from the slaves on Winthrop's plantations.[51]

Judith noted other environmental influences that explained her nephews' failings. Their peers at Exeter and Harvard led them astray. Whenever David or William had promised to reform, they were sincere. But a single encounter with one of their partners in crime inevitably resulted in a resumption of their rebellious ways. William fell in with an especially bad lot. Many of his friends were South Carolinians, but the ringleader of his little group of rebels was Augustus Thorndike, the son of a wealthy Boston merchant. Thorndike, Judith noted sarcastically, had attended "the virtuous Seminary of Edinburgh"—an institution that Winthrop always praised—and had returned to Massachusetts less moral than when he left. "So notorious is the dissipation prevalent in Edinburgh," she informed her brother, "that an education there is become extremely hazardous to the morals of the young."[52]

Significantly, whenever she discussed her nephews' peccadilloes, Judith always held out hope. Even the reprehensible Sinisterus Courtland had eventually reformed. While boys often had a hard time resisting temptation, she thought that most of them developed into fine, upstanding adults. Only an adult male had the strength to resist licentiousness. Judith always referred to her nephews' worst behavior as "errors," or as temporary aberrations. Their tender age might have made them vulnerable, but it also allowed them to learn from their mistakes. Everyone knew that youth was "the season of caprice." And while "seeds early sown" often appeared dead to worried parents, in the end they developed into hardy plants. Because the boys were weak but not evil, they could correct their errors without doing any irreparable damage to their reputation. In fact,

Judith insisted that her nephews' problems might well be a blessing in disguise. Was it not, she wondered, better for them to suffer a few setbacks when they were young than to make serious mistakes when they were older and more accountable for their actions? Just as some people thought the reformed rake made the best husband, so it was possible that the prodigal son—who learned from his behavior—became the most virtuous adult.[53]

Judith was not talking in mere abstractions. She knew countless men whose early years were marked by indiscretion, but who had become virtuous members of adult society. A youthful John Murray had enjoyed a "life of dissipation," in London. Yet no one questioned his probity as an adult. Lucius Manlius had been more incorrigible than any of her nephews. After Harvard's governors had voted to suspend him, he had contemptuously torn up the bill of particulars in front of them, vowing never to return to Cambridge. He was now esteemed in the literary world and known far and wide for his virtue.[54] Winthrop himself, of course, had enjoyed his share of wine and women, if not song, at Harvard. Nevertheless, he had become a military hero and governor of the Mississippi Territory. Surely his sons would fare as well.

Judith blamed her nephews' erratic behavior on their upbringing, their classmates, and their youth. But in her mind, there was one more important—perhaps essential—part of the equation. Her experience proved in a perverse way that as long as women were denied a proper education and not accorded the respect all humans deserved, America's future was at risk. One of her earliest encounters with William was a case in point. She was sitting at her desk, and in her "slow, circumulatory manner" was doing some simple addition. Observing her halting efforts, William intervened, showing her a faster and more accurate method of compiling sums. Defensive, Judith explained that in her day it was not "the fashion" to teach girls arithmetic. The incident had been humiliating. How could any woman expect deference from children who knew more than she did? Judith usually held her own in the beginning. As soon as her nephews began studying the classics, however, she was out of her depth. She could complain as often as she liked that their concentration on Latin and Greek led inevitably to "carelessness" in all other subjects. The fact remained. Because of her ignorance, her authority inevitably diminished. When William began his peripatetic ways, wandering Boston's streets looking for adventure, she could not even follow him and bring him home. A mere boy was free to roam freely. A grown woman was not.[55]

Judith saw her frustrations as symptomatic of a fundamental problem. "Among the weeds which infest the garden of science," she told Winthrop, "a contempt for the female world is of a growth astonishingly rampant, and a

Woman, especially an *old Woman* is considered the most inefficient and insignificant being in the human family." Each of her nephews in turn had rebelled against her tutelage, proclaiming a disdain for "petticoat government." Even the relatively docile Washington became "a little wild, and uncontroulable" the longer he remained under Judith's care. The "authority of a woman, an elderly Woman," simply did not exist. "I am," she told her brother, "old, I am feeble, I am a woman."[56]

*   *   *

In the beginning, Judith had been confident of her ability as a mother and a teacher. By the time William and Washington left Boston and headed for home, she was not so sure. None of her nephews had lived up to her expectations. At least for a while, she thought she had succeeded in turning Julia Maria and Anna into model republican daughters. Even that solace was eventually called into question. When Winthrop observed the fruits of Anna's expensive education, he was not pleased, convinced that his sister had failed to acquaint his stepdaughter with the basic skills she needed as a housewife. Even worse, despite all Judith's work and all of her sacrifices, Julia Maria's adult life in no way resembled that of the redoubtable Margaretta. Judith rationalized her failures with her nephews; she was unapologetic as she defended the choices she had made with Anna. She had a much more difficult time explaining Julia Maria's behavior after her daughter committed one of the most devastating errors a genteel woman could make. Judith's very efforts to salvage her daughter's reputation, however, served only to accentuate the gender differences against which she had fought her entire life. Moreover, her attempts to defend Julia Maria revealed just how traditional her own views of gender were. Judith may have demanded intellectual equality with men, but in fact she judged her daughter by different, much more exacting and unforgiving standards than she did her nephews. If she had believed that education was the means by which women could become men's equals, her daughter's plight should have caused her to question the maxims upon which her entire adult life had rested.

Judith had worked hard to make sure that her daughter would not be encumbered by the limitations that she herself faced. Julia Maria was well educated and would never be embarrassed because her sons knew more than she did. She had even fulfilled one of her mother's most cherished dreams, learning the rudiments of Latin from Mr. Bigelow, a tutor Judith had hired for just that purpose.[57] Still, no matter how often she proclaimed that girls should transcend the artificial obstacles that circumscribed their dreams, Judith was influenced by the prejudices of her day. Although she claimed that girls should disregard gender-based custom, she always made sure that both Anna and Julia Maria were proper ladies, that their reputations were unsullied and they were prepared to take their place in respectable society.

Indeed, whenever the desire for excellence and the need to observe strict decorum clashed, decorum usually won. This was never so obviously the case as it was in the fall of 1803, when the Murrays decided that they no longer wanted Julia Maria to take part in oratorical exhibitions. Judith was invariably pleased whenever one of her nephews was invited to speak in public. What was laudable for men, however, was suspect for genteel women. "As the regulations established in our Country, will not admit a *Woman's* chief excellence to consist in this confessedly beautiful accomplishment," Judith explained, " we are not very anxious she should progress further in this line." Thus, she said, "we think a modest adherence to the rules prescribed to her sex, will not allow a *personal* solicitation of public attention." She did not appear to realize that she was imitating her own parents' example, deferring to irrational custom instead of encouraging Julia Maria to develop a skill she clearly enjoyed, and to defy the sort of rules she herself had always resented.[58] An "extensive" education was fine. But propriety could not be disregarded lightly.

Judith was also careful to make sure that Julia Maria and Anna—like Margaretta—were prepared to occupy "that useful domestic sphere in which custom, and perhaps nature, has designed they should move." She wanted them to be comfortable "at the wash tub" or with "the mop, or scrubbing brush" in their hands. She also initiated them into the "mysteries of the kitchen." If she had to choose between preparing Julia Maria to be a good housewife or being proficient in those areas "termed polite," she insisted that she would always choose the former. Fortunately, she thought no such choice was necessary, for the "knowledge of every thing in the domestic line" could be acquired as easily in six months as in six years. "Female avocations," she sniffed, were "not designed to fill the immortal mind." Housewifery might be important—she never denied that it was—but it was mindless work that any girl could learn.[59]

No matter how disappointed Judith was with her abortive efforts to earn fame with her pen, no matter how much she resented the genteel poverty that appeared to be her lot, only one thing really counted. If Julia Maria became a true "Margaretta," a rational and virtuous woman of the republic, then none of her other failures mattered. Despite all the sacrifices she made in order to give her daughter the most extensive education possible, however, Julia Maria's story did not have the happy ending that should by all rights have been hers. Her education did not prepare Julia Maria for independence. Nor did she become a decorous and rational wife and mother, using her knowledge to improve the lives of her husband and children. To achieve that genteel and traditional end, Julia Maria needed a spotless reputation. If conventional wisdom had it that children were humans whose reason was at yet unformed, then, theoretically, indiscretions committed in youth should not leave an enduring mark. This was true for prodigal sons, who could rise above their youthful follies and marry whomever they wanted. Benjamin Franklin was only one of many boys who overcame their little "errata" to become great men. Girls—particularly elite girls—were, like the fictional Eliza Wharton of *The Coquette*, doomed to be punished for their indiscretions.[60]

It all started in 1806, when Mississippian Adam Lewis Bingaman arrived at Franklin Place. Six months Julia Maria's junior, Adam was the oldest son of Charlotte and Adam Bingaman. His father was a planter, rancher, and merchant whose property in land and slaves made him one of Natchez's wealthiest citizens. When Winthrop had first met Adam, Sr., he had been impressed. Granted, his neighbor lacked education and polish, but that would not be the case for his firstborn son. Adam would study with the finest classics teachers in Boston before entering Harvard College.[61] Acting on Winthrop's recommendation, the Bingamans decided that their son could have no better guardian than Judith Sargent Murray.

Almost from the day Adam moved into Franklin Place, Judith was charmed by the newest member of her household. Bright, handsome, quietly confident, a third-generation member of Natchez's planter aristocracy, Adam compared favorably with all her nephews and was everything Judith had once hoped her own son would be. Julia Maria was also enchanted by Adam, and he had every reason to be drawn to her. Gilbert Stuart's portrait of her depicts a young woman as attractive as her mother had been at her age. Clad in a revealing gown, her bare head framed with artfully arranged auburn ringlets, she holds a few sheets of music, reminding observers that she is not only beautiful but genteel. Julia Maria and Adam relished one another's company. They had similar tastes; both of them loved languages and literature; they even painted in the same style. They took music and drawing lessons together and often could be found side by side, as Adam recited poetry to his entranced audience of one. When Julia Maria composed an elaborate acrostic of Adam's last name, Judith tried to dismiss it as the mere "effusions of an innate admiration of Genius, and talents." Still, she confided that a "very strong, and mutual attachment" existed between Adam and her daughter. The relationship, she hastened to add, was intellectual, not carnal. "The idea of sexual distinctions," Judith observed, "seems never to have obtained in their minds." Indeed, the two saw one another as brother and sister. Nevertheless, while she claimed to trust both Adam and her "almost faultless child," she never let nature take its course. She kept the two "under my eye," and just to be safe, Julia Maria still slept in her parents' bed each night.[62]

By March 1809, Judith was almost relieved that Adam was about to leave Franklin Place. A year earlier, she had made light of the growing affection between Adam and her daughter. Now, she claimed to be stunned when Adam openly declared his love for Julia Maria. She could no longer pretend that the relationship was merely fraternal. Thus, Judith redoubled her efforts to keep Julia Maria's reputation unsullied, watching her daughter with "unremitting vigilance, advice, caution," refusing to let her out of her sight. "The appearance of a young lady without a suitable escort," she explained, "would justly subject her to the accusation of indiscretion."[63]

Judith's "unremitting vigilance" and her fear that someone might accuse Julia Maria of "indiscretion" say a great deal about the uneasy relationship between gender ideal and sexual reality at the beginning of the nineteenth century. Especially in elite, New England circles, many were inching toward notions of "true womanhood," including the belief that women were naturally less interested in sex than men. At the very least, the responsibility for enforcing sexual boundaries increasingly devolved upon women. Nevertheless, Judith knew perfectly well that in the real world, if not on the pages of romantic novels, women as well as men might welcome a sexual encounter. While premarital pregnancies had peaked in America between 1761 and 1800, they had not declined precipitously, much less disappeared. Men and women did not live in separate spheres. They interacted on a daily basis, and they did not always have a chaperone. The belief that a virtuous woman was a passionless woman may have been advanced in some quarters by the time Adam Bingaman entered the Murray household. But no prudent mother would allow her daughter to face sexual temptation in the real world.

Judith revealed something of the ambivalence with which she viewed the question of women's sexual nature in a letter to a young friend in 1797. On the one hand, she praised her correspondent as a "discreet young Woman" who deported herself with "propriety and genuine delicacy." Such a demeanor was, she asserted, a "sexual trait." At the same time, however, she suggested that the attributes she described were evidence of good breeding, not innate virtue. Whatever the case, one thing was sure. If Julia Maria succumbed to temptation, she, not her lover, would face assaults on her character both as a woman and as a worthy member of genteel society.[64]

Though Judith was determined to protect her daughter, she welcomed the prospect of having Adam Bingaman as a son-in-law and gave the couple every reason to believe that she and John would approve their marriage. Indeed, there was very little in Adam to criticize. Possessed of "uncommon sensibility," he also had an "uncommon power of commanding his feelings." This alone was high praise. But there was more. Adam was kind and attentive. He was also wealthy, although Judith would never admit that she wanted either riches or social status for her daughter. And he was intelligent. J. S. J. Gardiner, declared that Adam was by far the most gifted student he had ever taught.[65] Poetry and forensics came easily to him and he was blessed with an "astonishing" memory. Judith was pleased but hardly surprised when Adam sailed through his college entrance exams. He easily earned the admiration of his tutors, and he began to collect honors almost as soon as he commenced his studies. He joined a number of literary societies, including the prestigious Phi Beta Kappa, and he was selected to recite a Latin ode he had composed in honor of John Kirkland's installation as president. If anything, Judith sometimes worried that Adam studied too hard, as she observed that he was "too ambitious, too capacious for his constitution."[66]

If Judith worked behind the scenes to smooth the way for a possible marriage between her daughter and Adam, on one point she was adamant. Julia Maria could not marry Adam if his parents objected. Anyone who had read *The Gleaner* knew that she disapproved of parents who compelled a loveless marriage. At the same time, however, she always urged young people to seek their parents' blessing before they wed.[67] Thus she wrote to Charlotte Bingaman in January of 1811, asking whether she should be Adam's "advocate" with her daughter. For whatever reason, the Bingamans did not reply for almost a year, and Adam began his last year at Harvard without having heard from his parents.[68]

When Judith finally did receive a letter from Adam's father, she was reasonably pleased. Granted, Mr. Bingaman was cautious. Although he was sure that Julia Maria was everything that he could want in a daughter-in-law, he made it clear that Adam had "no prospect of an establishment." He also worried that the young people were acting a little hastily, a sentiment with which Judith agreed. She had always hoped that Julia Maria would not confront the "cares which are consequent upon a wedded life at an early period." Her own experience proved that age brought judgment that youth simply did not have. Nevertheless, Judith discarded her long held prejudice against early marriages with amazing ease. "There is," she calmly observed, "no general rule which does not admit an exception." Besides, after Adam graduated from Harvard in August, he planned to return home for a long visit. No one was proposing a rush to the altar. Maturity and distance might well make hearts grow less fond, in which case both Adam and Julia Maria would avoid a dreadful mistake.[69]

Both the Murrays and the Bingamans felt as though they were entering dangerous territory. Readers of romantic novels were all too aware of the dangers posed by strangers.[70] In Judith's own *Gleaner*, the nefarious Sinisterus Courtland had managed to deceive any number of people who knew nothing of his unsavory past. Margaretta's parents had embraced Edward Hamilton at least partly because he was a known commodity. Adam was no stranger, of course. He had come to Boston highly recommended by Judith's own brother. He had lived at Franklin Place for years and Judith surely thought she knew him very well. Still, she had never met the Bingamans, and she had no idea what sort of life her daughter could expect if she married Adam, especially if they moved to Natchez. The Bingamans were at a far greater disadvantage. Adam's parents were aware of the Murrays' precarious economic position, and they knew that men, like women, could be victims of conniving fortune hunters. Thus, while they did not directly oppose the marriage, they did want to disabuse Julia Maria of any material expectations she harbored. The Bingamans may have been comforted by Judith's claim that her daughter had no interest in a "splendid establishment," but they were even more relieved to learn that no one was pushing for an immediate marriage.[71]

Adam left Harvard in the summer of 1812. His hard work had paid off, for he graduated first in his class. Soon thereafter, he headed for home. Judith assumed that he was leaving without being formally engaged to Julia Maria. As she contemplated her daughter's future, she had only one real concern. She would be devastated if Adam insisted that Julia Maria move with him to Mississippi. Thus, Judith used what little material and moral resources she possessed to assure what she saw as a happy outcome for herself and her daughter. In August she wrote to Adam's father with an intriguing suggestion. Predicting that her holdings in the Massachusetts State Bank might soon pay a handsome dividend, she offered to use her anticipated profits to set her future son-in-law up in business in Boston or, if he preferred, to read law with one of the city's eminent lawyers. She would view her investment either as a loan to Mr. Bingaman or as a gift to Adam. She also said that Adam could live at Franklin Place free of charge.[72]

When Adam left Boston, he promised to write often and to return to Franklin Place as soon as he could. Instead, August became September, and September became October and no one at Franklin Place received a single letter from Mississippi. Almost as worrisome, Mr. Bingaman owed the Murrays over $800 for his son's expenses, and he gave every indication that he thought Judith's meticulous efforts to account for every penny she spent on Adam's behalf were inadequate, even insinuating that he thought she was inflating her claims. Judith indignantly challenged him to allow anyone of his choosing to inspect her books, which, she insisted, were in perfect order. Moreover, she hinted that Adam had something he needed to tell his parents. She would not, she added obliquely, admit responsibility "*for any act of his* which you may think proper to censure." In the meantime, she worried about her daughter, whose health was declining. By the fall of 1812, Julia Maria was so ill that she traveled to Glouces-ter, hoping the sea breezes there would cure her physical if not her emotional malaise. Both she and Judith continued to write to Natchez, but their letters re-mained unanswered.[73]

Judith learned only in bits and pieces the reason for her daughter's unhap-piness. At first, Julia Maria told her that she and Adam, "softened by mutual ten-derness, mutual regrets, and mutual despondence," had exchanged—"*without my knowledge*, the most solemn, and sacred vows" before Adam had left for home. The vows were not legally binding, of course; they were, like the prom-ises Mary Wollstonecraft had once exchanged with Gilbert Imlay, registered only in heaven. Still, Julia Maria viewed herself as a "*wedded* although a virgin bride." Before long, however, Judith had to alter her story. While she was "not yet at lib-erty *to be more explicit*," she told Winthrop, the "engagement had been *more obligatory more solemn than had entered even into my imagination*." In the spring of 1813, Judith finally shared the sorry chain of events with her brothers. Before Adam had left Boston, he and Julia Maria had married—secretly. To complicate matters, Adam had not been old enough to procure a wedding license. Thus, al-though they had a marriage certificate, their vows might not actually be legal. Still worse, Julia Maria was pregnant. Judith put the best face on the situation, framing her daughter as an innocent and naive girl, suggesting that she was so ignorant of sexual matters that it had been months before she even realized that she was expecting a child.[74]

No matter how Judith tried to explain her daughter's plight, she could not escape the fact that this was hardly the behavior one would expect from Con-stantia's daughter. *The Gleaner* had unambiguously condemned secret mar-riages. Margaretta may have been vulnerable, but she would never have deceived her parents as Julia Maria had done. Judith had repeatedly railed against a sex-ual double standard that allowed women to make no mistakes while offering re-formed rakes absolution for their sins. But she had never denied the existence of that standard and had always urged her daughter and nieces to observe its stric-tures. Her warnings had fallen on deaf ears. Julia Maria's experience was more akin to the fictional Frances Wellwood's than it was to Margaretta's. And unlike Frances, Julia Maria was not an orphan. She really had no excuse.

Judith desperately defended her daughter. Julia Maria had never lied to her parents before; she had done so on this occasion only because she did not want her parents, whom she viewed with "filial affection," to worry unnecessarily. While she had invariably behaved with the utmost "prudence and discretion," in this single and uncharacteristic instance, her heart simply got the best of her. Moreover, it was Adam's persistence that led to the catastrophe. On his commencement day, Adam had begged his fiancée to marry him. When she refused, he was "wretched," fearing that time and distance would not make Julia Maria's heart grow fonder and that she would marry someone else. In the end, she was "softened by the sufferings of the Man to whom she had surrendered her whole heart." Sensibility had trumped judgment.[75]

This was one version of events, and it was one from which Judith never deviated. Genteel women were not aggressive suitors. Their power, such as it was, lay solely in their ability to accept or reject a proposal. Only once had Judith directly challenged conventional wisdom on courtship. Even then she had done so privately; she was invariably more circumspect in her public pronouncements. "Custom," she had suggested to a friend, "hath erected around our sex barriers which we may not leap with impunity: Man, so says the despot, must make his approaches, proposals must come from him, while we with apparent reluctance, accede to his wishes." Yet, she continued, she thought that women too readily accepted mere social conventions. There were times when women should defy the arbitrary rules that hemmed them in. Ultimately, however, she retreated from her own logic. "Eccentricity is always suspicious," she conceded. Before we "bid deviance to time honored rules, or neglect to observe those directions adopted by discretion, and established and rendered familiar by habit, we should deliberately weigh, ponder, and reflect." Custom might be despotic; but even at her most audacious, Judith knew women could ignore it only at their peril.[76]

Alas, Judith could not stop some observers from offering a less sympathetic version of her daughter's tale. There were too many people who were more than willing to see Adam as the unwitting victim of Julia Maria's seductive powers. Lucius Manlius snickered with ill-disguised disdain as he described his cousin's low-cut dresses and her efforts to capture the attentions of vulnerable male suitors. He hinted—with no apparent evidence to back him up—that Adam married Julia Maria only because she was pregnant. Motivated by a strong sense of honor, said Lucius Manlius, Adam simply did the honorable thing. The Bingamans arrived at the same conclusion. If they had initially given the couple their blessing, it did not take them long to develop a distaste for the "alliance" or to imply that mother and daughter had trapped their son. Winthrop, too, always suspected that Julia Maria was not the innocent that Judith described. In time, he grew more critical. He suggested that his niece's behavior had not been "immaculate," that she was, in fact, a sexual aggressor. Ironically, the more the attacks on her daughter mounted, the more Judith took refuge in common stereotypes. She had once praised Adam for the care he took to protect Julia Maria's reputation. He had refused, for instance, to allow her to travel to Cambridge alone, for he knew that a "young Lady in a crowd, without a Patron, or some other guardian Matron, seems not to be moving in her appropriate sphere." Now, however, Judith declared that she herself had erected every obstacle before Adam, as she tried "to stem the torrent of his uncontroullable wishes." It was Adam's "indefatigable and close pursuit," she said, that had ultimately led Julia Maria to yield to his demands.[77]

In June, after "hours of peril"—some forty-eight in all—and "indescribable agonies," Julia Maria gave birth to a healthy baby girl. She was named Charlotte, after Adam's mother.[78] Judith adored her granddaughter, of course, but could not help but note that the child's presence would put more pressure on the family's shrinking budget. In the short run, Adam visited his wife and daughter on rare occasions, but he spent most of his time in Natchez, helping his family run the plantation and reading law on the side. If the Bingamans were rich in land and slaves, they had little ready cash. And while Adam declared that he was "miserably disappointed" by his current condition, he claimed to be helpless to rectify it. He later lamented that it was money—or the lack thereof—that lay at the heart of his family's quarrels with Judith and he was probably right.[79] Once again, Judith could not prevent economic reality from poisoning her relationships with people she cared about most.

*   *   *

Judith had always feared that her daughter would one day be thrown upon the doubtful mercies of a heartless world. Her quarrel with Samuel Jackson had been about much more than money. As Judith saw it, Jackson had stolen Julia Maria's future, limiting her choices, robbing her of security and independence. She had invariably justified her plans for her daughter's education with the assertion that it would give her the ability to shape her own destiny, no matter what life might have in store for her. Now it appeared that marriage had not given Julia Maria the security women expected in exchange for dependence. Instead, she suffered all the liabilities of a feme covert without enjoying any of the perquisites of a protected wife.

In 1814 Judith made one last desperate attempt to secure a measure of autonomy for her daughter. Although Julia Maria was shocked when her mother mentioned the plan, Judith would not be dissuaded. Twenty years earlier, John had written a will leaving virtually all his property—real and personal—to his wife. He had also left Julia Maria ten dollars "as a small token of my affection." The will had been something of a triumph for Judith who probably had encouraged John to devise it. Both her father and her first husband had died intestate, causing no end of problems. She did not want to be stuck with her "widow's thirds" at John Murray's death. Nor did she want whatever property she inherited to be merely for "her use." When John wrote the will, of course, Julia Maria was a child and he assumed his wife would take care of his daughter's needs.[80]

Now, however, Julia Maria was an adult with a husband of uncertain prospects and a child of her own. Judith begged John to alter his will in light of their daughter's situation. John was reluctant, not because he was averse to helping Julia Maria but because he had "an abhorence of property, and of all questions relative thereto." Nevertheless, Judith prevailed. In August of 1814, John added a codicil to his will. The codicil employed a device that had become more common after the Revolution, as fathers sought to protect their daughters from the coercive authority of their husbands, giving them at least some control over their assets. Common law was no help in this regard. In Massachusetts, such provisions were especially necessary because the state remained reluctant to embrace equity law.[81]

John began by declaring his confidence in the ability and integrity of his "beloved son in law." He asked Adam to excuse him for "indulging my parental affection" by providing for Julia Maria's security. As he knew only too well, misfortunes occurred even to honorable men. Thus he intended to prepare for any contingency. The new document protected Julia Maria by creating a trusteeship for her, composed of three men in whose judgment and integrity John had absolute confidence. At John's death, the trustees would, with Julia Maria's "approbation"—but not with Adam's—sell what remained of the family estate, investing it advantageously. Once a year, she would receive "for her own use" the income those investments earned. Should Julia Maria want to share her assets, she could do so. But the decision would be hers. She retained the right to dispose of her property and to name her own beneficiaries in any way she deemed appropriate. If she died intestate, her property would automatically descend to her children. The same procedure would be used for succeeding generations. Finally, John named his wife as his executor.[82]

The amended will served as the equivalent of a separate estate. Julia Maria controlled everything. John appointed no one in Mississippi as his daughter's trustee. Her children, not Adam, would receive what remained of her inheritance. If Adam failed to support his family, then Judith intended to make sure that her daughter could support herself, not by taking in sewing or opening a school, but by living off the fruits of her parents' investments. It would be wrong, she told Winthrop, "to render her during her whole life powerless." Had Adam been worthy of her confidence, Judith might not have felt so strongly. But under the circumstances, the will was Julia Maria's best—perhaps her only— protection. Judith had always warned that marriage did not guarantee a happy ending—especially for women. Brides lost a great deal when they wed. They abandoned their name, the family of their birth, their very identity, when they entered a new home and adopted new loyalties. If they married well, they would enjoy the "highest state of friendship." If they did not, Judith reminded Anna Williams with more feeling than usual, they would endure a relationship that was synonymous with "*Master* and *Slave*." In the ideal world, "equality should be the motto of wedded life." In reality, husbands could be masters and women could do little to avoid slavery.[83]

In fact, the will did not guarantee Julia Maria the independence Judith wanted. Adam could challenge it in court—and he had a reasonable chance of winning. Massachusetts did not give the Supreme Judicial Court jurisdiction to enforce trusts until 1818. Even then, many husbands obtained through informal means what prudent fathers tried to deny them. There was nothing to stop Adam from giving Julia Maria "advice" about her property, and nothing to keep her from accepting his judgment.[84]

*   *   *

By 1815, Judith felt totally helpless. John, Esther, and Maria were all gone. Fitz William seldom left home and never wrote. She knew that no matter how often he considered it, Winthrop would never leave Natchez. Her daughter and grand-daughter were all she had left, the only physical reminder of John that remained. Even that comfort might not last. The Bingamans wanted Julia Maria and Charlotte to move to Mississippi, and Adam seemed to agree with his parents. Judith knew that no one, least of all the courts, would "controvert a husband's right to rule." The law, she pointed out, "has placed the destiny of my only child, and now of a darling grand child, in his power—he can, if he pleases, remove them *forever* from my view." No matter how many odes to companionate marriage Judith might write, she knew that Adam's authority over his family was absolute. Mother and daughter ultimately had only one resource, one that women had employed to varying effect from time immemorial. They could exercise their feminine wiles. We can, Judith said, try to "soothe him to our wishes." Ultimately, some fortunate women had influence; none had power. Thus, while Julia Maria expressed the "strongest aversion, even to horror, at the idea of a residence in Natchez," if Adam demanded it, she would obey. Judith, moreover, would accompany her. She desperately wanted to remain in Franklin Place, dying on the bed upon which John had drawn his last breath. The thought of traveling 3,000 miles only to live in "uncertain dependence" in someone else's home was unbearable. But, she said, "my wishes are impotent." In the meantime, both women existed in limbo, enduring long stretches when they did not know whether Adam was even alive. Increasingly, Judith distrusted a man she had once described as nearly perfect. Whenever she discussed Adam, her writing, usually so neat and precise, became scrawls, her periods became dashes, and her spelling disintegrated. His neglect of his little family, Judith said, was "shocking truly shocking."[85]

In the meantime, Julia Maria was a virtual recluse. She spent most of her time "gloomily alone" in the "melancholy apartment, sitting by the fire, grieving over her father's death and her husband's absence, writing to Adam, reading and rereading the few letters her husband bothered to send her, convinced that mean-spirited gossips were enjoying the depths to which she had fallen. She occasionally visited Fitz William and Anna. Other than that, she scarcely left home, not even to attend church. Plays, balls, an occasional quiet social visit were out of the question. When Judith suggested that the two of them visit Saratoga, whose waters might alleviate the worst symptoms of Julia Maria's rheumatism, she insisted that it would be "improper" to appear in public "without her *legal* Protector." Despite Judith's protests that people would know that she went only in "pursuit of health," Julia Maria would not budge.[86]

In time, Judith began to refer to the relationship between Julia Maria and her husband as an "apparent estrangement." Over and over she desperately enumerated Adam's superior qualities, trying to convince herself that "Virtue can never die." Perhaps, she thought, her son-in-law's dependence on his parents had destroyed his confidence. She had watched both her husbands suffer the indignity of financial embarrassment. She knew that if a mere woman cherished independence, a man was even more humiliated when he could not provide for his own family. When Adam had urged Julia Maria to marry him, he had been young, confident, a little brash, blind to the pitfalls that could destroy the plans of an honorable man. While marrying for love was a noble ideal, the most enamored couples could not live on love alone. Although she was "tortured by suspense and agonized by apprehension," Judith was reasonably confident that her son-in-law was not addicted to any "degrading vices," nor had he formed an "illicit sexual attachment." For more than that, she dared not hope. Without hope, she admitted, she would become a "confirmed maniac."[87]

Occasionally Adam made the long trip to Boston, but he never stayed long.

When he was there, he and Julia Maria fell easily into their old ways. They were, as they once had been, not only "*one heart*, but *one soul*." Adam spent the nights reading law or translating odes, making a present of them to his wife. When his eyes grew tired, Julia Maria read aloud to him. Judith, however, no longer smiled upon appearances of marital bliss; she did not trust Adam to act with honor, much less affection. She had become cautious and a bit cynical in her old age.[88]

Judith's hopes for her own and her daughter's happiness were dormant. She would not be a famous playwright or a revered author. If she was careful and just a little lucky, she might be able to satisfy her little family's material needs. But she would never be wealthy, or even secure. Most of her closest friends and relatives were dead. She had offended those few who were among the living. True, Julia Maria and Charlotte still resided with her. But for how long? And under what circumstances? Perhaps happiness was too much to expect in this life. Still, while she struggled to accept her lot, she never quite managed to accept what the fates offered her without a fight.

Epilogue

In 1818, Judith confided to a close relative that she was exhausted, the victim of the succession of "mortifications" and "sufferings" she had endured over the last few years. Her confidence was low, and she could not help but wonder if God was sending tribulations her way in order to "wean" her from her dependence on earthly pleasures. Heaven had never looked so inviting. She was heartbroken by yet another serious "estrangement" from Winthrop. She worried constantly about Julia Maria's plight and was especially unhappy because she knew that her daughter's anomalous position would only be resolved if she joined Adam in Natchez. Nor was there a single minister in Boston to whom she could go for comfort or inspiration. Finally, she had abandoned all thought of publishing any more during her own lifetime. She wished the city's editors good fortune. But she had no work of her own to fill their pages.[1]

Despite her unhappiness, Judith admitted that a few pleasures remained. "I delight in the cultivation of the human mind," she had once assured Winthrop. She often claimed that she was a mere housewife with few skills and no education to speak of, but in fact she acted as the preceptress of a substantial number of children—mostly boys—in the twilight of her years. Although she received no remuneration for her efforts, she still believed that the task of preparing young people to assume their rightful positions as virtuous members of the republic was an exalted one. Thus, even before Washington left for Harvard, she had accepted another Mississippian into her household.[2]

Winthrop Sargent Harding, son of the first attorney general of Mississippi, arrived in Boston in the fall of 1814, to begin studying Latin with John Gardiner. Two years later, yet another Mississippian, David Urquhart, also moved into 5 Franklin Place. Judith worried that she might not meet the expectations of her charges' parents. Still, she was determined to do what she could to implant the seeds of "integrity and honour" in the boys' hearts. She clung stubbornly to her own principles, indicating that she would be "liberal of applause," which she still saw as "one of the best incentives to rectitude." Nevertheless, she often thought that she was getting too old to handle young boys very effectively, and she hesitated to correct them, feeling that to do so "would be an awkward assumption of power." Thus she promised that if she sensed that she was losing control of either boy, she would immediately put "the reins in more energetic hands." In her more confident moments, however, she could not help but assure both sets of parents that "I have sufficient vanity to think that I can manage them."[3]

Her confidence in the future was surely not helped by the emotional distance that had gradually divided Judith and Winthrop. Winthrop blamed his sister for much of what had gone so wrong with William. He admitted that his oldest son was a difficult child and it was possible that no one could control him. "God only knows," he sighed, "when he shall cease aberrance." Still, he was sure that Judith's misguided kindness had made matters worse. As she endured her brother's criticisms, Judith despaired. She already knew far too much about Winthrop's unbending nature. She had suffered for years because he opposed her marriage to John Murray. She had also watched helplessly as Julia Maria shrank from her uncle's haughty gaze. Now she feared that Winthrop's disapproval of the way she had raised his children would drive a permanent wedge between them. The breach, she observed, is "wide, *very wide*." She had once seen writing and receiving correspondence as a way to nurture the ties binding her to friends and family. Now, whenever she saw a missive from her brother, she almost feared to open it. "Reason begins to sicken at letters," she said. "They make rich promises to the eye which they rarely keep to the heart." When she began to contemplate moving to Natchez, she hesitated, fearing that Winthrop would actually "bar [his] doors" against her. She tried to dismiss her apprehensions as silly, but she knew that "things as strange have happened." A woman's world was always small. She feared that her own universe was about to become smaller.[4]

Her anxiety was not without foundation. The relationship between the siblings had always been conflicted, and while Judith often begged Winthrop to move to Massachusetts, she had secretly feared that she and her brother might not get along if they lived in close proximity. She was right. At first, Winthrop had been delighted to see her when he came to Cambridge, determined to take charge of his sons' education. By the time he left for home, he was barely speaking to his sister. Whatever had driven him over the edge, his frustration had been steadily mounting for years. He was unhappy about more than his sister's failures with William. The two also quarreled about money. Throughout the years, Winthrop had often come to Judith's financial aid, but he no doubt resented her chronic demands on his pocketbook. He had predicted this would happen when she married John Murray, and he was not reluctant to point out that he was right. He was less irritated by her requests for money, however, than he was by her constant complaining. She always maintained that she wanted nothing but "independence" and a "competence," saying that if only she were free from debt she would rest content. Anyone who had read the thirty-third entry of *The Gleaner* knew that Judith wanted much more than that. The essay described in loving detail the tale of "Hortensius," an "upright and important magistrate" who came to the rescue of his sister, a poor widow whose husband had died leaving her penniless. Hortensius provided her with an "elegant habitation" and was the "guardian, the support, and the preceptor of her children." He saw to it that his sister's children had "the most liberal" education possible. His nieces married into the "genteelest families" while his nephew became an eminent barrister.[5]

At some point during Winthrop's sojourn in Massachusetts Judith had tried to give her brother an exact account of her precarious financial situation, no doubt hoping he would see fit to emulate Hortensius's excellent example. Instead, he exploded. Not only did he refuse to give her any more money, he claimed that she already owed him more than she could ever repay. She had, he said, dipped freely and often into the funds earmarked for his own children that he had sent her over the years. He also told her that he was tired of her self-pity. She did nothing, he said, but talk about her poverty. He had heard enough.[6]

When Judith made one desperate attempt to defend herself from her brother's accusations, she only made matters worse. She was devastated by Winthrop's accusation that she had spent his money unwisely and improperly, perhaps even dishonestly. The accusation stung, for it was the same one she heard all too often from the Boston Universalists, who were convinced that she mixed her brother's money liberally with her own. True enough, Winthrop had occasionally offered to pay her for taking care of his children, and while she preferred to treat her nieces and nephews as guests, she had reluctantly accepted some compensation. She also admitted that despite her best efforts, she did not always keep the most accurate records. I am not an accountant, she cried. She purchased everything at the lowest prices; she spent no money frivolously. Still, although she was confident that she had never acted unethically, Winthrop's attack threw her off balance.[7]

Judith later conceded that Winthrop had sent her "thousands and thousands of dollars" over the years, but she had never—or almost never—used any of it for herself. She may have occasionally taken a little from his coffer to pay her bills and to put food on the table. But she thought she had earned the right to do so. Sometimes, moreover, Winthrop had owed *her*. When his money did not arrive in a timely fashion, she had paid for preceptors' fees, books, paper, and clothing out of her own pocket—this when Boston prices were steadily rising. She had also assumed responsibility for more than her share of William's debts.[8]

Perhaps most important, Judith had worked diligently, even aggressively to augment her brother's $6,000 nest egg, investing it where it would get the highest return at a time when making money in Massachusetts was no easy feat. She did so despite the tendency of most men to avoid transacting business with women, whom they assumed were simply not up to the task. In April 1803, for instance, Judith informed Winthrop that his money was "laying in an unproductive state." The Bank of Boston had just been incorporated, but she had been unable to invest in the new venture. "Certain characters," she explained, enjoyed a monopoly of the shares. She briefly considered investing in another promising bank, but abandoned the project when her uncle Daniel advised her against it. Instead, she gave Daniel permission to put half of Winthrop's money in the new Suffolk Marine Insurance Company. A month later, he doubled the investment. She hoped that she was not acting with too much "temerity," but, she told Winthrop, she had never seen the point of putting money in a trunk when it could be put to productive uses. Moreover, Epes was the company's president. To Judith, this was proof enough that the venture was safe. A year and a half later she was delighted to report that Winthrop's Suffolk funds were, "in the technical phraseology, looking up" and would soon produce a solid dividend. Later on, however, when the value of his shares plummeted and Winthrop received no dividends at all, she advised him not to sell. There was, she sighed, no better place for his money, so he might as well keep it where it was. In the short run, she had to borrow on her brother's account to pay for her nephews' expenses. Still her advice was on the mark. In February of 1807, Winthrop received a nice dividend, nearly $450, on his Suffolk funds, and his navy securities earned another $1,100. Unfortunately, Judith had to spend it all as fast as it came in.[9]

Judith quarreled about money with all of her siblings. Whenever she did so, both her insecurity and her sense of entitlement revealed themselves. She was insecure because as a woman she never felt totally comfortable or welcome in the financial world. Despotic custom, of course, often kept her from doing what she felt she had to do to survive; she could not even sue Samuel Jackson without her husband's permission. She knew that all too often, people thought she was pushy, hysterical, or simply traveling beyond her sphere. Others cavalierly dismissed her concerns, seeing them as silly or naive. And she always feared that her ignorance would lead her to make a costly error. She suspected as well that sophisticated men often took advantage of her inexperience and she knew that they never took her seriously. Ignorance and powerlessness invariably went hand in hand, and both were the lot of women. Judith had tried, valiantly, to earn a living with her writing. She had been only marginally successful. Thus, she was forced to rely on the men in her life to take care of her. Unfortunately, neither John Stevens nor John Murray had been dependable. They both wanted to be good providers, but they had failed. Winthrop was successful. Although he *could* be her savior, he refused.

At the same time that she struggled against the prejudices of a hostile world, Judith was doggedly determined to get what she thought she deserved. She had never become accustomed to the status to which her marriages had consigned her. Nor had she forgotten what it meant to be a Sargent. True enough, she lived better than the vast majority of Americans. She received some $800 a year from her various investments and she was aware that she was "ungrateful" not to recognize how fortunate she was. Still, she never truly compared herself to "most" Americans. When she contemplated her assets, she only knew that her siblings, her cousins, virtually everyone with whom she identified, were much better off than she would ever be. "We are," she reminded Winthrop, "the children of the same Parents, and my wishes for *ease* and *affluence* are similar to your own." She acknowledged that if she watched her pennies, she would have enough to live on. But she had a "very opulent brother" who could make her life so much better, so much what it *should* be. She did not truly believe that she was being unreasonable to hope that Winthrop would keep her in the "style of a Lady." She may not have had a legal claim to her brother's beneficence, but the ties of blood and "affection" surely meant something. If their situation was reversed, she insisted, she would be delighted to elevate Winthrop to the eminence he deserved. She had assumed that he felt the same way. Perhaps, she dreamed, he would hire a manservant for her who would serve her a glass of wine each afternoon. Perhaps he would give her the funds to rent an occasional hack. People often accused her of being a "romantic," she said. Her fantasies proved them right.[10]

Winthrop was furious with his sister for seeking more than he was willing to give. The more she talked of her woes, the angrier he became. Eventually, all his pent-up frustration rose to the surface, and he berated her for every slight, every mistake, he had suffered at her hands over the years. When he left Franklin Place for the last time, he rode as quickly as he could, vowing to have nothing more to do with anyone in that house again.

Judith made a real effort not to think too much about Winthrop's disapproval, but she was obviously pained by her brother's efforts to keep himself and the rest of his family at arm's length. Although he allowed his sister to manage Washington's finances so long as his son remained at Harvard, he refused to let the boy visit Boston, even during vacations. Nor did he ask Judith about

Washington's scholastic progress. Instead, he received regular reports directly from Levi Hedge, his son's tutor, who always informed him that he wished Washington had a "little more zeal for his studies, and less fondness for amusements." Still, although Hedge predicted that the boy would never "rank as a scholar" he was fairly sure that he would "at least, pass reputably through his Collegiate course." Judith, too, hoped her nephew would graduate "without censure" but even she admitted that just before he left Franklin Place he had suddenly become "rather wild, and a little uncontroulable." Still, she thought he was by no means immune to reason.[11]

Judith's reaction to her brother's silence was uncharacteristically subdued. Deferring to Winthrop's wishes, she carefully addressed her Mississippi letters to Mary, and she clung gratefully to whatever news Natchez residents gave her about her brother and sister-in-law. Her position was awkward. Winthrop had not relieved her of responsibility for his various investments. She promised to follow his orders "scrupulously" but this was difficult to do since he absolutely refused to write to her. This was especially true after Epes stepped down from his position as president of the Suffolk company, and Winthrop's affairs there became increasingly complicated. Try as she might to unravel a tangled web of paper certificates and Suffolk dividends, she felt vulnerable without her brother's instructions. It did not help matters, of course, that the cashier at the Boston bank refused to deal directly with a woman.[12]

Still, Judith refused to beg for a rapprochement. She did warn Winthrop that, should she ever visit Natchez, "nothing short of your express prohibition, personally enforced, shall bar your doors against me." Increasingly she thought—sometimes with hope, usually with fear—that she might, indeed, be in a position to test her brother's willingness to receive her. In October of 1817, Julia Maria got a letter from Adam indicating that he might send for her the following summer. If her daughter left Boston, Judith saw no reason to remain there. The thought of leaving everything and everyone she knew and loved was daunting. But there were good reasons to sell Franklin Place and set out for a place unknown. Her "little tenement" was heavily taxed. She was estranged from the Boston Universalists, and thus did not feel as though she was leaving a loving community of fellow religionists behind. When the society built a new meetinghouse, she attended the dedication of the building but did not purchase a pew there. Gloucester minister Thomas Jones—who owed his very position to John—officiated at the ceremony and barely mentioned her husband's name. Her old nemesis Hosea Ballou also preached at the dedication. He said a few things that Judith found "unfamiliar," but none that were totally irrational or unscriptural. Still, she said, in an obvious understatement, Ballou was not Murray.[13]

By February, Judith had left her old church for Ballou's Second Universalist Society, although she remained troubled by much of what she heard from the pulpit. She told Anna Sargent that she entered the minister's meetinghouse each Sunday, prepared to listen to the "blessed truths he *may* utter." He was, she admitted, "*not all I wish.*" At times, Ballou did not even seem to be a Christian. He denied the existence of the Trinity. He saw Christ, not as God, but as a mere example to humankind. He did not believe in the "judgment to come." Although Judith did not absent herself from church altogether, she found herself attending services only occasionally. We cannot, she sighed, derive pleasure from hearing doctrine to which we are opposed. If Ballou was the best Boston had to offer, leaving would not be difficult.[14]

Deciding where to go was more difficult than Judith had once thought it would be. Sometimes she considered simply moving to the country—perhaps finding a place near Fitz William and Anna. At the very least, rural life had the virtue of being relatively inexpensive. She briefly contemplated going to New York where she could attend Edward Mitchell's church. There she could spend her last days near a minister who preached the "glad tidings" of true Universalism. She went so far as to ask Mitchell how much she would need to live comfortably in the city, but as she did with so many of her plans, she rejected this one almost as quickly as it entered her head. Even more fantastically, she entertained the possibility of fleeing America altogether. One of John's relatives had invited her to Dublin, and the idea was intriguing. She had always longed to visit the country where John had spent his formative years. She had, moreover, envied the freedom with which her father, brothers, and husbands had all roamed the world. She was an old woman now, and she could move where and when she wanted without regard to the clicking of censorious tongues. In the end, however, while her desire to travel abroad was "irrepressible," she knew that it, too, was "romantically fanciful."[15]

When it became clear that Julia Maria and Charlotte were actually, at long last, moving to Mississippi, Judith jettisoned all her vague plans and began preparing in earnest to accompany daughter and granddaughter to Natchez. She wrote to Mary Sargent, seeking her candid advice. She did not want to make the trip if her brother would not welcome her. He had recently sent her some oranges. Did that gift, perhaps, represent a softening of his anger? She also had to decide whether to travel by land or by ocean. Each alternative had its drawbacks. A trip by land would be long, hazardous, and expensive. An "arduous voyage" would mean that she would suffer from her dreaded seasickness. No matter which mode she chose, she would make the trip "without a male escort." She once had called a relative of hers a "complete Heroine" because she had braved the winter sea alone. Judith doubted that she possessed similar courage.[16] There was also the question of living in someone else's home. She had always feared ending her days as a dependent, existing on the questionable mercies of a benevolent relative. She had steadfastly resisted such a fate ever since she had left her parents' home. Now, however, she had little choice, unless she was willing to face the prospect of never seeing Julia Maria or Charlotte again. That, she was not prepared to do.

Even after she moved to Natchez, Judith could not abandon her connections to her New England roots. In her last will, written less than three months before her death, she referred to herself as "Judith Murray, commonly called J. Sargent Murray, of Boston." She indicated that she lived "at present" in Mississippi, but she still identified herself as a resident of "Boston, County of Suffolk, State of Massachusetts, New England." She did not sell her house on Franklin Place. And she thought that there was a good chance that she might die, not in Natchez, but in her native land. If that happened, she wanted, "for *special reasons*, not necessary to assign," to be buried in the vault that contained her "very dear sister's" ashes.[17]

Somehow, grandmother, daughter, and granddaughter survived the trip to Mississippi. How they went, what they saw along the way, what their reactions to their new and very different life were—all of these remain a mystery. Was she welcome in Winthrop's home? Did she find Natchez exotic and interesting? Or was she homesick in an alien environment, filled with slaves and heat and humidity? Did Winthrop tell her that he had decided to have all of his slaves sold after he and Mary died? And if she knew, was she pleased?[18] Did the trip destroy her health immediately? Or did she have a few months to enjoy the countryside and take in the sights of a world that looked like nothing she had seen before?

Only one, tantalizing sentence in her will provides even a clue about Judith's emotional reaction to Mississippi. Should she die in Natchez, she said, she wanted her survivors to "select some sequestered spot," secure from "the invasions of the Planter, or from intrusion of any description, in which to deposit my remains." It was, moreover, her "express wish, that said spot be inclosed by a decent railing." And she wanted her grave marked with a "monumental marble" that would announce her parents' names and the place of her birth. Perhaps Natchez seemed too wild, too forbidding to this woman whose idealized notion of nature was redolent of fields tamed by the plow, of well-tended orchards and land marked by neatly defined boundaries. At any rate, she hoped the "decent railing" would protect her from the human and animal "intrusions" that might destroy the peace of her final resting place.[19]

Other than that, only a few things are clear about Judith's brief time in Mississippi. She had looked forward to seeing Anna Williams Thompson again, and she probably did so. How often she visited David and James is less certain. David witnessed the will she devised in Natchez. But the boys were estranged from their parents, and were "going to Law" with Mary and Winthrop over the disposition of "what they call their Father's Estate." Mary thought that the entire matter would not be settled before she and Winthrop died, and she worried that in the end their half brothers would rob both William and Washington of their "patrimonial Inheritance." Nor do we know whether Judith and Winthrop reconciled. He did not witness her will. But in his own final testament he left a substantial bequest to his "beloved Sister Mrs. Murray," an indication that they arrived at some rapprochement. Winthrop was once more confined to his bedroom, in excruciating pain, the result of gout and dropsy. Alienated from so many members of his Natchez family, he may actually have welcomed his sister, if not his niece and her husband, into his home.[20]

Even if she visited Winthrop and Mary at Gloster Place, Judith probably resided with Adam, Julia Maria, and Charlotte at Oak Point Plantation. Adam, Sr., died in October of 1819, leaving his oldest son the lion's share of his extensive estate. Adam was at last independent, able to provide for his wife and child in grand fashion. That was just as well. Julia Maria would not have inherited much from her own parents. And while her uncle's will left a little something for the children of Esther and Fitz William, it pointedly excluded Judith's daughter.[21]

Her last will offers some evidence that Judith and Adam were reconciled, even as it underscores her continued determination to secure at least a measure of independence for Julia Maria. She left her son-in-law half of her bank stock, her loan office certificates, her stock in the Marine and Fire Insurance Company of Boston, and money from the sale of the Ohio land she still owned. Julia Maria got the other half. Moreover, Judith was not above offering Adam the benefit of her advice, even from the grave. If, she intoned, he truly had an "*honorable mind*," he would make sure that her daughter would be left with "the *full, free, and independent* use" of the property she had bequeathed to him; "in case of *accident* to himself it may be some *little minimal aid to them both*." Nor did Adam get all her property. Franklin Place went to Charlotte, and eventually to Charlotte's children. If her granddaughter had no heirs, then the property would be divided among the legal heirs of her "late honored Father." Her "love of justice," Judith explained, told her that her house, which was "principally purchased with monies received from my Father," should remain in the Sargent family.[22]

She also made some sentimental bequests. Charlotte got her watch, some silver objects, Goldsmith's *History of England*, and her beloved *Clarissa*. Julia Maria received the rest of her books, her plate, clothes, pictures, needlework, and "furniture of every description." At Julia Maria's death, all the family pictures would go to Fitz William and Winthrop—except for Stuart's portrait of Julia Maria. That, Judith conceded, Julia Maria could dispose of as she wished.[23]

As for the many other people to whom she was "*tenderly attached*," Judith could offer most of them only her "most affectionate benedictions." Even as she faced her death, she could not resist reminding her survivors that she was not "possessed of opulence." She would like to leave all her friends and relatives something. But they were all "*comparatively* affluent," and her own estate was minuscule. She managed to give $200 to her niece, Anna, "*as a small token* of that love with which she was for many happy years most tenderly cherished." She also bequeathed $200 to the poor of the town of Gloucester, her "native Place." The day before she died, Judith was still fine tuning her bequests.[24] Sadly, Judith's carefully devised plans were irrelevant so far as her daughter and granddaughter were concerned. Judith was the first member of her family to be buried in the Bingaman family plot near Fatherland Plantation, but not the last. Charlotte died two months after her grandmother. Julia Maria followed her two years later.

Judith Sargent Murray died at age sixty-nine, on July 6, 1820, having lived less than two years in her new home.[25] Her survivors obeyed her instructions, erecting a sturdy iron fence around the graveyard, making a feeble attempt to encircle her resting place and to protect her remains from desecration. Her tombstone, at least, reminded future generations that in spirit—which was surely all that mattered—she remained true to her heritage. She was the daughter of Winthrop Sargent of Gloucester, Massachusetts, and the widow of the Reverend John Murray of Boston. "Dear Spirit," it read, "the monumental stone can never speak thy worth."

It was not her "monumental stone," however, that would provide succeeding generations with evidence of Judith Sargent Murray's "worth." Today, the Bingaman family graveyard is accessible only to the most determined sojourners, those who are willing to ford the strong currents of St. Catherine's Creek to pay homage to Judith, her daughter and granddaughter. Still, Judith did her best to see that what really mattered would survive her own death. She took only a few prized items with her when she left Franklin Place for Natchez. She took the family Bible, of course, whose faithful record of the births and deaths of the members of her immediate family served as a physical reminder of her Gloucester roots. She probably brought some clothes, leaving behind the heaviest winter garments that had served her in good stead over the years. Her furniture did not make the trip. But her precious Letter Books, all twenty of them, did. They contained Judith's memories, some good, some bad, all important; they were her way of representing herself to subsequent generations. Taken as a whole, her letters were a carefully crafted story of her life. The countless poems and essays, some of which had been published and others never seen the light of day, reminded the world that she not only had existed, but had once been a member of the new nation's republic of letters. And they gave her a chance to remain in the public eye, to continue to influence the course of American history long after her own mortal body had entered its narrow tenement and turned to dust.

Afterword

Biographies nearly always end on a subdued and disquieting note. Granted, there are always those fortunate people who manage to avoid dying in their prime and are able to look back on their lives with a sense of satisfaction, a feeling that their time on this earth has been well spent. But many more are like Judith Sargent Murray, melancholy and vaguely disappointed, comparing the dreams of their youth with the reality of their old age. Even those who are content with their achievements generally long to do just a little more. Thus it seems only fair—to Judith and to those of us who want to understand and appreciate her place in her world—to remind ourselves of her importance as a member of her nation's "Republic of Letters." If she left this world disappointed and a little bitter, the very fact that she set her sights so high gives us some sense of just how unusual she was.

Indeed, it is easy to underestimate Judith Sargent Murray and her accomplishments, to emphasize her many limitations rather than to talk of her participation in a conversation about gender roles and identities that permeated her world and resonates even today. Observing her from the perspective of the twenty-first century, we can see her inconsistencies, her doubts, and above all the blinders she wore as the result of her elite status. And yet to see only her obvious weaknesses is to ignore her very real strengths, to forget that this was, indeed, an extraordinary woman.

Granted, Murray "failed" to demand the right to vote or hold office for women. Granted, too, that her paeans to motherhood sound saccharine, even reactionary, to modern ears. Nevertheless, her view of gender roles and possibilities was unusual for her time. It anticipated rather than mimicked the arguments of her more well-known contemporaries. She wrote "The Sexes" in 1779, and published her "Desultory Thoughts" in 1784. Both pieces centered on a forthright defense of women's intellectual abilities. Both were written well before Mary Wollstonecraft published *A Vindication of the Rights of Woman* in 1792. Her "On the Equality of the Sexes" appeared in print the same year that Catharine Macaulay published her *Letters on Education*. Clearly Murray was in the forefront of those eighteenth-century women on both sides of the Atlantic who were beginning to challenge traditional views of women's place.

In America, Murray was rivaled by none in her defense of women's rights. More than any of her contemporaries, she put the leaders of the republic on notice, calling upon them to examine and defend their assumptions about gender inequality in a nation that professed to be founded on egalitarian principles. Sarah Wentworth Morton was more popular in her own time than Judith Sargent Murray was. But it is Murray's work, not Morton's, that remains fresh, speaking to us across the centuries in language that we understand. Abigail Adams is a name most people recognize today, but however admirable this wife and mother of presidents might be, she was not interested in achieving literary fame, nor did she think systematically about the role of women in her society. Mercy Otis Warren was a talented playwright, poet, and historian, but she shrank from asserting her rights as a woman. In her plays, Susanna Rowson implicitly challenged gender conventions, but she did not take on the male establishment with the rigor or determination that characterized so much of the work of Judith Sargent Murray.

Murray's literary achievements speak for themselves. Her Universalist *Catechism*, published in 1782, directly challenged gender conventions, claiming that women need not apologize for intruding upon the "masculine" territory of theology. Both her "Desultory Thoughts" (1784) and her "On the Equality of the Sexes" (1790) argued that it was nurture, not nature, that made women *appear* to be men's intellectual inferiors. Her plays, *The Medium* (1795), or *Virtue Triumphant*, and *The Traveller Returned* (1796) were performed at Boston's Federal Street Theater. No matter how disappointed she was at the critical reception her plays received, the fact remains: Murray was the first American woman to have a play produced in the Massachusetts capital. And then, of course, there was her magnum opus, her three-volume book of essays, poems, and plays, *The Gleaner* (1798). The book was extraordinary on many levels. Most important, it contained Murray's famous four-part essay "Observations on Female Abilities," which marshaled a large body of evidence to prove that women were capable of any task—from running their own businesses to heading governments, to leading armies. Not only did Murray write the book, but she was its most tireless promoter. If some people laughed at her unabashed craving for fame, she pretended not to care, as she garnered subscriptions for her volumes, negotiated terms with her printers, and collected payment from recalcitrant customers.

Throughout her long literary career, Judith Sargent Murray never deviated from the views she developed in the 1770s. While she agreed that men and women were different in some ways, she always sought to blur gender differences and to emphasize the common humanity that both sexes shared. Her belief that women should be "independent," that they should be prepared to take care of their own economic needs should they be widowed or choose not to marry, was especially audacious, at a time when economic independence was recognized as the ultimate prerequisite for political rights. Her insistence that women, like men, should share the fruits of the American Revolution allowed her to think in universal rather than gendered terms about the promises Thomas Jefferson had made in his preamble to the Declaration of Independence.

Judith Sargent Murray failed to receive either the adulation of the literary community she had hoped for or the economic recompense for her efforts that she thought she deserved and so desperately needed. After 1798, her efforts to write for public consumption dwindled, although they never died. Suffering from the "backlash" against women's rights that pervaded the American intellectual landscape after the turn of the century, unable to see beyond her own elite status or to identify with *all* women, not just the privileged few, and faced with more than her share of personal traumas, she never truly scaled the heights that had seemed so accessible to her in her youth. Even though her experience was uniquely hers and hers alone, she can be seen as a "representative" woman, if not a "typical" one. For if Murray's experience illuminates the possibilities that seemed to beckon to American women who came of age during the last half of the eighteenth century, it also acknowledges the very real limits that continued to circumscribe the aspirations of any woman, no matter how ambitious or talented she might be.

Archival Sources

Cape Ann Historical Society, Gloucester, Massachusetts
    Gloucester Church Records
    Record Book of the Free and Independent Church of Christ
    Records of the Meetings and Actions of the First Parish in Gloucester
City Hall, Gloucester, Massachusetts
    Gloucester Town Meeting Records
Harvard Archives, Pusey Library, Cambridge, Massachusetts
    Faculty Records
Historical Society of Pennsylvania
    Samuel Shaw Papers
    Simon Gratz Papers
    Pennsylvania Population Land Company
    Population Treasury Book
    Benjamin Rush, MSS.
Massachusetts Archives, Boston, Massachusetts
    Estate of Epes Sargent, Jr.
    Estate of John Stevens
Massachusetts Historical Society
    Winthrop Sargent Papers (Seven Microfilm Reels)
    Sargent Murray Gilman Hough Papers
    George Lyman Paine Autograph Collection, 1660–1828
    Proceedings of the Proprietors of the First Universalist Church in Boston
    Frothingham Papers
    Warren-Adams Papers
Mississippi Archives, Jackson, Mississippi
    Judith Sargent Murray, Letter Books
    Judith Sargent Murray, Repository
    Judith Sargent Murray Papers
    Judth Sargent Murray, Poetry
    Papers of the Rev. John Murray

New-York Historical Society
    William Palmer Papers
    Jacob Clinch Papers
Peabody Essex Institute, Salem, Massachusetts
    William Stevens, Probate Records

Notes

Preface

1. See, especially, Linda K. Kerber, *Women of the Republic: Intellect and Ideology in Revolutionary America* (Chapel Hill: University of North Carolina Press, 1980); Mary Beth Norton, *Liberty's Daughters: The Revolutionary Experience of American Women, 1750–1800* (Boston: Little Brown, 1980).

2. Vena Bernadette Field, *Constantia: A Study of the Life and Works of Judith Sargent Murray, 1751–1820* (Orono: University of Maine Press, 1931).

3. Ibid., 51. Field relied for this information on A. Corbett, "Famous Women in New England History," in Corbett, *Original Studies in Local History* (1903).

4. Judith Sargent Murray, *The Gleaner* (1798), rep. with introductory essay by Nina Baym (Schenectady, N.Y.: Union College Press, 1992), 132.

Part I Introduction

1. Judith Stevens to John Murray, summer 1777, Judith Sargent Murray, Letter Book 1: 68, Mississippi Archives.

2. "Curiosity," 1777, Judith Sargent Murray, Repository, 34, 35, Mississippi Archives. Mary Beth Norton has pointed out that eighteenth-century women who wished to defend "the sex" from charges of inferiority usually took one of two approaches. Either they argued—as Judith did in "Curiosity" that an allegedly inferior quality was actually an asset, or they argued—as Judith did in a number of cases—that men were equally guilty of that quality. Norton, *Liberty's Daughters: The Revolutionary Experience of American Women, 1730–1800* (Boston: Little, Brown, 1980), 239.

3. Murray, "The Sexes," Repository, 225.

4. Judith Stevens to Winthrop Sargent, 3 July, 10 August 1778, Murray, Letter Book 1: 122, 142.

5. Murray, "The Sexes," 230. She wryly observed, however, that women would waive any claim to superiority if men would only grant them a measure of equality.

6. Ibid., 225, 226.

7. Ibid., 226.

8. Ibid., 226.

9. It was partly for this reason that Judith disliked Rousseau, who tried to "fetter" the "*free Born female Mind*" (emphasis original throughout) by denying women's capacity for judgment. Judith Stevens to John Murray, 1 November 1779, Letter Book 1: 250.

10. Murray, "The Sexes," 226–27.

11. Ibid., 227–28.

12. Ibid., 226, 229, 232.

13. She made an identical argument in a letter to Noah Parker in 1780. Judith Stevens to Noah Parker, 16 December 1780, Letter Book 1: 305.

14. "The Sexes," 229, 231.

15. Ibid., 232.

16. Ibid., 233.

17. See, for instance, Judith Stevens to Maria Sargent, 6 April 1781, Letter Book 1: 327.

18. Norton, *Liberty's Daughters*, 238.

19. "The Sexes," Murray, 232. In this, she echoed the views of other women who recognized that the wartime experience created a huge chasm between men and women. See Nina Baym, "Mercy Otis Warren's Gendered Melodrama of Revolution," *South Atlantic Quarterly* 90 (1991): 532–33; Mary Kelley, "'Vindicating the Equality of Female Intellect': Women and Authority in the Early Republic," *Prospects: An Annual of American Cultural Studies* 17 (1992): 8.

20. See Nathan O. Hatch, "The Democratization of Christianity and the Character of American Politics," in Mark A. Noll, ed., *Religion and American Politics: From the Colonial Period to the 1980s* (New York: Oxford University Press, 1990), 93.

21. Alfred F. Young, "The Women of Boston: 'Persons of Consequence' in the Making of the American Revolution, 1765–1776, in H. B. Applewhite and Darlene G. Levy, eds., *Women and Politics in the Age of the Democratic Revolution* (Ann Arbor: University of Michigan Press, 1990), 189–90.

22. Linda K. Kerber, "The Revolutionary Generation: Ideology, Politics and Culture in the Early Republic," in Eric Foner, ed., *The New American History* (Philadelphia: Temple University Press, 1990), 37. See also Nathan O. Hatch, "Elias Smith and the Rise of Religious Journalism in the Early Republic," in William L. Joyce, David D. Hall, and Richard D. Brown, eds., *Printing and Society in Early America* (Worcester, Mass.: American Antiquarian Society, 1983), 251–52. Of course, as Christopher Hill points out, the Puritans— against whose tradition Judith ultimately rebelled—had done much the same thing a century earlier, as they defied the corporate feudalism of the past in favor of a religion that was ultimately individualistic and even bourgeois. Hill, "Clarissa Harlow and Her Times," in Robert Donald Spector, ed., *Essays on the Eighteenth-Century Novel* (Bloomington: Indiana University Press, 1965), 48–50.

23. Laurel Thatcher Ulrich, "'Daughters of Liberty': Religious Women in Revolutionary New England," in Ronald Hoffman and Peter J. Albert, eds., *Women in the Age of the American Revolution* (Charlottesville: University Press of Virginia), 211.

Chapter 1. *"This Remote Spot"*

1. Murray, Repository, 26–28. Probably written in 1775, at the death of Judith's five-year-old sister, the piece appeared in her "Repository" essays in *Massachusetts Magazine* (June 1794): 369; Judith Sargent Murray to Epes Sargent, 5 July 1790, Letter Book 4: 156; Independent Christian Society, Gloucester Massachusetts, Records. See

also John J. Babson, *History of the Town of Gloucester* (Gloucester, Mass.: Proctor Brothers, 1860), 151.

2. Murray, "Nature, Commerce, Good and Evil," Repository, 55; Murray, "Commerce," in Poetry 1: 222. See also Andrew Burstein, *Sentimental Democracy: The Evolution of America's Romantic Self-Image* (New York: Hill and Wang, 1999), 200–201; John Fea, "The Way of Improvement Leads Home: Philip Vickers Fithian's Rural Enlightenment," *Journal of American History* 90 (2003): 465; Ralph Lerner, *The Thinking Revolutionary: Principle in the Republic* (Ithaca, N.Y.: Cornell University Press, 1987), 204–7; Carroll Smith-Rosenberg, "Domesticating 'Virtue': Coquettes and Revolutionaries in Young America," in Elaine Scarry, ed., *Literature and the Body: Essays on Populations and Persons* (Baltimore: Johns Hopkins University Press, 1988), 164; Caleb Crain, *American Sympathy: Men, Friendship, and Literature in the New Nation* (New Haven, Conn.: Yale University Press, 2001), 20; T. H. Breen and Timothy Hall, "Structuring Provincial Imagination: The Rhetoric and Experience of Social Change in Eighteenth-Century New England," *American Historical Review* 103 (December 1998): 144; Christine Leigh Heyrman, *Commerce and Culture: The Maritime Communities of Colonial Massachusetts, 1690–1750* (New York: Norton, 1984), 161–65.

3. See Heyrman, *Commerce and Culture*, chap. 1.

4. Judith Stevens to Miss Tracy, [?] September 1769, to Esther Ellery, 25 March 1776, Letter Book 1: 3, 39; Babson, *Gloucester*, 1, 3, 16, 18, 215.

5. Babson, *Gloucester*, 215; Heyerman, *Commerce and Culture*, 156.

6. For an analysis of the meaning of eighteenth-century portraits, see Carrie Rebora et al., *John Singleton Copley in America* (New York: Metropolitan Museum of Art, 1995), 186–87; T. H. Breen, "The Meaning of Likeness: American Portrait Painting in an Eighteenth-Century Consumer Society," *Word and Image* 6 (1990): 325–50. Emma Worcester Sargent, *Epes Sargent of Gloucester and His Descendants* (Boston: Houghton Mifflin, 1923), 6, 8–9; Richard J. Morris, "Social Change, Republican Rhetoric, and the American Revolution: The Case of Salem, Massachusetts," *Journal of Social History* 31 (1997): 420; Gloucester Church Records, 17 April 1745; and Heyrman, *Commerce and Culture*, 72–73, 165, 165n, 197.

7. Charles Edward Mann, *The Sargent Family and the Old Sargent Homes* (Lynn, Mass.: Frank S. Whitten, 1919), 15, 63; Babson, *Gloucester*, 318, 385; Jules David Prown, *John Singleton Copley in America, 1738–1774* (Cambridge, Mass.: Harvard University Press, 1966), 40–41; Rebora, *Copley*, 150, 197.

8. Winthrop Sargent, *Early Sargents of New England* (privately printed, 1922), 31; Sargent, *Epes Sargent of Gloucester*, 134–38.

9. Judith Stevens to Winthrop Sargent, 31 August 1787, Letter Book 3: 223; Heyrman, *Commerce and Culture*, 75, 165; Babson, *Gloucester*, 153–54, 242, 385.

10. For the struggle to build the new church, see Richard Eddy, "Mrs. Judith Sargent Murray," *Universalist Quarterly* 18 (1882): 212; JSM to Winthrop Sargent, 5 March 1786, Letter Book 2: 7; Records of the Meetings and Actions of the First Parish in Gloucester, Begun Jan. 29, 1728/9, 5–6, 26–36, 51; Babson, *Gloucester*, 311–14, 453. For Epes Sargent's largess, see Gloucester Church Records, passim; First Parish Meetings and Actions, 74–77. For the meaning and importance of pew membership in eighteenth-century America, see Heyrman, *Commerce and Culture*, 160–71. David S. Shields, *Civil Tongues and Polite Letters in British America* (Chapel Hill: University of North Carolina Press, 1997), 280.

11. Babson, *Gloucester*, 497–99. As Barbara Smith points out, this was a society built upon reciprocal, but not equal, relationships. Barbara Clark Smith, "Food Rioters and the American Revolution," *William and Mary Quarterly* 3rd ser. 51 (1994): 30.

12. JSM to Sarah Ellery, 21 June 1790, Letter Book 4: 128–129. For the importance of family hierarchy, see Stuart Blumin, *The Emergence of the Middle Class: Social Experience in the American City, 1760–1900* (New York: Cambridge University Press, 1989), 21–26, 39–46, 75, and Elaine Forman Crane, *Ebb Tide in New England: Women, Seaports, and Social Change, 1630–1800* (Boston: Northeastern University Press, 1998), 100. For "refinement," see Richard Bushman, *The Refinement of America: Persons, Houses, Cities* (New York: Knopf, 1992), 25, 182–83. See also Stephanie Coontz, *The Social Origins of Private Life: A History of American Families, 1600–1900* (London: Verso Press, 1988), 3, 12–14; Peter Dobkin Hall, "Marital Selection and Business in Massachusetts Merchant Families, 1700–1900," in Michael Gordon, ed., *The American Family in Social-Historical Perspective* (New York: St. Martin's Press, 1978), 101; Michael Grossberg, *Governing the Hearth: Law and the Family in Nineteenth-Century America* (Chapel Hill: University of North Carolina Press, 1985), 4–5; Mary Ryan, *The Empire of the Mother: American Writing About Domesticity, 1830–1860* (New York: Hayworth Press, 1982), 8.

13. Letter Book 1: Introduction. Memory, we know, is a very tricky thing. It is highly selective, and people often blend their memories of their past with their perceptions of the present. Thus, if Judith "remembered" that even as a child she resented her comparatively poor education, this may well have been because, as an adult, she grew to resent that education and saw in it a symbol of all the limitations her society placed on women's lives. See Robert E. McGlone, "Deciphering Memory: John Adams and the Authorship of the Declaration of Independence," *Journal of American History* 85 (September 1998): 411–38.

14. Judith Stevens to Winthrop Sargent, 17 May 1780, Letter Book 1: 279; JSM to Anna Sargent, 12 January 1796, Letter Book 10: 3; John Murray to Mr. Redding, 15 December, 1794, in "John Murray," *Universalist Quarterly* 25 (October 1868): 471.

15. Sargent, *Epes Sargent of Gloucester*, 50–51; Judith Stevens to Judith Sargent, [?] February, [2] April 1776, Letter Book 1: 29, 40; to Winthrop Sargent, 7 January 1784, Letter Book 2: 186; JSM to Anna Sargent, 12 January 1796, Letter Book 10: 3; to David and James Williams, 29 January 1802, Letterbook 11: 334; to Winthrop Sargent, 4 June 1803, Letterbook 12: 851.

16. Babson, *Gloucester*, 232; Sargent, *Epes Sargent of Gloucester*, 50–51; John Murray to William Palmer, 22 February 1799, William Palmer Papers.

17. Judith Stevens to a widowed and unfortunate Uncle, [?] October 1769, to Miss Goldthwait, 5 April, 6 June 1777, Letter Book 1: 4, 61, 63; to Winthrop Sargent, 17 May 1780, Letter Book 2: 283; Sargent, *Epes Sargent of Gloucester*, 137–138.

18. Ibid., See Ruth H. Bloch, "Untangling the Roots of Modern Sex Roles: A Survey of Four Centuries of Change," *Signs* 4 (1978): 242; John Demos, "The Changing Faces of Fatherhood: A New Exploration in American Family History," in Stanley H. Cath, Alan R. Gurwitt, and John Munder Ross, eds., *Father and Child: Developmental and Clinical Perspectives* (Boston: Little Brown, 1982), 427–29; Mark E. Kann, *A Republic of Men: The American Founders, Gendered Language, and Patriarchal Politics* (New York: New York University Press, 1998), 12–14; E. Anthony Rotundo, *American Manhood: Transformations in Masculinity from the Revolution to the Modern Era* (New York: Basic Books, 1993), 11–13; Daniel Blake Smith, "The Study of the Family in Early America: Trends, Problems,

and Prospects," *William and Mary Quarterly* 3rd ser. 39 (January 1982): 13. This retention of patriarchy was, if anything, stronger in the Puritan households of New England than it was in any other part of colonial America.

19. Paul Gilje, *Liberty on the Waterfront: American Maritime Culture in the Age of Revolution* (Philadelphia: University of Pennsylvania Press, 2004), 35, 43–44, 53, 57, 59; Murray, "Nature, Commerce, Good and Evil," Repository, 55; Lisa Norling, "Ahab's Wife: Women and the American Whaling Industry, 1820–1870," in Margaret Creighton and Lisa Norling, eds., *Iron Men, Wooden Women: Gender and Seafaring in the Atlantic World, 1700–1920*, (Baltimore: Johns Hopkins University Press 1996), 73–81.

20. Judith Sargent to Aunt P____, 15 April 1768, Judith Stevens to a widowed and unfortunate Uncle, [?] October 1769, to Winthrop Sargent, 3 July 1778, Letter Book 1: 1, 4, 122; to Winthrop Sargent, 12 October 1782, to Fitz William Sargent, 8 March 1783, Letter Book 2: 70, 117; JSM to Winthrop Sargent, 1 May 1788, Letter Book 3: 303; to Master Winthrop Sargent, 21 December 1799, Letter Book 11: 102; Sargent, *Epes Sargent of Gloucester*, 51; Winthrop Sargent, Unbound Diary, 1814–1820, 31 May 1816, Sargent Papers.

21. Judith Stevens to Winthrop Sargent, 18 April 1783, Letter Book 2: 140. See Nancy Armstrong, *Desire and Domestic Fiction: A Political History of the Novel* (New York: Oxford University Press, 1987), 28; William C. Dowling, *Literary Federalism in the Age of Jefferson: Joseph Dennie and the Port Folio, 1801–1812* (Columbia: University of South Carolina Press, 1999), 36–39, 74–75; Robert Middlekauff, *Ancients and Axioms: Secondary Education in Eighteenth-Century New England* (New York: Arno Press, 1971), 122; Ronald Story, *The Forging of an Aristocracy: Harvard and the Boston Upper Class, 1800–1870* (Middletown, Conn.: Wesleyan University Press, 1980), 105; Harry S. Stout, "Religion, Communication, and the Ideological Origins of the American Revolution," *William and Mary Quarterly* 3rd ser. 34 (October 1977): 532; Ronald J. Zboray, *A Fictive People: Antebellum Economic Development and the Reading Public* (New York: Oxford University Press, 1993), 93–94; Sara Delamont and Lorna Duffin, eds., *The Nineteenth-Century Woman: Her Cultural and Physical World* (New York: Barnes and Noble, 1978), 18.

22. Judith Stevens to Winthrop Sargent, 17 May 1780, Letter Book 1: 282; to Winthrop Sargent, 25 July 1784, Letter Book 2: 253; JSM to Epes Sargent, 20 May, 1801, Letter Book 11: 289; Faculty Records 3: 16–22, 113, 126, 142, 152–54, Harvard Archives; Joseph F. Kett, *Rites of Passage: Adolescence in America, 1790 to the Present* (New York: Basic Books, 1977), 21; Emory Elliott, *Revolutionary Writers: Literature and Authority in the New Republic, 1725–1810* (New York: Oxford University Press, 1986), 35.

23. Estimates of literacy in colonial America vary. A few assertions can be safely made. Access to education depended upon class, gender, and region. Elite colonists were more likely to be literate than poor and middling sorts. Men were generally more literate than women. And New Englanders were the most literate Americans. We also know that more women could read than could write. And women, even in New England, seldom received formal schooling. They were taught at home, largely by their mothers. See David D. Hall, "The Uses of Literacy in New England, 1600–1860." in Joyce et al., eds, *Printing and Society in Early America*, 1–47; Kenneth Lockridge, *Literacy in Colonial new England* (New York: Norton, 1974); Gloria L. Main, "An Inquiry Into When and Why Women Learned to Write in Colonial New England," *Journal of Social History* 24 (1990–1991): 579–89; E. Jennifer Monaghan, "Literacy Instruction and Gender in Colonial New England," *American Quarterly* (March 1988): 18–41.

24. Richard D. Brown, *Knowledge Is Power: The Diffusion of Information in Early America, 1700–1865* (New York: Oxford University Press, 1989), 162; Thomas Woody, *A History of Women's Education in the United States*, 2 vols. (New York: Science Press, 1929), 1:137–45.

25. Patricia Cleary, "Making Men and Women in the 1770s: Culture, Class and Commerce in the Anglo-American World," in Laura McCall and Donald Yacovne, eds., *A Shared Experience: Men, Women, and the History of Gender* (New York: New York University Press, 1998), 100; Crane, *Ebb Tide*, 215–31; Barbara Miller Solomon, *In the Company of Educated Women: A History of Women and Higher Education in America* (New Haven, Conn.: Yale University Press, 1985), 6, 13; David W. Robson, *Educating Republicans: The College in the Era of the American Revolution, 1750–1800* (Westport, Conn.: Greenwood Press, 1985), 12; Middlekauff, *Ancients and Axioms*, 71; Shields, *Civil Tongues*, 120; Zboray, *A Fictive People*, 85; Nancy Armstrong and Leonard Tennenhouse, eds., *The Ideology of Conduct: Essays on Literature and the History of Sexuality* (New York: Methuen, 1987), 10. There were, of course, seventeenth-century women who would use the same language that Judith Sargent Murray employed a century later to demand educational opportunities for themselves. At the very least, Judith could claim to be part of a vibrant—although small—intellectual tradition when she took up the cause of women's education. See Laurel Thatcher Ulrich, " 'Vertuous Women Found': New England Ministerial Literature, 1668–1735," *American Quarterly* 28 (1976): 20–40.

26. Even in 1805, for instance, Boston's Lynn Academy promised to teach men all branches of knowledge, while offering women "the cultivation of polite manners and correct morals, of useful knowledge and refined education." *Columbian Centinel*, 20 November 1805.

27. Judith Stevens to John Murray, 1 October 1775, to Miss Goldthwait, 5 January 1778, Letter Book 1: 24, 82; to Fitz William Sargent, 8 November 1782, to Catherine Osborne Sargent, 5 June 1784, Letter Book 2: 87, 332; to Mrs. Pilgrim of London, 2 September 1786, Letter Book 3: 139; JSM to Winthrop and Judith Sargent, 16 October 1790, Letter Book 4: 254; to Epes Sargent, 22 June 1795, Letter Book 8: 319; to Epes Sargent, 11 January 1799, Letter Book 10: 331; to Miss Eliza Payne, 7 December 1802, Letter Book 12: 797; to Winthrop Sargent, 22 January 1810, Letter Book 16: n.p. See Solomon, *In the Company of Educated Women*, 13. David Shields points out that musical ability, especially for women, was a sign of gentility and a way of asserting cultural power in the eighteenth century. Judith would clearly need to find other venues to exhibit her genteel nature. Shields, *Civil Tongues*, 153–56.

28. Judith Stevens, Note (n.d.), Letter Book 1: 58; to Mrs. Pilgrim of Old England, 2 September 1786, to Winthrop Sargent, 28 November 1786, Letter Book 3: 139–140, 296; JSM to Winthrop Sargent, September 1803, Letter Book 12: [878]. See Kathryn Kish Sklar, "The Schooling of Girls and Changing Community Values in Massachusetts Towns, 1750–1820," *History of Education Quarterly* 33 (1993): 524–25 for the relationship between education, gender, and power. Many historians have repeated biographer Vena Bernadette Fields's assertion that Murray was tutored in Latin and Greek along with her brother. Murray's letters prove that assertion to be unfounded. Field, *Constantia*, 15. See also Sharon M. Harris, in Judith Sargent Murray, *Selected Writings of Judith Sargent Murray*, ed. Sharon M. Harris (New York: Oxford University Press, 1995), xvi.

29. Judith Stevens to Mrs. Pilgrim of London, 2 September 1786, Letter Book 3: 139.

See also Notes of Compliment and Friendship, Letter Book 1: 57, 60. Ruth H. Bloch, "Religion, Literary Sentimentalism, and Popular Revolutionary Ideology," in Ronald Hoffman and Peter J. Albert, eds., *Religion in a Revolutionary Age: Perspectives on the American Revolution* (Charlottesville: University Press of Virginia, 1994), 312; Stephen Botein, "The Anglo-American Book Trade Before 1776: Personnel and Strategies," in Joyce et al., eds., *Printing and Society in Early America*, 64, 81; Elliott, *Revolutionary Writers*, 26; Ruth Perry, *Women, Letters, and the Novel* (New York: AMS Press, 1980), xi; Robert B. Winans, "The Growth of a Novel-Reading Public in Late-Eighteenth-Century America," *Early American Literature* 9 (1975): 268; Zboray, *A Fictive People*, 184.

   30. See Judith Stevens, Note, Letter Book 1: 57; JSM to Mrs. David Urquhart, 21 October 1805, Letter Book 13: [60]; Elisabeth B. Nichols, "'Pray Don't Tell Anybody That I Write Politics': Private Expressions and Public Admonitions in the Early Republic" (Ph.D. dissertation, University of New Hampshire, 1997), 77, 79, 104, 113–16, 140–43; Cathy N. Davidson, *Revolution and the Word: The Rise of the Novel in America* (New York: Oxford University Press, 1986), 112–13; William J. Gilmore, *Reading Becomes a Necessity of Life: Material and Cultural Life in Rural New England, 1780–1830* (Knoxville: University of Tennessee Press, 1989), 128, 131, 194, 237–48, 255, 265; Michael Warner, *The Letters of the Republic: Publication and the Public Sphere in Eighteenth Century America* (Cambridge, Mass.: Harvard University Press, 1990), 16–17; Winans, "The Growth of a Novel-Reading Public," 268–69; Zboray, *A Fictive People*, 133; Ronald Story, "Class and Culture in Boston: The Athenaeum, 1807–1860," *American Quarterly* 27 (1975): 196; Nancy Cott, *The Bonds of Womanhood: "Women's Sphere" in New England, 1780–1835* (New Haven, Conn.: Yale University Press, 1977), 52.

   31. Judith Stevens, Note, to Mr. Murray, 16 August, 28 October, 1 November, 8 November 1779, to Mr. Parker, 11 May 1780, to Mr. Murray, 9 November 1781, Letter Book 1: 57, 206, 245, 248–50, 252, 273–75, 362; to Winthrop Sargent, 12 October 1782, to Miss Mary Parker, 8 September, 1784, Letter Book 2: 70, 272; Mary Rose Kasraie, "Left to 'affectionate partiality': An Authoritative Edition of Selected Letters by Judith Sargent Murray" (Ph.D. dissertation, Georgia State University, 2001), 83; Robert Markley, "Sentimentality as Performance: Shaftsbury, Sterne, and the Theatrics of Virtue," in Felicity Nussbaum and Laura Brown, eds., *The New Eighteenth Century* (New York: Methuen, 1987), 217; Perry, *Women, Letters, and the Novel*, 147–49; Barbara Sickerman, "Sense and Sensibility: A Case Study of Women's Reading in Late Victorian America," in Dorothy O. Helly and Susan M. Reverby, eds., *Connected Domains: Beyond the Public\Private Dichotomy in Women's History* (Ithaca, N.Y.: Cornell University Press, 1992), 75; Kathryn Shevelov, "Fathers and Daughters: Women as Readers of the *Tatler*," in Elizabeth A. Flynn and Patrocinio P. Schweickart, eds., *Gender and Reading: Essays on Readers, Texts, and Contexts* (Baltimore: Johns Hopkins University Press, 1986), 107.

   32. *The Gleaner*, 724–25; Eva Martin Sartori and Dorothy Wynne Zimmerman, eds., *French Women Writers: A Biographical Source Book* (New York: Greenwood Press, 1991), 432–35. See also "Madeleine de Scudéry," in William Rose Benét et al., eds., *Benét's Readers' Encyclopedia*, 3rd ed. (New York: Harper and Row, 1987), 878; Davidson, *Revolution and the Word*, 130; Perry, *Women, Letters, and the Novel*, 146; Katherine M. Rogers, ed., *Before Their Time: Six Women Writers of the Eighteenth Century* (New York: Frederick Ungar, 1979), ix, 1–2, 28–35; Janet Todd, ed., *British Women Writers: A Critical Reference Guide* (New York: Continuum, 1989), 19–20, 287, 420; Sheila L. Skemp, *Judith Sargent*

Murray: A Brief History with Documents (Boston: Bedford Press, 1998), 14. The message that Judith received from the work of women like Mary Astell was ambivalent and conflicted. Astell could never wholly escape the traditional view of women that dominated her world. While she railed against the despotism of the past, she also urged women to be self-effacing, to suppress their desires—especially their sexual desires—and to strive always for propriety. In her own work, written nearly a century later, Judith Sargent Murray would do much the same thing. See Mary Poovey, *The Proper Lady and the Woman Writer: Ideology as Style in the Works of Mary Wollstonecraft, Mary Shelley, and Jane Austen* (Chicago: University of Chicago Press, 1984), 4.

33. See Irvin Ehrenpreis and Robert Halsband, *The Lady of Letters in the Eighteenth Century: Papers Read at a Clark Library Seminar, January 18, 1969* (Los Angeles: William Andrews Clark Memorial Library, 1969), 33–46; Rogers, *Before Their Time*, 48, 49; Todd, *British Women Writers*, 30, 38–39, 296–99, 357, 480–85; Sartori and Zimmerman, *French Women Writers*, 180–83; Skemp, *Judith Sargent Murray*, 14, 15.

34. Judith Stevens to Miss Goldthwait, 5 January 1778, Letter Book 1: 82; JSM to Mr. Parker, 5 September 1784, Letter Book 2: 263; to Sarah Sargent, 15 August 1806, Letter Book 13: 189. See also Judith Stevens to Anna, 8 October 1786, Letter Book 3: 159.

35. Historians are divided over the meaning of novels for eighteenth-century women. See Burstein, *Sentimental Democracy*, 312–13; Bloch, "Religion, Literary Sentimentalism, and Popular Revolutionary Ideology," 318–20; Davidson, *Revolution and the Word*, 45–49; Henri Petter, *The Early American Novel* (Columbus: Ohio State University Press, 1971), 47–48, 78–80; Jay Fliegelman, *Prodigals and Pilgrims: The American Revolution Against Patriarchal Authority, 1750–1800* (New York: Cambridge University Press, 1982), 26.

36. Judith Stevens to John Murray, 28 November 1779, to Mrs. Sargent, 6 April 1781, Letter Book 1: 258, 328; Ehrenpreis and Halsband, *The Lady of Letters*, 7–8; Nichols, " 'Pray Don't Tell Anybody,' " 80–81; Davidson, *Revolution and the Word*, 66–69; Davidson, "Mothers and Daughters in the Fiction of the New Republic," in Cathy N. Davidson and E. M. Broner, eds., *The Lost Tradition: Mothers and Daughters in Literature* (New York: Frederick Ungar, 1980), 117–18; John Preston, *The Created Self: The Reader's Role in Eighteenth-Century Fiction* (London: Heinemann Press, 1970), 3.

37. Armstrong, *Desire and Domestic Fiction*, 4; Ernest Earnest, *The American Eve in Fact and Fiction, 1775–1914* (Urbana: University of Illinois Press, 1974), 10, 30–34.

38. The literature on the meaning of novel-reading for women is voluminous. See especially Bloch, "Religion, Literary Sentimentalism, and Popular Revolutionary Ideology," 316, 328; Davidson, *Revolution and the Word*, 41–43, 126–28; Davidson, "Mothers and Daughters," 118; Davidson, "Toward a History of Books and Readers," in Cathy N. Davidson, ed., *Reading in America: Literature and Social History* (Baltimore: Johns Hopkins University Press, 1989), 162; Gilmore, *Reading Becomes a Necessity*, 37–40; Susan K. Harris, " 'But Is It Any Good?': Evaluating Nineteenth-Century American Women's Fiction," in Joyce W. Warren, ed., *The (Other) American Traditions: Nineteenth-Century Women Writers* (New Brunswick, N.J.: Rutgers University Press, 1993), 265–68; Mary Kelley, "Designing a Past for the Present: Women Writing Women's History in Nineteenth-Century America," *Proceedings of the American Antiquarian Society* 105, Part 2 (1996): 319; Janice A. Radway, *Reading the Romance: Women, Patriarchy, and Popular Literature* (Chapel Hill: University of North Carolina Press, 1984), 3–18; Rotundo, *American Manhood*, 17–18;

Sickerman, "Sense and Sensibility," 79–80; Preston, *The Created Self*, 2–7; Nichols, "'Pray Don't Tell Anybody,'" 77, 87–88.

39. Chandos Michael Brown, "Mary Wollstonecraft, or, the Female Illuminati: The Campaign Against Women and 'Modern Philosophy' in the Early Republic," *Journal of the Early American Republic* 15 (Fall 1995): 402–3; Gilmore, *Reading Becomes a Necessity*, 44, 123–34; Kelley, "'Vindicating the Equality of Female Intellect,'" 4–6; Patrice Clark Koelsch, "Public and Private: Some Implications for Feminist Literature and Criticism," in Janet Sharistanian, ed., *Gender, Ideology, and Action: Historical Perspectives on Women's Public Lives* (Westport, Conn.: Greenwood Press, 1986), 16–19; Radway, *Reading the Romance*, 220–21; Sickerman, "Sense and Sensibility," 72; Zboray, *A Fictive People*, 181–83; Judith Stevens to Winthrop Sargent, 31 July 1783, Letter Book 10: 57.

40. Judith Stevens to Fitz William Sargent, 1 June 1782, Letter Book 2: 10; JSM to Winthrop Sargent, 10 October 1787, Letter Book 3: 233; to Mary A____, 2 March 1795, Letter Book 8: 271–72.

41. Judith Sargent to Winthrop Sargent, Sr., 3 November 1765, Judith Stevens, Note, Letter Book 1: 1, 55; Judith Stevens to Winthrop Sargent, 12 October 1782, Letter Book 2: 70; JSM to the Rev. William Emerson, 21 November 1805, to Mr. Thomas A. Cooper, 13 December 1805, Letter Book 13: [76], 91–[92]. As early as 1779, she had begun to refer to herself as "Constantia" in her private correspondence, even though it would be years before she would use her favorite pseudonym in the public arena. Judith Stevens to John Murray, 28 October 1779, Letter Book 1: 245.

42. Monaghan, "Literacy," 27–28; Ryan, *The Empire of the Mother*, 7.

43. Susan Clair Imbarrato, *Declarations of Independency in Eighteenth-Century American Autobiography* (Knoxville: University of Tennessee Press, 1998), xiii xvii, 21–23; Catherine E. Kelly, *In the New England Fashion: Reshaping Women's Lives in the Nineteenth Century* (Ithaca, N.Y.: Cornell University Press, 1999), 6, 59; Pattie Cowell, "Early New England Women Poets' Writing as a Vocation," *Early American Literature* 29 (1994): 104.

44. Rhys Isaac, "Stories and Constructions of Identity: Folk Tellings and Diary Inscriptions in Revolutionary Virginia," in Ronald Hoffman, Mechal Sobel, and Fredrika J. Teute, eds., *Through a Glass Darkly: Reflections on Personal Identity in Early America* (Chapel Hill: University of North Carolina Press, 1977), 216; Laurel Thatcher Ulrich, *Good Wives: Image and Reality in the Lives of Women in Northern New England, 1650–1750* (New York: Knopf, 1982), 51–67; Imbarrato, *Declarations*, x, xix, 9; Rogers, *Before Their Time*, xi. Indeed, Patricia Meyer Spacks argues that for most women in this period, writing represented "the only viable possibility for freedom." Spacks, *The Female Imagination* (New York: Knopf, 1975), 159–60, 315. See also Gregory Paul Polly, "Private and Public Letters: Epistolary Negotiations in the Early Republic" (Ph.D. dissertation, Harvard University, 1977), 36–37, 43.

45. Nor was this uncommon. See Howard Anderson and Irvin Ehrenpreis, "The Familiar Letter in the Eighteenth Century: Some Generalizations," in Howard Anderson, Philip B. Daghlian, and Irvin Ehrenpreis, eds., *The Familiar Letter in the Eighteenth Century* (Lawrence: University Press of Kansas, 1966), 269, 280–81; Imbarrato, *Declarations*, 9; Patricia Meyer Spacks, *Gossip* (New York: Knopf, 1985), 162–63; Zboray, *A Fictive People*, 118–19. For an excellent example of a letter that emulates fiction, complete with dialogue, see Judith Stevens to John Murray, 3–6 April 1778, Letter Book 1: 102.

46. Murray, Letter Fragment [1790], Letter Book 6: 372; Virginia Elsie Radatz Stewart, "The Intercourse of Letters: Familiar Correspondence and the Transformation of American Identity in the Eighteenth Century" (Ph.D. dissertation, Northwestern University, 1997), 4; Polly, "Private and Public Letters," 36–37, 43.

47. Anderson and Ehrenpreis, "The Familiar Letter," 272, 279; Joan B. Landes, *Women and the Public Sphere in the Age of the French Revolution* (Ithaca, N.Y.: Cornell University Press, 1988), 63; Brown, *Knowledge Is Power*, 169–70; Shields, *Civil Tongues*, 319–20; Spacks, *Gossip*, 162–63; Zboray, *A Fictive People*, 113–15, 117; Stewart, "The Intercourse of Letters," 2, 3; Nichols, " 'Pray Don't Tell Anybody,' " 28, 50, 57–58; Polly, "Private and Public Letters," 36; Fea, "The Way of Improvement," 486.

48. Julia A. Stern, *The Plight of Feeling: Sympathy and Dissent in the Early American Novel* (Chicago: University of Chicago Press, 1997), 17; Frank Shuffelton, "In Different Voices: Gender in the American Public of Letters," *Early American Literature* 25 (1990): 289; Nichols, " 'Pray Don't Tell Anybody,' " 31, 72, 227n, 275, 347; Polly, "Private and Public Letters," 15, 17; Judith Stevens to Winthrop Sargent, 5 April 1780, Letter Book 1: 272; JSM to Maria Sargent, 30 October 1791, 14 July 1794, Letter Book 8: 10, 15; Sharon M. Harris, ed., *American Women Writers to 1800* (New York: Oxford University Press, 1996), 27. These letters were, like diaries, acts of self-examination, and—when they were read in chronological order—provided a story, however incomplete, that even humble women could publish or at least pass down from one generation to the next. See Barbara E. Lacey, 'The World of Hannah Heaton: The Autobiography of an Eighteenth-Century Connecticut Farm Woman," *William and Mary Quarterly* 3rd ser. 45 (1988): 282.

49. Judith Stevens, Note, to Winthrop Sargent, 8 May 1779, Letter Book 1: 55, 183; JSM to John Murray, 13 September 1794, Letter Book 2: 276. See Imbarrato, *Declarations*, 5.

50. Letter Book 1: Introduction; Judith Stevens to Dr. Plummer [November or December 1776], to Mr. Sewall, 15 July 1781, Letter Book 1: 59, 340.

51. The fact that Judith had the time to write and rewrite her letters and then copy them into her letter books advertised her as a lady of leisure. She was neither a merchant, who wrote in a bold, masterful style, nor a tradesman. Her ornamental hand was a reflection of both her class and her gender. Tamara Plakins Thornton, *Handwriting in America: A Cultural History* (New Haven, Conn.: Yale University Press, 1996), 35–40; Nina Baym, *American Women Writers and the Work of History, 1790–1860* (New Brunswick, N.J.: Rutgers University Press, 1995), 93.

52. JSM to Epes Sargent, 11 January 1799, Letter Book 10: 330; Zboray, *A Fictive People*, 113–19; Bushman, *Refinement in America*, 90–95; Alvaro Riberiro, "Real Business, Elegant Civility and Rhetorical Structure in Two Letters by Charles Burney," in Alan T. McKenzie, ed., *Sent as a Gift: Eight Correspondences from the Eighteenth Century* (Athens: University of Georgia Press, 1993), 10, 94, 103, 105; Anderson and Ehrenpreis, "The Familiar Letter," 271–75; Janet Gurkin Altman, "Political Ideology in the Letter Manual (France, England, New England)," *Studies in Eighteenth-Century Culture* 18 (1988): 19, 28; Spacks, *Gossip*, 70, 73; Nichols, " 'Pray Don't Tell Anybody,' " 75; Toby L. Ditz, "Secret Selves, Credible Personas: The Problematics of Trust and Public Display in the Writing of Eighteenth-Century Philadelphia Merchants," in Robert Blair St. George, ed., *Possible Pasts: Becoming Colonial in Early America* (Ithaca, N.Y.: Cornell University Press, 2000), 230–31.

53. Judith Stevens to her Aunt E. S., 5 July 1782, Letter Book 2: 43; Prown, *John Singleton Copley in America*, 42, 57; Breen, "The Meaning of Likeness," 325–50; Rebora, *Copley*, 53–54, 94; Margaret M. Lovell, "Bodies of Illusion: Portraits, People, and the Construction of Memory," in St. George, ed., *Possible Pasts*, 295, 299.

54. Judith Stevens to her Aunt E. S., 5 July 1782, Letter Book 2: 43; Justin Winsor, ed., *The Memorial History of Boston, Including Suffolk County Massachusetts, 1630–1880*, vol. 4, *The Last One Hundred Years* (Boston: James R. Osgood, 1881), 386–87; Rebora, *Copley*, 60–62; Murray, *Selected Writings*, 39; Lovell, "Bodies of Illusion," 297.

55. The average age of marriage for women at the time of the Revolution was twenty-three. Men were just a little older. Nancy Cott, "Passionless: An Interpretation of Victorian Sexual Ideology, 1790–1850," *Signs* 4 (1978): 229; Ellen K. Rothman, *Hands and Hearts: A History of Courtship in America* (New York: Basic Books, 1984), 23; Kelly, *In the New England Fashion*, 102–4; Peter Dobkin Hall, "Family Structure and Economic Organization: Massachusetts Merchants, 1700–1850," in Tamara K. Herevon, ed., *Family and Kin in Urban Communities, 1700–1930* (New York: New Viewpoints, 1977), 44; Story, *The Forging of an Aristocracy*, 5.

56. William Stevens, Probate Records nos. 344–47, Peabody Essex Institute; Babson, *Gloucester*, 55–56, 164–68, 187–89; Babson, *Notes and Additions to the History of Gloucester, Part First, Early Settlers* (Gloucester, Mass.: M.V.B. Perley Telegram Office, 1876), 75–80; Gloucester Town Meeting Records, 3: 1–4. The marriage of Judith's sister Esther to John Stevens Ellery was an even better example of the intricate relationships of Gloucester's elite. Ellery was John Stevens's cousin and Esther's second cousin. Sargent, *Epes Sargent of Gloucester*, 74.

57. Judith Stevens to Winthrop Sargent, 10 August 1778, 5 April, 8 May 1779, 17 May 1780, Letter Book 1: 142, 174, 181, 277; JSM to Judith and Winthrop Sargent, 16 October 1790, Letter Book 4: 166; to Eliza Sargent, 26 November 1804, Letter Book 12: 965–967; to Winthrop Sargent, 3 March 1816, Letter Book 20: 12.

58. Judith Stevens to Winthrop Sargent, 17 May 1780, Letter Book 1: 277; to Madam Walker, 8 October 1783, to Mr. Parker, 5 September 1784, to Miss Goldthwait, 5 December 1784, Letter Book 2: 170, 263, 297; JSM to Miss Saltonstall of New London, 27 May 1797, Letter Book 10: 120; Babson, *Gloucester*, 432n. See also Henrik Hartog, *Man and Wife in America: A History* (Cambridge, Mass.: Harvard University Press), 42; Rothman, *Hands and Heart*, 68–71.

59. Judith Stevens to Winthrop Sargent, 8 May 1779, Letter Book 1: 180–81; to Anna, 8 October 1786, JSM to Maria Sargent, 15 April 1788, Letter Book 3: 159, 293–94; to Anna, 11 October 1790, Letter Book 4: 253; to Miss Abby Saltonstall of New London, 27 May 1797, Letter Book 10: 120–21.

60. Judith Stevens to John Murray, 18 February 1786, Letter Book 3: 63; Crane, *Ebb Tide*, 223–26; Bloch, "Untangling the Roots of Modern Sex Roles," 238–43; Hill, "Clarissa Harlowe and Her Times," 31; Lonna M. Malmsheimer, "Daughters of Zion: New England Roots of American Feminism," *New England Quarterly* 50 (1977): 498.

61. Because marriage was based on individual emotional needs, it was, as Shields points out, profoundly individualistic and self-interested. Private decisions could now disrupt community expectations and destroy traditional community hierarchy. Shields, *Civil Tongues*, 137.

62. Cott, *The Bonds of Womanhood*, 83; Hall, "Family Structure and Economic

Organization," 45; Kann, *Republic of Men*, 8–10; Steven Mintz and Susan Kellogg, *Domestic Revolutions: A Social History of American Family Life* (New York: Free Press, 1988), 46–47; D. B. Smith, "The Study of the Family in Early America," 18, 23; Jan Lewis, "The Republican Wife: Virtue and Seduction in the Early Republic," *William and Mary Quarterly* 3rd ser. 44(1987): 693–95; Hill, "Clarissa Harlowe and Her Times," 40–54; Fliegelman, *Prodigals and Pilgrims*, 27–29.

63. Judith Stevens to Winthrop Sargent, [?] October 1769, Murray, Letter Book 1: 6. See Esther Edwards Burr, *The Journal of Esther Edwards Burr, 1754–1757*, ed. Carol F. Karlsen and Laurie Crumpacker (New Haven, Conn.: Yale University Press, 1984), 199; Kelly, *In the New England Fashion*, 131–32; Suzanne Lebsock, *The Free Women of Petersburg: Status and Culture in a Southern Town, 1784–1860* (New York: Norton, 1985), 25; Rothman, *Hands and Hearts*, 73; Mary Ryan, *Women in Public: Between Banners and Ballots, 1825–1880* (Baltimore: Johns Hopkins University Press, 1990), 8.

64. Judith Stevens to John Murray, 12, 16 August 1779, Letter Book 1: 199, 206; Lebsock, *The Free Women of Petersburg*, 18; Burr, *Journal*, 265; Crane, *Ebb Tide*, 226; Gordon Wood, *The Radicalism of the American Revolution* (New York: Vintage, 1991), 58; Elizabeth Barnes, *States of Sympathy: Seduction and Democracy in the American Novel* (New York: Columbia University Press, 1997), 43; Mintz and Kellogg, *Domestic Revolutions*, 47.

65. Hartog, *Man and Wife*, 42. For women's loss of power, see Cott, "Passionless," 228.

66. Judith Stevens to Winthrop Sargent, October 1769, to Judith Sargent, 9 April 1778, Letter Book 1: 6, 104.

67. Murray, "Cleora," 31 May 1777, Repository, 124; Judith Stevens to Esther Ellery, March or April 1778, Letter Book 1: 97; to Winthrop Sargent, 7 January 1784, Letter Book 2: 186; JSM to Winthrop Sargent, 4 June 1803, Letter Book 12: 851.

68. Demos, "The Changing Faces of Fatherhood," 430; Richard W. Wertz and Dorothy C. Wertz, *Lying-In: A History of Childbirth in America* (New York: Free Press, 1977), 2, 3; Elaine Tyler May, *Barren in the Promised Land: Childless Americans and the Pursuit of Happiness* (New York: HarperCollins, 1995), 24–27; Susan Klepp points out that women's self-image was "inextricably tied to their fecundity." Klepp, "Revolutionary Bodies: Women and the Fertility Transition in the Mid-Atlantic Region, 1760–1820," *Journal of American History* 85 (December 1998): 920, 926.

69. Ruth H. Bloch, "American Feminine Ideals in Transition: The Rise of the Moral Mother, 1785–1815," *Feminist Studies* 4 (1978): 116; Bloch, "Untangling the Roots of Modern Sex Roles," 250–51; Carl Degler, *At Odds: Women and the Family in America from the Revolution to the Present* (New York: Oxford University Press, 1980), 55; Sylvia D. Hoffert, *Private Matters: American Attitudes Toward Childbearing and Infant Nurture in the Urban North, 1800–1860* (Urbana: University of Illinois Press, 1989), 1, 2; Perry, *Women, Letters, and the Novel*, 145; Catherine M. Scholten, *Childbearing in American Society, 1650–1850* (New York: New York University Press, 1985), 51–57; Ulrich, " 'Virtuous Women Found,' " 39–40; May, *Barren in the Promised Land*, 37–43; Margaret Marsh and Wanda Ronner, *The Empty Cradle: Infertility in America from Colonial Times to the Present* (Baltimore: Johns Hopkins University Press, 1996), 16–19.

70. Judith Stevens to Judith Sargent, April 1776, Letter Book 1: 42. See especially Jeanne Boydston, *Home and Work: Housework, Wages, and the Ideology of Labor in the Early Republic* (New York: Oxford University Press, 1990), 11–15.

Chapter 2. Universal Salvation

1. Gloucester Church Records, 25. John Stevens was not on the list. This may have been because he was at sea during the period and thus not considered "delinquent" in the usual sense. He did, indeed, leave the First Parish Church with this wife, and there is no reason to suppose that the two disagreed on religious matters. See Judith Stevens to John Murray, 14 November 1774, Letter Book 1: 15.

2. Richard D. Brown, "The Emergence of Urban Society in Rural Massachusetts, 1760–1820," *Journal of American History* 61 (June 1974): 34–35; Jane C. Nylander, *Our Own Snug Fireside: Images of the New England Home, 1760–1860* (New York: Knopf, 1993), 10; Gerald F. Moran and Maris A. Vinovskis, "The Puritan Family and Religion: A Critical Reappraisal," *William and Mary Quarterly* 3rd ser. 39 (January 1982): 34–35.

3. Nathan O. Hatch, *The Democratization of American Christianity* (New Haven, Conn.: Yale University Press, 1989), 126; Ernest Cassara, *Universalism in America: A Documentary History* (Boston: Beacon Press, 1971), 4; Heyrman, *Commerce and Culture*, 88, 92; Patricia Bonomi, "Religious Dissent and the Case for American Exceptionalism," in Hoffman and Albert, eds., *Religion in a Revolutionary Age*, 42; Ulrich, " 'Daughters of Liberty,' " 225.

4. John Murray, *The Life of Rev. John Murray, Preacher of Universal Salvation, written by himself with a continuation by Mrs. Judith Sargent Murray* (Boston: Universalist Publishing House, 1869), 16, 19, 23, 25, 59; George H. Williams, "American Universalism: A Bicentennial Essay," *Journal of the Universalist Historical Society* 9 (1971): 44.

5. Murray, *Life*, 48–49; Babson, *Gloucester*, 429; Ezra Stiles to Rev. Forbes, 24 December 1777, and "An Answer to a Piece Entitled 'An Appeal to the Impartial Publick, by an Association' Calling Themselves 'Christian Independents in Glocester,' " both in Richard Eddy, *Universalism in Gloucester, Massachusetts* (Gloucester: Proctor Brothers, 1892), 162, 172.

6. Murray, *Life*, 8, 35, 158; Russell E. Miller, *The Larger Hope: The First Century of the Universalist Church in America* (Boston: Unitarian Universalist Association, 1979), 8; John Murray, *Letters and Sketches of Sermons*, 3 vols. (Boston: Joshua Belcher, 1812), 3: 387.

7. Murray, *Life*, 165–77, 186.

8. Ibid., 187; Miller, *The Larger Hope*, 12–13. See Ezra Stiles to the Rev. Forbes, 24 December 1777, in Eddy, *Universalism in Gloucester*, 163, for Stiles's extremely derogatory characterization of Murray.

9. Babson, *Gloucester*, 429; Clarence R. Skinner and Alfred S. Cole, *Hell's Ramparts Fell: The Life of John Murray* (Boston: Universalist Publishing House, 1941), 98; Eddy, *Universalism in Gloucester*, 10, 11; Cassara, *Universalism in America*, 74–75; Timothy D. Hall, *Contested Boundaries: Itinerancy and the Reshaping of the Colonial American Religious World* (Durham, N.C.: Duke University Press, 1994), 17–40; Breen and Hall, "Structuring Provincial Imagination," 1427–31; Kann, *Republic of Men*, 65; Hatch, *The Democratization of American Christianity*, 134; "An Answer to a Piece," in Eddy, *Universalism in Gloucester*, 160; John Murray to a Lady, n.d., *Letters and Sketches*, 1: 34.

10. Murray, *Life*, 12; P. Elton Carpenter, "John Murray and the Rise of Liberal Religion" (M.A. thesis, Columbia University, 1937), 17, 83; Winsor, *Memorial History of Boston*, 489; Murray, *Letters and Sketches*, 3: 50; Ernest Cassara, "John Murray and the Origins of Universalism in New England: A Commentary on Peter Hughes's 'Religion

Without a Founder,'" *Journal of Unitarian-Universalist History* 26 (1999): 73; Cassara, *Universalism in America*, 23; "An Answer to a Piece"; Ezra Stiles to the Rev. Forbes, 24 December 1777, in Eddy, *Universalism in Gloucester*, 158, 163; John Murray to Robert Redding, 30 March 1795, "John Murray Letters," *Universalist Quarterly* 25 (1868): 36; John Murray to William Palmer, 19 March 1799, Palmer Papers; Judith Stevens to John Murray, 4 September 1779, Letter Book 1: 227.

11. Murray, *Letters and Sketches*, 1: 317–18; John Murray to E. Forbes, 5 January 1778, John Murray to Ezra Stiles, 20, 22 January, 1778, Noah Parker to Epes Sargent, 1778, John Murray, Correspondence 1: 1–22, Papers of the Rev. John Murray.

12. Murray, *Letters and Sketches*, 1: 289, 319; Miller, *The Larger Hope*, 16, 17; Peter Hughes, "Early New England Universalism: A Family Religion," *Journal of Universalist-Unitarian History* 26 (1999): 1089; John Murray to Robert Redding, 29 December 1795, "John Murray Letters," *Universalist Quarterly* 6 (January 1869): 29.

13. Meetings and Actions, 121; Murray, *Life*, 295–98; "An Answer to a Piece," in Eddy, *Universalism in Gloucester*, 158.

14. "An Answer to a Piece," 158; Murray, *Life*, 298; Judith Stevens to John Murray, 6 December 1774, to Catherine Sargent, 10 April 1778, Letter Book 1: 14, 107; to John Murray, 30 October 1785, Letter Book 3: 24.

15. Judith Stevens to John Murray, 14 November, 6 December 1774, Letter Book 1: 13–15; Perry, *Women, Letters, and the Novel*, 132–33.

16. Murray, *Life*, 314; Babson, *Gloucester*, 328–29; "An Answer to a Piece," 159–60.

17. Jon Butler, "Coercion, Miracle, Reason: Rethinking the American Religious Experience in the Revolutionary Age," in Hoffman and Albert, eds., *Religion in a Revolutionary Age*, 6, 7. Not surprisingly, Universalists were most successful in those towns where they garnered support from inhabitants of high social standing. See Hughes, "Early New England Universalism," 109.

18. John Cleaveland, *An Attempt to Nip in the Bud the Unscriptural Doctrine of Universal Salvation . . . which a certain Stranger, who calls himself John Murray, has of late been endeavoring to spread in the First Church of Gloucester* (Salem, Mass.: E. Russell, 1776); Gloucester Church Records, 24 August 1775; Babson, *Gloucester*, 402, 406; Dissenters to Rev. Eli Forbes, 4 April 1776, Rev. Eli Forbes to Dissenters, 8 April 1776, to First Parish, 11 April 1776, Independent Christian Society, Letters.

19. Murray, *Life*, 312, 364–66; Stephen A. Marini, *Radical Sects of Revolutionary New England* (Cambridge, Mass.: Harvard University Press, 1982), 107; Murray, *Letters and Sketches*, 1; Judith Stevens to John Murray, 28 November 1779, Letter Book 1: 228; See also JSM to John Murray, 9 April 1789, Letter Book 4: 19–22.

20. Babson, *Gloucester*, 432, 432n; Judith Stevens to John Murray, 8 August, to Miss Parker, 13 August 1778, to John Murray, 2 September, 1778, to Mr. Parker, 25 September 1778, to Mr. Cleveland of Norwich, 15 October 1778, to John Murray, 26 August, 16 September 1779, 21 September 1780, Letter Book 1: 140, 143, 153, 162, 166, 220, 232, 290; Murray, "Suffering by comparison," Repository, 60; Murray, "Attending at Church during the absence of our spiritual guide," Poetry 1: 236.

21. Gloucester Church Records, 26–27. See also Judith Stevens to John Murray, 30 October 1785, Letter Book 3: 24.

22. Gloucester Church Records, 28–29.

23. Eddy, *Universalism in Gloucester*, 19–20; Miller, *The Larger Hope*, 21; Babson, *Gloucester*, 439. Daniel and Mary Sargent never joined the Universalist congregation. But the land on which the first church was built belonged to Daniel, who had left Gloucester for Boston in 1778.

24. Heyrman, *Commerce and Culture*, 96–142; Cassara, *Universalism in America*, 5; Cassara, "John Murray and the Origins of Universalism," 87; Ann Lee Bressler, *The Universalist Movement in America, 1770–1880* (New York: Oxford University Press, 2001), 22–23. See also Miller, *The Larger Hope*, 58; Hatch, *The Democratization of American Christianity*, 23ff, 40; Hughes, "Early New England Universalism," 95, 106; James R. Rohrer, *Keepers of the Covenant: Frontier Missions and the Decline of Congregationalism, 1774–1818* (New York: Oxford University Press, 1995), 7; Marini, *Radical Sects of Revolutionary New England*, 95, 100.

25. Judith Stevens to John Murray, 16 September 1779, Letter Book 1: 233. See Mechal Sobel, "The Revolution in Selves: Black and White Inner Aliens," in Hoffman, Sobel, and Teute, eds., *Through a Glass Darkly*, 163, 174; Fea, "The Way of Improvement," 467; R. Lawrence Moore, *Religious Outsiders and the Making of Americans* (New York: Oxford University Press, 1986), xi–xii, 3–9.

26. JSM to Miss E____ S____, 30 July 1790, Letter Book 4: 188; Murray, "After attending a Modern sermon—1781," Poetry 3: 130–31; Murray, "Christmas Day," Repository, 145–53.

27. Judith Stevens to Fitz William Sargent, 18 July 1778, Letter Book 1: 130–31. The following summary of Murray's religious beliefs comes from Bressler, *The Universalist Movement*, 17–19; Cassara, *Universalism in America*, 5–6, 13–17, 71–73; Cassara, "John Murray and the Origins of Universalism in New England," 73–75; Marini, *Radical Sects of Revolutionary New England*, 68–69, 134, 144–47; Williams, "American Universalism," 6–7; Eddy, *Universalism in Gloucester*, 142–44.

28. Murray, "To a Lady," "To a Friend," in Murray, *Letters and Sketches*, 1: 44, 231–32; Judith Stevens to Mrs. D____ S____, [19] July 1775, Letter Book 1: 20; John Murray, *Universalism Vindicated* (Charlestown, Mass.: B.J. Lamson, n.d.), xiii.

29. Judith Stevens to Noah Parker, [?] 1777, Repository, 40; Judith Stevens to Miss Goldthwait, 5 January 1778, Letter Book 1: 82; JSM to Mrs. Lewis, 12 February 1802, Letter Book 11: 336; Gloucester Church Records, 6 September 1772; Murray, "Wedded life," 1777, Repository, 44, 45; Bressler, *The Universalist Movement*, 9, 14, 20–21; Hughes, "The Origins of New England Universalism: Religion Without a Founder," *Journal of Unitarian-Universalist History* 24 (1997): 55.

30. Elaine Forman Crane, "Religion and Rebellion: Women of Faith in the American War for Independence," in Hoffman and Albert, eds., *Religion in a Revolutionary Age*, 81; Crane, Ebb Tide, 29, 64; Mary Maples Dunn, "Saints and Sisters: Congregational and Quaker Women in the Early Colonial Period," *American Quarterly* 30 (1978): 584, 590; Linda K. Kerber, "Can a Woman Be an Individual? The Limits of the Puritan Tradition in the Early Republic," *Texas Studies in Literature and Language* 25 (Winter 1983): 167; Margaret Masson, "The Typology of the Female as a Model for the Regenerate: Puritan Preaching, 1690–1730," *Signs* 2 (1976): 305, 307; Rosemary Skinner Keller, "New England Women: Ideology and Experience in First-Generation Puritanism (1630–1650)," in Rosemary Radford Ruether and Rosemary Skinner Keller, eds., *Women and Religion in America*, vol. 2, *The Colonial and Revolutionary Periods* (New York: Harper and Row, 1983), 137;

Marilyn J. Westerkamp, *Women and Religion in Early America, 1600–1850: The Puritans and Evangelical Traditions* (London: Routledge, 1999), 24; Amanda Porterfield, "Women's Attraction to Puritanism," *Church History* 60 (1991): 199–208.

31. Crane, *Ebb Tide*, 60; Ulrich, " 'Vertuous Women Found,' " 29–30; Ulrich, " 'Daughters of Liberty,' " 213; Westerkamp, *Women and Religion in Early America*, 26; Hartog, *Man and Wife in America*, 42.

32. Boydston, *Home and Work*, 4; Nancy Isenberg, *Sex and Citizenship in Antebellum America* (Chapel Hill: University of North Carolina Press, 1998), 42–48; Malmsheimer, "Daughters of Zion," 485–88; Gayle Rubin, "The Traffic in Women: Notes on the 'Political Economy' of Sex," in Rayna R. Reiter, ed., *Towards an Anthropology of Women* (New York: Monthly Review Press, 1975), 280–82; Keller, "New England Women," 132–36; Ulrich, " 'Vertuous Women Found,' " 38–40; Westerkamp, *Women and Religion in Early America*, 51–55; Demos, "Changing Faces of Fatherhood," 427.

33. Bloch, "Untangling the Roots of Modern Sex Roles," 239; Masson, "The Typology of the Female as a Model for the Regenerate," 308–14; Moran and Vinovskis, "The Puritan Family and Religion," 60–61; Westerkamp, *Women and Religion in Early America*, 4–5, 20–21; J. R. Brink, ed., *Female Scholars: A Tradition of Learned Women Before 1800* (Montreal: Eden Press, 1980), 2; Crane, *Ebb Tide*, 57–59, 62–85; Dunn, "Saints and Sisters," 583–93; Kerber, "Can a Woman Be an Individual?" 167, 178; Demos, "Changing Faces of Fatherhood," 427; Gloucester Church Records, passim.

34. Williams, "American Universalism," 44; Bressler, *The Universalist Movement*, 89; Murray, *Letters and Sketches*, 1: 51.

35. Miller, *The Larger Hope*, 534, 555; Murray, "On an insult offer'd to our friend," Poetry 1: 248; Bonomi, "Religious Dissent and the Case for American Exceptionalism," 44–45; Lee Virginia Chambers-Schiller, *Liberty, a Better Husband: Single Women in America: The Generations of 1780–1840* (New Haven, Conn.: Yale University Press, 1984), 86; Cott, "Passionless," 226–27; Cott, *Bonds of Womanhood*, 145; Crane, *Ebb Tide*, 86–87; Crane, "Religion and Rebellion," 68–69, 75; Philip Gould, *Covenant and Republic: Historical Romance and the Politics of Puritanism* (Cambridge: Cambridge University Press, 1996), 105–6; Sobel, "The Revolution in Selves," 173–74; Hartog, *Man and Wife in America*, 43–44; Joan Hoff-Wilson, "The Illusion of Change: Women and the American Revolution," in Alfred F. Young, ed., *Beyond the American Revolution: Explorations in the History of American Radicalism* (Dekalb: Northern Illinois University Press, 1976), 409–10; Kelly, *In the New England Fashion*, 142–43; Lacey, "The World of Hannah Heaton," 280–304; Judith Stevens to John Murray, 3 April 1778, Letter Book 1: 100; to Mrs. Barrell of Old York, 31 January 1784, to John Murray, 25 June 1785, Letter Book 2: 193, 344.

36. Londa Schiebinger, *The Mind Has No Sex? Women in the Origins of Modern Science* (Cambridge, Mass.: Harvard University Press, 1989), 165; John Murray, "To a Friend," "Letter to Mr. I. T., *Letters and Sketches*, 1: 236, 2: 356; *The Gleaner*, 132.

37. Murray, "Isabella," Repository, 111; "Several Chapters of Isaiah Paraphrased or Rather Versified, 1778," Repository, 95; *The Gleaner*, 707–9. For the notion of woman as "body" see especially Elizabeth Kowalski-Wallace, *Consuming Subjects: Women, Shopping, and Business in the Eighteenth Century* (New York: Columbia University Press, 1997), 148. See E. Anthony Rotundo, "Body and Soul: Changing Ideals of American Middle-Class Manhood, 1770–1920," *Journal of Social History* 16 (1983): 23–38, for an analysis of the "shift from manhood of the soul to manhood of the body" in this period.

See also Carole Pateman, *The Sexual Contract* (Stanford, Calif.: Stanford University Press, 1988), 17.

38. Murray, "On the emancipation of an inquiring mind—led by conviction to embrace the salutary doctrine of universalism, 1781," Poetry 3: 103; Karen L. Schiff, "Objects of Speculation: Early Manuscripts on Women and Education by Judith Sargent (Stevens) Murray," *Legacy* 17 (2000): 216; Judith Stevens to Miss Parker, 13 August 1778, to John Tyler, 9, 15 May 1779, Letter Book 1: 147–48, 184–87.

39. Judith Stevens to John Murray, 28 March 1776, 13 August 1779, Letter Book 1: 92–3, 202–3; to Winthrop Sargent, 28 March 1785, Letter Book 2: 322.

40. Judith Stevens to John Murray, Summer, 1777, 8 August, 2, 17, 23 September 1778, Letter Book 1: 72, 140, 153, 156, 158–60; Murray, "Death of an unbeliever, 1775," Repository, 32–33. Throughout her biography of John Murray, she seized every opportunity to mention the "respectable" men and women who flocked to John's side.

41. Judith Stevens to John Murray, 12 September 1775, to Miss Goldthwait, 3 March 1776, to John Murray, 23 November 1776, Summer 1777, 17 September 1778, 15 August, 16 September 1779, Letter Book 1: 22–23, 34, 52, 65–66, 155, 205, 233.

42. Judith Stevens to John Murray, 17 September 1778, 18 October, 8 November 1779, Letter Book 1: 155, 240, 251. See also, Judith Stevens to John Murray, 17 November 1779, Letter Book 1: 252–53; Murray, "Upon the effects of the salutary truths of Revelation addressed to a Preacher," 1780, Poetry 3: 45–49.

43. Judith Stevens to John Murray, 5 August 1779, 8, 18 October 1779, 6, 21 November 1781, Letter Book, 1: 198, 236, 240, 359, 369; JSM to Maria Sargent, 15 April 1788, Letter Book 3: 295.

44. Judith Stevens to Dr. Plummer, [November or December] 1776, to Winthrop Sargent, 5 December 1779, 5 April 1780, to John Murray, 6 November 1781, to Maria Sargent, 5 December 1781, Letter Book 1: 60, 238, 266, 272, 359, 372.

45. Judith Stevens to John Murray, 29 December 1780, Letter Book 1: 317. Her letter referred to a "Lady Rachel M," but the context indicates that she had Mary Montague in mind. See also Note to Mr. Martin [n.d.], Letter Book 1: 58.

46. Judith Stevens to Mr. Parker, 5 October 1777, Mr. Sewall of Portsmouth, 15 August 1778, to John Murray, 26 August 1779, 29 December 1780, Letter Book 1: 75, 149, 220, 317. See also, Judith Stevens to John Murray, 8 October 1779, Letter Book 1: 237.

47. Judith Stevens to Mr. Sewall of Portsmouth, 15 August 1778, Letter Book 1: 149; to Mr. Sewall of Portsmouth, 15 July 1781, to John Murray, 20 July 1782, to Mrs. Osborne of Boston, 23 June 1785, Letter Book 2: 56, 339, 340.

48. Judith Stevens to Mr. Parker, 31 January 1782, to Winthrop Sargent, 12 October 1782, to Rev. William Emerson, 21 November 1805, Letter Book 2: 1, 71; Letter Book 13: 76.

49. Judith Stevens to Winthrop Sargent, 5 April 1780, to Mr. Sewall, 15 July 1781, Letter Book 1: 271, 339; to Mr. Parker, 31 January 1782, to John Murray, 28 June 17[82], to Winthrop Sargent, 12 October 1782, Letter Book 2: 1, 36, 70. Jean-Christophe Agnew, *Worlds Apart: The Market and the Theater in Anglo-American Thought, 1550–1750* (New York: Cambridge University Press, 1986), 181; Warner, *The Letters of the Republic*, 137, 141–42, 148; Nancy Fraser, "Rethinking the Public Sphere: A Contribution to the Critique of Actually Existing Democracy," in Bruce Robbins, ed., *The Phantom Public Sphere* (Minneapolis: University of Minnesota Press, 1993), 19.

50. [Judith Stevens], *Some Deductions from the System Promulgated in the Page of*

Divine Revelation, Ranged in the Order and Form of a Catechism. Intended as an Assistant to the Christian Parent or Teacher (Norwich: John Trumbell, 1782), 27–30, 35 (hereafter *Catechism*).

51. Ibid., 8; Judith Stevens to Mr. Parker, 15 April 1782, Letter Book 2: 3, 4.

52. Judith Stevens to Mr. Parker, 9 June 1782, to John Murray, 20 July 1782, to Winthrop Sargent, 12 October 1782, Letter Book 2: 14, 55, 70. This was the first Universalist Catechism printed in America. A second, also Rellyan in principle, written by Boston Universalist Shippie Townshend, was published in 1794. Richard Eddy, *Universalist Quarterly* 12 (1875): 450, 450n.

53. Judith Stevens to Mr. Parker, [Fall] 1782, Letter Book 2: 74.

54. Judith Stevens to Madam Walker, 16 October 1782, Letter Book 2: 77.

55. *Catechism*, iii. See Susan Juster, *Disorderly Women: Sexual Politics and Evangelicalism in Revolutionary New England* (Ithaca, N.Y.: Cornell University Press, 1994).

56. *Catechism*, iii–iv.

57. *Ibid.*, iv–v.

58. Murray, "Upon printing my little catechism—1782," Poetry 3: 148–49.

59. Judith Stevens to Mrs. Barrell of Old York, 31 January 1784, Letter Book 2: 195.

Chapter 3. Independence

1. See Heyrman, *Commerce and Culture*, 193–94 for evidence that their vulnerability made many Gloucester merchants more committed to tradition, less comfortable with the outside world than ever.

2. Judith Stevens to Winthrop Sargent, 8 January 1774, to John Murray, 1 October 1775, Letter Book 1: 10, 25.

3. Judith Stevens to John Murray, 11 August 1778, to Winthrop Sargent, 28 October 1781, Letter Book 1: 143–45, 358; JSM to Miss Pierce of Plymouth, England, 16 July 1788, Letter Book 3: 333.

4. Nathan Hatch argues that this tendency to hear terms associated with secular Whig ideology in a religious context was true of many New Englanders, men as well as women. See Hatch, *The Sacred Cause of Liberty: Republican Thought and the Millennium in Revolutionary New England* (New Haven, Conn.: Yale University Press, 1977), especially chap. 2.

5. Lester H. Cohen, "Mercy Otis Warren: The Politics of Language and the Aesthetics of Self," *American Quarterly* 35 (1983): 202; Elaine F. Crane, "Dependence in the Era of Independence: The Role of Women in a Republican Society," in Jack Green, ed., *The American Revolution: Its Character and Limits* (New York: New York University Press, 1987), 257; Wilson, "The Illusion of Change," 419–20; Norton, *Liberty's Daughters*, 238; Ulrich, "'Daughters of Liberty,'" 214–37. In fact, Gloucester did have one such spinning bee in November 1768, at the home of Rev. Chandler. Whether Judith attended is unclear. Ulrich, "'Daughters of Liberty,'" 216.

6. Judith Stevens to John Murray, 29, 30 July 1778, Letter Book 1: 136–38. See Crane, *Ebb Tide*, especially 205–43; Edith B. Gelles, *Portia: The World of Abigail Adams* (Bloomington: Indiana University Press, 1992), 37–56; Gelles, "The Abigail Industry," *William and Mary Quarterly* 3rd ser. 45 (October 1988): 656–83; Wilson, "The Illusion of Change," 424–25.

7. Gelles, *Portia*, 41–47.

8. Rosemarie Zagarri, *A Woman's Dilemma: Mercy Otis Warren and the American Revolution* (Wheeling, Ill.: Harlan Davidson, 1995), 18–107.

9. Gloucester, Town Records, 3: 160; Sargent, *Epes Sargent of Gloucester*, 11; Judith Stevens to Miss Goldthwait, 5 January 1778, Letter Book 1: 83.

10. Judith Stevens to John Murray, 1 October 1775, Letter Book 1: 143–45, 358; JSM to Mrs. Lewis, 12 February 1802, Letter Book 11: 336; Murray, "To the Reverend Doctor Byles . . . ," Poetry, 1: 55, 60. See also Murray, "To a young Lady who informed me she was seeking to engraft sweet hope upon the root of despair! Written on the commencement of the Revolutionary War," Poetry 1: 19–20.

11. Judith Stevens to John Murray, 17 June 1775, Letter Book 1: 16, 17; Murray, "Reflecting, during a Fine Morning, upon Existing Circumstances, 1775," Repository, 19, 20.

12. Murray, *Life*, 314–16; Miller, *The Larger Hope*, 17; Eddy, *Universalism in Gloucester*, 16–18; Babson, *Gloucester*, 433; Judith Stevens to Winthrop Sargent, 25 February 1778, Murray, Letter Book 1: 89.

13. Murray, *Life*, 315–17.

14. Miller, *The Larger Hope*, 18; Babson, *Gloucester*, 434; Gloucester Town Records, 1: 161, 3: 174; Murray, *Life*, 318–23.

15. John Murray Papers, 324.

16. Judith Stevens to Winthrop and Judith Sargent, 15 August 1769, to John Murray, 16 September 1779, Letter Book 1: 21, 235; Kerber, *Women of the Republic*, 76–78.

17. Judith Stevens to Judith Sargent, [?] January 1776, to Esther Ellery, 25 March 1776, to Judith Sargent, [April 1776], [?] 1776, to John Murray, 15 July 1776, to Winthrop Sargent, 1 October 1776, Letter Book 1: 26–27, 40, 42, 49, 51.

18. Murray, *Life*, 318; Babson, *Gloucester*, 397–98; Judith Stevens to John Murray, 28 July, 1 October 1775, to Judith Sargent, [April 1776], Letter Book 1: 20–22, 41, 42. Between 1775 and 1779, the ratable polls in Gloucester declined by almost half. Paper money steadily depreciated. The cost of poor relief began to rise as early as 1775, and at one point one-sixth of the town's population was on the charity roles. Babson, *Gloucester*, 357, 397–401, 418.

19. Judith Stevens to John Murray, 1 October 1775, to Judith Sargent, [?] November 1775, to Esther Ellery, [?] January 1776, to Judith Sargent, [?] January 1776, to Miss Goldthwait, [?] February 1776, to Mrs. S____, 5 March 1776, to Judith Sargent, [?] [April 1776, [?] May 1776, to John Murray, 2 September 1778, Letter Book 1: 24–28, 31–32, 35, 41–42, 153; Murray, "Reflections during a fine Morning upon existing circumstances," 1775, Repository, 19; "Written at an early period of the Revolutionary War," Poetry 1: 235. See Carol Berkin, *Revolutionary Mothers: Women in the Struggle for America's Independence* (New York: Knopf, 2005), 26–49 for an excellent description of the way the war affected ordinary women—especially those women who lived along the coast.

20. Judith Stevens to Judith Sargent, [?] January 1776, to Esther Ellery, [?] January 1776, Letter Book 1: 28. By March, Judith was urging her mother to return to Gloucester, keeping the Chebacco residence in reserve as a "place of refuge." And by the end of April, Judith, Sr., was back home. Judith Stevens to Judith Sargent, 16 March 1776, [?] April 1776, Letter Book 1: 37, 41.

21. Judith Stevens to John Murray, Summer 1777, to Mrs. Perkins of Boston, 31 December 1777, to Mr. Parker, 25 September 1778, to Winthrop Sargent, 8 September 1779,

to Mr. Allen, [16] October 1779, to Mr. Murray, 28 October 1779, Letter Book 1: 68, 79, 162, 232, 239, 246. The literature dealing with women's "contributions" to the war effort is voluminous. See Paula Baker, "The Domestication of American Politics: Women and American Political Society, 1780–1920," *American Historical Review* 89 (June 1984): 624; Susan Branson, *These Fiery Frenchified Dames: Women and Political Culture in Early National Philadelphia* (Philadelphia: University of Pennsylvania Press, 2001), 9–11; Elizabeth Comitti, "Women and the American Revolution," *New England Quarterly* 20 (September 1947): 342–43; Kerber, " 'History Can Do It No Justice': Women and the Reinterpretation of the American Revolution," in Hoffman and Albert, eds., *Women in the Age of the Revolution*, 14, 38–39; Kerber, *Women of the Republic*, chaps. 2, 3; Norton, *Liberty's Daughters*, chaps. 6–9. Drew Gilpin Faust's "Altars of Sacrifice: Confederate Women and the Narratives of War," *Journal of American History* 76 (March 1990): 1200–1228 argues that the Civil War was unique in the "extraordinary level" of women's participation, in extremely gendered ways, in the war effort. In fact, much of what she discusses is applicable to women's experiences in the American Revolution.

22. Judith Stevens to Winthrop Sargent, 24 August, 8 September 1779, Letter Book 1: 214, 230; Henry Pleasants, Jr., *Winthrop Sargent: Patriot and Pioneer* (Philadelphia [?]: Society of Colonial Wars of Pennsylvania, 1944), 5, 6; Charles Sprague Sargent, "Winthrop Sargent," *Ohio Archaeological and Historical Publications* 33 (1924): 229–30.

23. Judith Stevens to Winthrop Sargent, [?] November 1777, to Mr. Tyler of Norwich, [Fall 1778], to Winthrop Sargent, 1 December 1779, Letter Book 1: 78, 169, 263; Murray, "Upon a Disappointment," "News from my Brother," Poetry 1: 245–47; "Acknowledgments upon the receipt of letters," "A letter from my brother, 1777," Repository, 35, 198. See also Murray, "Written at a period of the American contest replete with uncertainty," Poetry 1: 171; "Pleasures as well as Pains," Repository, 78.

24. Judith Stevens to Winthrop Sargent, 3 July 1778, Letter Book 1: 123; Margaret R. Higonnet, Jane Jenson, Sonya Michel, and Margaret Collins Weitz, eds., *Behind the Lines: Gender and the Two World Wars* (New Haven, Conn.: Yale University Press, 1987), 1.

25. Lydia Minturn Post put it well. Describing a Quaker neighbor, who took neither "part nor lot" in the war, she found his behavior "strange," indeed. In her mind, it was impossible "*To be a man, and remain neutral!*" Harris, ed., *American Women Writers to 1800*, 297.

26. Judith Stevens to Esther Ellery, 9 April 1778, Letter Book 1: 105–6. See Ruth H. Bloch, "The Gendered Meanings of Virtue in Revolutionary America," *Signs* 13 (Fall 1987): 42–45; Baker, "The Domestication of American Politics," 624; Linda K. Kerber, "The Republican Ideology of the Revolutionary Generation," *American Quarterly* 37 (1985): 484; Kerber, " 'May All Our Citizens Be Soldiers and All Our Soliders Citizens': The Ambiguities of Female Citizenship in the New Nation," in Joan R. Challiner and Robert L. Beisner, eds., *Arms At Rest: Peacemaking and Peacekeeping in American History Challinor* (Westport, Conn.: Greenwood Press, 1987), 5; J. G. A. Pocock, *The Machiavellian Moment: Florentine Political Thought and the Atlantic Republican Tradition* (Princeton, N.J.: Princeton University Press, 1975), 41; Lawrence D. Criss, *Citizens in Arms: The Army and the Militia in American Society in the War of 1812* (Chapel Hill: University of North Carolina Press), 4, 5; Charles Royster, *A Revolutionary People at War: The Continental Army and American Character, 1775–1783* (New York: Norton, 1997), 6.

27. Judith Stevens to Winthrop Sargent, [?] November, 1777, 1 December 1779, Let-

ter Book 1: 79, 262; Higonnet et al., *Behind the Lines*, 4, 5; Kerber, "'History Can Do It No Justice,'" 32; Royster, *A Revolutionary People at War*, 205–6.

28. Judith Stevens to John Murray, 11 August 1778, Letter Book 1: 145; Murray, "A letter from my brother," 1777, Repository, 35.

29. Judith Stevens to Winthrop Sargent, 25 February, 3 July 1778, 8 May, 1 December 1779, 5 April 1780, Letter Book 1: 88, 122, 183, 262, 271; Wayne Bodle, "Soldiers in Love: Patrolling the Gender Frontiers of the Early Republic," in Merril D. Smith, ed., *Sex and Sexuality in America* (New York: New York University Press, 1998), 221; Samuel J. Watson, "Flexible Gender Roles During the Market Revolution: Family, Friendship, Marriage, Masculinity among U.S. Army Officers, 1815–1846," *Journal of Social History* 29 (1995): 82; John Ferling, "The New England Soldier: A Study in Changing Perceptions," *American Quarterly* 33 (Spring 1981): 35, 36; Kann, *Republic of Men*, 41–43. See also Fred W. Anderson, "The Hinge of the Revolution: George Washington Confronts a People's Army, July 3, 1775," *Massachusetts Historical Review* 1 (1999): 34, 35.

30. Kerber, "'History Can Do It No Justice,'" 26; Nina Baym, "Mercy Otis Warren's Gendered Melodrama," 542.

31. Judith Stevens to John Murray, 28 July 1775, 6 September 1779, Letter Book 1: 21, 227–29.

32. Judith Stevens to John Murray, Summer 1777, Letter Book 1: 68–69. See Berkin, *Revolutionary Mothers*, 31–33; Comitti, "Women and the American Revolution," 329–37; Faust, "Altars of Sacrifice," 1200; Higonett, et al., eds., *Behind the Lines*, 1–7; Kerber, "'History Can Do It No Justice,'" 20–22, 38–39; Kerber, "'May All Our Citizens Be Soldiers,'" 7; Joan W. Scott, "Gender: A Useful Category of Historical Analysis," *American Historical Review* 91 (December 1986): 1073; Nina Baym, *Feminism and American Literary History: Essays* (New Brunswick, N.J.: Rutgers University Press, 1992), 133; Baym, "Mercy Otis Warren," 539; George C. Calou, "Women in the American Revolution: Vignettes or Profiles?" in Mabel E. Deutrich and Virginia C. Purdy, eds., *Clio Was a Woman: Studies in the History of Women* (Washington D.C.: Howard University Press, 1980), 83; Ulrich, "'Daughters of Liberty,'" 231, 234.

33. Judith Stevens to Winthrop Sargent, 31 December 1779, 17 May 1780, Letter Book 1: 270, 279.

34. Judith Stevens to John Murray, 24, 25 December 1780, Letter Book 1: 307–10.

35. Judith Stevens to John Murray, 26, 27, 28 December 1780, to Maria Sargent, 28 December 1780, Letter Book 1: 311–16.

36. Judith Stevens to John Murray, 28 December 1780, 2, 3, 7 January 1781, to Winthrop Sargent, 18 April, 8, 15 May 1781, Letter Book 1: 313, 318–22, 330–33.

37. Judith Stevens to Winthrop Sargent, 25 February, 1778, to John Murray, 3 January 1781, Letter Book 1: 88–89, 320–21; Samuel Shaw to Winthrop Sargent, 25 January 1781, Shaw Papers, Murray; "To my brother dangerously ill abroad"; "Wrote at Medfield December 25th 1780 to which place I was unexpectedly summoned two days before to attend my eldest Brother apprehended dangerously ill," Poetry 1: 259; 3: 89.

38. Judith Stevens to Winthrop Sargent, 15 May, 16 July, 1 September 1781, Letter Book 1: 334, 341, 347; to Esther Ellery, 4 July 1782, Letter Book 2: 42; Mann, *The Sargent Family*, 57.

39. Judith Stevens to Winthrop Sargent, Sr., 3 August 1781, to Winthrop Sargent, 25 August, 1 September 1781, Letter Book 1: 342, 346–47.

40. Judith Stevens to Winthrop Sargent, 17 May 1780, 25 August 1781, Letter Book 1: 278, 346.

41. Judith Stevens to Winthrop Sargent, 1 October 1776, 25 February 1778, 25 August 1781, Letter Book 1: 51, 90, 346; to John Murray, 28 June 17 [82], Letter Book 2: 37, 38; Murray, "Sentiments," Poetry 1: 136; Samuel Shaw to Winthrop Sargent, 1 October 1779, Shaw Papers. See Ulrich, " 'Daughters of Liberty,' " 239–43; Kerber, " 'History Can Do It No Justice,' " 14; Harris, ed., *American Women Writers*, 298; Richard Vetterli and Gary Bryner, *In Search of the Republic: Public Virtue and the Roots of American Government* (Lanham, Md.: Rowman and Littlefield, 1996), 52.

42. See Lacy, "The World of Hannah Heaton," 301–2; Ulrich, " 'Daughters of Liberty,' " 234–35, 237; Harris, *American Women Writers*, 167–68; Harry S. Stout, "Rhetoric and Reality in the Early Republic: The Case of the Federalist Clergy," in Noll, ed., *Religion and American Politics*, 66; Linda Kerber, " 'I Have Don . . . much to Carrey on the War': Women and the Shaping of Republican Ideology After the American Revolution," in Applewhite and Levy, eds., *Women and Politics in the Age of the Democratic Revolution*, 246–47.

43. Judith Stevens to Winthrop Sargent, 1 October 1776, to John Murray, 8 October 1779, Letter Book 1: 51, 237. See Nina Baym, "Between Enlightenment and Victorian: Toward a Narrative of American Women Writers Writing History," *Critical Inquiry* 18 (1991): 32; Baym, "Mercy Otis Warren," 535; Baym, *American Women Writers and the Work of History*, 32–33.

44. Watson, "Flexible Gender Roles During the Market Revolution," 86–88; Judith Stevens to John Murray, 16 September 1779, to Winthrop Sargent, 20 July, 25 August 1781, Letter Book 1: 235, 342, 346.

45. Judith Stevens to John Murray, 30 November 1780, Letter Book 1: 298; to Winthrop Sargent, Sr., 15 June 1782, Letter Book 2: 18; Murray, "A Party of Pleasure," Repository, 361–62.

46. Judith Stevens to John Murray, 21 August, 16 September 1779, Letter Book 1: 213, 235; Murray, "Lines penned under the shade of a spreading Oak, the environs of which exhibited the scenes of my infantile amusement," Poetry 1: 66–68; "Upon the approach of the Chatham Man of war to our harbour's mouth—May 4, 1782," Poetry 3: 155; Anna Matilda, "Stanzas to Della Crusca," "Vanity," Poetry 4: 10, 43.

47. Crain, *American Sympathy*, 2–10; Judith Stevens to Mrs. Wheat of New London, 17 September 1786, Letter Book 3: 151; Murray, "Arnold," "Andre," Repository, 79–81; Murray, "Written upon seeing some letters addressed to Miss Seward by Major Andre—with an extract from her elegant and pathetic hand upon the death of that Hero—1781," Poetry 3: 132–33; "Penned after spending an evening in the course of which the fate of Major Andre was with coming sorrow deplored, 1781," Poetry 3: 124–[125]. At some point Judith scrawled a large "X" across the second poem.

48. Judith Stevens to John Murray, 31 August 1778, Letter Book 1: 151.

49. Judith Stevens to John Murray, 11, 31 August 1778, 18 October 1779, Letter Book 1: 143–44, 151–52, 241–42; to Winthrop Sargent, Sr., 15 June 1782, Letter Book 2: 18; Murray, "Vicissitudes," "Birth of the Dauphin, 1782," Repository, 61–62, 287; Murray, "Written at a period of the American contest replete with uncertainty," Poetry 1: 169–70; "On the Uncertainty of Popular Applause—1781," "To a friend—upon reading the proceedings of the Government against the Abbe Raynal—1781," Poetry 3: 96–98, [142]–45; Babson, *Gloucester*, 347.

50. Judith Stevens to Winthrop Sargent, 28 October 1781, Letter Book 1: 357–58; to Winthrop Sargent, 5 September 1782, Letter Book 2: 65. See especially Edwin C. Burrows and Michael Wallace, "The American Revolution: The Ideology and Practice of National Liberation," *Perspectives in American History* 6 (1972): 167–306.

51. Murray, "Birth of the Dauphin, 1782," Repository, 286–88; Judith Stevens to John Murray, 11 August 1778, Letter Book 1: 143–45; to Mrs. Pilgrim of Old England, 31 October 1784, Letter Book 2: 291; JSM to Mrs. Gardiner, 4 April 1788, to Miss Pierce of Plymouth England, 16 July 1788, Letter Book 3: 291, 333.

52. Judith Stevens to John Murray, 28 June 17[82], Letter Book 2: 34–35; Murray, "Lavinia," Repository, 326–329. See also Murray, "British Clemency, 1782," Repository, 313–14.

53. This discussion is drawn from both the essay and the poem, Murray, "Charles I of England," Repository, 258–63 and "The Martyred Prince of England-1781," Poetry 1: 312–15. Both are found in *The Gleaner*, 52.

54. Gould, *Covenant and Republic*, 74; Mark Gerzon, *A Choice of Heroes: The Changing Faces of American Manhood* (Boston: Houghton Mifflin, 1982), 31–37; Baym, *Feminism and American Literary History*, 134; Baym, "Mercy Otis Warren's Gendered Melodrama," 536–55.

55. Nina Baym, "Women and the Republic: Emma Willard's Rhetoric of History," *American Quarterly* 43 (1991): 15–16; Baym, "Mercy Otis Warren's Gendered Melodrama," 551; Murray, "Cathon and Colonel, 1779," "Lines Occasioned by reflecting upon the ingratitude of America to her Soldiery, 1784," Poetry 2: 217, 240.

56. Judith Stevens to Winthrop Sargent, 25 February 1778, 25 August 1781, Letter Book 1: 90, 346; JSM to Winthrop and Judith Sargent, 12 October 1788, Letter Book 3: 350; *The Gleaner*, 452–53.

57. Judith Stevens to John Murray, 17 June 1775, to Winthrop Sargent, 25 February 1778, Letter Book 1: 17, 18, 88; to John Murray, 18 June 1784, to Winthrop Sargent, 25 December 1784, Letter Book 2: 247, 309. See Kerber, *Women of the Republic*, 35–36.

58. Judith Stevens to John Murray, 28 December 1780, to Mr. Sewall, 15 July 1781, to Winthrop Sargent, 25 August 1781, Letter Book 1: 313, 339, 346; Murray, "Line addressed to my mother upon the death of the last of her brothers who died abroad attended only by a nephew, 2 November 1782," "News from my Brother," Poetry 1: 45, 247.

59. Murray, "On reading the institution of the Cincinnati, January 28, 1784," Poetry 3: 183. See Baym, *American Women Writers*, 29.

Chapter 4. Creating a Genteel Nation

1. See Judith Stevens to Mr. Parker, 31 January 1782, Letter Book 2: 1; Note to Dr. Plummer, n.d., Letter Book 1: 60.

2. See Blanche Glassman Hersh, "The 'True Woman' and the 'New Woman' in Nineteenth-Century America: Feminist Abolitionists and a New Concept of True Womanhood," in Mary Kelley, ed., *Woman's Being, Woman's Place: Female Identity and Vocation in American History* (Boston: G.K. Hall, 1979), 273, who argues that many women saw their primary identity as "human" and in that sense, they claimed the same rights and

duties as any citizen. Their secondary identity was gendered, and in this capacity they served as wives, mothers, and nurturers.

3. Murray, "Freedom," Poetry 1: 309. See Betsy Erkkila, "Revolutionary Women," *Tulsa Studies in Women's Literature* 6 (1987): 192, 211–19; Coontz, *The Social Origins of Private Life*, 146–47, 152–53; Joan Cashin, "Introduction to Special Issue on Gender in the Early Republic," *Journal of the Early Republic* 15 (1995): 354–56; Thomas Laqueur, *Making Sex: Body and Gender from the Greeks to Freud* (Cambridge, Mass.: Harvard University Press, 1990), 194; Smith-Rosenberg, "Domesticating 'Virtue': Coquettes and Revolutionaries in Young America," in Elaine Scarry, ed., *Literature and the Body: Essays on Populations and Persons* (Baltimore: Johns Hopkins University Press, 1988), 161–62; Kerber, "Separate Spheres, Female Worlds, Women's Place: The Rhetoric of Women's History," *Journal of American History* 75 (1988): 20; Kerber, *Women of the Republic*, 82; Mary Beth Norton, "The Evolution of White Women's Experience in Early America," *American Historical Review* 89 (1984): 614; Scott, "Gender: A Useful Category of Historical Analysis," 1073–74; Susan Juster, " 'Neither Male Nor Female': Jemima Wilkinson and the Politics of Gender in Post-Revolutionary America," in St. George, ed., *Possible Pasts*, 366–68. JSM to Mrs. H_____, 25 November 1800, to Mrs. Tenney of Exeter, 5 January 1802, Letter Book 11: 228, 323; *Boston Gazette* 13 June, 5 September 1796; *Salem Mercury*, 21 October 1788; Kerber, " 'History Can Do It No Justice,' " 34; Jan Lewis, " 'Of Every Age, Sex & Condition': The Representation of Women in the Constitution," *Journal of the Early Republic* 15 (1995): 363–68; Rosemarie Zagarri, "The Rights of Man and Woman in Post-Revolutionary America," *William and Mary Quarterly* 3rd ser. 55 (1998): 216–17, 224–29; David Waldstreicher, *In the Midst of Perpetual Fetes: The Making of American Nationalism, 1776–1820* (Chapel Hill: University of North Carolina Press, 1997), 223, 234–46; Branson, *These Fiery Frenchified Dames*, passim. For an example of doubts about the impermeability of race, see *Boston Gazette*, 25 July 1796.

4. Gould, *Covenant and Republic*, 68, 88; Joan R. Gundersen, "Independence, Citizenship, and the American Revolution," *Signs* 13 (1987): 60, 65, 71–76; Sharon M. Harris, "Hannah Webster Foster's *The Coquette*: Critiquing Franklin's America," in Harris, ed., *Redefining the Political Novel: American Women Writers, 1797–1901* (Knoxville: University of Tennessee Press, 1995), 4; Crane, *Ebb Tide*, 175, 207; Zagarri, "The Rights of Man and Woman," 203; Kerber, " 'I Have Don . . . Much,' " 228–35, 251; Kerber, " 'History Can Do It No Justice,' " 30–32; Linda K. Kerber, "A Constitutional Right to Be Treated like American Ladies: Women and the Obligations of Citizenship," in Linda K. Kerber, Alice Kessler-Harris, and Kathryn Kish Sklar, eds., *U.S. History as Women's History: New Feminist Essays* (Chapel Hill: University of North Carolina Press, 1995), 19–25; Kerber, "The Revolutionary Generation," 30; Kerber, " 'May All Our Citizens Be Soldiers,' " 11; Kerber, "The Republican Ideology of the Revolutionary Generation," 487–88; Pateman, *The Sexual Contract*, 21; Karin Wulf, *Not All Wives: Women of Colonial Philadelphia* (Ithaca, N.Y.: Cornell University Press, 2000).

5. Michelle Rosaldo, "The Use and Abuse of Anthropology: Reflections on Feminism and Cross-Cultural Understanding," *Signs* 5 (1980): 395–98; Crane, *Ebb Tide*, 209–12; Kann, *Republic of Men*, 26–27, 99; Catherine A. Brekus, *Strangest Pilgrims: Female Preaching in America, 1740–1845* (Chapel Hill: University of North Carolina Press, 1998), 72–73; Isaac, "Stories and Constructions of Identity," 221; Kerber, "Separate Spheres," 31–32; Coontz, *Social Origins of Private Life*, 133–34; Zagarri, "The Rights of Man and Woman," 219–22.

6. Judith Stevens to Miss Mary Parker, 1 January 1785, Letter Book 2: 311–12; to Mr. ____ of ____, 5 September 1787, Letterbook 3: 226; JSM to Mrs. Pilgrim of Old England, 7 November 1789, Letterbook 4: 57.

7. Judith Stevens to Winthrop Sargent, 8 September 1779, Letter Book 1: 232; Judith Stevens to Madam Walker, 8 October 1783, Letter Book 2: 171. See Babson, *Gloucester*, 412–13, 440, 441; Sargent, *Epes Sargent of Gloucester*, 49 for evidence that all of Gloucester was suffering from the vicissitudes of trade throughout the war.

8. John H. Sheppard, *Reminiscences of Lucius Manlius Sargent* (Boston: David Clapp and Sons, 1871), 7, 8; Judith Stevens to Esther Sargent, 2 June 1776, to John Murray, 28 October 1779, Letter Book 1: 43–44, 246.

9. Judith Stevens to Mr. Parker, 9 June 1782, Letter Book 2: 14–15. There is some uncertainty about the origins of the house. Some historians claim that Stevens bought it from John and James Babson. Others say that Winthrop, Sr., gave the home to John and Judith. Judith's own letters indicate that they either built the house or at the very least extensively remodeled it. See Mann, *The Sargent Family*, 37.

10. The quote comes from Field, *Constantia*, 17. See Carole Shammas, *The Pre-Industrial Consumer in England and America* (Oxford: Clarendon Press, 1990), 165–68, 187; Bushman, *Refinement*, 5; Nylander, *Our Own Snug Fireside*, 246–48, for a description of New England housing in this period.

11. John F. Kasson, *Rudeness and Civility: Manners in Nineteenth-Century Urban America* (New York: Hill and Wang, 1990), 170; Mann, *The Sargent Family*, 34; Sargent, *Epes Sargent of Gloucester*, 50, 51. The Stevens house (known now as the Sargent House) is still standing, on 49 Middle Street in Gloucester. For the furniture that graced the "mansion," see the 1789 photocopy of John Stevens's probate records, available upon request from the Sargent House Museum. For the meaning of the consumer items that graced the Stevens home—as well as of the architectural structure of the house, see especially Grant McCracken, *Culture and Consumption: New Approaches to the Symbolic Character of Consumer Goods and Activities* (Bloomington: Indiana University Press, 1988), 33–41; Kevin M. Sweeney, "High-Style Vernacular: Lifestyles of the Colonial Elite," in Cary Carson, Ronald Hoffman and Peter J. Albert, eds., *Of Consuming Interests: The Style of Life in the Eighteenth Century* (Charlottesville: University Press of Virginia, 1994), 1–58; Cary Carson, "The Consumer Revolution in Colonial British America: Why Demand?" in ibid., 483–700; and Bushman, *Refinement*, 50–58.

12. Judith Stevens to John Murray, 20 September, 21 November 1781, Letter Book 1: 349, 369; to John Murray, 17 June 1782, to Maria Sargent, 5 September 1782, Letter Book 2: 26–27, 64.

13. Judith Stevens to Madam Walker, [?] January 1783, to Mr. Parker, 5 September 1784, Letter Book 2: 92, 263; to Winthrop Sargent, 10 October 1787, Letterbook 3: 233.

14. Judith Stevens to Maria Sargent, 24 March 1781, Letter Book 1: 323; to John Murray, 20 July 1782, to Mrs. Walker, 8 April 1783, to Esther Ellery, 2 June, 21 June 1783, 2 July 1785, to Mrs. Barrell of Old York, 15 July 1785, Letterbook 2: 53, 139, 145, 155, 353–54, 359; "Returning from a Visit to the Metropolis," Murray, Poetry 1: 259–60; Sargent, *Epes Sargent of Gloucester*, 134, 136; Rebora et al., *John Singleton Copley*, 194; Chambers Schiller, *Liberty a Better Husband*, 42; Carroll Smith-Rosenberg, "Hearing Women's Words," in Carroll Smith-Rosenberg, ed., *Disorderly Conduct: Visions of Gender in Victorian America* (New York: Knopf, 1985), 37ff.; Kelly, *In the New England Fashion*, 69.

15. Shields, *Civil Tongues*, 38–39; Wood, *Radicalism*, 41; Judith Stevens to John Murray, 24 August, 30 October 1779, Letter Book 1: 217, 246; to Fitz William Sargent, 25 May 1782, to John Murray, 11 June 1782, Letter Book 2: 9, 15; Murray, "Pity & Condescension," "Duty to Servants," Repository, 223–25, 242–46.

16. See Jacqueline Reinier, *From Virtue to Character: American Childhood, 1775–1850* (New York: Twayne, 1996), 18, for a concise description of the "enlightened" child-rearing techniques Judith was inclined to embrace.

17. The quote is from John Demos, *A Little Commonwealth: Family Life in Plymouth Colony* (New York: Oxford University Press, 1970), 134–35; JSM to Winthrop Sargent, 8 September 1779, Letter Book 1: 231. See Lawrence A. Cremin, *American Education: The Colonial Experience, 1607–1783* (New York: Harper and Row, 1970), 361–70; Wood, *Radicalism*, 151–52; Gould, *Covenant and Republic*, 38; Fliegelman, *Prodigals and Pilgrims*, 212. An emphasis on education by example was no more egalitarian than education by stern precept had been. While it rejected force as a weapon, it presumed an elite, hierarchical society where superiors taught, controlled, and shaped inferiors.

18. Judith Stevens to John Murray, 11 August 1778, Letter Book 1: 143; Solomon, *In the Company of Educated Women*, 5; Hatch, *The Sacred Cause of Liberty*, 93–96; Wood, *Radicalism*, 215–20; Bloch, "The Gendered Meanings of Virtue," 49–50; Rosemarie Zagarri, "Morals, Manners and the Republican Mother," *American Quarterly* 44 (1992): 26–43; Fliegelman, *Prodigals and Pilgrims*, 23, 26; Burstein, *Sentimental Democracy*, 187.

19. Fliegelman, *Prodigals and Pilgrims*, 25; Klepp, "Revolutionary Bodies," 916; Isenberg, *Sex and Citizenship*, 44–45; Lewis, "Mother Love: The Construction of an Emotion in Nineteenth-Century America," in Andrew E. Barnes and Peter N. Stearns, eds., *Social History and Issues in Human Consciousness: Some Interdisciplinary Connections* (New York: New York University Press, 1989), 213–15; Regina Markell Morantz, "Making Women Modern: Middle Class Women and Health Reform in Nineteenth-Century America," *Journal of Social History* 10 (1977): 493; Wood, *Radicalism*, 150–52, 215–18, 240, 356–57; Waldstreicher, *In the Midst of Perpetual Fetes*, 172; Zagarri, "Morals, Manners and the Republican Mother," 27–29, 38; Gould, *Covenant and Republic*, 97, 102; Marion Rust, "'Women Were Born for Universal Sway': Susanna Rowson, Algerian Captivity and the Making of a Citizen," paper presented at Omohundro Institute of Early American History and Culture Conference on Sexuality in America, Philadelphia, 4 April 2000, 13.

20. Murray, "Locke, 1781," Repository, 281–83. Indeed, as she had pointed out in "Curiosity" and "The Sexes," there were those who thought women were innately more curious than men.

21. Daniel Kilbride, "Cultivation, Conservatism, and the Early National Gentry: The Manigault Family and Their Circle," *Journal of the Early Republic* 19 (1999): 225, 238, 242.

22. Murray, "Cleora," 21 May 1777, Repository, 33–34; Judith Stevens to Miss Goldthwait, 6 June 1777, Letter Book 1: 64.

23. Marsh and Ronner, *The Empty Cradle*, 10, 17–18; May, *Barren in the Promised Land*, 30; Murray, Repository, 8; *Massachusetts Magazine*, April 1793, 196–97; Judith Stevens to Mrs Sayward of Old York, 8 September 1780, to John Murray, 2 December 1780, Letter Book 1: 287, 301. The record concerning Anna and Mary is fuzzy. Even Anna's last name is unknown—it was either "Plummer" or "O'Dell." Sometimes Judith referred to both girls as her nieces; other times she implied that only Anna was related to John. Moreover, while she wrote many letters to Anna, and remembered her in her will, she

never kept any letters to Mary, nor did she mention her very often. Still, on occasion, she referred to her "two orphans"—surely meaning Mary and Anna. There is some evidence that the girls were sisters. In the end, the identities of both girls remains something of a mystery. See Judith Sargent Murray, *From Gloucester to Philadelphia in 1790: Observations, anecdotes, and thoughts from the 18th-century letters of Judith Sargent Murray*, ed. Bonnie Hurd Smith (Cambridge, Mass.: Judith Sargent Murray Society, 1998), 25–26.

24. Judith Stevens to John Murray, 24 August 1779, to Mrs. Parker, 15 October 1779, to Maria Sargent, 5 August 1781, to John Murray, 12 November 1781, Letter Book 1: 216–19, 239, 344, 366; to Mrs. Barrell of Old York, 31 January 1784, Letter Book 2: 192–93, 222; to Aunt Prentiss of Boston, 15 May 1784, to Winthrop Sargent, 26 December 1785, Letter Book 3: 32; to Maria Sargent, 6 April 1790, Letter Book 4: 79; Murray, "Pity and Condescension," Repository, 223; Fliegelman, *Prodigals and Pilgrims*, 51, 53, 215. See also Davidson, "Mothers and Daughters," 119–20.

25. Judith Stevens to John Murray, 2 December 1780, Letter Book 1: 300; Murray, "In answer to a friend who supposed me solicitous to take upon myself the charge of a female orphan—1780," Poetry 3: 63–66; Murray, "Remarks occasioned by meeting with an Old Lady," [1782?], Repository, 315; Murray, "Upon the introduction of a female Orphan into my family the care of whom was to devolve upon me—1780," Poetry, 3: 87.

26. Judith Stevens to John Murray, 2 December 1780, Letter Book 1: 301–2.

27. Murray, "Pleasures as well as Pains," Repository, 79; Judith Stevens to John Murray, 20 September 1781, Letter Book 1: 350; to Winthrop Sargent, 26 December 1785, Letter Book 3: 32.

28. Judith Stevens to John Murray, 23 November 1781, Letter Book 1: 370; to Anna, 2 June 1783, Letterbook 2: 147–48; to Winthrop Sargent, 26 December 1785, Letterbook 3:32; Murray, "Copies for Miss A's Writing Book," Poetry 1: 98–100. Judith later reworked some letters she wrote to Anna for her *Gleaner* essays. See especially the letter to Miss Sophia Aimwell, in *The Gleaner*, 444–47.

29. Judith Stevens to Anna, 16 June 1782, 23 June 1785, Letter Book 2: 22–23, 340–41; to Maria Sargent, 15 October 1785, to Anna, 19 October 1785, Letter Book 3: 16, 21; Murray, "Pity & Condescension," Repository, 222. See Poovey, *The Proper Lady*, 24, for attitudes toward female orphans.

30. Woody, *History of Women's Education* 1: 145–46; Judith Stevens to Aunt E____ S____, 26 June 1786, Letter Book 3: 105.

31. Judith Stevens to Miss Johnson of Boston, [?] May 1773, Letter Book 1: 9; to Anna, 23, 28 June 1782, 2 June 1783, Letter Book 2: 29, 33–34, 145, 147. See Perry, *Women, Letters and the Novel*, 50–51 for other evidences of women who were concerned with the antics of coquettes.

32. Poovey, *The Proper Lady*, 18–24; Klepp, "Revolutionary Bodies," 937; C. Dallett Hemphill, *Bowing to Necessities: A History of Manners and Morals in America, 1620–1860* (New York: Oxford University Press, 1999), 110–21; Cott, "Passionless," 223–24; Perry, *Women, Letters, and the Novel*, 23; Spacks, *Gossip*, 31–32; Hill, "Clarissa Harlow," 52–54; Rothman, *Hands and Hearts*, 51; Judith Stevens to Miss Palfrey, 24 November 1776, Letter Book 1: 54; to Winthrop Sargent, 22 April 1782, to Anna, 23 June 1782, to Anna, 23 June 1785, Letter Book 2: 5, 28–29, 341–42; Murray, "The Martyr of Sensibility, 10 November 1781," Repository, 82–83; "Slander," Repository, 56; Murray, "Lines Occasioned by the misfortunes of a Friend, 1780," Poetry 3: 62, 63; "Copies Composed for the writing book of

Miss [Anna] P_____"; "To the same, by way of conclusion to her Sampler," Poetry 1: 90, 96; Jan Lewis points out that chastity for women was the equivalent of bravery for men. But while the wartime experience proved that even good soldiers could be afraid, for women, chastity was an absolute moral category. Lewis, "The Republican Wife," 716, 719. These attitudes were especially crucial to women like Judith Stevens, who had claims to social respectability. For less well-situated women, especially those who lived in rural areas, sexual dalliances were much less likely to raise eyebrows. See Clare Lyons, *Sex Among the Rabble: An Intellectual History of Gender and Power in the Age of Revolution* (Chapel Hill: University of North Carolina Press, 2006), Part III, and Laurel Thatcher Ulrich, and Lois K. Stabler, " 'Girling of It' in Eighteenth-Century New Hampshire," in Peter Benes, ed., *Families and Children*, Dublin Seminar of New England Folklife (Cambridge, Mass.: Boston University, 1987), 24–36.

33. Judith Stevens to Anna, 23 June 1785, Letter Book 2: 341. Godbeer notes that the didactic literature advising women to avoid sex before marriage preceded any change in women's sexual activity. Richard Godbeer, *Sexual Revolution in Early America* (Baltimore: Johns Hopkins University Press, 2002), 229, 238, 246, 265, 278–80. For the classic analysis of "passionlessness," see Cott, "Passionless," 219–36.

34. Judith Stevens to Esther Ellery, 21 March 1776, to Miss Palfrey, 24 November 1776, Letter Book 1: 39, 53, 54; to Anna, 9 July 1782, to Mr. _____ of _____ 31 July 1784, to Anna, 23 June 1785, Letter Book 2: 47, 254–55, 342; Murray, "Melancholy consequences of a single Error," 1775, Repository, 16–18. She published the essay in the *Massachusetts Magazine* in January 1794. See also Murray, "Lines Occasioned by the misfortunes of a friend," Poetry 3: 59–63; Marion Rust, "What's Wrong with *Charlotte Temple*?" *William and Mary Quarterly* 3rd ser. 60 (2003): 104, 106.

35. Spacks, *Gossip*, 150–52; Poovey, *The Proper Lady*, 21–24; Hemphill, *Bowing to Necessities*, 104–8; Judith Stevens to Anna, 3 July 178 [2], Letter Book 2: 39, 40; to Anna, 18 November 1786, Letter Book 3: 181; JSM to my niece, 14 December 1795, Letter Book 8: 361.

36. Judith Stevens to Anna, 2 June 1783, Letter Book 2: 145, 147.

37. Judith Stevens to Anna, 16, 28 June, 3, 9 July 1782, Letter Book 2: 22, 24, 32–33, 38, 45; to Anna, 18 October 1785, Letter Book 3: 21.

38. Judith Stevens to Winthrop Sargent, 8 September 1779, Letter Book 1: 231; to Fitz William Sargent, 18 May 1782, Letterbook 2: 8. Fitz William's complaints were not uncommon. Boys often complained about the drudgery of academic life. Ironically, women were usually grateful for any educational opportunity, and seldom rebelled against the tedium their schooling entailed. See Mary Kelley, *Learning to Stand and Speak: Women, Education, and Public Life in America's Republic* (Chapel Hill, N.C.: University of North Carolina Press, 2006), 94–95.

39. Judith Stevens to Winthrop Sargent, 8 September, 5 December 1779, Letter Book 1: 231, 232, 264, 266; to Winthrop Sargent, 8 July, 5 September 1782, Letter Book 2: 45, 65. Robert Middlekauff's description of educational practices provides explanation enough of why Fitz William hated his studies. Middlekauff, *Ancients and Axioms*, 82–83.

40. Judith Stevens to Winthrop Sargent, 8 September 1779, Letter Book 1: 231–32; to Winthrop Sargent, 8 July 1782, to Fitz William Sargent, 9 November 1782, Letter Book 2: 44, 88.

41. Judith Stevens to Winthrop Sargent, 5 December 1779, 17 May 1780, to Winthrop Sargent, Sr., [31?] December [1781], Letter Book 1: 264, 266, 279–82, 377.

42. Judith Stevens to Winthrop Sargent, 5 December, 1779, Letter Book 1: 265; to Winthrop Sargent, 8 July 1782, to Fitz William Sargent, 9 November 1782, Letterbook 2: 43–44, 87.

43. Judith Stevens to John Murray, 12 August 1779, to Judith Sargent, 13 August 1779, to Winthrop Sargent, 5 December 1779, 17 May 1780, Letter Book 1: 200–201, 266, 280.

44. Judith Stevens to Winthrop Sargent, 25 August 1781, to Fitz William Sargent, [?] November 1781, Letter Book 1: 346, 367; to Fitz William Sargent, 25 May, 24 October, 9 November 1782, Letter Book 2: 18, 83, 89.

45. Judith Stevens to Mrs. Perkins of Boston, 31 December 1777, to John Murray, 28 November 1779, Letter Book 1: 80, 258; to Fitz William Sargent, 17 October 1782, Letterbook 2: 78; Murray, "Flattery," [1777], Repository, 48–49; Murray, "Upon flattery—addressed to a friend—1779," Poetry 3: 35–38.

46. Judith Stevens to Fitz William Sargent, 4 June, 17 October 1782, Letter Book 2: 10, 78. For evidence of Fitz William's reluctance to write any of his siblings, see Judith Stevens to Winthrop Sargent, 31 August 1787, Letter Book 3: 222; to Anna Sargent, 15 April 1799, Letter Book 11: 8; to Winthrop Sargent, July [1804], Letter Book 12: [936]–37; Fitz William Sargent to Winthrop Sargent, 8 October 1795, Sargent Murray Gilman Hough Papers, Box 1, 1799–1850.

47. Cremin, *American Education: The Colonial Experience*, 362; Judith Stevens, Note to Doctor [Plummer?], n.d., Letter Book 1: 57; Judith Stevens to Fitz William Sargent, 15 March 1783, Letter Book 2: 121–23.

48. Judith Stevens to Fitz William Sargent, 18 May 1782, Letter Book 2: 6–8.

49. Judith Stevens to Fitz William Sargent, [?] November 1781, Letter Book 1: 367; to Fitz William Sargent, 18, 25, May, 27 July, 17 October 1782, Letter Book 2: 6, 9, 57–58, 77–78.

50. Judith Stevens to Fitz William Sargent, 24 October, 2 November 1782, Letter Book 2: 82, 84–86.

51. Judith Stevens to Maria Sargent, 5 September 1782, to Fitz William Sargent, 17 October, 1782, 5 April 1783, Letter Book 2: 60, 79, 135.

52. Benjamin Rush, *Thoughts upon the Mode of Education Proper in a Republic* (Philadelphia, 1786) in Frederick Rudolph, ed., *Essays on Education in the Early Republic* (Cambridge, Mass.: Harvard University Press, 1965), 13–16; Cremin, *American Education: The National Experience, 1783–1876* (New York: Harper and Row, 1980), 124–25. Judith's gendered expectations and advice was typical. Courtesy books warned women about the dangers of sexual activity and gave them very specific advice about how to interact with men. They were much less likely to give men similar warnings or advice. Hemphill, *Bowing to Necessities*, 120–21.

53. Judith Stevens to Winthrop Sargent, 15 May 1785, Letter Book 2: 333; to Maria Sargent, 6 April 1790, Letter Book 4: 79; to Mrs. Williams, 26 July 1817, Letter Book 20: 57; Fraser, "Rethinking the Public Sphere," 23–26; Burstein, *Sentimental Democracy*, 290, 293,-94, 300–305; Crain, *American Sympathy*, 2, 21; Fea, "The Way of Improvement," 481, 486–87; Gould, *Covenant and Republic*, 26, 114–18; Lewis, "Mother Love," 213–15; Morantz, "Making Women Modern," 493; Shields, *Civil Tongues* 103–4; Waldstreicher, *In the Midst of Perpetual Fetes*, 172; Warner, *Letters of the Republic*, 173–75; Wood, *Radicalism*, 150–51.

54. Judith Stevens to a widowed and unfortunate Uncle, [?] September 1769, to Mrs. D.S., [19] July 1775, to John Murray, 1 October 1775, Letter Book 1: 4, 19, 24. She drew the line where benevolence was concerned. She helped the "industrious poor" but she did

not heed the pleas of the "every day clamorous beggar." Murray, "Prudence & Charity," "System," Repository, 74, 115. See Markley, "Sentimentality as Performance," 211, for a brief discussion of the way benevolence could be used to exhibit social and moral superiority. Crain, *American Sympathy*, 2, 21 offers a succinct explanation of the noncorporal characteristics of sympathy.

55. Judith Stevens to Fitz William Sargent, 1 March 1783, Letter Book 2: 115; Murray, "Pity Condescension," Repository, 223; Kenneth A. Lockridge, "Colonial Self-Fashioning: Paradoxes and Pathologies in the Construction of Genteel Identity in Eighteenth-Century America," in Hoffman, Sobel, and Teute, eds., *Through a Glass Darkly*, 281; Bushman, *Refinement*, 127–28, 182–83; Juster, "'Neither Male Nor Female,'" 375.

56. Judith Stevens to Winthrop Sargent, 5 December 1779, Letter Book 1: 266; Murray, "Sentiments," Poetry 1: 156; Erkkila, "Revolutionary Women," 215–19; Nichols, "'Pray Don't Tell Anybody,'" 284–85, 292–94; Nylander, *Our Own Snug Fireside*, 10.

57. Judith Stevens to John Murray, 15 October, 9 November 1781, Letter Book 1: 354, 363; to Anna, 2 June 1783, Letter Book 2: 145; Warner, *The Letters of the Republic*, 134–42; Bushman, *Refinement*, 25; Spacks, *Gossip*, 148–49; Shields, *Civil Tongues*, 9, 42, 46, 99–102; Wood, *Radicalism*, 193–96; Zagarri, "Morals, Manners and the Republican Mother," 32, 33; Kasson, *Rudeness and Civility*, 4, 58; Imbarrato, *Declarations of Independency*, 11–12; Kann, *A Republic of Men*, 110. Such notions of middle-class gentility existed in England as well as America. The *Tattler* and the *Spectator* both tended to conflate birth and worth, offering middle-class readers a significant cultural role. Merchants and gentlemen could see themselves as partners with true aristocrats in the effort to preserve and even expand morality and decorum in the world at large. See Markley, "Sentimentality as Performance," 217–19.

58. One way to make sure that gentility was real, not superficial, was to practice it even in the privacy of one's own home. We must, thought Judith, always act the part, never appearing "*undressed*," even before members of the family. Only then would gentility become "second nature." JSM to Esther Sargent, 17 September 1790, Letter Book 4: 235. See also Daniel Kilbride, "Cultivation, Conservatism, and the Early National Gentry," 241, 249; Lockridge, "Colonial Self-Fashioning," 279; Judith Stevens to John Murray, 8 November 1779, Letter Book 1: 252.

59. See Bushman, *Refinement*, 43–46, 63–68, 81–83, 96–99; Shields, *Civil Tongues*, 16, 31–36; Hemphill, *Bowing to Necessities*, 68–77; Armstrong and Tennenhouse, eds., *The Ideology of Conduct*, 2–5; Judith Stevens to Esther Sargent, [?] November 1770, to John Murray, Summer, 1777, 28 August 1779, Letter Book 1: 8, 72, 223–24; to Fitz William Sargent, 1, 8, 15 February 1783, Letter Book 2: 101, 106–8, 111.

60. Judith Stevens to John Murray, 3 April, 28 July 1778, Letter Book 1: 101, 135; to Anna, 23 June 1782, to John Murray, 16 July 1782, Letter Book 2: 28, 48; Murray, "Taking a journey from Gloucester to Boston," Poetry 1: 253; "Wishes for retirement—while upon a visit to a gay Metropolis," 1782, Poetry 3: 167–68.

61. Judith Stevens to Anna, 9 July 1782, to Fitz William Sargent, 22 February 1 March 1783, Letter Book 2: 45–46, 111–15. See also Judith Stevens to John Murray, 1 December 1780, Letter Book 1: 299; Murray, "Whispering," Repository, 321–22. David Shields points out, however, that most people saw cards as yet another symbol of the ability to engage in polite social interaction. Shields, *Civil Tongues*, 159–60.

62. See Kilbride, "Cultivation, Conservatism, and the Early National Gentry," 222–23; Shields, *Civil Tongues*, 6.

Part II Introduction

1. See Harold Milton Ellis, "Joseph Dennie and His Circle: A Study in American Literature from 1792–1812," *Bulletin of the University of Texas* 40 (1915): 78–79; Carol Sue Humphrey, *The Press of the Young Republic, 1783–1833* (Westport, Conn.: Greenwood Press, 1996), 145, for a discussion of the growth in the number and availability of magazines in this period.

2. Richard D. Brown, "From Cohesion to Competition," in Joyce et al., eds. *Printing*, 301–7; David Paul Nord, "A Republican Literature: A Study of Magazine Reading and Readers in Late Eighteenth-Century New York," *American Quarterly* 40 (1988): 42–64; Lewis, "Republican Wife," 692; *Gentleman and Lady's Town and Country Magazine*, May 1784, 3–4.

3. *Gentleman and Lady's Town and Country Magazine*, May 1784, 12–13, 20–22, 27–28.

4. "Desultory Thoughts," ibid. (June 1784), n.p.; Judith Stevens to Madam Walker, 8 June 1784, Letter Book 2: 234. The first draft of the essay is in her Repository. She underlined the title twice—not her usual practice, and put it in quotes as well. Repository, 352–56. As Karen L. Schiff points out, the expression was one she had used before, one she had borrowed from Edward Young's 1759 "Conjectures on Original Composition." See Schiff, "Objects of Speculation," 221; Murray, "Dr. Young," Repository, 172–75.

5. Murray, "Reverence Thy Self," Repository, 352, 355–56. Judith had, of course, sung the importance of praise on many occasions already. And just four months after her essay appeared in print, she wrote to Mary Parker, paraphrasing herself when she insisted that even undeserved flattery, in careful hands, "acts as a stimulus." Judith Stevens to Miss Mary Parker of Portsmouth, 8 September 1784, Letter Book 2: 268.

6. See, for example, Bruce Burgett, *Sentimental Bodies: Sex, Gender, and Citizenship in the Early Republic* (Princeton, N.J.: Princeton University Press, 1998), 46; Mary Kelley, "The Sentimentalists: Promise and Betrayal in the Home," *Signs* 4 (1979): 438; Poovey, *The Proper Lady*, 57; Shuffelton, "In Different Voices," 230, 291; Warner, *Letters of the Republic*, xiii; Edward Watts, *Writing and Postcolonialism in the Early Republic* (Charlottesville: University of Virginia Press, 1998), 53.

Chapter 5. "Sweet Peace"

1. Judith Stevens to Maria Sargent, 15 October 1783, Letter Book 2: 175.

2. Judith Stevens to Madam Walker, 16 December 1784, 15 January, 18 April 1785, Letter Book 2: 306–7, 314–15, 327. Heterosocial reading groups were an excellent means by which women like Judith Stevens could cultivate and display their intellectual ability before their peers. See Kelly, *In the New England Fashion*, 197.

3. Judith Stevens to John Murray, 9 November 1781, Letter Book 1: 362–63; to Mrs. Barrell of Old York, 31 January, 18 May 1784, to John Murray, 18 June 1784, to Mrs. Barrell of Old York, 8 October 1784, to Winthrop Sargent, 13 January 1785, Letter Book 2: 195, 228, 244–45, 313.

4. Ironically, if she was less likely to engage in "productive" household manufacturing

and purchased more goods than her mother would have done, some historians argue that she actually lost a certain authority in the process. She was a mere consumer, who spent money that was often hard to come by, rather than producing goods. This idea reinforced if it did not create the idea that women were extravagant and luxury-loving creatures who could not be trusted. See Boydston, *Home and Work*, 35, 41–43; Smith, "Food Rioters and the American Revolution," 12.

5. Judith Stevens to Maria Sargent, 24 March 1781, to John Murray, 4 October, 9 November 1781, Letter Book 1: 324, 351–52, 362; Judith Stevens to Mrs. Barrell of Old York, 8 October 1784, to Miss Mary Parker of Portsmouth, 10 February, 1785, Letter Book 2: 284, 318–19; to Miss Mary Sargent Allen, 15 September 1785, Letter Book 3: 13; Murray, "The Sick Domestic," "Dissimulation again," Repository, 53, 57; Murray, "Petulant lines complaining of being absorbed in family cares occasioned by several additions to my household among whom were those whom I found it impossible to please," Poetry 1: 269–70. For the burdens of housework in the late eighteenth century, see Nylander, *Our Own Snug Fireside*, 50, 105, 117, 131, 150; Shammas, *The Pre-Industrial Consumer*, 62; Laurel Thatcher Ulrich, *A Midwife's Tale: The Life of Martha Ballard, Based on Her Diary, 1785–1812* (New York: Random House, 1990); Boydston, *Home and Work*, 17–18; Carroll Smith-Rosenberg, "Hearing Women's Words: A Feminist Reconstruction of History," in Smith-Rosenberg, *Disorderly Conduct*, 11–52.

6. Judith Stevens to Miss Mary Parker of Portsmouth, 8 September 1784, to Winthrop Sargent, 5 February 1785, Letter Book 2: 270, 316–17.

7. Judith Stevens to Winthrop Sargent, 15 July, 25 July, 16 October, 8 November 1784, Letter Book 2: 251–52, 287, 293; to Winthrop Sargent, 15 March 1786, Letter Book 3: 77; Kann, *Republic of Men*, 69–71; Burstein, *Sentimental Democracy*, 121, 123; John Resch, *Suffering Soldiers: Revolutionary War Veterans, Moral Sentiment, and Political Culture in the Early Republic* (Amherst: University of Massachusetts Press, 1999), 4, 71. Winthrop's fellow officers agreed that they suffered unfairly. As George Turner put it, when "public Faith and Gratitude are not in the Government, we cannot expect Integrity in its Citizens." George Turner to Winthrop Sargent, 29 November 1787, Sargent Papers, Correspondence, vol. 1.

8. Wood *Radicalism*, 241; Kann, *Republic of Men*, 71; Judith Stevens to Winthrop Sargent, 29 January, 18 February, 1784, Letter Book 2: 187, 199–200; Murray, "On reading the institution of the Cincinnati, January 28, 1784," Poetry 3: 181–91. See also "On being told that the Citizens of Columbia were opposing themselves to her Warriors," Poetry 1: 270–71.

9. Judith Stevens to Winthrop Sargent, 18 February, 28 February, 28 April 1784, Letter Book 2: 196–99, 201–2, 214.

10. Murray, "Lines Occasioned by reflecting upon the Ingratitude of America to her Soldiery, 1784," Poetry 2: 234–63.

11. Judith Stevens to Winthrop Sargent, 18 February, 13 April 1784, Letter Book 2: 196, 200, 208.

12. *Gentleman and Lady's Town and Country Magazine*, May 1784, 3–4; Judith Stevens to Mrs. Barrell of Old York, 18 May 1784, to Mr. Parker, 5 September 1784, Letter Book 2: 228, 266–67.

13. Constantia, "Desultory Thoughts . . . ," *Gentleman and Lady's Town and Country Magazine*, October 1784, 251–53.

14. Judith Stevens to Mrs. Barrell of Old York, 8 October 1784, Letter Book 2: 286.

15. Schiff, "Objects of Speculation," 219–21; Murray, "Reverence Thy Self," 356; Constantia, "Desultory Thoughts," *Gentleman and Lady's Town and Country Magazine* (May 1784), 253.

16. Judith Stevens to Winthrop Sargent, 25 October 1784, to Mr. _____ of _____, 31 March 1785, Letter Book 2: 290, 323; to Mrs. Barrell of Old York, 2 September 1786, Letter Book 3: 142.

17. Kann, *Republic of Men*, 7–8, 52–57, 79–83; Rotundo, *American Manhood*, 59, 112; Thomas A. Foster, *Sex and the Eighteenth-Century Man: Massachusetts and the History of Sexuality in America* (Boston: Beacon Press, 2006), chaps. 1, 5; Samuel B. Webb to Winthrop Sargent, 26 August 1787, Sargent Papers, Correspondence, vol. 1. In a sense, men *needed* women if they were to earn the respect of their community, if people were to view them as adults. It would not be surprising if some men, at least, did not resent women under such circumstances. See Lockridge, "Colonial Self-Fashioning," passim.

18. Judith Stevens to Winthrop Sargent, 15 November, 15 December, 31 December 1782, 28 January, 9 March 1783, 5 April 1783, Letter Book 2: 89, 91–92, 100, 119–20, 135–36.

19. For the suffering of Gloucester's merchant community at war's end, see Babson, *Gloucester*, 399–401, 466. For changing relationships between fathers and sons see Coontz, *The Social Origins of Private Life*, 126–27; Rotundo, *American Manhood*, 16–17.

20. E. Anthony Rotundo, "Learning About Manhood: Gender Ideals and the Middle-Class Family in Nineteenth-Century America," in J. A. Mangan and James Walvin, *Manliness and Morality* (New York: St. Martin's Press, 1987), 36–39; Rotundo, "Body and Soul," 24–25; Rotundo, *American Manhood*, 3, 12–13, 15; Michael S. Kimmel, *Manhood in America: A Cultural History* (New York: Free Press, 1996), 19, 26.

21. Judith Stevens to Winthrop Sargent, 18 April 1783, 13, 28 April 1784, to Maria Sargent, 15 June 1784, to John Murray, 18 June 1784, to Winthrop Sargent, 25 July, 16 October 1784, 28 March 1785, Letter Book 2: 141, 208–9, 212, 238, 246, 252, 288, 322. Winthrop was probably even more bitter when he saw that some of the officers who had served beside him in the war—William Cooper, for instance, or Henry Knox—were, indeed, moving up in the world. They were not members of the colonial elite. Yet they were succeeding where he—who was certainly more worthy by any traditional yardstick—was failing. See Alan Taylor, "From Fathers to Friends of the People: Political Personae in the Early Republic," in Doron Ben-Atar and Barbara B. Oberg, *Federalists Reconsidered* (Charlottesville: University of Virginia Press, 1998), 225.

22. See, for instance, Joy Day Buel and Richard Buel, Jr., *The Way of Duty: A Woman and Her Family in Revolutionary America* (New York: Norton, 1984), 226–35; Alfred F. Young, *Masquerade: The Life and Times of Deborah Sampson, Continental Soldier* (New York: Vintage, 2004), 246–47.

23. B. H. Pershing, "Winthrop Sargent" (Ph.D. dissertation, University of Chicago, 1934), 4, 5; Judith Stevens to Winthrop Sargent, [?] October 1769, Letter Book 1: 5; to Winthrop Sargent, 15 June 1782, 25 April 1783, Letter Book 2: 17, 141–42; to Winthrop Sargent, 31 August 1787, Letter Book 3: 223; Esther Ellery to Winthrop Sargent, 27 December 1788, Sargent Murray Gilman Hough Papers. For the tendency of military officers to dabble in land speculation, see R. L. Cayton, "Radicals in the 'Western World': The Federalist Conquest of Trans-Appalachian North America," in Ben-Atar and Oberg, eds., *Federalists Reconsidered*, 79.

24. Judith Stevens to Winthrop Sargent, 3 July 1786, Letter Book 3: 111; Pershing,

"Winthrop Sargent," 4–5, 22, 24; Burstein, *Sentimental Democracy* 45; Taylor, "From Fathers to Friends of the People," 231; Sargent, *Epes Sargent of Gloucester*, 58; Charles Sprague Sargent, "Winthrop Sargent," 233; Pleasants, *Winthrop Sargent*, 10, 11, 15; Cayton, "Radicals in the 'Western World,'" 80–81; Manasseh Cutler to Winthrop Sargent, 6 October 1786, Sargent Papers Correspondence, vol. 1.

25. Judith Stevens to John Murray, 12 September 1775, Letter Book 1: 22–23; to Winthrop Sargent, 28 June, 31 August 1787, to Maria Sargent, 6 September 1787, to Winthrop Sargent, 1 May 1788, Letter Book 3: 209, 222, 229, 304; Bodle, "Soldiers in Love," 219, 228; Resch, *Suffering Soldiers*, 4, 71; Kann, *Republic of Men*, 75; Frances Paul Prucha, *Sword of the Republic: The U.S. Army on the Frontier, 1783–1846* (Lincoln: University of Nebraska Press, 1969), 5–6, 9; Pleasants, *Winthrop Sargent*, 10–11; Burstein, *Sentimental Democracy*, 123. See also Esther Ellery to Winthrop Sargent, 27 December 1788, Sargent Murray Gilman Hough Papers.

26. Judith Stevens to John Murray, 17 May 1784, Letter Book 2: 223–24.

27. Judith Stevens to Winthrop Sargent, 31 July 1783, 8 June 1785, Letter Book 2: 164, 334; to Madam Walker, 5 May 1786, to Winthrop Sargent, 15 May 1786, to John Murray, 27 May 1786, to Doctor Potter of Wallingford, 8 April 1787, Letter Book 3: 82–84, 202; Gelles, *Portia*, 123–25; Zboray, *A Fictive People*, 112; Shields, *Civil Tongues*, 319–20.

28. Judith Stevens to Winthrop Sargent, 1 December 1779, Letter Book 1: 262; Estate of Epes Sargent, Jr., no. 24611, vol. 353: 383, 447–49, vol. 355: 263–64; vol. 356: 158–63, vol. 359: 406–9; Babson, *Gloucester*, 267.

29. Judith Stevens to Mrs. Walker, 8 October, 18 December 1783, to Winthrop Sargent, 29 January 1784, Letter Book 2: 171, 183, 186.

30. John Stevens, "Address to Creditors," Letter Book 3: 37; Babson, *Gloucester*, 396–401, 409–13; Judith Stevens to Mrs. Walker, 8 October 1783, Letter Book 2: 171.

31. Judith Stevens to Winthrop Sargent, 28 January 1783, to Daniel Sargent, 18 March 1783, to Winthrop Sargent, 28 June 1783, to Captain _____, 18 August 1783, to Mrs. N____ of Philadelphia, 18 April 1785, Letter Book 2: 100, 125, 162, 166–67, 330. See Ulrich, *Good Wives*, 36–50 for the classic formulation of the "deputy husband." See also, Rotundo, *American Manhood*, 135; Kelly, *In the New England Fashion*, 36; Lisa Waciega, "A 'Man of Business': The Widow of Means in Southeastern Pennsylvania, 1750–1850," *William and Mary Quarterly* 3rd ser. 44 (1987): 40–64; Susan Branson, "Women and the Family Economy in the Early Republic: The Case of Elizabeth Meredith," *Journal of the Early Republic* 18 (1996): 47–71 for evidence that women were often knowledgeable about and involved in their own or their husband's business affairs.

32. Judith Stevens to Winthrop Sargent, 8 December 1783, 7 January 1784, Letter Book 2: 179, 184; to D. Rogers of Gloucester, 5 March 1786, Letter Book 3: 72.

33. Judith Stevens to Noah Parker, 15 December 1783, to Madam Walker, 18 December 1783, to Winthrop Sargent, 29 January 1784, to Miss Goldthwait, 16 June 1784, Letter Book 2: 180–81, 183, 186, 243. See also Murray, "To Edwin inclosing some grey hairs which I had unexpectedly discovered—1784," Poetry 3: 237.

34. Judith Stevens to John Murray, 25, 31 January, 1786, to Mr. D. Rogers of Gloucester, 5 March 1786, to Mrs. Gardiner, 5 March 1786, Letter Book 3: 51, 57, 72, 74; Stevens, "Address to Creditors," Letter Book 3: 38.

35. Judith Stevens to John Murray, 13 September 1784, to Winthrop Sargent, 25 September 1784, to John Murray, 2 June 1785, Letter Book 2: 276, 280, 334.

36. Judith Stevens to Maria Sargent, 8 May 1785, to John Murray, 17 June, 7 July 1785, Letter Book 2: 331–32, 336, 356–57. The mall was probably located on the eastern edge of Boston Commons. Kasraie, "Left to 'affectionate partiality,'" 337n. For evidence that Boston's 1783 celebration of independence was in the hands of conservatives, who made sure that all the events were respectable, orderly, and hierarchical, see Alfred Young, *The Shoemaker and the Tea Party* (Boston: Beacon Press, 1999), 110–12.

37. Judith Stevens to Winthrop Sargent, 28 November 1785, to Miss Mary Parker of Portsmouth, 5 December 1785, to Madam Walker, 5 December 1785, to Winthrop Sargent, 26 December 1785, Letter Book 3: 27–30, 33; Files of the Court of Common Pleas, Essex Square Court House, Salem, Massachusetts, vol. 10: 368, 379, 391, 536.

38. Judith Stevens to Winthrop Sargent, 3, 5 January 1786, to Mr. Murray, 11, 14, 22 January 1786, to Madam Walker, 31 January 1786, to D. Rogers of Gloucester, 5 March 1786, Letter Book 3: 35–36, 39, 41, 49, 54, 72. Husbands had to secure their wives' written permission before they alienated property that might affect a wife's dower. In many states, women were questioned publically, so that the courts could be sure that a woman gave her permission without coercion. She could not actually stop her husband from selling his or their land. But if he died she could sue to receive her portion of this property. Consequently, most buyers were reluctant to proceed without a wife's written permission. In Massachusetts, the law did not recognize the possibility of fraud or force, and so women could sign deeds at home. In Judith's case, it is clear that she understood her husband's circumstances and gave her permission willingly. See Marylynn Salmon, *Women and the Law of Property in Early America* (Chapel Hill: University of North Carolina Press, 1986), 16, 22–24.

39. Judith Stevens to Winthrop Sargent, 5 January 1786, to John Murray, 14, 20, 21, 22 January 1786, Letter Book 3: 36, 41–42, 45, 49; Stevens, "Address to Creditors," Letter Book 3: 37–38. Given John's aversion to writing, it is likely that Judith composed the piece herself, even though she was not at all confident that it would succeed. Judith Stevens to Winthrop Sargent, 5 March 1786, Letter Book 3: 70.

40. Judith Stevens to John Murray, 22 January 1786, to Winthrop Sargent, 28 February 1786, to John Murray, 2 August 1788, Letter Book 3: 49, 68, 341.

41. See Wood, *Radicalism*, 140; Peter J. Coleman, *Debtors and Creditors in America: Insolvency, Imprisonment for Debt, and Bankruptcy, 1607–1900* (Madison: State Historical Society of Wisconsin, 1974), 255–57, 259–60; Ditz, "Secret Selves, Credible Personas," 220–21, 233; Smith-Rosenberg, "Black Gothic: The Shadowy Origins of the American Bourgeoisie," in St. George, *Possible Pasts*, 245. At least his creditors did not demand that John be confined to jail.

42. Judith Stevens to John Murray, 31 January, 12, 18, 19 February 1786, Letter Book 3: 57, 61, 63–64.

43. Judith Stevens to Judith Sargent, 1 January 1786, to John Murray, 14, 24–26 January 1786, to Madam Walker, 31 January 1786, to Winthrop Sargent, 15 February 1786, Letter Book 3: 34, 40, 50–54, 62.

44. See Crane, "Dependence in the Era of Independence," 259–64; MaryLynn Salmon, "Republican Sentiment, Economic Change and the Property Rights of Women in American Law," in Hoffman and Albert, eds., *Women in the Age of the American Revolution*, 449, 451; Salmon, *Women and the Law of Property*, xv–xvii, 7–8, 14–15, 122–23; Salmon, "'Life, Liberty, and Dower': The Legal Status of Women After the American

Revolution," in Carol R. Berkin and Clara M. Lovett, eds., *Women, War, and Revolution* (New York: Holmes and Meier, 1980), 86–88; Joan R. Gunderson and Gwen Victor Gampel, "Married Women's Legal Status in Eighteenth-Century New York and Virginia," *William and Mary Quarterly* 3rd ser. 39 (January 1982): 130–33; Boydston, *Home and Work*, 8, 11, 25, 28; Branson, "Women and the Family in the Economy," 48; Pateman, *The Sexual Contract*, 31; D. Kelly Weisberg, ed., *Women and the Law: The Social Historical Perspective*, vol. 2, *Property, Family, and the Legal Profession* (Cambridge, Mass.: Schenkman Press, 1982), 95; Kerber, *Women of the Republic*, 139, 153; Kerber, "A Constitutional Right," 21–23.

45. Judith Stevens to Maria Sargent, 15 June 1784, Letter Book 2: 237; to Judith Sargent, 1 January 1786, to Winthrop Sargent, 5 January 1786, Letter Book 3: 34, 36; Lewis, "The Republican Wife," 711–12; Gloria L. Main, "Widows in Rural Massachusetts on the Eve of the Revolution," in Hoffman and Albert, eds., *Women in the Age of the American Revolution*, 68, 69.

46. Judith Stevens to John Murray, 12 September 1775, Letter Book 1: 23; to Winthrop Sargent, 29 January 1784, to Aunt Olive, 1 May 1784, to Madam Walker, 8 June 1784, to Maria Sargent, 15 June 1784, Letter Book 2: 187–88, 217, 234, 236. See Boydston, *Home and Work*, 156; Cynthia Kierner, "'The Dark and Dense Cloud Perpetually Lowering over us': The Decline of the Gentry in Post-Revolutionary Virginia," *Journal of the Early Republic* 20 (2000): 209; Claudia Goldin, "The Economic Status of Women in the Early Republic: Quantitative Evidence," *Journal of Interdisciplinary History* 16 (1986): 396–97. Aunt Allen remained a boarder in the Stevens house for well over a year. The pittance she donated toward her own upkeep did not, in Judith's mind, compensate for the burden she represented. Judith Stevens to Miss Goldthwait, 16 June 1784, Letter Book 2: 242.

47. Judith Stevens to Winthrop Sargent, 15 May 1783, to Maria Sargent, 15 October 1783, 15 June 1784, Letter Book 2: 143–44, 175, 237; to Judith Sargent, 1 January 1786, Letter Book 3: 34–35. See Phyllis Whitman Hunter, *Purchasing Identity in the Atlantic World: Massachusetts Merchants, 1670–1780* (Ithaca, N.Y.: Cornell University Press, 2001), 88–90, 98–99. Hunter argues that this emphasis on fashion declined with the Revolution. Judith's letters suggest that this was not always the case.

48. Judith Stevens to Madam Walker, 9 September 1784, Letter Book 2: 273; See Armstrong, *Desire and Domestic Fiction*, 76, 77; Isenberg, *Sex and Citizenship*, 49; Kelly, *In the New England Fashion*, 183, 219, 229; Nylander, *Our Own Snug Fireside*, 152–54; Smith-Rosenberg, "'Domesticating 'Virtue,'" 165–66.

49. Judith Stevens to Mr. ____, 31 January 1786, to Winthrop Sargent, 6 February 1786, to John Murray, 20 February 1786, to D. Rogers of Gloucester, 5 March 1786, Letter Book 3: 55, 60–61, 64, 72; Kowaleski-Wallace, *Consuming Subjects*, 2–9. For other examples of elite women who were devastated by the gap between their expectations and their postwar reality, see Joann Gillespie, "Filiopietism," *Early American Literature* 29 (1994): 147, 156; Kierner, "'The Dark and Dense Cloud,'" 195, 199; Sarah Eve Edward, in Harris, ed., *Writings*, 49. As Nancy Armstrong points out, in this era many observers were beginning to argue that genteel women were especially able to curb both their own desires, and the desires of their husbands. They were not merely inferior men, but moral instructors. Judith subscribed to this view, even when she was not always able to achieve it. See Armstrong, "The Rise of the Domestic Women," 122, 129–30.

50. Judith Stevens to Winthrop Sargent, 6 February 1786, to Mrs. Gardiner, 5 March 1786, to Maria Sargent, 8 April 17[8]6, Letter Book 3: 61, 74, 78–79.

51. Judith Stevens to Mr. ____, 31 January 1786, to Mr. Joseph Russell, 31 January 1786, to John Murray, 18 February 1786, to Mr. D. Rogers of Gloucester, 5 March 1786, to Winthrop Sargent, 15, 28 March 1786, Letter Book 3: 55, 58, 63, 71, 76–77.

52. Judith Stevens to Mr. Joseph Russell, 31 January 1786, to Winthrop Sargent, 31 January 1786, to Mr. Pierce of Gloucester, 6 March 1786, to Winthrop Sargent, 15 March 1786, Letter Book 3: 58–59, 75–76.

53. Kann, *Republic of Men*, 2, 6; Boydston, *Home and Work*, 44; Rotundo, *American Manhood*, 2, 3; Foster, *Sex and the Eighteenth-Century Man*, 33.

54. Judith Stevens to Winthrop Sargent, 6 Feburary 1786, Letter Book 3: 60. See Toby L. Ditz, "Shipwrecked; or, Masculinity Imperiled: Mercantile Representations of Failure and the Gendered Self in Eighteenth-Century Philadelphia," *Journal of American History* 81 (1994): 51–80; Wood, *Radicalism*, 140; Ruth Wallis Herndon, "The Domestic Cost of Seafaring: Town Leaders and Seamen's Families in Eighteenth-Century Rhode Island," in Creighton and Norling, eds., *Iron Men*, 57, 61, 64.

55. Judith Stevens to Winthrop Sargent, 21 April 1786, to Madam Walker, 5 May 1786, Letter Book 3: 81–82.

56. Field, *Constantia*, 22; Judith Stevens to Madam Walker, 5 May 1786, to Winthrop Sargent, 15 May 1786, to John Murray, 27 May 1786, Letter Book 3: 82–84.

57. Judith Stevens to Winthrop Sargent, 8, 15 June 1786, to Winthrop Sargent, Sr., 23 June 1786, to my Aunt E____ S____, 26 June 1786, to Winthrop Sargent, 18 July 1786, Letter Book 3: 91, 93, 96–98, 106, 118.

58. Judith Stevens to Winthrop Sargent, Sr., 23 June 1786, to Fitz William Sargent, 24 June 1786, to Winthrop Sargent, 25 June 1786, to Judith Sargent, 5 July 1786, Letter Book 3: 98, 101–2, 107–8, 115; Stevens, Journal, 18, 19 October 1786, Letter Book 3: 169. One sign that Judith's spirits had lifted was her desire to write letters virtually every day.

59. Judith Stevens to Winthrop Sargent, Sr., 23 June 1786, to Judith Sargent, 30 July 1786, to Winthrop Sargent, Sr., 30 July 1786, to Winthrop Sargent, 5 August 1786, Letter Book 3: 98, 127–28, 130.

60. Judith Stevens to Mrs. Walker, 18 August 1785, to Mrs. Barrell of Old York, 2 September 1786, to Mrs. Walker, 25 October 1786, Letter Book 3: 6, 141, 175.

61. Judith Stevens to Winthrop Sargent, 2 January 1787, Letter Book 3: 192.

62. Judith Stevens to Winthrop Sargent, 15 January 1787, Letter Book 3: 193; Main, "Widows in Rural Massachusetts on the Eve of the Revolution," 71, 73.

63. Judith Stevens to Madam Walker, 13 April 1787, to Winthrop Sargent, 5 May 1787, Letter Book 3: 203, 205.

64. Judith Stevens to Winthrop Sargent, 5 May 1787, Letter Book 3: 205.

65. Judith Stevens to Madam Barrell of Old York, 12 September 1787, Letter Book 3: 230; Murray, "On being inform'd that a very happy couple had dwindled into mere Man and Wife," 1782, Poetry 3: 164–65. See Bridget Hill, ed., *Eighteenth-Century Women: An Anthology* (London: Allen and Unwin, 1984), 134; Mary Beth Norton, "Reflections on Women in the Age of the American Revolution," in Hoffman and Albert, eds., *Women in the Age of the American Revolution*, 487; Daniel Scott Smith, "Inheritance and the Social History of Early American Women," in Hoffman and Albert, eds., *Women in the Age of the American Revolution*, 55–57; Alexander Keyssar, "Widowhood in Eighteenth-Century Massachusetts: A Problem in the History of the Family," *Perspectives in American History* 8 (1974): 88–98.

66. Judith Stevens to Mrs. L. S., 5 June 1780, Letter Book 1: 286; to Mrs. Gardiner, 15 December 1787, Letter Book 3: 251; Murray, "Sentiments," Repository, 66; Crane, *Ebb Tide*, 116; Gunderson, "Independence," 73. For examples of her determination throughout her life to help women left destitute by the death of their husbands, see JSM to Esther Ellery, 24 March 1800, to Miss N____, 11 September, 3 November 1800, Letter Book 11: 153–56, 191, 220; to Anna Sargent, 22 September 1804, Letter Book 12: 951.

67. Judith Stevens to Winthrop Sargent, 15 February 1786, Letter Book 3: 62. See Crane, *Ebb Tide*, 145; Smith, "Inheritance and the Social History of Early American Women," 64–65; Stanley Katz, "Republicanism and the Law of Inheritance in the American Revolution," *Michigan Law Review* 76 (1977): 3, 7, 12–17, 25; Pauline Maier, "The Transforming Impact of Independence Reaffirmed: 1776 and the Definition of American Social Structure," in James Henretta, Michael Kammen, and Stanley Katz, eds., *The Transformation of Early American History* (New York: Knopf, 1991), 194–217.

68. See Richard H. Chused, "Married Women's Property and Inheritance by Widows in Massachusetts: A Study of Wills Probated between 1800 and 1850," *Berkeley Women's Law Journal* 2 (1986): 42, 42n; Keyssar, "Widowhood in Eighteenth-Century Massachusetts," 109–10; Salmon, *Women and the Law of Property*, 141–44; Main, "Widows in Rural Massachusetts," 79, 85–89; Carole Shammas, "Early American Women and Control over Capital," in Hoffman and Albert, eds., *Women in the Age of the American Revolution*, 137–44.

69. Norton, "The Evolution of White Women's Experience," 605; Chused, "Married Women's Property," 42, 49; Crane, *Ebb Tide*, 158, 172; Keyssar, "Widowhood in Eighteenth-Century Massachusetts," 101; Salmon, *Women and the Law of Property*, 82, 133, 143; Main, "Widows in Rural Massachusetts," 73.

70. Judith Stevens to Winthrop Sargent, 28 June, 13 August 1787, to Judith Sargent, 23 October 1787, to Winthrop Sargent, Sr., 29 October 1787, to Mrs. Gardiner, 6 November, 15 December 1787, Letter Book 3: 209, 210, 213, 239, 241, 242, 251; Esther Ellery to Winthrop Sargent, 27 December 1788, Sargent Murray Gilman Hough Papers, Box 1.

71. Judith Stevens to Winthrop Sargent, 31 July, 1785, Letter Book 2: 363; to Judith Sargent, 1 January 1786, to Winthrop Sargent, 5 March 1786, to Mrs. Barrell of Old York, 12 September 1787, JSM to Winthrop Sargent, 17 January 1788, Letter Book 3: 34–35, 70, 231, 257. She was clearly flouting tradition when she refused to move in with her parents. Brown, *Knowledge Is Power*, 176–79; Chambers-Schiller, *Liberty, a Better Husband*, 107–13.

72. Just why she thought she would get the entire house is unclear. The law clearly gave her only one-third for her own use. Perhaps, because her father had title to the house, she thought he would ignore legalities and give the entire property to her. Her father was in this case, as he had been when she begged for a better education, a slave to custom.

73. Judith Stevens to Mrs. Barrell of Old York, 12 September 1787, to Winthrop Sargent, 17 January 1788, Letter Book 3: 231, 257–58; Daniel Scott Smith, "Female Householding in Late Eighteenth-Century America and the Problem of Poverty," *Journal of Social History* 28 (1994): 86.

74. Judith Stevens to Madam Walker, 2 June 1786, to John Murray, 2 August 1788, to Winthrop Sargent, 22 September 1788, Letter Book 3: 89, 341, 345.

75. JSM to [?], 10 September 1807, Letter Book 14: 74; Estate of John Stevens, no. 26364, vol. 360, 453.

76. Judith Stevens to Mrs. Wheat of New London, 17 September 1786, to Mrs. Barrell of Old York, 12 September 1787, to Winthrop Sargent, 17 January 1788, Letter Book 3: 150, 231, 258–59. See Smith, "Female Householding," 86, 97–98; Goldin, "The Economic Status of Women in the Early Republic," 396–97, 400, 404; Kierner, "'The Dark and Dense Cloud,'" 211; Smith, "Inheritance," 61; Kerber, *Women of the Republic*, 153–54; Cott, *The Bonds of Womanhood*, 42. See *The Gleaner*, 730–31 for her tale of the woman from St. Sebastian who supported herself and her daughters, avoided dependence, and did not "unsex" herself in the process. To be sure there *were* women who were actively involved in business affairs, no matter what the pious platitudes of the age indicated. Still, this was becoming rarer with each passing year. See Branson, "Women and the Family Economy," 47–71; Crane, *Ebb Tide*, 129–33.

Chapter 6. A Belle Passion

1. Judith Stevens to Maria Sargent, 21 March 1788, Letter Book 3: 282; Chambers-Schiller, *Liberty, a Better Husband*, 33.

2. Marini, *Radical Sects of Revolutionary New England*, 109; Record Book of the Free and Independent Church of Christ, 35–36; Gloucester Church Records, 1779–1838, 139.

3. Hatch, *The Sacred Cause of Liberty*, 99, 110–16; William E. Nelson, *Americanization of the Common Law: The Impact of Legal Change on Massachusetts Society, 1760–1830* (Cambridge, Mass.: Harvard University Press, 1975), 104–5; Eddy, *Universalism in Gloucester*, 22; John D. Cushing, "Notes on Disestablishment in Massachusetts, 1780–1833," *William and Mary Quarterly* 3rd ser. 16 (1969): 171, 173; Hughes, "Early New England Universalism," 101; Breen and Hall, "Structuring Provincial Imagination," 424. See Nathan O. Hatch, "In Pursuit of Religious Freedom: Church, State, and People in the New Republic," in Greene, ed., *The American Revolution*, 395, for the democratic implications of sectarianism in the post-Revolutionary era. See Richard Shiels, "The Feminization of American Congregationalism, 1730–1835," *American Quarterly* 33 (1981): 61 and Brekus, *Strangest Pilgrims*, 14, for a discussion of the way separation of church and state threatened the position, and even the identity, of Congregational men in particular. So concerned were most people in Massachusetts about the implications of Universalism that they argued that Universalists (like women) should not be allowed to sit on juries or to testify in court. Cassara, *Universalism in America*, 32.

4. Stephen A. Marini, "Religion, Politics, and Ratification," in Hoffman and Albert, eds., *Religion in a Revolutionary Age*, 194; "An Answer to a Piece Entitled 'An Appeal to the Impartial Publick,' by an Association Calling themselves Christian Independents, in Gloucester," in Eddy, *Universalism in Gloucester*, 171, 174–75.

5. Judith Stevens to John Murray, [20?] October 1785, Letter Book 3: 24–25; Cushing, "Notes on Disestablishment," 173–74; [Epes Sargent,] "An Appeal to the Impartial Publick by the Society of Christian Independents, Congregating in Gloucester," in Eddy, *Universalism in Gloucester*, 141; "An Answer to a Piece," 174–76.

6. Judith Stevens to Mrs. Gardiner, 4 April 1788, Letter Book 3: 290. The First Parish Church described the series of events quite differently. It claimed that the Universalists

wanted a test case and actually asked the authorities to tax them. It also claimed that it tried to return some money to the Universalists because the auction brought in more than the members owed. But the Universalists refused the offer, preferring to call the entire affair "oppression" and "injury." "An Answer to a Piece," 166–67.

7. Murray, *Life*, 328–29; Eddy, *Universalism in Gloucester*, 23; Cushing, "Notes on Disestablishment," 174.

8. Judith Stevens to John Murray, 25 June 1785, to Mr. Right, a Native of Copenhagen, 1 July 1785, Letter Book 2: 344, 349–50; Williams, "American Universalism," 28; Murray, *Life*, 331; Cushing, "Notes on Disestablishment," 176.

9. Judith Stevens to Miss Goldthwait, 6 June 1777, Letter Book 1: 64–65; to Mrs. Barrell of Old York, 8 October 1784, Letter Book 2: 285; Cushing, "Notes on Disestablishment," 176; Murray, *Life*, 326; "An Appeal to the Impartial Publick," 138–44; Carpenter, "John Murray and the Rise of Liberal Religion," 45.

10. Judith Stevens to John Murray, 15 August 1785, Letter Book 3: 4; *Catechism*, v.

11. Cushing, "Notes on Disestablishment," 179, 180; Eddy, *Universalism in Gloucester*, 26, 27; Murray, *Life*, 335–36; Judith Stevens to Mr. Right, a Native of Copenhagen, 1 July 1785, Letter Book 2: 349; to Winthrop Sargent, Sr., 21 July 1786, to Mrs. Pilgrim of London, [?] August 1787, Letter Book 3: 123, 217. Clearly, the Massachusetts Universalists in general—and Judith in particular—saw no distinction between their religious beliefs and the ideals of the Enlightenment, as they spearheaded the drive for religious equality in the state throughout the 1780s. Bloch, "Religion, Literary Sentimentalism, and Popular Revolutionary Ideology," 323–25, Jon Butler, "Coercion, Miracle, Reason: Rethinking the American Religious Experience in the Revolutionary Age," in Hoffman and Albert, eds., *Religion in a Revolutionary Age*, 28–29.

12. Murray, *Life*, 327–28; Cushing, "Notes on Disestablishment," 180–81; Eddy, *Universalism in Gloucester*, 28–29; Judith Stevens to John Murray, 22 January 1788, to the Honorable J. Sullivan, esq. of Boston [n.d.], Letter Book 3: 263, 274–75.

13. Judith Stevens to Mr. Russell of Boston, 25 February 1788, to the Honorable Thomas Dawes, Esq., 2 April 1788, to Mr. Dawes, [n.d.], Letter Book 3: 277, 286, Appendix I: 367.

14. Judith Stevens to John Murray, 15 January 1788, Letter Book 3: 254.

15. Judith Stevens to John Murray, 15, January 1788, to Mr. Russell of Boston, 18 January 1788, to John Murray, 21, 22 January 1788, Letter Book 3: 256, 260, 263–64.

16. Judith Stevens to Mrs. Wheat of New London, 17 September 1786, to John Murray, 11 November 1786, 16 October 1787, to Maria Sargent, 15 April 1788, Letter Book 3: 150, 178, 236, 294. See Burr, *Journal*, 15, for an example of another woman who was always on guard for fear of the malicious gossips who watched her every move.

17. Murray, "Detraction," Repository, 357–58; Judith Stevens to Winthrop Sargent, 18 April 1788, Letter Book 3: 299. See Spacks, *Gossip*, 5–7, 128, 159–60.

18. Unattached women who took in male boarders were always suspect. People could not help but wonder if they were promiscuous or immoral. If John Murray was a nonpaying guest in Judith's home, his situation may well have seemed especially irregular. See Kierner, " 'The Dark and Dense Cloud,' " 209.

19. Judith Stevens to Mr. Russell, 3 April 1788, to Maria Sargent, 15 April 1788, to Mrs. Pilgrim of England, 31 July 1788, Letter Book 3: 288, 294, 338. See also JSM to Mrs. Barrell of Old York, 1 November 1793, Letter Book 8: 165.

20. Judith Stevens to Maria Sargent, 15 April 1788, Letter Book 3: 294–95.

21. Judith Stevens to John Murray, 22 January 8 May 1788, Letter Book 3: 264, 309.

22. Judith Stevens to Winthrop Sargent, 18 April 1788, Letter Book 3: 299. The main offender was probably her cousin Catherine Goldthwait Gardiner. The two had become estranged for religious reasons.

23. Judith Stevens to Winthrop Sargent, 11 August 1787, 21 February, 18 April, 8 July 1788, Letter Book 3: 211, 269–70, 300, 328–29; Grossberg, *Governing the Hearth*, 21.

24. Judith Stevens to Maria Sargent, 15 April 1788, Letter Book 3: 294.

25. Judith Stevens to Mr. Parker, 5 October 1777, Letter Book 1: 76; to Epes Sargent, 6 June 1783, Letter Book 2: 150; Fliegelman, *Prodigals and Pilgrims*, 41; Lebsock, *Free Women of Petersburg*, 53; "Comparison Between the Sexes," *Gentleman's and Lady's Town and Country Magazine*, September 1787, 200–201. For evidence that most people were beginning to demand more than friendship in their marriages, see Rothman, *Hands and Hearts*, 36, 37.

26. Judith Stevens to John Murray, 16 August 1779, Letter Book 1: 206; Journal of trip to Portsmouth and Old York, 12 October 1786, Letter Book 3: 164; JSM to Miss Pilgrim of Plymouth, Old England, 20 May 1789, to John Murray, 10 June 1789, Letter Book 4: 36, 45; to Mr. Holderness of Wexford, Ireland, 11 August 1798, Letter Book 10: 266; "Unison of Sentiment," Murray, Repository, 12; Murray, "Upon Love—1779," Poetry 3: 35; Murray, Life, 407. See also "On Connubial Bliss," *Gentleman's and Lady's Town and Country Magazine*, July 1784, 103.

27. Barnes, *States of Sympathy*, 2–3; Burstein, *Sentimental Democracy*, 20–21; Cohen, "Mercy Otis Warren," 482; Karen A. Wyler, "'The Fruit of Unlawful Embraces,': Sexual Transgression and Madness in Early American Sentimental Fiction," in Smith, ed., *Sex and Sexuality*, 290; Gould, *Covenant and Republic*, 121; Rothman, *Hands and Hearts*, 39; Schiebinger, *The Mind Has No Sex*, 230–31; Westerkamp, *Women and Religion in Early America*, 133. For an alternative view of the emotions, see Bloch, "The Gendered Meanings of Virtue," 48–49.

28. Jean Bethke Elshtain, *Public Man, Private Woman: Women in Social and Political Thought* (Princeton, N.J.: Princeton University Press, 1981), 118–19, 127; Crane, *Ebb Tide*, 223, 234; Thomas Laqueur, *Making Sex*, 196–97.

29. Delamont and Duffin, *The Nineteenth-Century Woman*, 23; Burgett, *Sentimental Bodies*, 115, 123–28; Rothman, *Hands and Hearts*, 39–41.

30. See Coontz, *The Social Origins of Private Life*, 146–48; Kerber, "Separate Spheres, Female Worlds, Women's Place," 20; Harris, "Hannah Webster Foster's *The Coquette*," 3, 4. For an analysis of the way that an emphasis on class differences was put on the defensive after the Revolution, even as "natural" differences based on gender were reaffirmed, see Maier, "The Transforming Impact of Independence, Reaffirmed."

31. Laqueur, *Making Sex*, 5, 6, 149–56; Scheibinger, *The Mind Has No Sex*, 189–93, 224–26; Ruth H. Bloch, "Changing Conceptions of Sexuality and Romance in Eighteenth-Century America," *William and Mary Quarterly* 3rd ser. 60 (2003): 34–38; Bloch, "Untangling the Roots of Modern Sex Roles," 237–52. For an example of the complimentarian approach, see B. W. "On Matrimonial Felicity," *Gentleman and Lady's Town and Country Magazine*, September 1784, 193–94.

32. Lockridge, "Colonial Self-Fashioning," 279–91; Kowaleski-Wallace, *Consuming Subjects*, 148; Jane Tompkins, "Susanna Rowson, Father of the American Novel," in Warren,

ed., *The (Other) American Traditions*, 35, 36; Laqueur, *Making Sex*, 5, 6; Lavater, "General Remarks on Women," *Massachusetts Magazine* 6 (January 1794): 20–21.

33. Armstrong, "The Rise of the Domestic Woman," in Armstrong and Tennenhouse, *The Ideology of Conduct*, 13, 118–19; Felicity Nussbaum, "Heteroclites: The Gender of Character in Scandalous Memoirs," in Nussbaum and Brown, eds., *The New Eighteenth Century*, 155; Judith Stevens to Winthrop Sargent, 28 November 1782, Letter Book 2: 90; "Desultory Thoughts, *Gentleman and Lady's Town and Country Magazine*, May 1784, 251. Virtually everyone—including Mary Wollstonecraft—accepted male standards of excellence in the eighteenth century. To share the rights of man, women had to acquire the skills of men. Schiebinger, *The Mind Has No Sex*, 230–31.

34. Samuel Shaw to Winthrop Sargent, 23 August 1779, Shaw Papers; JSM to Winthrop Sargent, 21 December 1788, Letter Book 3: 363; Eddy, *Universalism in Gloucester*, 129–30.

35. Judith Stevens to Winthrop Sargent, 18 April 1788, Letter Book 3: 299, 300.

36. Judith Stevens to Maria Sargent, 15 April 1788, to Winthrop Sargent, 11 June 1788, Letter Book 3: 296, 322–25.

37. Judith Stevens to John Murray, 18 May 1788, to Mrs. Pilgrim of England, 31 July 1788, Letter Book 3: 316–17, 338.

38. Murray, "The Family Picture," 1782, Repository, 289–90; Judith Stevens to Fitz William Sargent, 1 March 1783, Letter Book 2: 115; to Mrs. Gardiner, 4 April 1788, to Winthrop and Judith Sargent, 5 July 1788, to Miss Pierce of Plymouth, England, 16 July 1788, Letter Book 3: 291–92, 326–27, 332; Eddy, *Universalism in Gloucester*, 130–31.

39. On eighteenth-century notions of courtship, see Fliegelman, *Prodigals and Pilgrims*, 125, 132; Fliegelman, "Familial Politics, Seduction, and the Novel: The Anxious Agenda of an American Literary Culture," in Greene, ed., *The American Revolution*, 341–42; Grossberg, *Governing the Hearth*, 6, 19–21; Kelly, *In the New England Fashion*, 145; Lebsock, *The Free Women of Petersburg*, 16–17; Lewis, "The Republican Wife," 696; Rothman, *Hands and Hearts*, 36. Judith Stevens to Mrs. Gardiner, 4 April 1788, to Maria Sargent, 16 July 1788, Letter Book 3: 291–92, 334; to "Zerviah," 29 May 1789, Letter Book 4: 40; Murray, "Ingratitude," Repository, 192.

40. Judith Stevens to Maria Sargent, 30 July 1788, to Mrs. Pilgrim of old England, 31 July 1788, Letter Book 3: 337–38.

41. Judith Stevens to John Murray, 8 May, 1 August 1788, Letter Book 3: 310, 340.

42. Judith Stevens to John Murray, 26 September 1788, Letter Book 3: 346.

43. Judith Stevens to John Murray, 26 September, 1 October 1788, Letter Book 3: 346. Judith's aversion to the month of October may have had something to do with "the approach of a dreary Winter" that inevitable followed in the wake of New England's fall splendors. Even in September, the chill in the air reminded her of the winter to come. Judith Stevens to John Murray, 12 September 1775, Letter Book 1: 23. Moreover, she had lost both a baby sister and a close friend in October of 1775. See Murray, "On the Demise of an Infant Sister," and "On the Death of a Friend," Repository, [369], 433–34.

44. Judith Stevens to Mrs. Plummer of Salem, 4 October 1788, to Winthrop and Judith Sargent, 5 October 1788, JSM to Maria Sargent, 13 October 1788, Letter Book 3: 347–48, 350–52.

45. JSM to Judith and Winthrop Sargent, 12, 27 October 1788, to Anna, 7 November 1788, Letter Book 3: 350, 353, 356.

46. Murray, "Happiness," Repository, 176; Judith Stevens to John Murray, 29 June 1785, Letter Book 2: 346; JSM to Maria Sargent, 13 October 1788, Letter Book 3: 351; to John Murray, 9 January, 6 April 1789, to Mrs. Barrell of Old York, 8 May 1789, to John Murray, 10 June 17[89], Letter Book 4: 1–2, 19, 30, 45.

47. JSM to Winthrop Sargent, 21 December 1788, to Maria Sargent, 28 December 1788, Letter Book 3: 363–365; to Maria Sargent, 27 January, 15 March, 15 July 1789, Letter Book 4: 3, 15, 51; Pleasants, *Winthrop Sargent*, 17.

48. JSM to Mrs. Powell, 23 April 1789, to Maria Sargent, 25 April, 7 May 1789, Letter Book 4: 23–25, 28.

49. Judith Stevens to Mrs. Barrell of Old York, 8 October 1784, Letter Book 2: 283.

50. See especially Juster, *Disorderly Women*; Skemp, *Judith Sargent Murray*, 22.

51. Eddy, *Universalism in Gloucester*, 192–93; Murray, *Life*, 406; Gloucester Church Records, 1779–1838, 1–4, 45.

52. Murray, *Life*, 75, 123; JSM to John Murray, 26 February, 5 April, 11 May 1789, Letter Book 4: 11, 19, 32.

53. JSM to Maria Sargent, 10 June 1788, Letter Book 3: 320; to Maria Sargent, 27 January 1789, to John Murray, 26 February 1789, Letter Book 4: 3, 11.

54. See Bloch, "American Feminine Ideals in Transition,"101–8; Scholten, *Childbearing in American Society*, 58–64; Ryan, *The Empire of the Mother*, 56; Westerkamp, *Women and Religion in Early America*, 26–27.

55. Judith Stevens to Winthrop Sargent, 5 August 1786, Letter Book 3: 128. Granted, this was not a view that everyone accepted in its entirety. Winthrop Sargent, for instance, continued to believe that women were too tender to be adequate disciplinarians, as he warned his sister Esther "not to let a weak fondness operate to the prejudice" of her son Jack. Esther's response was typical. Any mother, she asserted, would "willingly sacrifice her own happiness to promote that of her Children." Esther Ellery to Winthrop Sargent, 27 December 1788, Sargent Murray Gilman Hough Papers.

56. Judith Stevens to Aunt E____ S____, 15 July 1785, Letter Book 2: 361; to Winthrop Sargent, 5 August 1786, Letter Book 3: 128. See Nylander, *Our Own Snug Fireside*, 32.

57. Melvin Yazawa, "Creating a Republican Citizenry," in Greene, ed., *The American Revolution*, 201–303; Kerber, "'I Have Don . . . Much,'" 244; Lewis, "Mother Love," 210–11, 214; Jacqueline S. Reinier, "Raising the Republican Child: Attitudes and Practices in Post-Revolutionary Philadelphia," *William and Mary Quarterly* 3rd ser. 39 (1982): 151–52, 156–58. It is true that the notion that women should teach sons Christian virtue existed in the seventeenth century, particularly in Puritan households. Thus "republican motherhood" was in some ways a secularized version of old habits. Still, eighteenth-century families were much more likely to trust women to inculcate virtue in their sons than they had been in the seventeenth century. See Dunn, "Saints and Sisters," 594; Crane, *Ebb Tide*, 207–9, 212–16.

58. Reinier, *From Virtue to Character*, 47–48.

59. Judith Stevens to Fitz William Sargent, 24 June 1786, Letter Book 3: 104; JSM to Maria Sargent, 23 February 1789,Letter Book 4: 8; to Anna Sargent, 28 February 1799, Letter Book 10: 361; Baym, "Between Enlightenment and Victorian," 26; Armstrong and Tennenhouse, *The Ideology of Conduct*, 9.

60. JSM to Mrs. Epes Sargent, 22 June 1790, Letter Book 4: 133; Boydston, *Home and Work*, xi; Michelle Rosaldo, "Women, Culture, and Society: A Theoretical Overview," in

Michelle Rosaldo and Louise Lamphere, eds., *Women, Culture, and Society* (Stanford, Calif.: Stanford University Press, 1974), 21–26; Lewis, "Mother Love," 209–10; Landes, *Women and the Public Sphere*, 138, 148; Hoffert, *Private Matters*, 1; Bloch, "American Feminine Ideals in Transition," 116–20. As Elaine Crane has astutely pointed out, moreover, the rhetoric investing women with special and important tasks as mothers probably did little to change a woman's real life. It may have given women a more palatable identity, but it was still a confining identity, "inextricably linked to gender." Crane, "Dependence in the Era of Independence," 268.

61. Klepp, "Revolutionary Bodies," 910–11, 926–39; Nancy Schrom Dye and Daniel Blake Smith, "Mother Love and Infant Death, 1750–1920," *Journal of American History* 73 (1986): 337–40; Mintz and Kellogg, *Domestic Revolutions*, 21; Wilson, "The Illusion of Change," 401–3.

62. Judith Stevens to Maria Sargent, 5 September 1782, to Madam Walker, 18 April 1785, Letter Book 2: 60, 327; JSM to Maria Sargent, 28 December 1788, Letter Book 3: 366; to Maria Sargent, 27 January 1789, to Mrs. Barrell of Old York, 8 May 1789, to John Murray, 10 June 17[89], to Maria Sargent, 15 July 1789, Letter Book 4: 3, 29, 45, 51; to Esther Ellery, 23 February 1796, Letter Book 10: 8; Wertz and Wertz, *Lying In*, 20–21; Judith Walzer Leavitt, "Under the Shadow of Maternity: American Women's Responses to Death and Disability in Nineteenth-Century Childbirth," *Feminist Studies* 12 (1986): 133–36, 140–41; Ulrich, *A Midwife's Tale*, 169–70; Scholten, *Childbearing in American Society*, 21–22.

63. John Murray to Thomas Fitzgerald, 8 June 1789, Gratz Papers; JSM to Maria Sargent, 15, 25 March 1789, to John Murray, 11 May 1789, Letter Book 4: 16, 18, 32; Leavitt, "Under the Shadow of Maternity," 144; Wertz and Wertz, *Lying In*, 1, 4; Kierner, " 'The Dark and Dense Cloud,' " 203.

64. Klepp, "Revolutionary Bodies," 927; Scholten, *Childbearing in American Society*, 16.

65. JSM to Maria Sargent, 25 March, 15 July 1789, Letter Book 4: 18, 52; Hoffert, *Private Matters*, 41, 46.

66. Brothers Samuel and Joshua Plummer were both doctors, and either may have been Judith's physician. Their nephew David was a Universalist. Babson, *Gloucester*, 279; Kasraie, "Left to 'Affectionate Partiality,' " 326n. For an understanding of the reasons some women sought doctors rather than midwives see Scholten, " 'On the Importance of the Obstetrick Art': Changing Customs of Childbirth in America, 1760–1825," *William and Mary Quarterly* 3rd ser. 34 (1977): 434–45; Wertz and Wertz, *Lying In*, 1, 4, 6, 13, 21–23; Degler, *At Odds*, 56. See also Burr, *Journal*, 142.

67. Hoffert, *Private Matters*, 21–24, 47, 63–65, 68, 107; Scholten, *Childbearing in American Society*, 31–34, 37, 39; Scholten, " 'The Obstetrick Art,' " 427–29, 437, 439–41; Wertz and Wertz, *Lying In*, 24, 33.

68. Scholten, " 'The Obstetrick Art,' " 439, 442–43; Scholten, *Childbearing in American Society*, 37, 46–48; Hoffert, *Private Matters*, 23–24; JSM to Maria Sargent, 15 July 1789, Letter Book 4: 51.

69. John Murray to Colonel Paul Dudley Sargent, 1 October 1789, transcript in Sargent House Museum, Gloucester, Massachusetts; JSM to Mrs. Pilgrim of Old England, 7 November 1789, to Mrs. Lucy Sargent of Sullivan, 6 May 1790, to Winthrop and Judith Sargent, 12 June 1790, Letter Book 4: 55, 83, 109; Murray, *The Gleaner*, 3: 197.

70. Sargent, *Epes Sargent of Gloucester*, 53; John Murray to Colonel Paul Dudley Sargent, 1 October 1789; JSM to Maria Sargent, 3, 22 November 1789, Letter Book 4: 54–55, 59, 61. Even when a pregnancy had a happier outcome, elite women often endured a long, painful recovery. Both psychologically and physically, Judith's suffering was particularly difficult. See Leavitt, "Under the Shadow of Maternity," 140.

71. John Murray to Colonel Paul Dudley Sargent, 1 October 1789; JSM to Maria Sargent, 3, 22 November 1789, Letter Book 4: 54, 59–60. At least by the 1840s, people often talked about deceased children as angels who went to heaven to prepare a place for the rest of the family. They also talked of "angelic beings" who surrounded infants, guarding them from harm. Judith's vision was unusual only because it came so early. See Hoffert, *Private Matters*, 183.

72. John Murray to Colonel Paul Dudley Sargent, 1 October 1789; JSM to Mrs. Pilgrim of Old England, 7 November 1789, to Maria Sargent, 24 December 1789, 18 January 1790, to Mrs. Lucy Sargent of Sullivan, 6 May 1790, to Esther Ellery, 29 July 1790, Letter Book 4: 56, 65, 67, 83, 186–87.

73. Dye and Blake, "Mother Love," 329–32; Hoffert, *Private Matters*, 170–80. Nor was the anger of women such as Judith always unfair. Eighteenth-century physicians often *did* use forceps clumsily or inappropriately, feeling almost compelled to take heroic measures when none were required. See Wertz and Wertz, *Lying In*, 37, 64–66; Dye, "History of Childbirth in America," *Signs* 6 (1980): 102–3.

Chapter 7. A Wider World

1. JSM to Mrs. Pilgrim of Old England, 7 November 1789, Letter Book 4: 57.

2. JSM to Mrs. Pilgrim of Old England, 3 November 1790, Letter Book 4: 262.

3. JSM to Fitz William Sargent, 20 January, 17 September, 1790, Letter Book 4: 71–73, 234; to Winthrop Sargent, 18 January 1791, Letter Book 5: 365.

4. JSM to the Rev. Doctor Moore, 12 September 1795, Letter Book 8: 349; Armstrong, *Desire and Domestic Fiction*, 31, 130; Crane, "Dependence in the Era of Independence," 256; Rosaldo, "Women, Culture, and Society," 32; Lewis, "Republican Wife," 689–93, 708–10, 720–21; Herbert Ross Brown, *The Sentimental Novel in America*, 1789–1860 (Durham, N.C.: Duke University Press, 1940), 100. As Elisabeth Griffith has pointed out, even in the mid-nineteenth century, American feminists continued to decry the powerless position married women occupied in a patriarchal society. Griffith, "Elizabeth Cady Stanton on Marriage and Divorce: Feminist Theory and Domestic Experience," in Kelley, ed., *Woman's Being, Woman's Place*, 235–51.

5. Zagarri, *A Woman's Dilemma*, 91–94; Abigail Adams to John Adams, 31 March 1776, in L. H. Butterfield et al., eds., *Adams Family Correspondence*, 4 vols. (Cambridge, Mass.: Harvard University Press, 1973), 1: 370. Livingston's words are cited in Harris, *American Women Writers*, 65.

6. JSM to Winthrop and Judith Sargent, 23 March 1790, to Winthrop Sargent, 15 April 1790, Letter Book 4: 78, 81–82.

7. JSM to Maria Sargent, 18 January 1789, to Winthrop Sargent, 24 October 1790, Letter Book 4: 67, 260; to Maria Sargent, 10 November 1790, to Winthrop Sargent, 23

November 1790, Letter Book 5: 361, 363; to Winthrop Sargent, 18 January 1791, Letter Book 6: 375.

8. JSM to Mrs. Barrell, 8 May 1789, to John Murray, 2 December 1789, Letter Book 4: 30, 62; to John Murray, 29 January, 26 April 1791, Letter Book 5: 349, 353; to Maria Sargent, 23 December 1790, Letter Book 6: 400.

9. JSM to John Murray, 18, 19 June 1791, to Winthrop Sargent, 23 November 1791, Letter Book 5: 356, 362.

10. Judith Stevens to Winthrop Sargent, 15 May 1786, Letter Book 3: 84; JSM to Maria Sargent, 19 January 1790, to Madam Walker, 19 January 1790, to Fitz William Sargent, 20 January 1790, Letter Book 4: 68, 70–71, 73. For American attitudes toward the theater, see Kenneth Silverman, "The Economic Debate over the Theater in Revolutionary America," in Paul J. Korshin, ed., *The American Revolution and Eighteenth-Century Culture: Essays from the 1976 Bicentennial Conference of the American Society for Eighteenth-Century Studies* (New York: AMS Press, 1976), 219–40; Ann Fairfax Withington, *Toward a More Perfect Union: Virtue and the Formation of American Republics* (New York: Oxford University Press, 1991), especially 20–47.

11. JSM to , 18 January 1790, to Madam Walker, 19 January 1790, to Fitz William Sargent, 20 January 1790, Letter Book 4: 68, 71, 73.

12. The Epilogue appeared in the March 1790 edition of *Massachusetts Magazine*, 186–87.

13. JSM to Maria Sargent, 19 January 1790, to Madam Walker, 19 January 1790, Letter Book 4: 68, 70–71.

14. JSM to [?], 30 December 1790, to [?] Pearson, 31 December 1790, Letter Book 7: 24, 25; to John Murray, 1 January 1791, Letter Book 5: 347; to Fitz William Sargent, 17 January 1791, to Maria Sargent, 25 January 1791, Letter Book 6: 407, 409; to John Murray, 3 February 1791, Letter Book 5: 350; to [?], [?] August 1792, Letter Book 7: 27; Apology for an Epilogue and Valedictory Prologue, *Massachusetts Magazine*, May 1791, 307–8; Murray, Prologue and Epilogue to the *West Indian*, Poetry 1: 348–52.

15. JSM to John Murray, 10 April 1789, to Madam Walker, 19 January 1790, to John Murray, 23 January 1790, to Winthrop and Judith Sargent, 23 March 1790, Letter Book 4: 20–21, 70, 74, 78.

16. Cassara, "John Murray and the Origins of Universalism," 86; John Murray to Thomas Fitzgerald, 8 June 1789, Gratz Papers; JSM to John Murray, 6 February 1789, to Winthrop and Judith Sargent, 23 March 1790, Letter Book 4: 7, 78.

17. Cassara, *Universalism in America*, 29; Cassara, "John Murray and the Origins of Universalism," 82–83; Marini, *Radical Sects of Revolutionary New England*, 107, 109; Record Book of the Free and Independent Church of Christ, 37r.

18. Bressler, *The Universalist Movement*, 33; John Murray to Israel Israel, 30 November 1789, Rush MSS, 22: 86.

19. JSM to Anna, 15 June, 23 August, 20 September, 11 October 1790, Letter Book 4: 112, 219–20, 241–42, 253; Journal, 15, 16, 22 May, 5 June 1790, Letter Book, 4: 87–88, 90, 92, 105–6.

20. Murray, "To Anna P____ written in an Inn while upon a journey in consequence of hearing the young Lady express uncommon satisfaction in our little tour," Poetry 1: 97; JSM to Mrs. Pilgrim of Hampstead, England, 14 June 1792, Letter Book 8: 54; John Murray to Mr. Redding, 9 June 1794, *Universalist Quarterly* 6 (1869): 419.

21. Sara Mills, *Discourses of Difference: An Analysis of Women's Travel Writing and Colonialism* (New York: Routledge, 1991), 42, 85, 95–97, 103–4; Baym, *American Women Writers*, 133. Judith re-wrote and published one of her letters, a "Description of BETHLEHEM; in the STATE of PENNSYLVANIA," *Massachusetts Magazine*, June 1791, 365–70.

22. See Baym, *American Women Writers*, 133–34; Mills, *Discourses of Difference*, 28; Judith Stevens to Madam Walker, 13 September 1782, Letter Book 2: 67.

23. Ulrich, *A Midwife's Tale*, 167; Young, *Masquerade*, 192–224.

24. For the beginnings of tourism, see Dean MacConnell, *The Tourist: A New Theory of the Leisure Class* (New York: Schocken Books, 1976), 41–42. Tourism was much more prevalent in the early nineteenth century than in 1790, but it had its roots in this earlier period. See also Imbarrato, *Declarations of Independence*, 40–41, 44, 53.

25. Journal, 29 May 1790, Letter Book 4: 98–101.

26. Ibid., 12, 26 June, 3, 10, 17 July 1790, Letter Book 4: 108, 146, 153, 163–65, 173, 175.

27. Ibid., 12 June 1790, Letter Book 4: 107. Dr. Alexander Hamilton's description of Philadelphia at mid-century offers an unusually negative assessment. Alexander Hamilton, *Gentleman's Progress: The Itinerarium of Dr. Alexander Hamilton, 1744*, ed. Carl Bridenbaugh (Chapel Hill: University of North Carolina Press, 1948), 20–23, 192–93. Other visitors were much kinder. See James Birket, *Some Cursory Remarks Made by James Birket in His Voyage to North America 1750–1751* (New Haven, Conn.: Yale University Press, 1916), 63, 67, 69; Andrew Burnaby, *Travels Through the Middle Settlements in North-America in the Years 1759 and 1760*, 2nd ed. (Ithaca, N.Y.: Cornell University Press 1963), 53–56; Peter Kalm, *Travels into North America* (Barre, Mass.: Imprint Society, 1972), 8, 20–33. For the "other" Philadelphia, see Billy G. Smith, *The "Lower Sort": Philadelphia's Laboring People, 1750–1800* (Ithaca, N.Y.: Cornell University Press, 1990), 165; Lyons, *Sex Among the Rabble*, Part II.

28. Journal, 19 June, 10 July 1790, Letter Book 4: 125–26, 165–66.

29. Waldstreicher, *In the Midst of Perpetual Fetes*, 208; Journal, 24 June, 10 July 1790, Letter Book 4: 143, 160.

30. Journal, 12 June, 17 July 1790, Letter Book 4: 107, 169–70. See Hamilton, *Itinerarium*, 18, 21; Birket, *Some Cursory Remarks*, 63–69; Burnaby, *Travels*, 55.

31. Journal, 12 June, 3, 17 July 1790, Letter Book 4: 108, 150, 174. For the "republican" atmosphere of the city, see Burnaby, *Travels*, 97. For Quaker ties to other elite Americans, see Kilbride, "Cultivation, Conservatism, and the Early National Gentry," 236.

32. JSM to Esther Ellery, 14 June 1790, to Aunt Allen, 16 June 1790, Letter Book 4: 111–12, 116–17. At least one historian agrees that Judith was correct in attributing the distrust of the theater to Quaker influence. Glenn Hughes, *A History of the American Theatre, 1700–1950* (New York: Samuel French, 1951), 52.

33. Journal, 10 July 1790, Letter Book 4: 160–63.

34. JSM to Mrs. Epes Sargent, 22 June 1790, Letter Book 4: 130, 136. While it was founded in 1742, it was not until 1785 that Bethlehem welcomed outsiders. Woody, *History of Women's Education*, 1: 333.

35. JSM to Mrs. Epes Sargent, 22 June 1790, Letter Book 4: 132–35.

36. Ibid., 133–34, 136. Although Judith did not mention it, the students even produced and performed plays. Woody, *History of Women's Education*, 1: 333, 399.

37. JSM to Mrs. Epes Sargent, 22 June 1790, Letter Book 4: 133; Woody, *History of Women's Education*, 1: 96–97.

38. Journal, 12 June 1790, JSM to Esther Ellery, 14 June 1790, to Aunt Prentiss, 16 June 1790, to Epes Sargent, 5 July 1790, to Esther Ellery, 29 July 1790, to Miss Allen, 30 July 1790, Letter Book 4: 108, 111, 117, 156, 187, 190.

39. Journal, 24 July, 31 July, 7 August 1790, Letter Book 4: 181, 183, 192–95, 202–3.

40. Ibid., 14 August 1790, Letter Book 4: 205–10.

41. Ibid., 4: 208–9. Judith's reaction to Martha Washington mirrors the view of Mercy Otis Warren—no Federalist by any means—who was impressed by Washington's intelligence as well as her determination to avoid pretentious airs. Earnest, *The American Eve*, 16.

42. Journal, 21, 28 August, 4 September, 2 October 1790, Letter Book 4: 214–16, 221–29, 248.

43. JSM to Maria Sargent, 15 September 1790, Letter Book 4: 233; Murray, "Wedded Discord," Repository, 52. Judith's description of Connecticut's divorce laws is a reflection of her social conservatism. Massachusetts and Connecticut had always had slightly more flexible divorce laws than either England or the other colonies. After the Revolution, it became a bit easier in both states for women to sue for divorce. In Connecticut, women could get a divorce on the basis of cruelty, desertion, or nonsupport. In Massachusetts, women had to add infidelity to the mix—something Connecticut laws did not demand. Nancy Cott suggests that changes in the divorce laws after the Revolution may have had something to do with the rhetoric of equality and independence that permeated the war years. Others, notably Elaine Crane, point out that the divorce rate throughout America remained minuscule. Clearly Judith exaggerated the prevalence of divorce in Connecticut. See Cott, "Divorce and the Changing Status of Women in Massachusetts, *William and Mary Quarterly* 3rd ser. 33 (1976): 586–614; Crane, *Ebb Tide*, 190–96, 212; Salmon, " 'Life, Liberty, and Dower,' " 61–73, 80; Barbara E. Lacey, "Women in the Era of the American Revolution: The Case of Norwich, Connecticut," *New England Quarterly* 53 (1990): 537.

44. JSM to Esther Ellery, 29 July 1790, to Maria Sargent, 11, 12 September 1790, to Judith and Winthrop Sargent, 18, 25 September, 16 October 1790, Letter Book 4: 186, 231–32, 238, 244–45, 252.

45. Journal, 23 October 1790, Letter Book 4: 257, 259.

46. To Maria Sargent, 1 November 1790, Letter Book 4: 260; Letter Fragment, 1790, Letter Book 6: 372.

47. Eddy, *Universalism in Gloucester*, 31, 32; Gloucester Church Records, 49; Gloucester, Town Records, Book 3, 487.

48. JSM to Maria Sargent, 18 January 1790, to Anna, 15 June 1790, Journal, 3 July, 17 July 1790, Letter Book 4: 67, 113, 150–51, 174; to Winthrop Sargent, Sr., 23 November 1790, Letter Book 5: 361 . Peale painted the picture Judith described in 1772, and added the baby and a table filled with medicine bottles four years later in an effort to dramatize the pain parents suffered when they lost their children to the dreaded disease of smallpox. Reinier, *From Virtue to Character*, 41.

49. JSM to Maria Sargent, 9 October 1790, Letter Book 4: 249; to Judith Sargent, 25 March 1791, Letter Book 6: 419.

50. JSM to Winthrop and Judith Sargent, 3 March 1791, to Winthrop Sargent, Sr., 8 March 1791, to Judith Sargent, 25 March 1791, to Mrs. Barrell of Old York, 23 June 1791, Letter Book 6: 412–13, 419, 433.

51. JSM to John Murray, 11, 14 March 1791, to Winthrop Sargent, 15 June 1791, Letter Book 5: 351–52, 373; to Winthrop Sargent, Sr., 25 March 1791, to Mrs. Mackie of Philadelphia, 21 June 1791, Letter Book 6: 422, 431.

52. JSM to Maria, 11 July 1791, Letter Book 6: 438–39; to John Murray, 22 July 1791, Letter Book 5: 356–58.

53. JSM to Maria, 8 August 1791, Murray, Letter Book 6: 440–41; to Winthrop Sargent, 16 August 1791, Letter Book 5: 380. At least she had a child to honor the Sargent women. It was Fitz William, not Judith, who had a "little namesake" to honor Winthrop Sargent. Fitz William Sargent to Winthrop Sargent, 5 May 1792, Sargent Murray Gilman Hough Papers.

54. JSM to Judith Sargent, 22 September 1791, to Maria Sargent, 25 October 1791, Letter Book 8: 2–6.

55. JSM to Maria Sargent, 25, 30 October 1791, Letter Book 8: 7, 9; to John Murray, 4 November 1791, Letter Book 5: 359; to Winthrop Sargent, 7 March 1796, Letter Book 9: 543.

56. See Bloch, "American Feminine Ideals in Transition," 109–13; Coontz, *The Social Origins of Private Life*, 127; Cott, *The Bonds of Womanhood*, 87; Demos, "The Changing Faces of Fatherhood," 431–33; Mintz and Kellogg, *Domestic Revolutions*, 47, 59; Boydston, *Home and Work*, 81; Rotundo, *American Manhood*, 26–29; Melissa A. Butler, "Early Liberal Roots of Feminism: John Locke and the Attack on Patriarchy," *American Political Science Review* 72 (1978): 142–48; Samuel Harrison Smith, "Remarks on Education" (Philadelphia: John Omrod, 1798), in Rudolph, *Essays on Education*, 205. For comments on motherhood as a job that required expertise, see Reinier, "Raising the Republican Child," 153, 156; Hoffert, *Private Matters*, 3, 143–54; Scholten, *Childbearing in American Society*, 11, 68, 75, 90–91.

57. JSM to Maria Sargent, 30 October 1791, 8 August 1792, to Mrs. Pilgrim of Hampstead England, 15 November 1794, to Anna Sargent, 27 July 1795, Letter Book 8: 11, 59, 60, 244, 338. See Dye and Smith, "Mother Love," 337–45 for a discussion of the intense, emotional relationship mothers often had with their children in this period.

58. JSM to Mrs. W____ of Philadelphia, 8 June 1792, to Mrs. Pilgrim of Hampstead, England, 15 November 1794, Letter Book 8: 48, 243–44; to Anna Sargent, 17 October 1800, Letter Book 11: 210–11. Advice books recommended weaning somewhere between the ninth and twelfth months, but Judith was not unusual in prolonging the process. Reinier, *From Virtue to Character*, 54–55.

59. Hoffert, *Private Affairs*, 147; Reinier, "Raising the Republican Child," 152; Reinier, *From Virtue to Character*, 10, 54–55; Smith, "The Study of the Family in Early America," 16; Bloch, "American Feminine Ideals in Action," 110; JSM to Esther Ellery, 29 March, 15 May, 10 November 1797, Letter Book 10: 92–93, 116, 174.

60. JSM to Mrs. Barrell of Old York, 24 December 1792, Letter Book 8: 87; to Anna Sargent, 17 October 1800, Letter Book 11: 210–11; Rosaldo, "The Use and Abuse of Anthropology," 397; Hoffert, *Private Affairs*, 153–55; Smith, "The Study of the Family in Early America," 16. See Crane, *Ebb Tide*, 213–14 and Brown, "Mary Wollstonecraft," 394, for the confining and restrictive aspects of breast-feeding.

61. JSM to Winthrop Sargent, 30 January 1791, Letter Book 5: 366–369.

62. JSM to Winthrop Sargent, 30 January, 4 April 1791, Letter Book 5: 370; to Maria Sargent, 8 August 1791, Letter Book 6: 442, 443; to Winthrop Sargent, 9 August 1791, Letter Book 5: 376; to Maria Sargent, 22 January 1792, Letter Book 8: 24.

63. Frazer Ells Wilson, "St. Clair's Defeat," *Ohio Archaeological and Historical Publications* 11 (1903): 30; Donald J. Ratcliffe, *Party Spirit in a Frontier Republic: Democratic Politics in Ohio, 1793–1821* (Columbus: Ohio State University Press, 1998), 22; Prucha, *Sword of the Republic*, 21–26; Winthrop Sargent, "Extracts from Winthrop Sargent's Diary, 1793–1795," *Ohio Archaeological and Historical Publications* 33 (1924): 241–42. See also Armstrong Starkey, *European and Native American Warfare, 1675–1815* (Norman: University of Oklahoma Press, 1998),146–47; William H. Denny, ed., "Military Journal of Major Ebenezer Denny," *Memoirs of the Historical Society of Pennsylvania* 7 (1860): 374–75.

64. James R. Jacobs, *The Beginning of the U.S. Army, 1783–1812* (Princeton, N.J.: Princeton University Press, 1947), 85, 91, 105, 110; Frazer Ells Wilson, *Arthur St. Clair* (Richmond, Va.: Garrett and Maisie, 1944), 31–34; Thomas P. Slaughter, *The Whiskey Rebellion: Frontier Epilogue to the American Revolution* (New York: Oxford University Press, 1986), 105–7; Pleasants, *Winthrop Sargent*, 18–19; Starkey, *European and Native American Warfare*, 146–47; Sargent, "Extracts," 240–41, 246–48, 258–69.

65. *Columbian Centinel*, 7 December 1791; JSM to Maria Sargent, 28 December 1791, 22 January 1792, Letter Book 8: 17–18, 25.

66. JSM to Maria Sargent, 6 May, 8, 31 August, 1 October 1792, Letter Book 8: 39, 62, 64, 71; Winthrop Sargent to Judge John Symmes, 10 May 1792, to Captain Pierce, 8 September, 1794, William Henry Smith, ed., *The St. Clair Papers: The Life and Public Services of Arthur St. Clair* (Cincinnati: Robert Clarke, 1882), 2: 287–99, 301, 327–29; Sargent, "Winthrop Sargent," 233; Prucha, *Sword of the Republic*, 29–34; Pleasants, *Winthrop Sargent*, 22–23; Pershing, "Winthrop Sargent," 45, 84–88, 132; Jacobs, *The Beginning of the U.S. Army*, 117–21; Willa B. Low, *Winthrop Sargent, Soldier and Statesman* (Gloucester, Mass.: Sargent-Murray-Gilman-Hough House Associates, 1976), 11.

Chapter 8. A Career of Fame

1. See especially JSM to John Murray, 7 January 1791, Murray, Letter Book 5: 348; to Judith Sargent, 25 March, 2 April 1791, Letter Book 6: 419–21, 423–24; Shields, *Civil Tongues*, 311; Davidson, *Revolution and the Word*, 32. Her defense of Philenia in this regard was a bit more complicated because of the sexual scandal that permeated the Morton household. The affair is described in Emily Pendleton and Harold Milton Ellis, *Philenia: The Life and Works of Sarah Wentworth Morton, 1759–1846* (Orono: University of Maine Studies, 1931), 33–39.

2. JSM to Madam Walker, 16 December 1784, Letter Book 2: 306; to John Murray, 1 August 1788, Letter Book 3: 340; Letter Fragment, 1790, JSM to Mrs. Barrell of Old York, 23 June 1791, to Maria Sargent, 30 October 1791, to Anna Sargent, 5 June 1793, Letter Book 6: 373, 432–33; Letter Book 8: 10, 114; *Massachusetts Magazine*, January 1789.

3. *Massachusetts Magazine*, January 1790. See Shields, *Civil Tongues*, 265, 311; Jacqueline Hornstein, "Sarah Wentworth Morton," in Lena Manero, ed., *American Women Writers: A Critical Reference Guide from Colonial Times to the Present* (New York: Frederick Unger, 1981), 3: 230–32; Field, *Constantia*, 24–25.

4. Pendleton and Ellis, *Philenia*, 43, 52; JSM to the Editors of the *Massachusetts Magazine*, Repository 1; "Lines to Philenia," *Massachusetts Magazine*, April 1790, 248–49.

5. JSM to Mrs. Barrell of York, 24 December 1792, Letter Book 8: 87–88; *Massachusetts Magazine*, January 1790, 57–58; February 1790, 120; March 1790, 186; June 1790, 37; March 1791, 181–82; May 1791, 307–8; Murray, "Desultory Thoughts," 251. "On the Domestic Education of Children" appeared in May 1790, 275–77; "Description of Bethlehem" was published in June 1791, 365–70.

6. William J. Free, *The Columbian Magazine and American Literary Nationalism* (Paris: Mouton, 1968), 70–71; Murray, "The Sexes," Repository, 226–27; "On the Equality of the Sexes," *Massachusetts Magazine*, March 1790, 133; Letter Book 4: 36; JSM to Miss P____ of Plymouth, Old England, 20 May 1789, to [?], 15 June 1793, Letter Book 7: 28, 45.

7. "On the Equality of the Sexes," *Massachusetts Magazine*, March 1790, 132.

8. Pauline Schloesser says that the letter was written to John Murray. This is not the case. Schloesser, *The Fair Sex: White Women and Racial Patriarchy in the Early American Republic* (New York: New York University Press, 2002), 226n; "On the Equality of the Sexes," *Massachusetts Magazine*, April 1790, 224; Judith Stevens to Miss Goldthwait, 6 June 1777, Letter Book 1: 63.

9. "On the Equality of the Sexes," *Massachusetts Magazine*, April 1790, 224–25.

10. JSM to Mrs. Barrell of Old York, 23 June 1791, Letter Book 6: 433.

11. JSM to Mrs. Barrell of Old York, 1 November 1793, Letter Book 8: 165. See Kirstin Wilcox, "The Scribblings of a Plain Man and the Temerity of a Woman: Gender and Genre in Judith Sargent Murray's *The Gleaner*," *Early American Literature* 30 (1995): 143–44, for the argument that Murray used Margaretta to persuade readers to read her other essays.

12. Although approximately a quarter of the *Spectator* essays speak directly to women, they are written from a male perspective. Reinier, *From Virtue to Character*, 6–7. Judith Stevens to Mrs. Barrell of Old York, 8 July 1785, Letter Book 2: 357; "The Gleaner," no. 5, *Massachusetts Magazine*, July 1792, 418; no. 6, August 1792, 476; Agnew, *Worlds Apart*, 162, 172; Mary Crawford and Roger Chaffin, "The Reader's Construction of Meaning: Cognitive Research on Gender and Comprehension," and Kathryn Shevelow, "Fathers and Daughters: Women as Readers of the *Tatler*," in Elizabeth A. Flynn and Patrocinio P. Schweickart, eds., *Gender and Reading: Essays on Readers, Texts, and Contexts* (Baltimore: Johns Hopkins University Press, 1986), 3, 21, 24; 110–21; Watts, *Writing and Post Colonialism*, 52, 56.

13. "The Gleaner," no. 2, *Massachusetts Magazine*, March 1792, 151; no. 7, September 1792, 549–51. For the social value of "accomplishments," see Kelley, *Learning to Stand and Speak*, 69. See also Landes, *Women and the Public Sphere*, 177–81; Ryan, *Women in Public*, 8; Hanna Scolnicov, *Woman's Theatrical Space* (New York: Cambridge University Press, 1994), 8.

14. "The Gleaner," no. 2, *Massachusetts Magazine*, November 1792, 675–76. See Malmsheimer, "Daughters of Zion," 500, 503; Lewis, "The Republican Wife," 700–702; Rotundo, *American Manhood*, 3–4; Nussbaum, "Heteroclites," 154; Sklar, "The Schooling of Girls," 536; Davidson, *Revolution and the Word*, 107–8; Rodney Hessinger, " 'Insidious Murders of Female Innocence': Representations of Masculinity in the Seduction Tales of the Late Eighteenth Century," in Smith, ed., *Sex and Sexuality in Early America*, 263–72; Westerkamp, *Women and Religion in Early America*, 134.

15. Compare this, for instance, to the epic struggles between Clarissa and Lovelace, or Charles Brockten Brown's Ormond and Constantia. "The Gleaner," no. 2, *Massachusetts*

Magazine, March 1792, 148; no. 7, November 1792, 676–79; no. 9, December 1792, 713–18. See Wilcox, "The Scribblings of a Plain Man," 134–35 for comments on Margaretta's meek acceptance of her father's request. See also Leslie A. Fiedler, *Love and Death in the American Novel* (New York: Stein and Day, 1966), 71–76, 89 and W. M. Sale, Jr., "From Pamela to Clarissa," in Spector, ed., *Essays on the Eighteenth-Century Novel*, 19, 23–24, for analyses of the way the English and American versions of the seduction motif differ. The "Margaretta" story gives added impetus to Nancy Cott's warning to avoid the tendency to reify the notion of separate spheres. They were, in the end, "ideological constructions about propriety," not physical spheres. And in particular, the home remained the man's domain. Mr. Vigillius dominated his home, despite his respect for Mary's innate good sense. The "private" spaces women occupy can always be penetrated by men. Cott, "On Men's and Women's History," in Mark C. Carnes and Clyde Griffen, eds., *Meanings for Manhood: Constructions of Masculinity in Victorian America* (Chicago: University of Chicago Press, 1990), 206–7. See also, Ryan, *Women in Public*, 5.

16. The argument is uncannily similar to Ormond's in Charles Brockden Brown's *Ormond: Or The Secret Witness*, published a half a decade later. Interestingly, Brown's heroine is named "Constantia."

17. "The Gleaner," no. 11, *Massachusetts Magazine*, February 1793, 80–84. See Lewis, "The Republican Wife," 713–15 and Godbeer, *Sexual Revolution in Early America*, 284, for analyses of the ultimately weak situation in which women found themselves in this period.

18. This is not atypical. As Rodney Hessinger points out, most novels reflected the real fears that parents and their daughters had in a mobile society, filled with strangers, where danger seemingly confronted single women everywhere. Thus, while parents did not want to make the mistake of Clarissa's family, neither were they comfortable allowing their daughters to make their own choices. Hessinger, "'Insidious Murderers,'" 271–72. Compare this interpretation to Kerber, "'I Have Don . . . Much,'" 251; Bloch, "Changing Conceptions of Sexuality and Romance," 25; Davidson, *Revolution and the Word*, 113, 129; Harris, in Murray, *Selected Writings*, xxxiii.

19. For the way seduction novels can be seen as political tracts, see especially Lewis, "The Republican Wife," 713; James Jasinski, "The Feminization of Liberty, Domesticated Virtue, and the Reconstruction of Power and Authority in Early American Political Discourse," *Quarterly Journal of Speech* 79 (1993): 157–58.

20. "The Gleaner," no. 10, *Massachusetts Magazine*, January 1793, 15–20; no. 12, March, April 1793, 141, 205, 209; no. 17, October 1793, 587, 589. Jean N. Dorgan argues that *The Gleaner* implied that an egalitarian marriage was the first step for women who hoped for equality in the public sphere. This may have been true of some of the Gleaner essays, but not in the Margaretta story. Jean Nostrand Dorgan, "Eighteenth-Century Voices of Educational Change: Mary Wollstonecraft and Judith Sargent Murray" (Ph.D. dissertation, Rutgers University, 1976), 89. Wilcox notes that a "tension" exists between Mary's insistence on equality and her belief in hierarchy and order. Ultimately, the balance is tipped away from equality and toward subordination. Wilcox, "The Scribblings of a Plain Man," 137, 141.

21. "The Gleaner," no. 18, *Massachusetts Magazine*, November 1793, 649–56; no. 25, June 1794, 354–58.

22. JSM to Maria Sargent, 16 March 1793, Letter Book 8: 101; "The Gleaner," no. 25,

Massachusetts Magazine, June 1794, 354–55. See Armstrong, *Desire and Domestic Fiction*, 59–60, 72; Kathryn Shevelow, *Women and Print Culture: The Construction of Feminity in the Early Periodical* (New York: Routledge, 1989), 4, 12–13.

23. See Shevelow, *Women and Print Culture*, 1–7, 54–57.

24. "The Gleaner," no. 2, *Massachusetts Magazine*, March 1792, 147–48; no. 6, August 1792, 476; no. 7, September 1792, 549. See also Harris, *American Women Writers*, 135. For Judith's aversion to public speaking and her comfort using the pen, see Judith Stevens to Winthrop Sargent, 28 March 1785, Letter Book 2: 322.

25. "The Gleaner," no. 15, *Massachusetts Magazine*, August 1793, 460–61. See Chambers-Schiller, *Liberty, a Better Husband*, 16–17, 24–26; Burr, *Journal*, 145; Brown, *The Sentimental Novel*, 107, for attitudes toward the single life in this period.

26. "The Gleaner," no. 15, *Massachusetts Magazine*, August 1793, 464–68. See Bushman, *Refinement*, 302–3.

27. "The Gleaner," no. 4, *Massachusetts Magazine*, May 1792, 298–303. For a discussion of the assault on the classics, see Linda K. Kerber, *Federalists in Dissent: Imagery and Ideology in Jeffersonian America* (Ithaca, N.Y.: Cornell University Press, 1970). Kerber does not discuss the gendered implications of such an assault. Moreover, she finds that it was Jeffersonian Republicans, not Federalists, who generally entered the fray.

28. "The Gleaner," no. 1, *Massachusetts Magazine*, February 1792, 96; no. 5, July 1792, 420–21; no. 6, August 1792, 476; no. 14, July 1793, 394–96. The emphasis in her comments on the Masons, is Judith's.

29. For the classic depiction of the view of liberty as a helpless woman, see Bernard Bailyn, *Ideological Origins of the American Revolution* (Cambridge, Mass.: Belknap Press, 1967). See also Jasinski, "Feminization," 148–49, 153–58.

30. "The Gleaner," no. 23, *Massachusetts Magazine*, April 1794, 137–39. See Landes, *Women and the Public Sphere*, 159, 162, 166 for a discussion of the way that even the most positive depictions of liberty after the French Revolution clung to traditional gender stereotypes.

31. Schloesser, *The Fair Sex*, 158–59, 178; Schiebinger, *The Mind Has No Sex*, 285, 291; Kowaleski-Wallace, *Consuming Subjects*, 148; Tompkins, "Susannah Rowson," 35–36; Laqueur, *Making Sex*, 5–6; Murray, "Materialism," 1784, Repository, 341; JSM to Winthrop Sargent, 15 July 1796, Letter Book 9: 590.

32. Thornton, *Handwriting in America*, 25–26, 31–33, 37–38. For this very reason, many people distrusted the printed word. Designing people could use it to deceive people, to conceal their identity, to pretend to be disinterested even as they had very interested motives for writing. Thus, many still preferred oratory to print. When people spoke in person, their gestures, their stance, their voice all expressed their individuality. The speaker became at least as important as the message. But oratory was for men, not for women. And Judith had no desire to call attention to her person in any event. Handwriting, not print, was "the medium of the self" (31–33).

33. Shevelow, *Women and Print Culture*, 73; Judith Stevens to Winthrop Sargent, 16 October 1784, Letter Book 2: 288.

34. Shields, *Civil Tongues*, 265, 273; Wilcox, "The Scribblings of a Plain Man," 127–28; "The Gleaner," no. 6, *Massachusetts Magazine*, August 1792, 477.

35. "The Gleaner," no. 5, *Massachusetts Magazine*, August 1792, 476–77. See also "The Repository," no. 2, *Massachusetts Magazine*, October 1792, 614.

36. "The Gleaner," no. 12, *Massachusetts Magazine*, March 1793, 137–38. For a discussion of the way that Americans were beginning to change their attitudes toward the use of pseudonyms see Warner, *Letters of the Republic*, 38, and Waldstreicher, *In the Midst of Perpetual Fetes*, 63. See also Burgett, *Sentimental Bodies*, 124–30; Agnew, *Worlds Apart*, 167. "The Gleaner," no. 12, *Massachusetts Magazine*, March 1794, 156–57, provides an especially good example of the way the styles of the "gleaner" and Mr. Vigilius are blurred. For examples of her introduction of other characters, see "The Gleaner," no. 6, August 1792, 468–90.

37. JSM to [?], 15 June 1793, Letter Book 7: 28; Spacks, *The Female Imagination*, 12, 20; Davidson, *Revolution and the Word*, 97–98; Watts, *Writing and Post-Colonialism*, 42; Hannah More, *Strictures on the Modern System of Female Education*, 2nd ed. (London: T. Cadell, Jr. and W. Davies, 1799), 2: 13–14.

38. See Wood, *Radicalism of the American Revolution*, 39–40. In fact, she anticipated by more than a decade the "Federalist feminism" of Joseph Dennie's *Port Folio*, which proclaimed that women's minds had been ignored too long, even as it argued that intellect was the only yardstick by which a society could measure merit. Dowling, *Literary Federalism*, 80–81, 84; Waldstreicher, *In the Midst of Perpetual Fetes*, 67–68, 71. For a discussion of one woman who argued that both class *and* gender distinctions were unjust, see Donna Landry, "The Resignation of Mary Collier: Some Problems in Feminist Literary History," in Nussbaum and Brown, eds., *The New Eighteenth Century*, 105. For an indication that JSM was not alone in her identification with elite men and her desire to separate herself from lower-class women, see Smith-Rosenberg, "Hearing Women's Words," 42; Ryan, *Women in Public*, 74.

39. Nord, "A Republican Literature," 48, 50; David Jaffee, "The Village Enlightenment in New England, 1760–1820," *William and Mary Quarterly* 3rd ser. 47 (1990): 327–29. For an alternative interpretation, see Watts, *Writing and Postcolonialism*, 55; Harris in Murray, *Selected Writings*, xxxi.

40. "The Gleaner," no. 24, *Massachusetts Magazine*, May 1794, 275. See Carroll Smith-Rosenberg, "Bourgeois Discourse and the Age of Jackson: An Introduction," in Smith-Rosenberg, ed., *Disorderly Conduct*, 85 for a nice analysis of the differences between eighteenth-and early nineteenth-century views of heterogeneity.

41. "The Gleaner," no. 24, *Massachusetts Magazine*, May 1794, 276–77. For examples of other eighteenth-century writers—including Mary Wollstonecraft—who saw class and gender issues in a similar way, see Poovey, *The Proper Lady*, 31–33; Sylvana Tomaselli, "The Enlightenment Debate on Women," *History Workshop* 20 (1985): 107–12; Landes, *Women and the Public Sphere*, 148–51, 170–72.

42. "The Repository," no. 1, *Massachusetts Magazine*, September 1792, 568.

43. "The Repository," no. 17, *Massachusetts Magazine*, February 1794, 89–91; no. 18, May 1794, 260–61.

44. "The Repository," no. 2, *Massachusetts Magazine*, January 1792, 18; Murray, "Friendship," Repository, 5, 6; "The Repository," no. 3, "Friendship," *Massachusetts Magazine*, November 1792, 667–68; Murray, "Sentiments on Christian Amity," Repository, 97; "The Repository," no. 6, "Platonism," *Massachusetts Magazine*, February 1793, 73; JSM to Maria Sargent, 9 November 1790, Letter Book 6: 375; to Maria Sargent, 29 May 1794, Letter Book 8: 198–201.

45. JSM to Epes Sargent, 22 June 1795, Letter Book 8: 316; Proceedings of the Pro-

prietors of the First Universalist Church in Boston, vol. 1, 1792–1803; Charles A. Howe, "How Human an Enterprise: The Story of the First Universal Society in Boston During John Murray's Ministry," *Proceedings of the Unitarian Universalist Society* (1990–1991): 19; Murray, *Life*, 339n; Winsor, *The Memorial History of Boston*, 448. Elbridge Gerry Brooks, "Letters of Murray and Richards," *Universalist Quarterly* 9 (July 1872): 141.

46. Proceedings of the Proprietors 1: 2 March, 5 April 1792; 18 August, 20, 24 October 1793; Howe, "How Human an Enterprise," 19; John Murray to Mr. Redding, 15 December 1794, *Universalist Quarterly* 25 (1968): 471–72; Boston Church to the Brethren of the Universal Profession, Philadelphia, 12 May 1792, *Universalist Quarterly* 12 (1875): 472.

47. JSM to Maria Sargent, 12 June 1793, to Miss Abby Saltonstall of New London, 2 November 1793, Letter Book 8: 121–22, 168.

48. JSM to Maria Sargent, 7 August 1793, to Winthrop Sargent, Sr., 8 August 1793, Letter Book 8: 130–31, 134–35.

49. JSM to Maria Sargent, 28 August, 2, 25 December 1793, 5 January 1794, to Miss Saltonstall of New London, 28 January 1795, Letter Book 8: 147–48, 169–71, 175, 254–55.

50. John Murray to Mr. Redding, 9 June 1794, *Universalist Quarterly* 6 (1869): 422; JSM to Maria Sargent, 24, 27, 28 March, to Winthrop Sargent, 24 September 1794, Letter Book 8: 181–82, 186–88, 191–92.

Chapter 9. "A School of Virtue"

1. JSM to [?], 29 April 1794, Murray, Letter Book 8: 195.

2. JSM to Maria Sargent, 21 June 1794, Letter Book 8: 210.

3. Bushman, *Refinement of America*, 354–55; Harold Kirker and James Kirker, *Bulfinch's Boston, 1797–1817* (New York: Oxford University Press, 1964), 12, 16, 21, 54; Young, *The Shoemaker and the Tea Party*, 121–27; Harlow Elizabeth Walker Sheidley, "Sectional Nationalism: The Culture and Politics of the Massachusetts Conservative Elite, 1815–1836" (Ph.D. dissertation, University of Connecticut, 1990), 20, 28; *Columbian Centinel*, 4 March, 11 April 1795; Josiah Quincy, *A Municipal History of the Town and City of Boston During Two Centuries, From September 17, 1630 to September 17, 1830* (Boston: Charles C. Little and James Brown, 1852), 35.

4. Kirker and Kirker, *Bulfinch's Boston*, 39, 40, 65–67; Harold Kirker, *The Architecture of Charles Bulfinch* (Cambridge, Mass.: Harvard University Press, 1969), 89; Frank Chouteau Brown, "The First Boston Theatre on Federal Street," *Old Time New England* 36 (1945): 2; Ellen Susan Bulfinch, ed., *The Life and Letters of Charles Bulfinch, Architect* (New York: Burt Franklin 1973), 98–102; *Columbian Centinel*, 5 October 1791; Winsor, *Memorial History of Boston*, 474, 474n; Young, *The Shoemaker and the Tea Party*, 126; *Federal Orrery* (4 May 1795): 222; Reinier, *From Virtue to Character*, 50.

5. JSM to Esther Ellery, 19 September 1794, to Mrs. P____ of Hampstead, England, 15 November 1794, Letter Book 8: 224, 244; to Winthrop Sargent, 24 September 1794, 9, 16 August 1796, Letter Book 9: 491–93, 593; *Massachusetts Magazine*, February 1794, 67. See also Kirker and Kirker, *Bulfinch's Boston*, 40–46; Kirker, *The Architecture of Charles Bulfinch*, 89–90; Bushman, *The Refinement of America*, 101–3; 113–14, 354–55. Henry Sargent's painting, *The Dinner Party*, created about 1821, gives an idea of the dining area in

the houses. Now hanging in the Boston Museum of Fine Arts, this picture of Sargent's home, 10 Franklin Place, depicts a gathering of the Wednesday Evening Club. The dining room has a carpeted floor and a table big enough for fifteen people. It has two windows and a fireplace. Its tall ceilings give the room an airy look; the decorative molding around the top of the wall adds a genteel touch.

6. JSM to Esther Ellery, 19 September 1794, to Mrs. S____ of Hampstead, England, 19 September 1794, Letter Book 8: 224, 228; Goldin, "The Economic Status of Women in the Early Republic," 398.

7. JSM to Miss Saltonstall of New London, 28 January 1795, Letter Book 8: 255; to Winthrop Sargent, 24 September 1794, Letter Book 9: 290; to Mrs. W____ of Philadelphia, 11 June 1797, to Maria Sargent, 1 October 1798, to Miss E____ S____ of Hampstead, 11 December 1798, Letter Book 10: 126, 286–87, 313.

8. Kasson, *Rudeness and Civility*, 117; Ryan, *Women in Public*, 60–63; *Columbian Centinel*, 4 March 1795; *Boston Gazette*, 28 December 1795.

9. JSM to Maria Sargent, 24, 27, 28 March 1794, n.d., 10 August 1794, to the two Girls, Mary Sargent Allen and Sarah Sargent Ellery, 21 July 1795, to Esther Ellery, 24 July 1795, to Miss Sarah Ellery, 25 August 1795, to Epes Sargent, 21 September 1795, to Miss A____, 26 September 1795, Letter Book 8: 181–82, 186–88, 191–92, 218, 220, 329, 335, 342–43, 353–54; to Winthrop Sargent, 16 August 1796, Letter Book 9: 594; to Maria Sargent, 6 October 1796, Letter Book 10: 43; *Boston Gazette*, 12 June 1797; *Federal Orrery* (18 May 1795): 235. Even a century later, almost 36% of Boston's children died before the age of ten. Reinier, *From Virtue to Character*, 62.

10. Gilmore, *Reading Becomes a Necessity of Life*, 21, 25; *Columbian Centinel*, 12 September 1795; Kilbride, "Cultivation, Conservatism, and the Early National Gentry," 226; *Boston Gazette*, 28 December 1795, 15 April 1797; JSM to Miss Saltonstall of New London, 28 January 1795, to Mrs. Barrell of York, 29 January 1795, to Miss Allen, 2 February 1795, to the Two Girls, Mary Sargent Allen and Sarah Sargent Ellery, 21 July 1795, Letter Book 8: 256–57, 263, 332–34.

11. Winsor, *Memorial History of Boston*, 242; Quincy, *Municipal History*, 20–21; *Federal Orrery* (1 June 1795): 254; *Boston Gazette*, 28 March 1796; *Columbian Centinel*, 14 March, 1, 29 April, 2 December 1795; JSM to Maria Sargent, 6 May 1792, to Mrs. W____ of Philadelphia, 8 March 1793, Letter Book 8: 38, 95; to the Mother of Mr. Murray, 10 October 1796, Letter Book 10: 45.

12. Anne C. Rose, "Social Sources of Denominationalism Reconsidered: Post-Revolutionary Boston as a Case Study," *American Quarterly* 38 (1986): 249, 252; Proceedings of the Proprietors, vol. 1: 7 April 1794, 18 October 1795, 1 May 1796; *Federal Orrery* (24 March 1796): 189; Murray, *Life of John Murray*, 369; Howe, "How Human an Enterprise," 20, 25.

13. John Murray to a Friend, Murray, *Letters and Sketches of Sermons* 1: 293; John Murray to Mrs. Y____, Murray, *Letters and Sketches of Sermons*, 2: 261; JSM to Epes Sargent, 22 June 1795, Letter Book 8: 316.

14. Nylander, *Our Own Snug Fireside*, 230; Burr, *Journal*, 15; JSM to Mrs. W____ of Philadelphia, 11 June 1797, Letter Book 10: 126. Even the fictionalized Eliza Wharton in Hannah Foster's *Coquette* resisted becoming a minister's wife, knowing that such a position would not only "confine" her to a domestic life but make her dependent upon her husband's parishioners, who would feel free to use her behavior her as a convenient means to attack their minister. Smith-Rosenberg, "Domesticating 'Virtue,'" 173.

15. Howe, "How Human an Enterprise," 21; JSM to the Two Girls Mary Sargent Allen and Sarah Sargent Ellery, 21 July 1795, Letter Book 8: 329–30; to Mrs. W____ of Philadelphia, 11 June 1797, to Maria Sargent, 1 October 1798, Letter Book 10: 126, 287; Murray, Repository, 120.

16. JSM to Miss Mary A____, 27 December 1794, Letter Book 8: 249.

17. JSM to Winthrop Sargent, 30 November 1795, Letter Book 9: 496; Esther Sargent to Winthrop Sargent, 15 October 1795, Sargent Murray Gilman Hough House Papers.

18. JSM to Miss Mary Allen, 2 Feburary 1795, to Esther Ellery, 3 March 1795, Letter Book 8: 262, 274–75; to Winthrop Sargent, 30 November 1795, Letter Book 9: 496.

19. JSM to the Two Girls, Mary Sargent Allen and Sarah Sargent Ellery, 21 July 1795, Letter Book 8: 328; to Winthrop Sargent, 29 February 1796, Letter Book 9: 541; *Boston Gazette*, 14 December 1795, 11 July 1796; Ryan, *Women in Public*, 64–66; Cott, "Passionless," 225; Branson, *These Fiery Frenchified Dames*, 55–100; Rosemarie Zagarri, "Gender and the First Party System," in Ben-Atar and Oberg, eds., *Federalists Reconsidered*, 118–34; Waldstreicher, *In The Midst of Perpetual Fetes*, 171; Barbara Laslett, "The Family as a Public and Private Institution: An Historical Perspective," *Journal of Marriage and the Family* 35 (1973): 489, 492.

20. In France many people recognized that the Revolution, at least in the short run, opened up public spaces for women. Landes, *Women and the Public Sphere*, 147. Judith did not seem to notice this. She talked of the Revolution's class, not its gender implications, which does a great deal to explain her hostility.

21. JSM to Mrs. Pilgrim of London, 25 December 1792, to Maria Sargent, 24 March 1793, Letter Book 8: 91, 108–9.

22. JSM to Maria Sargent, 5 January 1794, Letter Book 8: 178; to Winthrop Sargent, 30 November 1795, Letter Book 9: 495.

23. JSM to Winthrop Sargent, 18 January 1796, Letter Book 9: 528. For discussions of the profound uneasiness with which Federalists viewed the competitive and individualistic wave of the future, see Poovey, *The Proper Lady*, xvi, 30; Brown, "Mary Wollstonecraft," 400, 403; Robert E. Shallope, "Republicanism, Liberalism, and Democracy: Political Culture in the Early Republic," *Proceedings of the American Antiquarian Society* 102 (1992): 149. Poovey discusses the anti-feminist "backlash" that followed in the wake of the French Revolution. Poovey, *The Proper Lady*, 131–33.

24. JSM to the Reverend Doctor Moore, 12 September 1795, Letter Book 8: 352; to Winthrop Sargent, 30 November 1795, 28 January, 13 February, 12 April 1796, Letter Book 9: 495, 533, 535–37, 572; "The Gleaner," 23, 24, *Massachusetts Magazine*, April, May 1794.

25. JSM to Winthrop Sargent, 4 April, 1 May 1796, Letter Book 9: 567–78.

26. JSM to Winthrop Sargent, 23 April, 6 June 1796, Letter Book 9: 574–76, 588. See Morton Borden, *Parties and Politics in the Early Republic, 1789–1815* (Arlington Heights, Ill.: Harlan Davidson, 1967), 48–50, for a concise summary of the congressional reaction to the Jay Treaty.

27. JSM to Anna Sargent, 20 June 1793, Letter Book 8: 115; to Winthrop Sargent, 28 January, 8 May, 15, 16 August 1796, 13 January 1797, Letter Book 9: 533, 583–84, 593, 605.

28. JSM to Winthrop Sargent, 15 March 1787, Letter Book 3: 195; to Maria Sargent, 2 December 1793, 21 June, 14 July 1794, Letter Book 8: 210, 215–16; to Winthrop Sargent, 19 January, 14 February, 8, 9 June 1795, Letter Book 9: 500, 504, 511, 514.

29. JSM to Anna Sargent, 30 October 1795, Letter Book 8: 355; to Winthrop Sargent,

15 August 1796, 13 January 1797, Letter Book 9: 592, 604; Governor St. Clair to Secretary Sargent, 28 August, 6 September 1796, to James Ross, 6 September 1796, Smith, ed., *St. Clair* Papers, 2: 405–6, 410.

30. Caroline Turner Smith, *Caroline Augusta Sargent Turner, Daughter of Gov. Winthrop Sargent (1795–1844)* (Chatham, N.J.: self-published, 1995), 12–15.

31. JSM to Winthrop Sargent, 21 March, 15 July, 1 November 1796, 2 February, 27 April, 11 June, 1 August 1797, Letter Book 9: 561, 592, 598–99, 607, 613, 615, 619.

32. JSM to Winthrop Sargent, 1 November 1796, 2 February 1797, Letter Book 9: 598–99, 617.

33. John Murray to Robert Redding, 23 May 1796, in Skinner and Cole, *Hell's Ramparts*, 154; JSM to Anna Sargent, 2 February 1795, to Mr. S____, 13 February 1795, to Anna Sargent, 10 June 1795, Letter Book 8: 261, 270, 309; to Winthrop Sargent, 30 November, Letter Book 9: 496, 498; to Winthrop Sargent, 31 December 1795 to Anna Sargent, 19 May 1796, Letter Book 10: 22–23; to Winthrop Sargent, 13 October 1796, 13 January 1797, Letter Book 9: 597, 604; Mann, *The Sargent Family*, 37. Interestingly, when Judith signed the deed to the Gloucester house "in her own right," in April 1797, she signed it Judith Sargent—not Judith Stevens or Judith Murray.

34. JSM to Esther Ellery, 3 March 1795, to Epes Sargent, 4 May 1795, to Anna Sargent, 27 July 1795, to Epes Sargent, 31 August 1795, Letter Book 8: 275, 297, 338, 347; to Winthrop Sargent, 28 January, 22 February 1796, Letter Book 9: 532, 538; to Mr. S____ and Lady, 14 March 1797, Letter Book 10: 91; to Winthrop Sargent, 24 April 1797, Letter Book 9: 611; to Miss [Esther] Sargent of Hampstead, 8 May 1797, Letter Book 10: 111. See Bulfinch, ed., *Life and Letters of Charles Bulfinch* (New York: Burt Franklin, 1973), 90, 98–99, for details concerning the Tontine Crescent's financial difficulties.

35. John Murray to William Palmer, 20 August 1800, Palmer Papers; Proceedings of the Proprietors, vol. 1, 17 June 1798.

36. John Murray to John West, 16 November 1795, George Lyman Paine, Autograph Collection, 1660–1828; John Murray to Robert Redding, 8 November 1797, *Universalist Quarterly* 6 (1869): 425; JSM to Winthrop Sargent, 28 January 1796, Letter Book 9: 531; to Mrs. P____ of Plymouth in England, 23 May 1796; to Miss Catherine Sargent, 13 July 1796; to Mrs. Barrell of York, 31 January 1798; Letter Book 10: 25, 37, 193; *Columbian Centinel*, 24 September 1791.

37. JSM to Maria Sargent, 14 July 1794, to Anna Sargent, 20 January 1795, to Miss Saltonstall, 28 January 1795, to Miss Allen, 2 March 1795, to Esther Ellery, 3 March 1795, to Miss Allen, 26 April 1795, Letter Book 8: 215, 251, 256, 271–72, 274, 296.

38. JSM to Mr. Paine, Editor of the *Federal Orrery*, 15 October 1794, Letter Book 8: 237–39. See Ellis, "Joseph Dennie," 69.

39. "The Reaper," no. 1 *Federal Orrery* (20 October 1794): 2; "The Reaper," no. 3, "Androgeny," *Federal Orrery* (17 November 1794); "The Reaper," no. 2, *Federal Orrery* (27 October 1794); 10. "Androgeny" is also in Murray, Repository, 122; "The Reaper," no. 2, appears in Repository, 121–22.

40. JSM to Mr. Paine, Editor of the *Federal Orrery*, 11 November 1794, Letter Book 8: 241, 242. For her fears of being accused of plagiarism see JSM to Epes Sargent, 4 May 1795, Letter Book 8: 302.

41. JSM to Miss Saltonstall, 28 January 1795, to Epes Sargent, 4 May 1795, Letter Book 8: 256, 301.

42. *Columbian Centinel*, 12 September 1795; JSM to Esther Ellery, 3 March 1795, Letter Book 8: 276; to Epes Sargent, 1 March 1796, Letter Book 10: 11–12. As Sharon Harris has pointed out, both men and women in the eighteenth century became playwrights in part because they did not find the genre intimidating. Because they used dialogue in their poetry and their short sketches, it seemed a logical step. Many teachers used dialogue, as Judith did in her *Catechism*, as a pedagogical tactic. Harris, *American Women Writers*, 170; see also Baym, *American Women Writers*, 190.

43. See Silverman, "Economic Debate over the Theater," 219–40; Withington, *Toward a More Perfect Union* especially 11, 13, 20–47.

44. See Silverman, "The Economic Debate over the Theater," 222–33; Kenneth Silverman, *A Cultural History of the American Revolution: Painting, Music, Literature, and the Theatre in the Colonies and the United States from the Treaty of Paris to the Inauguration of George Washington, 1763–1789* (New York: T.Y. Crowell, 1976), 546–51; Joseph J. Ellis, *After the Revolution: Profiles of Early American Culture*, 35, 129–32; David Grimsted, *Melodrama Unveiled: American Theater and Culture, 1800–1850* (Chicago: University of Chicago Press, 1968), 85, 87; Withington, *Toward a More Perfect Union*, chap. 2.

45. See Ryan, *Women in Public*, 67, 71; Richard Butsch, "Bowery B'hoys and Matinee Ladies: The Re-Gendering of Nineteenth-Century American Theater Audiences," *American Quarterly* 46 (1994): 374–75, 379, 381, 400; Faye E. Dudden, *Women in the American Theater: Actresses and Audiences, 1790–1870* (New Haven, Conn.: Yale University Press, 1994), 3, 5, 15.

46. "The Gleaner," no. 21 *Massachusetts Magazine*, February 1794, 95–105; Pendleton and Ellis, *Philenia*, 51; Kirker and Kirker, *Bulfinch's Boston*, 57–58; *Columbian Centinel*, 12 November 1791; Ruth Michael, "A History of the Professional Theatre in Boston from the Beginning to 1816" (Ph.D. dissertation, Radcliffe, 1941), 1: 31; Silverman, *A Cultural History of the American Revolution*, 547–53; JSM to Maria Sargent, 6 October 1796, Letter Book 10: 43.

47. Michael, "History of the Professional Theatre in Boston," 34; Dorothy M. Bonawitz, "The History of the Boston Stage from the Beginning to 1812" (Ph.D. dissertation, Pennsylvania State College, 1936), 45–46; G. Thomas Tanselle, *Royall Tyler* (Cambridge, Mass.: Harvard University Press, 1967), 50; Ryan, *Women in Public*, 62, 67, 71; Grimsted, *Melodrama Unveiled*, 53; Dudden, *Women in the American Theater*, 25–26; "The Reaper," no. 4 *Federal Orrery* (20 November 1794): 38; *Columbian Centinel*, 22 February 1794, 27 March, 23 May 1795.

48. *Federal Orrery* (10 November 1794). See also Michael, "History of the Professional Theatre in Boston," 51–54; Kirker, *The Architecture of Charles Bulfinch*, 67.

49. "The Gleaner," no. 21, *Massachusetts Magazine*, February 1794, 100–105; Michael, "History of the Professional Theatre in Boston," 59–61; JSM to Maria Sargent, 27 March 1794, to Esther Ellery, 3 March 1795, to Anna Sargent, 5 March 1795, Letter Book 8: 190, 275–81, 283.

50. Landes, *Women and the Public Sphere*, 52; Zoe Detsi-Diamanti, *Early American Women Dramatists, 1775–1860* (New York: Garland, 1988), 6–9; Dudden, *Women in the American Theater*, 17–18; Preston, *Created Self*, 197. Mercy Otis Warren had qualms about writing political plays, even when they would be read, not performed, because she feared losing her "femininity." Judith's efforts were much more audacious, and thus more open to attack. Shuffelton, "In Different Voices," 291, 298.

51. Ehrenpreis and Halsband, *The Lady of Letters*, 32, 38, 44, 47; Margarete Rubik, *Early American Dramatists, 1550–1800* (New York: St. Martin's Press, 1998), 144–45, 167–84; Charles Lowell Lees, "An Introductory Study of the American People of the Eighteenth Century Through Their Drama and Theatrical Study" (Ph.D. dissertation, University of Wisconsin, 1934); Walter J. Meserve, *An Emerging Entertainment: The Drama of the American People to 1828* (Bloomington: Indiana University Press, 1977), 117–18; Baym, "Between Enlightenment and Victorian," 36; Amelia Howe Kritzer, ed., *Plays by Early American Women, 1775–1850* (Ann Arbor: University of Michigan Press, 1995), 2; Susan Coultrap-McQuin, *Doing Literary Business: American Women Writers in the Nineteenth Century* (Chapel Hill: University of North Carolina Press, 1990), 194. Rogers, *Before Their Time*, vii–viii, gives a slightly more upbeat assessment of eighteenth-century women who wrote for money.

52. JSM to Epes Sargent, 4 May 1795, Letter Book 8: 301; to Winthrop Sargent, 21 March 1796, Letter Book 9: 559; John Murray to Robert Redding, 26 February 1799, *Universalist Quarterly* 6 (1869): 427.

53. See especially Rust, "'Women Were Born for Universal Sway,'" 5, 8, 10–11, 20. See also Wendy Martin, "Profile: Susanna Rowson, Early American Novelist," *Women's Studies* 2 (1974): 1–8; Christopher Castiglia, "Susanna Rowson's *Reuben and Rachel*: Captivity, Colonization, and the Domestication of Columbus," in Harris, ed., *Redefining the Political Novel*, 23–42; Detsi-Diamanti, *Early American Women Dramatists*, 64–65.

54. Rust, "'Women Were Born for Universal Sway,'" 2, 3, 9, 30–31; Dudden, *Women in the American Theater*, 2, 3, 14–16; Kathy Peiss, "Going Public: Women in Nineteenth-Century Cultural History," *American Literary History* 3 (1991): 822; Isenberg, *Sex and Citizenship*, 42–44.

55. Mary Ann Schofield and Cecilia Macheski, eds., *Curtain Calls: British and American Women and the Theater, 1660–1820* (Athens: Ohio University Press, 1991), xvi; Kritzer, "Playing with Republican Motherhood," 151; Cathy Davidson, "The Life and Times of Charlotte Temple," in Davidson, ed., *Reading in America*, 160.

56. *Federal Orrery* (26 February 1795): 151; (2 March 1795): 155; (5 March 1795): 160; *Columbian Centinel*, 4 March 1795. For discussions of women playwrights who did—or did not—use pseudonyms see Kritzer, "Playing with Republican Motherhood," 164n; Detsi-Diamanti, *Early American Women Dramatists*, 10; Poovey, *Proper Lady*, 41; Meserve, *An Emerging Entertainment*, 127.

57. JSM to Epes Sargent, 4 May 1795, to Mrs. Bache of Philadelphia, 19 June 1795, Letter Book 8: 301, 312; Bonawitz, "History of the Boston Stage," 66; Grimsted, *Melodrama Unveiled*, 145.

58. *Columbian Centinel*, 11 March 1795.

59. Nor, did it really deserve to be. Detsi-Diamanti argues that it showed "little dramatic skill," that its style was "stilted and dull," and its stock characters were pale reflections of similar American "types" in Royall Tyler's *The Contrast*. Detsi-Diamanti, *Early American Women Dramatists*, 32.

60. JSM to Mrs. Sargent, 22 June 1795, to Epes Sargent, 31 August 1795, Letter Book 8: 318, 347; to Winthrop Sargent, 7 March, 13 April 1796, Letter Book 9: 544, 573–74.

61. JSM to Epes Sargent, 4, 8 May 1795, to Mrs. Bache of Philadelphia, 19 June 1795, Letter Book 8: 300–301, 312; to Winthrop Sargent 7 March 1796, Letter Book 9: 555; Dudden, *Women in the American Theater*, 12–13; Grimsted, *Melodrama Unveiled*, 141–46; *Fed-*

eral Orrery (19 January 1795): 107; Jeffrey H. Richards, "How to Write an American Play: Murray's *Traveller Returned* and Its Sources," *Early American Literature* 33 (1998), 288n; Meserve, *An Emerging Enlightenment*, 127–28; Rust, "'Women Were Born for Universal Sway,'" 9n. For indications that Judith's experience with Powell was not singular, see Weldon B. Durham, ed., *American Theatre Companies, 1749–1887* (New York: Greenwood Press, 1986), 75–76; Michael, "History of the Professional Theatre in Boston," 42–47, 75–80; George O. Seilhamer, *History of the American Theatre* (Philadelphia: Globe Printing House, 1891), 3: 228–31.

62. JSM to Mrs. Bache of Philadelphia, 19 June 1795, to Epes Sargent, 22 June 1795, Letter Book 8: 311–13, 317; to Winthrop Sargent, 21, 28 March, 13 April 1796, Letter Book 9: 559–60, 563, 574. When she referred to the Chestnut Theater's willingness to produce new plays, she may very well have had Rowson's recent success in mind.

63. JSM to Winthrop Sargent, 30 November 1795, 21 March 1796, Letter Book 9: 520–21, 559–60. In America, to have one's play performed as few as seven times was a real sign of success. Judith was by no means the only native author who failed to reap the financial awards or critical acclaim of a Royall Tyler or Susanna Rowson. Arthur Hobson Quinn, *A History of the American Drama from the Beginning to the Civil War* (New York: Harper and Brothers, 1923), 76. See also Grimsted, *Melodrama Unveiled*, 63.

64. JSM to Epes Sargent, 4 May, 22 June 1795, to Mrs. P____, 30 June 1795, Letter Book 8: 302, 317, 322; to Winthrop Sargent, 9, 25 January, 8 May 1796, Letter Book 9: 525–26, 530, 579–80.

65. JSM to Mr. Powell, 16 May 1795, Letter Book 8: 304.

66. Ibid., 304–6.

67. JSM to Epes Sargent, 9 January 1796, Letter Book 10: 2; *Columbian Centinel*, 25 May, 26 September, 1795; *Federal Orrery* (12, 21, 25 May, 24 September 1795). Tyler was Royall Tyler's brother. Durham, *American Theater Companies*, 75–76; Michael, "History of the Professional Theater in Boston," 98–99.

68. JSM to Epes Sargent, 9 January 1796, to Anna Sargent, 26 March 1796, to Maria Sargent, 8 October 1798, Letter Book 10: 2–3, 13, 296; *Columbian Centinel*, 7 November 1795.

69. JSM to Esther Ellery, 28 March 1796, Letter Book 10: 15. The *Centinel* advertised the play, characterizing it as an "American Production," on 9 March 1796.

70. JSM to Epes Sargent, 2 April 1796, Letter Book 10: 19; Michael, "A History of the Professional Theatre in Boston," 78; Ellis, "Joseph Dennie," 69, 70.

71. JSM to Esther Ellery, 28 March 1796, to Epes Sargent, 2 April 1796, Letter Book 10: 15–16, 18.

72. *Federal Orrery* (17 March 1796): 171; JSM to Esther Ellery, 28 March 1796, Letter Book 10: 16. Judith's reaction to Paine's critique was not especially unusual. See, for instance, Thadeus Harris to Richard Devens, 1 August, 1 September, 1795, Richard Devens to Thadeus Harris, 31 August, 3 September 1795, Frothingham Papers, Box 1, Folder 17.

73. *Federal Orrery* (21 March 1796), 175.

74. *Federal Orrery* (24 March 1796); *Columbian Centinel* 26 March 1796.

75. JSM to Epes Sargent, 2 April 1796, Letter Book 10: 18–20.

76. JSM to Anna Sargent, 26 March 1796, to Esther Ellery, 28 March 1796, to Epes Sargent, 2 April 1796, Letter Book 10: 13–15, 18, 19.

77. Richards, "How to Write an American Play," 288n; JSM to Esther Ellery, 28 March 1796, to Epes Sargent, 2 April 1796, Letter Book 10: 15, 19. See *Federal Orrery* (8, 18,

22 December 1794): 59, 70, 74; (8, 19, 26 January 1795): 94, 107, 115; (12 November 1795): 25–26, for examples of Thespiad's negative reviews.

78. William Cobbett, *Peter Porcupine in America: Pamphlets on Republicanism and Revolution*, ed. David A. Wilson (Ithaca, N.Y.: Cornell University Press, 1994), 131; *The Traveller Returned* in *The Gleaner*, 670.

79. Seilhamer, *History of the American Theater*, 3: 248; Detsi-Diamanti, *Early American Women Dramatists*, 32–33; Meserve, *An Emerging Entertainment*, 154–55. Jeffrey Richards makes a persuasive argument that Judith used *The West Indian*—a play performed by the Gloucester thespians—as her model for *The Traveller Returned*. Richards, "How to Write an American Play," 277–82.

80. *The Traveller Returned*, 655. See Richards, "How to Write an American Play," 284.

81. *The Traveller Returned*, 655. Emily is the eighteenth-century ideal. Harriot is too sentimental, while Mrs. Montague is too rational. In terms that Ralph Maitland would have found appealing, Emily is the "happy medium."

82. *Virtue Triumphant* in *The Gleaner*, 554, 562, 565, 578, 608; Kritzer, "Playing with Republican Motherhood," 153–54, 162; Kritzer, "Comedies by Early American Women," in Brenda Murphy, ed., *The Cambridge Companion to American Women Playwrights* (Cambridge: Cambridge University Press, 1999), 12.

83. *Virtue Triumphant*, 561, 569, 605; *The Traveller Returned*, 650, 663–64; Kritzer, "Comedies," 9, 12–13; Kritzer, "Playing with Republican Motherhood," 153–57; Kritzer, *Plays by Early American Women*, 15; Richards, "How to Write an American Play," 282–83. Kritzer argues that Judith's depiction of the "female rake reformed" was unique. Kritzer, *Plays by Early American Women*, 15. Judith had, of course, played with this idea already in her treatment of Frances Wellwood. Admittedly Frances was no rake; she was a deceived innocent. Yet she lived a "life of sin" and surely was as deserving of punishment as Clarissa Harlowe or Charlotte Temple. Instead she was rewarded with a husband and a comfortable living, and even managed to recover her social standing. See also Kritzer, "Playing with Republican Motherhood," 154–55, 157.

84. *The Traveller Returned*, 647, 651, 655, 659, 661–63. Harris argues that JSM "obviously" preferred Harriot to Emily. Perhaps. Modern readers surely find her the more attractive character. Judith was probably less certain, and surely found Emily less "stodgy" and more admirable than this argument implies. Harris, in Murray, *Selected Writings*, xxxviii.

85. JSM to Winthrop Sargent, 11 June 1797, Letter Book 9: 614; *The Traveller Returned*, 649, 663; *Virtue Triumphant*, 603–6.

86. *Virtue Triumphant*, 589; *The Traveller Returned*, 648; Kritzer, "Playing with Republican Motherhood," 157–58. Judith's validation of the single life echos her advice to her niece, Anna. JSM to Anna, 11 October 1790, Letter Book 4: 253.

87. *The Traveller Returned*, 641.

88. Her ambivalence was apparent three years later when she found it difficult to respond to a young friend who, like Eliza, was "warmly against disproportioned, or unequal marriages." JSM to Miss C____ of L____, 7 March 1797, Letter Book 10: 87.

89. *Virtue Triumphant*, 560, 561, 572, 586, 590.

90. Ibid., 600, 601.

91. *The Traveller Returned*, 660; Kritzer, "Playing with Republican Motherhood,"

153; Kritzer, "Comedies," 3, 11; Detsi-Diamanti, *Early American Women Dramatists*, 50–53; Grimsted, *Melodrama Unveiled*, 127.

92. Seilhamer, *History of the American Theatre*, 3: 306; Michael, "History of the Professional Theatre in Boston," 133; JSM to Winthrop Sargent, 8, 21 May 1796, Letter Book 9: 580, 585–86; JSM to Anna Sargent, 19 May 1786, to Maria Sargent, 8 October 1798, Letter Book 10: 21, 296–97.

93. JSM to Winthrop Sargent, 21 May 1796, Letter Book 9: 585–86; to Mr. Thomas A. Cooper, 17 December 1805, Letter Book 13: [92].

Chapter 10. Federalist Muse

1. See, for instance, Norton, *Liberty's Daughters*, 230, 247; Kerber, *Women of the Republic*, 11, 228; Patricia Jewell McAlexander, "The Creation of the American Eve: The Cultural Dialogue on the Nature and Role of Women in Late Eighteenth-Century America," *Early American Literature* 9 (1975): 255–57.

2. JSM to Winthrop Sargent, 13 April 1796, Letter Book 9: 573; to Mrs. Jackson of Philadelphia, 15 October 1796, to the Rev. Robert Redding, Truro, England, 14 December 179[6], Letter Book, 10: 49, 68–69; JSM to Mercy Otis Warren, 4 March 1796, Warren-Adams Papers.

3. John Murray to Robert Redding, 29 December 1795, 26 February 1799, *Universalist Quarterly* 26 (1869): 32, 426.

4. Shields, *Civil Tongues*, 262.

5. *The Gleaner*, 806; *Massachusetts Magazine*, December 1795, n.p.

6. JSM to Rev. Mr. Harris, 13 February 1796, to Epes Sargent, 15 July, 15 August, 30 September, 6 November 1797, Letter Book 10: 7, 136, 137, 140, 141, 155 172.

7. JSM to Epes Sargent, 6 November 1797, to Mrs. W[arren?] of P____, 4 December 1797, Letter Book 10: 172, 180; see Davidson, *Revolution and the Word*, 16–30; Matthew J. Bruccoli, ed., *The Profession of Authorship in America, 1800–1870: The Papers of William Charvat* (Columbus: Ohio State University Press, 1968), 6–11; Hellmut Lehmann-Haupt, with Lawrence C. Wroth and Rollo G. Silver, *The Book in America: A History of the Making and Selling of Books in the United States*, 2nd ed. (New York: Bowker, 1951), 51.

8. Gelles, *Portia*, 13, 15, 127, 129; Zagarri, *A Woman's Dilemma*, 63, 147–49.

9. Pendleton and Ellis, *Philenia*, 99; Anne M. Ousterhout, *The Most Learned Woman in America: A Life of Elizabeth Graeme Fergusson* (University Park: Pennsylvania State University Press, 2004), 318, 327–30.

10. Patricia L. Parker, *Susanna Rowson* (Boston: Twayne, 1986), 26–27, 84, 88. The prolific Hannah Adams—whose decision to publish was based solely on her need to support herself—comes close to Judith's businesslike efforts to sell subscriptions to *The Gleaner*. Even Adams tended to rely on the patronage—which she aggressively sought out—of well-placed men. Gary D. Schmidt, *A Passionate Usefulness: The Life and Literary Labors of Hannah Adams* (Charlottesville: University of Virginia Press, 2004).

11. JSM to Mrs. Jackson of Philadelphia, 15 October 1796, to John Adams, Esq., Vice President of the United States, 1 November 1796, to His Excellency George Washington, President of the United States, [1796], to General Henry Knox, 6 March 1797, to General

Lincoln, 6 March 1797, to His Excellency Governor Sumner, 1 August 1797, Letter Book 10: 49, 55–56, 60, 84–85, 139.

12. JSM to Winthrop Sargent, 31 December 1796, Letter Book 9: 602; to Mrs. Jackson of Philadelphia, 4 January 1797, to Epes Sargent, 10 May, 15 July 1797, Letter Book 10: 72, 112, 136. For examples of her use of Washington's and Adams's names, see JSM to Mrs. Jackson of Philadelphia, 15 October 1796, to Mr. the Honorable Mr. G____, 24 November 1796, to Col. G____ of Exeter, 4 January 1797, to Col. Marshall, 5 June 1797, Letter Book 10: 49, 64, 74, 123, and passim.

13. Zagarri, *A Woman's Dilemma*, 135–39; JSM to Mercy Otis Warren, 4 March 1796, Letter Book 10: 183–84. The original is in the Warren-Adams Papers.

14. JSM to Mrs. Barrell of York, 31 October 1796, to Mrs. Jackson of Philadelphia, 4 January 1797, to the Rev. Mr. Harris, 4 March 1797, to Mr. Dennie, 9 April 1797, to Mrs. Morton, 4 May 1797, to Mr. and Mrs. Morton, 5 June 1797, to the Rev. Doctor Morse of Charlestown, 26 June 1797, Letter Book 10: 53–54, 72, 84, 98–99, 107, 124, 130. The Mortons, Sally Barrell, Jedidiah Morse and the Rev. Harris all purchased copies of *The Gleaner*. Dennie's name does not appear on the subscription list. For Anne Bingham, see Branson, *These Fiery Frenchified Dames*, 6, 133–34.

15. JSM to Winthrop Sargent, 1 November 1796, 28 April 17[9]8, Letter Book 9: 599, 639; to Esther Ellery, 24 February 1797, Letter Book 10: 77. Winthrop did purchase a book, but he bought it too late to have his name listed among *The Gleaner's* subscribers.

16. JSM to Colonel G____ of Exeter, 4 January 1797, to Mr. E____ of Newport, 4 January 1797, to Mr. C____ of Providence, 5 January 1797, to Colonel W____ of N____, 3 March 1797, to Samuel Brown Esquire, 6 March 1797, to Mrs. A____, 7 March 1797, to JFS of G____, 29 March 1797, to Mr. And Mrs. S____, 2 April 1797, to the Rev. Mr. G____, 7 April 1797, to Doctor J____, 5 June 1797, to Mr. And Mrs. Cobb of Taunton, 5 June 1797, to Mr. B____ of Hartford, 3 July 1797, to Col. W____, 13 July 1797, Letter Book 10: 74–75, 80, 85, 92, 96–97, 122, 125, 134–35. See Ellis, *After the Revolution*, ix, x, for evidence that many American authors were beginning to doubt their ability to create a truly native literary culture.

17. JSM to Mr. A____ of Gloucester, 24 February 1797, to Mrs. S____ of S____, 3 March 1797, to Mr. and Mrs. S____, 2 April 1797, Letter Book 10: 78, 82, 96.

18. JSM to Miss Abby Saltonstall of New London, 4 November 1796, to Miss Nancy Turner of Norwich, 24 May 1797, to Abby Saltonstall of New London, 27 May 1797, Letter Book 10: 58–59, 118–19, 121.

19. JSM to Mrs. Jackson of Philadelphia, 15 October 1796, 4 January, 25 April 1797, Letter Book 10: 49, 72, 106.

20. JSM to Miss C____ of L____, 7 March 1797, to Mrs. JFS of G____, 29 March 1797, Letter Book 10: 87, 92.

21. JSM to Mrs. Barrell of York, 31 October 1796, to Monsieurs Thomas & Andrews, 26 July 1797, Letter Book 10: 54, 138–39. Elizabeth Graeme was experiencing the same high prices in Philadelphia. Ousterhout, *The Most Learned Woman in America*, 330.

22. JSM to Winthrop Sargent, 28 August 1797, Letter Book 9: 621–23; Esther Ellery to Winthrop Sargent, 20 February 1798, Sargent Murray Gilman Hough Papers.

23. JSM to Winthrop Sargent, 4 September 1797, Letter Book 9: 625–26; Esther Ellery to Winthrop Sargent, 20 February 1798, 29 June 1800, Sargent Murray Gilman Hough Papers.

24. JSM to Epes Sargent, 30 September 1797, to Monsiers Thomas and Andrews, 2, 3 October 1797, to Esther Ellery, 20 October 1797, Letter Book 10: 155–58, 164.

25. JSM to Monsieurs Thomas and Andrews, n.d., to Mrs. Jackson of Philadelphia, 31 October 1797, Letter Book 10: 159, 170; to Winthrop Sargent, 28 April 17[9]8, Letter Book 9: 639.

26. JSM to Epes Sargent, 10 May 1797, Letter Book 10: 112.

27. JSM to Mr. and Mrs. S____, 2 April 1797, Letter Book 10: 96–97; Kelly, *The New England Fashion*, 7; Burr, *Journal*, ix–x, 5; Schiebinger, *The Mind Has No Sex*, 231; Betty Rizzo, "The Dash and Its Grammar," in McKenzie, ed., *Sent as a Gift*, 82–84. For a different explanation, one that probably did not apply to Judith, see Harris, *American Women Writers*, 22.

28. JSM to Maria Sargent, 1 October 1798, Letter Book 10: 289–90; Benjamin Rush, *Thoughts upon Female Education, Accommodated to the Present State of Society, Manners, and Government in the United States of America* (Boston: Samuel Hall, 1787), in Rudolph, ed., *Essays on Education in the Early Republic*, 28–29; Sheidley, "Sectional Nationalism," 191–92; Smith-Rosenberg, "Hearing Women's Words," 47–48; Free, *The Columbian Magazine*, 57–59.

29. Tompkins, "Susannah Rowson," 35; Gilmore, *Reading Becomes a Necessity*, 49, 109.

30. JSM to Epes Sargent, 10 May, 6 November 1797, Letter Book 10: 113–15, 173; Free, *The Columbian Magazine*, 57. See also JSM to Alexis Eustaphieve, Esq., 18 February 1817, Letter Book 20: 45–46.

31. JSM to Winthrop Sargent, 21 March 1798, Letter Book 9: 637. In fact, she—or the printers—altered this plan in the end.

32. JSM to Epes Sargent, 15 July, 30 September, 6 November 1797, to Mrs. W[arren?] of P____, 4 December 1797, to Epes Sargent, 24 December 1797, Letter Book 10: 136, 156, 172, 180, 186.

33. JSM to Mrs. Jackson of Philadelphia, 30 November 1797, to Mrs. W[arren?] of P____, 4 December 1797, to Mr. Manning, 8 December 1797, to Epes Sargent, 24 December 1797, to Mrs. Barrell of York, 31 January 1798, Letter Book 10: 179–80, 182, 186, 192; John Murray to Robert Redding, 29 December 1795, *Universalist Quarterly* (1869): 32.

34. JSM to Mrs. Jackson of Philadelphia, 30 November 1797, to Mrs. Barrell, 31 January 1798, to Mr. Manning, [?] March 1798, Letter Book 10: 180, 192, 196; to Winthrop Sargent, 21 March 1798, Letter Book 9: 636.

35. JSM to Mrs. Jackson of Philadelphia, 31 October 1797, Letter Book 10: 169–70.

36. JSM to Mrs. Barrell of York, 31 October 1796, to Miss Turner of Norwich, 10 April 1798, to Miss Saltonstall of new London, 10 April 1798, to Colonel W____ of ____, 23 April 1798, to Monsieurs John and Daniel Russell Esq., 7 May 1798, to the Rev. Mr. Warren of Portland, 15 May 1798, Letter Book 10: 54, 55, 208–9, 213–14, 219; Card for the *Centinel*, Letter Book 10: 200.

37. JSM to Mrs. Jackson of Philadelphia, 2 June 1798, to Mr. Wescott of Philadelphia, 2 June 1798, to Esther Ellery, 12 June 1798, to Mrs. Jackson of Philadelphia, 18 June, 13 December 1798, Letter Book 10: 225, 227–30, 238, 317; to Mrs. Jackson of Philadelphia, 25 February 1800, Letter Book 11: 140.

38. JSM to Esther Ellery, 12 June 1798, to Mrs. Jackson of Philadelphia, 18 June 1798, to Mr. C____ of Norfolk, Virginia, 18 December 1798, to Mrs. Jackson of Philadelphia, 9 March 1799, Letter Book 10: 229–30, 238, 320–21, 368–69.

39. Dorgan, "Eighteenth-Century Voices of Educational Change," 10, 14; JSM to Epes Sargent, 8 August 1798, to the Mother of Mr. Murray, 10 August 1798, to Mr. Bowen, [?] January 1799, Letter Book 10: 260, 263, 345; to Epes Sargent, 3 May 1799, to Mr. D. S., Junior, 1 January 1800, to Mrs. D____ of Philadelphia, 21 April 1800, Letter Book 11: 21, 114, 161. See also JSM to Mr. G____ of Boston, 25 June 1798, to Epes Sargent, 2 October 1798, Letter Book 10: 243, 292. Four years after *The Gleaner* appeared, Judith continued to give away copies of the book. JSM to Mr. Roland of Exeter, 19 January 1802, Letter Book 11: 324.

40. JSM to the Rev. Robert Redding, Truro, England, 14 December 179[6], Letter Book 10: 68; to Winthrop Sargent, 21 March 1798, Letter Book 9: 637; to Nancy Turner, 10 April 1798, to Mrs. S____ of G____, 14 May 1798, Letter Book 10: 208, 217–18. In "The Gleaner Unmasked," she referred directly to "the uniformity of my plan." *The Gleaner*, 807.

41. See, for instance, Philip F. Gura, "Early American Literature at the New Century," David S. Shields, "Joy and Dread Among the Early Americanists," *William and Mary Quarterly* 3rd ser. 57 (2000): 599–620; 635–40.

42. *The Gleaner*, 636; Spacks, *The Female Imagination*, 227–29; Baym, *American Women Writers*, 153–56; Baym, *Feminism and American Literary History*, 122. For an alternative reading of *The Gleaner* see Watts, *Writing and Postcolonialism*, 64–65.

43. *The Gleaner*, 805; Watts, *Writing and Postcolonialism*, 56.

44. *The Gleaner*, 13–14. See also Madelon Jacoba, "The Novella as Political Message: The Margaretta Story," *Studies in the Humanities* 18 (1991): 150–51; Watts, *Writing and Postcolonialism*, 57.

45. *The Gleaner*, 804–5; Wilcox, "The Scribblings of a Plain Man," 127.

46. JSM to Epes Sargent, 15 August 1797, Letter Book 10: 141; *The Gleaner*, 805; Watts, *Writing and Postcolonialism*, 59.

47. Mary Wollstonecraft, *A Vindication of the Rights of Woman*, ed. Carol H. Poston (New York: Norton, 1988), 7; *The Gleaner*, 287–88, 294–98. For the conventions of the educational novel, which Judith adopted as her own, see Anne Schofield, *Masking and Unmasking the Female Mind: Disguising Romances in Feminine Fiction, 1713–1799* (Newark: University of Delaware Press), 111, 113.

48. See Davidson, "Mothers and Daughters in the Fiction of the New Republic," 117, 118; Jacoba, "The Novella as Political Message," 153.

49. Gould, *Covenant and Republic*, 58; Kelley, "Designing a Past for the Present," 345; Baym, "Between Enlightenment and Victorian," 26.

50. Watts, *Writing and Postcolonialism*, 62; Wilcox, "The Scribblings of a Plain Man," 125; *The Gleaner*, 428, 441.

51. *The Gleaner*, 373, 381–85, 439.

52. Ibid., 387–419. For a discussion of other women historians of the period who condemned Elizabeth's "murder" of the near saintly Mary, see Baym, *American Women Writers*, 143; Kelley, "Designing a Past for the Present," 329, 346. Carole Levin points out that in their own day Mary Queen of Scots and Elizabeth I had a difficult time balancing kingly (masculine) qualities with their feminine role and image. Thus it is probably not surprising that eighteenth-century women had a similar problem. Levin, "Queens and Claimants: Political Insecurity in Sixteenth-Century England," in Sharistanian, ed., *Gender, Ideology, and Action*, 43.

53. *The Gleaner*, 702, 727–28.

54. Ibid., 728–30. The widow did not prepare her sons for a merchant's life. Rather, she sent them to the army, where they served their country in an honorable—manly— fashion.

55. Ibid., 726, 730–31.

56. For two—in most ways competing—rationales women used to achieve power, see Laqueur, *Making Sex*, 197, and Rosaldo, "Women, Culture, and Society," 338. For an especially restrictive definition of politics and gender relations, which maintains that only 7 percent of the book deals with gender issues and that most of it is extremely conventional, even conservative, see Schloesser, *The Fair Sex*, 157. A more thoughtful and even-handed approach is Jeanne Boydston, "Making Gender in the Early Republic: Judith Sargent Murray and the Revolution of 1800," in James Horn, Jan Ellen Lewis, and Peter S. Onuf, eds., *The Revolution of 1800; Democracy, Race, and the New Republic* (Charlottesville: University of Virginia Press, 2002), 240–66. For an argument that both Wollstonecraft and Murray were "primitive" and "hesitant" in their attempt to form a connection between the private and public worlds, see Kerber, "A Constitutional Right," 24–25.

57. *The Gleaner*, 212–13; Judith Stevens to John Murray, 17 June 1775, to Winthrop Sargent, 15 May 1781, Letter Book 2: 16, 333. The problem with that assertion, of course, as Boydston points out, was that it had less and less appeal. Federalist leaders clung to it longer than anyone, but even they had to give way to the demands of Jeffersonian Republicans who were privileging the vote and were increasingly likely to construct citizenship in gendered and racial terms. Boydston, "Making Gender," 258–62.

58. See Jan Lewis, "'Of Every Age Sex & Condition,'" 367–68; Waldstreicher, *In the Midst of Perpetual Fetes*, 109–11; Jürgen Habermas, *The Structural Transformation of the Public Sphere: An Inquiry into a Category of Bourgeois Society*, trans. Thomas Berger (Cambridge, Mass.: Harvard University Press, 1989). See also Fraser, "Rethinking the Public Sphere," 10–11; Zagarri, "Gender and the First Party System," 124, 126, 131, 133; Chalou, "Women in the American Revolution," 75–86; Elliott, *Revolutionary Writers*, 46.

59. JSM to Mrs. Barrell of York, 25 November 1800, to Anna Sargent, 28 November 1808, Letter Book 11: 228; Letter Book 15: [66].

60. Jacoba, "The Novella as Political Message," 152–53; JSM to Epes Sargent, 2 October 1798, Letter Book 10: 293. Of course her eagerness to see Abigail Adams as president had a great deal to do with the fact that Thomas Jefferson was the nation's vice president. A Federalist woman from Massachusetts was surely superior to a Republican man from Virginia!

61. *The Gleaner*, 337, 340. See Perry, *Women, Letters, and the Novel*, 129, 162–63; Harris, *American Women Writers to 1800*, 171; Brown, *The Sentimental Novel*, 52, 54, 63, 66, 72; Spacks, *Gossip*, 164. As both Perry and Brown point out, most people believed that spontaneous letters were a more accurate gauge of truth than face-to-face discussions.

62. *The Gleaner*, 762–64.

63. Ibid., 777–80; see Nina Baym's introduction, xvi xvii. Jay Fliegelman points out that the eighteenth-century metaphor of the enclosed grotto symbolized the individual who was protected from outside corruption, who remained innocent and pure despite the existence of evil in the world. Fliegelman *Prodigals and Pilgrims*, 30.

64. *The Gleaner*, 790, 792, 796–801; Ann Kirschner, "'Tending to Edify, Astonish,

and Instruct': Published Narratives of Spiritual Dreams and Visions in the Early Republic," *Early American Studies* 1 (2003): 226.

65. *The Gleaner*, 801–2, 804, 807.

66. Lyndall Gordon, *Vindication: A Life of Mary Wollstonecraft* (New York: Harper Collins, 2005), 152; John Murray to Winthrop Sargent, 7 December 1798, Winthrop Sargent Papers, Reel 4; Sarah W. Morton to Joseph Dennie, 27 March 1797, Dennie Papers, Harvard University Library; JSM to Epes Sargent, 2 October 1798, Murray, Letter Book 10: 292; to Epes Sargent, 3 May 1799, to John James, 24 August 1799, Letter Book 11: 21–22, 52.

67. *The Gleaner*, 11; JSM to Mr. C_____ of Richmond, Virginia, 18 May 1798, to Esther Ellery, 12 June 1798, to Maria Sargent, 17 September 1798, Letter Book 10: 223, 230, 277. Judith had tried to win over a few of her Virginia subscribers in her 99th *Gleaner* essay, when she wrote a flattering account of the hospitality for which the state was justly known. This was not enough to soothe the anger of many Virginians, however, most of whom probably had quit reading the book long before they would have encountered the piece. *The Gleaner*, 787.

68. Anonymous, Review of *The Gleaner, Monthly Register Magazine and Review of the United States* (Charleston, S.C., December 1806): 21–27, esp. 25–27. I am grateful to Rosemarie Zagarri of George Mason University for pointing me to this review.

69. JSM to the Rev. Mr. Gardiner, Letter Book 13: 82; Ellis, "Joseph Dennie and His Circle," 76; *Monthly Anthology* 2 (December 1805): 630–32. Many modern critics of *The Gleaner* are equally unimpressed with its literary value, claiming the writing is stilted, self-conscious, and "rather pedestrian." See, for instance, Petter, *The Early American Novel*, 72–73; Earnest, *The American Eve*, 31–33.

70. *The Gleaner*, 12; JSM to C. D. Ebeling, Professor of the Greek language and of geography in Hamburgh, 22 July 1799, Letter Book 11: 38–39.

71. *The Gleaner*, 448–53, 710.

72. Ibid., 703–9, 716, 720.

73. Ibid., 723, 727.

74. See, for example, Kelley, " 'Vindicating the Equality of the Female Intellect,' " 1–27; McAlexander, "The Creation of the American Eve," 252–66; Davidson, *Revolution and the Word*, 88, 129–30; Kerber, " 'History Can Do It No Justice,' " 36.

75. Gordon, *Vindication*, 14, 20, 21; Mary Wollstonecraft to William Godwin, 4 September 1796, in *Godwin and Mary: Letters of William Godwin and Mary Wollstonecraft*, ed. Ralph M. Wardle (Lawrence: University of Kansas Press, 1966), 28; Wollstonecraft, *Vindication*, 16–17.

76. Emily W. Sunstein, *A Different Face: The Life of Mary Wollstonecraft* (New York: Harper and Row, 1995), 255; JSM to Mr. Redding of Falmouth, England, 7 May 1801, Letter Book 11: 287–88.

Part III Introduction

1. See Dowling, *Literary Federalism*, 68, 70; Ellis, *After the Revolution*, 213–15. For Judith's retreat in particular, see Jeanne Boydston, "Making Gender," 240–66; Larry E. Tise,

The American Counter Revolution: A Retreat from Liberty, 1783–1800 (Mechanicsburg, Pa.: Stackpole Books, 1998), 278–93.

2. JSM to David Williams, 18 November 1803, to Mrs. David Urquardt, 21 October 1805, Letter Book 12: [892], Letter Book 13: [63].

3. William Godwin, *Memoirs of the Author of Vindication of the Rights of Woman* (London: Printed for J. Johnson . . . and G.G. and J. Robinson, 1798). For the term "rights talk" and the discussion of the prevalence of such talk see Zagarri, "The Rights of Man and Woman," 203–30.

4. Marcelle Thiebaux, "Mary Wollstonecraft in Federalist America: 1791–1802," in Ronald H. Reiman, Michael C. Jaye, and Betty T. Bennett, eds., *The Evidence of the Imagination: Studies of Interactions Between Life and Art in English Romantic Literature* (New York: New York University Press, 1978), 196, 200; Norton, *Liberty's Daughters*, 251; R. M. Janes, "On the Reception of Mary Wollstonecraft's *A Vindication of the Rights of Woman*," *Journal of the History of Ideas* 39 (1978): 293–302; John Adams, *Letters of John Adams, Addressed to His Wife*, ed. Charles Francis Adams, 3rd ed. (Boston: Little and Brown, 1841), 2: 139; Elizabeth Drinker, *The Diary of Elizabeth Drinker: The Life Cycle of an Eighteenth-Century Woman*, ed. Elaine Forman Crane (Boston: Northeastern University Press, 1994), 163.

5. Godwin, *Memoirs*, 112, 114, 155.

6. Mary Wollstonecraft., *A Wollstonecraft Anthology*, ed. Janet M. Todd (Bloomington: Indiana University Press, 1977), 1; Sunstein, *A Different Face*, 351; Cott, *Bonds of Womanhood*, 202–3; Kerber, *Women of the Republic*, 225; Chandos Michael Brown, *Benjamin Silliman: A Life in the Young Republic* (Princeton, N.J.: Princeton University Press, 1989), 46, 71–74; *Columbian Centinel*, 21 June 1800.

7. JSM to Mrs. Barrell of York, 25 November 1800, Letter Book 11: 229, 232.

8. See Brown, "Mary Wollstonecraft," 407; Lucy M. Freibert and Barbara A. White, eds., *Hidden Hands: An Anthology of American Writers, 1790–1870* (New Brunswick, N.J.: Rutgers Univesity Press, 1985), 55–56; Richard D. Birdsall, "Sally Sayward Barrell Keating Wood,"in Edward T. Wilson and Janet Wilson James, eds., *Notable American Women: A Biographical Dictionary* (Cambridge, Mass.: Belknap Press, 1971), 3: 649–50; Wyler, "'The Fruit of Unlawful Embraces,'" 285, 296–97.

9. JSM to Maria Sargent, 8, 15 November 1800, Letter Book 11: 224; JSM to Mrs. Barrell of York, 25 November 1800, Letter Book 11: 226, 232–33.

10. JSM to Miss B____, 1 April 1801, to Mrs. K____, 21 April 1802, Letter Book 11: 280, 343, 353.

11. JSM to Miss B____ 1 April 1801, to Mrs. K____, 21 April 1802, Letter Book 11: 280, 343–45.

12. JSM to Mrs. K____, 21 April 1802, Letter Book 11: 350.

13. JSM to Miss B____ 1 April 1801, to Mrs. K____ 21 April 1802, Letter Book 11: 281, 351–53.

14. JSM to Mrs. K____, 21 April 1802, Letter Book 11: 348–50.

15. Ibid., 348. See Kelley, "'Vindicating the Equality of Female Intellect,'"1–27, for an excellent discussion of the dilemma faced by those who wished to argue that women were different from yet equal to men.

16. Laqueur, *Making Sex*, 5, 6; Tise, *The American Counter Revolution*, 279–94; Lavater, "General Remarks on Women," *Massachusetts Magazine*, January 1794, 20–21;

"Comparison between the Sexes," *Gentleman and Lady's Town and Country Magazine*, September 1784, 200.

17. JSM to Miss M____, 20 October 1802, Letter Book 12: 770. See also JSM to Mrs. Saltonstall of New London, [?] March 1799, Letter Book 10: 379; to Mrs. Abbie H____, 10 February 1800, to Mrs. Lewis, 12 February 1802, to Mrs. S____, 22, 25 September 1800, Letter Book 11: 130, 136–37, 192.

Chapter 11. *"We Are Fallen on Evil Times"*

1. JSM to Winthrop Sargent, 26 January 1805, Letter Book 12:977; to [?], 6 May 1805, Letter Book 13: 3.

2. JSM to Esther Ellery, 23 December 1799, to Epes Sargent, 26 December 1799, to Esther Ellery, 18 January 1800, to L. Sargent of Sullivan, 25 February 1801, Letter Book 11: 104–5, 108, 118–20, 263; to Winthrop Sargent, 14 December 1804, Letter Book 12: [970].

3. JSM to Mr. Hodgdon of Philadelphia, 18 May 1798, to Anna Sargent, 12 June 1798, to Esther Ellery, 14 July 1798, Letter Book 10: 221, 234, 247; Winthrop Sargent to Timothy Pickering, 16 June 1798, in Dunbar Rowland, ed., *The Mississippi Territorial Archives, 1798–1803: Executive Journals of Governor Winthrop Sargent and Governor William Charles Cole Claiborne* (Nashville, Tenn.: Brandon Printing Co., 1905), 1: 22. See Jacobs, *The Beginning of the U.S. Army*, 214; Prucha, *Sword of the Republic*, 55–59; John Hebron Moore, *The Emergence of the Cotton Kingdom in the Old Southwest: Mississippi, 1770–1860* (Baton Rouge: Louisiana University Press, 1988), 2–8, for a description of the early Mississippi Territory.

4. Winthrop Sargent to Timothy Pickering, 20 August, 18 September 1798, 21 March 1799, Rowland, *Mississippi Territorial Archives*, 1: 30–33, 48; JSM to Fitz William Sargent, 5 November 1798, Letter Book 10: 306–7.

5. JSM to Colonel Hodgdon of Philadelphia, 29 December 1800, Letter Book 11: 236; For Winthrop's problems in Mississippi, see Winthrop Sargent to John Marshall, 15 June 1800, Rowland, *Mississippi Territorial Archives*, 1: 245; JSM to Anna Sargent, 10 October 1800, Letter Book 11: 200. For JSM's efforts on Winthrop's behalf, see JSM to Colonel Hodgdon of Philadelphia, 17 January 1801, to the Honourable Mr. Thatcher, 22, 26, January, 31 March 1801, to Mr. D____ S____ Jr., 24 January 1801, to Fitz William Sargent, 2 February 1801, to Esther Ellery, 11 February 1801, to Anna Sargent, 11 February 1801, to Colonel Hodgdon of Philadelphia, 31 March 1801, Letter Book 11: 237–49, 255–56, 273–74. Rumor had it that Claiborne got the job due to a bribe. John Murray to Winthrop Sargent, 14 January 1802, Sargent Murray Gilman Hough Papers. The letter announcing his termination was written in May f 1801.

6. JSM to [?], 12 December 1805, to Winthrop Sargent, 28 December 1805, Letter Book 13: [90], [108]; to Winthrop Sargent, 18 September 1806, Letter Book 14: [16]; John Murray to William Palmer, 12 March 1802, Palmer Papers; JSM to Winthrop Sargent, 22 November 1802, Letter Book 12: [790]; to Mr. J____ G____, 5 September 1797, Letter Book 10: 147; to Esther Ellery, 24 March 1800, Letter Book 11: 151. See Howe, "How Human an Enterprise," 23; JSM to Mr. J____ G____, 5 September 1797, to the Mother of Mr. Murray, 10 August 1798, Letter Book 10: 147, 263; to Esther Ellery, 24 March 1800, Letter Book

11: 152; to Anna Sargent, 28 November 1808, Letter Book 15: [66] for information on the Murrays' own problems.

7. JSM to Winthrop Sargent, 26 June, 17 December 1808, 4 February, 7 May 1809, to Anna Williams, 1 January 1809, Letter Book 15: [32], 79, 87 [88], 93, 107.

8. Hughes, "The Origins of New England Universalism," 12, 13; Babson, *Gloucester*, 510, 511; JSM to Winthrop and Mary Sargent, 6 June 1812, to Winthrop Sargent, 3 August, 19 October, 17 November 1812, Letter Book 17: 119, [126], 161, 173; to Winthrop Sargent, 7 October 1813, Letter Book 18: 37 [38]; to Winthrop Sargent, 1 October 1814, Letter Book 19: 13.

9. JSM to Winthrop Sargent, 4, 19 October 1812, Letter Book 17: [158] 61; to Winthrop Sargent, 7 October 1813, 20 January 1814, Letter Book 18: 37, 57; to Winthrop Sargent, 12, 17 October 1814, Letter Book 19: 17, 19. True, the fortunes of many commercially oriented Americans were changing in this period, disrupting communities and families and making way for an ethos based on competition and risk taking. The war, however, hastened what was probably an inevitable trend. Hall, "Family Structure and Economic Organization," 47–48.

10. JSM to Winthrop Sargent, 8 September, 1 October 1814, Letter Book 19: 9, [14].

11. JSM to Winthrop Sargent, 29 January 1813, Letter Book 17: [192]; to Winthrop Sargent, 13 February 1815, Letter Book 19: [58]; Epes Sargent to Winthrop Sargent, 1 September 1815, Sargent Murray Gilman Hough Papers; Sargent unbound diary, 1814–1820, 23 October 1815, Winthrop Sargent Papers. For Judith's health problems see JSM to Maria Sargent, 19 October 1799, to Epes Sargent, 24 May 1800, to Anna Sargent, 12 January 1803, Letter Book 11: 71, 162, 326; to Winthrop Sargent, 25 April, 30 July 1803, Letter Book 12: [810] 11, [840], [868].

12. JSM to [?], 14 July, 1806, Letter Book 13: 183 [184]; to [?], July 1808, to Winthrop Sargent, 20 February 1809, Letter Book 15: 33, 94–95; Howe, "How Human an Enterprise," 23; Nylander, *Our Own Snug Fireside*, 86; Skinner, *Hell's Ramparts*, 154–55; Proceedings of the Proprietors, 1: 14 September 1799, 30 June 1800, 10, 28 February, 28 June 1801; John Murray to William Palmer, 27 January, 11 February 1801, Palmer Papers; John Murray to Thomas Fitzgerald, 8 June 1798, Gratz Papers; JSM to Miss Lucy Sargent of Sullivan, 4 February 1799, Letter Book 10: 354; George Richards to Edward Turner, 14 July 1802, Brooks, "Letters of Murray and Richards," *Universalist Quarterly* 9 (1872): 281–82; John Murray to Jacob Clinch, 7 February, 1799, 6 April, 23 December 1801, 12 October 1802, 29 January, 1803, Clinch Papers. To add insult to injury, the Rev. Thomas Jones, whom John had handpicked to replace him in Gloucester, got a raise virtually every year, received a salary for life, and was the recipient of occasional "liberal gifts" as well. Babson, *Gloucester*, 481.

13. John Murray to William Palmer, 16 April 1803, Palmer Papers. He also contributed to the upkeep of his widowed mother. JSM to Mr. ____.G.____ 5 September 1797, Letter Book 10: 146.

14. Mann, *The Sargent Family and the Old Sargent Homes*, 60; JSM to Fitz William Sargent, 4, 18 November 1806, 31 March 1810, Letter Book 14: [36] 39; 16: n.p. See Chambers-Schiller, *Liberty, a Better Husband*, 44 for an account of the way in which women, single or married, quarreled with friends and relatives over "trifling amounts of money."

15. JSM to Maria Sargent 16 March 1793, Letter Book 7: 101; to Miss A____, 2 February 1795, Letter Book 8: 262; to Mr. J____ G____, 5 September 1797, Letter Book 10: 146;

to John Murray, 27 August 1805, Letter Book 13: [42]; to [Mr. Mitchell], 6 June 1810, Letter Book 16: n.p.; John Murray to William Palmer, 16 April 1803, Palmer Papers.

16. JSM to Esther Ellery, 23 November 1799, to Elizabeth Jackson, 25 February 1800, 31 March 1801, Letter Book 11: 86, 87, 140, 276; to Winthrop Sargent, 31 January 1806, Letter Book 13: 119.

17. JSM to Mr. J____ G____, 5 September 1797, Murray, Letter Book 10: 147–48; to Epes Sargent of Hampstead, 31 July 1799, to Mrs. L. Sargent, 12 December 1799, to Esther Ellery, 24 March 1800, to Epes Sargent of Hampstead, 21 September 1801, to Esther Sargent, 26 January 1802, Letter Book 11: 41, 94–95, 152, 294, 325–26; to Anna Sargent, 5 July 1803, Letter Book 12: [860].

18. JSM to Fitz William Sargent, 18 January 1800, Letter Book 11: 117. On at least one other occasion, Fitz William invested in an "adventure" on behalf of his sister. JSM to Anna Sargent, 26 October 1801, Letter Book 11: 310.

19. For her positive moments, see JSM to Anna Sargent, 12 January 1796, to Mr. J____ G____, 5 September 1797, Letter Book 10: 4, 146; to [?], 17 September, 12 December, [December], 17, 18 December 1810, Letter Book 16: n.p.; to [?], 1 [October 1811], 8 February, 24 August 1812, to Winthrop Sargent, 31 August 1812, Letter Book 17: 25 [26], [78] [80], [130], 131 [138]. For less successful experiences, see JSM to Winthrop Sargent, 19 August 1806, Letter Book 13: 191; to Mr. Parkman, 17 August 1808, to General J. Wilkins, 23 August 1808, to [?], 21 December 1808, Letter Book 15:39–41, 79, [80]; to [?], 17 September, 12 December, [December], 17, 18 December 1810, to [?], 16 August, [October], 1811, to [?] 18 February, 24 August 1812, Letter Book 16: n.p. See Waciega, "A 'Man of Business,'" 51, 53 for proof that Judith's understanding of the complexities of banks, stocks, and investments was by no means unique.

20. JSM to Elizabeth Jackson, 25 February 1800, 31 March 1801, Letter Book 11: 137–38, 276; John Murray to Robert Redding, 23 May 1799, *Universalist Quarterly* 8 (1871): 223.

21. John Murray to Robert Redding, 23 May 1799, *Universalist Quarterly* 8 (1871), 223; JSM to Elizabeth Jackson, 31 October 1797, Letter Book 10: 171; to Elizabeth Jackson, 25 February 1800, Letter Book 11: 138.

22. See Robert Nelson Hale, "Pennsylvania Population Company" (Ph.D. dissertation, University of Pittsburgh, 1950); Elizabeth K. Henderson, "The Northwestern Lands of Pennsylvania, 1790–1812," *Pennsylvania Magazine of History and Biography* 60 (1936): 130–60; Enoch Marvin to Thomas Astley, 3 April 1798, Pennsylvania Population Land Company, Box 3, Folder 1. Samuel Jackson was not one of the big players in the Company, but the records indicate that he was, nevertheless, heavily involved. Population Treasury Book.

23. John Murray to Winthrop Sargent, 7 December 1798, Winthrop Sargent Papers, Reel 4; John Murray to Robert Redding, 23 May 1799, *Universalist Quarterly* 8 (1871): 223–24; JSM to Elizabeth Jackson, 10 March, 2 June 1798, Letter Book 10: 195, 226; JSM to Epes Sargent, 13 March 1799, to Elizabeth Jackson, 25 February 1800, Letter Book 11: 3, 139–40.

24. JSM to Elizabeth Jackson, 10 March 1798, Letter Book 10: 195. See Kierner, "'The Dark and Dense Cloud,'" for an indication of the sense of profound loss that affected members of gentry families as they lost both money and status in the postwar years.

25. For evidence that Judith was probably right, see Hale, "Pennsylvania Population

Company," 231; Josiah Lewis to S. Baird, 2 January 1807, Pennsylvania Population Land Company, Box 4, Folder 6.

26. JSM to Winthrop Sargent, 23 November 1790, Letter Book 5: 362; to Horace Binney, 16 September 1809, to Samuel Jackson, 28 September 1809, Letter Book 15: [134] 35, 141 [142]; to Mr. and Mrs. Jackson, 7 July 1810, to [?], 26 February 1811, Letter Book 16: n.p.; to Winthrop Sargent, 15 February 1814, Letter Book 18: [70]; to Mr. Thompson, 20 April 1816, Letter Book 20: 18.

27. JSM to Mr. J____ H____, 5 November 1799, to the Rev. Mr. Redding, 7 May 1801, Letter Book 11: 76, 77, 286, 287; to [?], 4 February 1804, to the Rev. Mr. Redding, 4 June 1806, Letter Book 12: [908], [160], 161; Eddy, *Universalism in Gloucester*, 189.

28. JSM to [?], 6 October 1808, Letter Book 15: 61.

29. JSM to Monsieurs Belcher and Armstrong, 7, 16 June 1806, Letter Book 13: 165–67; to [?] 29 August 1806, to Maria Sargent, 10 November 1806; Letter Book 14: [6], 37 [38]; to Winthrop Sargent, 6 August 1814, Letter Book 18: [106]; Sheppard, "Reminiscences."

30. JSM to [?], 29 August 1806, to Maria Sargent, 10 November 1806, Letter Book 14: [6], 37 [38].

31. Bonawitz, "The History of the Boston Stage," 216–17; Michael, "A History of the Professional Theater in Boston," 119; Seilhamer, *History of the American Theater*, 341; JSM to Mrs. P____, [March 1798], Letter Book 10: 197; to Miss C____ S____ of Hampstead, 4 May 1799, Letter Book 11: 23; to Mr. Paine, 6 September 1804, Letter Book 12: 947.

32. JSM to Mr. Paine, 6 October 1804, Letter Book 12: [952] 53; to Mr. T. A. Cooper, 17 December 1805, Letter Book 13: 93; to the Manager of the Boston Theater, [? February 1807], Letter Book 14: 59.

33. JSM to Mr. Paine, 3 January 1805, Letter Book 12: 975; to Mr. T. A. Cooper, 17 December 1805, Letter Book 13: [94]. Again, it is fair to ask whether or not Judith really wanted to remain anonymous. Why make an anagram of one of her own pseudonyms? Why not adopt yet another name for herself?

34. Hughes, *A History of the American Theatre*, 17, 84; JSM to Mr. Paine, 6 October 1804, to Winthrop Sargent, 23 March 1805, Letter Book 12: 953 [954], 995 [996]; to Mr. Powell, 7 December 1805, to [?], [?] March 1806, Letter Book, 13: 83, 133.

35. Hughes, *A History of the American Theatre*, 78; JSM to Mrs. David Urquhart of New Orleans, 21 October 1805, to Mr. Powell, 7 December 1805, to to T. A. Cooper, 12, 17, 18, 24 December 1805, Letter Book 13: 59, 75, [84] [86], [90], [92] [96], 99 [100], 113 [114].

36. JSM to the Manager of the Boston Theater, [? February 1807], to Mr. Bernard, 6 March 1807, [?] March [1807], Letter Book 14: 59, 60, [64], [66].

37. JSM to Anna Williams, 2 May 1808, Letter Book 15: 25.

38. JSM to Alexis Eustaphieve Esquire, Russian Counsel, 20 January 1817, Letter Book 20:42. The review appeared in *The Emerald*, 9 January 1808, 124–26. No copy of *The African* seems to exist. Judith asked the theater to return all copies to her. It may well have been among the many manuscripts that she consigned to the flames in later years.

39. JSM to Mr. Sewall, 7 July 1806, Letter Book 13: [180]; Skinner and Cole, *Hell's Ramparts*, 155.

40. Hughes, "The Origins of New England Universalism," 24; JSM to Epes Sargent, 11 January 1799, Letter Book 10: 335.

41. Hughes, "The Origins of New England Universalism," 1; Winsor, *Memorial*

History of Boston, 492–96; Howe, "How Human an Enterprise," 24; JSM to Epes Sargent, 11 January 1799, Letter Book 10: 335–36. For particulars on Judith's theological disagreements with Ballou, see Sketch of Mr. Ballou's Sermon, January 1799, Letter Book 10: 337–39; Murray, "Mr. Ballou," Repository, 154–57.

42. JSM to Winthrop Sargent, 31 January 1804, to Anna Sargent, 20 February, 1805, Letter Book 12: 387 [388], 907; to Anna Sargent, 5 June 1809, Letter Book 15: 115.

43. JSM to Miss N[ancy] P____, 19 October 1801, Letter Book 11: 305–8.

44. JSM to Maria Sargent, 1, 8 October 1798, Letter Book 10: 284–86, 294–95; to Mrs. L. Sargent Sullivan, 12 December 1799, Letter Book 11: 95–96; to Mrs. L. Sargent Sullivan, 17 November 1803, Letter Book 12: 889 [890].

45. JSM to Winthrop Sargent, 20 June [1814], Letter Book 18: [94]. Gilbert Stuart had painted her picture in 1806. While it portrayed a dignified woman comfortable with fine lace and all the trappings of bourgeois respectability, observers would see only a slight resemblance between that painting and the one Copley had painted before Judith's first marriage. See Lawrence Park, comp., *Gilbert Stuart: An Illustrated Descriptive List of His Works* (New York: William Edwin Rudge, 1926). Vol. 2: 543 describes the portrait; vol. 4 has a black and white copy.

46. Judith Stevens to John Murray, 1 September 1779, Letter Book 2: 226; to [?], Spring 1818, Letter Book 20: 91. See also Murray, "Respect Due to the Weight of years," Repository, 247–48.

47. JSM to Anna Sargent, 7 May 1803, to Esther Ellery, 24 May 1803, to Winthrop Sargent, 29 August 1803, Letter Book 12: 847 [848], 873; to Winthrop Sargent, 28 July 1806; Letter Book 13: 185; to Fitz William Sargent, 4 November 1806; to Winthrop and Mary Sargent, 12 October 1807, Letter Book 14: [36], [88]; to Winthrop Sargent, 8 December 1811, Letter Book 17: 41–43; to Winthrop Sargent, 6 December 1813, Letter Book 18: [48] 49.

48. John Murray to Winthrop Sargent, 2 December 1801, Sargent Murray Gilman Hough Papers; JSM to Epes Sargent, 4 December 1799, 21 September 1801, to the Mother of my Husband, 6 November 1801, Letter Book 11: 90, 296, 313. John did take her on a seven week trip to Philadelphia in the fall of 1807. JSM to [?], 30 November 1807, Letter Book 12: 109–11.

49. JSM to Anna Sargent, 15 April 1799, to Esther Ellery, 17 April, 1 May 1799, to Epes Sargent, 3 May 1799, to Fitz William Sargent, 3 June 1799, to Epes Sargent, 13 June 1799, to Mrs. Lewis, granddaughter of Mrs. Washington, 12 February 1802, Letter Book 11: 8, 15–16, 20, 25, 27, 335; John Murray to William Palmer, 16 May 1799, Palmer Papers; John Murray to Jacob Clinch, 20 November 1802, Clinch Papers.

50. John Murray to Jacob Clinch, 18 February 1803, 5, 19 April 1808, Clinch Papers; George Richards to Edward Turner, 17 August 1807, Brooks, "Letters of Murray and Richards," 451; Proceedings of the Proprietors, 2: 30 May 1807; Howe, "How Human an Enterprise," 26; JSM to Winthrop Sargent, 26 June 1808, to Miss Turner, 30 December 1808, Letter Book 15: [30], [84].

51. John Murray to Jacob Clinch, 5 May, 7 July, 27 or 28 October 1809, Clinch Papers; John Murray to William Palmer, 21 September 1809, Palmer Papers; Howe, "How Human an Enterprise," 26–27; JSM to Winthrop Sargent, 19 November 1809, Letter Book 15: [158]; to Anna Sargent, 27 November 1809, to Mrs. Leonard, 25 June 1810, Letter Book 16: n.p.

52. Proceedings of the Proprietors, 2: 22, 29 October 1809; John Murray to Jacob

Clinch, 18 February 1803, Clinch Papers; George Richards to Edward Turner, 17 August 1807, Brooks, "Letters of Murray and Richards," 451; JSM to Winthrop Sargent, 19 November 1809, Letter Book 15: [158]; to [?], 15 January, 19 February 1810, to Lucius Manlius, 16 December 18[10], to Mrs. Leonard, 25 June 1810, to [?], 14 March 1811, Letter Book 16:n.p.; to Winthrop Sargent, 20 June 1814, Letter Book 18: 95.

53. Proceedings of the Proprietors, 2: 6 May, 24 June 1810; Howe, "How Human an Enterprise," 27; JSM to [?], 3 April 1810, to Winthrop Sargent, 23 April, 8 May 1810, to Mr. and Mrs. Jackson, 7 July 1810, to Winthrop Sargent, 1 October 1810, Letter Book 16: n.p. Judith paid $1 a week each to a hired girl and to a woman to help in the kitchen. Thus $1 an hour for a hack was indeed expensive. JSM to Mrs. Leonard, 25 June 1810, Letter Book 16: n.p.

54. James Thomas Flexner, *History of American Painting: The Light of Distant Skies, 1760–1835* (New York: Dover, 1954), 74, 80, 82, 200–201; JSM to [?], [?] February 1810, to Anna Sargent, 31 March 1810, Winthrop Sargent, 1 October 1810, Letter Book 16: n.p.; to Winthrop Sargent, 30 October 1815, Letter Book 19: 175; to Julia Maria Bingaman, 22 July 1816, Letter Book 20: 24, 25. For evidence that her investments did not always pan out, see JSM to Fitz William Sargent, 5 August 1809, Letter Book 15: 121, to Winthrop Sargent, 30 October 1815, Letter Book 19: 175.

55. JSM to [?], 16 September 1810, to Mr. Greene, 16 September 1810, to Winthrop Sargent, 1 October 1810, to Mrs. Mitchell, 18 October 1810, Letter Book 16: n.p; to Winthrop Sargent, 20 January 1814, Letter Book 18: [60].

56. Howe, "How Human an Enterprise," 29, 30; Hughes, "Origins of New England Universalism," 10, 11; *Proceedings of the Proprietors*, 2: 10, 20 October, 24 November 1812; 2 January, 4 April 1813; JSM to Winthrop Sargent, 1 October 1810, Letter Book 16: n.p.; to Winthrop Sargent, 21 December 1811, Letter Book 17: 53; to the Rev. Mr. [?], 23 April, 15 July 1815 to Mrs. Terrell, 24 June 1815, to the Rev. Mr. Mitchell, 4 November 1815, Letter Book 19: 95, 119, 135, [180].

57. Proceedings of the Proprietors, 2: 5 April 1812; JSM to Mr. Russell, 27 April 1812, to Winthrop Sargent, 8 May 1812, Letter Book 17: 101 [102]; to Winthrop Sargent, 8 August 1815, Letter Book 19: 143 [144]; to Mrs. Leonard, 15 March 1817, Letter Book 20: 50; Klepp, "Revolutionary Bodies," 930–31.

58. JSM to [?], 6 October 1808, to Miss Turner, 30 December 1808, Letter Book 15: 61, 83; to Anna Sargent, 14 January 1811, to Mrs. Urquhart, 17 January 1811, to Winthrop Sargent, 31 January 1811, to [?], [?] March 1811, Letter Book 16: n.p.; to Julia Maria Sargent, 12 May 1812, Letter Book 17: [112]; to Mrs. Sewall, 15 July 1815, to Mr. Mitchell, 4 November 1815, Letter Book 19:[136], [182].

59. JSM to Jonathan Belcher, 11 April 1812, Letter Book 17: 99; to John Adams, 11 August 1813, to [?] Sargent, 12 September 1813, to Winthrop Sargent, 12 September 1813, to [?], 29 September 1813, to [?], 13, 21 December 1813, to Mr. Alexander Richards, 7 February 1814, Letter Book 18: [22], [26] 27, 29, [32], 53 [54], 63; to Mrs. Terrell, 24 June 1815, Letter Book 19: [120]; to [?], 12 August 1816, Letter Book 20: 27–28.

60. JSM to Winthrop Sargent, 30 July 1815, to William Surget, 27 August 1815, to Winthrop Sargent, 11 September 1815, to the Rev. Mr. [?], 28 September 1815, to Winthrop Sargent, 31 December 1815, Letter Book 19: 141, [152], [154], [156], [170] 71, [214]; Howe, "How Human an Enterprise," 30; Keyssar, "Widowhood in Eighteenth-Century Massachusetts," 112–14.

61. JSM to Winthrop Sargent, 23 September 1816, Letter Book 20: 33.

Chapter 12. Republican Daughters, Republican Sons

1. JSM to Mrs. Pilgrim of London, 8 November 1791, to Maria Sargent, 6 May 1792, to Mrs. W_____ of Philadelphia, 8 March 1793, Letter Book 8: 16, 38, 94; to Julia Maria, 18 May 1810, Letter Book 16: n.p.

2. JSM to Mrs. Barrell of York, 29 January 1795, Letter Book 8: 258.

3. JSM to Colonel Hodgdon, 28 January 1799, to Esther Ellery, 30 January 1799, to Fitz William Sargent, 30 January 1799, Letter Book 10: 344–348; to Mr. Payne, [?] October 1801, Letter Book 11: 309; JSM to Epes Sargent, 1 February 1799, Sargent Papers, Reel 4; William C. Davis, *A Way Through the Wilderness: The Natchez Trace and the Civilization of the Southern Frontier* (New York: Harper Collins, 1995), 161; Clayton James, *Antebellum Natchez* (Baton Rouge: Louisiana State University Press, 1968), 217.

4. John Murray to Winthrop Sargent, 14 January 1802, Sargent Murray Gilman Hough Papers; JSM to Miss Saltonstall of New London, 4 November 1796, Letter Book 10: 58; to Winthrop Sargent, 2 February 1797, Letter Book 9: 606–7; to Winthrop Sargent, 31 January, 26 May 1804, Letter Book 12: 907, 931.

5. JSM to Fitz William Sargent, 4 June [1782], Letter Book 2: 10; to Winthrop Sargent, 19 October 1812, Letter Book 17: 161; to the Rev. Mr. [?], 28 February 1815, to Winthrop Sargent, 27 February, 29 April, 5 June 1815, Letter Book 19: 75, [68], 97 [98], 112; to Winthrop Sargent, 3 March 1816, to Mr. Harding, 12 October 1816, Letter Book 20: 12, 36. For references to children as "seeds," see Murray, "Martesia," "The Preceptor," Repository, 193–97, 777; Murray, "Severity to Children," Poetry 1: 297; Renier, *From Virtue to Character*, 5–9, 27.

6. See Kerber, "The Republican Ideology of the Revolutionary Generation."

7. See especially Chodorow, "Family Structure and Feminine Personality," in Rosaldo and Lamphere, *Women, Culture, and Society*, 44–54.

8. Smith-Rosenberg, "Hearing Women's Words," 31–33; JSM to Esther Ellery, 28 February 1799, Letter Book 10: 358; to John James, 16 September 1799, to Mr. David and James Williams, 28 January 1802, Billet to Mr. F. A. of Boston, 17 August 1802, Letter Book 11: 57, 332–33, 361; to Winthrop Sargent, 30 September 1802, 31 January 1805, to Eliza Payne, 27 March 1805, Letter Book 12: 762, [980], [998]; Anna Williams to Winthrop and Mary Sargent, 26 June, 2 December 1802, Sargent Murray Gilman Hough Papers.

9. See Laura Thatcher Ulrich, "Hannah Barnard's Cupboard: Female Property and Identity in Eighteenth-Century New England," in Hoffman, Sobel, and Teute, *Through a Glass Darkly*, 269.

10. Judith Stevens to Esther Ellery, 27 June 1782, Letter Book 2: 31; JSM to Winthrop Sargent, 23 December 1814, 8 August 1815, Letter Book 19: 35 [38], 143.

11. E. Anthony Rotundo, "Boy Culture: Middle-Class Boyhood in Nineteenth-Century America," in Carnes and Griffen, eds., *Meanings for Manhood*, 16–17, 19; Rotundo, *American Manhood*, 34, 37, 47; Rosaldo, "Women, Culture, and Society," 28; Mintz and Kellogg, *Domestic Revolutions*, 44; Demos, "Changing Faces of Fatherhood," 436–37; Renier, *From Virtue to Character*, 58–59; Anya Jabour, "Masculinity and Adolescence in Antebellum America: Robert Wirt at West Point, 1820–1821," *Journal of Family History* 23 (1998): 396.

12. JSM to Winthrop Sargent, 8 May 1813, Letter Book 18: 5; Rotundo, "Learning about Manhood," 47; Rotundo, "Boy Culture," 32, 33; Rotundo, "Body and Soul," 3–32;

Daniel A. Cohen, "Arthur Mervyn and His Elders: The Ambivalence of Youth in the Early Republic," *William and Mary Quarterly* 3rd ser. 43 (1986): 363–68; Kett, *Rites of Passage*, 11, 16–17; Joe Dubbert, *A Man's Place: Masculinity in Transition* (Englewood Cliffs, N.J.: Prentice-Hall, 1979), 17–18. Michael Paul Rogin also points out that children separated from their fathers sensed that they were adrift and felt a little alienated. In some children this led, as it seems to have done in William's case, to alcoholism. Rogin, *Fathers and Children: Andrew Jackson and the Subjugation of the American Indian* (New York: Knopf, 1975).

13. JSM to Winthrop Sargent, 8 May, 1 October, 6 December 1810, Letter Book 16: n.p.; to Winthrop Sargent, 19 October 1812, to Anna Sargent, 17 April 1813, Letter Book 17: 161, [206]; to Winthrop Sargent, 23 November 1813, Letter Book 18: 45 [46]; to Winthrop Sargent, 22 August 1814, 30 July 1815, Letter Book 19: [4], 141.

14. JSM to Mrs. Tenney, 19 March 1805, to Winthrop Sargent, 23 March 1805, Letter Book 12: 991, [994]; to Winthrop Sargent, 20 May 1806, Letter Book 13: [156].

15. JSM to Judge Tenney, 3 October 1803, Letter Book 12: 885; to David Williams, 4 June 1805, to Winthrop Sargent, 12 August 1805, Letter Book 13: 13, [36]. See also JSM to Winthrop Sargent, Fall 1803, Letter Book 12: [874]-877; to Mrs. Tenney, 13 May 1805, to Judge Tenney, 3 June 1805, to David Williams, 4 June 1805, Letter Book 13: 5–6, 9–11.

16. JSM to Maria Sargent, 6 May 1792, Letter Book 8: 38; "Extract," *Boston Gazette*, 24 April 1797. See, Barnes, *States of Sympathy*, 59; Cott, *Bonds of Womanhood*, 104–5; Madelon Cheek, "'An Inestimable Prize,' Educating Women in the New Republic: The Writings of Judith Sargent Murray," *Journal of Thought* 20 (1985); M. F. Heiser, "The Decline of Neoclassicism, 1801–1848," in Harry Hayden Clark, ed., *Transitions in American Literary History* (New York: Farrar, Straus and Giroux, 1975), 147n; Davidson, *Revolution and the Word*, 13; Rush, *Thoughts upon Female Education*, 27–40, especially 36; Simeon Doggett, "A Discourse on Education," and Noah Webster, *On the Education of Youth in America*, 44–77, in Rudolph, ed., *Essays on Education*, 147–66, 44–77.

17. See Kelley, "'Vindicating the Quality of Female Intellect,'" 6–8, 13; Crane, *Ebb Tide*, 215–22; Jacoba, "The Novella as Political Message," 147, 155; Armstrong, "The Rise of the Domestic Woman," 97; Gould, *Covenant and Republic*, 100; Davidson, *Revolution and the Word*, 62–65; Sara Delamont, "The Contradictions in Ladies' Education," in Delamont and Duffin, eds., *The Nineteenth-Century Woman*, 139, 163; Cott, *Bonds of Womanhood*, 108–9, 118, 123–24; Mintz and Kellogg, *Domestic Revolutions*, xix; "Essay on Education," *Massachusetts Magazine* 1 (1789): 28–29; "On the Female Accomplishments Most Agreeable to a Husband," *Massachusetts Magazine* 6 (1794): 38–39, Rush, *Thoughts upon Female Education*, 28–29.

18. Wilson, "Illusion of Change," 412; Rush, *Thoughts upon Female Education*, 38; Bushman, *Refinement of America*, 300; Coontz, *Social Origins of Private Life*, 151; Cott, *Bonds of Womanhood*, 123–24; Cleary, "Making Men and Women in the 1770s," 101, 104. An advertisement for "The Portsmouth Miscellany: Or Ladies Library, improved," that appeared in the 5 January 1805 issue of the *Columbian Centinel* said it all. The table of contents included "On the Danger of Sentimental or Romantic Connections," "A Letter to a Very Young Lady on her Marriage," "Studies Most Ornamental to the Fair Sex," and the ubiquitous "Dr. Gregory's Legacy to his Daughters."

19. Billet to Miss Payne, [n.d.], Letter Book 11: 304; JSM to Winthrop Sargent, 5 March 1803, to Sarah and Lucy _____, 26 January 1805, Letter Book 12: [828], [976]; to

Winthrop Sargent, 6 December 1810, Letter Book 16: n.p.; to Winthrop Sargent, 7, 29 October 1811, Letter Book 17: [22], [28] 29. See also Lerner, *The Thinking Revolutionary*, 211. She had no such reservations with her nephews, all of whom she encouraged to compete for academic recognition.

20. JSM to Maria Sargent, 21 June 1794, to Mrs. Barrell of York, 29 January 1795, to Esther Ellery, 3 March 1795, Letter Book 8: 207, 259, 275; to the Mother of Mr. Murray, 10 October 1796, Letter Book 10: 45; to Esther Ellery, 24 March 1800, Letter Book 11: 53; to Winthrop Sargent, [?] September 1803, Letter Book 12: 878. See Reinier, *From Virtue to Character*, 158–59.

21. JSM to Anna Sargent, 27 January 1802, to David and James Williams, 28 January 1802, Letter Book 11: 328–29, 331–32; to David and James Williams, 13 July 1803, to David Williams, 18 November 1803, Letter Book 12: [864], 891.

22. Murray, "Education," Repository, 163–65.

23. Nancy Cott, "Eighteenth-Century Family and Social Life Revealed in Massachusetts Divorce Records," *Journal of Social History* 10 (1976): 29; Mintz and Kellogg, *Domestic Revolutions*, 52; JSM to Maria Sargent, 16 March 1793, to Mrs. Barrell of York, 29 January 1795, Letter Book 8: 101, 258; to the Mother of Mr. Murray, 10 October 1796, to Esther Ellery, 20 October 1797, to Mr. and Mrs. S____, 2 April 1797, Letter Book 10: 45, 96, 166; to Anna Sargent, 17 October 1800, Letter Book 11: 212; John Murray to William Palmer, 19 March 1799, Palmer Papers; John Murray to Jacob Clinch, 20 November 1802, Clinch Papers. See also JSM to Winthrop Sargent, 18 January 1796, Letter Book 9: 527; John Murray to Robert Redding, 29 December 1795, *Universalist Quarterly* 6 (1869): 32, 33.

24. Woody, *History of Women's Education* 1: 146; Anne F. Scott, "What, Then, Is This American: This New Woman?" *Journal of American History* 65 (1978), 681; Solomon, *In the Company of Educated Women*, 15, 17–18; Kritzer, "Playing with Republican Motherhood," 152; Detsi-Diamanti, *Early American Women Dramatists*, 26; Seilhamer, *History of the American Theatre*, 353; JSM to Winthrop Sargent, 21 March 1796, Letter Book 9: 560–61.

25. JSM to Winthrop Sargent, 21 March 1796, Letter Book 9: 560; Billet to Maria, 26 February 1801, Billet to Mr. Parsons, 26 February 1801, Advertisement for Miss McGeorge, n.d.; JSM to Epes Sargent of Hampstead, 15 April 1801, Letter Book 11: 226–27, 282; JSM to Mrs. Saunders, 29 November 1802, 3, 12 January 1803, 7 February 1803, to Mrs. Saunders and Miss Beach, 23 March 1803, Letter Book 12: 792–93, [808], [812]. [822], [834].

26. JSM to Winthrop Sargent, 21 March 1796, Letter Book 9: 560; to Mrs. Barrell of York, 31 January 1798, to My Daughter's Preceptor, [?] December 1798; to Epes Sargent, 1 February, Letter Book 10: 193, 313, 351; to Epes Sargent, 26 December 1799, Letter Book 11: 114; to Winthrop Sargent, Fall 1803, Letter Book 12: [878]. See also *The Gleaner*, 735.

27. JSM to the Mother of Mr. Murray, 10 October 1796, to Mr. Payne, Preceptor of the Academy in Federal Street, 15 May 1798, to Miss ____, 5 September 1798, to Epes Sargent, 1 February 1799, Letter Book 10: 45, 220, 275, 350; to Miss C____ S____, 4 May 1799, Letter Book 11: 24; Kirker and Kirker, *Bullfinch's Boston*, 68. The "grammar" was no doubt Webster's *A Grammatical Institute, of the English Language, Comprising An easy, consise and systematic Method of Education . . .*, later simply known as *The American Spelling Book* or the "Blue-Black Speller." See Ellis, *After the Revolution*, 172.

28. JSM to my daughter's Preceptor, 15 October 1798, Letter Book 10: 299; to Epes Sargent, 21 October 1799, Billet to Mr. Payne, my daughter's Preceptor, [?] 1800, JSM to

Mr. B____, 28 February 1800, to Miss Payne, assistant to my daughter's Preceptor, 12 February 1801, Letter Book 11: 75, 145, 160, 258; to Miss Elisa Payne, 17 February, 10 December 1804, Letter Book 12: [912], 969. So long as Julia Maria continued to study at the Federal Street School, Judith continued to offer pointed suggestions, usually to little avail. See Billet to Mr. Payne, 16 July 1802, Letter Book 11: 359–60.

29. Esther Sargent to Winthrop Sargent, 27 December 1788, Sargent Murray Gilman Hough Papers; Samuel Knox, "An Essay on the Best System of Liberal Education," and Amable-Louis-Rose de Lafitte du Courteil, "Proposal to Demonstrate the Necessity of a National Institution in the United States of America for the Education of Both Sexes" (1797), in *Education in the Early Republic*, ed. Rudolph, 303–7, 243; Yazawa, "Creating a Republican Citizenry," 301–3.

30. JSM to the Rev. Mr. Eaton, 28 July 1815, Letter Book 19: [138] 39. As Reinier points out, the ramifications of an education that taught children to deny their own desires and subdue their own passions had ramifications beyond the effect on an individual child. In a republic with no king, no tradition, and a weak government, citizens needed to control their own worst impulses if the country was not going to descend into chaos. Reinier, *From Virtue to Character*, 4, 33.

31. JSM to Winthrop Sargent, 4 July, Fall 1803, 26 May 1804, Letter Book 12: [858], [878], 931.

32. JSM to Winthrop Sargent, [?] September 1803, Letter Book 12: 875–77; to Winthrop Sargent, 8 May 1813, Letter Book 18: 5. See Rotundo, *American Manhood*, 34, 37, 47; Rotundo, "Boy Culture," 32–33; Jabour, "Masculinity and Adolescence," 398–99, 405.

33. JSM to Fitz Winthrop Sargent at Billerica, 29 March, 13 April 1799, Letter Book 11: 5–6, 332; to David and James Williams, 28 January 1802, 13 July 1803, to David Williams, 18 November 1803, to James Williams, 18 February, 16 March 1805, to Mrs. Tenney, 19 March 1805, Letter Book 12: 863–65, 891, [984], 989, [992]. Virtually every letter Judith sent to the boys was filled with complaints and corrections. See, for example, JSM to David and James Williams, 28 January 1802, to David Williams, 2 November 1801, 12 July, to Master Winthrop Sargent, 18 September 1802, to David Williams, 9 October 1802, Letter Book 11: 331–32, 311–12, 358, 363–65; to James Williams, 5 June 1805, Letter Book 13: [14].

34. JSM to Esther Ellery, 7 August 1798, Letter Book 10:252; to Judge Tenney, 5 May 1804, to Winthrop Sargent, 26 May 1804, Letter Book 12: 925 [930]; to Winthrop Sargent, 28 December 18[05], 31 January, 28 April, 1 May 1806, to David Williams, 1, 20 May, 6 June 1806, to Winthrop Sargent, 20 June, Letter Book 13: [102], 120, 147, 151, 153–54, 157, [162–64], 171–73; to Winthrop Sargent, 18 September 1806, to Mr. Bigelow, 24 September 1806, to Mr. Dearborn, 24 September 1806, to Winthrop Sargent, 3 November 1806, 9 February 1807, to [?], 16 February 1807, Letter Book 14: 15, 17 [18], [20] 23, [30] [32], 53–55; to Winthrop Sargent, 26 August 1808, Letter Book 15: [46]; Faculty Records, Harvard Archives 8: 83, 86–87.

35. JSM to Winthrop Sargent, 26 August 1808, to Anna Sargent, 31 August 1808, Letter Book 15: [46] 51, [54]. David arrived in New Orleans a month later. David Williams to Winthrop Sargent, 26 September 1808, Sargent Murray Gilman Hough Collection.

36. JSM to Miss Elisa Payne, 23 September 1807, to Winthrop Sargent, 29 September 1807, to Miss Eliza Payne, 22 December1807, Letter Book 14: 75 [78], [122].

37. JSM to Maria Sargent, 29 May 1794, Letter Book 8: 202–3; to Winthrop Sargent, 29 September, 5 December 1807, to Winthrop and Mary Sargent, 22 December 1807,

Letter Book 14: [78], [112], [122]; to Winthrop Sargent, 7 March 1808, to Winthrop and Mary Sargent, 23 July 1808, Letter Book 15: [10] 11, [34].

38. JSM to Winthrop Sargent, 3 December 1808, 27 May 1809, to Adam Bingaman, 4 October 1809, to Winthrop Sargent, 15 October 1809, Letter Book 15: [74], 109, 143–45, 151 [152]; to Winthrop Sargent, 2 October 1811, 22 February, 7 December 1812, Letter Book 17: [18], 81, [180]; to Winthrop Sargent, 11 August 1813, Letter Book 18: 23; to Winthrop Sargent, 5 June 1815, Letter Book 19: [108]; *Columbian Centinel*, 13 June 1795. See also David F. Allmendinger, Jr., *Paupers and Scholars: The Transformation of Student Life in Nineteenth-Century New England* (New York: St. Martin's Press, 1975), 9–10; Kett, *Rites of Passage*, 41, 51–56; Story, *The Forging of an Aristocracy*, 62.

39. Faculty Records 8: 265, 365–68, Harvard Archives; JSM to Winthrop Sargent, 22 February 1812, to Mr. Ware, 9, 20 November 1812, Letter Book 17: [82], 165 [166], [174].

40. JSM to Mr. Ware, 20 November 1812, Letter Book 17: 174; to Winthrop Sargent, 27 July 1813, Letter Book 18: 19. Throughout Spring 1813, she wrote, unsuccessfully, to a number of people, begging them to allow William to stay under their roof, asking, as well, for help in finding a suitable tutor. JSM to [?], [?] May 1813, to [?] 15 May 1813, to the Rev. Mr. Hedge, 2 June, 21 June 1813, Letter Book 18: [10] [14].

41. JSM to Mr. Ware, 20 November 1812, to Winthrop Sargent, 7 December 1812, 4 January, 8 March 1813, to President Kirkland, 16 April 1813, Letter Book 17: [174], [180], [182], 193, 205; to Winthrop Sargent, 8 May 1813, 24 March, 6 August 1814, Letter Book 18: 5, [6], [74], [106]; Faculty Records 8: 9, 9: 6, Harvard Archives.

42. JSM to Winthrop Sargent, 27 November 1814, Letter Book 19: [28], 29.

43. JSM to Winthrop Sargent, 3, 23 December 1814, to the Rev. Mr. [?], 28 February 1815, to Winthrop Sargent, 8 August 1815, to the Rev. Mr. Clarke, 2, November 1815, Letter Book 19: 33, 35 [38], [74] [76], 143, [176–78].

44. JSM to Winthrop Sargent, 23 December 1814, Letter Book 19: 35 [38]. Judith was by no means the only parent or guardian in these days who suspected that male children were "insane." The transition from childhood to adulthood was extremely difficult for both parents and sons. As boys' personalities changed, as they became totally different people, mothers and fathers could not help but imagine that their sons were suffering from a species of madness. Jabour, "Masculinity and Adolescence," 411.

45. JSM to Winthrop Sargent, 5 January 1815, to the Rev. Mr. Eaton, 9 January 1815, to the Rev. Mr. Sewall, 10 January 1815, to President Kirkland, 11 January 1815, to the Rev. Mr. Chickering, 13 January 1815, to Winthrop Sargent, 5 June, 30 October 1815, to the Rev. Mr. Clarke, 2, 20 November 1815, Letter Book 19: 41, 43 [46], [96] 105, [172] 173, [176–78].

46. JSM to Winthrop Sargent, 5 June, 31 December 1815, Letter Book 19: [106–12], 209; to [?] 31 May, 5 June 1816, to the Rev. Mr. Clarke, 6 June 1816, to Anna Williams Thompson, 8 July 1816, Letter Book 20: 20, 21, 23 Sargent, Unbound Diary, 23, 24, 27 April, 27, 30, 31 May, 1–9 June 1816.

47. Sargent, Unbound Diary, 4 July, 18 September 1816;.C. K. Shipton, *Sibley's Harvard Graduates* (Boston: Massachusetts Historical Society, 1975) 17: 626. Washington was admitted to Harvard on 27 September at age 14 and graduated without major incident in 1820. Although he was punished for minor pranks—carrying canes around Harvard yard, failing to attend chapel or class, exhibiting an "improper attitude at public worship"—he was never rusticated. JSM to Winthrop Sargent, 23 September, Letter Book 20: 32; Faculty Records 9: 82–83, 85, 88 163, 168, 176, Harvard Archives.

48. Sargent, Unbound Diary, 13 June 1817; Faculty Records 9: 95, 100, Harvard Archives. Indeed, he obtained the degree in 1817, apparently without ever returning to Cambridge. Shipton, *Sibley's Harvard Graduates*, 626.

49. JSM to Winthrop Sargent, 27 February, to the Rev. Mr. [?], 28 February 1815, to Winthrop Sargent, 29 April, 5 June 1815, Letter Book 19: [68], 75, 97 [98], 105; to Mr. Harding, 12 October 1816, to the Rev. Mr. Gardiner, 21 December 1816, to Mr. Harding, 17 January 1818, Letter Book 20: 12, 35–36, 41, 74. Rotundo argues that in effect the two cultures—male and female—were at war in this period. Rotundo, *American Manhood*, 49.

50. JSM to Mrs. Tenney, 20 May 1806, Letter Book 13: [156]; to Mrs. Webber, 6 October 1807, Letter Book 14: 85; to Winthrop Sargent, 23 October 1813, Letter Book 18: 41; to Winthrop Sargent, 29 April 1815, Letter Book 19: 97. Yale and Princeton, as well as Harvard, blamed self-indulgent southern students for the misbehavior that characterized their students. Brown, *Benjamin Silliman*, 143; Richard Bushman, "A Poet, a Planter, and a Nation of Farmers," *Journal of the Early Republic* 19 (1999): 13.

51. JSM to Winthrop Sargent, 26 May 1804, Letter Book 12: 931; to Winthrop Sargent, 4 October 1812, Letter Book 17: [156]; 29 April 1815, Letter Book 19: 97.

52. JSM to Winthrop Sargent, 11 August 1813, 20 January 1814, Letter Book 18: 25, [58]; to Winthrop Sargent, 3 December 1814, 5 June 1815, Letter Book 19: [32], [108]; Faculty Records 8: 7, 8; 9: 20, 40, 46, 47, 60, Harvard Archives.

53. JSM to Fitz Winthrop Sargent, 10 April 1798, Letter Book 10: 210; to Winthrop Sargent, 11 August, 30 September 1813, Letter Book 18: 23 [26], 33–35; to Winthrop Sargent, 3 December 1814, 5 January, 13 February 1815, to William Sargent, 4 March 1815, to Mary Sargent, 15 March 1815, to Winthrop Sargent, 30 July, 8 August 1815, to the Rev. Mr. Clarke, 2, November 1815, to Winthrop Sargent, 16 November 1815, Letter Book 19: 31, 41, [58], 77, 81, 141 [142], [176–78], [186–90]. See Kaan, *Republic of Men*, 158; Mintz and Kellogg, *Domestic Revolutions*, 47–49. If childhood was a distinct stage where children learned to control their impulses and prepare to govern themselves, then what was a mortal sin for an adult was only venial for a child.

54. Murray, *Life of the Rev. John Murray*, 112; JSM to Winthrop Sargent, 27 Feburary 1815, Letter Book 19: 67.

55. JSM to Winthrop Sargent, 22 January 1810, Letter Book 16: n.p.; 21 January 1813, Letter Book 17: 189; 8 August 1815, Letter Book 19: 143.

56. JSM to Winthrop Sargent, 27 November 1814, to the Rev. Mr. Eaton, 9 January 1815, the Rev. Mr. Chickering, 27 May 1815, to Winthrop Sargent, 5 June, 16 November 1815, Letter Book 19: 29, [42], 103, [112], [188]; to Winthrop Sargent, 23 September 1816, Letter Book 20: 32.

57. JSM to Mr. Bigelow, 23 September 1806, Letter Book 14: 21.

58. JSM to [?], 18 March 1803, Letter Book 12: [888]; to John Murray, 27 August 1805, to Winthrop Sargent, 27 August, 19 October 1805, Letter Book 13: 39, 43, 57; to Winthrop Sargent, 7 March 1808, Letter Book 15: [10].

59. JSM to Mrs. David Urquahart, 21 October 1805, Letter Book 13: 61; to Winthrop Sargent, 15 April 1807, 17 December 1808, Letter Book 15: [76] 77; to Winthrop Sargent, 7 October 1811, Letter Book 17: [20] 21.

60. Fliegelman, "Familial Politics: Seduction and the Novel," 340; Harris, "Hannah Webster Foster's *The Coquette*, 6. See also Fliegelman, *Prodigals and Pilgrims*, 76, 88.

61. Adam had probably arrived in Boston in 1806, for Judith mentioned his instal-

lation at Harvard in June of that year. JSM to Miss Eliza Payne, 12 June 1806, Letter Book 13: [170]; Winthrop Sargent to John Marshall, 12 November 1800, Rowland, *Mississippi Territorial Archives*, 307; see David G. Sansing, Sim C. Callon, and Carolyn Vance Smith, *Natchez: An Illustrated History* (Natchez, Miss.: Plantation Publication Company, 1992), 79, 86–88, and Cecilia M. Shulman, "The Bingamans of Natchez," *Journal of Mississippi History* 63 (2001): 285–316 for excellent discussions of Adam Bingaman and his place in early Natchez.

62. JSM to Winthrop Sargent, 24 September 1808, Letter Book 15: 57 [60]; to Julia Maria, 18 May 1810, Letter Book 16: n.p.; Sargent, *Epes Sargent of Gloucester*, 55; Park, comp., *Gilbert Stuart*, 2: 544.

63. JSM to Winthrop Sargent, 18 March 1809, to Mr. Bingaman, 14 October 1809, Letter Book 15: [96] 97, [148]; to Winthrop Sargent, 1 June 1811, Letter Book 16: n.p. See also, JSM to Sarah and Judith Sargent, 22 May 1810, to Adam Bingaman, 2 June 1810, to Mr. Lathrop, [March 1811], Letter Book 16: n.p.

64. Hemphill, *Bowing to Necessity*, 112–13; Hoff-Wilson, "The Illusion of Change," 404, 405; Rothman, *Hands and Hearts*, 49–51; Cott, "Passionless," 219–236; JSM to Miss C____ of L____, 1 January 1797, Letter Book 10: 70.

65. JSM to Mrs. Bingaman, 2 May 1808, Letter Book 15: [20–22]. Gardiner was the highest of high Federalists. After his marriage in 1794, he opened a classics school in Boston, which he ran for a little over a decade. Thereafter, he tutored "selected pupils" in preparation for admission to Harvard. Lewis P. Simpson, ed., *The Federalist Literary Mind* (Baton Rouge: Louisiana State University Press, 1962), 24–25; Ellis, "Joseph Dennie and His Circle," 72, 81–82.

66. JSM to Winthrop Sargent, 13 August 1808, to Mr. Bingaman 14 October 1809, to Winthrop Sargent, 15 October 1809, Letter Book 15: 43, 147–49, [152]; to Julia Maria, 5 June, [?] October 1810, to Mr. Bingaman, 1 October 1810, to Winthrop Sargent, 6 December 1810, Letter Book 16: n.p.; to Winthrop Sargent, 7, 29 October 1811, to Mr. Bingaman, 4 January, 6 June 1812, to Winthrop Sargent 8 March 1813, Letter Book 17: [22], 29, 61 [62], 115, [194]–195; Faculty Records 8: 244, 235, Harvard Archives.

67. By the beginning of the eighteenth century, of course, more and more young people were marrying without parental consent. Still, in cases where marriage meant the transfer of land or property to the next generation, sons in particular were wise not to wed against the wishes of their family. Mintz and Kellogg, *Domestic Revolutions*, 20.

68. JSM to Mrs. Bingaman, 26 January, Letter Book 16: n.p.; to Mrs. Bingaman, 2 September 1811, Letter Book 17: 5–7. See Fliegelman, *Prodigals and Pilgrims*, 95 for a succinct explanation of the obligations to their parents that society expected from young people.

69. JSM to Mr. Bingaman, 31 December 1811, 4 January 1812, to Winthrop Sargent, 22 February 1812, Letter Book 17: 57–59, 61–63, 83. At least in the abstract, Judith's opposition to early marriages remained strong. While she was pleased to hear that "many beaus" were "fluttering" around Anna Williams, for instance, she advised the girl to let years "elapse before you select a partner for life." JSM to Anna Williams, 2 May 1808, Letter Book 15: [26].

70. Hessinger, " 'Insidious Murderers of Female Innocence,' " 271–72.

71. Ibid.; JSM to Mr. Bingaman, 31 December 1811, Letter Book 17: 59. They would have been less happy had they read the poem Judith sent to her daughter in May of 1812,

which praised the "virtues" of "*Bingaman*," and anticipated Julia Maria's "bright prospects." JSM to Julia Maria, 12 May 1812, Letter Book 17: [112].

72. JSM to Winthrop Sargent, 24 September 1808, Letter Book 15: 59; to Mr. Bingaman, 24 August 1812, Letter Book 17: 127 [130].

73. JSM to Mary Allen, 29 August 1812, to Mr. Bingaman, 21 October 1812, to Winthrop Sargent, 27 October 1812, to Julia Maria, 11, 12 November 1812, Letter Book 17: 137, [162–64], [166], [168] 69.

74. JSM to Winthrop Sargent, 7 December 1812, to Adam Bingaman, 11 January 1813, to Winthrop Sargent, 18 January 1813, Letter Book 17: 177 [180], 187 [192]; to Anna Sargent, 3 May 1813, to Winthrop Sargent, 8 May 1813, Letter Book 18: 1–3, 6–9.

75. JSM to Anna Sargent, 3 May 1813, to Winthrop Sargent, 8 May 1813, Letter Book 18: 1–3, 6–9.

76. Rothman, *Hands and Hearts*, 34, 35; JSM to Miss C____ of L____, 1 January 1797, Letter Book 10: 70.

77. JSM to Winthrop Sargent, 1 June, 31 July, Letter Book 16: n.p.; to Winthrop Sargent, 7 October 1811, to Julia Maria, 12 May 1812, to Winthrop Sargent, 8 March 1813, Letter Book 17: [22] 23, 113, 195; to Lewis Bingaman, 5 September 1816, to Winthrop Sargent, 28 September 1817, Letter Book 20: 30, 65; Sheppard, "Reminiscences"; Harris, in Murray, *Selected Writings*, xli.

78. Judith never said anything about the choice of Charlotte as a name for her granddaughter. She did not like the name Judith. "Julia" had been an acceptable modification of her own name; Maria, of course, had been a relative and her closest friend when her daughter was born. The name may have been Julia Maria's peace offering to her new in-laws. Or it may have been Adam's way of asserting his own patriarchal authority. At any rate, the decision to name the baby in honor of a woman neither Judith nor Julia Maria had ever met may have rankled.

79. JSM to Winthrop Sargent, 19 April 1814, Letter Book 18: 83; to Winthrop Sargent, 11 September 1815, Letter Book 19: 157; to [?], 23 October 1817, Letter Book 20: 71.

80. Will of John Murray, 1794, Suffolk County Records 23754: 468.

81. JSM to Winthrop Sargent, 19 April, 6 August 1814, Letter Book 18: 83 [84], [106] 7; Will of John Murray, 468. Carole Shammas, Marylynn Salmon, and Michael Dahlin, *Inheritance in America from Colonial Times to the Present* (New Brunswick, N.J.: Rutgers University Press, 1987), 75–76; Chused, "Married Women's Property," 44–45.

82. Will of John Murray, 469–72.

83. JSM to Abby Saltonstall of New London, 27 May 1797, Letter Book 10: 119–21; to Anna Williams, 14 February 1814, Letter Book 18: 66; to Winthrop Sargent, 31 December 1815, Letter Book 19: [212] 13; Will of John Murray, 470.

84. Shammas, Salmon, and Davis, *Inheritance in America*, 75; Chused, "Married Women's Property," 43–44, 52. Even the 1818 law limited married women's ability to own separate estates and the power they could actually exercise. All separate estates had to include provisions for a trusteeship.

85. JSM to Abby Saltonstall of New London, 27 May 1797, Letter Book 10: 120; to Winthrop Sargent, 22 June 1813, 19 July 1814, Letter Book 18: 16, 83; to Winthrop Sargent, 8 August, Letter Book 19: [146]; to Winthrop Sargent, 27 January, 8 April 1816, to Adam Bingaman, [?] October 1816, to [?], 23 October 1817, Letter Book 20: 5, 14, 35, 71; Esther Ellery to Winthrop Sargent, 15 October 1795, Sargent Murray Gilman Hough Papers.

86. JSM to Winthrop Sargent, 31 December 1815, Letter Book 19: 207 [208].

87. JSM to Winthrop Sargent, 19 April, 28 May, 20 June, 6 August 1814, Letter Book 18: [82] 83, [92], [98], 105; to Winthrop Sargent, 8 September 1814, to Adam Bingaman, 8 September 1814, to Winthrop Sargent, 12 October 1814, 29 April 1815, 19 December 1815, Letter Book 19: [8–12], [16], [100], 207 [208].; to Julia Maria, 22 July 1816, to Mr. Mitchell, 7 May 1818, to [?], 18 June 1818, Letter Book 20: 24, 85, 91. Rothman, *Hands and Hearts*, 31, 59. Marrying for love—or at least demanding love as a precondition for marriage—was, it turned out, a more complicated matter than most people had predicted. See Mintz and Kellogg, *Domestic Revolutions*, 57.

88. JSM to Winthrop Sargent, 4 January 1813, Letter Book 17: 185; to Winthrop Sargent, 9 April 1816, Letter Book 20: 16.

Epilogue

1. JSM to [Publishers of *Boston Weekly Magazine*], 29 March 1817, to [her "highly esteemed Aunt"], 23 February 1818, to Mary Sargent, Spring 1818, Letter Book 20: 54, 78, 89.

2. JSM to Winthrop Sargent, 26 May 1804, Letter Book 12: 931.

3. JSM, Acknowledgment, 19 September 1814, to Mr. Harding, 30 December 1815, to the Rev. Mr. Gardiner, 21 December 1816, to Mr. Harding, 22 March 1817, Letter Book 19: n.p., 203 [206]; Letter Book 20: 41, 53; Rowland, *Mississippi Territorial Archives*, 173, 173n.

4. JSM to William Sargent, 28 July, 28 September 1817, to Winthrop Sargent, 29 September 1817, Letter Book 20: 59–62, 66–67; Sargent, Unbound Diary, 25 October 1817.

5. JSM to Winthrop Sargent, 20 June 1814, 23 September 1816, to William Sargent, 28 July, 28 September 1817, to Winthrop Sargent, 29 September 1817, Letter Book 18: 97; Letter Book 20: 33, 59–62, 66, 67; *The Gleaner*, 252–53.

6. JSM to Julia Maria Bingaman, 22 July 1816, to Winthrop Sargent, 28 September 1817, Letter Book 20: 25, 64.

7. JSM to Winthrop Sargent, 20 September 1804, 12 August 1805, 28 April, 19 August 1806, 29 October 1811, 30 October 1815, 28 September, 1817, Letter Book 10: [948]; Letter Book 13: 37, 147, 191; 17: [28]; Letter Book 19: 175; 20: 64–65.

8. JSM to Winthrop Sargent, 20 September 1804, 29 October 1811, 30 October 1815, 28 September 1817, Letter Book 10: [948]; 17: [28]; 19: 175, 20: 64–65.

9. JSM to Winthrop Sargent, 25 April 1803, 19 June, 4 July, 21 September 1803, 21 December 1804; to Anna Sargent, 5 January 1805; to Winthrop Sargent, 8 December 1805; to Gilbert and John Aspinwall, [?] January 1806; to Winthrop Sargent, 19 August 1806, 9 February 1807, Letter Book 12: 843 [844], 855, 859, [880] 881; Letter Book 10: 975; Letter Book 12: 980; Letter Book 13: [108], [114], [192]; Letter Book 14: 53.

10. JSM to Winthrop Sargent, 28 September 1817, Letter Book 20: 63.

11. JSM to Winthrop Sargent, 23 September 1816, to Mary Sargent, [n.d. 1818], to Anna Williams Thompson, [Spring 1818], to Mary Sargent, [Spring 1818], Letter Book 20: 32, 82, 87, 89; Levi Hedge to Winthrop Sargent, 22 November 1817, 27 April, 24 July, 1 September, 29 October 1818, Sargent Papers, Reel 7. In fact, Washington was rusticated on two separate occasions. See Faculty Records 9: 218, 225, Harvard Archives.

12. JSM to Mr. Urquhart, 17 January 1818, Mary Sargent, [?], [Spring], 14 August 1818, Letter Book 20: 74, 82–83, 88, 96.

13. JSM to Winthrop Sargent, 29 September 1817, to the Rev. Mr. Mitchell, 22 October, 1817, to [?], 23 October 1817, to [?], 18 June 1818, Letter Book 20: 66, 70–72, 90.

14. JSM to the Rev. Mr. Mitchell, 19 February 1818, to Anna Sargent, 25 February 1818, to the Rev. Mr. Mitchell, 7 May 1818, to [?], 13 May 1818, Letter Book 20: 78, 80, 85, 86.

15. JSM to Mr. Urquhart, 21 October 1817, to [?], 16 March 1818, to [?] 11 April 1818, to the Rev. Mr. Mitchell, 7 May 1818, to Mary Sargent, Spring 1818, Letter Book 20: 70, 81, 84, 85, 89.

16. JSM to Winthrop Sargent, 19 October 1805, to [?], 18 February 181[6], to [her "highly esteemed Aunt"], to Anna Williams Thompson, Spring 1818, to Mary Sargent, Spring 1818, Letter Book 13: [56]; 20: 10, 79, 87, 89.

17. Judith Sargent Murray, Last Will and Testament, 30 March 1820, Adams County Probate Court, Box 27, Microfilm Roll, 367.

18. See the Codicil to Winthrop Sargent Will, written 21 November 1819.

19. JSM, Will.

20. Ibid; Mary Sargent to William Sargent, 1 October 1818, Sargent Papers, Reel 7; Winthrop Sargent Will, 1 October 1818, Sargent Papers, Reel 7.

21. Shulman, "The Bingamans of Natchez," 298; Winthrop Sargent Will.

22. JSM, Will.

23. Ibid.

24. Ibid.

25. *Mississippi State Gazette*, 8 July 1820.

Index

Illustrations are indexed using the abbreviation "fig."

Acknowledgments

This book has been a long time—much too long a time—in the making. As a result, it has profited from the advice of a large and diffuse group of scholars. A number of historians have read all or parts of this manuscript, offering their suggestions for shaping, improving, refining its arguments, and—perhaps most helpful of all—cutting it. I especially thank Carol Berkin, Holly Brewster, Nancy Cott, Elaine Crane, Edie Gelles, Joan Gundersen, Linda Kerber, and Rosemarie Zagarri. Perhaps more important, many of these fine scholars have formed a supportive network of women whose interest in Judith—feigned or not—gave me the encouragement I needed to continue the often tedious process or writing, editing, and writing again, a process that I thought, on many occasions, would never end. I can't help but believe that if Judith had enjoyed the support and friendship of such intelligent and sympathetic women, her life would have been much different, her prospects much improved. Other scholars, too, have asked incredibly useful questions about my perspective on Murray, forcing me on more than one occasion to rethink my approach or to sharpen my analysis. Particularly valuable in this regard are Wayne Bodle, Mary Kelley, Fredrika Teute, Al Young, and the 2006 members of the Advisory Council for the Omohundro Institute of Early American History and Culture.

I have been fortunate to have worked with a number of excellent graduate students, who have been of enormous help to me as I completed this manuscript. Susan Curry—whose seminar paper on Judith Sargent Murray sparked my early interest in this subject, and Suzanne Farmer and Stephanie Harper—who saved me from making countless footnote errors—deserve special mention. Martha Oakes, curator of the Sargent House Museum in Gloucester, has provided countless services and in the summer of 1996 gave me a wonderfully informative tour of Murray's Gloucester home. Joan Ciolino, director of the Sargent House Museum, helped me find pictures of both the exterior and the interior of Judith's "mansion house" on Middle Street. Bonnie Hurd Smith, independent scholar and founder of the Judith Sargent Murray Society, continues to transcribe, edit, and publish bits and pieces of Murray's correspondence, giving scholars easy access to the corpus of Judith Sargent Murray's written work. Thanks, also, to the National Endowment for the Humanities, the Liberal Arts

Development Fund, the Graduate School, and the Department of History at the University of Mississippi, all of whom helped me finance the research trips and conference presentations that made this book possible.

The folks at the University of Pennsylvania Press have been wonderfully helpful and supportive. Bob Lockhart, my editor, has the patience of a saint. I will never be able to thank him sufficiently for his smart, kind, and thoughtful reading of my manuscript in its many permutations. Of course I groaned at some of his suggestions, as he encouraged me to hit the delete button more often than I would have liked. But he was almost invariably right on target. Kathy Brown also read the last version of this book—on "vacation" no less!—offering a number of useful comments and criticisms. And Chris Hu became my computer guru, as he walked me through the vagaries of the online world, helping me do what was no doubt obvious to him, but was a total mystery to me. Alison Anderson, managing editor, and Jennifer Shenk, copyeditor, have both been indispensable. Their close reading of the manuscript has saved me from countless errors; their suggestions were invaluable.

Finally, this book owes its very existence to one man, the Reverend Gordon Gibson. Had it not been for this Unitarian-Universalist minister's dedicated and determined effort to locate Judith Sargent Murray's Letter Books, this effort—literally—would not have been possible. Thanks to him, the Murray Papers reside in the Mississippi Archives in Jackson, safe from the ravages of the elements that came close to destroying them.